Selected Readings in Sociobiology

— WALDROP '79

Selected Readings in Sociobiology

James H. Hunt
University of Missouri—St. Louis

McGraw-Hill Book Company

New York St. Louis San Francisco Auckland Bogotá Hamburg
Johannesburg London Madrid Mexico Montreal New Delhi
Panama Paris São Paulo Singapore Sydney Tokyo Toronto

SELECTED READINGS IN SOCIOBIOLOGY

1 2 3 4 5 6 7 8 9 0 DODO 8 9 8 7 6 5 4 3 2 1 0

This book was set in Times Roman by Cobb/Dunlop Publisher Services Incorporated.
The editor was James E. Vastyan; the production supervisor was Donna Piligra.
R. R. Donnelley & Sons Company was printer and binder.

Library of Congress Cataloging in Publication Data

Main entry under title:

Selected readings in sociobiology.

    1. Social behavior in animals—Addresses, essays, lectures. 2. Sociobiology—Addresses, essays, lectures. 3. Behavior evolution—Addresses, essays, lectures. I. Hunt, James H.
QL775.S42   304   80-10671
ISBN 0-07-031308-3

for Nile and Lucile Hunt

they supported and encouraged
the education of a biologist

I want to be scene,
Not herd, said a wayward
Young springbok, as it split.
Know your place, said
The leader, which is together,
And clubbed the errant back,
Giving it the Gesellschaft.

John M. Burns
Conform

Contents

2

SOCIAL INSECTS

3

4

5

Introduction

My attention was generally first called to them by the twittering of some small birds, belonging to several different species, that follow the ants in the woods. On approaching to ascertain the cause of this disturbance, a dense body of the ants, three or four yards wide, and so numerous as to blacken the ground, would be seen moving rapidly in one direction, examining every cranny, and underneath every fallen leaf. On the flanks, and in advance of the main body, smaller columns would generally first flush the cockroaches, grasshoppers, and spiders. The pursued insects would rapidly make off, but many, in their confusion and terror, would bound right into the midst of the main body of ants. A grasshopper, finding itself in the midst of its enemies, would give vigorous leaps, with perhaps two or three of the ants clinging to its legs. Then it would stop a moment to rest, and that moment would be fatal, for the tiny foes would swarm over the prey, and after a few more ineffectual struggles it would succumb to its fate, and soon be bitten to pieces and carried off to the rear.

Thomas Belt
The Naturalist in Nicaragua *

*John Murray, London, 1874.

Social behavior in nonhuman species has long fascinated inquisitive naturalists. For ants, literary similes as well as good descriptions of social behaviors can be found in Greek, Roman, and other classical literatures. Precise, scientific studies of social behavior are, of course, much more recent. Evolutionary biology dates from a clear milestone—the publication of Darwin's *On the Origin of Species* in 1859. The fundamental principles of natural selection presented in that work still stand as the central dogma of the discipline. Mendelian genetics subsequently explained the major mode of inheritance of traits, and molecular genetics has elucidated the chemical framework of inheritance, but Darwinian principles are still the clearest guide to understanding the evolutionary interaction of organisms and their environments. The role of natural selection in the evolution of social species has, however, posed certain problems. The existence of sterile castes in social insects and of altruistic behavior in many animal species are two outstanding cases.

In an often quoted passage from the *Origin,* Darwin noted that social insects posed a "special difficulty" that could weaken or even dismantle the principles of natural selection. The problem was to explain the existence of sterile workers in ants, bees, wasps, and termites, and, in particular, to explain their morphological divergence from the reproductive castes. These workers contribute mightily to the success of their kind, but, being sterile, they do not reproduce themselves. How can their behavior or morphology be naturally selected if they do not reproduce? After posing the dilemma, Darwin presented a resolution: that natural selection acts on these insects not at the level of the individual but rather at the level of the family (which, in social insects, is expressed in the form of a colony). Differential success among colonies of a social insect species can often be measured by size and/or longevity, both of which may relate directly to the number of virgin reproductives produced by a colony. The virgin reproductives are very close kin (usually siblings) of the sterile workers, and through relatedness, the action of natural selection on the sterile castes is passed to succeeding generations. The family level selection hypothesis served well enough for over a century; contemporary theorists have augmented and clarified it.

Altruistic behavior, in which an individual animal behaves in some manner that benefits one or more neighbors but at some cost to itself, is much less easily explained. Costs and benefits are measured solely in terms of individual offspring surviving to reproductive maturity. The beneficiaries of altruistic behavior may include not only near kin but also distant relatives and even those that are not related. The family level selection hypothesis cannot, therefore, be immediately applied. The challenge to natural selection theory was to explain the evolution and continued existence of altruistic behaviors. Most attempted explanations, until recently, invoked selection acting on groups of individuals.

W. C. Allee, in *The Social Life of Animals* (1938), developed the thesis that there is a natural cooperation among animals that is in opposition to the "intense and frequently very personal struggle for existence" of natural selection. Arguments in favor of such natural cooperation had their roots in the writings of the nineteenth-century French biologist Espinas, and, before Allee, these arguments appeared notably in the work of the Russian anarchist Kropotkin and others who stood in opposition to the social Darwinists of the late nineteenth and early twentieth centuries. These early writings on natural cooperation are anecdotal and rely on inference for support of their thesis, but a major work appeared in 1962 that abruptly ended that course. V. C. Wynne-Edwards' *Animal Dispersion in Relation to Social Behavior* attempted to advance the thesis of natural cooperation by clearly identifying and directly addressing group selection as the mechanism that would foster it. Wynne-Edwards suggested that many social behaviors serve primarily to provide information to members of a society on the density of their breeding population. Individuals could then adjust their reproductive efforts accordingly to engender an optimum balance between population density and resource abundance. Social groups containing nonaltruists (that is, individuals bent on maximizing their Darwinian fitness) would soon overpopulate in relation to available resources and become extinct. Selection between groups of all altruists and groups containing nonaltruists was specifically postulated as the means of maintaining population stability.

This proposition stimulated spirited controversy and a period of research and writing that reaffirmed the primacy of natural selection in the evolution of the social displays and other behaviors cited by Wynne-Edwards. Several theorists convincingly demonstrated that group selection can occur, but only under very restrictive conditions. Current debate focuses on the extent, if any, to which group selection may occur in nature, but notions of natural cooperation on a large scale, as envisioned by Wynne-Edwards, have been dispelled. This group selection controversy did not resolve the problem of the evolution of altruism.

The major advance in the analysis of the evolution of altruism occurred during the same period, but the key hypothesis came from a new source. In papers published in 1963 and 1964, W. D. Hamilton presented and developed a novel extension of natural selection theory. The primary currency of natural selection is reproductively successful offspring. Success in natural selection is, however, more generally measured by contribution to the gene pool of a species, which is termed fitness. Hamilton's contribution was to point out that fitness can have two components: successfully reproducing offspring plus successfully reproducing kin who have genes in common with the individual whose fitness is being measured. The key concept, then, is of inclusive fitness, which combines a classical Darwinian component (offspring) and a kinship component. An altruist can sacrifice its own reproduction but, nonetheless, have positive fitness if the beneficiaries of the altruism are kin and if certain additional conditions are met. Hamilton argued that altruism can be selected for if the inequality $k > 1/r$ is satisfied, where k equals the ratio of benefit to the beneficiary to cost to the altruist of the altruistic act, and r is Sewall Wright's coefficient of relatedness between the altruist and beneficiary. If the inequality is satisfied, the altruist nonetheless derives positive fitness from its act by means of inclusive fitness. In that the beneficiary of the altruism shares genes with the altruist, the altruistic trait can conceivably be maintained in the gene pool and passed to succeeding generations. Hamilton's model is not unlike Darwin's family level selection idea. Hamilton's signal conceptual contribution, however, was to specify precise conditions under which altruism may be selected for. The inclusive fitness concept has become a cornerstone of the emerging discipline of sociobiology.

Sociobiology, broadly defined, is the biological study of social behavior, encompassing the entire range of animal species that exhibit sociality. The emergence of sociobiology as a recognized area of academic inquiry was heralded in 1975 by the publicity that accompanied publication of E. O. Wilson's *Sociobiology: The New Synthesis.* Wilson accurately sensed the coalescing interests of diverse zoologists, entomologists, anthropologists, sociologists, and others who were involved in studies of animal and/or human sociality. He sought to review the extensive available literature and, wherever possible, to identify common themes or unifying principles. In particular, he tried to unite principles of ethology, genetics, population biology, and ecology in the study of social species. The success of Wilson's attempt cannot yet be fully measured, but the impact of his volume has clearly been substantial. Response to the book ranged from generally laudatory in the popular media to highly critical, even caustic, in some sociological and anthropological writings, with most biologists taking some intermediate position. At the very least, the book catalyzed fruitful discussions, debates, and research endeavors on the nature and evolution of sociality.

Use of the term sociobiology is, at present, imprecise. Early use generally implied study of social behavior in an ethological context. E. O. Wilson's use implied a broad discipline spanning the entire range of topics covered in his 1975 book; this use encompassed a diversity of concerns ranging from those of natural historians and ethnographers to the concerns of mathematical modelers and theoretical geneticists. An interest in social species was sufficient for inclusion in the confraternity. This broad definition of the term has not been generally applied, however, and two narrower interpretations are recognizable. Among biologists studying nonhuman social species, the term sociobiology seems at present to be particularly applied to work that invokes inclusive fitness as a paradigm for social evolution. Among human biologists, the term sociobiology is reserved largely for studies that are concerned directly with the identification and assessment of the role of genetic factors in human sociality. Each of these narrower usages is associated with particular points of view in fields where several points of view have adherents. Thus, the term sociobiology has negative connotations to some workers, especially in human biology. It does not seem likely at present, then, that use of the term sociobiology in the broad, nonrestrictive sense will gain easy acceptance. The study of social species will doubtless continue, however, nomenclatural problems and philosophical debates notwithstanding.

This volume is intended as a contribution to the field of sociobiology as it was broadly conceptualized in Wilson's 1975 treatise. Papers selected for inclusion range from theory to natural history, though greatest emphasis has been placed on theory and on synthesis of new and existing data. Emphasis has also been placed on more recent work, with only two papers from the 1960s and two from the 1950s included. The preponderance of more recent papers has yielded an emphasis on genetic theories and on discussions of genetic factors in sociality which reflects the majority of contemporary work in the field. Balanced coverage of topics and of points of view in sociobiology has been attempted, but a truly comprehensive treatment of such a large and rapidly developing discipline is not possible. In general, papers have been chosen that cover interest areas and organisms more familiar to biologists than to sociologists, psychologists, or anthropologists. Papers in the final section of this volume have been included to clearly indicate that some principles of sociobiology have potential use—or misuse—beyond the halls of academe.

Further developments in sociobiological theory will undoubtedly extend the existing horizons. At the present time, however, abundant opportunity exists for significant contributions by insightful researchers in almost all facets of the field. Theoretical development has largely proceeded well beyond the existing data base. Careful reading of the papers presented here should show the way to many avenues of much needed and potentially fruitful research.

ACKNOWLEDGMENTS

Numerous people have helped in various ways to bring this volume into being and into its final form. A partial listing includes M. Bekoff, R. Berkelhamer, J. L. Brown, G. J. Gamboa, Z. T. Halpin, B. Y. Pleasants, J. Pleasants, C. Stratton, and M. J. West-Eberhard. I express my sincere thanks to all these friends and colleagues. Selection of papers has been the sole prerogative of the editor, and responsibility for errors of omission and commission as well as for any errors of substance in the editorial comments rests squarely on my shoulders. The illustrations preceding each section and the cover were executed by Thomas Waldrop. I especially appreciate the valuable technical assistance and invaluable moral support of Jane A. Stevens.

James H. Hunt

Selected Readings in Sociobiology

Part One

Elements of Sociality

A model is built by a process of abstraction which defines a set of sufficient parameters on the level of study, a process of simplification which is intended to leave intact the essential aspects of reality while removing distracting elements, and by the addition of patently unreal assumptions which are needed to facilitate study.

Richard Levins
*Evolution in Changing Environments**

Progress in science is frequently achieved through testing alternate hypotheses, discarding those that do not fit observed phenomena, refining and retesting the remaining hypotheses, and so on. Distinctions between so-called hard and soft sciences generally turn on the degree to which hypotheses can be made quantitative and on the accuracy with which phenomena may be predicted by those hypotheses. Most scientists would agree that biochemistry falls toward the hard end of the spectrum and cultural anthropology toward the soft. Evolutionary biology, encom-

*Princeton University Press, Princeton, N.J., 1968.

passing sociobiology, falls somewhere in between. Testable hypotheses and predictive models in sociobiology are frequently presented in quantitative form, but the accuracy of sociobiological predictions has been, at the very least, difficult to measure in real situations. The difficulties of assessing sociobiological predictions will be directly addressed in following sections of this reader, but these difficulties do not diminish the intrinsic values of the models themselves and of the hypotheses that have been presented.

In recent years, many models have been developed that focus directly on aspects of sociality. Among these, perhaps none has had such profound impact and pervasive influence on the development of subsequent thinking as has W. D. Hamilton's model of inclusive fitness. The germ of the idea, the model itself, and examination of its implications were developed by Hamilton in a series of papers. Of these, the first full formulation of the model in 1964 has become one of the most frequently cited references in sociobiology. That model is reprinted here in full. In a companion article, Hamilton developed various hypotheses and implications generated by the model. The initial portion of that work, developing general implications, is also reprinted here. Another portion that develops special implications of inclusive fitness with regard to social insects is included in the second section of this reader.

Kin selection is a widely used concept in contemporary sociobiology. Some authors loosely, and incorrectly, equate kin selection with inclusive fitness. Though they are closely linked, the two concepts are not equivalent. J. Maynard Smith's introduction of the term kin selection and its meaning is presented in the second selection. Maynard Smith's article also includes a model of group (interdemic) selection with a discussion of the constraints that affect that process.

Hamilton's original formulation of inclusive fitness employed Sewall Wright's coefficient of relatedness to assess relative value of kin in the fitness measurement. In a brief note reprinted here, M. Milinski suggests that R. A. Fisher's concept of reproductive value should also be considered in assessing relative value of kin. To do so should improve the heuristic value and predictive ability of the inclusive fitness model.

Though the kin selection concept had signal success in resolving the evolution of altruism where beneficiaries are kin, problems involving altruism nonetheless remained. In particular, there are occasional, clear instances of true altruism, in which the beneficiary is so distantly related (if at all) to the altruist that kin selection cannot apply. Robert Trivers, a prominent sociobiological theorist, directly addressed this problem. In a 1971 paper reprinted here, he introduced the concept of reciprocal altruism. In Trivers's view, even apparently pure altruism can be seen as selfish and ultimately self-serving if two conditions are met: that there be assymetrical cost/benefit ratios associated with the altruistic act, and that there be individual reciprocity of altruistic acts. If reciprocal altruism, in fact, occurs, then group selection need not be invoked to explain the evolution of altruism.

The fifth selection, by M. J. West Eberhard, discusses, at length, kin selection theory and its application to various aspects of the evolution of altruism in social behavior. Also discussed are mutualism, parental manipulation, and reciprocal altruism. A major section of this paper that discusses the evolution of social insects is reserved for Part Two of this reader.

Though group selection need not be applied to the evolution of altruism, group selection should not be excluded from consideration in evolutionary biology. Several published models have convincingly demonstrated that group selection can theoretically occur. However, most of these models invoke severe constraints on the system, including small group size, low intergroup migration, and high rates of group extinction, as noted in Maynard Smith's contribution. These constraints have been seen to be so restrictive as to raise serious doubts about the incidence of group selection in nature. A model with more relaxed constraints and allowing individual dispersal was presented by D. S. Wilson in 1975 and is reprinted here. The Wilson model is one of intrademic selection, as opposed to Maynard Smith's interdemic model.

The closing paper in this section addresses an entirely different aspect of social behavior. Sociobiology, broadly defined, includes in its purview social interactions in courtship and reproduction. Among these, sexual selection and breeding systems have received extensive attention. These topics are treated in Part Three of this volume. Social behavior in established family units, especially patterns of parental care and of juvenile behavioral ontogeny, have also been intensively studied by ethologists and comparative psychologists. Since the introduction of Hamilton's inclusive fitness model, numerous investigators have undertaken analysis of intrafamilial social behaviors in terms of strategy analysis. This work has sought to identify and assess the impact of particular behaviors on the performer's inclusive fitness. The approach has had varied success, with perhaps the more general papers generating the more thought provoking insights. Among these, Robert Trivers's discussion of parent-offspring conflict is reprinted here.

The Genetical Evolution of Social Behaviour. I

W. D. Hamilton

Galton Laboratory, University College, London

A genetical mathematical model is described which allows for interactions between relatives on one another's fitness. Making use of Wright's Coefficient of Relationship as the measure of the proportion of replica genes in a relative, a quantity is found which incorporates the maximizing property of Darwinian fitness. This quantity is named "inclusive fitness". Species following the model should tend to evolve behaviour such that each organism appears to be attempting to maximize its inclusive fitness. This implies a limited restraint on selfish competitive behaviour and possibility of limited self-sacrifices.

Special cases of the model are used to show (a) that selection in the social situations newly covered tends to be slower than classical selection, (b) how in populations of rather non-dispersive organisms the model may apply to genes affecting dispersion, and (c) how it may apply approximately to competition between relatives, for example, within sibships. Some artificialities of the model are discussed.

1 INTRODUCTION

With very few exceptions, the only parts of the theory of natural selection which have been supported by mathematical models admit no possibility of the evolution of any characters which are on average to the disadvantage of the individuals possessing them. If natural selection followed the classical models exclusively, species would not show any behaviour more positively social than the coming together of the sexes and parental care.

Sacrifices involved in parental care are a possibility implicit in any model in which the definition of fitness is based, as it should be, on the number of adult offspring. In certain circumstances an individual may leave more adult offspring by expending care and materials on its offspring already born than by reserving them for its own survival and further fecundity. A gene causing its possessor to give parental care will then leave more replica genes in the next generation than an allele having the opposite tendency. The selective advantage may be seen to lie through benefits conferred indifferently on a set of relatives each of which has a half chance of carrying the gene in question.

From this point of view it is also seen, however, that there is nothing special about the parent-offspring relationship except its close degree and a certain fundamental asymmetry. The full-sib relationship is just as close. If an individual carries a certain gene the expectation that a random sib will carry a replica of it is again

From *The Journal of Theoretical Biology 7:* 1–25. Reprinted with permission from The Journal of Theoretical Biology. Copyright by Academic Press Inc. (London) Ltd.

one-half. Similarly, the half-sib relationship is equivalent to that of grandparent and grandchild with the expectation of replica genes, or genes "identical by descent" as they are usually called, standing at one quarter; and so on.

Although it does not seem to have received very detailed attention the possibility of the evolution of characters benefitting descendants more remote than immediate offspring has often been noticed. Opportunities for benefitting relatives, remote or not, in the same or an adjacent generation (i.e. relatives like cousins and nephews) must be much more common than opportunities for benefitting grandchildren and further descendants. As a first step towards a general theory that would take into account all kinds of relatives this paper will describe a model which is particularly adapted to deal with interactions between relatives of the same generation. The model includes the classical model for "non-overlapping generations" as a special case. An excellent summary of the general properties of this classical model has been given by Kingman (1961b). It is quite beyond the author's power to give an equally extensive survey of the properties of the present model but certain approximate deterministic implications of biological interest will be pointed out.

As is already evident the essential idea which the model is going to use is quite simple. Thus although the following account is necessarily somewhat mathematical it is not surprising that eventually, allowing certain lapses from mathematical rigour, we are able to arrive at approximate principles which can also be expressed quite simply and in non-mathematical form. The most important principle, as it arises directly from the model, is outlined in the last section of this paper, but a fuller discussion together with some attempt to evaluate the theory as a whole in the light of biological evidence will be given in the sequel.

2 THE MODEL

The model is restricted to the case of an organism which reproduces once and for all at the end of a fixed period. Survivorship and reproduction can both vary but it is only the consequent variations in their product, net reproduction, that are of concern here. All genotypic effects are conceived as increments and decrements to a basic unit of reproduction which, if possessed by all the individuals alike, would render the population both stationary and non-evolutionary. Thus the fitness $a^{\bullet}$ of an individual is treated as the sum of his basic unit, the effect δa of his personal genotype and the total e° of effects on him due to his neighbours which will depend on their genotypes:

$$a^{\bullet} = 1 + \delta a + e^{\circ}. \tag{1}$$

The index symbol $^{\bullet}$ in contrast to $^{\circ}$ will be used consistently to denote the inclusion of the personal effect δa in the aggregate in question. Thus equation (1) could be rewritten

$$a^{\bullet} = 1 + e^{\bullet}.$$

In equation (1), however, the symbol * also serves to distinguish this neighbour modulated kind of fitness from the part of it

$$a = 1 + \delta a$$

which is equivalent to fitness in the classical sense of individual fitness.

The symbol δ preceding a letter will be used to indicate an effect or total of effects due to an individual treated as an addition to the basic unit, as typified in

$$a = 1 + \delta a.$$

The neighbours of an individual are considered to be affected differently according to their relationship with him.

Genetically two related persons differ from two unrelated members of the population in their tendency to carry replica genes which they have both inherited from the one or more ancestors they have in common. If we consider an autosomal locus, not subject to selection, in relative B with respect to the same locus in the other relative A, it is apparent that there are just three possible conditions of this locus in B, namely that both, one only, or neither of his genes are identical by descent with genes in A. We denote the respective probabilities of these conditions by c_2, c_1 and c_0. They are independent of the locus considered; and since

$$c_2 + c_1 + c_0 = 1,$$

the relationship is completely specified by giving any two of them. Li & Sacks (1954) have described methods of calculating these probabilities adequate for any relationship that does not involve inbreeding. The mean number of genes per locus i.b.d. (as from now on we abbreviate the phrase "identical by descent") with genes at the same locus in A for a hypothetical population of relatives like B is clearly $2c_2+c_1$. One half of this number, $c_2+\frac{1}{2}c_1$, may therefore be called the expected fraction of genes i.b.d. in a relative. It can be shown that it is equal to Sewall Wright's Coefficient of Relationship r (in a non-inbred population). The standard methods of calculating r without obtaining the complete distribution can be found in Kempthorne (1957). Tables of

$$f = \tfrac{1}{2}r = \tfrac{1}{2}(c_2 + \tfrac{1}{2}c_1) \text{ and } F = c_2$$

for a large class of relationships can be found in Haldane & Jayakar (1962).

Strictly, a more complicated metric of relationship taking into account the parameters of selection is necessary for a locus undergoing selection, but the following account based on use of the above coefficients must give a good approximation to the truth when selection is slow and may be hoped to give some guidance even when it is not.

Consider now how the effects which an arbitrary individual distributes to the population can be summarized. For convenience and generality we will include at this stage certain effects (such as effects on parents' fitness) which must be zero under the restrictions of this particular model, and also others (such as effects on offspring) which although not necessarily zero we will not attempt to treat accurately in the subsequent analysis.

The effect of A on specified B can be a variate. In the present deterministic treatment, however, we are concerned only with the means of such variates. Thus the effect which we may write $(\delta a_{\text{father}})_A$ is really the expectation of the effect of A upon his father but for brevity we will refer to it as the effect on the father.

The full array of effects like $(\delta a_{\text{father}})_A$, $(\delta a_{\text{specified sister}})_A$, etc., we will denote

$$\{\delta a_{\text{rel.}}\}_A$$

From this array we can construct the simpler array

$$\{\delta a_{r, c_2}\}_A$$

by adding together all effects to relatives who have the same values for the pair of coefficients (r, c_2). For example the combined effect $\delta a_{\frac{1}{4}, 0}$ might contain effects actually occurring to grandparents, grandchildren, uncles, nephews and half-brothers. From what has been said above it is clear that as regards changes in autosomal gene-frequency by natural selection all the consequences of the full array are implied by this reduced array—at least, provided we ignore (a) the effect of previous generations of selection on the expected constitution of relatives, and (b) the one or more generations that must really occur before effects to children, nephews, grandchildren, etc., are manifested.

From this array we can construct a yet simpler array, or vector,

$$\{\delta a_r\}_A,$$

by adding together all effects with common r. Thus $\delta a_{\frac{1}{4}}$ would bring together effects to the above-mentioned set of relatives and effects to double-first cousins, for whom the pair of coefficients is $(\frac{1}{4}, 1/16)$.

Corresponding to the effect which A causes to B there will be an effect of similar type on A. This will either come from B himself or from a person who stands to A in the same relationship as A stands to B. Thus corresponding to an effect by A on his nephew there will be an effect on A by his uncle. The similarity between the effect which A dispenses and that which he receives is clearly an aspect of the problem of the correlation between relatives. Thus the term e° in equation (1) is not a constant for any given genotype of A since it will depend on the genotypes of neighbours and therefore on the gene-frequences and the mating system.

Consider a single locus. Let the series of allelomorphs be G_1, G_2, G_3, $\ldots$, G_n, and their gene-frequencies $p_1, p_2, p_3, \ldots, p_n$. With the genotype G_iG_j associate the array $\{\delta a_{\text{rel.}}\}_{ij}$; within the limits of the above-mentioned approximations natural selections in the model is then defined.

If we were to follow the usual approach to the formulation of the progress due to natural selection in a generation, we should attempt to give formulae for the neighbour modulated fitnesses a_{ij}. In order to formulate the expectation of that element of e_{ij}^o which was due to the return effect of a relative B we would need to know the distribution of possible genotypes of B, and to obtain this we must use the double measure of B's relationship and the gene-frequencies just as in the problem of the correlation between relatives. Thus the formula for e_{ij}^o will involve all the arrays $\{\delta a_{r,c}\}_{ij}$ and will be rather unwieldy (see Section 4).

An alternative approach, however, shows that the arrays $\{\delta a_r\}_{ij}$ are sufficient to define the selective effects. Every effect on reproduction which is due to A can be thought of as made up of two parts: an effect on the reproduction of genes i.b.d. with genes in A, and an effect on the reproduction of unrelated genes. Since the coefficient r measures the expected fraction of genes i.b.d. in a relative, for any particular degree of relationship this breakdown may be written quantitatively:

$$(\delta a_{rel.})_A = r(\delta a_{rel.})_A + (1-r)(\delta a_{rel.})_A .$$

The total of effects on reproduction which are due to A may be treated similarly:

$$\sum_{rel.} (\delta a_{rel.})_A = \sum_{rel.} r(\delta a_{rel.})_A + \sum_{rel.} (1-r)(\delta a_{rel.})_A ,$$

or

$$\sum_r (\delta a_r)_A = \sum_r r(\delta a_r)_A + \sum_r (1-r)(\delta a_r)_A ,$$

which we rewrite briefly as

$$\delta T_A^{\bullet} = \delta R_A^{\bullet} + \delta S_A^{o} ,$$

where $\delta R_A^{\bullet}$ is accordingly the total effect on genes i.b.d. in relatives of A, and δS_A is the total effect on their other genes. The reason for the omission of an index symbol from the last term is that here there is, in effect, no question of whether or not the self-effect is to be in the summation, for if it is included it has to be multiplied by zero. If index symbols were used we should have $\delta S_A^{\bullet} = \delta S_A^{o}$, whatever the subscript; it therefore seems more explicit to omit them throughout.

If, therefore, all effects are accounted to the individuals that cause them, of the total effect $\delta T_{ij}^{\bullet}$ due to an individual of genotype G_iG_j a part $\delta R_{ij}^{\bullet}$ will involve a specific contribution to the gene-pool by this genotype, while the remaining part δS_{ij} will involve an unspecific contribution consisting of genes in the ratio in which the gene-pool already possesses them. It is clear that it is the matrix of effects $\delta R_{ij}^{\bullet}$ which determines the direction of selection progress in gene-frequencies; δS_{ij} only influences its magnitude. In view of this importance of the $\delta R_{ij}^{\bullet}$ it is convenient to give some name to the concept with which they are associated.

In accordance with our convention let

$$R_{ij}^{\bullet} = 1 + \delta R_{ij}^{\bullet};$$

then $R_{ij}^{\bullet}$ will be called the *inclusive fitness*, $\delta R_{ij}^{\bullet}$ the *inclusive fitness effect* and δS_{ij} the *diluting effect*, of the genotype G_iG_j.

Let

$$T^{\bullet}_{ij} = 1 + \delta T^{\bullet}_{ij}.$$

So far our discussion is valid for non-random mating but from now on for simplicity we assume that it is random. Using a prime to distinguish the new gene-frequencies after one generation of selection we have

$$p'_i = \frac{\sum_j p_i p_j \underline{R}^{\bullet}_{ij} + p_i \sum_{j,k} p_j p_k \underline{\delta S}_{jk}}{\sum_{j,k} p_j p_k T^{\bullet}_{jk}} = p_i \frac{\sum_j p_j R^{\bullet}_{ij} + \sum_{j,k} p_j p_k \underline{\delta S}_{jk}}{\sum_{j,k} p_j p_k T^{\bullet}_{jk}}.$$

The terms of this expression are clearly of the nature of averages over a part (genotypes containing G_i, homozygotes G_iG_i counted twice) and the whole of the existing set of genotypes in the population. Thus using a well known subscript notation we may rewrite the equation term by term as

$$p'_i = p_i \frac{R^{\bullet}_{i.} + \delta S_{..}}{T^{\bullet}_{..}}$$

$$\therefore \ p'_i - p_i = \Delta p_i = \frac{p_i}{T^{\bullet}_{..}} (R^{\bullet}_{i.} + \delta S_{..} - T^{\bullet}_{..})$$

or

$$\Delta p_i = \frac{p_i}{R^{\bullet}_{..} + \delta S^{\bullet}_{..}} (R^{\bullet}_{i.} - R^{\bullet}_{..}). \tag{2}$$

This form clearly differentiates the roles of the $R^{\bullet}_{ij}$ and $\delta S^{\bullet}_{ij}$ in selective progress and shows the appropriateness of calling the latter diluting effects.

For comparison with the account of the classical case given by Moran (1962), equation (2) may be put in the form

$$\Delta p_i = \frac{p_i}{T^{\bullet}_{..}} \left(\frac{1}{2} \frac{\partial R^{\bullet}_{..}}{\partial p_i} - R^{\bullet}_{..} \right)$$

where $\partial/\partial p_i$ denotes the usual partial derivative, written d/dp_i by Moran.

Whether the selective effect is reckoned by means of the $a^{\bullet}_{ij}$ or according to the method above, the denominator expression must take in all effects occurring during the generation. Hence $a^{\bullet}_{..} = T^{\bullet}_{..}$.

As might be expected from the greater generality of the present model the extension of the theorem of the increase of mean fitness (Scheuer & Mandel, 1959; Mulholland & Smith, 1959; a much shorter proof by Kingman, 1961a) presents certain difficulties. However, from the above equations it is clear that the quantity that will tend to maximize, if any, is $R^{\bullet}_{..}$, the mean inclusive fitness. The following brief discussion uses Kingman's approach.

The mean inclusive fitness in the succeeding generation is given by

$$R_{..}^{\bullet\prime} = \sum_{i,j} p_i' p_j' R_{ij}^{\bullet} = \frac{1}{T_{..}^{\bullet 2}} \sum_{i,j} p_i p_j R_{ij}^{\bullet} (R_{i.}^{\bullet} + \delta S_{..})(R_{.j}^{\bullet} + \delta S_{..}).$$

$$\therefore \ R_{..}^{\bullet\prime} - R_{..}^{\bullet} = \Delta R_{..}^{\bullet} = \frac{1}{T_{..}^{\bullet 2}} \left\{ \sum_{i,j} p_i p_j R_{ij}^{\bullet} R_{i.}^{\bullet} R_{.j}^{\bullet} + \right.$$

$$\left. + 2\delta S_{..} \sum_{i,j} p_i p_j R_{ij}^{\bullet} R_{i.}^{\bullet} + R_{..}^{\bullet} \delta S_{..}^2 - R_{..}^{\bullet} T_{..}^{\bullet 2} \right\}$$

Substituting $R_{..}^{\bullet} + \delta S_{..}$ for $T_{..}^{\bullet}$ in the numerator expression, expanding and rearranging:

$$\Delta R^{\bullet} = \frac{1}{T_{..}^{\bullet 2}} \left\{ \left(\sum_{i,j} p_i p_j R_{ij}^{\bullet} R_{.j}^{\bullet} - R_{..}^{\bullet 3} \right) + \right.$$

$$\left. + 2\delta S_{..} \left(\sum_{i,j} p_i p_j R_{ij}^{\bullet} R_{i.}^{\bullet} - R_{..}^{\bullet 2} \right) \right\}.$$

We have ( ) $\geqslant 0$ in both cases. The first is the proven inequality of the classical model. The second follows from

$$\sum_{i,j} p_i p_j R_{ij}^{\bullet} R_{i.}^{\bullet} = \sum_i p_i R_{i.}^{\bullet 2} \geqslant \left(\sum_i p_i R_{i.}^{\bullet} \right)^2 = R_{..}^{\bullet 2}.$$

Thus a sufficient condition for $\Delta R_{..}^{\bullet} \geqslant 0$ is $\delta S_{..} \geqslant 0$. That $\Delta R_{..}^{\bullet} \geqslant 0$ for positive dilution is almost obvious if we compare the actual selective changes with those which would occur if $\{R_{ij}^{\bullet}\}$ were the fitness matrix in the classical model.

It follows that $R_{..}^{\bullet}$ certainly maximizes (in the sense of reaching a local maximum of $R_{..}^{\bullet}$) if it never occurs in the course of selective changes that $\delta S_{..} < 0$. Thus $R_{..}^{\bullet}$ certainly maximizes if all $\delta S_{ij} \geqslant 0$ and therefore also if all $(\delta a_{rel.})_{ij} \geqslant 0$. It still does so even if some or all δa_{ij} are negative, for, as we have seen δS_{ij} is independant of δa_{ij}.

Here then we have discovered a quantity, inclusive fitness, which under the conditions of the model tends to maximize in much the same way that fitness tends to maximize in the simpler classical model. For an important class of genetic effects where the individual is supposed to dispense benefits to his neighbours, we have formally proved that the average inclusive fitness in the population will always increase. For cases where individuals may dispense harm to their neighbours we merely know, roughly speaking, that the change in gene frequency in each generation is aimed somewhere in the direction of a local maximum of average inclusive fitness,[†] but may, for all the present analysis has told us, overshoot it in such a way as to produce a lower value.

As to the nature of inclusive fitness it may perhaps help to clarify the notion if we now give a slightly different verbal presentation. Inclusive fitness may be imagined as the personal fitness which an individual actually expresses in its production of adult offspring as it becomes after it has been first stripped and then augmented in a certain way. It is stripped of all components which can be considered as due to the individual's social environment, leaving the fitness which he would express if not exposed to any of the harms or benefits of that environment. This quantity is then augmented by certain fractions of the quantities of harm and benefit which the individual himself causes to the fitnesses of his neighbours. The fractions in question are simply the coefficients of relationship appropriate to the neighbours whom he affects: unity for clonal individuals, one-half for sibs, one-quarter for half-sibs, one-eighth for cousins, ... and finally zero for all neighbours whose relationship can be considered negligibly small.

Actually, in the preceding mathematical account we were not concerned with the inclusive fitness of individuals as described here but rather with certain averages of them which we call the inclusive fitnesses of types. But the idea of the inclusive fitness of an individual is nevertheless a useful one. Just as in the sense of classical selection we may consider whether a given character expressed in an individual is adaptive in the sense of being in the interest of his personal fitness or not, so in the present sense of selection we may consider whether the character or trait of behaviour is or is not adaptive in the sense of being in the interest of his inclusive fitness.

3 THREE SPECIAL CASES

Equation (2) may be written

$$\Delta p_i = p_i \frac{\delta R_{i.}^{\bullet} - \delta R_{..}^{\bullet}}{1 + \delta T_{..}^{\bullet}}. \tag{3}$$

Now

$$\delta T_{ij}^{\bullet} = \sum_r (\delta a_r)_{ij}$$

is the sum and

$$\delta R^{\bullet} = \sum_r r(\delta a_r)_{ij}$$

is the first moment about $r = 0$ of the array of effects $\{\delta a_{\text{rel.}}\}_{ij}$ cause by the genotype G_iG_j; it appears that these two parameters are sufficient to fix the progress of the system under natural selection within our general approximation.

Let

[†]That is, it is aimed "uphill": that it need not be at all directly towards the local maximum is well shown in the classical example illustrated by Mulholland & Smith (1959).

$$r^{\bullet}_{ij} = \frac{\delta R^{\bullet}_{ij}}{\delta T^{\bullet}_{ij}}, \qquad (\delta T^{\bullet}_{ij} \neq 0); \tag{4}$$

and let

$$r^{\circ}_{ij} = \frac{\delta R^{\circ}_{ij}}{\delta T^{\circ}_{ij}}, \qquad (\delta T^{\circ}_{ij} \neq 0). \tag{5}$$

These quantities can be regarded as average relationships or as the first moments of reduced arrays, similar to the first moments of probability distributions.

We now consider three special cases which serve to bring out certain important features of selection in the model.

(a) The sums $\delta T^{\bullet}_{ij}$ differ between genotypes, the reduced first moment $r^{\bullet}$ being common to all. If all higher moments are equal between genotypes, that is, if all arrays are of the same "shape," this corresponds to the case where a stereotyped social action is performed with differing intensity or frequency according to genotype.

Whether or not this is so, we may, from equation (4), substitute $r^{\bullet}\delta T^{\bullet}_{ij}$ for $\delta R^{\bullet}_{ij}$ in equation (3) and have

$$\Delta p_i = p_i r^{\bullet} \frac{\delta T^{\bullet}_{i.} - \delta T^{\bullet}_{..}}{1 + \delta T^{\bullet}_{..}}.$$

Comparing this with the corresponding equation of the classical model,

$$\Delta p_i = p_i \frac{\delta a_{i.} - \delta a_{..}}{1 + \delta a_{..}}. \tag{6}$$

we see that placing genotypic effects on a relative of degree $r^{\bullet}$ instead of reserving them for personal fitness results in a slowing of selection progress according to the fractional factor $r^{\bullet}$.

If, for example, the advantages conferred by a "classical" gene to its carriers are such that the gene spreads at a certain rate the present result tells us that in exactly similar circumstances another gene which conferred similar advantages to the sibs of the carriers would progress at exactly half this rate.

In trying to imagine a realistic situation to fit this sort of case some concern may be felt about the occasions where through the probabilistic nature of things the gene-carrier happens not to have a sib, or not to have one suitably placed to receive the benefit. Such possibilities and their frequencies of realization must, however, all be taken into account as the effects $(\delta a_{\text{sibs}})_A$, etc., are being evaluated for the model, very much as if in a classical case allowance were being made for some degree of failure of penetrance of a gene.

(b) The reduced first moments $r^{\bullet}_{ij}$ differ between genotypes, the sum $\delta T^{\bullet}$ being common to all. From equation (4), substituting $r^{\bullet}_{ij} \delta T^{\bullet}$ for $\delta R^{\bullet}_{ij}$ in equation (3) we have

$$\Delta p_i = p_i \frac{\delta T^\bullet}{T^\bullet} (r^\bullet_{i.} - r^\bullet_{..}).$$

But it is more interesting to assume δa is also common to all genotypes. If so it follows that we can replace $\bullet$ by $\circ$ in the numerator expression of equation (3). Then, from equation (5), substituting $r^\circ_{ij} \, \delta T^\circ$ for δR_{ij}, we have

$$\Delta p_i = p_i \frac{\delta T^\circ}{T^\bullet} (r^\circ_{i.} - r^\circ_{..}).$$

Hence, if a giving-trait is in question (δT° positive), genes which restrict giving to the nearest relative (r°_i greatest) tend to be favoured; if a taking-trait (δT° negative), genes which cause taking from the most distant relatives tend to be favoured.

If all higher reduced moments about $r = r^\circ_{ij}$ are equal between genotypes it is implied that the genotype merely determines whereabouts in the field of relationship that centres on an individual a stereotyped array of effects is placed.

With many natural populations it must happen that an individual forms the centre of an actual local concentration of his relatives which is due to a general inability or disinclination of the organisms to move far from their places of birth. In such a population, which we may provisionally term "viscous," the present form of selection may apply fairly accurately to genes which affect vagrancy. It follows from the statements of the last paragraph but one that over a range of different species we would expect to find giving-traits commonest and most highly developed in the species with the most viscous populations whereas uninhibited competition should characterize species with the most freely mixing populations.

In the viscous population, however, the assumption of random mating is very unlikely to hold perfectly, so that these indications are of a rough qualitative nature only.

(c) $\quad \delta T^\bullet_{ij} = 0$ for all genotypes.

$\therefore \quad \delta T^\circ_{ij} = -\delta a_{ij}$

for all genotypes, and from equation (5)

$$\delta R^\circ_{ij} = -\delta a_{ij} r^\circ_{ij}.$$

Then, from equation (3), we have

$$\Delta p_i = p_i (\delta R^\bullet_{i.} - \delta R^\bullet_{..}) = p_i \left\{ (\delta a_{i.} + \delta R^\circ_{i.}) - (\delta a_{..} + \delta R^\circ_{..}) \right\}$$

$$= p_i \left\{ \delta a_{i.} (1 - r^\circ_{i.}) - \delta a_{..} (1 - r^\circ_{..}) \right\}.$$

Such cases may be described as involving transfers of reproductive potential. They are especially relevant to competition, in which the individual can be considered as endeavouring to transfer prerequisites of survival and reproduction from his competitors to himself. In particular, if $r^\circ_{ij} = r^\circ$ for all genotypes we have

$$\Delta p_i = p_i (1 - r^\circ)(\delta a_{i.} - \delta a_{..}).$$

Comparing this to the corresponding equation of the classical model (equation (6)) we see that there is a reduction in the rate of progress when transfers are from a relative.

It is relevant to note that Haldane (1923) in his first paper on the mathematical theory of selection pointed out the special circumstances of competition in the cases of mammalian embryos in a single uterus and of seeds both while still being nourished by a single parent plant and after their germination if they were not very thoroughly dispersed. He gave a numerical example of competition between sibs showing that the progress of gene-frequency would be slower than normal.

In such situations as this, however, where the population may be considered as subdivided into more or less standard-sized batches each of which is alloted a local standard-sized pool of reproductive potential (which in Haldane's case would consist almost entirely of prerequisites for pre-adult survival), there is, in addition to a small correcting term which we mention in the short general discussion of competition in the next section, an extra overall slowing in selection progress. This may be thought of as due to the wasting of the powers of the more fit and the protection of the less fit when these types chance to occur positively assorted (beyond any mere effect of relationship) in a locality; its importance may be judged from the fact that it ranges from zero when the batches are indefinitely large to a halving of the rate of progress for competition in pairs.

4   ARTIFICIALITIES OF THE MODEL

When any of the effects is negative the restrictions laid upon the model hitherto do not preclude certain situations which are clearly impossible from the biological point of view. It is clearly absurd if for any possible set of gene-frequencies any $a_{ij}^{\bullet}$ turns out negative; and even if the magnitude of δa_{ij} is sufficient to make $a_{ij}^{\bullet}$ positive while $1+e_{ij}^{\bullet}$ is negative the situation is still highly artificial, since it implies the possibility of a sort of overdraft on the basic unit of an individual which has to be made good from his own takings. If we call this situation "improbable" we may specify two restrictions: a weaker, $e_{ij}^{\circ} > -1$, which precludes "improbable" situations; and a stronger, $e_{ij}^{\bullet} > -1$, which precludes even the impossible situations, both being required over the whole range of possible gene-frequencies as well as the whole range of genotypes.

As has been pointed out, a formula for $e_{ij}^{\bullet}$ can only be given if we have the arrays of effects according to a double coefficient of relationship. Choosing the double coefficient (c_2, c_1) such a formula is

$$e_{ij}^{\bullet} = \underset{c_2,c_1}{\Sigma^{\bullet}} \ [c_2 \operatorname{Dev}(\delta a_{c_2,c_1})_{ij} + \tfrac{1}{2}c_1 \{ \operatorname{Dev}(\delta a_{c_2,c_1})_{i.} + \operatorname{Dev}(\delta a_{c_2,c_1})_{.j} \}] + \delta T^{\circ}_{..}$$

where

$$\operatorname{Dev}(\delta a_{c_2,c_1})_{ij} = (\delta a_{c_2,c_1})_{ij} - (\delta a_{c_2,c_1})_{..} \quad \text{etc.}$$

Similarly

$$e_{ij}^{\circ} = \Sigma^{\circ} \ [\ '' \ ] + \delta T^{\circ}_{..} \ ,$$

the self-effect $(\delta a_{1,0})_{ij}$ being in this case omitted from the summations.

The following discussion is in terms of the stronger restriction but the argument holds also for the weaker; we need only replace $^{\bullet}$ by $^{\circ}$ throughout.

If there are no dominance deviations, i.e. if

$$(\delta a_{\text{rel.}})_{ij} = \tfrac{1}{2}\left\{(\delta a_{\text{rel.}})_{ii} + (\delta a_{\text{rel.}})_{jj}\right\} \qquad \text{for all } ij \text{ and rel.},$$

it follows that each ij deviation is the sum of the $i.$ and the $j.$ deviations. In this case we have

$$e^{\bullet}_{ij} = \Sigma^{\bullet} r \operatorname{Dev} (\delta a_r)_{ij} + \delta T^{\bullet}_{..} \;.$$

Since we must have $e^{\bullet}_{..} = \delta T^{\bullet}_{..}$, it is obvious that some of the deviations must be negative.

Therefore $\delta T^{\bullet}_{..} > -1$ is a necessary condition for $e^{\bullet}_{ij} > -1$. This is, in fact, obvious when we consider that $\delta T^{\bullet}_{..} = -1$ would mean that the aggregate of individual takings was just sufficient to eat up all basic units exactly. Considering that the present use of the coefficients of relationships is only valid when selection is slow, there seems little point in attempting to derive mathematically sufficient conditions for the restriction to hold; intuitively however it would seem that if we exclude over- and under-dominance it should be sufficient to have no homozygote with a net taking greater than unity.

Even if we could ignore the breakdown of our use of the coefficient of relationship it is clear enough that if $\delta T^{\bullet}_{..}$ approaches anywhere near -1 the model is highly artificial and implies a population in a state of catastrophic decline. This does not mean, of course, that mutations causing large selfish effects cannot receive positive selection; it means that their expression must moderate with increasing gene-frequency in a way that is inconsistent with our model. The "killer" trait of *Paramoecium* might be regarded as an example of a selfish trait with potentially large effects, but with its only partially genetic mode of inheritance and inevitable density dependance it obviously requires a selection model tailored to the case, and the same is doubtless true of most "social" traits which are as extreme as this.

Really the class of model situations with negative neighbour effects which are artificial according to a strict interpretation of the assumptions must be much wider than the class which we have chosen to call "improbable." The model assumes that the magnitude of an effect does not depend either on the genotype of the effectee or on his current state with respect to the prerequisites of fitness at the time when the effect is caused. Where taking-traits are concerned it is just possible to imagine that this is true of some kinds of surreptitious theft but in general it is more reasonable to suppose that following some sort of an encounter the limited prerequisite is divided in the ratio of the competitive abilities. Provided competitive differentials are small however, the model will not be far from the truth; the correcting term that should be added to the expression for Δp_i can be shown to be small to the third order. With giving-traits it is more reasonable to suppose that if it is the nature of the prerequisite to be transferable the individual can give away whatever fraction of his own property that his instincts incline him to. The model was designed to illuminate altruistic behaviour; the classes of selfish and competitive behaviour which it can also usefully illuminate are more restricted, especially where selective differentials are potentially large.

For loci under selection the only relatives to which our metric of relationship is strictly applicable are ancestors. Thus the chance that an arbitrary parent carries a gene picked in an offspring is ½, the chance that an arbitrary grandparent carries it is ¼, and so on. As regards descendants, it seems intuitively plausible that for a gene which is making steady progress in gene-frequency the true expectation of genes i.b.d. in a n-th generation descendant will exceed $½^n$, and similarly that for a gene that is steadily declining in frequency the reverse will hold. Since the path of genetic connection with a simple same-generation relative like a half-sib includes an "ascending part" and a "descending part" it is tempting to imagine that the ascending part can be treated with multipliers of exactly ½ and the descending part by multipliers consistently more or less than ½ according to which type of selection is in progress. However, a more rigorous attack on the problem shows that it is more difficult than the corresponding one for simple descendants, where the formulation of the factor which actually replaces ½ is quite easy at least in the case of classical selection, and the author has so far failed to reach any definite general conclusions as to the nature and extent of the error in the foregoing account which his use of the ordinary coefficients of relationship has actually involved.

Finally, it must be pointed out that the model is not applicable to the selection of new mutations. Sibs might or might not carry the mutation depending on the point in the germ-line of the parent at which it had occurred, but for relatives in general a definite number of generations must pass before the coefficients give the true—or, under selection, the approximate—expectations of replicas. This point is favourable to the establishment of taking-traits and slightly against giving-traits. A mutation can, however, be expected to overcome any such slight initial barrier before it has recurred many times.

5 THE MODEL LIMITS TO THE EVOLUTION OF ALTRUISTIC AND SELFISH BEHAVIOUR

With classical selection a genotype may be regarded as positively selected if its fitness is above the average and as counter-selected if it is below. The environment usually forces the average fitness $a_{..}$ towards unity; thus for an arbitrary genotype the sign of δa_{ij} is an indication of the kind of selection. In the present case although it is $T^{\bullet}_{..}$ and not $R^{\bullet}_{..}$ that is forced towards unity, the analogous indication is given by the inclusive fitness effect $\delta R^{\bullet}_{ij}$, for the remaining part, the diluting effect δS_{ij}, of the total genotypic effect $\delta T^{\bullet}_{ij}$ has no influence on the kind of selection. In other words the kind of selection may be considered determined by whether the inclusive fitness of a genotype is above or below average.

We proceed, therefore, to consider certain elementary criteria which determine the sign of the inclusive fitness effect. The argument applies to any genotype and subscripts can be left out.

Let

$$\delta T^\circ = k\delta a.$$

According to the signs of δa and δT° we have four types of behaviour as set out in the following diagram:

Neighbours

	gain; δT°+ve	lose; δT°−ve
gains; δa+ve	k+ve *Selected*	k−ve Selfish behaviour ?
loses; δa−ve	k−ve Altruistic behaviour ?	k+ve *Counterselected*

Individual

The classes for which k is negative are of the greatest interest, since for these it is less obvious what will happen under selection. Also, if we regard fitness as like a substance and tending to be conserved, which must be the case in so far as it depends on the possession of material prerequisites of survival and reproduction, k −ve is the more likely situation. Perfect conservation occurs if $k = -1$. Then $\delta T = 0$ and $T^\circ = 1$: the gene-pool maintains constant "volume" from generation to generation. This case has been discussed in Case (c) of section 3. In general the value of k indicates the nature of the departure from conservation. For instance, in the case of an altruistic action $|k|$ might be called the ratio of gain involved in the action: if its value is two, two units of fitness are received by neighbours for every one lost by an altruist. In the case of a selfish action, $|k|$ might be called the ratio of diminution: if its value is again two, two units of fitness are lost by neighbours for one unit gained by the taker.

The alarm call of a bird probably involves a small extra risk to the individual making it by rendering it more noticeable to the approaching predator but the consequent reduction of risk to a nearby bird previously unaware of danger must be much greater.[†] We need not discuss here just how risks are to be reckoned in terms of fitness: for the present illustration it is reasonable to guess that for the generality of alarm calls k is negative but $|k| > 1$. How large must $|k|$ be for the benefit to others to outweigh the risk to self in terms of inclusive fitness?

$$\begin{aligned}\delta R^{\bullet} &= \delta R^\circ + \delta a\\ &= r^\circ \delta T^\circ + \delta a \qquad\qquad \text{from (5)}\\ &= \delta a(kr^\circ + 1). \qquad\qquad \text{from (7).}\end{aligned}$$

[†]The alarm call often warns more than one nearby bird of course—hundreds in the case of a flock —but since the predator would hardly succeed in surprising more than one in any case the total number warned must be comparatively unimportant.

Thus of actions which are detrimental to individual fitness (δa −ve) only those for which

$$-k > \frac{1}{r}\raisebox{0.6ex}{$\circ$}$$

will be beneficial to inclusive fitness (δR^{*} +ve).

This means that for a hereditary tendency to perform an action of this kind to evolve the benefit to a sib must average at least twice the loss to the individual, the benefit to a half-sib must be at least four times the loss, to a cousin eight times and so on. To express the matter more vividly, in the world of our model organisms, whose behaviour is determined strictly by genotype, we expect to find that no one is prepared to sacrifice his life for any single person but that everyone will sacrifice it when he can thereby save more than two brothers, or four half-brothers, or eight first cousins ... Although according to the model a tendency to simple altruistic transfers ($k = -1$) will never be evolved by natural selection, such a tendency would, in fact, receive zero counter-selection when it concerned transfers between clonal individuals. Conversely selfish transfers are always selected except when from clonal individuals.

As regards selfish traits in general (δa +ve, k −ve) the condition for a benefit to inclusive fitness is

$$-k > \frac{1}{r}\raisebox{0.6ex}{$\circ$} \ .$$

Behaviour that involves taking too much from close relatives will not evolve. In the model world of genetically controlled behaviour we expect to find that sibs deprive one another of reproductive prerequisites provided they can themselves make use of at least one half of what they take; individuals deprive half-sibs of four units of reproductive potential if they can get personal use of at least one of them; and so on. Clearly from a gene's point of view it is worthwhile to deprive a large number of distant relatives in order to extract a small reproductive advantage.

REFERENCES

Haldane, J. B. S. (1923). *Trans. Camb. phil. Soc.* **23**, 19.

Haldane, J. B. S. & Jayakar, S. D. (1962). *J. Genet.* **58**, 81.

Kempthorne, O. (1957). "An Introduction to Genetical Statistics." New York: John Wiley & Sons, Inc.

Kingman, J. F. C. (1961a). *Quart. J. Math.* **12**, 78.

Kingman, J. F. C. (1961b). *Proc. Camb. phil. Soc.* **57**, 574.

Li, C. C. & Sacks, L. (1954). *Biometrics,* **10**, 347.

Moran, P. A. P. (1962). *In* "The Statistical Processes of Evolutionary Theory," p. 54. Oxford: Clarendon Press.

Mulholland, H. P. & Smith, C. A. B. (1959). *Amer. math. Mon.* **66**, 673.

Scheuer, P. A. G. & Mandel, S. P. H. (1959). *Heredity,* **31**, 519.

The Genetical Evolution of Social Behaviour. II (*extract*)

W. D. Hamilton
Galton Laboratory, University College, London

Grounds for thinking that the model described in the previous paper can be used to support general biological principles of social evolution are briefly discussed.

Two principles are presented, the first concerning the evolution of social behaviour in general and the second the evolution of social discrimination. Some tentative evidence is given.

More general application of the theory in biology is then discussed, particular attention being given to cases where the indicated interpretation differs from previous views and to cases which appear anomalous. A hypothesis is outlined concerning social evolution in the Hymenoptera; but the evidence that at present exists is found somewhat contrary on certain points. Other subjects considered include warning behaviour, the evolution of distasteful properties in insects, clones of cells and clones of zooids as contrasted with other types of colonies, the confinement of parental care to true offspring in birds and insects, fights, the behaviour of parasitoid insect larvae within a host, parental care in connection with monogyny and monandry and multi-ovulate ovaries in plants in connection with wind and insect pollination.

1 INTRODUCTION

In the previous paper (Hamilton, 1964) a genetical mathematical model was used to deduce a principle concerning the evolution of social behaviour which, if true generally, may be of considerable importance in biology. It has now to be considered whether there is any logical justification for the extension of this principle beyond the model case of non-overlapping generations, and, if so, whether there is evidence that it does work effectively in nature.

In brief outline, the theory points out that for a gene to receive positive selection it is not necessarily enough that it should increase the fitness of its bearer above the average if this tends to be done at the heavy expense of related individuals, because relatives, on account of their common ancestry, tend to carry replicas of the same gene; and conversely that a gene may receive positive selection even though disad-

The work presented in these two papers was carried out during tenure of a Leverhulme Research Studentship at the London School of Economics and a Medical Research Council Scholarship.

The author has to thank Mr. J. Hajnal and Dr. C. A. B. Smith for much helpful discussion and advice concerning the analytical parts, and also Professor O. W. Richards for reading the first draft of Part II. It is also a pleasure to thank Professor W. E. Kerr for his helpful comments on the present version of Part II and for the kind hospitality of his laboratory in Brazil.

vantageous to its bearers if it causes them to confer sufficiently large advantages on relatives. Relationship alone never gives grounds for *certainty* that a person carries a gene which a relative is known to carry except when the relationship is "clonal" or "mitotic" (e.g. the two are monozygotic twins)—and even then, strictly, the possibility of an intervening mutation should be admitted. In general, it has been shown that Wright's Coefficient of Relationship r approximates closely to the chance that a replica will be carried. Thus if an altruistic trait is in question more than $1/r$ units of reproductive potential or "fitness" must be endowed on a relative of degree r for every one unit lost by the altruist if the population is to gain on average more replicas than it loses. Similarly, if a selfish trait is in question, the individual must receive and use at least a fraction r of the quantity of "fitness" deprived from his relative if the causative gene is to be selected.

For a more critical explanation of these ideas and of the important concept of "inclusive fitness", which will be freely referred to in what follows, the reader is referred to the previous paper.

2 THE GROUNDS FOR GENERALIZATION

It is clear that in outline this type of argument is not restricted to the case of non-overlapping generations nor to the state of panmixia on which we have been able to base a fairly precise analysis. The idea of the regression, or "probabilistic dilution", of "identical" genes in relatives further and further removed applies to all organisms performing sexual reproduction, whether or not their generations overlap and whether or not the relatives considered belong to the same generations.

However perhaps we should not feel entirely confident about generalizing our principle until a more comprehensive mathematical argument, with inclusive fitness more widely defined, has been worked out. But even from this point of view there does seem to be good reason for thinking that it can be generalized—reason about as good, at least, as that which is supposed to give foundation to certain principles of the classical theory.

Roughly speaking the classical mathematical theory has developed two parallel branches which lie to either side of the great range of reproductive schedules which organisms actually do manifest. One is applicable to once-and-for-all reproduction (e.g. Kingman, 1961); and this form is actually exhibited by many organisms, notably those with annual life-cycles. The other is applicable to "continuous" reproduction (e.g. Kimura, 1958). This involves a type of reproductive process which is strictly impossible for any organism to practice, but which for analytic purposes should be approximated quite closely by certain species, for example, some perennial plants. Our model is a generalization in the former branch and there seems little reason to doubt that it can be matched by a similar model in the latter.

Even in the classical theory itself difficulties still face generalization between the two branches, and yet their continuance does not seem to cause much worry. For instance there does not seem to be any comprehensive definition of fitness. And, perhaps in consequence of this lack, it rather appears that Fisher's Fundamental Theorem of Natural Selection has yet to be put in a form which is really as general as Fisher's original statement purports to be (Fisher, 1930, p. 37, see points raised by Moran, 1962, pp. 60, 66). On the other hand, the clarity of Fisher's statement must surely, for general usefulness, have far out-weighed its defects in rigour.

3 VALUATION OF THE WELFARE OF RELATIVES

Altogether then it would seem that generalization would not be too foolhardy. In the hope that it may provide a useful summary we therefore hazard the following generalized unrigorous statement of the main principle that has emerged from the model.

> The social behavior of a species evolves in such a way that in each distinct behaviour-evoking situation the individual will seem to value his neighbours' fitness against his own according to the coefficients of relationship appropriate to that situation.

The aspect of this principle which concerns altruism seems to have been realized by Haldane (1955) as is shown in some comments on whether a genetical trait causing a person to risk his life to save a drowning child could evolve or not. His argument, though not entirely explicit and apparently restricted to rare genes, is essentially the same as that which we have outlined for altruism in the Introduction.

Haldane does not discuss the question which his remarks raise of whether a gene lost in an adult is worth more or less than a gene lost in a child. However, this touches an aspect of the biological accounting of risks which together with the whole problem of the altruism involved in parental care is best reserved for separate discussion.

The principle was also foreshadowed much earlier in Fisher's (1930, p. 177 *et seq.*) discussion of the evolution of distastefulness in insects. That this phenomenon presents a difficulty, namely an apparent absence of positive selection, is obvious as soon as we reject the pseudo-explanations based on the "benefit to the species", and the problem is of considerable importance as distastefulness, construed in a wide sense, is the basis not only of warning coloration but of both Batesian and Mullerian mimicry. The difficulty of explaining the evolution of warning coloration itself is perhaps even more acute here; *a priori* we would expect that at every stage it would be the new ultra-conspicuous mutants that suffered the first attacks of inexperienced predators. Fisher suggested a benefit to the nearby siblings of the distasteful, or distasteful and conspicuous insect, and gave some suggestive evidence that these characters are correlated with gregariousness of the larvae. He remarked that, "the selective potency of the avoidance of brothers will of course be only half as great as if the individual itself were protected; against this is to be set the fact that it applies to the whole of a possibly numerous brood." He doubtlessly realized that further selective benefit would occur through more distant relatives but probably considered it negligible. He realized the logical affinity of this problem with that of the evolution of altruistic behaviour, and he invokes the same kind of selection in his attempt to explain the evolution of the heroic ideal in barbaric human societies.

Another attempt to elucidate the genetical natural selection of altruistic behaviour occurring within a sibship was published by Williams & Williams in 1957. Although their conclusions are doubtlessly correct the particular form of analysis they adopted seems to have failed to bring out the crucial role of the two-fold factor in this case.

A predator would have to taste the distasteful insect before it could learn to avoid the nearby relatives. Thus despite the toughness and resilience which is supposed to characterize such insects (qualities which the classical selectionists may have been tempted to exaggerate), the common detriment to the "altruist" must be high and the ratio of gain to loss (k) correspondingly low. The risks involved in giving a warning signal, as between birds, must be much less so that in this case, as indicated in the previous paper, it is more credible that the condition

$$k > \frac{1}{r}$$

is fulfilled even when cases of the parents warning their young and the young each other up to the time of their dispersal are left out of account. The average relationship within a rabbit-warren is probably quite sufficient to account for their "thumping" habit (for relevant observations see Thompson & Worden, 1956, pp. 104, 217). Ringing experiments on birds indicate that even adult territorial neighbours must often be much closer relatives than their powers of flight would lead us to expect (e.g. Lack, 1953, pp. 114–16); a fact that may be of significance for the interpretation of the wider comity of bird behaviour.

The phenomena of mutual preening and grooming may be explained similarly. The mild effort required must stand for a diminution of fitness quite minute compared to the advantage of being cleansed and cleared of ectoparasites on parts of the body which the individual cannot deal with himself. Thus the degree of relationship within the flocks of birds, troupes of monkeys and so on where such mutual help occurs need not be very high before the condition for an advantage to inclusive fitness is fulfilled; and for grooming within actual families, of monkeys for instance, it is quite obviously fulfilled.

An animal whose reproduction is definitely finished cannot cause any further self-effects. Except for the continuing or pleiotropic effects of genes which are established through an advantage conferred earlier in the life-history, the behaviour of a post-reproductive animal may be expected to be entirely altruistic, the smallest degree of relationship with the average neighbour being sufficient to favour the selection of a giving trait. Blest (1963) has recently shown that the post-reproductive behaviour of certain saturnid moths is indeed adaptive in this way. His argument may be summarized in the present terminology as follows. With a species using cryptic resemblance for its protection the very existence of neighbours involves a danger to the individual since the discovery of one by a predator will be a step in teaching it to recognize the crypsis. With an aposematic species on the other hand, the existence of neighbours is an asset since they may well serve to teach an inexperienced predator the warning pattern. Thus with the cryptic moth it is altruistic to die immediately after reproduction, whereas with the warningly-coloured moth it is altruistic to continue to live at least through the period during which other moths may not have finished mating and egg-laying. Blest finds that the post-reproductive life-spans of the moths he studied are modified in the expected manner, and that the cryptic species even show behaviour which might be interpreted as an attempt to destroy their cryptic pattern and to use up in random flight activity the remainder of their vital reserves. The selective forces operating on the post-reproductive life-span are doubtless generally weak; they will be strongest when the average relationship of neighbours is highest, which will be in the most viscous populations. It would be interesting to know how behaviour affecting gene-dispersion correlates with the degree of the effects which Blest has observed.

4 DISCRIMINATION IN SOCIAL SITUATIONS

Special case (b) of the previous paper has shown explicitly that a certain social action cannot in itself be described as harmful or beneficial to inclusive fitness; this depends on the relationship of the affected individuals. The selective advantage of genes which make behaviour conditional in the right sense on the discrimination of factors which correlate with the relationship of the individual concerned is therefore obvious. It may be for instance, that in respect of a certain social action performed towards neighbours indiscriminately, an individual is only just breaking even in terms of inclusive fitness. If he could learn to recognize those of his neighbours who really were close relatives and could devote his beneficial actions to them alone an advantage to inclusive fitness would at once appear. Thus a mutation causing such discriminatory behaviour itself benefits inclusive fitness and would be selected. In fact, the individual may not need to perform any discrimination so sophisticated as we suggest here; a difference in the generosity of his behaviour according to whether the situations evoking it were encountered near to, or far from, his own home might occasion an advantage of a similar kind.

Although this type of advantage is itself restricted to social situations, it can be compared to the general advantage associated with making responses conditional on the factors which are the most reliable indicators of future events, an advantage which must for instance have been the basis for the evolution of the seed's ability to germinate only when conditions (warmth, moisture, previous freezing, etc.) give real promise for the future survival and growth of the seedling.

Whether the trend implied could ever spread very far may be doubted. All kinds of evolutionary changes in behaviour, especially those subject to the powerful forces of individual advantage, are liable to disrupt any *ad hoc* system of discrimination.

This is most true, however, for discrimination in the range of distant relationships where the potential gains are least. The selective advantage when a benefit comes to be given to sibs only instead of to sibs and half-sibs indifferently is more than four times the advantage when a benefit of the same magnitude is given to cousins only instead of to cousins and half-cousins indifferently.

Nevertheless, if any correlate of relationship is very persistent, long-continued weak selection could lead to the evolution of a discrimination based on it even in the range of distant relationships. One possible factor of this kind in species with viscous populations, and one whose persistence depends only on the viscosity and therefore may well be considerably older than the species in question, is familiarity of appearance. For in a viscous population the organisms of a particular neighbourhood, being relatives, must tend to look alike and an individual which used the restrained symbolic forms of aggressive behaviour only towards familiar-looking rivals would be effecting a discrimination advantageous to inclusive fitness.

In accordance with the hypothesis that such discriminations exist it should turn out that in a species of resident bird, strongly territorial and minimally vagrant, the conflicts which proved least readily resolved by ritual behaviour and in which consequent fighting was fiercest were between the rivals that had the most noticeable differences in plumage and song. Whether much evidence of this nature exists I do not know. The rather uncommon cases of interspecific territory systems in birds, as recently reviewed by Wynne-Edwards (1962, p. 391), seem to be contrary. If differences between interspecific and conspecific encounters were noticed by the original observers they are not mentioned by Wynne-Edwards; and in any case, the very existence of these situations, taken at face value and assumed to be stable and of long standing, is as contrary to the present theory as it is to Gause's principle. Likewise, the positive indications I can bring forward are rather few and feeble. Tinbergen (1953, p. 49) has observed a hostile reaction by Herring Gulls towards members of their colony forced to behave abnormally (caught in a net) and states that a similar phenomenon is sometimes observed with other social species. Personal observations on colonies of the wasps *Polistes canadensis* and *P. versicolor* have shown a very strong hostility when a wasp taken off a nest, is returned to it in a wet and bedraggled condition. This type of reaction after a member of the colony has been much handled seems to be quite common in the social insects. It is perhaps specifically aroused by certain acquired odours, or these combined with the odour of venom. That bird-ringers, who would surely have noticed any social stigma that fell upon birds carrying their often very conspicuous rings, usually report that the rings were no apparent inconvenience to the birds is a counter-indication whose force is slightly reduced by the fact that in passerines and most other common birds the legs are unimportant in social communication. It is similarly fortunate for the insect ethologist that spots of fresh oil-paint by themselves on bees and wasps seem to provoke very little reaction. Butterflies of the family *Lycaenidae,* especially males, are often to be seen jostling one another in the air, sometimes in groups of more than two. The function of this behaviour is obscure; the species do not seem to be at all strongly territorial. According to Ford (1945, p. 256) lepidopterists find that a bunch of jostling butterflies is rather apt to contain an unusual variety.

With the higher animals we may perhaps appeal to evidence of discrimination based on familiarity of a more intimate kind. Animals capable of forming a social hierarchy presumably have some ability to recognize one another as individuals, and with this present it is not necessary for the discrimination to be on the basis of "racialistic" differences of appearance, voice or smell. An individual might look extremely like certain members of a group and lie within the group's range of variation in every one of his perceptible characters and yet still be known for a stranger. Speaking from a wide knowledge of just such social animals Wynne-Edwards (1962, p. 136) refers to "the widespread practice of attacking and persecuting strangers and relegating newcomers to the lowest social rank" and gives several references. The antagonistic nature of this discrimination is of course just what we expect.

As might be expected the evidence in the cases of closest relationship is much more impressive. Tinbergen (1953, p. 224 *et seq.*) investigated the ability of Herring Gulls to recognize their own chicks by observing the reaction to strange chicks placed amongst them. He found that during the first two or three days after hatching strange chicks are accepted, but by the end of the first week they are driven away. Herring Gulls will sometimes form the habit of feeding on the live chicks as well as on the eggs in their own breeding colony when they can catch them unattended, but Tinbergen records no case where an intruded chick was killed although this probably sometimes happens; the hostile behaviour he observed was half-hearted at first but became more definite as the age of the gull's own brood advanced. During the days which follow hatching, the chicks become progressively more mobile and the chance that they will wander into neighbouring nest-territories must increase. Therefore it seems a reasonable hypothesis that the ability to discriminate "own young" advances in step with the chance that without such discrimination strange chicks would be fostered and the benefits of parental care wasted on unrelated genes. Supporting this hypothesis are the findings quoted by Tinbergen (p. 228) of Watson and Lashley on two tropical species of tern: "The Noddies nesting in trees do not recognize their young at any age, whereas the ground-nesting Sooties are very similar to Herring Gulls in that they learn to recognize their own young in the course of four days." House Sparrows will accept strange young of the right age placed in the nest but after the nestlings have flown "they will not, in normal circumstances, feed any but their own young." (Summers-Smith, 1963, p. 50). Not all observations are as satisfactory for the theory as these however; we may mention the positive passion for fostering said to be shown by Emperor Penguins that have lost their own chick (Prevost, 1962). This and some other similar anomalies will be briefly discussed in the last section.

Tinbergen showed that Herring Gulls discriminate eggs even less than chicks, the crudest egg-substitutes being sufficient to release brooding behaviour providing certain attributes of shape and colour are present. This is what we would expect in view of the fact that eggs do not stray at all. It is in striking contrast with the degree of egg-discrimination which is shown by species of birds subject to cuckoo parasitism.

The theoretical principle which these observations seem largely to support is supplementary to the previous principle and we may summarize it in a similar statement.

The situations which a species discriminates in its social behaviour tend to evolve and multiply in such a way that the coefficients of relationship involved in each situation become more nearly determinate.

In situations where relationship is not variable, as for example between the nestlings in an arboreal nest, there still remains a discrimination which, if it could be made could greatly benefit inclusive fitness. This is the discrimination of those individuals which do carry one or both of the behaviour-causing genes from those which do not. Such an ability lies outside the conditions postulated in the previous paper but the extended meaning of inclusive fitness is obvious enough. That genes could cause the perception of the presence of like genes in other individuals may sound improbable; at simplest we need to postulate something like a supergene affecting (a) some perceptible feature of the organism, (b) the perception of that feature, and (c) the social response consequent upon what was perceived. However, exactly the same *a priori* objections might be made to the evolution of assortative mating which manifestly has evolved, probably many times independently and despite its obscure advantages.

If some sort of attraction between likes for purposes of co-operation can occur the limits to the evolution of altruism expressed by our first principle would be very greatly extended, although it should still never happen that one individual would value another more highly than itself, fitness for fitness. And if an individual can be attracted towards likes when it has positive effects—benefits—to dispense, it can presumably be attracted the other way, towards unlikes, when it has negative effects to dispense (i.e. when circumstances arise which demand combat, suggest robbery, and so on).

REFERENCES

Blest, A. D. (1963). *Nature,* **197,** 1183.
Fisher, R. A. (1930). "The Genetical Theory of Natural Selection". New York: Dover (1958).
Ford, E. B. (1945). "Butterflies". London: Collins.
Haldane, J. B. S. (1955). *New Biol.* **18,** 34.
Hamilton, W. D. (1964). *J. Theoret. Biol.* 7, 1.
Kimura, M. (1958). *Heredity,* **12,** 145.
Kingman, J. F. C. (1961). *Proc. Camb. phil. Soc.* **57,** 574.
Lack, D. (1953). "The Life of the Robin". Pelican.

Moran, P. A. P. (1962). "The Statistical Processes of Evolutionary Theory". Oxford: Claren-
    don Press.
Prevost, J. (1962). *New Scient.* **16,** 444.
Summers-Smith, D. (1963). "The House Sparrow". London: Collins.
Taber, S. & Wendel, J. (1958). *J. econ. Ent.* **51,** 786.
Thompson, H. V. & Worden, A. N. (1956). "The Rabbit". London: Collins.
Tinbergen, N. (1953). "The Herring Gull's World". London: Collins.

Group Selection and Kin Selection

J. Maynard Smith
Department of Zoology, University College, London

Wynne-Edwards [1,2] has argued persuasively for the importance of behaviour in regulating the density of animal populations, and has suggested that since such behaviour favours the survival of the group and not of the individual it must have evolved by a process of group selection. It is the purpose of this communication to consider how far this is likely to be true.

The strongest arguments for believing that conventional behaviour is the immediate cause regulating population density concern cases of territorial behaviour, particularly in birds. But it does not follow that such behaviour has evolved by group selection, because territorial behaviour capable of adjusting the population density to the available food supply could evolve by selection acting at the level of the individual rather than of the group. The appropriate degree of aggression would evolve if: (1) individuals which are too aggressive raise fewer offspring, either because they suffer physical damage or because they waste in display time and energy which should be spent in raising their young; (2) individuals which are too timid either fail to establish a territory or establish one too small to contain an adequate food supply for the young. Further, the degree of 'choosiness'—that is, the readiness to fight for a territory in one kind of area rather than put up with one in a less favourable area —will evolve by individual selection in such a way as to lead to an efficient distribution in space. This will happen because if, on one hand, individuals are too 'choosy', territories in the favoured areas will become too small in relation to the food supply, so that less choosy individuals breeding in the less favoured but more sparsely inhabited areas will leave more offspring, whereas if individuals are too little choosy, selection will act in the reverse direction.

Thus there is no need to invoke group selection to explain the evolution of individual breeding territories, or the adjustment of territory size to food supply or to variations in the habitat. But there are other characteristics of animals which are more difficult to explain by individual selection; sex is an obvious and important example, but difficulties also arise in explaining the evolution of 'altruistic' characters, such as alarm notes or injury-feigning in birds.

It is possible to distinguish two rather different processes, both of which could cause the evolution of characteristics which favour the survival, not of the individual, but of other members of the species. These processes I will call kin selection and group selection, respectively. Kin selection has been discussed by Haldane[3] and by Hamilton[4].

By kin selection I mean the evolution of characteristics which favour the survival of close relatives of the affected individual, by processes which do not

From *Nature 201:* 1145–46. Reprinted by permission of Macmillan Journals Limited.

require any discontinuities in population breeding structure. In this sense, the evolution of placentæ and of parental care (including 'self-sacrificing' behaviour such as injury-feigning) are due to kin selection, the favoured relatives being the children of the affected individual. But kin selection can also be effective by favouring the siblings of the affected individuals (for example, sterility in social insects, inviability of cotton hybrids due to the 'corky' syndrome[5]) and presumably by favouring more distant relatives. There will be more opportunities for kin selection to be effective if relatives live together in family groups, particularly if the population is divided into partially isolated groups. But such partial isolation is not essential. In kin selection, improbable events are involved only to the extent that they are in all evolutionary change—in the origin of genetic differences by mutation.

If groups of relatives stay together, wholly or partially isolated from other members of the species, then the process of group selection can occur. If all members of a group acquire some characteristic which, although individually disadvantageous, increases the fitness of the group, then that group is more likely to split into two, and in this way bring about an increase in the proportion of individuals in the whole population with the characteristic in question. The unit on which selection is operating is the group and not the individual. The only difficulty is to explain how it comes about that all members of a group come to have the characteristic in the first place. If genetically determined, it presumably arose in a single individual. It cannot be pictured as spreading to all members of a group by natural selection, because if it could do that, it could equally well spread in a large population—either by individual selection or kin selection—and there is no need to invoke a special mechanism of group selection to explain it. Hence the only way in which such a characteristic could spread to all members of a group would be by genetic drift. (There is also the possibility that it might spread through a group by cultural transmission, but this is unlikely to be important in animals other than man.) If this were to happen at all often, then the groups must be small (or else commonly re-established by single fertilized females or single pairs), the disadvantage of the characteristic to the individual slight, and the gene flow between groups small, because every time a group possessing the socially desirable characteristic is 'infected' by a gene for anti-social behaviour, that gene is likely to spread through the group. These conditions are severe, although they may sometimes be satisfied.

The distinction between kin selection and group selection as here defined is that for kin selection the division of the population into partially isolated breeding groups is a favourable but not an essential condition, whereas it is an essential condition for group selection, which depends on the spread of a characteristic to all members of a group by genetic drift.

Wynne-Edwards[2] points out that birds may return after migration to the precise spot where they were raised, and argues that this would favour the operation of group selection. This is not so. What is required for group selection is that the species should be divided into a large number of local populations, within which there is free interbreeding, but between which there is little gene flow. The mere fact that many birds breed near where they were born does not bring about this situation; it would favour the operation of kin selection, but it is difficult to see how kin selection could bring about the evolution of many of the types of population-regulating behaviour which Wynne-Edwards believes he has discovered.

Wynne-Edwards also argues that the behavioural mechanisms he hypothesizes would be proof against the occurrence by mutation and subsequent spread of anti-social behaviour patterns because of genetic homœostasis. This is a piece of special pleading: it also shows a misunderstanding of the situations in which homœostasis of this kind is to be expected. Both genetical theory and the experimental evidence suggest that if natural selection has been pushing a character in a given direction for a long time, it will be difficult for selection to produce further change in the same direction, but comparatively easy to produce a change in the reverse direction. Thus it would only be plausible to suggest that there are genetic reasons why anti-social behaviour should not increase if it were also suggested that selection had already produced an extreme degree of anti-social behaviour, and this is precisely what Wynne-Edwards denies. In fact, 'anti-social' mutations will occur, and any plausible model of group selection must explain why they do not spread.

There is one special form of group selection which is worth considering in more detail, because it can, perhaps, explain the evolution of 'self-sterilizing' behaviour; that is, behaviour which leads an individual not to breed in circumstances in which other members of the species are breeding successfully. (This is quite different from behaviour which leads individuals not to breed when other members of the species are attempting unsuccessfully to breed, or to produce fewer offspring when conditions are such that they would be unable to raise a larger number; such behaviour, although of great interest, presents no special difficulty to a selectionist.) The difficulty is that if the difference between breeders and non-breeders is genetically determined, then it is the breeders whose genotype is perpetuated.

A possible explanation is that what is inherited is the level of responsiveness to the presence of other breeding individuals. Thus suppose that there are aggressive A individuals which continue to breed or to attempt to breed at high densities, and timid a individuals, which are discouraged from breeding when the density of breeding individuals reaches a certain level, the difference between A and a being genetically determined. In a mixed group of A and a individuals, if the density is high, only A will breed, and a will be lost from the group. In a group of A individuals at high density all will attempt to breed, with the consequence that the food supply may be exhausted and the group produce few progeny. In a group consisting entirely of a individuals, at high densities some will breed and some will not, the difference between breeding and non-breeding individuals being due to age, to previous environmental history, or even to chance. Consequently, an a group is less likely to outstrip its food supply, and so will leave more progeny. The difference between A and a groups at high densities is an example of the difference between a scramble (A) and a contest (a) (ref. 6).

Given such a behavioural difference, the following conditions seem necessary if a is to increase under natural selection:

1 Groups must for a time be reproductively isolated, because a is eliminated from mixed groups.

2 Groups must be started by one or a few founders, since otherwise groups consisting entirely of a individuals would never come into existence.

3 When a group of A individuals outstrips its food supply, it must not immediately encroach on the food supply of neighbouring a groups, for if it did so, the advantage of a groups would disappear. This is a difficult condition to meet, and appears to rule out this mechanism in cases in which the population is divided into herds, flocks, troops or colonies, each group having a joint feeding territory which borders that of neighbouring groups. The condition is most likely to be met when the food supply is discontinuous in space, each patch of food supporting its own group.

A greatly oversimplified model of this type of selection will now be given. To fix ideas, suppose that there exists a species of mouse which lives entirely in haystacks. A single haystack is colonized by a single fertilized female, whose offspring form a colony which lives in the haystack until next year, when new haystacks are available for colonization. At this time, mice migrate, and may mate with members of other colonies before establishing a new colony. The population consists of aggressive A and timid a individuals, timidity being due to a single Mendelian recessive; a/a are timid, and A/a and A/A aggressive.

Only when a colony is started by an a/a female fertilized by an a/a male will it consist finally of a individuals; all other colonies will lose the a gene by selection, and come to consist entirely of A individuals. Thus at the time when colonies are about to break up, there are only two kinds of colony, A and a. It is assumed that an a colony contributes $1 + K$ times as many mice to the migrating population as does an A colony, and has a proportionately greater chance of having a daughter colony.

In one summer, let the frequency of a colonies be P_0. Then, in the migrating population, the proportion of a/a individuals is:

$$\frac{P_0(1+K)}{P_0(1+K)+1-P_0} = \frac{P_0(1+K)}{1+KP_0} = p \text{ say}$$

It is assumed that a proportion r of all migrating female mice mate with males from their own colony, the remaining $(1-r)$ mating at random. Hence the frequency of $a/a \times a/a$ mating as a fraction of all matings is

$$rp + (1-r)p^2 = P_1$$

where P_1 is the frequency of a colonies in the next summer.

Hence the condition for the evolutionary spread of 'timid' behaviour—that is, of the a gene—is:

$$rp + (1-r)p^2 > P_0 \quad \text{where} \quad p = \frac{P_0(1+K)}{1+KP_0}$$

This reduces to

$$r(1 + K) - (1 - P_0 K^2) > 0$$

Thus when P_0 is large ($P_0 \simeq 1$),

$$r + K > 1$$

and when P_0 is small ($P_0 \simeq 0$),

$$r(1 + K) > 1$$

Thus, if there is little or no interbreeding between colonies even at migration ($r \simeq 1$), timid behaviour will evolve provided it is an advantage to the group; this corresponds to the case in which the population is divided into more or less permanently isolated groups, which are periodically reduced to very small numbers, and which may either become extinct or split to give rise to two groups. However, the conclusion that timid or altruisitic behaviour can readily evolve if there is no interbreeding between groups means little, since it is unlikely that species are often divided into a large number of small and completely isolated groups.

If there is fairly free interbreeding between colonies at regular intervals (that is, if r is small), selection could maintain the gene for timidity once it had become the common allele in the population. For example, if there were random mating, $r = 0$, between members of different colonies at the time of migration, then selection could maintain a as the common allele if a colonies had a twofold advantage. But, with random mating, selection could not cause a to increase if it were initially rare: if $r = 0$, the condition $r(1 + K) > 1$ cannot be satisfied.

With an intermediate amount of gene flow between colonies, selection could both establish and maintain timid or altruistic behaviour, provided that colonies with altruistic behaviour have a large selective advantage and that colonies are founded by very few individuals.

The model is too artificial to be worth pursuing further. It is concluded that if the admittedly severe conditions listed here are satisfied, then it is possible that behaviour patterns should evolve leading individuals not to reproduce at times and in circumstances in which other members of the species are reproducing successfully. Whether this is regarded as an argument for or against the evolution of altruistic behaviour by group selection will depend on a judgment of how often the necessary conditions are likely to be satisfied.

REFERENCES

1 Wynne-Edwards, V. C., *Animal Dispersion in Relation to Social Behaviour* (Oliver and Boyd, Edinburgh and London, 1962).
2 Wynne-Edwards, V. C., *Nature,* **200,** 623 (1963).
3 Haldane, J. B. S., *New Biology,* **18,** 34 (1955).
4 Hamilton, W. D., *Amer. Nat.,* **97,** 354 (1963).
5 Stephens, S. G., *J. Genet.,* **50,** 9 (1950).
6 Nicholson, A. J., *Austral. J. Zool.,* **2,** 9 (1955).

Kin Selection and Reproductive Value

Manfred Milinski
Workforce for Behavior Research, Division of Biology, Ruhr
University, Bochem

Kin selection theory, foreshadowed by Fisher (1930) and elaborated by Hamilton (1964), explains altruistic behaviour towards relatives as selfish, since the altruist promotes the propagation of his own genes through his relatives. For example, an altruist maximises his own fitness when sacrificing his life if, by doing so, the lives of more than two of his full siblings are saved, each of them sharing, on the average, half his genes. Altruism should increase with the degree of relatedness of the aided kin. Thus, a brother can be expected to be helped twice as often as an uncle. These ideas are widely accepted today and are employed to account for such phenomena as the sterility of worker bees.

There is, however, a complication concerning the age of the recipient and that of the altruist, as was pointed out by Emlen (1970) and by Dawkins (1976). Namely, it is quite possible that the net benefit of aiding a young although distant relative exceeds the net benefit of assisting an older, even more closely related one, since the latter may have much less chance of producing offspring. Hence, the altruist must concern himself not only with the degree of relatedness, but also with the probability of the recipient's producing offspring.

The likelihood that an individual of a given age is expected to contribute to future generations was termed "reproductive value" by Fisher (1930). This value normally has its maximum at the onset of the individual's reproductive phase, since at that time the number of his expected offspring is greatest. For the remainder of his ontogeny the reproductive value decreases until it reaches zero at the end of the reproductive phase. At birth it is less than the maximum value due to potential intervening mortality prior to reproductive age. Several examples for the relationship between reproductive value and age are given by Pianka (1974).

Hence the degree of altruism should reflect the receiver's reproductive value with the degree of relatedness being constant. More generally, the extent of altruism should be a function of the product of the receiver's reproductive value and his degree of relatedness to the altruist; this product could be influenced by changing risks, in terms of his physical capabilities, for the altruist during ontogeny. Note that altruism should cease altogether, if only one of the two factors becomes zero.

The degree of altruism is also dependent upon the reproductive value of the *altruist.* Natural selection measures the costs of an altruistic act in terms of the risk

I am indebted to Prof. Dr. E. Curio for criticism and for encouraging me to publish my ideas. I thank Dr. M. Shalter also for criticism and for his kind improvement of my English.

From *Zeitschrift fur Tierpsychologie 47:* 328–29. Reprinted by permission of the author and Verlag Paul Parey.

to the altruist's own offspring. Hence, the costs depend on the number of the altruist's own expected offspring, i.e. his own reproductive value. Thus, the degree of altruism should also reflect the altruist's own reproductive value. He should be minimally altruistic when his reproductive value is at peak, whereas he should be maximally altruistic when his reproductive value approaches zero, i.e. at the end of his reproductive phase. There should be a second although less than maximal peak of altruism in early infancy long before the start of the reproductive phase, assuming that the ability to perform an altruistic act is present.

There is a third influence of the reproductive value on the extent of altruism towards relatives: The costs of altruism depend on the absolute number of one's own expected offspring, i.e. the *absolute* reproductive value. A ♂ that is going to found a harem has a greater reproductive value than each of his ♀♀. The same altruistic act is more costly for him than for any of his ♀♀, all other things being equal. Thus, a ♀ should be more inclined than the ♂ to aid a relative. In a recent paper, Sherman (1977) showed for female ground squirrels, *Spermophilus beldingi,* that the probability of uttering alarm calls depends on the number of related ♀♀ inhabiting adjacent burrows. Mature ♂♂ very seldom emit alarm calls; they leave their native colony when adult and, hence, do not encounter relatives in their new colony. Sherman explained this behaviour in terms of kin selection. One phenomenon he did not explain, however, is why young ♂♂ voice fewer alarm calls than their sisters, even though both are surrounded by the *same* number of close relatives. This can be explained, I think, by the different subjective reproductive values of the sexes: A young ♂ who is a potential "pasha" risks more potential offspring than does a young ♀ in giving an alarm call. A young ♂ who is not quite sure of his prospect to found a harem in later years does best in behaving like a potential pasha. It may be that the few observed young ♂♂ that did call were the weakest, and thus had the lowest reproductive values.

It might well be that reproductive value has an even greater influence on the propensity for altruism to occur than merely the degree of relatedness.

LITERATURE CITED

Dawkins, R. (1976): The selfish gene. Oxford Univ. Press.
Emlen, J. M. (1970): Age specifity and ecological theory. Ecology 51, 588–601.
Fisher, R. A. (1930): The genetical theory of natural selection. Clarendon Press, Oxford.
Hamilton, W. D. (1964): The genetical theory of social behaviour. J. theor. Biol. 7, 1–53.
Pianka, E. R. (1974): Evolutionary ecology. Harper and Row, New York.
Sherman, P. W. (1977): Nepotism and the evolution of alarm calls. Science 197, 1246–1253.

The Evolution of Reciprocal Altruism

Robert L. Trivers
Biological Laboratories, Harvard University

A model is presented to account for the natural selection of what is termed reciprocally altruistic behavior. The model shows how selection can operate against the cheater (non-reciprocator) in the system. Three instances of altruistic behavior are discussed, the evolution of which the model can explain: (1) behavior involved in cleaning symbioses; (2) warning cries in birds; and (3) human reciprocal altruism.

Regarding human reciprocal altruism, it is shown that the details of the psychological system that regulates this altruism can be explained by the model. Specifically, friendship, dislike, moralistic aggression, gratitude, sympathy, trust, suspicion, trustworthiness, aspects of guilt, and some forms of dishonesty and hypocrisy can be explained as important adaptations to regulate the altruistic system. Each individual human is seen as possessing altruistic and cheating tendencies, the expression of which is sensitive to developmental variables that were selected to set the tendencies at a balance appropriate to the local social and ecological environment.

INTRODUCTION

Altruistic behavior can be defined as behavior that benefits another organism, not closely related, while being apparently detrimental to the organism performing the behavior, benefit and detriment being defined in terms of contribution to inclusive fitness. One human being leaping into water, at some danger to himself, to save another distantly related human from drowning may be said to display altruistic behavior. If he were to leap in to save his own child, the behavior would not necessarily be an instance of "altruism"; he may merely be contributing to the survival of his own genes invested in the child.

Models that attempt to explain altruistic behavior in terms of natural selection are models designed to take the altruism out of altruism. For example, Hamilton (1964) has demonstrated that degree of relationship is an important parameter in predicting how selection will operate, and behavior which appears altruistic may, on knowledge of the genetic relationships of the organisms involved, be explicable in terms of natural selection: those genes being selected for that contribute to their own perpetuation, regardless of which individual the genes appear in. The term "kin

I thank W. H. Drury, E. Mayr, I. Nisbet, E. E. Williams and E. O. Wilson for useful comments on earlier drafts of this paper, and I thank especially I. DeVore and W. D. Hamilton for detailed comment and discussion. I thank A. Rapoport and D. Krebs for access to unpublished material. This work was completed under a National Science Foundation pre-doctoral fellowship and partially supported by grant number NIMH 13156 to I. DeVore.

From *The Quarterly Review of Biology* 46:35–57. Reprinted by permission of the author and *The Quarterly Review of Biology*.

selection" will be used in this paper to cover instances of this type—that is, of organisms being selected to help their relatively close kin.

The model presented here is designed to show how certain classes of behavior conveniently denoted as "altruistic" (or "reciprocally altruistic") can be selected for even when the recipient is so distantly related to the organism performing the altruistic act that kin selection can be ruled out. The model will apply, for example, to altruistic behavior between members of different species. It will be argued that under certain conditions natural selection favors these altruistic behaviors because in the long run they benefit the organism performing them.

THE MODEL

One human being saving another, who is not closely related and is about to drown, is an instance of altruism. Assume that the chance of the drowning man dying is one-half if no one leaps in to save him, but that the chance that his potential rescuer will drown if he leaps in to save him is much smaller, say, one in twenty. Assume that the drowning man always drowns when his rescuer does and that he is always saved when the rescuer survives the rescue attempt. Also assume that the energy costs involved in rescuing are trivial compared to the survival probabilities. Were this an isolated event, it is clear that the rescuer should not bother to save the drowning man. But if the drowning man reciprocates at some future time, and if the survival chances are then exactly reversed, it will have been to the benefit of each participant to have risked his life for the other. Each participant will have traded a one-half chance of dying for about a one-tenth chance. If we assume that the entire population is sooner or later exposed to the same risk of drowning, the two individuals who risk their lives to save each other will be selected over those who face drowning on their own. Note that the benefits of reciprocity depend on the unequal cost/benefit ratio of the altruistic act, that is, the benefit of the altruistic act to the recipient is greater than the cost of the act to the performer, cost and benefit being defined here as the increase or decrease in chances of the relevant alleles propagating themselves in the population. Note also that, as defined, the benefits and costs depend on the age of the altruist and recipient (see *Age-dependent changes* below). (The odds assigned above may not be unrealistic if the drowning man is drowning because of a cramp or if the rescue can be executed by extending a branch from shore.)

Why should the rescued individual bother to reciprocate? Selection would seem to favor being saved from drowning without endangering oneself by reciprocating. Why not cheat? ("Cheating" is used throughout this paper solely for convenience to denote failure to reciprocate; no conscious intent or moral connotation is implied.) Selection will discriminate against the cheater if cheating has later adverse affects on his life which outweigh the benefit of not reciprocating. This may happen if the altruist responds to the cheating by curtailing all future possible altruistic gestures to this individual. Assuming that the benefits of these lost altruistic acts outweigh the costs involved in reciprocating, the cheater will be selected against relative to individuals who, because neither cheats, exchange many altruistic acts.

   This argument can be made precise. Assume there are both altruists and non-altruists in a population of size N and that the altruists are characterized by the fact that each performs altruistic acts when the cost to the altruist is well below the benefit to the recipient, where cost is defined as the degree to which the behavior retards the reproduction of the genes of the altruist and benefit is the degree to which the behavior increases the rate of reproduction of the genes of the recipient. Assume that the altruistic behavior of an altruist is controlled by an allele (dominant or recessive) a_2, at a given locus and that (for simplicity) there is only one alternative allele, a_1, at that locus and that it does not lead to altruistic behavior. Consider three possibilities: (1) the altruists dispense their altruism randomly throughout the population; (2) they dispense it nonrandomly by regarding their degree of genetic relationship with possible recipients; or (3) they dispense it nonrandomly by regarding the altruistic tendencies of possible recipients.

1   Random Dispensation of Altruism

There are three possible genotypes: a_1a_1, a_2a_1, and a_2a_2. Each allele of the heterozygote will be affected equally by whatever costs and benefits are associated with the altruism of such individuals (if a_2 is dominant) and by whatever benefits accrue to such individuals from the altruism of others, so they can be disregarded. If altruistic acts are being dispensed randomly throughout a large population, then the typical a_1a_1 individual benefits by $(1/N)\Sigma b_i$, where b_i is the benefit of the ith altruistic act performed by the altruist. The typical a_2a_2 individual has a net benefit of $(1/N)\Sigma b_i$ $-(1/N)\Sigma c_j$, where c_j is the cost to the a_2a_2 altruist of his jth altruistic act. Since $-(1/N)\Sigma c_j$ is always less than zero, allele a_1 will everywhere replace allele a_2.

2   Nonrandom Dispensation by Reference to Kin

This case has been treated in detail by Hamilton (1964), who concluded that if the tendency to dispense altruism to close kin is great enough, as a function of the disparity between the average cost and benefit of an altruistic act, then a_2 will replace a_1. Technically, all that is needed for Hamilton's form of selection to operate is that an individual with an "altruistic allele" be able to distinguish between individuals with and without this allele and discriminate accordingly. No formal analysis has been attempted of the possibilities for selection favoring individuals who increase their chances of receiving altruistic acts by appearing as if they were close kin of altruists, although selection has clearly sometimes favored such parasitism (e.g., Drury and Smith, 1968).

3   Nonrandom Dispensation by Reference to the Altruistic Tendencies of the Recipient

What is required is that the net benefit accruing to a typical a_2a_2 altruist exceed that accruing to an a_1a_1 non-altruist, or that

$$(1/p^2)(\Sigma b_k - \Sigma c_j) > (1/q^2)\Sigma b_m,$$

where b_k is the benefit to the $a_2 a_2$ altruist of the kth altruistic act performed toward him, where c_j is the cost of the jth altruistic act by the $a_2 a_2$ altruist, where b_m is the benefit of the mth altruistic act to the $a_1 a_1$ nonaltruist, and where p is the frequency in the population of the a_2 allele and q that of the a_1 allele. This will tend to occur if Σb_m is kept small (which will simultaneously reduce Σc_j). And this in turn will tend to occur if an altruist responds to a "nonaltruistic act" (that is, a failure to act altruistically toward the altruist in a situation in which so doing would cost the actor less than it would benefit the recipient) by curtailing future altruistic acts to the non-altruist.

Note that the above form of altruism does not depend on all altruistic acts being controlled by the same allele at the same locus. Each altruist could be motivated by a different allele at a different locus. All altruistic alleles would tend to be favored as long as, for each allele, the net average benefit to the homozygous altruist exceeded the average benefit to the homozygous nonaltruist; this would tend to be true if altruists restrict their altruism to fellow altruists, regardless of what allele motivates the other individual's altruism. The argument will therefore apply, unlike Hamilton's (1964), to altruistic acts exchanged between members of different species. It is the *exchange* that favors such altruism, not the fact that the allele in question sometimes or often directly benefits its duplicate in another organism.

If an "altruistic situation" is defined as any in which one individual can dispense a benefit to a second greater than the cost of the act to himself, then the chances of selecting for altruistic behavior, that is, of keeping $\Sigma c_j + \Sigma b_m$ small, are greatest (1) when there are many such altruistic situations in the lifetime of the altruists, (2) when a given altruist repeatedly interacts with the same small set of individuals, and (3) when pairs of altruists are exposed "symmetrically" to altruistic situations, that is, in such a way that the two are able to render roughly equivalent benefits to each other at roughly equivalent costs. These three conditions can be elaborated into a set of relevant biological parameters affecting the possibility that reciprocally altruistic behavior will be selected for.

1 *Length of lifetime.* Long lifetime of individuals of a species maximizes the chance that any two individuals will encounter many altruistic situations, and all other things being equal one should search for instances of reciprocal altruism in long-lived species.

2 *Dispersal rate.* Low dispersal rate during all or a significant portion of the lifetime of individuals of a species increases the chance that an individual will interact repeatedly with the same set of neighbors, and other things being equal one should search for instances of reciprocal altruism in such species. Mayr (1963) has discussed some of the factors that may affect dispersal rates.

3 *Degree of mutal dependence.* Interdependence of members of a species (to avoid predators, for example) will tend to keep individuals near each other and thus increase the chance they will encounter altruistic situations together. If the benefit of the mutual dependence is greatest when only a small number of individuals are together, this will greatly increase the chance that an individual will repeatedly interact with the same small set of individuals. Individuals in primate troops, for example, are mutually dependent for protection from predation, yet the optimal troop size for foraging is often small (Crook, 1969). Because they also meet the other conditions outlined here, primates are almost ideal species in which to search for reciprocal altruism. Cleaning symbioses provide an instance of mutual dependence between members of different species, and this mutual dependence appears to have set the stage for the evolution of several altruistic behaviors discussed below.

4 *Parental care.*   A special instance of mutual dependence is that found between parents and offspring in species that show parental care. The relationship is usually so asymmetrical that few or no situations arise in which an offspring is capable of performing an altruistic act for the parents or even for another offspring, but this is not entirely true for some species (such as primates) in which the period of parental care is unusually long. Parental care, of course, is to be explained by Hamilton's (1964) model, but there is no reason why selection for reciprocal altruism cannot operate between close kin, and evidence is presented below that such selection has operated in humans.

5 *Dominance hierarchy.*   Linear dominance hierarchies consist by definition of asymmetrical relationships; a given individual is dominant over another but not vice versa. Strong dominance hierarchies reduce the extent to which altruistic situations occur in which the less dominant individual is capable of performing a benefit for the more dominant which the more dominant individual could not simply take at will. Baboons (*Papio cynocephalus*) provide an illustration of this. Hall and DeVore (1965) have described the tendency for meat caught by an individual in the troop to end up by preemption in the hands of the most dominant males. This ability to preempt removes any selective advantage that food- sharing might otherwise have as a reciprocal gesture for the most dominant males, and there is no evidence in this species of any food-sharing tendencies. By contrast, Van Lawick-Goodall (1968) has shown that in the less dominance-oriented chimpanzees more dominant individuals often do not preempt food caught by the less dominant. Instead, they besiege the less dominant individual with "begging gestures," which result in the handing over of small portions of the catch. No strong evidence is available that this is part of a reciprocally altruistic system, but the absence of a strong linear dominance hierarchy has clearly facilitated such a possibility. It is very likely that early hominid groups had a dominance system more similar to that of the modern chimpanzee than to that of the modern baboon (see, for example, Reynolds, 1966).

6 *Aid in combat.*   No matter how dominance-oriented a species is, a dominant individual can usually be aided in aggressive encounters with other individuals by help from a less dominant individual. Hall and DeVore (1965) have described the tendency for baboon alliances to form which fight as a unit in aggressive encounters (and in encounters with predators). Similarly, vervet monkeys in aggressive encounters solicit the aid of other, often less dominant, individuals (Struhsaker, 1967). Aid in combat is then a special case in which relatively symmetrical relations are possible between individuals who differ in dominance.

The above discussion is meant only to suggest the broad conditions that favor the evolution of reciprocal altruism. The most important parameters to specify for individuals of a species are how many altruistic situations occur and how symmetrical they are, and these are the most difficult to specify in advance. Of the three instances of reciprocal altruism discussed in this paper only one, human altruism, would have been predicted from the above broad conditions.

The relationship between two individuals repeatedly exposed to symmetrical reciprocal situations is exactly analogous to what game theorists call the Prisoner's Dilemma (Luce and Raiffa, 1957; Rapoport and Chammah, 1965), a game that can be characterized by the payoff matrix

	A_2	C_2
A_1	R, R	S, T
C_1	T, S	P, P

where $S < P < R < T$ and where A_1 and A_2 represent the altruistic choices possible for the two individuals, and C_1 and C_2, the cheating choices (the first letter in each box gives the payoff for the first individual, the second letter the payoff for the second individual). The other symbols can be given the following meanings: R stands for the reward each individual gets from an altruistic exchange if neither cheats; T stands for the temptation to cheat; S stands for the sucker's payoff that an altruist gets when cheated; and P is the punishment that both individuals get when neither is altruistic (adapted from Rapoport and Chammah, 1965). Iterated games played between the same two individuals mimic real life in that they permit each player to respond to the behavior of the other. Rapoport and Chammah (1965) and others have conducted such experiments using human players, and some of their results are reviewed below in the discussion of human altruism.

W. D. Hamilton (pers. commun.) has shown that the above treatment of reciprocal altruism can be reformulated concisely in terms of game theory as follows. Assuming two altruists are symmetrically exposed to a series of reciprocal situations with identical costs and identical benefits, then after 2n reciprocal situations, each has been "paid" nR. Were one of the two a nonaltruist and the second changed to a non-altruistic policy after first being cheated, then the initial altruist would be paid $S + (n - 1)P$ (assuming he had the first opportunity to be altruistic) and the non-altruist would recieve $T + (n - 1)P$. The important point here is that unless T $\gg$ R, then even with small n, nR should exceed $T + (n - 1)P$. If this holds, the nonaltruistic type, when rare, cannot start to spread. But there is also a barrier to the spread of altruism when altruists are rare, for $P > S$ implies $nP > S + (n - 1)P$. As n increases, these two total payoffs tend to equality, so the barrier to the spread of altruism is weak if n is large. The barrier will be overcome if the advantages gained by exchanges between altruists outweigh the initial losses to non-altruistic types.

Reciprocal altruism can also be viewed as a symbiosis, each partner helping the other while he helps himself. The symbiosis has a time lag, however; one partner helps the other and must then wait a period of time before he is helped in turn. The return benefit may come directly, as in human food-sharing, the partner directly returning the benefit after a time lag. Or the return may come indirectly, as in warning calls in birds (discussed below), where the initial help to other birds (the warning call) sets up a causal chain through the ecological system (the predator fails to learn useful information) which redounds after a time lag to the benefit of the caller. The time lag is the crucial factor, for it means that only under highly specialized circumstances can the altruist be reasonably guaranteed that the causal chain he initiates with his altruistic act will eventually return to him and confer, directly or indirectly, its benefit. Only under these conditions will the cheater be selected against and this type of altruistic behavior evolve.

Although the preconditions for the evolution of reciprocal altruism are specialized, many species probably meet them and display this type of altruism. This paper will limit itself, however, to three instances. The first, behavior involved in cleaning symbioses, is chosen because it permits a clear discrimination between this model and that based on kin selection (Hamilton, 1964). The second, warning calls in birds, has already been elaborately analyzed in terms of kin selection; it is discussed here to show how the model presented above leads to a very different interpretation of these familiar behaviors. Finally, human reciprocal altruism is discussed in detail because it represents the best documented case of reciprocal altruism known, because there has apparently been strong selection for a very complex system regulating altruistic behavior, and because the above model permits the functional interpretation of details of the system that otherwise remain obscure.

ALTRUISTIC BEHAVIOR IN CLEANING SYMBIOSES

The preconditions for the evolution of reciprocal altruism are similar to those for the operation of kin selection: long lifetime, low dispersal rate, and mutual dependence, for example, tend to increase the chance that one is interacting with one's close kin. This makes it difficult to discriminate the two alternative hypotheses. The case of cleaning symbiosis is important to analyze in detail because altruistic behavior is displayed that cannot be explained by kin selection, since it is performed by members of one species for the benefit of members of another. It will be shown instead that the behavior can be explained by the model presented above. No elaborate explanation is needed to understand the evolution of the mutually advantageous cleaning symbiosis itself; it is several additional behaviors displayed by the host fish to its cleaner that require a special explanation because they meet the criteria for altruistic behavior outlined above—that is, they benefit the cleaner while apparently being detrimental to the host.

Feder (1966) and Maynard (1968) have recently reviewed the literature on cleaning symbioses in the ocean. Briefly, one organism (e.g., the wrasse, *Labroides dimidiatus*) cleans another organism (e.g., the grouper, *Epinephelus striatus*) of ectoparasites (e.g., caligoid copepods), sometimes entering into the gill chambers and mouth of the "host" in order to do so. Over forty-five species of fish are known to be cleaners, as well as six species of shrimp. Innumerable species of fish serve as hosts. Stomach analyses of cleaner fish demonstrate that they vary greatly in the extent to which they depend on their cleaning habits for food, some apparently subsisting nearly entirely on a diet of ectoparasites. Likewise, stomach analyses of host fish reveal that cleaners differ in the rate at which they end up in the stomachs of their hosts, some being apparently almost entirely immune to such a fate. It is a striking fact that there seems to be a strong correlation between degree of dependence on the cleaning way of life and immunity to predation by hosts.

Cleaning habits have apparently evolved independently many times (at least three times in shrimps alone), yet some remarkable convergence has taken place. Cleaners, whether shrimp or fish, are distinctively colored and behave in distinctive ways (for example, the wrasse, *L. dimidiatus,* swims up to its host with a curious dipping and rising motion that reminds one of the way a finch flies). These distinctive features seem to serve the function of attracting fish to be cleaned and of inhibiting any tendency in them to feed on their cleaners. There has apparently been strong selection to avoid eating one's cleaner. This can be illustrated by several observations. Hediger (1968) raised a grouper (*Epinephelus*) from infancy alone in a small tank for six years, by which time the fish was almost four feet in length and accustomed to snapping up anything dropped into its tank. Hediger then dropped a small live cleaner (*L. dimidiatus*) into the grouper's tank. The grouper not only failed to snap up the cleaner but opened its mouth and permitted the cleaner free entry and exit.

> Soon we watched our second surprise: the grouper made a movement which in the preceding six years we had never seen him make: he spread the right gill-covering so wide that the individual gill-plates were separated from each other at great distances, wide enough to let the cleaner through (translated from Hediger, 1968 p. 93).

When Hediger added two additional *L. dimidiatus* to the tank, all three cleaned the grouper with the result that within several days the grouper appeared restless and nervous, searched out places in the tank he had formerly avoided, and shook himself often (as a signal that he did not wish to be cleaned any longer). Apparently three cleaners working over him constantly was too much for him, yet he still failed to eat any of them. When Hediger removed two of the cleaners, the grouper returned to normal. There is no indication the grouper ever possessed any edible ectoparasites, and almost two years later (in December, 1968) the same cleaner continued to "clean" the grouper (pers. observ.) although the cleaner was, in fact, fed separately by its zoo-keepers.

Eibl-Eibesfeldt (1959) has described the morphology and behavior of two species (e.g., *Aspidontus taeniatus*) that mimic cleaners (e.g., *L. dimidiatus*) and that rely on the passive behavior of fish which suppose they are about to be cleaned to dart in and bite off a chunk of their fins. I cite the evolution of these mimics, which resemble their models in appearance and initial swimming behavior, as evidence of strong selection for hosts with no intention of harming their cleaners.

Of especial interst is evidence that there has been strong selection not to eat one's cleaner even after the cleaning is over. Eibl-Eibesfeldt (1955) has made some striking observations on the goby, *Elacitinus oceanops:*

> I never saw a grouper snap up a fish after it had cleaned it. On the contrary, it announced its impending departure by two definite signal movements. First it closed its mouth vigorously, although not completely, and immediately opened it wide again. Upon this intention movement, all the gobies left the mouth cavity. Then the grouper shook its body laterally a few times, and all the cleaners returned to their coral. If one frightened a grouper it never neglected these forewarning movements (translated from Eibl-Eibes-feldt, 1955, p. 208).

Randall has made similar observations on a moray eel (*Gymnothorax japonicus*) that signalled with a "sharp lateral jerk of the eel's head," after which "the wrasse fairly flew out of the mouth, and the awesome jaws snapped shut" (Randall, 1958, 1962). Likewise, Hediger's Kasper Hauser grouper shook its body when it had enough of being cleaned.

Why does a large fish not signal the end to a cleaning episode by swallowing the cleaner? Natural selection would seem to favor the double benefit of a good cleaning followed by a meal of the cleaner. Selection also operates, of course, on the cleaner, and presumably favors mechanisms to avoid being eaten. The distinctive behavior and appearance of cleaners has been cited as evidence of such selection. One can also cite the distinctive behavior of the fish being cleaned. Feder (1966) has pointed out that hosts approaching a cleaner react by "stopping or slowing down, allowing themselves to assume awkward positions, seemingly in a hypnotic state." Fishes sometimes alter their color dramatically before and while being cleaned, and Feder (1966) has summarized instances of this. These forms of behavior suggest that natural selection has operated on cleaners to avoid attempting to clean fish without these behaviors, presumably to avoid wasting energy and to minimize the dangers of being eaten. (Alternatively, the behaviors, including color change, may aid the cleaners in finding ectoparasites. This is certainly possible but not, I believe, adequate to explain the phenomenon completely. See, for example, Randall, 1962.)

Once the fish to be cleaned takes the proper stance, however, the cleaner goes to work with no apparent concern for its safety: It makes no effort to avoid the dangerous mouth and may even swim inside, which as we have seen, seems particularly foolhardy, since fish being cleaned may suddenly need to depart. The apparent unconcern of the cleaner suggests that natural selection acting on the fish being cleaned does not, in fact, favor eating one's cleaners. No speculation has been advanced as to why this may be so, although some speculation has appeared about the mechanisms involved. Feder advances two possibilities, that of Eibl-Eibesfeldt (1955) that fish come to be cleaned only after their appetite has been satisfied, and one of his own, that the irritation of ectoparasites may be sufficient to inhibit hunger. Both possibilities are contradicted by Hediger's observation, cited above, and seem unlikely on functional grounds as well.

A fish to be cleaned seems to perform several "altruistic" acts. It desists from eating the cleaner even when it easily could do so and when it must go to special pains (sometimes at danger to itself) to avoid doing so. Furthermore, it may perform two additional behaviors which seem of no direct benefit to itself (and which consume energy and take time), namely, it signals its cleaner that it is about to depart even when the fish is not in its mouth, and it may chase off possible dangers to the cleaner:

> While diving with me in the Virgin Islands, Robert Schroeder watched a Spanish hogfish grooming a bar jack in its bronze color state. When a second jack arrived in the pale color phase, the first jack immediately drove it away. But later when another jack intruded on the scene and changed its pale color to dark bronze it was not chased. The bronze color would seem to mean "no harm intended; I need service" (Randall, 1962, p. 44).

The behavior of the host fish is interpreted here to have resulted from natural selection and to be, in fact, beneficial to the host because the cleaner is worth more to it alive than dead. This is because the fish that is cleaned "plans" to return at later dates for more cleanings, and it will be benefited by being able to deal with the same individual. If it eats the cleaner, it may have difficulty finding a second when it needs to be cleaned again. It may lose valuable energy and be exposed to unnecessary predation in the search for a new cleaner. And it may in the end be "turned down" by a new cleaner or serviced very poorly. In short, the host is abundantly repaid for the cost of its altruism.

To support the hypothesis that the host is repaid its initial altruism, several pieces of evidence must be presented: that hosts suffer from ectoparasites; that finding a new cleaner may be difficult or dangerous; that if one does not eat one's cleaner, the same cleaner can be found and used a second time (e.g., that clean-ers are site-specific); that cleaners live long enough to be used repeatedly by the same host; and if possible, that individual hosts do, in fact, reuse the same cleaner.

1 *The cost of ectoparasites.* It seems almost axiomatic that the evolution of cleaners entirely dependent on ectoparasites for food implies the selective disadvantage for the cleaned of being ectoparasite-ridden. What is perhaps surprising is the effect that removing all cleaners from a coral reef has on the local "hosts" (Limbaugh, 1961). As Feder (1966) said in his review:

> Within a few days the number of fishes was drastically reduced. Within two weeks almost all except territorial fishes had disappeared, and many of these had developed white fuzzy blotches, swellings, ulcerated sores, and frayed fins (p. 366).

Clearly, once a fish's primary way of dealing with ectoparasites is by being cleaned, it is quickly vulnerable to the absence of cleaners.

2 *The difficulty and danger of finding a cleaner.*   There are naturally very few data on the difficulty or danger of finding a new cleaner. This is partially because, as shown below, fish tend repeatedly to return to familiar cleaners. The only observation of fish being disappointed in their search for cleaners comes from Eibl-Eibesfeldt (1955): "If the cleaners fail to appear over one coral in about half a minute, the large fishes swim to another coral and wait there a while" (translated from p. 210). It may be that fish have several alternative cleaning stations to go to, since any particular cleaning station may be occupied or unattended at a given moment. So many fish tend to be cleaned at coral reefs (Limbaugh, 1961, observed a cleaner service 300 fish in a 6-hour period), that predators probably frequent coral reefs in search of fish being cleaned. Limbaugh (1961) suggested that good human fishing sites are found near cleaning stations. One final reason why coming to be cleaned may be dangerous is that some fish must leave their element to do so (Randall, 1962):

> Most impressive were the visits of moray eels, which do not ordinarily leave their holes in the reef during daylight hours, and of the big jacks which swam up from deeper water to the reef's edge to be "serviced" before going on their way (p. 43).

3 *Site specificity of cleaners.*   Feder (1966) has reviewed the striking evidence for the site specificity of cleaners and concludes:

> Cleaning fishes and cleaning shrimps have regular stations to which fishes wanting to be cleaned can come (p. 367).

Limbaugh, Pederson, and Chase (1961) have reviewed available data on the six species of cleaner shrimps, and say:

> The known cleaner shrimps may conveniently be divided into two groups on the basis of behavior, habitat and color. The five species comprising one group are usually solitary or paired. . . . All five species are territorial and remain for weeks and, in some cases, months or possibly years within a meter or less of the same spot. They are omnivorous to a slight extent but seem to be highly dependent upon their hosts for food. This group is tropical, and the individuals are brightly marked. They display themselves to their hosts in a conspicuous manner. They probably rarely serve as prey for fishes. A single species, *Hippolysmata californica,* comprises the second group. . . . This species is a gregarious, wandering, omnivorous animal . . . and is not highly dependent upon its host for survival. So far as is known, it does not display itself to attract fishes (p. 238).

It is *H. californica* that is occasionally found in the stomachs of at least one of its hosts. The striking correlation of territoriality and solitariness with cleaning habits is what theory would predict. The same correlation can be found in cleaner fish. *Labroides,* with four species, is the genus most completely dependent on cleaning habits. No *Labroides* has ever been found in the stomach of a host fish. All species are highly site-specific and tend to be solitary. Randall (1958) reports that an individual *L. dimidiatus* may sometimes swim as much as 60 feet from its cleaning station, servicing fish on the way. But he notes,

> This was especially true in an area where the highly territorial damsel fish *Promacentris nigricans* (Lepede) was common. As one damsel fish was being tended, another nearby would assume a stationary pose with fins erect and the *Labroides* would move on to the latter with little hesitation (p. 333).

Clearly, what matters for the evolution of reciprocal altruism is that the same two individuals interact repeatedly. This will be facilitated by the site specificity of either individual. Of temperate water cleaners, the species most specialized to cleaning is also apparently the most solitary (Hobson, 1969).

   4 *Lifespan of cleaners.*   No good data exist on how long cleaners live, but several observations on both fish and shrimp suggest that they easily live long enough for effective selection against cheaters. Randall (1958) repeatedly checked several ledges and found that different feeding stations were occupied for "long periods of time," apparently by the same individuals. One such feeding station supported two individuals for over three years. Of one species of cleaner shrimp, *Stenopus hispidus,* Limbaugh, Pederson, and Chase (1961) said that pairs of individuals probably remain months, possibly years, within an area of a square meter.

   5 *Hosts using the same cleaner repeatedly.*   There is surprisingly good evidence that hosts reuse the same cleaner repeatedly. Feder (1966) summarizes the evidence:

> Many fishes spend as much time getting cleaned as they do foraging for food. Some fishes return again and again to the same station, and show a definite time pattern in their daily arrival. Others pass from station to station and return many times during the day; this is particularly true of an injured or infected fish (p. 368).

Limbaugh, Pederson, and Chase (1961) have presented evidence that in at least one species of cleaner shrimp (*Stenopus scutellus*), the shrimp may reservice the same individuals:

> One pair was observed in the same football-sized coral boulder from May through August 1956. During that period, we changed the position and orientation of the boulder several times within a radius of approximately seven meters without disturbing the shrimp. Visiting fishes were momentarily disturbed by the changes, but they soon relocated the shrimps (p. 254).

Randall (1958) has repeatedly observed fish swimming from out of sight directly to cleaning stations, behavior suggesting to him that they had prior acquaintance with the stations. During two months of observations at several feeding stations, Eibl-Eibesfeldt (1955) became personally familiar with several individual groupers (*Epinephelus striatus*) and repeatedly observed them seeking out and being cleaned at the same feeding stations, presumably by the same cleaners.

In summary, it seems fair to say that the hosts of cleaning organisms perform several kinds of altruistic behavior, including not eating their cleaner after a cleaning, which can be explained on the basis of the above model. A review of the relevant evidence suggests that the cleaner organisms and their hosts meet the preconditions for the evolution of reciprocally altruistic behavior. The host's altruism is to be explained as benefiting him because of the advantage of being able quickly and repeatedly to return to the same cleaner.

WARNING CALLS IN BIRDS

Marler (1955, 1957) has presented evidence that warning calls in birds tend to have characteristics that limit the information a predator gets from the call. In particular, the call characteristics do not allow the predator easily to determine the location of the call-giver. Thus, it seems that giving a warning call must result, at least occasionally, in the otherwise unnecessary death of the call-giver, either at the hands of the predator that inspired the call or at the hands of a second predator formerly unaware of the caller's presence or exact location.

Given the presumed selection against call-giving, Williams (1966) has reviewed various models to explain selection for warning cries:

1   Warning calls are functional during the breeding season in birds in that they protect one's mate and offspring. They have no function outside the breeding season, but they are not deleted then because "in practice it is not worth burdening the germ plasm with the information necessary to realize such an adjustment" (Williams, 1966, p. 206).
2   Warning calls are selected for by the mechanism of group selection (Wynne-Edwards, 1962).
3   Warning calls are functional outside the breeding season because there is usually a good chance that a reasonably close kin is near enough to be helped sufficiently (Hamilton, 1964; Maynard Smith, 1964). Maynard Smith (1965) has analyzed in great detail how closely related the benefited kin must be, at what benefit to him the call must be, and at what cost to the caller, in order for selection to favor call-giving.

The first is an explanation of last resort. While it must sometimes apply in evolutionary arguments, it should probably only be invoked when no other explanation seems plausible. The second is not consistent with the known workings of natural selection. The third is feasible and may explain the warning calls in some species and perhaps even in many. But it does depend on the somewhat regular nearby presence of closely related organisms, a matter that may often be the case but that has been demonstrated only as a possibility in a few species and that seems very unlikely in some. A fourth explanation is suggested by the above model:

4 Warning calls are selected for because they aid the bird giving the call. It is disadvantageous for a bird to have a predator eat a nearby conspecific because the predator may then be more likely to eat him. This may happen because the predator will

    i   be sustained by the meal,
    ii be more likely to form a specific search image of the prey species,
    iii be more likely to learn the habits of the prey species and perfect his predatory techniques on it,
    iv be more likely to frequent the area in which the birds live, or
    v be more likely to learn useful information about the area in which the birds live.

In short, in one way or another, giving a warning call tends to prevent predators from specializing on the caller's species and locality.

There is abundant evidence for the importance of learning in the lives of predatory vertebrates (see, for example, Tinbergen, 1960; Leyhausen, 1965; Brower and Brower, 1965). Rudebeck (1950, 1951) has presented important observations on the tendency of avian predators to specialize individually on prey types and hunting techniques. Owen (1963) and others have presented evidence that species of snails and insects may evolve polymorphisms as a protection against the tendency of their avian predators to learn their appearance. Similarly, Kuyton (1962; cited in Wickler, 1968) has described the adaptation of a moth that minimizes the chance of its predators forming a specific search image. Southern (1954), Murie (1944), and numerous others have documented the tendency of predators to specialize on certain localities within their range. Finally, Blest (1963) has presented evidence that kin selection in some cryptic saturnid moths has favored rapid, post-reproductive death to minimize predation on the young. Blest's evidence thus provides an instance of a predator gaining useful information through the act of predation.

It does not matter that in giving a warning call the caller is helping its non-calling neighbors more than it is helping itself. What counts is that it outcompetes conspecifics from areas in which no one is giving warning calls. The non-calling neighbors of the caller (or their offspring) will soon find themselves in an area without any caller and will be selected against relative to birds in an area with callers. The caller, by definition, is always in an area with at least one caller. If we assume that two callers are preferable to one, and so on, then selection will favor the spread of the warning-call genes. Note that this model depends on the concept of *open* groups, whereas "group selection" (Wynne-Edwards, 1962) depends partly on the concept of closed groups.

It might be supposed that one could explain bird calls more directly as altruistic behavior that will be repaid when the other birds reciprocate, but there are numerous objections to this. It is difficult to visualize how one would discover and discriminate against the cheater, and there is certainly no evidence that birds refrain from giving calls because neighbors are not reciprocating. Furthermore, if the relevant bird groupings are very fluid, with much emigration and immigration, as they often are, then cheating would seem to be favored and no selection against it possible. Instead, according to the model above, it is the mere fact that the neighbor survives that repays the call-giver his altruism.

It is almost impossible to gather the sort of evidence that would discriminate between this explanation and that of Hamilton (1964). It is difficult to imagine how one would estimate the immediate cost of giving a warning call or its benefit to those within earshot, and precise data on the genetic relationships of bird groupings throughout the year are not only lacking but would be most difficult to gather. Several lines of evidence suggest, however, that Hamilton's (1964) explanation should be assumed with caution:

1   There exist no data showing a decrease in warning tendencies with decrease in the genetic relationship of those within earshot. Indeed, a striking feature of warning calls is that they are given in and out of the breeding season, both before and after migration or dispersal.

2   There do exist data suggesting that close kin in a number of species migrate or disperse great distances from each other (Ashmole, 1962; Perdeck, 1958; Berndt and Sternberg, 1968; Dhont and Hublé, 1968).

3   One can advance the theoretical argument that kin selection under some circumstances should favor kin dispersal in order to avoid competition (Hamilton, 1964, 1969). This would lead one to expect fewer closely related kin near any given bird, outside the breeding season.

The arguments advanced in this section may also apply, of course, to species other than birds.

HUMAN RECIPROCAL ALTRUISM

Reciprocal altruism in the human species takes place in a number of contexts and in all known cultures (see, for example, Gouldner, 1960). Any complete list of human altruism would contain the following types of altruistic behavior:

1   helping in times of danger (e.g. accidents, predation, intraspecific aggression;

2   sharing food;

3   helping the sick, the wounded, or the very young and old;

4   sharing implements; and

5   sharing knowledge.

All these forms of behavior often meet the criterion of small cost to the giver and great benefit to the taker.

During the Pleistocene, and probably before, a hominid species would have met the preconditions for the evolution of reciprocal altruism: long lifespan; low dispersal rate; life in small, mutually dependent, stable, social groups (Lee and DeVore, 1968; Campbell, 1966); and a long period of parental care. It is very likely that dominance relations were of the relaxed, less linear form characteristic of the living chimpanzee (Van Lawick-Goodall, 1968) and not of the more rigidly linear form characteristic of the baboon (Hall and DeVore, 1965). Aid in intraspecific combat, particularly by kin, almost certainly reduced the stability and linearity of the dominance order in early humans. Lee (1969) has shown that in almost all Bushman fights which are initially between two individuals, others have joined in. Mortality, for example, often strikes the secondaries rather than the principals. Tool use has also probably had an equalizing effect on human dominance relations, and the Bushmen have a saying that illustrates this nicely. As a dispute reaches the stage where deadly weapons may be employed, an individual will often declare: "We are none of us big, and others small; we are all men and we can fight; I'm going to get my arrows," (Lee 1969). It is interesting that Van Lawick-Goodall (1968) has recorded an instance of strong dominance reversal in chimpanzees as a function of tool use. An individual moved from low in dominance to the top of the dominance hierarchy when he discovered the intimidating effects of throwing a metal tin around. It is likely that a diversity of talents is usually present in a band of hunter-gatherers such that the best maker of a certain type of tool is not often the best maker of a different sort or the best user of the tool. This contributes to the symmetry of relationships, since altruistic acts can be traded with reference to the special talents of the individuals involved.

To analyze the details of the human reciprocal-altruistic system, several distinctions are important and are discussed here.

1 *Kin selection.* The human species also met the preconditions for the operation of kin selection. Early hominid hunter-gatherer bands almost certainly (like today's hunter-gatherers) consisted of many close kin, and kin selection must often have operated to favor the evolution of some types of altruistic behavior (Haldane, 1955; Hamilton, 1964, 1969). In general, in attempting to discriminate between the effects of kin selection and what might be called reciprocal-altruistic selection, one can analyze the form of the altruistic behaviors themselves. For example, the existence of discrimination against non-reciprocal individuals cannot be explained on the basis of kin selection, in which the advantage accruing to close kin is what makes the altruistic behavior selectively advantageous, not its chance of being reciprocated. The strongest argument for the operation of reciprocal-altruistic selection in man is the psychological system controlling some forms of human altruism. Details of this system are reviewed below.

2 *Reciprocal altruism among close kin.* If both forms of selection have operated, one would expect some interesting interactions. One might expect, for example, a lowered demand for reciprocity from kin than from nonkin, and there is evidence to support this (e.g., Marshall, 1961; Balikci, 1964). The demand that kin show some reciprocity (e.g., Marshall, 1961; Balikci, 1964) suggests, however, that reciprocal-

altruistic selection has acted even on relations between close kin. Although interactions between the two forms of selection have probably been important in human evolution, this paper will limit itself to a preliminary description of the human reciprocally altruistic system, a system whose attributes are seen to result only from reciprocal-altruistic selection.

   3   *Age-dependent changes.* Cost and benefit were defined above without reference to the ages, and hence reproductive values (Fisher, 1958), of the individuals involved in an altruistic exchange. Since the reproductive value of a sexually mature organism declines with age, the benefit to him of a typical altruistic act also decreases, as does the cost to him of a typical act he performs. If the interval separating the two acts in an altruistic exchange is short relative to the lifespans of the individuals, then the error is slight. For longer intervals, in order to be repaid precisely, the initial altruist must receive more in return than he himself gave. It would be interesting to see whether humans in fact routinely expect "interest" to be added to a long overdue altruistic debt, interest commensurate with the intervening decline in reproductive value. In humans reproductive value declines most steeply shortly after sexual maturity is reached (Hamilton, 1966), and one would predict the interest rate on altruistic debts to be highest then. Selection might also favor keeping the interval between act and reciprocation short, but this should also be favored to protect against complete non-reciprocation. W. D. Hamilton (pers. commun.) has suggested that a detailed analysis of age-dependent changes in kin altruism and reciprocal altruism should show interesting differences, but the analysis is complicated by the possibility of reciprocity to the kin of a deceased altruist (see *Multi-party interactions* below).

   4   *Gross and subtle cheating.*   Two forms of cheating can be distinguished, here denoted as gross and subtle. In *gross cheating* the cheater fails to reciprocate at all, and the altruist suffers the costs of whatever altruism he has dispensed without any compensating benefits. More broadly, gross cheating may be defined as reciprocating so little, if at all, that the altruist receives less benefit from the gross cheater than the cost of the altruist's acts of altruism to the cheater. That is,

$$\sum_i c_{ai} > \sum_j b_{aj},$$

where C_{ai} is the cost of the ith altruistic act performed by the altruist and where b_{aj} is the benefit to the altruist of the jth altruistic act performed by the gross cheater; altruistic situations are assumed to have occurred symmetrically. Clearly, selection will strongly favor prompt discrimination against the gross cheater. *Subtle cheating,* by contrast, involves reciprocating, but always attempting to give less than one was given, or more precisely, to give less than the partner would give if the situation were reversed. In this situation, the altruist still benefits from the relationship but not as much as he would if the relationship were completely equitable. The subtle cheater benefits more than he would if the relationship were equitable. In other words,

$$\sum_{i,j} (b_{qi} - c_{qj}) > \sum_i (b_{qi} - c_{ai}) > \sum_{i,j} (b_{aj} - c_{ai})$$

where the ith altruistic act performed by the altruist has a cost to him of C_{ai} and a benefit to the subtle cheater of b_{qi} and where the jth altruist act performed by the subtle cheater has a cost to him of C_{qi} and a benefit to the altruist of b_{aj}. Because human altruism may span huge periods of time, a lifetime even, and because thousands of exchanges may take place, involving many different "goods" and with many different cost/benefit ratios, the problem of computing the relevant totals, detecting imbalances, and deciding whether they are due to chance or to small-scale cheating is an extremely difficult one. Even then, the altruist is in an awkward position, symbolized by the folk saying, "half a loaf is better than none," for if attempts to make the relationship equitable lead to the rupture of the relationship, the altruist, assuming other things to be equal, will suffer the loss of the substandard altruism of the subtle cheater. It is the subtlety of the discrimination necessary to detect this form of cheating and the awkward situation that ensues that permit some subtle cheating to be adaptive. This sets up a dynamic tension in the system that has important repercussions, as discussed below.

   5 *Number of reciprocal relationships.* It has so far been assumed that it is to the advantage of each individual to form the maximum number of reciprocal relationships and that the individual suffers a decrease in fitness upon the rupture of any relationship in which the cost to him of acts dispensed to the partner is less than the benefit of acts dispensed toward him by the partner. But it is possible that relationships are partly exclusive, in the sense that expanding the number of reciprocal exchanges with one of the partners may necessarily decrease the number of exchanges with another. For example, if a group of organisms were to split into subgroups for much of the day (such as breaking up into hunting pairs), then altruistic exchanges will be more likely between members of each subgroup than between members of different subgroups. In that sense, relationships may be partly exclusive, membership in a given subgroup necessarily decreasing exchanges with others in the group. The importance of this factor is that it adds further complexity to the problem of dealing with the cheater and it increases competition within a group to be members of a favorable subgroup. An individual in a subgroup who feels that another member is subtly cheating on their relationship has the option of attempting to restore the relationship to a completely reciprocal one or of attempting to join another subgroup, thereby decreasing to a minimum the possible exchanges between himself and the subtle cheater and replacing these with exchanges between a new partner or partners. In short, he can switch friends. There is evidence in hunter-gatherers that much movement of individuals from one band to another occurs in response to such social factors as have just been outlined (Lee and DeVore, 1968).

   6 *Indirect benefits or reciprocal altruism?* Given mutual dependence in a group it is possible to argue that the benefits (non-altruistic) of this mutual dependence are a positive function of group size and that altruistic behaviors may be selected for because they permit additional individuals to survive and thereby confer additional indirect (non-altruistic) benefits. Such an argument can only be advanced seriously for slowly reproducing species with little dispersal. Saving an individual's life in a hunter-gatherer group, for example, may permit non-altruistic actions such as cooperative hunting to continue with more individuals. But if there is an optimum group size, one would expect adaptations to stay near that size, with individuals joining groups when the groups are below this size, and groups splitting up when they are above this size. One would only be selected to keep an individual alive when the group is below optimum and not when the group is above optimum. Although an abundant literature on hunter-gatherers (and also nonhuman primates) suggests that adaptations exist to regulate group size near an optimum, there is no evidence that altruistic gestures are curtailed when groups are above the optimum in size. Instead, the benefits of human altruism are to be seen as coming directly from reciprocity—not indirectly through non-altruistic group benefits. This distinction is important because social scientists and philosophers have tended to deal with human altruism in terms of the benefits of living in a group, without differentiating between non-altruistic benefits and reciprocal benefits (e.g. Rousseau, 1954; Baier, 1958).

THE PSYCHOLOGICAL SYSTEM UNDERLYING HUMAN RECIPROCAL ALTRUISM

Anthropologists have recognized the importance of reciprocity in human behavior, but when they have ascribed functions to such behavior they have done so in terms of group benefits, reciprocity cementing group relations and encouraging group survival. The individual sacrifices so that the group may benefit. Recently psychologists have studied altruistic behavior in order to show what factors induce or inhibit such behavior. No attempt has been made to show what function such behavior may serve, nor to describe and interrelate the components of the psychological system affecting altruistic behavior. The purpose of this section is to show that the above model for the natural selection of reciprocally altruistic behavior can readily explain the function of human altruistic behavior and the details of the psychological system underlying such behavior. The psychological data can be organized into functional categories, and it can be shown that the components of the system complement each other in regulating the expression of altruistic and cheating impulses to the selective advantage of individuals. No concept of group advantage is necessary to explain the function of human altruistic behavior.

There is no direct evidence regarding the degree of reciprocal altruism practiced during human evolution nor its genetic basis today, but given the universal and nearly daily practice of reciprocal altruism among humans today, it is reasonable to assume that it has been an important factor in recent human evolution and that the underlying emotional dispositions affecting altruistic behavior have important genetic components. To assume as much allows a number of predictions.

1   *A complex, regulating system.*   The human altruistic system is a sensitive, unstable one. Often it will pay to cheat: namely, when the partner will not find out, when he will not discontinue his altruism even if he does find out, or when he is unlikely to survive long enough to reciprocate adequately. And the perception of subtle cheating may be very difficult. Given this unstable character of the

system, where a degree of cheating is adaptive, natural selection will rapidly favor a complex psychological system in each individual regulating both his own altruistic and cheating tendencies and his responses to these tendencies in others. As selection favors subtler forms of cheating, it will favor more acute abilities to detect cheating. The system that results should simultaneously allow the individual to reap the benefits of altruistic exchanges, to protect himself from gross and subtle forms of cheating, and to practice those forms of cheating that local conditions make adaptive. Individuals will differ not in being altruists or cheaters but in the degree of altruism they show and in the conditions under which they will cheat.

The best evidence supporting these assertions can be found in Kreb's (1970) review of the relevant psychological literature. Although he organizes it differently, much of the material supporting the assertions below is taken from his paper. All references to Krebs below are to this review. Also, Hartshorne and May (1928–1930) have shown that children in experimental situations do not divide bimodally into altruists and "cheaters" but are distributed normally; almost all the children cheated, but they differed in how much and under what circumstances. ("Cheating" was defined in their work in a slightly different but analogous way.)

2 *Friendship and the emotions of liking and disliking.* The tendency to like others, not necessarily closely related, to form friendships and to act altruistically toward friends and toward those one likes will be selected for as the immediate emotional rewards motivating altruistic behavior and the formation of altruistic partnerships. (Selection may also favor helping strangers or disliked individuals when they are in particularly dire circumstances.) Selection will favor a system whereby these tendencies are sensitive to such parameters as the altruistic tendencies of the liked individual. In other words, selection will favor liking those who are themselves altruistic.

Sawyer (1966) has shown that all groups in all experimental situations tested showed more altruistic behavior toward friends than toward neutral individuals. Likewise, Friedrichs (1960) has shown that attractiveness as a friend was most highly correlated among undergraduates with altruistic behavior. Krebs has reviewed other studies that suggest that the relationship between altruism and liking is a two-way street: one is more altruistic toward those one likes and one tends to like those who are most altruistic (e.g., Berkowitz and Friedman, 1967; Lerner and Lichtman, 1968).

Others (Darwin, 1871; Williams, 1966; and Hamilton, 1969) have recognized the role friendship might play in engendering altruistic behavior, but all have viewed friendship (and intelligence) as prerequisites for the appearance of such altruism. Williams (1966), who cites Darwin (1871) on the matter, speaks of this behavior as evolving

in animals that live in stable social groups and have the intelligence and other mental qualities necessary to form a system of personal friendships and animosities that transcend the limits of family relationships (p. 93).

This emphasis on friendship and intelligence as prerequisites leads Williams to limit his search for altruism to the Mammalia and to a "minority of this group." But according to the model presented above, emotions of friendship (and hatred) are not prerequisites for reciprocal altruism but may evolve *after* a system of mutual altruism has appeared, as important ways of regulating the system.

3   *Moralistic aggression.*   Once strong positive emotions have evolved to motivate altruistic behavior, the altruist is in a vulnerable position because cheaters will be selected to take advantage of the altruist's positive emotions. This in turn sets up a selection pressure for a protective mechanism. Moralistic aggression and indignation in humans was selected for in order

   a   to counteract the tendency of the altruist, in the absence of any reciprocity, to continue to perform altruistic acts for his own emotional rewards;
   b   to educate the unreciprocating individual by frightening him with immediate harm or with the future harm of no more aid; and
   c   in extreme cases, perhaps, to select directly against the unreciprocating individual by injuring, killing, or exiling him.

Much of human aggression has moral overtones. Injustice, unfairness, and lack of reciprocity often motivate human aggression and indignation. Lee (1969) has shown that verbal disputes in Bushmen usually revolve around problems of gift-giving, stinginess, and laziness. DeVore (pers. commun.) reports that a great deal of aggression in hunter-gatherers revolves around real or imagined injustices —inequities, for example, in food-sharing (see, for example, Thomas, 1958; Balikci, 1964; Marshall, 1961). A common feature of this aggression is that it often seems out of all proportion to the offenses committed. Friends are even killed over apparently trivial disputes. But since small inequities repeated many times over a lifetime may exact a heavy toll in relative fitness, selection may favor a strong show of aggression when the cheating tendency is discovered. Recent discussions of human and animal aggression have failed to distinguish between moralistic and other forms of aggression (e.g., Scott, 1958; Lorenz, 1966; Montague, 1968; Tinbergen, 1968; Gilula and Daniels, 1969). The grounds for expecting, on functional grounds, a highly plastic developmental system affecting moralistic aggression is discussed below.

4   *Gratitude, sympathy, and the cost/benefit ratio of an altruistic act.*   If the cost-/benefit ratio is an important parameter in determining the adaptiveness of reciprocal altruism, then humans should be selected to be sensitive to the cost and benefit of an altruistic act, both in deciding whether to perform one and in deciding whether, or how much, to reciprocate. I suggest that the emotion of gratitude has been selected to regulate human response to altruistic acts and that the emotion is sensitive to the cost/benefit ratio of such acts. I suggest further that the emotion of sympathy has been selected to motivate altruistic behavior as a function of the plight of the recipient of such behavior; crudely put, the greater the potential benefit to the recipient, the greater the sympathy and the more likely the altruistic gesture, even to strange or disliked individuals. If the recipient's gratitude is indeed a function of the cost/benefit ratio, then a sympa-

thetic response to the plight of a disliked individual may result in considerable reciprocity.

There is good evidence supporting the psychological importance of the cost/benefit ratio of altruistic acts. Gouldner (1960) has reviewed the sociological literature suggesting that the greater the need state of the recipient of an altruistic act, the greater his tendency to reciprocate; and the scarcer the resources of the donor of the act, the greater the tendency of the recipient to reciprocate. Heider (1958) has analyzed lay attitudes on altruism and finds that gratitude is greatest when the altruistic act does good. Tesser, Gatewood, and Driver (1968) have shown that American undergraduates thought they would feel more gratitude when the altruistic act was valuable and cost the benefactor a great deal. Pruitt (1968) has provided evidence that humans reciprocate more when the original act was expensive for the benefactor. He shows that under experimental conditions more altruism is induced by a gift of 80 per cent of $1.00 than 20 percent of $4.00. Aronfreed (1968) has reviewed the considerable evidence that sympathy motivates altruistic behavior as a function of the plight of the individual arousing the sympathy.

5 *Guilt and reparative altruism.* If an organism has cheated on a reciprocal relationship and this fact has been found out, or has a good chance of being found out, by the partner and if the partner responds by cutting off all future acts of aid, then the cheater will have paid dearly for his misdeed. It will be to the cheater's advantage to avoid this, and, providing that the cheater makes up for his misdeed and does not cheat in the future, it will be to his partner's benefit to avoid this, since in cutting off future acts of aid he sacrifices the benefits of future reciprocal help. The cheater should be selected to make up for his misdeed and to show convincing evidence that he does not plan to continue his cheating sometime in the future. In short, he should be selected to make a reparative gesture. It seems plausible, furthermore, that the emotion of guilt has been selected for in humans partly in order to motivate the cheater to compensate his misdeed and to behave reciprocally in the future, and thus to prevent the rupture of reciprocal relationships.

Krebs has reviewed the evidence that harming another individual publicly leads to altruistic behavior and concludes:

> Many studies have supported the notion that public transgression whether intentional or unintentional, whether immoral or only situationally unfortunate, leads to reparative altruism (p. 267).

Wallace and Sadalla (1966), for example, showed experimentally that individuals who broke an expensive machine were more likely to volunteer for a painful experiment than those who did not, but only if their transgression had been discovered. Investigators disagree on the extent to which guilt feelings are the motivation behind reparative altruism. Epstein and Hornstein (1969) supply some evidence that guilt is involved, but on the assumption that one feels guilt even when one behaves badly in private, Wallace and Sadalla's (1966) result contradicts the view that guilt is the only motivating factor. That private transgressions are not as likely as public ones to lead to reparative altruism is precisely what the model would predict, and it is possible that the common psychological assumption that one feels guilt even when one behaves badly in private is based on the fact that many transgressions performed in private are *likely* to become public knowledge. It should often be advantageous to confess sins that are likely to be discovered before they actually are, as evidence of sincerity (see below on detection of mimics).

6 *Subtle cheating: the evolution of mimics.*   Once friendship, moralistic aggression, guilt, sympathy, and gratitude have evolved to regulate the altruistic system, selection will favor mimicking these traits in order to influence the behavior of others to one's own advantage. Apparent acts of generosity and friendship may induce genuine friendship and altruism in return. Sham moralistic aggression when no real cheating has occurred may nevertheless induce reparative altruism. Sham guilt may convince a wronged friend that one has reformed one's ways even when the cheating is about to be resumed. Likewise, selection will favor the hypocrisy of pretending one is in dire circumstances in order to induce sympathy-motivated altruistic behavior. Finally, mimicking sympathy may give the appearance of helping in order to induce reciprocity, and mimicking gratitude may mislead an individual into expecting he will be reciprocated. It is worth emphasizing that a mimic need not necessarily be conscious of the deception; selection may favor feeling genuine moralistic aggression even when one has not been wronged if so doing leads another to reparative altruism.

Instances of the above forms of subtle cheating are not difficult to find. For typical instances from the literature on hunter-gatherers see Rasmussen (1931), Balikci (1964), and Lee and DeVore (1968). The importance of these forms of cheating can partly be inferred from the adaptations to detect such cheating discussed below and from the importance and prevalence of moralistic aggression once such cheating is detected.

7 *Detection of the subtle cheater: trust-worthiness, trust, and suspicion.*   Selection should favor the ability to detect and discriminate against subtle cheaters. Selection will clearly favor detecting and countering sham moralistic aggression. The argument for the others is more complex. Selection may favor distrusting those who perform altruistic acts without the emotional basis of generosity or guilt because the altruistic tendencies of such individuals may be less reliable in the future. One can imagine, for example, compensating for a misdeed without any emotional basis but with a calculating, self-serving motive. Such an individual should be distrusted because the calculating spirit that leads this subtle cheater now to compensate may in the future lead him to cheat when circumstances seem more advantageous (because of unlikelihood of detection, for example, or because the cheated individual is unlikely to survive). Guilty motivation, in so far as it evidences a more enduring commitment to altruism, either because guilt teaches or because the cheater is unlikely not to feel the same guilt in the future, seems more reliable. A similar argument can be made about the trustworthiness of individuals who initiate altruistic acts out of a calculating rather than a generous-hearted disposition or who show either false sympathy or false gratitude. Detection on the basis of the underlying psychological dynamics is only one

form of detection. In many cases, unreliability may more easily be detected through experiencing the cheater's inconsistent behavior. And in some cases, third party interactions (as discussed below) may make an individual's behavior predictable despite underlying cheating motivations.

The anthropological literature also abounds with instances of the detection of subtle cheaters (see above references for hunter-gatherers). Although I know of no psychological studies on the detection of sham moralistic aggression and sham guilt, there is ample evidence to support the notion that humans respond to altruistic acts according to their perception of the motives of the altruist. They tend to respond more altruistically when they perceive the other as acting "genuinely" altruistic, that is, voluntarily dispatching an altruistic act as an end in itself, without being directed toward gain (Leeds, 1963; Heider, 1958). Krebs (1970) has reviewed the literature on this point and notes that help is more likely to be reciprocated when it is perceived as voluntary and intentional (e.g., Goranson and Berkowitz, 1966; Lerner and Lichtman, 1968) and when the help is appropriate, that is, when the intentions of the altruist are not in doubt (e.g., Brehm and Cole, 1966; Schopler and Thompson, 1968). Krebs concludes that, "When the legitimacy of apparent altruism is questioned, reciprocity is less likely to prevail." Lerner and Lichtman (1968) have shown experimentally that those who act altruistically for ulterior benefit are rated as unattractive and are treated selfishly, whereas those who apparently are genuinely altruistic are rated as attractive and are treated altruistically. Berscheid and Walster (1967) have shown that church women tend to make reparations for harm they have committed by choosing the reparation that approximates the harm (that is, is neither too slight nor too great), presumably to avoid the appearance of inappropriateness.

Rapoport and Dale (1967) have shown that when two strangers play iterated games of Prisoner's Dilemma in which the matrix determines profits from the games played there is a significant tendency for the level of cooperation to drop at the end of the series, reflecting the fact that the partner will not be able to punish for "cheating" responses when the series is over. If a long series is broken up into subseries with a pause between subseries for totaling up gains and losses, then the tendency to cheat on each other increases at the end of each subseries. These results, as well as some others reported by Rapoport and Chammah (1965), are suggestive of the instability that exists when two strangers are consciously trying to maximize gain by trading altruistic gestures, an instability that is presumably less marked when the underlying motivation involves the emotions of friendship, of liking others, and of feeling guilt over harming a friend. Deutsch (1958), for example, has shown that two individuals playing iterated games of Prisoner's Dilemma will be more cooperative if a third individual, disliked by both, is present. The perceived mutual dislike is presumed to create a bond between the two players.

It is worth mentioning that a classic problem in social science and philosophy has been whether to define altruism in terms of motives (e.g., real vs. "calculated" altruism) or in terms of behavior, regardless of motive (Krebs, 1970). This problem reflects the fact that, wherever studied, humans seem to make distinctions about altruism partly on the basis of motive, and this tendency is consistent with the hypothesis that such discrimination is relevant to protecting oneself from cheaters.

8 *Setting up altruistic partnerships.*   Selection will favor a mechanism for establishing reciprocal relationships. Since humans respond to acts of altruism with feelings of friendship that lead to reciprocity, one such mechanism might be the performing of altruistic acts toward strangers, or even enemies, in order to induce friendship. In short, do unto others as you would have them do unto you.

The mechanism hypothesized above leads to results inconsistent with the assumption that humans always act more altruistically toward friends than toward others. Particularly toward strangers, humans may initially act more altruistically than toward friends. Wright (1942) has shown, for example, that third grade children are more likely to give a more valuable toy to a stranger than to a friend. Later, some of these children verbally acknowledged that they were trying to make friends. Floyd (1964) has shown that, after receiving many trinkets from a friend, humans tend to *decrease* their gifts in return, but after receiving many trinkets from a neutral or disliked individual, they tend to *increase* their gifts in return. Likewise, after receiving few trinkets from a friend, humans tend to increase their gifts in return, whereas receiving few trinkets from a neutral or disliked individual results in a decrease in giving. This was interpreted to mean that generous friends are taken for granted (as are stingy non-friends). Generosity from a non-friend is taken to be an overture to friendship, and stinginess from a friend as evidence of a deteriorating relationship in need of repair. (Epstein and Hornstein, 1969, provide new data supporting this interpretation of Floyd, 1964.)

9 *Multiparty interactions.*   In the close-knit social groups that humans usually live in, selection should favor more complex interactions than the two-party interactions so far discussed. Specifically, selection may favor learning from the altruistic and cheating experiences of others, helping others coerce cheaters, forming multiparty exchange systems, and formulating rules for regulated exchanges in such multiparty systems.

    i *Learning from others.*   Selection should favor learning about the altruistic and cheating tendencies of others indirectly, both through observing interactions of others and, once linguistic abilities have evolved, by hearing about such interactions or hearing characterizations of individuals (e.g., "dirty, hypocritical, dishonest, untrustworthy, cheating louse"). One important result of this learning is that an individual may be as concerned about the attitude of onlookers in an altruistic situation as about the attitude of the individual being dealt with.

    ii *Help in dealing with cheaters.*   In dealing with cheaters selection may favor individuals helping others, kin or non-kin, by direct coercion against the cheater or by everyone refusing him reciprocal altruism. One effect of this is that an individual, through his close kin, may be compensated for an altruistic act even after his death. An individual who dies saving a friend, for example, may have altruistic acts performed by the friend to the benefit of his offspring. Selection will discriminate against the cheater in this situation, if kin of the martyr, or others, are willing to punish lack of reciprocity.

iii *Generalized altruism.*   Given learning from others and multiparty action against cheaters, selection may favor a multiparty altruistic system in which altruistic acts are dispensed freely among more than two individuals, an individual being perceived to cheat if in an altruistic situation he dispenses less benefit for the same cost than would the others, punishment coming not only from the other individual in that particular exchange but from the others in the system.

iv *Rules of exchange.*   Multiparty altruistic systems increase by several-fold the cognitive difficulties in detecting imbalances and deciding whether they are due to cheating or to random factors. One simplifying possibility that language facilitates is the formulation of rules of conduct, cheating being detected as infraction of such a rule. In short, selection may favor the elaboration of norms of reciprocal conduct.

There is abundant evidence for all of the above multiparty interactions (see the above references on hunter-gatherers). Thomas (1958), for example, has shown that debts of reciprocity do not disappear with the death of the "creditor" but are extended to his kin. Krebs has reviewed the psychological literature on generalized altruism. Several studies (e.g., Darlington and Macker, 1966) have shown that humans may direct their altruism to individuals other than those who were hurt and may respond to an altruistic act that benefits themselves by acting altruistically toward a third individual uninvolved in the initial interaction. Berkowitz and Daniels (1964) have shown experimentally, for example, that help from a confederate leads the subject to direct more help to a third individual, a highly dependent supervisor. Freedman, Wallington, and Bless (1967) have demonstrated the surprising result that, in two different experimental situations, humans engaged in reparative altruism only if it could be directed to someone other than the individual harmed, or to the original individual only if they did not expect to meet again. In a system of strong multiparty interactions it is possible that in some situations individuals are selected to demonstrate generalized altruistic tendencies and that their main concern when they have harmed another is to show that they are genuinely altruistic, which they best do by acting altruistic without any apparent ulterior motive, e.g., in the experiments, by acting altruistic toward an uninvolved third party. Alternatively, A. Rapoport (pers. commun.) has suggested that the reluctance to direct reparative altruism toward the harmed individual may be due to unwillingness to show thereby a recognition of the harm done him. The redirection serves to allay guilt feelings without triggering the greater reparation that recognition of the harm might lead to.

10 *Developmental plasticity.*   The conditions under which detection of cheating is possible, the range of available altruistic trades, the cost/benefit ratios of these trades, the relative stability of social groupings, and other relevant parameters should differ from one ecological and social situation to another and should differ through time in the same small human population. Under these conditions one would expect selection to favor developmental plasticity of those traits regulating altruistic and cheating tendencies and responses to these tendencies in others. For example, developmental plasticity may allow the growing organism's sense of guilt to be educated, perhaps partly by kin, so as to permit those forms of cheating that local conditions make adaptive and to discourage those with more dangerous consequences. One would not expect any simple system regulating the development of altruistic behavior. To be adaptive, altruistic behavior must be dispensed with regard to many characteristics of the recipient (including his degree of relationship, emotional makeup, past behavior, friendships, and kin relations), of other members of the group, of the situation in which the altruistic behavior takes place, and of many other parameters, and no simple developmental system is likely to meet these requirements.

Kohlberg (1963), Bandura and Walters (1963), and Krebs have reviewed the developmental literature on human altruism. All of them conclude that none of the proposed developmental theories (all of which rely on simple mechanisms) can account for the known diverse developmental data. Whiting and Whiting (in prep.) have studied altruistic behavior directed towards kin by children in six different cultures and find consistent differences among the cultures that correlate with differences in child-rearing and other facets of the cultures. They argue that the differences adapt the children to different adult roles available in the cultures. Although the behavior analyzed takes place between kin and hence Hamilton's model (1964) may apply rather than this model, the Whitings' data provide an instance of the adaptive value of developmental plasticity in altruistic behavior. No careful work has been done analyzing the influence of environmental factors on the development of altruistic behavior, but some data exist. Krebs has reviewed the evidence that altruistic tendencies can be increased by the effects of warm, nurturant models, but little is known on how long such effects endure. Rosenhan (1967) and Rettig (1956) have shown a correlation between altruism in parents and altruism in their college-age children, but these studies do not separate genetic and environmental influences. Class differences in altruistic behavior (e.g., Berkowitz, 1968; Ugurel-Semin, 1952; Almond and Verba, 1963) may primarily reflect environmental influences. Finally, Lutzker (1960) and Deutsch (1958) have shown that one can predict the degree of altruistic behavior displayed in iterated games of Prisoner's Dilemma from personality typing based on a questionnaire. Such personality differences are probably partly environmental in origin.

It is worth emphasizing that some of the psychological traits analyzed above have applications outside the particular reciprocal altruistic system being discussed. One may be suspicious, for example, not only of individuals likely to cheat on the altruistic system, but of any individual likely to harm oneself; one may be suspicious of the known tendencies toward adultery of another male or even of these tendencies in one's own mate. Likewise, a guilt-motivated show of reparation may avert the revenge of someone one has harmed, whether that individual was harmed by cheating on the altruistic system or in some other way. And the system of reciprocal altruism may be employed to avert possible revenge. The Bushmen of the Kalahari, for example, have a saying (Marshall, 1959) to the effect that, if you wish to sleep with someone else's wife, you get him to sleep with yours, then neither of you goes after the other with poisoned arrows. Likewise, there is a large literature on the use of reciprocity to cement friendships between neighboring groups, now engaged in a common enterprise (e.g., Lee and DeVore, 1968).

The above review of the evidence has only begun to outline the complexities of the human altruistic system. The inherent instability of the Prisoner's Dilemma, combined with its importance in human evolution, has led to the evolution of a very complex system. For example, once moralistic aggression has been selected for to protect against cheating, selection favors sham moralistic aggression as a new form of cheating. This should lead to selection for the ability to discriminate the two and to guard against the latter. The guarding can, in turn, be used to counter real moralistic aggression: one can, in effect, *impute* cheating motives to another person in order to protect one's own cheating. And so on. Given the psychological and cognitive complexity the system rapidly acquires, one may wonder to what extent the importance of altruism in human evolution set up a selection pressure for psychological and cognitive powers which partly contributed to the large increase in hominid brain size during the Pleistocene.

LIST OF LITERATURE

Almond, G. A., and S. Verba. 1963. *The Civic Culture.* Princeton University Press, Princeton, N.J.

Aronfreed, J. 1968. *Conduct and Conscience.* Academic Press, N.Y.

Ashmole, M. 1962. Migration of European thrushes: a comparative study based on ringing recoveries. *Ibis,* 104:522–559.

Baier, K. 1958. *The Moral Point of View.* Cornell University Press, Ithaca, N.Y.

Balikci, A. 1964. Development of basic socioeconomic units in two Eskimo communities. National Museum of Canada Bulletin No. 202, Ottawa.

Bandura, A., and R. H. Walters. 1963. *Social Learning and Personality Development.* Holt, Rinehart and Winston, N.Y.

Berkowitz, L. 1968. Responsibility, reciprocity and social distance in help-giving: an experimental investigation of English social class differences. *J. Exp. Soc. Psychol.,* 4:664–669.

Berkowitz, L., and L. Daniels. 1964. Affecting the salience of the social responsibility norm: effects of past help on the response to dependency relationships. *J. Abnorm. Soc. Psychol.,* 68:275–281.

Berkowitz, L., and P. Friedman. 1967. Some social class differences in helping behavior. *J. Personal. Soc. Psychol.,* 5:217–225.

Berndt, R., and H. Sternberg. 1968. Terms, studies and experiments on the problems of bird dispersion. *Ibis,* 110:256–269.

Berscheid, E., and E. Walster. 1967. When does a harm-doer compensate a victim? *J. Personal. Soc. Psychol.,* 6:435–441.

Blest, A. D. 1963. Longevity, palatability and natural selection in five species of New World Saturuiid moth. *Nature,* 197:1183–1186.

Brehm, J. W., and A. H., Cole. 1966. Effect of a favor which reduces freedom. *J. Personal. Soc. Psychol.,* 3:420–426.

Brower, J. V. Z., and L. P. Brower. 1965. Experimental studies of mimicry. 8. *Am. Natur.,* 49:173–188.

Campbell, B. 1966. *Human Evolution.* Aldine, Chicago.

Crook, J. H. 1969. The socio-ecology of primates. In J. H. Crooke (ed.), *Social Behavior in Birds and Mammals,* p. 103–166. Academic Press, London.

Darlington, R. B., and C. E. Macker. 1966. Displacement of guilt-produced altruistic behavior. *J. Personal. Soc. Psychol.,* 4:442–443.

Darwin, C. 1871. *The Descent of Man and Selection in Relation to Sex.* Random House, N.Y.

Deutsch, M. 1958. Trust and suspicion. *J. Conflict Resolution,* 2:267–279.

Dhont, A. A., and J. Hublé. 1968. Fledging-date and sex in relation to dispersal in young Great Tits, *Bird Study,* 15:127–134.

Drury, W. H., and W. J. Smith. 1968. Defense of feeding areas by adult herring gulls and intrusion by young. *Evolution,* 22:193–201.

Eibl-Eibesfeldt, I. 1955. Über Symbiosen, Parasitismus und andere besondere zwischenartliche Beziehungen tropischer Meeresfische. *Z. f. Tierpsychol.,* 12:203–219.

———. 1959. Der Fisch *Aspidontus taeniatus* als Nachahmer des Putzers *Labroides dimidiatus. Z. f. Tierpsychol.,* 16:19–25.

Epstein, Y. M., and H. A. Horstein. 1969. Penalty and interpersonal attraction as factors influencing the decision to help another person. *J. Exp. Soc. Psychol.,* 5:272–282.

Feder, H. M. 1966. Cleaning symbioses in the marine environment. In S. M. Henry (ed.), *Symbiosis,* Vol. 1, p. 327–380. Academic Press, N.Y.

Fisher, R. A. 1958. *The Genetical Theory of Natural Selection,* Dover, N.Y.

Floyd, J. 1964. Effects of amount of award and friendship status of the other on the frequency of sharing in children. Unpublished doctoral dissertation. University of Minnesota. (Reviewed in Krebs, 1970.)

Freedman, J. L., S. A. Wallington, and E. Bless. 1967. Compliance without pressure: the effect of guilt. *J. Personal. Soc. Psychol.,* 7:117–124.

Friedrichs, R. W. 1960. Alter versus ego: an exploratory assessment of altruism. *Am. Sociol. Rev.,* 25:496–508.

Gilula, M. F., and D. N. Daniels. 1969. Violence and man's struggle to adapt. *Science,* 164:395–405.

Goranson, R., and Berkowitz. 1966. Reciprocity and responsibility reactions to prior help. *J. Personal. Soc. Psychol.,* 3:227–232.

Gouldner, A. 1960. The norm of reciprocity: a preliminary statement. *Am. Sociol. Rev.,* 47:73–80.

Haldane, J. B. S. 1955. Population genetics. *New Biology,* 18:34–51.

Hall, K. R. L., and I. DeVore. 1965. Baboon social behavior. In I. DeVore (ed.), *Primate Behavior: Field Studies of Monkeys and Apes,* pp. 53–110. Holt, Rinehart and Winston, N.Y.

Hamilton, W. D. 1964. The genetical evolution of social behavior. *J. Theoret. Biol.,* 7:1–52.

———. 1966. The moulding of senescence by natural selection. *J. Theoret. Biol.,* 12:12–45.

———. 1969. Selection of selfish and altruistic behavior in some extreme models. Paper presented at "Man and Beast Symposium" (in press, Smithsonian Institution).

Hartshorne, H., and M. A. May. 1928–1930. *Studies in the Nature of Character. Vol. 1, Studies in Deceit; Vol. 2, Studies in Self-Control: Vol. 3, Studies in the Organization of Character.* Macmillan, N.Y.

Hediger, H. 1968. Putzer-fische im aquarium. *Natur und Museum,* 98:89–96.

Heider, F. 1958. *The Psychology of Interpersonal Relations.* Wiley, N.Y.

Hobson, E. S. 1969. Comments on certain recent generalizations regarding cleaning symbioses in fishes. *Pacific Science,* 23:35–39.

Kohlberg. L. 1963. Moral development and identification. In H. W. Stevenson (ed.), *Yearbook of the National Society for the Study of Education. Part 1. Child Psychology,* p. 277–332. University of Chicago Press, Chicago.

Krebs, D. 1970. Altruism—an examination of the concept and a review of the literature. *Psychol. Bull.,* 73:258–302.

Kuyton, P. 1962. Verhalten-becobachtungen an der Raupe des Kaiseratlas. *Z. d. Entomol.,* 72:203–207.

Lee, R. 1969. !Kung Bushman violence. Paper presented at meeting of American Anthropological Association, Nov. 1969.

Lee, R., and I. DeVore. 1968. *Man the Hunter.* Aldine, Chicago.

Leeds, R. 1963. Altruism and the norm of giving. *Merrill-Palmer Quart.,* 9:229–240.

Lerner, M. J., and R. R. Lichtman. 1968. Effects of perceived norms on attitudes and altruistic behavior toward a dependent other. *J. Personal. Soc. Psychol.,* 9:226–232.

Leyhausen, P. 1965. Über die Funktion der relativen Stimmungshierarchie (dasgestellt am Beispiel der phylogenetischen und ontogenetischen Entwicklung des Beutefangs von Raubtieren. *Z. f. Tierpsychol.,* 22:412–494.

Limbaugh, C. 1961. Cleaning symbioses. *Scient. Am.,* 205:42–49.

Limbaugh, C., H. Pederson, and F. Chase. 1961. Shrimps that clean fishes. *Bull. Mar. Sci. Gulf Caribb.,* 11:237–257.

Lorenz, K. 1966. *On Aggression.* Harcourt, Brace and World, N.Y.

Luce, R. D., and H. Raiffa, 1957. *Games and Decisions.* Wiley, N.Y.

Lutzker, D. 1960. Internationalism as a predictor of cooperative game behavior. *J. Conflict Resolution,* 4:426–435.

Marler, P. 1955. The characteristics of certain animal calls. *Nature,* 176:6–7.

———. 1957. Specific distinctiveness in the communication signals of birds. *Behavior,* 11:13–39.

Marshall, L. K. 1959. Marriage among !Kung Bushmen. *Africa,* 29:335–365.

———. 1961. Sharing, talking and giving: relief of social tension among !Kung Bushmen. *Africa,* 31:231–249.

Maynard, E. C. L. 1968. Cleaning symbiosis and oral grooming on the coral reef. In P. Person (ed.), *Biology of the Month,* pp. 79–88. Philip Person, American Association for the Advancement of Science, Wash., D.C.

Maynard Smith, J. 1964. Kin selection and group selection. *Nature,* 201:1145–1147.

———. 1965. The evolution of alarm calls. *Amer. Natur.,* 99:59–63.

Mayr, E. 1963. *Animal Species and Evolution.* Belknap Press, Cambridge.

Montagu, F. M. A. 1968. *Man and Aggression.* Oxford University Press, N.Y.

Murie, A. 1944. *The Wolves of Mount McKinley.* Fauna of National Parks, Faunal Series #5; Wash., D.C.

Owen, D. F. 1963. Similar polymorphismas in an insect and a land snail. *Nature,* 198:201–203.

Perdeck, A. 1958. Two types of orientation in migrating starlings, *Starnus vulgaris* L., and chaffishes, *Fringilla coeleus* L., as revealed by displacement experiments. *Ardea,* 46:1–35.

Pruitt, D. G. 1968. Reciprocity and credit building in a laboratory dyad. *J. Personal. Soc. Psychol.,* 8:143–147.

Randall, J. E. 1958. A review of the Labrid fish genus *Labroides* with discriptions of two new species and notes on ecology. *Pacific Science,* 12:327–347.

————. 1962. Fish service stations. *Sea Frontiers,* 8:40–47

Rapoport, A., and A. Chammah. 1965. *Prisoner's Dilemma.* University of Michigan Press, Ann Arbor.

Rapoport, A., and P. Dale. 1967. The "end" and "start" effects in iterated Prisoner's Dilemma. *J. Conflict Resolution,* 10:363–366.

Rasmussen, K. 1931. The Netsilik Eskimos: social life and spiritual culture. Report of the Fifth Thule Expedition 1921–1924. Vol. 8(1,2). Gyldendalske Boghandel, Copenhagen.

Rettig, S. 1956. An exploratory study of altruism. *Dissert. Abstr.,* 16:2220–2230.

Reynolds, L. 1966. Open groups in hominid evolution. *Man,* 1:441–452.

Rosenhan, D. 1967. *The Origins of Altruistic Social Autonomy.* Educational Testing Service, Princeton, N.J.

Rousseau, J. J. 1954. *The Social Contract.* Henry Regnery Co., Chicago.

Rudebeck, G. 1950. The choice of prey and modes of hunting of predatory birds with special reference to their selective effort. *Oikos,* 2:65–88.

————. 1951. The choice of prey and modes of hunting of predatory birds, with special reference to their selective effort *(cont.) Oikos,* 3:200–231.

Sawyer, J. 1966. The altruism scale: a measure of cooperative, individualistic, and competitive interpersonal orientation. *Am. J. Social.* 71:407–416.

Schopler, J., and V. T. Thompson. 1968. The role of attribution process in mediating amount of reciprocity for a favor. *J. Personal. Soc. Psychol.,* 10:243–250.

Scott, J. P. 1958. *Aggression.* University of Chicago Press, Chicago.

Southern, H. N. 1954. Tawny owls and their prey. *Ibis,* 96:384–410.

Struhsaker, T. 1967. Social structure among vervet monkeys *(Cercopithecus aethiops). Behavior,* 29:83–121.

Tesser, A., R. Gatewood, and M. Driver. 1968. Some determinants of gratitude. *J. Personal. Soc. Psychol.,* 9:232–236.

Thomas, E. M. 1958. *The Harmless People.* Random House, N.Y.

Tinbergen, L. 1960. The dynamics of insect and bird populations in pine woods. 1. Factors influencing the intensity of predation by song birds, *Arch. Neerl. de Zool.,* 13:265–343.

Tinbergen, N. 1968. On war and peace in animals and man. *Science,* 160:1411–1418.

Ugurel-Semin, R. 1952. Moral behavior and moral judgment of children. *J. Abnorm. Soc. Psychol.,* 47:463–474.

VanLawick-Goodall, J. 1968. A preliminary report on expressive movements and communication in the Gombe Stream chimpanzees. In P. Jay (ed.), *Primates,* p. 313–374 Holt, Rinehart and Winston, N.Y.

Wallace J., and E. Sadalla. 1966. Behavioral consequences of transgression: the effects of social recognition. *J. Exp. Res. Personal.,* 1:187–194.

Wickler, W. 1968. *Mimicry in Plants and Animals.* McGraw-Hill, N.Y.

Williams, G. C. 1966. *Adaptation and Natural Selection.* Princeton University Press, Princeton, N.J.

Wright, B. 1942. Altruism in children and the perceived conduct of others. *J. Abnorm. Soc. Psychol.,* 37:218–233.

Wynne-Edwards, V. C. 1962. *Animal Dispersion in Relation to Social Behavior.* Hafner, N.Y.

The Evolution of Social Behavior by Kin Selection (*part*)

Mary Jane West Eberhard
Department of Biology, Universidad del Valle, Cali, Colombia,
and Smithsonian Tropical Research Institute, Balboa, Canal Zone

Kin-selection theory (Hamilton's "genetical theory") explains how aid that is self-sacrificing (in terms of classical individual fitness), or "altruism," can evolve if sufficiently beneficial to relatives. It is discussed here in order to clarify the meaning of kin selection and inclusive fitness (the total reproductive value of an individual, both its production of offspring and effects on the reproduction of relatives). Hamilton's condition $K > 1/r$, the relationship of benefit/cost and relatedness necessary for advantageous altruism, is reformulated so as to be applicable to altruism by descendents, and from the point of view of any member of a population (e.g., affected parties other than the altruist). A general expression is derived which defines inclusive fitness in terms of a classical and kinship component. A unit of inclusive fitness—"offspring equivalents"—is defined. An index of the likelihood that altruism will occur in different social and ecological situations, K_b is employed to evaluate conflicts of interest among the members of social groups.

Specific cases of altruism are discussed with attention to costs and benefits in order to show how kin selection can operate even among quite distant relatives. The probability of altruism is increased if the beneficiary stands to gain a great deal (e.g., in emergencies), if the cost is low (e.g., if the altruist is excluded from reproduction on his own or is in control of an abundant resource), or both; and if the donor is particularly efficient at giving aid or if the beneficiary is particularly efficient at using it, as in the case of the specialized workers and queens of social insects, or if both situations obtain. Phenomena discussed include social responses to food shortages in insects and primates; anti-predator responses of ungulates in variously structured social groups; social grooming and solicitude toward infants in primates; adoption of orphans in a phylogenetically diverse set of animals; "helpers" among birds, mammals, and insects; alarm calls of vertebrates; and dominance-subordinance interactions in vertebrates and invertebrates.

This paper began as a joint effort by Richard D. Alexander and the author to write a paper on modifiers of kin selection and (later) on the evolution of social behavior (see Alexander, 1974). Many of the ideas discussed here came originally from Alexander or were brought to my attention by him; indeed, I am not always sure where his originality left off and mine began on certain topics. The same is true of help I received in extensive discussions of some sections with William G. Eberhard. Mary L. Corn, William D. Hamilton, Egbert Leigh, Charles D. Michener, Martin H. Moynihan, Katherine M. Noonan, Michael J. Orlove, and Robert L. Trivers also read the manuscript and made stimulating and helpful criticisms. José Ignacio Borrero kindly allowed me to use his personal library of books on birds and mammals. Financial support was provided by William G. Eberhard.

From *The Quarterly Review of Biology 50:* 1–22, 31–33. Reprinted by permission of the author and *The Quarterly Review of Biology*.

Subordinant behavior among primates and other animals living in groups of relatives may sometimes represent a kind of altruism that is advantageous (in terms of inclusive fitness) to the subordinant individual, providing the subordinant individual is a reproductively inferior relative of the dominant individual and contributes sufficiently to the dominant individual's reproduction.

Mutualism (reciprocity and cooperation) and parental manipulation may produce beneficent behavior resembling that produced by kin selection. Mutually beneficent behavior can be maintained by reciprocal-altruistic selection, parental imposition, or the selfish advantageousness of acts incidentally benefiting neighbors, as well as by kin selection. Reciprocal altruism—temporary altruism with the expectation of more than compensating future aid (reciprocation) on the part of the beneficiary—requires meticulous contemporaneous controls on cheating and is therefore probably restricted to intelligent animals, the only documented example being in man.

Kin-selection theory outlines certain limits to selfishness as well as the conditions under which altruism is advantageous. Inclusive fitness, because it includes the effects of all selfish and social traits on the reproductive value of an individual, is capable of evaluating the selective significance (biological function) of any social act, whether selfish, altruistic, reciprocal, cooperative, or destructive in nature. Thus, it provides an approach which could serve as the basis for a general and comprehensive theory of social behavior.

INTRODUCTION

According to classical evolutionary theory every characteristic of an organism is a means and a consequence of reproductive competition among individuals, and there should be no example of behavior benefiting another individual at reproductive cost to the performer. Reproductive cost and benefit are measured in terms of *fitness,* the number of adult offspring left by an individual in the next generation in the absence of chance effects (see Williams, 1966). Hamilton (1964a) has recently extended the conventional theory to encompass behavior involving detriment to individual fitness ("altruism") by introducing the concept of *inclusive fitness.* Inclusive fitness consists of two parts: the individual's personal fitness, and his effects on the fitnesses of his neighbors multiplied by his respective fractional relatedness to them. It thus takes into account the individual's total lifetime effect on the gene pool of the succeeding generation(s), both through the production of the individual's own offspring and through effects on the reproduction of other individuals. According to Hamilton's genetical theory of social behavior (Hamilton, 1964a, b), a social act is favored by natural selection if it increases the inclusive fitness of the performer.

Hamilton's ideas are widely referred to as the theory of "kin selection" (Maynard Smith, 1964). I shall use the term kin selection to refer to the subclass of natural selection by which genetic alleles change in frequency in a population owing to effects on the reproduction of *relatives* of the individual(s) in which a character (allele) is expressed, rather than to effects on the personal reproduction of that individual itself (the domain of classical selection). Just as classical natural selection depends on the likelihood that offspring resemble (genetically) their parents, kin selection depends on the likelihood that other (near or distant) relatives resemble each other, i.e., bear a certain portion of genes identical by descent, so that increasing the reproduction of relatives increases the frequency of alleles like one's own genes in the population.

Kin-selection theory explains social behavior at the level of the individual rather than at the level of the group or the species. Although some authors (e.g., Wilson, 1973) have interpreted kin selection as group selection or "kingroup" selection (Brown, 1974), the idea of inclusive fitness clearly focuses on the contribution of *individuals* to changes in population gene frequencies, simply including effects on all relatives (rather than just offspring) in the estimation of individual reproductive value. Extensions of kin-selection theory to the group or family level apply only in special circumstances (see Lewontin, 1970, for a discussion of the conditions necessary for group selection in general). In attempting to make widely applicable generalizations about social behavior I have rejected explanations at the group or population level, such as those of Wynne-Edwards (1962) and others, for reasons discussed by Williams (1966), Trivers (1971), Eshel (1972), Maynard Smith (1972), and Alexander (1974). Although selection above the individual level may sometimes affect the frequency of a social gene, contributing to its persistence or extinction, the allele must first become established by selection at the individual level (see Rand, 1967; Levins, 1970; and Alexander, 1971).

In the literature on kin selection, Hamilton and subsequent authors have tended to neglect the idea of inclusive fitness, and have concentrated on the role of a single factor, the degree of relatedness, in the evolution of social behavior. Emphasis on the extraordinarily high relatedness of hymenopteran (wasp, ant, and bee) sisters has created the erroneous impression that very high relatedness is a prerequisite for the operation of kin selection, a view tending to discourage its application to other social animals (e.g., birds and mammals) in which interacting individuals are not always so highly related. This supposition may explain the surprising absence of any direct reference to kin selection in important recent discussions of the functions and evolution of social behavior in primates (e.g., Jolly, 1972; Rowell, 1972) and other vertebrates (e.g., Kruuk, 1972).

This review begins to remedy this problem by outlining social, ecological, and developmental factors which, along with relatedness, influence the evolution of beneficent social interactions. Kin selection has a much wider potential application than is generally believed. It is one of a small set of hypotheses (see below) that should be considered whenever the functional (adaptive) significance of a social interaction is analyzed.

The examples to be cited are intended to illustrate the use of kin selection theory in conjunction with other ideas in the analysis of animal sociality, and are not intended to "prove" the existence of kin selection nor to show that it is the only possible explanation of the examples given. Some readers will consider certain examples "already explained" by some other plausible hypothesis. They are urged to realize that a single behavior can serve more than one function at once—the benefit to inclusive fitness through aid rendered to a near or distant relative can be an advantage over and above a selfish advantage. The claim that a farmer who saves his brother's life benefits by the consequent increase of genetic alleles like his in the population, through kin selection, does not detract from the biological validity of the farmer's assertion that he did it to get help milking the cows.

Although this review focuses primarily on the evolution of beneficence and altruism, I believe that a model like that presented here—beginning with Hamilton's idea of inclusive fitness—could serve as the basis for a general and comprehensive theory of social behavior capable of evaluating the selective significance of any social act, whether selfish, altruistic, reciprocal, cooperative, or destructive in nature, and at any degree of genetic relatedness. Applications of Hamilton's genetical theory to social phenomena other than altruism are to be found in Hamilton (1970, 1971, 1972), Trivers (1974), and Alexander (1974).

HAMILTON'S THEORY

Hamilton defined altruism as behavior benefiting another individual while detrimental to the performer, the benefit and the detriment being defined in terms of personal fitness. He originally (1963) stated that the condition necessary for advantageous altruism is

$$K > \frac{1}{r}$$

in which K is the ratio of gain to loss in fitness resulting from the altruism, and r the genetic relatedness (fraction of genes identical by descent) of the two individuals.

According to Hamilton's theory, then, three variables affect the likelihood of altruistic behavior between individuals:

1 *The closeness of genetic relatedness* between the aiding and the aided individual. Unreciprocated aid is more likely to occur among relatives, and the more closely related they are the more likely it is to occur.
2 *The magnitude of the benefit* to the aided individual, expressed in terms of the consequent increase in his fitness, or reproductive output. The greater the benefit derived from the aid, the more likely it is to be given.
3 *The magnitude of the cost* to the altruist in terms of his consequent loss in fitness. The more costly an altruistic act, the less likely it is to occur.

Hamilton (1964b, p. 19) gave the following "generalized unrigorous statement" of the main principle emerging from his model:

The social behavior of a species evolves in such a way that in each behaviour-evoking situation the individual will seem to value his neighbours' fitness against his own according to the coefficients of relationship appropriate to that situation.

REFORMULATION OF HAMILTON'S THEORY

Hamilton's expression, $K > 1/r$, while attractively compact, cannot be applied directly to all cases of altruism (see below), and tends to obscure the significance of inclusive fitness. The following reformulation modifies $K > 1/r$ in a series of steps so as to make it both more general and more easily analyzed in terms of classical and inclusive fitness.

Extension to Include Altruism by Descendents

The condition $K > 1/r$ assumes that the relatedness of the altruist and the young of the beneficiary is as one-half r. This is not true for direct ancestors of the altruist, the most important example being parents: in diploid animals, r with a full sibling is ½, not one-half of r with the parent (r with the parent is ½, and ½ r is thus ¼). Thus, the form $K > 1/r$ does not apply directly to the matrifilial societies of social insects, the most discussed application of the genetical theory. (Hamilton, in a personal communication, points out that in such cases the condition does yield proper values if both parents are considered beneficiaries and their degrees of relatedness are summed. However, it seems preferable to have an expression in which both terms can be applied uniformly to any case.) In more recent publications Hamilton (1971–74) has dropped the original $K > 1/r$ and has substituted another form,

$$K > \frac{1 + F_A}{2r_{AB}},$$

in which F_A is the inbreeding coefficient for individual A (the likelihood that two homologous genes in A, the altruist, are replicates) and r_{AB} is the probability that a gamete of A has the same gene as a gamete of B. Uniform application of the new expression requires the same assumption—that altruist and beneficiary's young are related as one-half the relatedness of the altruist and the beneficiary ("beneficiary" referring to the individual whose reproduction, or fitness, is favorably affected). A more generally and uniformly applicable procedure is to use values of

$$r_{AB,}$$

the relatedness of the altruist and the *young* of the beneficiary. In an outbreeding population the condition thus becomes

$$K > \frac{1}{2r_{AB,}} \tag{1}$$

This modification, while less compact, is perhaps intuitively easier to apply in addition to being more general, since it refers directly to the fitnesses affected and to the relative values of the individuals (young) whose production is altered.

Viewpoints of Non-donors

Hamilton's condition, like formula (1), applies only to the decision of a *donor* regarding the profitableness of altruism. The degree to which it can be used to predict the results of natural selection depends, among other things, on the degree to which the donor individual is in control of his own reproductive behavior. We must therefore consider the possibility that selection operating on individuals other than the donor might influence the probability of his becoming an altruist—that his altruism might sometimes be forced, reinforced, curtailed, or prohibited through selection operating on influential individuals such as parents (Alexander, 1974) or other members of a cohabiting group. It is even possible that at certain values of K and r_{AB}, a beneficiary might advantageously refuse aid—for example, if it were to exact too much from a close relative. (A case in which selection on the beneficiary might limit altruism—that of robbed wasps of the genus *Trigonopsis*—is given in the section on reciprocal altruism, below.) It is therefore useful to make a version of formulation (1) giving the condition for advantageous altruism from the point of view of any given member ("Ego") of a population:

$$K > \frac{r_{A_y}}{r_{B_y}} \tag{2}$$

where r_{A_y} and r_{B_y} are respectively the probabilities of Ego having a given gene in common by descent with the young of the donor *(A)* or with the young of the beneficiary *(B)*.

Expression in Terms of Fitness

Expressed in terms of fitness, a

$$K \equiv \frac{a_{B_2} - a_{B_1}}{a_{A_1} - a_{A_2}}, \text{ or } -\frac{\Delta a_B}{\Delta a_A}$$

where a_{A_1} and a_{B_1} are the would-be personal fitness of donor and beneficiary without altruism, a_{A_2} and a_{B_2} their fitnesses following altruism by A.

By substitution, we can rewrite formulation (2) as

$$r_{A_y}\Delta a_A + r_{B_y}\Delta a_B > 0.$$

This form applies to both beneficent (Δa_B positive) and harmful (Δa_B negative) acts, whether selfish (Δa_A positive) or altruistic (Δa_A negative), whatever the degree of relatedness of performer *(A)* and affected individual *(B)*.

Since animals that live in groups often perform behavior (such as alarm calls or cooperative hunting) that benefits more than one individual simultaneously, a more general expression is

$$r_{A_y}\Delta a_A + \sum_{i=1}^{n} (r_{B_y}\Delta a_B)_i > 0 \tag{3}$$

which sums the effects on the fitnesses of n individuals of an act by individual A. Since the most commonly considered point of view is that of the performer of a social act, the most commonly useful form of this expression is that in which A and Ego are identical and $r_{A,}$ is the average relatedness of the performer and his own young ($=\frac{1}{2}$):

$$\frac{1}{2}\Delta a_A + \sum_{i=1}^{n} (r_{B,}\Delta a_B)_i > 0 \tag{3a}$$

For the case in which Ego is a third party (neither the altruist nor the beneficiary) the condition is:

$$r_{A,}\Delta a_A + \sum_{i=1}^{n} (r_{B,}\Delta a_B) - \Delta a_E/2 > 0 \tag{3b}$$

in which Δa_E is the change in Ego's personal fitness due to intervention ($\Delta a_E/2 =$ cost of intervention).

Dilution Factor

I will next try to show how altruism can be advantageous even at relatively low values of $r_{AB,}$. Williams (1966) has objected to explanations involving aid given distant relatives on the grounds that such relatives carry a large portion of competing genes. This raises a very important point. For kin selection to operate positively at low values of r, r_{AB}, must be greater than the average relatedness of A with all other individuals in the population as a whole $(\bar{r})$. Above this value, as Hamilton (1964a, 1970) has pointed out, the unlike fraction acts to slow (or dilute) the progress of selection but does not alter its direction. This is because the fraction of a beneficiary's genotype that is not identical by descent contains a random collection of the alleles present in the population at large and therefore neither augments nor diminishes the relative frequency of genes like the altruist's in the gene pool. These nonidentical alleles, therefore, should not be thought of as "competing" genes in the sense that somehow they would oppose or cancel out the positive contribution of the fraction that is identical. For, if this were so, sexual reproduction in outbreeding organisms would be fruitless to an individual, since the non-identical half of its offspring's genes (those from the parent's mate) would exactly cancel out the positive contribution of the identical half. It is important to realize that any small above-average degree of relatedness can in fact serve as the basis for kin selection. As long as the relatedness of beneficiary and altruist is even slightly above average, any (even a small) increase in fitness (a_B) is profitable to A (providing the ecological cost of A of adding individuals to the population is not too great—see "Cheap Aid and the Effects of Ecological Competition," below; and Alexander, 1974).

Thus it would be more precise to write condition (3) by taking the dilution factor, $\bar{r}$, into account as follows:

$$(r_{A,}-\bar{r})\Delta a_A + \sum_{i=1}^{n} [(r_{B,}-\bar{r})\Delta a_B] > 0 \tag{4}$$

The left side of this expression is like the "inclusive fitness effect" of Hamilton (1964a) except for the involvement of $\bar{r}$, the significance of which Hamilton did not discuss until later (Hamilton, 1970).

The consideration of $\bar{r}$ is complicated by the difficulty of knowing how to define the relevant population to which it should refer—whether that population should be the whole species or some more closely interbreeding (and intercompeting) relatively isolated subunit of the species. As Hamilton has pointed out, it is probably realistic to assume that $r_{AB}, > \bar{r}$ in most social situations: with common patterns of dispersal the unrecognized individuals most likely to be encountered are the ones likely to be most related (here he evidently takes $\bar{r}$ to refer to the species as a whole, but the same assumption should hold for subpopulations also). Numerical values of r given in this paper and in the literature assume a large panmictic population in which $\bar{r}$ is negligible.

The Meaning of Inclusive Fitness

Expressions (1) through (4) simply restate the basic theorem of Hamilton's genetical theory of social behavior: for a given act (or gene) to be selectively advantageous to a given individual it must cause a net gain in the *inclusive fitness* of that individual. In formulation (3a), effects on the personal (classical) fitness of the performer are represented by the first term; kinship effects are represented by the second term. The sum of the two terms—the entire left side of expressions (3) through (4)—is the effect of the behavior in question on the inclusive fitness of A.

Inclusive fitness (a_i), then, is personal (classical) fitness (a) plus the lifetime sum of effects on the fitness of relatives $(\Sigma \Delta a_B)$, with each effect weighted according to the degree of relatedness of the individual affected. I shall call this second component of inclusive fitness the "kinship component" (a_k) to distinguish it from the personal (classical) component:

inclusive fitness = classical fitness + kinship component

$$a_i \quad = \quad a \quad + \quad a_k$$

The kinship component is calculated as follows:

$$a_k = 2 \sum_{i=1}^{n} [(r_{B_y} - \bar{r}) \Delta a_B],$$

in which n is the total number of individuals whose fitnesses are affected by the individual in question during his lifetime, and Δa_B is his total lifetime effect on the fitness of each one (B). (The sum is multiplied by two to make the units of the kinship component comparable to the units of classical fitness—each adult offspring or its equivalent in terms of genes identical by descent $= 1.0$.)

The unit of classical fitness is adult offspring. I shall call the unit of inclusive fitness "offspring equivalents," valuing each relative (or fraction thereof) added to, or subtracted from, the population according to its relatedness compared to the young of the individual in question. For example, in a diploid organism each offspring is on an average one-half genetically identical by descent to its parent, and its value in terms of classical fitness is 1.0. A sibling, also related by 0.5, is genetically equivalent to an offspring, or worth 1.0 offspring equivalents.

A nephew ($r = \frac{1}{4}$) is worth 0.5 offspring equivalents; a cousin ($r = \frac{1}{8}$) 0.25; a grandchild ($r = \frac{1}{4}$) 0.5; and so forth. Suppose an individual raises three offspring to reproductive maturity and in addition gives altruistic aid adding 0.5 to his mother's fitness and 1.0 to his brother's fitness. The aid given his mother is worth 0.5 offspring equivalents and that given his brother is worth 0.5 (r with the brother's offspring—nieces and nephews—is $\frac{1}{4}$, or 0.25). So this individual's classical component is 3.0; his kinship component is 1.0 (i.e., 0.5 + 0.5); and his inclusive fitness is 4.0.

In accordance with the present formulation, we can classify all social behavior into two major groups corresponding to the two components of inclusive fitness: first, the primarily "selfish," contributing primarily to the personal fitness component; and second, the primarily "altruistic," contributing primarily to the kinship component by means of positive effects on others. Classified in this way—according to the mode of action of natural selection—"selfish" social behavior includes both overt selfishness, such as aggressiveness and territoriality, and quasi-altruistic selfishness, such as cooperation and reciprocal (temporary) altruism. However, it should be common to find both components of inclusive fitness augmented simultaneously by a single act.

As pointed out by various authors (e.g., Lin and Michener, 1972) there is ultimately no such thing as biological altruism. Obviously, "altruism" as defined here is ultimately selfish in leading to the spread of alleles like those of the performer in the population. Problems in defining altruism are discussed by Orlove (1974). I shall use the word "beneficent" to describe any behavior raising the fitness of others regardless of its evolutionary basis.

The Threshold Value of *K* for Advantageous Altruism (K_t) as an Index of the Likelihood that Altruism Will Occur

Expression (2), above, defines the level of K (the benefit/cost ratio) above which altruism is advantageous. We can call this level K_t—the threshold value of K for advantageous altruism. When the benefit/cost ratio for a given altruistic act is higher than K_t from a given individual's point of view, then the altruism is advantageous to that individual. K_t is calculated by dividing the relatedness of the concerned individual to the young of the altruist (r_{A_y}) by his relatedness with the young of the beneficiary (r_{B_y}):

$$K_t = \frac{r_{A_y}}{r_{B_y}} \; .$$

The numerical value of K_t gives the number of extra young that must be produced by the beneficiary to just compensate every one lost to the altruist. This number must be exceeded if a given act of altruism is to be considered advantageous to the individual from whose point of view K_t is calculated. So the lower the value of K_t the more likely is the altruism to occur or to be encouraged as the result of natural selection on that individual or class of individuals. Because it can be applied to the point of view of any individual, K_t is particularly useful for analyzing conflicts of interest among individuals regarding the desirability of a given kind of social behavior or organization (see Table 1, and the discussion of insect sociality, below).

According to kin-selection theory, a donor is expected to be more altruistic toward close relatives than toward distant ones. But it must be common for altruism to occur in social groups of variously related individuals in which the altruist is unable to distinguish its different degrees of relatedness with others. The theory then predicts that *within groups of variously related individuals who are unable to distinguish between near and distant relatives, altruism will be performed as if* r_{B_y} *were equal to* r_{G_x}—*the average of all values of* r_{B_y} *for the possible beneficiaries in an average group of that kind.* In such cases $K_t = r_A/\bar{r}_{G_y}$

This version of K_t can be used as an index of the likelihood of observing a given kind of behavior in a given kind of group. For example, suppose we are interested in estimating the likelihood that orphans will be adopted by subadult females in a species living in nuclear family groups (parents and full sibs) as compared to a species forming clans containing equal numbers of infant siblings and cousins of the potential foster parent. From the adopting female's point of view, K_t in the nuclear family is 1.00 ($r_{A_y} = r$ with her own young $= 0.50$; $r_{B_y} = r$ with a full sib $= 0.50$); whereas in the clan, K_t is 1.33 ($r_{A_y} = 0.50$; $\bar{r}_{G_y} =$ average relatedness with full sibs, 0.50, and with cousins $0.25 = 0.375$; $0.50/0.375 = 1.33$). In other words, in order to be advantageous to the altruist in terms of inclusive fitness, adoption in the clan must be a third again more profitable (or less costly) than in the nuclear family.

THE IMPORTANCE OF COST AND BENEFIT

Hamilton (1963–72) has presented evidence that altruism occurs among close relatives, and has discussed various factors contributing to a high degree of genetic relatedness among the members of social groups. Alexander (unpub.) discusses kin selection among humans. Most examples cited as "problems" for the genetical theory, e.g., alarm calls which carry large distances, and human altruism, involve altruism at relatively low degrees of genetic relatedness. In this section I intend to show that such cases are often the exceptions that prove the rule: when r is relatively low, the other factors contributing to inclusive fitness are relatively high. That is, the act is either basically selfish (see "Reciprocal Altruism and Cooperation," below), or is forced (e.g., by parental manipulation—see below), or involves large gains to the beneficiary at relatively small cost to the performer. For example, a trained lifeguard who saves a drowning child (non-relative) can at very little risk to himself salvage the child's entire future reproductive effort (a_B) without altruism $= 0$). Theoretically, the most willing lifeguard should be a physically fit eunuch or post-reproductive individual (who has nothing to lose in terms of personal fitness), and

Table 1 K_t for Different Kinds of Social Organization from Different Points of View

	Diploid species		Haploid species	
	K_t from point of view of:		K_t from point of view of:	
Kind of society	Altruist	Altruist's mother	Altruist	Altruist's mother
Solitary Parental (A cares for own young)	1.00	1.00	1.00	1.00
Filial (A helps siblings)	2.00	1.00	1.33	1.00
Patri-filial A helps parent; brood 50% male, 50% female	1.00	0.50	1.00	0.50

Note $K_t = r_{E A_V}/r_{E B_V}$ = lowest possible benefit/cost ratio for the social organization (type of altruism) cited to be considered advantageous from "Ego's" (E's) point of view. A = altruist; B = beneficiary.

with few living relatives (little to lose in terms of future gains to inclusive fitness through aid to close kin). A good beneficiary is one with high reproductive value (Fisher, 1930), such as a pregnant low-income Catholic teenager about to produce her first child. So costs and benefits to fitness of a given act are age-dependent (Emlen, 1970); and a large number of other developmental, social, and ecological factors must affect the probability of altruism through their effects on the terms ΔA_B and Δa_A (K of Hamilton). It is thus ironic that these terms have generally been neglected in discussions of kin selection.

In general, the greater the ratio of benefit to cost *(K)* the more likely is the altruism, and the lower is the value of r necessary for positive selection. There are three obvious general situations in which K might be large enough to make altruism advantageous at low values of r: cases of great need (much to gain) on the part of the beneficiary; cases of cheap aid (little to lose on the part of the altruist); and cases in which a small amount of help has a great effect, either because the donor is especially efficient at giving aid (a "super-donor") or because the beneficiary is particularly efficient at utilizing it.

To simplify the discussion, I shall use Hamilton's K—the benefit/cost ratio—to refer to the total changes in fitness caused by a social act or role possibly affecting numerous individuals, even though strictly speaking it is only meaningfully applied to interactions between just two individuals having a given r.

Aid During Emergencies

The probability of altruism among somewhat related individuals is increased in urgent situations, when aid has a large positive effect on the beneficiary's fitness (he stands to lose a lot if not aided) and hence on the altruist's inclusive fitness. Kin-selection theory predicts that altruism toward relatives outside the immediate (nuclear) family may occur during emergencies even in species normally showing little altruistic behavior; and that unusual (extreme) altruism may occur among relatives under stress.

A possible example of the extreme altruism among relatives in an emergency is provided by Eickwort (1973) in one of the few published discussions of the role of changes in fitness in kin selection. She assesses the adaptiveness of cannibalism among chrysomelid beetles *(Labidomera clivicollis),* in which eggs and newly hatched larvae are sometimes eaten by older sibs (or half sibs). She defines the conditions under which such cannibalism would be adaptive (from the victim's point of view), and concludes that "cannibalism is most readily accounted for at [those] points in the life cycle where either the nutritional benefits are great or mortality is high for any reason" (p. 453). Alexander (pers. commun.) points out that such behavior may be the product of selection on the mother beetle, as he compares it to other animals in which parents sacrifice one offspring in favor of another during periods of food scarcity. Indeed, the threshold K for advantageous cannibalism (K_t) is only 1.0 from the mother's point of view, whereas it is 2.0 from the larva's point of view (assuming larvae to be full sibs), a difference that makes it perhaps more likely to evolve by selection on the parent. However, at values of K (the benefit/cost ratio) greater than 1.0 but less than 2.0 there would be a conflict of interest between parent and larva, and if K were often at this level larvae might be expected to evolve resistance to cannibalism. Above $K = 2.0$, cannibalism is desirable from both points of view.

Other kinds of "altruistic" responses to food shortage have been observed in insects. I have studied a colony of the tropical social wasp *Metapolybia aztecoides* during a period of nutritional crisis—when most of the original (swarm) workers had died or disappeared, and the first offspring workers had not yet emerged to replace them in feeding the numerous large larvae and idle queens present on the nest. The result was that some queens become workers (foragers), evidently in direct response to (i.e., immediately following) strong food-soliciting behavior on the part of hungry nestmates. Not only were the beneficiaries of this behavior experiencing an emergency, but there is evidence that the queens-turned-workers (altruists) were those among the original queens who had the lowest relative reproductive capacity (and hence stood to lose least by becoming non-reproducing workers): They were subordinates in their dominance interactions with other queens, a quality associated with lesser ovarian development in wasps (see Pardi, 1948; West, 1967). Eberhard (1972, 1974) found that nesting females of a primitively social sphecid wasp, *Trigonopsis cameronii,* are allowed in times of need to steal prey from cells stocked by relatives (stealing occurs when the robber has had poor hunting success). The restriction of stealing to periods of necessity may raise K sufficiently to make it advantageous for the robbed female to permit the robbery even though, in terms of r alone, she should prefer to keep the prey for her own young ($r = \frac{1}{2}$; stolen prey are used to rear young related to her by only $\frac{3}{8}$, if the associated females are sisters, which is the most closely related they could be as members of the same generation—see Eberhard, 1974). Some responses of primates to nutritional (ecological) stress, also possibly explainable in terms of kin selection, are discussed in the subsequent section on dominance and subordinance.

In many species of social insects the period of founding of the nest is a time of high colony mortality (see Brian, 1965; West Eberhard, 1969; Wilson, 1971), and in some species cooperation and altruism occur during that period among more distant relatives than is usual. In various species of tropical wasps new nests are founded by swarms containing several egg-laying queens and a staff of workers who attend the combined brood, for which the highest possible worker-brood relatedness ($r_{AB,}$, queens and workers being assumed to be sisters) is only ¼. There is evidence that in some species, once the initial high-risk period is over, the colonies return to the matrifilial condition, and a high $r_{AB,}$ (½ if queens mate only once) is restored (West Eberhard, 1973). A similar phenomenon has been noted by Pisarski (1972, 1973) in long-term observations of formicine ants. Certain species of the subgenera *Formica* and *Coptoformica* live in nesting associations called "polycalic" colonies, in which the members of several individual subcolonies inhabiting separate nests are somewhat related, all of them being ultimately descended (by repeated budding off of polygynous groups) from a single original monogynous nest (queen). Mature, established subcolonies of the polycalic colony function independently, but newly founded ones receive a massive influx of aid (workers) from other nests (i.e., from peripheral relatives), so that there is a rapid initial growth. When a subcolony for some reason begins to decline, its workers move brood and reproductives to another nest, where they are received ("adopted"?) without animosity.

Attack by predators, a kind of emergency common in nature, often summons aid from group members who are not the attacked individual's parents and who are not altruistic in other situations. Beneficiaries of such aid are commonly young (helpless) individuals. Janzen (1970) saw several adult coatis (*Nasua narica*) come to the aid of a young adult male who was being attacked by a *Boa constrictor*. Female coatis and their young live in rather changeable groups usually showing little cooperation or altruism but likely to be members of the same family or extended family (Kaufmann, 1962). Kruuk's (1972) comparative study of group-living ungulates under attack by hyenas amounts to a natural experiment in which he observed different degrees of altruism in the responses of differently structured groups to a "constant" strong predator. It is thus a useful test of kin selection theory, although Kruuk did not directly discuss this aspect. He found a "relation between group size and cohesion and the anti-predator response" (p. 206). Thompson's gazelles, which live in large amorphous herds, generally do not assist each other in defense against predators; whereas eland and buffalo, living in fairly small to large herds (clearly discrete units) show aggression and mutual assistance in their reactions against hyenas; and the families and stallion bands of zebras, small and very distinctive units, show high aggression in defense of their own unit but not of others. Kruuk (1972, p. 205) found it "hard to see why zebra mares should defend only their own foals, whereas eland come to the assistance of calves which are not necessarily their own (but in the same herd)." But the different degrees of altruism seem to correlate, as predicted by kin-selection theory, with the different degrees of genetic identity likely to exist within the groups described. Zebra families and bands roam independently, so that neighboring families are not likely to be relatives. Eland families, in contrast, are part of a stable group more likely to be composed of somewhat related subunits. Opportunities for reciprocation (see Trivers, 1971, and below) would also be more common among eland than among zebra.

Wounded or temporarily disabled individuals are given extra attention in many species. Wounded Bonnet macaques receive intensive grooming by many fellow group members in succession. Dirt and other foreign matter are picked out of wounds and the wounds are licked clean. There seems to be a direct relationship between the seriousness of the wound and the amount of grooming activity (Simonds, 1965). Wild dogs regurgitate food to cripples, infants, and nursing mothers who don't go out to feed; yet once the pups are weaned, food is refused the mother but given to the still relatively helpless pups (v. Lawick Goodall and v. Lawick Goodall, 1970). Similarly, infant, pregnant, and nursing wolves are regurgitated to by other members of a pack (Etkin, 1964). A mother and two calf zebras were aided by a group of ten adults when attacked by wild dogs, and a whole herd of fifty or so zebras will slow down to stay with a threatened foal (v. Lawick Goodall and v. Lawick Goodall, 1970).

Infant social primates are often helpless to the point of being unable to survive on their own, and can in that sense be considered to be in a constant state of emergency. They are commonly the objects of altruistic attention by adults other than their parents (see Carpenter, 1965; Jay, 1965; Simonds, 1965; review by Jolly, 1972). Attention to infants undoubtedly sometimes has selfish ulterior motives— other or additional selective advantages contributing to personal fitness, e.g., enhancing the social status of the donor (in rhesus monkeys—Jolly, 1972), providing practice in motherhood (in langurs—Jolly, 1972), or perhaps serving to help integrate (identify) the infant group member through intimate contact. But it is also likely to satisfy the conditions for profitable altruism when benefiting somewhat related infants, as in the species mentioned (see references cited). The famous "aunt behavior" of social primates (intense and repeated attention to infants by females other than their own mothers; see Jolly, 1972) may at least in part be due to benefits to the kinship component of the inclusive fitness of the so-called aunts (probably, in fact, relatives). The significance of infants as a class of suitable beneficiaries (individuals not yet competing with adults and with their entire reproductive lives ahead of them, hence with much to gain through altruistic aid) may be dramatized by Moynihan's (1970) observation that caged adult tamarin monkeys utter infantile cries when extremely frightened. This practice, if it occurs in nature, may represent mimicry of the infants' alarm cry and may serve to summon aid to adults (ordinarily less suitable beneficiaries, but possibly worth aiding in an extreme emergency).

A dramatic instance of dire emergency occurs when the dependent infant of a strongly parental species loses its mother. In such cases the infant will almost certainly die if left alone, so the potential gain in fitness for saving it is very high. In theory, whether or not such orphans are adopted depends on the social structure of the group in which they find themselves—whether or not they are likely to encounter a relative whose inclusive fitness might be increased by giving aid. In practice this seems to hold: adoption of orphans occurs in a taxonomically diverse set of animals, including chimpanzees (v. Lawick Goodall, 1968), baboons, macaques, and langur monkeys (see Jolly, 1972), wild dogs (v. Lawick Goodall and v. Lawick Goodall, 1970), coatis (Kaufmann, 1962), and a primitively social eumenid wasp, *Zethus miniatus* (West Eberhard, in prep.). In all of these cases the adopting individuals were either known siblings (chimpanzees) or other individuals likely to be somewhat closely related as members of extended families or clans (macaques, coatis, *Zethus miniatus*) or other relatively closed groups (langurs, wild dogs). Furthermore, in at least some of these cases the adopting individual was temporarily excluded from reproducing on its own—e.g., was a prereproductive young adult, or, in the case of the wasp, a female without a ready-made cell or larva —i.e., individuals with comparatively little to lose by being altruistic. Part (or all) of the adoptive parent's gain in inclusive fitness may, of course, be "selfish," e.g., as hypothesized by Kummer (1971), who has suggested that adoption of orphaned female infants by male Hamadrayas baboons sometimes serves as the first step toward building a harem.

By contrast, an outstanding refusal to adopt orphans is shown by wildebeest females: even lactating mothers who have lost their own calves refuse to accept bleating orphans who approach them and try to nurse from "udders bursting with milk" (v. Lawick Goodall and v. Lawick Goodall, 1970). Wildebeest cows also seldom show cooperative defense of calves (Kruuk, 1972). The failure to adopt orphans, like the lack of an altruistic anti-predator response, may be explained in terms of kin selection: wildebeests live in very large and amorphous herds, sometimes containing several hundred individuals. If the herds have no internal structure that would increase the likelihood that adjacent individuals are sufficiently related, then the relatedness of a cow with a nearby attacked or orphaned offspring may well be too low to justify whatever expenditure and risk are involved in saving its life. A similar refusal to adopt helpless orphans has been noted among flying foxes, bats —which, like wildebeest, are highly mobile parental animals living in very large groups, containing many thousands of individuals (Nelson, 1965)—, and in elephant seals (Williams, 1966), which also breed in huge groups evidently not showing internal subgroups beyond the nuclear-family level.

Cheap Aid and the Effect of Ecological Competition

It is obvious that if the benefit/cost ratio (K) must be above a certain level (K_t) for altruism to be advantageous, then the lower the cost of giving aid the more likely it is to occur, and the more likely it is to occur among relatively distant relatives. Hamilton (1964b) has given several illustrations of low-cost altruism, including alarm calls (see below), social grooming, and the length of post-reproductive lifespan in cryptically and aposematically colored moth species (see also Blest, 1963). Instances of "cheap aid" might occur (1) when an individual is itself incapable (or nearly incapable) of reproduction on its own—when it is idle, or has nothing or little to lose in terms of personal fitness through altruism (as in the case of postreproductive or sterile adults and those temporarily excluded from reproductive roles), or (2) when the altruism involves a non-storable essential resource that for the donor is in abundant supply.

Individuals temporarily excluded from reproducing, e.g., by virtue of their age or social position, stand to benefit through kin selection by helping reproducing relatives as long as the altruism does not cost too much in terms of their own future reproductive capacity—doing something is better than doing nothing, especially since there is always a certain probability that the "waiting" individual will die before reproducing. There are many examples of such altruism in a wide range of taxa. Among birds, the anis (*Crotophaga* spp.) and various species of jay have been cited as examples of altruistic care of young likely to be siblings by prereproductive adults (Hamilton, 1964b; Brown, 1970). Armstrong (1965) has listed eleven species of birds in which young individuals assist in rearing younger broods, including a swallow, mannikins, moorhens, wrens, tits, woodpeckers, and the Australian white-winged chough. "Supernumerary" adults reportedly help mated pairs feed the young in black-eared bush tits, banded cactus wrens, little bush tits, and variegated wrens (Armstrong, 1965). And young adult beavers still with their parents help to build and maintain dams prior to reproduction on their own (Bourlière, 1964).

Among primates, subordinate or young adult males are sometimes partly or entirely excluded (temporarily) from reproduction, yet participate in group defense and social grooming benefiting other individuals and their young (e.g., Hall and DeVore, 1965). While such behavior may have functions contributing to classical fitness (e.g., maintenance of a place in the group essential to future reproduction), part of the payoff would be in terms of the kinship component of inclusive fitness whenever the benefited individuals are likely to be relatives (for evidence that they are, see Jolly, 1972; Fox, 1972).

In temperate-zone populations of the social wasp *Polistes fuscatus* females which are physiologically capable of reproduction (mated, overwintered females with ovaries containing large eggs which they sometimes lay), but which emerge late from hibernation, become sterile workers on the nests of other females (West Eberhard, 1969). There seems to be a very high premium on starting colonies early: nearly all colonies are founded within two or three days in the spring, indicating that latecomers are at a marked reproductive disadvantage. They may have a lower personal fitness because of any one or a combination of such factors as the reduced availability of suitable nesting sites, the shorter length of the remaining growing season, the reduced chance of getting helpers, or physiological (reproductive) inferiority as indicated by their behavioral subordinance to queens (see West, 1967; West Eberhard, 1969). Such factors might make it preferable for them to help another rather than to go off on their own, even though the highest possible r_{AB}, ($\frac{3}{8}$) for doing so is slightly lower than the r ($\frac{1}{2}$) with their own young (all overwintered females are of the same generation; therefore the closest relationship they could share is that of sibling hymenopteran females: $r = \frac{3}{4}$; $\bar{r}$ with nieces and nephews $= \frac{3}{8}$).

The importance of the cost of altruism is indicated by the restraint sometimes shown in giving aid. Low-cost altruism occurs among groups in which individuals normally refuse to give high cost aid or give it only in situations of urgent necessity. *Metapolybia* (wasp) queens who become workers participate in relatively low risk activities (brood care and building on the comb), and undertake to forage (a higher risk activity, involving greater expenditure of energy and exposure to rain and predators) only when the colony is in a trophic crisis, as explained above. Gazelle females, which singly do not usually aid the offspring of other gazelles which are under attack by groups of hyenas, occasionally will do so in the company of others (e.g., several may perform distracting behavior near a fawn threatened by a single hyena) or in some less dangerous situation, e.g., when a fawn is injured but is not under attack (from Kruuk, 1972). Coatis who groom and guard the young of temporarily absent females do so with less intensity than they show to their own young (Kaufmann, 1962).

An example of category (2)—facultative low-cost altruism in times of abundance—may be represented by the feeding behavior of wild chimpanzees. When food is abundant the chimps make a lot of noise upon discovering a rich source of fruit, and thereby attract other groups to the site. However, when comparatively little fruit is available they forage on their own or in two's or three's (rather than in larger groups) and are quiet (Reynolds, 1970). Even if the noise arises from fighting over food rather than being an evolved signal, it constitutes an announcement that benefits the (presumably) rather unrelated individuals of other groups. That altruism should be more common when times are good is an idea quite natural and "obvious" to humans, which suggests that we go by the same rule.

The facultative nature of generosity in chimpanzees illustrates a further point. Just as the low cost of altruism in times of abundance makes altruism more likely, so should scarcity of a resource (the high cost of sharing) be associated with selfishness, even at high values of r. If there is a very strong competition for some resource, a potential donor should refuse to aid (and may even eliminate) its closest relative. Thus mammalian littermates and sibling nestlings among birds push each other aside even though they are (except for their parents) each other's closest relatives (see Alexander, 1974, for a discussion of this effect of ecological competition, and the possible role of parents in controlling such behavior). The cost of altruism (the denominator of K) is thus clearly a function of the intensity of competition between donor and beneficiary. In general, we should find that *the greater the intensity of reproductive or ecological competition between two individuals, the less the probability of altruism between them.* The probability of altruism thus depends on such ecological parameters as the so-called carrying capacity of the environment, population size, and population (or social) structure (since not all age or behavioral classes are equally competitive). This consideration immensely complicates the determination of K in nature. There is certainly no species for which the total ecological cost to conspecifics of adding another individual to the population (or subtracting one from it) is known.

Super-Donors and Super-Beneficiaries

The workers of social insect colonies are prime examples of super-donors. If it is advantageous to be a helper, it is probably more advantageous to be a more efficient helper; hence the extreme morphological and behavioral specializations of the sterile workers of some social insects can be viewed as products of selection on workers as individuals rather than as (or in addition to) products of selection at the level of the colony (selection on mothers), the traditional way of interpreting such adaptations (Darwin, 1859; Wilson, 1971). Although in most conditions the two kinds of selection would produce the same results, this is not always the case—see section on insect sociality (below). The beneficiary's capacity to use aid must keep pace with the donor's ability to provide it, or increased efficiency in giving aid will be selected against (will have no effect). It is therefore not surprising to find the most extreme examples of worker polymorphism accompanied by the most exaggerated super-reproductive queens (e.g., in the army ants, *Eciton*—see Wilson, 1971).

There is a corollary of this line of reasoning which helps dispense with some supposed problems for Hamilton's theory: the better the helper the more advantageous it is to be a helper rather than a reproductive individual, and the less important it is to be closely related to the beneficiary. That is, a worker, as a super-donor, is in a sense "trapped" in altruism, not only by being a relatively poor (or even sterile) reproductive individual, but also by being such a good donor that she cannot afford to be anything else if there is a relative ($r > \bar{r}$) around to be helped. Thus, if a worker's mother dies, and with her the worker's evolutionary raison d'être, she might be expected to serve a less closely related reproductive individual. If the altruist is completely sterile, as in the case of some social insects, the denominator of $K(a_A$ before altruism) goes to zero and K approaches infinity; so the sterile worker, while she will prefer to help her mother, should in the absence of the mother, or if unable to distinguish her from other reproductive females in the vicinity, finds it advantageous to help a female with any, even slight, degree of relatedness greater than $\bar{r}$—anything is better than nothing. This may help to explain the behavior of queenless army ant workers, which reportedly will join a passing colony and aid the "foreign" queen (Schnierla and Brown, in Lin and Michener, 1972). However, even in cases of complete sterility (laying workers are apparently unknown in army ants —see Lin and Michener, 1972), r_{AB}, of the orphaned worker and the adopted queen must be greater than $\bar{r}$ or it would be more advantageous for an orphan to die unemployed. It seems likely that this condition is satisfied in the case of the army ants, which represent a relatively "viscous" population, since the virgin queens are wingless and colonies reproduce by fission (Schnierla and Brown, 1950); hence an orphaned worker can be fairly certain that the first queen she encounters will be quite closely related to her on her mother's side.

The extremely high K of a super-donor may in some cases also help to explain the problematical existence in ants and polybiine wasps of multi-queen colonies, in which several queens band together, apparently in order to reap the advantages of rapid colony establishment, and the workers care for the broods of various females in addition to that of their mother. Strictly in terms of r, the worker's own mother is the only reproductive individual qualified as beneficiary. Accordingly, workers of multi-queen colonies should rebel and go off to reproduce on their own, or should learn to discriminate between their mother and other queens. However, in the case of a super-donor the choice is not between helping the mother or reproducing on her own; it is between helping the mother or some other, at least slightly related female, or nothing. Also it should be remembered that the worker is interested in maximizing the mother's reproduction, and if aiding other females contributes to the efficient integration of a multi-queen colony favorable to the mother it is likewise usually favorable from the worker's point of view. Thus, the multi-queen society can be viewed as a group of queens for whom cooperation (reciprocity) is advantageous to individual queens and, hence, to their workers.

Among vertebrates, various examples can be cited of altruism involving efficient beneficiaries, that is, superior reproductives or individuals in a relatively good position to capitalize on aid. Dominant individuals aided by subordinates will be discussed in a later section. Adults possessing an already established nest or territory are superior beneficiaries, especially if the nest is complicated or costly in terms of building time or energy (or both), or if suitable space is in short supply. At least some of the species already mentioned as having non-reproducing helpers make complicated nests or other structures connected with breeding—e.g., the anis, beavers, and *Polistes* wasps. Experienced males with established harems among baboons and macaques offer similar examples of individuals with a reproductive advantage who are sometimes the recipients of aid by reproductively excluded individuals (see Crook and Gartlan, 1966).

Alarm Calls

Alarm calls, which can confer great benefit at low cost, may sometimes be examples of altruism among individuals of low r. An individual under attack by a predator stands to lose his life if not warned; and various factors tend to reduce the likelihood of the alarmist himself being attacked. These factors include (1) the alarmist's awareness of the predator's presence before the predator is aware of or prepared to attack him; (2) the possibility that more than one individual may give the alarm (either through simultaneous perception of the predator or contagiousness of the alarm signal), and thus reduce the risk of alarm-giving by providing more than one distraction to the predator; and (3) the evolved ability, at least in some species, of alarmists to give signals difficult to localize (Marler, 1955, 1957). The combination of these factors acting to raise the value of K might make the value of r relatively unimportant in the evolution of alarm signals. Furthermore, any gain in the kinshi⌐

component of the alarmist's inclusive fitness would be multiplied if more than one somewhat related ($r>\bar{r}$) individual were helped simultaneously—a situation that is possible if the predator or parasite is capable of attacking more than one individual at a time or in quick succession.

Other explanations of alarm calls not involving kin selection are discussed by Maynard Smith (1965), Williams (1966), and Trivers (1971). Williams (1966) sees the warning signals of mammals (e.g., the raised white tails of deer) and of birds (e.g., the distraction and warning display of tail feathers in a bird taking flight) as primarily a device for protecting their own offspring, and he cites as evidence the fact that he knows of no such warning devices in species not showing well-developed parental care. He considers such signals non-adaptive (pathological or neutral) when given in the absence of the young. "As long as pathological social behavior is frequent (see Williams, 1966), it seems misguided to regard as adaptive any behavior that happens to benefit some individual. Selection in relation to low values of r must often be so weak that it gets lost in the evolutionary noise" (G. C. Williams, pers. commun.). Since other readers may share Williams' doubt concerning the importance of selection at low values of r, it seems worth pointing out that, while it may prove difficult to demonstrate—just as it is difficult to demonstrate any example of weak selection in nature—nevertheless weak kin selection, if and when it occurs, should follow the same rules as conventional natural selection. That is, a unit of inclusive fitness gained through aid to relatives is exactly equivalent to a unit of classical fitness in so far as prediction of the results of reproductive competition among individuals is concerned. My intention is mainly to point out that high values of r are not necessary for kin selection to be possible—that behaviors such as alarm signals have characteristics that might enable them to be selected positively through a contribution to the kinship component of inclusive fitness, whether or not they have originated or been maintained also, or even primarily, by selection in other contexts.

THE SIGNIFICANCE OF DOMINANCE AND SUBORDINANCE AMONG RELATIVES

Dominance-subordinance interactions are common among animals living in groups, including birds (see Collias, 1944; Watts and Stokes, 1971), mammals (see Etkin, 1964), and insects (see Pardi, 1948, 1950; Free, 1955). Among some primates dominance hierarchies seem to be important in determining the social and reproductive roles of individuals; so a proper interpretation of the functions of dominance and subordinance is critical to understanding primate social organization and, in turn, its relation to human society.

The selective advantage of being *dominant* is clear whenever, as commonly is the case, the dominant individual has improved access to some resource(s) (such as food, mates, or nesting sites—see above references) vital to or at least enhancing its survival, reproduction, or both. The significance or subordinance, however, is not so obvious, and remains the subject of controversy. Indeed, interpreting the significance of dominance hierarchies resolves to one question: why do certain individuals accept a subordinant social and reproductive role with respect to others when that means giving in to or even aiding a reproductive competitor? Answers commonly given to this question are: (1) that subordinance reduces the destructiveness of intragroup competition and is thus selectively advantageous to the group (e.g., Etkin, 1964); (2) that dominance relations serve to control population size by restricting breeding to a small number of individuals (e.g., Wynne-Edwards, 1962; Woolpy, 1968); and (3) that a dominance hierarchy (and subordinance) is the result of compromises among competitors (Williams, 1966), that is, the subordinate is a hopeful potential dominant who temporarily or permanently has lost out in competition with others.

Reasons for doubting the validity of interpretations like (1) and (2), based exclusively on group-selection, are given by Williams (1966) and Maynard Smith (1972). The present theory suggests a possible individual-level interpretation in addition to (3), namely, that in certain circumstances, submissive behavior may be a form of altruism that is advantageous to the subordinant individual by increasing its inclusive fitness.

In the case of a temporarily weak individual it seems obvious that avoiding fights might increase the chance of future reproductive success by reducing the risk of injury and the squandering of energy in prolonged conflict with a recognizable superior (see Maynard Smith, 1972). However, subordinance is not always passive. It often serves to channel the lower ranking individual into a different social role (see Markl, 1971, 1973), perhaps involving risky and energy-consuming altruism toward dominants and their young. For example, subordinate female *Polistes* wasps feed and defend the dominant queen and her larvae; subordinate male baboons participate in the care and defense of infants and mates not their own (Hall, 1960); and subordinate male flying foxes, excluded from reproduction for the year, stay at the periphery of the breeding group where they give alarm calls presumably benefiting dominant, breeding males (Nelson, 1965). Even passive deference to a competitor is a kind of altruism, since it allows the dominant individual prior access to resources which might be depleted by him, and there is a certain probability of the subordinate's death without reproduction (losing out in the waiting game). The present model enables us to specify the conditions under which advantageous altruistic subordinance could occur: if and when

    1   dominance reflects superior hereditary endowment (e.g., intelligence, experience, ability to produce or rear offspring, physical strength), or superior reproductive capacity, or both;
    2   the subordinate's behavior (deference or aid) contributes to the reproductive output of the dominant;
    3   the individuals involved are relatives ($r > \bar{r}$); and
    4   these factors (those affecting fitness and relatedness) are quantitatively related such that, following the period of subordinance (altruism), the theoretical conditions specified at the beginning of this paper (expressions 3 and 4) are satisfied.

The more closely related the members of a group, the more likely it is that subordinance functions in this way; but marked differences in reproductive capacity could lead to advantageous subordinance among quite distant relatives.

If dominance-subordinance relations function as hypothesized here, one would expect the evolution of an ability to discriminate the dominance interval (sufficient difference in dominance) necessary to indicate advantageous subordinance, individuals adopting the subordinate deference or aid behavioral syndrome whenever that level was surpassed. The required dominance differential should be adjustable to suit ecological conditions; e.g., in times of resource abundance, a relatively poor reproductive individual might better be able to make it on his (or her) own.

Evidence indicates that the model's conditions are satisfied in various phylogenetically diverse species, including social wasps, cercopithecoid primates (see below), bumblebees (Free, 1955), Welder brush turkeys (Watts and Stokes, 1971), kookaburras (Parry, 1972), and wolves (Woolpy, 1968). A quantitative test of the model has been made using data obtained in a study of dominance behavior and reproductive success in a natural population of *Polistes* wasps. In this case it was possible to show that subordinate females were very likely sisters of aided dominants, and that they did sufficiently better (in terms of inclusive fitness) than solitary reproductive individuals as to satisfy the conditions just outlined for advantageous subordinate altruism (West, 1967; West Eberhard, 1969).

The present hypothesis offers a possible explanation for the "wife sharing" of Tasmanian hens described by Maynard Smith and Ridpath (1972), since a pair of males forming a breeding group with a single female are brothers, and such "trios" have a higher productivity (1.45:1.0) than male-female pairs. In this case both males mate with the female, but the relative contributions of each as fathers is not known. Nor is it clear that dominance relations are established between them at some time, although the authors have stated that "it is certain that one of the males could drive out the other" (p. 449) if it were to his advantage to do so. If both gain equally by the arrangement, then I would regard this as a case of mutualism (reciprocal altruism or cooperation, see below) that does not necessarily involve altruism by kin selection.

Some primates have behavior and reproductive patterns which, in so far as they are known, fit the present interpretation remarkably well. For example, the dominance rank of male baboons depends on such factors as their health, fighting ability, ability to enlist the support of other males, and experience or intelligence (see discussion in Crook, 1972). That is, dominant males are likely to be "superior" individuals both in terms of inherited characteristics affecting their physical strength and intelligence, and in terms of their ability to protect and maintain a group of females and young. Fox (1972) discusses the evidence, in sum positive, that dominant baboons and macaques leave more offspring during their lifetimes than do subordinates. Thus the association of dominance, superior survival and reproductive capacity, and enhanced fitness required by the model is present. Furthermore, baboons and macaques tend to stay in groups of close relatives and are probably capable of recognizing at least some of their close kin (see Fox, 1972), a situation making advantageous altruistic deference or aid even more feasible. Unfortunately, the numerical data on kinship and individual reproductive success that would allow a quantitative test of the model are not available for any primate group.

This model also provides an interpretation for another dominance-related phenomenon observed in primates—the formation of one-male groups in regions or seasons of food scarcity, and the association sometimes observed between multi-male groups and food abundance (Crook and Gartlan, 1966). Crook (1972) points out that reducing the number of males present in a group is "adaptive," in that it allows a greater proportion of the available food to be apportioned to females responsible for rearing young, and he further discusses the advantage of the single-male social organization to the breeding individuals and to the group as a whole. But the explanation must ultimately focus on the males who leave the group in deference to the others: how could such behavior be advantageous to them as individuals? One obvious possibility is that during food scarcity males who break away from the breeding group get more to eat, either because they can forage more widely or effectively, or because they don't have to share with others. Solitary or small-group feeding in regions or in times of food scarcity occurs independent of dominance relations in chimpanzees (Reynolds, 1970), hyenas (Kruuk, 1972), and flying foxes (Nelson, 1965). The present model suggests an additional possible interpretation for species having dominance hierarchies: males who leave the breeding group may be subordinates who, having found reproductive deference to the dominant male advantageous, as just explained, find it advantageous to carry their altruism one step further and leave the group in time of food scarcity, thus increasing the dominant male's probability of reproductive success and therefore the subordinate's own inclusive fitness. When food is more abundant, and staying with the group would not cause undue nutritional stress, it might benefit the subordinate's inclusive fitness more to stay on as a defender. Crook (1972) has also discussed the theoretical relationship of group size, defense effectiveness, and resource availability per capita. He shows how, at some point, to add another male will not increase defense effectiveness, while it will be costly in terms of energy (resources) to the breeding individuals and their young. A subordinate male would also have to consider the effects of leaving or staying on his own chances of breeding in the future (e.g., the effects on his survival and well-being, social status, proximity to females, etc.).

Stated in terms of the general theory presented above, this model of dominance and subordinance predicts that a contending individual will profitably and willingly give in to a relative if dominance cues indicate that the benefit/cost ratio, K, is above a certain level (K_t from the subordinate altruist's point of view). What happens if that condition is not satisfied? One of two situations must then be true: either the individual in question is clearly dominant to the other, sufficiently so as to make the *other* a contented subordinate altruist; or there is a conflict of interest between the two, each one wanting the other to become altruistic and neither one wanting to concede because the benefit/cost for doing so is too low. Conflict of interest becomes more important among more distant relatives. For example, if the contenders are diploid siblings, conflict occurs whenever K is between 0.50 and 2.0, whereas, for cousins, the conflict range is considerably greater, including all situations for which K is between 0.125 and 8.0; and this range continues to increase as relatedness declines. Whenever there is a conflict of interest, fighting should escalate until one contender reaches the level at which the cost of continued fighting outweighs the potential benefit of winning, and the individual gives in. In this case the first to give in, the "subordinate," would not be expected to be altruistic. So it is of interest that in *Polistes* wasps close contenders are the most vicious and persistent fighters; and prolonged fighting among near equals can lead to one of the pair leaving an established nest and reproducing independently—giving in to, but not aiding, the other (West Eberhard, 1969).

The interpretation of dominance-subordinance interaction as a means of channelling individuals into the social (reproductive) roles most advantageous to them as individuals is not expected to apply to all the diverse examples of dominance-subordinance behavior found among animals. But it does seem necessary to revise hypotheses about the functions of dominance hierarchies by taking into account the possibility of individually advantageous subordinance.

KIN SELECTION IN RELATION TO OTHER FACTORS IN THE EVOLUTION OF ALTRUISM

Alexander (1974) points out that there are three general ways in which selection can act to produce beneficent social behavior: through kin selection, parental manipulation, and reciprocity. The second category is expanded here to include the additional possibility of altruism imposed by relatives other than parents, for example, by adults who adopt orphans or by socially dominant individuals in a position to manipulate the behavior and resources of others. I shall call such forced beneficence "imposed altruism." The purpose of this section and the next is to define the relations among kin selection, imposed altruism (particularly parental manipulation), and reciprocity, especially in the evolution of extreme altruism (worker sterility) in the social insects, where all three factors may have played a role.

Imposed Altruism

Altruism by parental manipulation is the only kind of beneficence imposed by selection on individuals other than the donor the theoretical nature of which has been discussed in the literature (Alexander, 1974; Trivers, 1974). It is probably by far the most common kind, because parents are often in a position to manipulate the phenotypes of offspring (see Alexander, 1974), and offspring are the individuals least likely to rebel inasmuch as their interests often coincide with those of their parents owing to the high degree of genetic similarity between them (see Table 1).

According to the parental-manipulation hypothesis (Alexander, 1974), altruism can sometimes be forced on individual offspring if parents with altruists among their brood reproduce more than parents with an entirely selfish brood, even when the altruism is disadvantageous to the altruist in terms of its own inclusive fitness. Illustrative examples include the trophic eggs of insects (crickets: West and Alexander, 1963; ants: Wilson, 1971), in which some gametes or zygotes are sacrificed to assist (feed) others, and the "controlled cannibalism" of hawks and owls in which larger young eat smaller ones in times of food shortage (Ingram, 1959, from Alexander, 1974).

In applying this hypothesis, it is critical to consider the extent to which offspring can be expected to rebel against parental manipulation. In what circumstances will there be a parent-offspring conflict regarding the advantageousness of altruism by offspring, and to what extent can offspring escape parental control? It is clear that parents and offspring will not always agree regarding the desirability of altruism, since K_t from the two points of view differs (see Table 1). Trivers (1974) has analyzed parent-offspring conflicts of interest and has emphasized the fact that offspring are expected actively to resist parental manipulation when it is counter to their own best interests. In cases of parent-offspring conflict, who can be expected to win? Alexander (1974) argues that the parent is likely to dominate the situation, being stronger and in control of resources on which the young are dependent, and in a position to manipulate the phenotypes of the young. Furthermore, he argues, offspring are future parents and are likely to be selected against as adults because they are likely to produce inferior (rebellious) broods. Trivers (1974) points out that although the contest is weighted in favor of the parent in cases of parent-offspring conflict, there are some signs of resistance in the behavior of offspring, e.g., during the weaning process in mammals. It seems clear that selection of offspring can favor an escape from parental manipulation as long as the benefit (increase in fitness because of rebellion when young) outweighs the cost of producing a rebellious brood as an adult (see Trivers, 1974).

Like altruism by kin selection, altruism imposed by parental control is only advantageous when the beneficiary is a relative—it will occur primarily among groups of kin. Exactly the same kinds of altruistic behavior can be produced by both kin selection and parental manipulation and the benefit/cost ratio at which they can advantageously occur overlaps (see Table 1). How, then, are we to know which kind of selection is responsible for a given case of altruism? Although it is possible to discuss in precise theoretical terms the conditions under which each kind of selection will occur and the situations in which conflict of interest is expected (see Trivers, 1974 and below), I know of no sure and practical way to distinguish all cases of kin selection from all cases of parental manipulation in nature. Presence or absence of the parent at the scene of the altruism is not an adequate criterion, since offspring altruism by selection on parents can theoretically occur even after the death or in the absence of the parent (see Alexander, 1974). The most that can be done is to discuss the various factors that make one explanation seem more likely than the other in a given case. For example, the "altruism" of a human infant sacrificed in favor of a sibling seems more likely properly explained by selection on parents (see Alexander, 1974) then by (kin) selection on offspring, considering the strength and influence of the parent and the physical helplessness of the human baby. On the other hand, similar sacrificing (cannibalism) of immature beetles can be explained credibly by either kin selection (Eickwort, 1973) or parental control. The two kinds of argument are illustrated in detail by parallel sets of interpretations applied to phenomena observed in social insects (see below).

An obvious opportunity for non-parents to impose altruism occurs when a peripheral relative adopts an orphan and assumes the manipulatory powers of parenthood without the same genetic responsibility. It seems likely that foster parents might sometimes impose altruism of a different kind or degree than that imposed by true parents. For instance, when the adoption occurs in a species that shows altruism characterized by parental manipulation favoring siblings, the foster parent could channel advantages to its own offspring that normally would have been destined for offspring of the true parents of the adopted individual.

To the degree that worker altruism is imposed by reproductive adults in social insects (see below), the conditions for control by relatives other than parents occur in several kinds of colonies. These cases differ from adoption in vertebrates in that control by non-parents is a regularly occurring part of the normal colony cycle, and could conceivably have preceded parental control in the evolutionary history of the species. In certain social wasps (e.g., *Polistes canadensis,* West Eberhard, 1969, and *Mischocyttarus drewsenii,* Jeanne, 1972) the reproductive cycle involves succession of a queen by a daughter of sibling who takes over a colony containing the ex-queen's workers and brood; and in *Polistes* species it is quite common for a newly founded nest to be conquered and controlled by a new arrival (possibly but not certainly a close relative of the original foundress) up to several weeks after nest initiation (Yoshikawa, 1955; West Eberhard, 1969, and pers. observ. on *P. carnifex* more than six weeks after nest founding), so that the first workers (altruists) are daughters of a deposed queen. The possibility of some degree of control of altruism by non-parents also exists in the polygynous (multi-queen) social Hymenoptera, in which there are complex interactions among the several queens and their immature and adult offspring (Naumann, 1970; West Eberhard, 1973); as well as in queen-recruiting ants (e.g., *Myrmica rubra*) in which the number of colony queens is augmented by the incorporation of additional gynes, at least sometimes sisters of those already present (Elmes, 1973).

In general, the same theoretical considerations regarding escape and rebellion that apply to parental manipulation should apply to control of altruism by other relatives. The more distantly related the dominating individual, the more the altruist is expected to resist imposed altruism. There should be very strong selection against altruism benefiting non-relatives without compensating beneficial consequences for the donor or its relatives—a kind of social parasitism which might sometimes evolve from relative-imposed altruism.

Intraspecific Mutualism

Mutualism or cooperation—a beneficent exchange in which both donors gain—can occur either among relatives or non-relatives. It seems useful to distinguish at least four kinds of intraspecific mutualism in order to analyze the way in which natural selection acts to maintain the performance of mutually beneficent acts:

1 *Mutualism maintained by reciprocal-altruistic selection.* Temporarily altruistic acts are performed mutually with each donor expecting more than compensating future beneficent behavior (reciprocation) on the part of the beneficiary, so as to result in a net gain in classical fitness of both participants. Possible example: reciprocity among humans (Trivers, 1971).

2 *Mutualism maintained by kin selection.* Each individual act is advantageous to the performer in terms of inclusive fitness—no reciprocation is required. However, individuals associate with kin because of the increased probability of being the recipients of similar ("reciprocal") aid. That is, the group owes its existence at least partly to the advantageousness of being able to dispense aid to (and receive it from) relatives. Possible examples: the sphecid wasp *Trigonopsis* (Eberhard, 1972, 1974); group-hunting species such as wolves (Woolpy, 1968) and wild dogs (van Lawick-Goodall and van Lawick-Goodall, 1970); communal nursing of young by lions (Schaller, 1972).

3 *Mutualism imposed by parents.* Mutualism among siblings could be the result of selection favoring parents whose offspring live together in cooperating groups (see Alexander, 1974). Possible example: "semisocial" groups of sisters in *Allodapula* bees (Michener, 1968).

4 *Mutualism maintained by ordinary selfish behavior incidentally benefiting neighbors.* The selfish behavior of an individual warning, feeding, or defending itself or its young can simultaneously benefit other individuals in the vicinity—e.g., by showing them the way to food, chasing off parasites, predators, or both; or by warning of danger. Groups may form and stay together because of this mutual advantage (see Williams, 1966). In this case the beneficent behavior costs the performer nothing beyond the expenditure justified by benefit to its own classical fitness. Possible examples: breeding aggregations of wildebeest (Kruuk, 1972); nesting aggregations and foraging flocks of colonial birds such as the piñon jay (see Brown, 1974); nesting aggregations of certain bees, *e.g., Lasioglossum zephyrum* (Batra, 1966; other examples in Michener, 1958, 1969; Lin, 1964).

Most mutualism among non-relatives or distant relatives is probably of type (4). Under special conditions (see Trivers, 1971, and below), non-relatives can also engage in reciprocal altruism (type 1). But mutualism maintained by reciprocal-altruistic selection alone is probably a rare or unstable phenomenon in most species, for reasons to be discussed below.

When mutualism occurs among relatives, it can be maintained by selection operating in any of the four ways listed, or in any combination of them; so for mutualistic groups of kin it will often be difficult to know for sure which kind(s) of selection are actually operating. This problem is illustrated by the following example. Eberhard (1972, 1974) has described the behavior of some primitively social sphecid wasps *(Trigonopsis cameronii)* in which females likely to be close relatives nest in small groups, each female provisioning her own cells but occasionally stealing prey from those of neighbors. Robbing females show altruistic restraint in not stealing at every opportunity, and apparently do so only in time of "need" (following poor hunting success). Robbed females are altruistic in permitting robberies, and only rarely attempt to prevent them even when present at the time of the robbery. Is such reciprocal pillage to be regarded as stealing or as sharing? At least three interpretations must be considered: (1) the behavior may represent reciprocal altruism (sensu Trivers, 1971), in which a female permits some stealing in the expectation of being able to get provisions in the same way on a future bad day; (2) it may be Hamiltonian altruism, in which each female permits limited (in accord with r) stealing by close relatives such as to benefit the kinship component of inclusive fitness, and limits her own stealing so as not to lower her inclusive fitness by excessively harming relatives (see Eberhard, 1972); or (3) it may be an instance of maternal control, in which a group of daughters distributes food among themselves in a manner that maximizes the total number of young produced by the sibling group.

Each of these three explanations is theoretically distinctive, in that each permits a different level of profit and loss due to stealing. These levels can be specified as follows. For an act by individual A (donor) benefiting individual B (beneficiary) let

B_b =   profit to B of aid,
C_b =   cost to B of reciprocation,
B_a =   profit to A from beneficent behavior of B,
C_a =   cost to A of original beneficent act,
$2r_{B_r}$ =   relatedness of and young of $B \times 2$ = increase in inclusive fitness of A for each offspring added to B's reproduction (expressed in offspring equivalents),

in which all costs and benefits are expressed in terms of fitness (offspring).

The conditions for positive selection are then:

1   For reciprocal altruism from the point of view of A:
   a.   Pure reciprocal altruism (kinship disregarded):

$$B_a > C_a$$

   b.   Reciprocal altruism among kin:

$$B_a > C_a - 2r_{B_r}(B_b - C_b)$$

   or, in species for which $r_{B_r} = r_B/2$ (e.g., outbreeding diploid animals):

$$B_a > C_a - r_B(B_b - C_b);$$

2 For mutualism maintained by kin selection, from the point of view of A:

    a. Altruism by A benefiting B:

$$B_b > C_a / 2r_{B},$$

    b. Altruism by B benefiting A (if not satisfied, A should refuse aid from B):

$$B_a > 2r_{B,}C_b$$

3 For reciprocal beneficence among siblings with parental control (condition for advantageous mutualism among brood from parent's point of view):

$$B_a + B_b > C_a + C_b$$

or

$$B_a > C_a - (B_b - C_b).$$

(Note that when $r_{B,} \equiv r_B/2$, as in the case of outbreeding diploid species, expression *(2a)* is identical to Hamilton's (1964b) $K > 1/r$. $B_b > C_a/2r_{B,}$ becomes $B_b > C_a/r_{B,}$ or $B_b/C_a > 1/r_{B,}$ in which $B_b/C_a + K$. Expression *(2b)* simplifies to $B_a/C_b > r_{B.}$

The brood-manipulating parent (case 3) is interested only in the summed individual fitnesses of the brood—the total number of grandchildren (descendents) produced—regardless of the kinship interactions and reciprocal debts important among the young themselves. Thus the evolution of mutualism may sometimes involve conflict of interest between parent and offspring. Selection on a parent might favor participation by offspring in a mutualistic group containing non-siblings (Alexander, 1974). Such a group could engage in mutual aid maintained by any one (or any combination) of the other three kinds of selection, and the above conditions (1, 2, and 4) would have to be satisfied from the *parent's* point of view.

Trivers (1971) has outlined and discussed the theoretical characteristics of "reciprocal altruism." He and later authors (Eshel, 1972; Hamilton, 1972; and Markl, 1973) have noted that reciprocal altruism and kin selection are likely under the same conditions (low dispersal rate; life in small stable groups; long period of parental care; and high benefit/cost ratio). Comparison of expressions (1a) and (1b), above, shows precisely how much kinship affects recipocal altruism, namely, by subtracting the quantity

$$2r_{B,}(B_b - C_b)$$

from the required reciprocal payoff. Note that for interspecific mutualism ($r_{B,} = 0$) this factor becomes zero, and this and the very special circumstance when $r_{B,} = \bar{r}$ are the only situations in which kinship effects can be ignored (when $\bar{r}$ is included in this expression it is subtracted from $r_{B,}$; so when $r_{B,} = \bar{r}$ the effect of kinship is zero). Even when reciprocal-altruistic selection is primarily responsible for a given beneficent act (e.g., in humans) the performer should demand more in return from a beneficiary of distant or unknown relatedness than from one of certain high relatedness. In view of these considerations it is probably an over-simplification to regard even human mutualism as resulting "only from reciprocal-altruistic selection" (Trivers, 1971, p. 46), especially since during the period of human history when biological selection was still operating to produce the basic characteristics of the human reciprocal system man probably lived in the kinds of groups favoring kin selection (Trivers, 1971, p. 45).

Maintenance of reciprocal altruism depends on some meticulous mechanism for recognizing and punishing a cheater *during its own lifetime.* Otherwise there is a premium on cheating among reciprocating members of the same species. Any small energy-saving or risk-avoiding failure to reciprocate to a beneficent conspecific individual is reproductively advantageous, and such cheating should become more and more exaggerated in successive generations until the system breaks down because of the disadvantage to those being cheated of continued association with cheaters.

It might be supposed that this eventual dissolution of the group would constitute adequate punishment of the cheater, whose descendents are deprived of the advantages of group living. But in this event the non-cheater, whose descendents are also deprived of mutualistic aid, actually loses more than the cheater, who at least gains (rather than loses) by the act of cheating. Inter-deme selection could eliminate cheating from a population by extinction of cheater-containing groups, but only if *all* of the following conditions were to hold: (1) group-living must be obligatory, so that cheaters lose as much by dissolution of the group as non-cheaters; (2) groups composing the population must be genetically isolated from each other (have a migration rate so low that it does not outweigh mutation rates), so that the temporarily successful cheaters are not able to infiltrate neighboring groups of non-cheaters before selection has operated to extinguish them along with their original group; and (3) non-cheaters must be able to colonize new areas with offshoot groups and thus propagate their kind, so that group-by-group extinction does not eventually lead to extinction of the entire population or species. Since such conditions are probably quite rare (conditions 2 and 3, for example, require both movement from place to place and genetic isolation), the reproductive advantages of failure to reciprocate should usually lead to the spread of this tendency whenever it occurs unchecked by contemporaries, even among species for which mutualism is essential to individual survival, since the long-term disadvantage—the breakdown of reciprocity and the extinction of descendents—cannot be foreseen.

In the case of humans, the problem of checks on cheating is resolved by the unusual development of human intelligence and memory, which makes it possible to discover cheaters and immediately limit reciprocation toward them (see Trivers, 1971). Human reciprocity is the only example of mutualism thus far shown to fit the conditions of reciprocal altruism as distinct from other kinds of intraspecific mutualism (Trivers, 1971). Trivers has considered one other possible example—the warning calls of birds, which he interprets as involving no reciprocally beneficent behavior by the beneficiary, and no checks against cheating. The mere survival of the warned individual repays the call-giver by preventing predators from specializing on the caller's species and locality. Viewed in this way, warning calls are not really *reciprocal* altruism, since only one member of the interacting pair (the alarm-giver) is temporarily altruistic; and no checks on cheating are required because the altruism is "automatically" repaid in the course of purely selfish behavior by the beneficiary. Hence the example does not really fit Trivers' model which, while not very explicit on this point, seems to require that *both* parties be (temporarily) altruistic. (See, for example, section 3, p. 37, of Trivers, 1971. The emphasis given checks on cheating throughout that paper also implies altruism by both parties, as just explained.) If the model in fact requires only one party to be temporarily altruistic, then it is trivially applicable to many phenomena clearly better considered as ordinary selfishness (e.g., mating behavior, in which a male donates sperm to a female, thereby enabling her to reproduce at the risk of wasting his effort unless she survives to provide the delayed payoff—his offspring).

Trivers has also applied the model to interspecific mutualism in a useful analysis of cleaning symbioses among fish. That discussion, again, involves an example of mutualism with only one party—the host fish—temporarily altruistic (the cleaner's contribution is seen as selfish feeding on the host's parasites), and Trivers' interpretation parallels those of other authors—e.g., Borradaile and Potts, 1958; Moynihan, 1962; Williams, 1966; and Janzen, 1966, 1967—who have explained interspecific mutualisms in terms of unadorned classical selection.

While Trivers (1971) expects reciprocal altruism to be found in many species, a model of reciprocal altruism requiring temporary altruism by both participants (and therefore contemporaneous controls against cheating) leads instead to the conclusion of Williams (1966) and Hamilton (1972) that the phenomenon is probably restricted to intelligent animals and, hence, to a few species of mammals (Williams, 1966). If reciprocal altruism does occur in non-humans it will probably be difficult to demonstrate, even in terms of checks against cheating. Differential beneficence by an individual toward different members of a group might not always indicate recognition of differentially reciprocating companions (or checks against cheating). It could represent control of other kinds of social parasitism, such as preemption by non-relatives or distant relatives of beneficence destined for relatives, or even outright stealing.

LIST OF LITERATURE

Alexander, R. D. 1971. The search for an evolutionary philosophy of man. *Proc. Roy. Soc. Vict.,* 84(1): 99–120.

———. 1974. The evolution of social behavior. *Ann. Rev. Syst. Ecol.,* 4:325–383.

Armstrong, E. A. 1965. *Bird Display and Behaviour.* Dover, N.Y.

Batra, S. W. T. 1966. The life cycle and behavior of the primitively social bee, *Lassioglossum zephyrum* (Halictidae). *Univ. Kansas Sci. Bull.,* 46(10): 359–423.

Blest, A. D. 1963. Longevity, palatability and natural selection in five species of New World saturniid moth. *Nature,* 197:1183–1186.

Borradaile, L. A., and F. A. Potts. 1958. *The Invertebrata.* Cambridge Univ. Press, Cambridge.

Bourlière, F. 1964. *The Natural History of Mammals.* Knopf, N.Y.

Brian, M. V. 1965. *Social Insect Populations.* Academic Press, London.

Brown, J. L. 1970. Cooperative breeding and altruistic behavior in the Mexican jay *(Aphelocoma ultramarina). Anim. Behav.,* 18:366–378.

———. 1974. Alternate routes to sociality in jays. With a theory for the evolution of altruism and communal breeding. *Am. Zool.,* 14: 63–80.

Carpenter, C. R. 1965. The howlers of Barro Colorado Island. In I. DeVore (ed.), *Primate Behavior,* p. 250–291. Holt, Rinehart and Winston, N.Y.

Collias, N. E. 1944. Aggressive behavior among vertebrate animals. *Physiol. Zool.,* 17: 85–123.

Crook, J. 1972. Sexual selection, dimorphism, and social organization in the primates. In B. G. Campbell (ed.), *Sexual Selection and the Descent of Man,* p. 231–281. Aldine, N.Y.

Crook, J., and J. S. Gartlan. 1966. Evolution of primate societies. *Nature,* 210: 1200–1203.

Darwin, C. D. 1859. *On the Origin of Species. A Facsimile of the First Edition* [1967]. Harvard Univ. Press, Cambridge.

Eberhard, W. G. 1972. Altruistic behavior in a sphecid wasp: support for kin-selection theory. *Science,* 172:1390–1391.

———. 1974. The natural history and behaviour of *Trigonopsis cameronii* Kohl (Sphecidae). *Trans. Roy. Ent. Soc. London,* 125(3): 295–328.

Eickwort, K. R. 1973. Cannibalism and kin selection in *Labidomera clivicollis* (Coleoptera: Chrysomelidae). *Am. Natur.,* 107(955): 452–453.

Elmes, G. W. 1973. Observations on the density of queens in natural colonies of *Myrmica rubra* L. (Hymenoptera:Formicidae). *J. Anim. Ecol.,* 42: 61–71.

Emerson, A. E. 1959. Social insects. *Encyclopaedia Britannica,* 20: 871–878.

Emlen, J. M. 1970. Age specificity and ecological theory. *Ecology,* 51(4): 588–601.

Eshel, I. 1972. On the neighbor effect and the evolution of altruistic traits. *Theoret. Pop. Biol.,* 3: 258–277.

Etkin, W. (ed.). 1964. *Social Behavior and Organization among Vertebrates.* Univ. Chicago Press, Chicago.

Fisher, R. A. 1930. *The Genetical Theory of Natural Selection.* 2nd Rev. Ed. [1958]. Dover, N.Y.

Fox, R. 1972. Alliance and constraint: sexual selection and the evolution of human kinship systems. In B. G. Campbell (ed.), *Sexual Selection and the Descent of Man,* p. 282–331. Aldine, N.Y.

Free, J. B. 1955. The behaviour of egg-laying workers of bumblebee colonies. *Brit. J. Anim. Behav.,* 3: 147–153.

Hall, K. R. L. 1960. Social vigilance behaviour in the Chacma baboon, *Papio ursinus. Behaviour,* 16: 261–294.

Hall, K. R. L., and I. DeVore. 1965. Baboon social behavior. In I. DeVore (ed.), *Primate Behavior,* p. 53–110. Holt, Rinehart and Winston, N.Y.

Hamilton, W. D. 1963. The evolution of altruistic behavior. *Am. Natur.,* 97: 354–356.

———. 1964a. The genetical theory of social behaviour. I. *J. Theoret. Biol.* 7: 1–16.

———. 1964b. The genetical theory of social behaviour. II. *J. Theoret. Biol.,* 7: 17–52.

———. 1970. Selfish and spiteful behavior in an evolutionary model. *Nature,* 228: 1218–1220.

————. 1971. Selection of selfish and altruistic behavior in some extreme models. In J. F. Eisenberg and W. S. Dillon (eds.), *Man and Beast: Comparative Social Behavior*, p. 57–91. Smithsonian Press, Washington, D.C.

————. 1972. Altruism and related phenomena mainly in the social insects. *Ann. Rev. Syst. Ecol.*, 3: 193–232.

————. 1974. Evolution sozialen Verhaltensweisen bei socialen Insekten. In G. H. Schmidt (ed.), *Soziale Insekten Kastenbildung-Polymorphismus*, Chapter 1. Wissenschaftliche Verlagsgesellschaft, Stuttgart. In press.

Ingram, C. 1959. The importance of juvenile cannibalism in the breeding biology of certain birds of prey. *Auk*, 76: 218–226.

Janzen, D. H. 1966. Coevolution of mutualism between ants and acacias in Central America. *Evolution*, 20(3): 249–275.

————. 1967. Interaction of the bull's-horn Acacia (*Acacia cornigera* L.) with an ant inhabitant (*Pseudomyrmex ferruginea* F. Smith) in eastern Mexico. *Kansas Univ. Sci. Bull.*, 47(6): 315–558.

————. 1970. Altruism by coatis in the face of predation by Boa constrictor. *J. Mammalogy*, 51(2): 387–389.

Jay, P. 1965. The common langur of North India. In I. DeVore (ed.), *Primate Behavior*, p. 197–249. Holt, Rinehart and Winston, N.Y.

Jeanne, R. L. 1972. Social biology of the neotropical wasp *Mischocyttarus drewseni*. *Bull. Mus. Comp. Zool.*, 144(3): 63–150.

Jolly, A. 1972. *The Evolution of Primate Behavior*. Macmillan, N.Y.

Kaufmann, J. H. 1962. Ecology and social behavior of the coati, *Nasua narica*, on Barro Colorado Island Panama. *Univ. Calif. Publ. Zoology*, 60(3): 95–222.

Kruuk, H. 1972. *The Spotted Hyena*. Univ. Chicago Press, Chicago.

Kummer, H. 1971. *Primate Societies*. Aldine, Atherton, N.Y.

Lawick-Goodall, H. van, and J. van Lawick-Goodall. 1970. *Innocent Killers*. Ballantine Books, N.Y.

Lawick-Goodall, J. van. 1968. The behaviour of free-living chimpanzees in the Gombe Stream Reserve. *Anim. Behav. Monogr.*, 1(3): 161–311.

Levins, R. 1970. Extinction. In *Some Mathematical Questions in Biology*, p. 77–107. Am. Math. Soc., Providence.

Lewontin, R. C. 1970. The units of selection. *Ann. Rev. Ecol. Syst.*, 1: 1–18.

Lin, N. 1964. Increased parasitic pressure as a major factor in the evolution of social behavior in halictine bees. *Insectes Soc.*, 11:187–192.

Lin, N., and C. D. Michener. 1972. Evolution of sociality in insects. *Quart. Rev. Biol.*, 47:131–159.

Markl, H. 1971. Vom Eigennutz des Uneigennützigen. *Naturw. Rdsch.* 24(7): 281–289.

————. 1973. Kin selection, altruism and aggression, with special reference to insects. Paper presented to the XIII. Int. Ethological Conference, Washington, D.C., August 1973. [Privately distributed.]

Marler, P. 1955. Characteristics of some animal calls. *Nature*, 176:6–8.

————. 1957. Specific distinctiveness in the communication signals of birds. *Behaviour*, 11:13–39

Maynard Smith, J. 1964. Kin selection and group selection. *Nature*, 201: 1145–1147.

————. 1965. The evolution of alarm calls. *Am. Natur.*, 99: 59–63.

———. 1972. Game theory and the evolution of fighting. In John Maynard Smith, *On Evolution*, p. 8–28. Edinburgh Univ. Press, Edinburgh.

Maynard Smith, J., and M. G. Ridpath. 1972. Wife-sharing in the Tasmanian native hens, *Tribonyx mortierii:* A case of kin selection? *Am. Natur.*, 106:447–452.

Michener, C. D. 1958. The evolution of social behavior in bees. *Proc. Tenth Int. Congr. Ent.*, Montreal, 2: 441–447.

———. 1968. Biological observations on primitively social bees *(Allodapula)* from Cameroon (Hymenoptera, Xylocopinae). *Insectes Soc.*, 15(4): 423–434.

———. 1969. Comparative social behavior of bees. *Ann. Rev. Entomol.*, 14: 299–342.

Moynihan, M. 1962. The organization and probable evolution of some mixed species flocks of neotropical birds. *Smithsonian Misc. Coll.*, 143(7): 1–140.

———. 1970. Some behavior patterns of platyrrhine monkeys II. *Saguinus geoffroyi* and some other tamarins. *Smithsonian Contr. Zool.*, No, 28: 1–77.

Naumann, M. 1970. The nesting behavior of *Protopolybia pumila* in Panama (Hymenoptera, Vespidae). Ph.D. Dissertation, Univ. Kansas.

Nelson, J. E. 1965. Behaviour of Australian Pteropodidae (Megachiroptera). *Behaviour*, 13(4): 544–557.

Orlove, M. J. 1974. A model of kin selection not invoking coefficients of relationship. *J. Theoret. Biol.*, in press.

Pardi, L. 1948. Dominance order in *Polistes* wasps. *Physiol. Zool.*, 21: 1–13.

——— 1950. Dominazione e gerarchia in alcuni invertebrati. *Coll. Intern. sur la Struct. et la Physiol. Sociétès animales, Paris*, p. 183–197.

Parry, V. A. 1972. *Koodaburras*, Taplinger, N.Y.

Pisarski, H. 1972. La structure des colonies polycaliques de *Formica (Coptoformica) exsecta* Nyl. *Ecologia Polska*, 20(12): 111–116.

———. 1973. Les principes d'organisation des colonies polycaliques des fourmis. *Proc. VII Int. Congr. IUSSI, London*, p. 311–316.

Rand, A. S. 1967. The adaptive significance of territoriality in iguanid lizards. In W. W. Milstead (ed.), *Lizard Ecology: A Symposium*, p. 106–115. Univ. Missouri Press, Columbia.

Reynolds, V. 1970. The "man of the woods." In *Field Studies in Natural History*, p. 202–210. Van Nostrand, N.Y.

Richards, O. W. and M. J. Richards. 1951. Observations on the social wasps of South America (Hymenoptera, Vespidae). *Trans. Roy. Ent. Soc. London*, 102: 1–167.

Rowell, T. 1972. *The Social Behaviour of Monkeys*. Penguin, Baltimore.

Schaller, G. B. 1972. *The Serengeti Lion*. Univ. Chicago Press, Chicago.

Schnierla, T. C., and R. Z. Brown. 1950. Army-ant life and behavior under dry-season conditions—4. *Bull. Am. Museum Natur. Hist.*, 95:269–353.

Simonds, P. E. 1965. The Bonnet Macaque in South India. In I. DeVore (ed.), *Primate Behavior*, p. 175–196. Holt, Rinehart and Winston, N.Y.

Trivers, R. L. 1971. The evolution of reciprocal altruism. *Quart. Rev. Biol.*, 46: 35–57.

———. 1972. Parental investment and sexual selection. In B. Campbell (ed.), *Sexual Selection and the Descent of Man 1871–1971*, p. 136–179. Aldine, Chicago.

———. 1974. Parent-offspring conflict. *Am. Zool*, 14: 249–264.

Watts, C. R., and A. W. Stokes. 1971. The social order of turkeys. *Sci. Amer.*, 224:112–118.

West, M. J. 1967. Foundress associations in polistine wasps: Dominance hierarchies and the evolution of social behavior. *Science*, 157: 1584–1585.

West, M. J., and R. D. Alexander, 1963. Subsocial behavior in a burrowing cricket *Anurogryllus muticus* (De Geer). (Orthoptera: Gryllidae). *Ohio Jour. Sci.,* 63:19–24.

West Eberhard, M. J. 1969. The social biology of polistine wasps. *Univ. Mich. Mus. Zool. Misc. Publ.,* 140:1–101.

———. 1973. Monogyny in "polygynous" social wasps. *Proc. VII Congr. IUSSI, London,* p. 396–403.

Wheeler, W. M. 1911. The ant-colony as an organism. *J. Morphol.,* 22:307–325.

———. 1928. *The Social Insects: Their Origin and Evolution.* Kegan Paul, Trench, Trubner and Co., London.

Williams, F. X. 1919. Philippine wasp studies. *Bull. Exp. Sta. Hawaiian Sugar Planters' Assoc.,* No. 114: 1–186.

Williams, G. C. 1966. *Adaptation and Natural Selection.* Princeton Univ. Press, Princeton.

Wilson, E. O. 1971. *The Insect Societies.* Belknap Press, Cambridge.

———. 1973. Group selection and its significance for ecology. *Bioscience,* 23(11): 631–638.

Woolpy, J. 1968. The social organization of wolves. *Natur. Hist.,* 77: 46–55.

Wynne-Edwards, V. C. 1962. *Animal Dispersion in Relation to Social Behaviour.* Oliver and Boyd, Edinburgh.

Yoshikawa, K. 1955. A polistine colony usurped by a foreign queen. Ecological studies of *Polistes* wasps II. *Insectes Soc.,* 2(3): 255–260.

A Theory of Group Selection

David Sloan Wilson
Department of Zoology, Michigan State University

In organisms possessing a dispersal phase the processes of mating, competition, feeding, and predation are often carried out within "trait-groups," defined as populations enclosed in areas smaller than the boundaries of the deme. A simple model shows that this can lead to the selection of "altruistic" traits that favor the fitness of the group over that of the individual. The extent of group selection that occurs depends mainly on the variation in the composition of genotypes between trait-groups. The traditional concepts of group and individual selection are seen as two extremes of a continuum, with systems in nature operating over the interval in between.

Most theories of group selection (1-6) postulate many groups fixed in space, with exchange by dispersers between groups. Within groups individual selection operates; an "altruist" trait can thus only become fixed by genetic drift. This requires the groups to be small, and dispersal between groups must be slight to prevent the reintroduction of "selfish" individuals. The "altruistic" groups could then serve as a stock for the recolonization of selfish groups that go extinct. See ref. 7 for a review.

The recent models of Levins (4), Boorman and Levitt (5), and Levin and Kilmer (6) make it plausible that this process can occur—the main question is to what extent the conditions for its operation (small group size, high isolation, high extinction rates) are met in nature. The current consensus is that the proper conditions are infrequent or at least limited to special circumstances such as the early stage of colonization of many populations (7).

This paper presents a theory of group selection based on a different concept of groups, perhaps more generally met in nature.

Most organisms have a dispersal stage—the seeds and pollen of plants, the post-teneral migratory phase of adult insects (8), the larvae of benthic marine life, the adolescents of many vertebrates. This means that individuals are spatially restricted during most of their life cycle, with the exception of their dispersal phase, when what was previously a boundary is easily transcended. As an example, a caterpillar is restricted to one or a few plants, but as a butterfly it spans whole fields.

Evolution's most easily conceived population unit is the deme, and it is determined by the movement occurring during the dispersal phase. Yet most ecological

I am indebted to Conrad Istock, E. O. Wilson, E. E. Werner, D. J. Hall, G. C. Williams, H. Caswell, F. M. Stewart, B. Levin, and the Ecology group at Michigan State for helpful criticism and discussion. This work was supported by National Science Foundation Grants GB35988 and BMS74-20550. This is contribution no. 267, Kellog Biological Station.

From *Proceedings of the National Academy of Sciences 72:* 143–46. Reprinted by permission of the author.

interactions, in terms of competition, mating, feeding and predation are carried out during the nondispersal stages in the smaller subdivisions, which I term "trait-groups." In some cases the trait-groups are discrete and easily recognized, such as for vessel-inhabiting mosquitoes and dung insects. In other cases they are continuous and each individual forms the center of its own trait-group, interacting only with its immediate neighbors, which comprise a small proportion of the deme. Two examples are plants and territorial animals. The following model treats only the discrete case, but the results can be generalized.

In order to determine if a heritable trait manifested within the trait-group will be favored in selection, the effect of that trait on relative fitnesses *within the trait-group* must be modelled, and the relative fitnesses for the deme obtained by taking the weighted average over all the trait-groups in the deme. Traditional models of selection neglect this; i.e., they assume that the trait-group equals the deme.

THE MODEL

Consider a single, haploid, randomly intermixing trait-group of organisms, composed of two types of individuals, A and B. These differ by only a single heritable trait, such as feeding rate, aggressiveness, or behavior under the threat of predation. Because the two types are identical in every other respect, they will have the same "baseline" fitness, and differences can be attributed solely to the effect of the trait. Haploidy and baseline fitness are of course artificial for most populations. They are used to simplify the argument, and the fundamental conclusions are not dependent upon them. Space does not permit a fuller treatment, which will be presented elsewhere.

By manifesting its trait, every A-individual changes its own fitness and often the fitness of the other animals in the trait-group by a certain increment or decrement. Call the individual manifesting the trait the donor, and all those affected by it (both A and B types) the recipients. These terms are commonly used for altruistic social behaviors, but here they are applied to all traits. For instance, an animal with a higher feeding rate deprives its neighbors of food that otherwise would be available to them. A positive fitness change is thus bestowed upon the donor and a negative fitness change to the recipients, even though the animals never interact behaviorally with each other.

Graphically, any trait can be portrayed as in Fig. 1. Each point on the graph represents a trait with its fitness change to the donor (f_d) and to each recipient (f_r). In the example just given the trait would lie somewhere in the fourth quadrant $(f_d$ positive, f_r negative). As another example, a warning cry might decrease the fitness of the caller $(f_d$ negative) and increase the fitness of those that hear the cry $(f_r$ positive), placing the trait somewhere in the second quadrant. In this model it is assumed that f_r is the same for both A and B types. While this will often be false in nature, it serves as a foundation for more realistic elaborations.

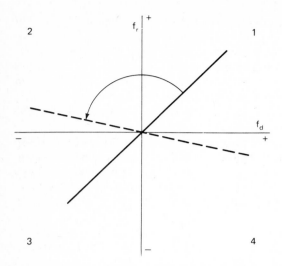

Figure 1 The entire set of traits giving fitness changes to the donor (f_d) and to each recipient (f_r). Any point to the right of the diagonal solid line is selected for; in the position shown the solid line represents the traditional concept of individual selection ($f_d > f_r$). Any point to the right of the broken line increases the fitness of the group ($f_d > -(N - 1)f_r$). As the variation in the composition of trait-groups increases, its effect on the selection of traits is to rotate the solid line until it is coincidental with the broken line (arrow).

If N is the total trait-group size and a,b the proportions of the A and B types, respectively, the average per capita fitness changes resulting from the trait can easily be calculated.

per capita fitness change to the A-type $= f_d + N(a - 1/N)f_r$
per capita fitness change to the B-type $= Naf_r$

Traditional selection models assume that the trait-group equals the deme. In this case the model is sufficient as stands and the A-individuals are selected for only if they have a higher per capita fitness change than the B-individuals.

$$f_d + N(a - 1/N)f_r > Naf_r \qquad\qquad [1]$$
$$f_d > Naf_r - N(a - 1/N)f_r$$
$$f_d > f_r \qquad\qquad [2]$$

Expression [2] is the traditional concept of individual selection, i.e., the trait must give the individual possessing the trait a higher relative fitness than the individuals not possessing the trait. This is portrayed in Fig. 1 by the solid line. Any point to the right of this line will be selected for by individual selection.

However, the A-trait increases the fitness of the trait-group only if:

$$f_d + (N-1)f_r > 0$$
$$f_d > -(N-1)f_r \tag{3}$$

Equation [3] represents the traditional concept of group selection, and is represented in Fig. 1 by the broken line. Any point to the right of (i.e., above) this line increases the fitness of the group.

Obviously, there is some overlap between Eqs. [2] and [3], that is some traits selected for by individual selection also increase the group's fitness. The problem of group selection is to determine if and how those traits that are advantageous to the group, yet outside the realm of individual selection, can be selected for, and conversely, how those traits that are disadvantageous to the group, yet within the realm of individual selection, can be blocked.

If the deme contains more than one trait-group (i.e., there is a dispersal phase), the per capita fitness changes of the A and B types for the *deme* are respectively:

$$\frac{\sum\limits_i Na_i[f_d + N(a_i - 1/N)f_r]}{\sum\limits_i Na_i} \quad \text{and} \quad \frac{\sum\limits_i Nb_i[Na_if_r]}{\sum\limits_i Nb_i}$$

These are simply the weighted averages of individual fitness changes over all the trait-groups in the deme. Each trait-group is assumed to have an equal overall density N and a_i, b_i are the proportions of the A and B types in each trait-group i.

As before, the A-type is selected for only if it has the highest per capita fitness.

$$\frac{\sum\limits_i Na_i[f_d + N(a_i - 1/N)f_r]}{\sum\limits_i Na_i} > \frac{\sum\limits_i Nb_i[Na_if_r]}{\sum\limits_i Nb_i} \tag{4}$$

$$\frac{\sum\limits_i Na_if_d}{\sum\limits_i Na_i} > \frac{\sum\limits_i Nb_ia_if_r}{\sum\limits_i b_i} - \frac{\sum\limits_i Na_i(a_i - 1/N)f_r}{\sum\limits_i a_i}$$

$$f_d > f_r \left[N\left(\frac{\sum\limits_i a_ib_i}{\sum\limits_i b_i} - \frac{\sum\limits_i a_i^2}{\sum\limits_i a_i} \right) + 1 \right] \tag{5}$$

Eq. [5] gives the condition for selection of the A-trait in the deme. It is the same as expression [2] with the exception of the term:

$$N\left(\frac{\sum\limits_i a_ib_i}{\sum\limits_i b_i} - \frac{\sum\limits_i a_i^2}{\sum\limits_i a_i} \right) \tag{6}$$

The value of this term depends on the compostion of the trait-groups. Given a single trait-group or trait-groups in which the proportions of A and B-types are identical, term [6] equals zero and Eq. [5] reverts to Eq. [2], the conditions for individual selection. If the types are completely segregated, such that any trait-group consists either entirely of A or entirely of B, then term [6] equals $-N$ and Eq. [5] reverts to Eq. [3], the conditions for pure group selection. Intermediate variation in trait-group composition yields intermediate solutions. Thus, the effect of increasing the variation in the composition of trait-groups is to push the system towards group selection. Graphically this is represented by rotating the solid line (giving the set of traits actually selected for) in Fig. 1 counter-clockwise, until it is coincidental with the broken line (arrow).

A variation greater than zero in the composition of trait-groups will be met by any stochastic process. If the placement of types into the trait-groups is randomly determined, then the variation in composition will follow the binomial distribution. In this case the expected value of term [6] is always -1 regardless of trait-group size (N) or the overall frequency of the A-type in the deme (a). Eq. [5] then becomes:

$$f_d > 0. \tag{7}$$

In other words, given a random distribution of types into trait-groups, any trait that increases the absolute fitness of the donor, *regardless of its relative fitness* will be selected for. Graphically, the solid line is rotated until it is coincidental with the y-axis. I am very grateful to F. M. Stewart for the proof of this, which will be presented elsewhere (the proof is not dependent on equal N in each trait-group).

If the variation in the composition of trait-groups is greater than random, term [6] yields values of less than -1, and altruistic traits that actually decrease the fitness of the donor can be selected for, such as alarm calls. This is also independent of A's frequency in the deme.

Kin that remain close to each other constitute one way of generating this greater than random variation (kin selection is thus a subset of this theory) but it is not the only way. Animal distributions are often found to be "patchy" or with a greater than random variation (9, 10). As one example, consider a situation in which larval insects are deposited into the trait-groups by adult females. The larvae upon hatching intermix within the trait-group, and so do not fall under the traditional concept of kin-selection. Assume that the females enter the trait-groups at random, N to a trait-group, so that as far as the *female* distributions of A and B types are concerned, term [6] equals -1. Each female then lays e eggs. Term [6] for the *larval* trait-group composition is now:

$$N \left(\frac{\sum_i a_i b_i}{\sum_i b_i} - \frac{\sum_i a_i^2}{\sum_i a_i} \right) = e(-1) \tag{8}$$

i.e., the proportions remain the same but the density is raised by a factor e, and the right hand side of Eq. [5] becomes $f_r(1-e)$, highly negative.

J. Maynard-Smith's (11) model of group selection is rather similar to the one presented here. He had the general concept of trait-groups, but apparently thought it was still necessary for altruistic traits to drift to fixation in some of the trait-groups for selection to occur. Genetic drift is not necessary for this model.

DISCUSSION

The process of group selection postulated here can be visualized in Fig. 2, showing two trait-groups with differing proportions of A and B types (2A). The A-trait is

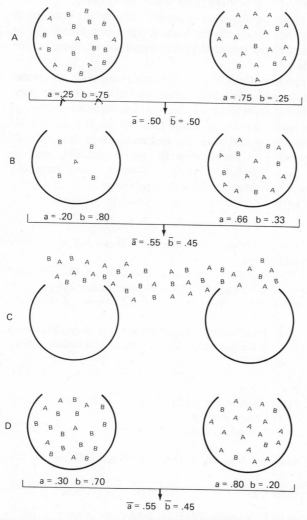

Figure 2 Illustration of the group selection process. See *text* for explanation.

an "altruistic" defense behavior, such as a warning cry. While the animals are in their trait-groups, predation occurs and within each trait-group the B's fare better than the A's. However, *considering both groups together the opposite is true, that is, the A's fare better than the B's* (2B). This is because due to the A-trait, the trait-group with the most A's has less overall predation upon it.

Were the groups to remain in isolation this would mean nothing, and the A's would rapidly be eliminated. However, all animals leave the trait-groups (2C), each has a single offspring, and the population settles back into the trait-groups (2D). The increased proportionality of the A-type for the entire system is now realized within each trait-group, and by this process B is eliminated from the system.

Notice that this form of group selection never really violates the concept of individual selection. It is always the type with the highest per capita fitness that is chosen, but when the effect of more than one trait-group is considered, these are the very types that behave altruistically.

The extent to which this process of group selection occurs depends on (1) the validity of the trait-group concept, and given this, (2) the variation in the composition of trait-groups. Both may be expected to vary widely among organisms, depending on behavior and habitat. In particular, small insular habitats might constrict the deme to the size of a single trait-group and push the system towards "individual" selection; and spatial heterogeneity, by partitioning the deme spatially, may be expected to enforce trait-groups and enhance group selection. In any case, the traditional concepts of group and individual selection appear to be two extremes of a continuum, with systems in nature operating in the interval in between.

REFERENCES

1   Wynne-Edwards, V. C. (1962) *Animal Dispersion in Relation to Social Behavior* (Oliver and Boyd, Edinburgh, Scotland), 653 pp.
2   Haldane, J. B. S. (1932) *The Causes of Evolution* (Longmans, Green & Co.; reprinted in 1966 by Cornell University Press, Ithaca, N.Y.; Cornell paperbacks), 235 pp.
3   Wright, S. (1945) "Tempo and mode in evolution: A critical review," *Ecology* 26, 415-419.
4   Levins, R. (1970) "Extinction," in *Some Mathematical Questions in Biology. Lectures on Mathematics in the Life Sciences,* ed. Gerstenhaber, M. (American Mathematical Society, Providence, R.I.), Vol. 2, pp. 77-107.
5   Boorman, S. A. & Levitt, P. R. (1973) "Group selection on the boundary of a stable population," *Theor. Pop. Biol.* 4, 85-128.
6   Levin, B. R. & Kilmer, W. L. (1974) "Interdemic selection and the evolution of altruism: a computer simulation study," *Evolution,* in press.
7   Wilson, E. O. (1973) "Group selection and its significance for Ecology," *BioScience* 23, 631-638.
8   Johnson, C. G. (1969) *Migration and Dispersal of Insects by Flight* (Methuen & Co., London), 763 pp.
9   Hutchinson, G. E. (1953) "The concept of pattern in ecology," *Proc. Acad. Natural Sci.,* Philadelphia, 105, 1-12.
10 Lloyd, M. (1967) "Mean crowding," *J. Anim. Ecol.* 36, 1-30.
11 Maynard-Smith, J. (1964) "Group selection and kin selection," *Nature* 201, 1145-1147.

Parent-Offspring Conflict

Robert L. Trivers
Museum of Comparative Zoology, Harvard University

When parent-offspring relations in sexually reproducing species are viewed from the standpoint of the offspring as well as the parent, conflict is seen to be an expected feature of such relations. In particular, parent and offspring are expected to disagree over how long the period of parental investment should last, over the amount of parental investment that should be given, and over the altruistic and egoistic tendencies of the offspring as these tendencies affect other relatives. In addition, under certain conditions parents and offspring are expected to disagree over the preferred sex of the potential offspring. In general, parent-offspring conflict is expected to increase during the period of parental care, and offspring are expected to employ psychological weapons in order to compete with their parents. Detailed data on mother-offspring relations in mammals are consistent with the arguments presented. Conflict in some species, including the human species, is expected to extend to the adult reproductive role of the offspring: under certain conditions parents are expected to attempt to mold an offspring, against its better interests, into a permanent nonreproductive.

In classical evolutionary theory parent-offspring relations are viewed from the standpoint of the parent. If parental investment (PI) in an offspring is defined as anything done by the parent for the offspring that increases the offspring's chance of surviving while decreasing the parent's ability to invest in other offspring (Trivers, 1972), then parents are classically assumed to allocate investment in their young in such a way as to maximize the number surviving, while offspring are implicitly assumed to be passive vessels into which parents pour the appropriate care. Once one imagines offspring as *actors* in this interaction, then conflict must be assumed to lie at the heart of sexual reproduction itself—an offspring attempting from the very beginning to maximize its reproductive success (RS) would presumably want more investment than the parent is selected to give. But unlike conflict between unrelated individuals, parent-offspring conflict is expected to be circumscribed by the close genetic relationship between parent and offspring. For example, if the offspring garners more investment than the parent has been selected to give, the offspring thereby decreases

I thank I. DeVore for numerous conversations and for detailed comments on the manuscript. For additional comments I thank W. D. Hamilton, J. Roughgarden, T. W. Schoener, J. Seger, and G. C. Williams. For help with the appendix I thank J. D. Weinrich. Finally, for help with the references I thank my research assistant, H. Hare, and the Harry Frank Guggenheim Foundation, which provides her salary. Part of this work was completed under an N.I.H. postdoctoral fellowship and partly supported by N.I.M.H. grant MH-13611 to I. DeVore.

From *American Zoologist 14:* 249–264. Reprinted by permission of the American Society of Zoologists and the author.

the number of its surviving siblings, so that any gene in an offspring that leads to an additional investment decreases (to some extent) the number of surviving copies of itself located in siblings. Clearly, if the gene in the offspring exacts too great a cost from the parent, that gene will be selected against even though it confers some benefit on the offspring. To specify precisely how much cost an offspring should be willing to inflict on its parent in order to gain a given benefit, one must specify how the offspring is expected to weigh the survival of siblings against its own survival.

The problem of specifying how an individual is expected to weigh siblings against itself (or any relative against any other) has been solved in outline by Hamilton (1964), in the context of explaining the evolution of altruistic behavior. An altruistic act can be defined as one that harms the organism performing the act while benefiting some other individual, harm and benefit being defined in terms of reproductive success. Since any gene that helps itself spread in a population is, by definition, being selected for, altruistic behavior in the above sense can be selected only if there is a sufficiently large probability that the recipient of the act also has the gene. More precisely, the benefit/cost ratio of the act, times the chance that the recipient has the gene, must be greater than one. If the recipient of the act is a relative of the altruist, then the probability that the recipient has the gene by descent from a common ancestor can be specified. This conditional probability is called the *degree of relatedness,* r_0. For an altruistic act directed at a relative to have survival value its benefit/cost ratio must be larger than the inverse of the altruist's r_0 to the relative. Likewise an individual is expected to forego a selfish act if its cost to a relative, times the r_0 to that relative, is greater than the benefit to the actor.

The rules for calculating degrees of relatedness are straightforward for both diploid and haplodiploid organisms, even when inbreeding complicates the relevant genealogy (see the addendum in Hamilton, 1971). For example, in a diploid species (in the absence of inbreeding) an individual's r_0 to his or her full-siblings is ½; to half-siblings, ¼; to children, ½; to cousins, ⅛. If in calculating the selective value of a gene one not only computes its effect on the reproductive success of the individual bearing it, but adds to this its effects on the reproductive success of related individuals, appropriately devalued by the relevant degrees of relatedness, then one has computed what Hamilton (1964) calls *inclusive fitness.* While Hamilton pointed out that the parent-offspring relationship is merely a special case of relations between any set of genetically related individuals, he did not apply his theory to such relations. I present here a theory of parent-offspring relations which follows directly from the key concept of inclusive fitness and from the assumption that the offspring is at all times capable of an active role in its relationship to its parents. The form of the argument applies equally well to haplodiploid species, but for simplicity the discussion is mostly limited to diploid species. Likewise, although many of the arguments apply to any sexually reproducing species showing parental investment (including many plant species), the arguments presented here are particularly relevant to understanding a species such as the human species in which parental investment is critical to the offspring throughout its entire prereproductive life (and often later as well) and in which an individual normally spends life embedded in a network of near and distant kin.

PARENT-OFFSPRING CONFLICT OVER THE CONTINUATION OF PARENTAL INVESTMENT

Consider a newborn (male) caribou calf nursing from his mother. The benefit to him of nursing (measured in terms of his chance of surviving) is large, the cost to his mother (measured in terms of her ability to produce additional offspring) presumably small. As time goes on and the calf becomes increasingly capable of feeding on his own, the benefit to him of nursing decreases while the cost to his mother may increase (as a function, for example, of the calf's size). If cost and benefit are measured in the same units, then at some point the cost to the mother will exceed the benefit to her young and the net reproductive success of the mother decreases if she continues to nurse. (Note that later-born offspring may contribute less to the mother's eventual RS than early-born, because their reproductive value may be lower [Fisher, 1930], but this is automatically taken into account in the cost function.)

The calf is not expected, so to speak, to view this situation as does his mother, for the calf is completely related to himself but only partially related to his future siblings, so that he is expected to devalue the cost of nursing (as measured in terms of future sibs) by his r_0 to his future sibs, when comparing the cost of nursing with its benefit to himself. For example, if future sibs are expected to be full-sibs, then the calf should nurse until the cost to the mother is more than twice the benefit to himself. Once the cost to the mother is more than twice the benefit to the calf, continued nursing is opposed by natural selection acting on both the mother and the calf. As long as one imagines that the benefit/cost ratio of a parental act changes continuously from some large number to some very small number near zero, then there must occur a period of time during which $\frac{1}{2} < B/C < 1$. This period is one of expected conflict between mother and offspring, in the sense that natural selection working on the mother favors her halting parental investment while natural selection acting on the offspring favors his eliciting the parental investment. The argument presented here is graphed in Figure 1. (Note, as argued below, that there are specialized situations in which the offspring may be selected to consume *less* PI than the parent is selected to give.)

This argument applies to all sexually reproducing species that are not completely inbred, that is, in which siblings are not identical copies of each other. Conflict near the end of the period of PI over the continuation of PI is expected in all such species. The argument applies to PI in general or to any subcomponent of PI (such as feeding the young, guarding the young, carrying the young) that can be assigned a more or less independent cost-benefit function. Weaning conflict in mammals is an example of parent-offspring conflict explained by the argument given here. Such conflict is known to occur in a variety of mammals, in the field and in the

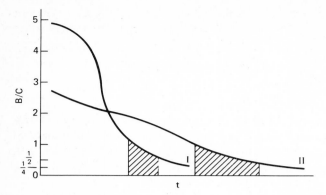

Figure 1 The benefit/cost ratio (B/C) of a parental act (such as nursing) toward an offspring as a function of time. Benefit is measured in units of reproductive success of the offspring and cost in comparable units of reproductive success of the mother's future offspring. Two species are plotted. In species I the benefit/cost ratio decays quickly; in species II, slowly. Shaded areas indicate times during which parent and offspring are in conflict over whether the parental care should continue. Future sibs are assumed to be full-sibs. If future sibs were half-sibs, the shaded areas would have to be extended until B/C = 1/4.

laboratory: for example, baboons (DeVore, 1963), langurs (Jay, 1963), rhesus macaques (Hinde and Spencer-Booth, 1971), other macaques (Rosenblum, 1971), vervets (Struhsaker, 1971), cats (Schneirla et al., 1963), dogs (Rheingold, 1963) and rats (Rosenblatt and Lehrman, 1963). Likewise, I interpret conflict over parental feeding at the time of fledging in bird species as conflict explained by the present argument: for example, Herring Gulls (Drury and Smith, 1968), Red Warblers (Elliott, 1969), Verreaux's Eagles (Rowe, 1947), and White Pelicans (Schaller, 1964).

Weaning conflict is usually assumed to occur either because transitions in nature are assumed always to be imperfect or because such conflict is assumed to serve the interests of both parent and offspring by informing each of the needs of the other. In either case, the marked inefficiency of weaning conflict seems the clearest argument in favor of the view that such conflict results from an underlying conflict in the way in which the inclusive fitness of mother and offspring are maximized. Weaning conflict in baboons, for example, may last for weeks or months, involving daily competitve interactions and loud cries from the infant in a species otherwise strongly selected for silence (DeVore, 1963). Interactions that inefficient *within* a multicellular organism would be cause for some surprise, since, unlike mother and offspring, the somatic cells within an organism are identically related.

One parameter affecting the expected length (and intensity) of weaning conflict is the offspring's expected r_o to its future siblings. The lower the offspring's r_o to its future siblings, the longer and more intense the expected weaning conflict. This suggests a simple prediction. Other things being equal, species in which different, unrelated males commonly father a female's successive offspring are expected to show stronger weaning conflict than species in which a female's successive offspring are usually fathered by the same male. As shown below, however, weaning conflict is merely a special case of conflict expected throughout the period of parental investment, so that this prediction applies to the intensity of conflict prior to weaning as well.

CONFLICT THROUGHOUT THE PERIOD OF PI OVER THE AMOUNT OF PI

In Figure 1 it was assumed that the amount of investment for each day (or moment in time) had already been established, and that mother and young were only selected to disagree over when such investment should be ended. But it can be shown that, in theory, conflict over the amount of investment that should at each moment be given, is expected throughout the period of PI.

At any moment in the period of PI the female is selected to invest that amount which maximizes the difference between the associated cost and benefit, where these terms are defined as above. The infant is selected to induce that investment which maximizes the difference between the benefit and a cost devalued by the relevant r_0. The different optima for a moment in time in a hypothetical species are graphed in Figure 2. With reasonable assumptions about the shape of the benefit and cost curves, it is clear that the infant will, at each instant in time, tend to favor greater parental investment than the parent is selected to give. The period of transition discussed in the previous section is a special case of this continuing competition, namely, the case in which parent and offspring compete over whether *any* investment should be given, as opposed to their earlier competition over *how much* should

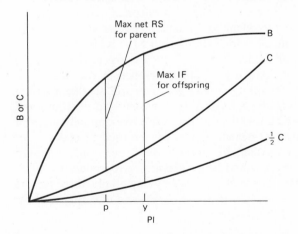

Figure 2 The benefit, cost, and half the cost of a parental act toward an offspring at one moment in time as a function of the amount the parent invests in the act (PI). Amount of milk given during one day of nursing in a mammal would be an example of PI. At p the parent's inclusive fitness (B–C) is maximized; at y the offspring's inclusive fitness (B – C/2) is maximized. Parent and offspring disagree over whether p or y should be invested. The offspring's future siblings are assumed to be full-siblings. IF = inclusive fitness.

be given. Since parental investment begins before eggs are laid or young are born, and since there appears to be no essential distinction between parent-offspring conflict outside the mother (mediated primarily by behavioral acts) and parent-offspring conflict inside the mother (mediated primarily by chemical acts), I assume that parent-offspring conflict may in theory begin as early as meiosis.

It must be emphasized that the cost of parental investment referred to above (see Fig. 2) is measured *only* in terms of decreased ability to produce *future* offspring (or, when the brood size is larger than one, decreased ability to produce *other* offspring). To appreciate the significance of this definition, imagine that early in the period of PI the offspring garners more investment than the parent has been selected to give. This added investment may decrease the parent's later investment in the offspring at hand, either through an increased chance of parental mortality during the period of PI, or through a depletion in parental resources, or because parents have been selected to make the appropriate adjustment (that is, to reduce later investment below what otherwise would have been given). In short, the offspring may gain a temporary benefit but suffer a later cost. This self-inflicted cost is subsumed in the benefit function (B) of Figure 2, because it decreases the benefit the infant receives. It is not subsumed in the cost function (C) because this function refers only to the mother's future offspring.

THE TIME COURSE OF PARENT OFFSPRING CONFLICT

If one could specify a series of cost-benefit curves (such as Fig. 2) for each day of the period of PI, then the expected time course of parent-offspring conflict could be specified. Where the difference in the offspring's inclusive fitness at the parent's optimum PI (p in Fig. 2) and at the offspring's optimum PI (y) is large, conflict is expected to be intense. Where the difference is slight, conflict is expected to be slight or nonexistent. In general, where there is a strong difference in the offspring's inclusive fitness at the two different optima (p and y), there will also be a strong difference in the parent's inclusive fitness, so that both parent and offspring will simultaneously be strongly motivated to achieve their respective optimal values of PI. (This technique of comparing cost-benefit graphs can be used to make other predictions about parent-offspring conflict, for example that such conflict should decrease in intensity with increasing age, and hence decreasing reproductive value, of the parent; see Figure 3.) In the absence of such day-by-day graphs three factors can be identified, all of which will usually predispose parent and offspring to show greater conflict as the period of PI progresses.

1 *Decreased chance of self-inflicted cost.* As the period of PI progresses, the offspring faces a decreased chance of suffering a later self-inflicted cost for garnering additional investment at the moment. At the end of the period of PI any additional investment forced on the parent will only affect later offspring, so that at that time the interests of parent and offspring are maximally divergent. This time-dependent

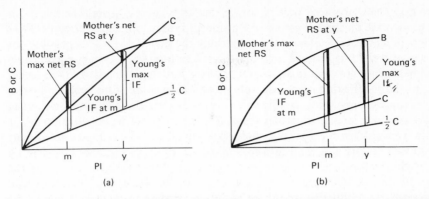

Figure 3 The benefit and cost of a parental act (as in Fig. 2) toward (*a*) an offspring born to a young female and (*b*) an offspring born to an old female. One assumes that the benefit to the offspring of a given amount of PI does not change with birth order but that the cost declines as a function of the declining reproductive value (Fisher, 1930) of the mother: she will produce fewer future offspring anyway. The difference between the mother's inclusive fitness at m and y is greater for (*a*) than for (*b*). The same is true for the offspring. Conflict should be correspondingly more intense between early born young and their mothers than between late born young and their mothers.

change in the offspring's chance of suffering a self-inflicted cost will, other things being equal, predispose parent and offspring to increasing conflict during the period of PI.

   2   *Imperfect replenishment of parental resources.*   If the parent is unable on a daily basis to replenish resources invested in the offspring, the parent will suffer increasing depletion of its resources, and, as time goes on, the cost of such depletion should rise disproportionately, even if the amount of resources invested per day declines. For example, a female may give less milk per day in the first half of the nursing period than in the second half (as in pigs: Gill and Thomson, 1956), but if she is failing throughout to replenish her energy losses, then she is constantly increasing her deficit (although at a diminishing rate) and greater deficits may be associated with disproportionate costs. In some species a parent does not feed itself during much of the period of PI and at least during such periods the parent must be depleting its resources (for example, female elephant seals during the nursing period: LeBoeuf et al., 1972). But the extent to which parents who feed during the period of PI fail to replenish their resources is usually not known. For some species it is clear that females typically show increasing levels of depletion during the period of PI (e.g., sheep: Wallace, 1948).

   3   *Increasing size of the offspring.*   During that portion of the period of PI in which the offspring receives all its food from its parents, the tendency for the offspring to begin very small and steadily increase in size will, other things being equal, increase the cost to the parent of maintaining and enlarging it. (Whether this is always true will depend, of course, on the way in which the offspring's growth rates changes as a function of increasing size.) In addition, as the offspring increases in size the relative energetic expense to it of competing with its parents should decline.

The argument advanced here is only meant to suggest a general tendency for conflict to increase during the period of PI, since it is easy to imagine circumstances in which conflict might peak several times during the period of PI. It is possible, for example, that weight at birth in a mammal such as humans is strongly associated with the offspring's survival in subsequent weeks, but that the cost to the mother of bearing a large offspring is considerably greater than some of her ensuing investment. In such circumstances, conflict *prior* to birth over the offspring's weight at birth may be more intense than conflict over nursing in the weeks after birth.

Data from studies of dogs, cats, rhesus macaques, and sheep appear to support the arguments of this and the previous section. In these species, parent-offspring conflict begins well before the period of weaning and tends to increase during the period of PI. In dogs (Rheingold, 1963) and cats (Schneirla et al., 1963) postnatal maternal care can be divided into three periods according to increasing age of the offspring. During the first, the mother approaches the infant to initiate parental investment. No avoidance behavior or aggression toward the infant is shown by the mother. In the second, the offspring and the mother approach each other about equally, and the mother shows some avoidance behavior and some aggression in response to the infant's demands. The third period can be characterized as the period of weaning. Most contacts are initiated by the offspring. Open avoidance and aggression characterize the mother.

Detailed quantitative data on the rhesus macaque (Hinde and Spencer-Booth, 1967, 1971), and some parallel data on other macaques (Rosenblum, 1971), demonstrate that the behavior of both mother and offspring change during the period of postnatal parental care in a way consistent with theory. During the first weeks after she has given birth, the rhesus mother's initiative in setting up nipple contacts is high but it soon declines rapidly. Concurrently she begins to reject some of the infant's advances, and after her own initiatives toward nipple contact have ceased, she rejects her infant's advances with steadily increasing frequency until at the end of the period of investment all of the offspring's advances are rejected. Shortly after birth, the offspring leaves the mother more often than it approaches her, but as time goes on the intiative in maintaining mother-offspring proximity shifts to the offspring. This leads to the superficially paradoxical result that as the offspring becomes increasingly active and independent, spending more and more time away from its mother, its initiative in maintaining mother-offspring proximity *increases* (that is, it tends to approach the mother more often than it leaves her). According to the theory presented here, this result reflects the underlying tendency of parent-offspring conflict to increase during the period of PI. As the interests of mother and offspring diverge, the offspring must assume a greater role in inducing whatever parental investment is forthcoming.

Data on the production and consumption of milk in sheep (Wallace, 1948) indicate that during the first weeks of the lamb's life the mother typically produces more milk than the lamb can drink. The lamb's appetite determines how much milk is consumed. But after the fourth week, the mother begins to produce less than the lamb can drink, and from that time on it is the mother who is the limiting factor in determining how much milk is consumed. Parallel behavioral data indicate that the mother initially permits free access by her lamb(s) but after a couple of weeks begins to prevent some suckling attempts (Munro, 1956; Ewbank, 1967). Mothers who are in poor condition become the limiting factor in nursing earlier than do mothers in good condition, and this is presumably because the cost of a given amount of milk is considerably higher when the mother is in poor condition, while the benefit to the offspring remains more or less unchanged. Females who produce twins permit either twin to suckle on demand during the first three weeks after birth, but in the ensuing weeks they do not permit one twin to suckle unless the other is ready also (Ewbank, 1964; Alexander, 1960).

DISAGREEMENT OVER THE SEX OF THE OFFSPRING

Under certain conditions a potential offspring is expected to disagree with its parents over whether it should become a male or a female. Since one can not assume that potential offspring are powerless to affect their sex, sex ratios observed in nature should to some extent reflect the offspring's preferred value as well as the parents'.

Fisher (1930) showed that (in the absence of inbreeding) parents are selected to invest as much in the total of their daughters as in the total of their sons. When each son produced costs on average the same as each daughter, parents are selected to produce a sex ratio of 50/50. In such species, the expected reproductive success (RS) of a son is the same as that of a daughter, so that an offspring should be indifferent as to its sex. But if (for example) parents are selected to invest twice as much in a typical male as in a typical female, then they will be selected to produce twice as many females as males, and the expected RS of each son will be twice that of each daughter. In such a species a potential offspring would prefer to be a male, for it would then achieve twice the RS it would as a female, without suffering a comparable decrease in inclusive fitness through the cost forced on its parents, because the offspring is selected to devalue that cost by the offspring's expected r_o to the displaced sibling. For the example chosen, the exact gain in the offspring's inclusive fitness can be specified as follows. If the expected RS of a female offspring is defined as one unit of RS, then, in being made male, the offspring gains one unit of RS, but it deprives its mother of an additional daughter (or half a son). This displaced sibling (whether a female or half of a male) would have achieved one unit of RS, but this unit is devalued from the offspring's standpoint by the relevant r_o. If the displaced sibling would have been a full sibling, then this unit of RS is devalued by ½, and the offspring, in being made a male, achieves a ½ unit net increase in inclusive fitness. If the displaced sibling would have been a half sibling, the offspring, in being made a male, achieves a ¾ unit net increase in inclusive fitness. The parent, on the other hand, experiences initially only a trivial decrease in RS, so that *initially* any gene in the offspring tending to make it a male against its parents' efforts would spread rapidly.

As a hypothetical gene for offspring control of sex begins to spread, the number of males produced increases, thereby lowering the expected RS of each male. This decreases the gain (in inclusive fitness) to the offspring of being made a male. If the offspring's equilibrial sex ratio is defined as that sex ratio at which an offspring is indifferent as to whether it becomes a male or a female, then this sex ratio can be calculated by determining the sex ratio at which the offspring's gain in RS in being made a male is exactly offset by its loss in inclusive fitness in depriving itself of a sister (or half a brother). The offspring's equilibrial sex ratio will depend on both the offspring's expected r_0 to the displaced siblings and on the extent to which parents invest more in males than in females (or vice versa). The general solution is given in the Appendix. Parent and offspring equilibrial sex ratios for different values of r_0 and different values of x (PI in a typical son/PI in a typical daughter) are plotted in Figure 4. For example, where the r_0 between siblings is ½ and where parents invest twice as much in a son as in a daughter (x=2), the parents' equilibrial sex ratio is 1:2 (males:females) while that of the offspring is 1:1.414.

As long as all offspring are fathered by the same male, he will prefer the same sex ratio among the offspring that the mother does. But consider a species such as caribou in which the female produces only one offspring a year and assume that a female's successive offspring are fathered by different, unrelated males. If the female invests more in a son than in a daughter, then she will be selected to produce more

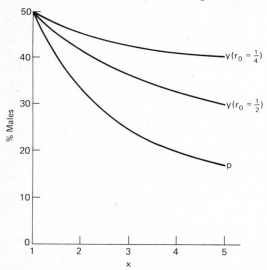

Figure 4 The optimal sex ratio (per cent males) for the mother (m) and the young (y) where the mother invests more in a son than in a daughter by a factor of x (and assuming no paternal investment in either sex). Two functions are given for the offspring, depending on whether the siblings it displaces are full-siblings (r_0 = 1/2) or half-siblings (r_0 = 1/4). Note the initial rapid divergence between the mother's and the offspring's preferred sex ratio as the mother moves from equal investment in a typical individual of either sex (x = 1) to twice as much investment in a typical male (x = 2).

daughters than sons. The greater cost of the son is not borne by the father, however, who invests nothing beyond his sperm, and who will not father the female's later offspring, so the father's equilibrial sex ratio is an equal number of sons and daughters. The offspring will prefer some probability of being a male that is intermediate between its parents' preferred probabilities, because (unlike the father) the offspring is related to the mother's future offspring but (unlike the mother) it is less related to them than to itself.

In a species such as just described (in which the male is heterogametic) the following sort of competitive interaction is possible. The prospective father produces more Y-bearing sperm than the female would prefer and she subjects the Y-bearing sperm to differential mortality. If the ratio of the sperm reaching the egg has been reduced to near the mother's optimal value, then the egg preferentially admits the Y-bearing sperm. If the mother ovulated more eggs than she intends to rear, she could then choose which to invest in, according to the sex of the fertilized egg, unless a male egg is able to deceive the mother about its sex until the mother has committed herself to investing in him. Whether such interactions actually occur in nature is at present unknown.

One consequence of the argument advanced here is that there is an automatic selective agent tending to keep maternal investment in a son similar to that in a daughter, for the greater the disparity between the investment in typical individuals of the two sexes, the greater the loss suffered by the mother in competitive interactions with her offspring over their preferred sex and in producing a sex ratio further skewed away from her preferred ratio (see Fig. 4). This automatic selection pressure may partly account for the apparent absence of strongly size-dimorphic young (at the end of PI) in species showing striking adult sexual dimorphism in size.

The argument presented here applies to any tendency of the parent to invest differentially in the young, whether according to sex or some other variable, except that in many species sex is irreversibly determined early in ontogeny and the offspring is expected at the very beginning to be able to discern its own sex and hence the predicted pattern of investment it will receive, so that, unlike other forms of differential investment, conflict is expected very early, namely, at the time of sex determination.

THE OFFSPRING AS PSYCHOLOGICAL MANIPULATOR

How is the offspring to compete effectively with its parent? An offspring can not fling its mother to the ground at will and nurse. Throughout the period of parental investment the offspring competes at a disadvantage. The offspring is smaller and less experienced than its parent, and its parent controls the resources at issue. Given this competitive disadvantage the offspring is expected to employ psychological rather than physical tactics. (Inside the mother the offspring is expected to employ chemical tactics, but some of the analysis presented below should also apply to such competition.) It should attempt to *induce* more investment than the parent wishes to give.

Since an offspring will often have better knowledge of its real needs than will its parent, selection should favor parental attentiveness to signals from its offspring that apprize the parent of the offspring's condition. In short, the offspring cries when hungry or in danger and the parent responds appropriately. Conversely, the offspring signals its parent (by smiling or wagging its tail) when its needs have been well met. Both parent and offspring benefit from this system of communication. But once such a system has evolved, the offspring can begin to employ it out of context. The offspring can cry not only when it is famished but also when it merely wants more food than the parent is selected to give. Likewise, it can begin to withhold its smile until it has gotten its way. Selection will then of course favor parental ability to discriminate the two uses of the signals, but still subtler mimicry and deception by the offspring are always possible. Parental experience with preceding offspring is expected to improve the parent's ability to make the appropriate discrimination. Unless succeeding offspring can employ more confusing tactics than earlier ones, parent-offspring interactions are expected to be increasingly biased in favor of the parent as a function of parental age.

In those species in which the offspring is more helpless and vulnerable the younger it is, its parents will have been more strongly selected to respond positively to signals of need emitted by the offspring, the younger that offspring is. This suggests that at any stage of ontogeny in which the offspring is in conflict with its parents, one appropriate tactic may be to revert to the gestures and actions of an earlier stage of development in order to induce the investment that would then have been forthcoming. Psychologists have long recognized such a tendency in humans and have given it the name of regression. A detailed functional analysis of regression could be based on the theory presented here.

The normal course of parent-offspring relations must be subject to considerable unpredictable variation in both the condition of the parent and (sometimes independently) the condition of the offspring. Both partners must be sensitive to such variation and must adjust their behavior appropriately. Low investment coming from a parent in poor condition has a different meaning than low investment coming from a parent in good condition. This suggests that from an early age the offspring is expected to be a psychologically sophisticated organism. The offspring should be able to evaluate the cost of a given parental act (which depends in part on the condition of the parent at that moment) and its benefit (which depends in part on the condition of the offspring). When the offspring's interests diverge from those of its parent, the offspring must be able to employ a series of psychological maneuvers, including the mimicry and regression mentioned above. Although it would be expected to learn appropriate information (such as whether its psychological maneuvers were having the desired effects), an important feature of the argument presented here is that the offspring cannot rely on its parents for disinterested guidance. One expects the offspring to be pre-programmed to resist some parental teaching while being open to other forms. This is particularly true, as argued below, for parental teaching that affects the altruistic and egoistic tendencies of the offspring.

If one event in a social relationship predicts to some degree future events in that relationship, the organism should be selected to alter its behavior in response to an initial event, in order to change the probability that the predicted events will occur. For example, if a mother's lack of love for her offspring early in its life predicts deficient future investment, then the offspring will be selected to be sensitive to such early lack of love, whether investment at that time is deficient or not, in order to increase her future investment. The best data relevant to these possibilities come from the work of Hinde and his associates on groups of caged rhesus macaques. In a series of experiments, a mother was removed from her 6-month-old infant, leaving the infant in the home cage with other group members. After 6 days, the mother was returned to the home cage. Behavioral data were gathered before, during, and after the separation (see points 1 and 2 below). In a parallel series of experiments, the infant was removed for 6 days from its mother, leaving her in the home cage, and the same behavioral data were gathered (see point 3 below). The main findings can be summarized as follows:

1 *Separation of mother from her offspring affects their relationship upon reunion.* After reunion with its mother, the infant spends more time on the mother than it did before separation—although, had the separation not occurred, the infant would have reduced its time on the mother. This increase is caused by the infant, and occurs despite an increase in the frequency of maternal rejection (Hinde and Spencer-Booth, 1971). These effects can be detected at least as long as 5 weeks after reunion. These data are consistent with the assumption that the infant has been selected to interpret its mother's disappearance as an event whose recurrence the infant can help prevent by devoting more of its energies to staying close to its mother.

2 *The mother-offspring relationship prior to separation affects the offspring's behavior on reunion.* Upon reunion with its mother, an infant typically shows distress, as measured by callings and immobility. The more frequently an infant was rejected *prior* to separation, the more distress it shows upon reunion. This correlation holds for at least 4 weeks after reunion. In addition, the more distressed the infant is, the greater is its role in maintaining proximity to its mother (Hinde and Spencer-Booth, 1971). These data support the assumption that the infant interprets its mother's disappearance in relation to her predeparture behavior in a logical way: the offspring should assume that a rejecting mother who temporarily disappears needs more offspring surveilance and intervention than does a nonrejecting mother who temporarily disappears.

3 *An offspring removed from its mother shows, upon reunion, different effects than an offspring whose mother has been removed.* Compared to an infant whose mother had been removed, an infant removed from its mother shows, upon reunion, and for up to 6 weeks after reunion, less distress and more time off the mother. In addition, the offspring tends to play a smaller role in maintaining proximity to its mother, and it experiences less frequent maternal rejections (Hinde and Davies, 1972

a,b). These data are consistent with the expectation that the offspring should be sensitive to the *meaning* of events affecting its relationship to its mother. The offspring can differentiate between a separation from its mother caused by its own behavior or some accident (infant removed from group) and a separation which may have been caused by maternal negligence (mother removed from group). In the former kind of separation, the infant shows less effects when reunited, because, from its point of view, such a separation does not reflect on its mother and no remedial action is indicated. A similar explanation can be given for differences in the mother's behavior.

PARENT OFFSPRING CONFLICT OVER THE BEHAVIORAL TENDENCIES OF THE OFFSPRING

Parents and offspring are expected to disagree over the behavioral tendencies of the offspring insofar as these tendencies affect related individuals. Consider first interactions among siblings. An individual is only expected to perform an altruistic act toward its full-sibling whenever the benefit to the sibling is greater than twice the cost to the altruist. Likewise, it is only expected to forego selfish acts when $C > 2B$ (where a selfish act is defined as one that gives the actor a benefit, B, while inflicting a cost, C, on some other individual, in this case, on a full-sibling). But parents, who are equally realted to all of their offspring, are expected to encourage all altruistic acts among their offspring in which $B > C$, and to discourage all selfish acts in which $C > B$. Since there ought to exist altruistic situations in which $C < B < 2C$, parents and offspring are expected to disagree over the tendency of the offspring to act altruistically toward its siblings. Likewise, whenever for any selfish act harming a full-sibling $B < C < 2B$, parents are expected to discourage such behavior and offspring are expected to be relatively refractory to such discouragement.

This parent-offspring disagreement is expected over behavior directed toward other relatives as well. For example, the offspring is only selected to perform altruistic acts toward a cousin (related through the mother) when $B > 8C$. But the offspring's mother is related to her own nephews and nieces by $r_0 = \frac{1}{4}$ and to her offspring by $r_0 = \frac{1}{2}$, so that she would like to see any altruistic acts performed by her offspring toward their maternal cousins whenever $B > 2C$. The same argument applies to selfish acts, and both arguments can be made for more distant relatives as well. (The father is unrelated to his mate's kin and, other things being equal, should not be distressed to see his offspring treat such individuals as if they were unrelated.)

The general argument extends to interactions with unrelated individuals, as long as these interactions have some effect, however remote and indirect, on kin. Assume, for example, that an individual gains some immediate benefit, B, by acting nastily toward some unrelated individual. Assume that the unrelated individual reciprocates in kind (Trivers, 1971), but assume that the reciprocity is directed toward both the original actor and some relative, e.g., his sibling. Assuming no other effects of the initial act, the original actor will be selected to perform the nasty act as long as $B>C_1+\frac{1}{2}(C_2)$, where C_1 is the cost to the original actor of the reciprocal nastiness he receives and C_2 is the cost to his sibling of the nastiness the sibling receives. The actor's parents viewing the interaction would be expected to condone the initial act only if $B>C_1 + C_2$. Since there ought to exist situations in which $C_1 + \frac{1}{2}(C_2)<B<C_1 + C_2$, one expects conflict between offspring and parents over the offspring's tendency to perform the initial nasty act in the situation described. A similar argument can be made for altruistic behavior directed toward an unrelated individual if this behavior induces altruism in return, part of which benefits the original altruist's sibling. Parents are expected to encourage such altruism more often than the offspring is expected to undertake on his own. The argument can obviously be extended to behavior which has indirect effects on kin other than one's sibling.

As it applies to human beings, the above argument can be summarized by saying that a fundamental conflict is expected during socialization over the altruistic and egoistic impulses of the offspring. Parents are expected to socialize their offspring to act more altruistically and less egoistically than the offspring would naturally act, and the offspring are expected to resist such socialization. If this argument is valid, then it is clearly a mistake to view socialization in humans (or in any sexually reproducing species) as only or even primarily a process of "enculturation," a process by which parents teach offspring their culture (e.g., Mussen et al., 1969, p. 259). For example, one is not permitted to assume that parents who attempt to impart such virtues as responsibility, decency, honesty, trustworthiness, generosity, and self-denial are merely providing the offspring with useful information on appropriate behavior in the local culture, for all such virtues are likely to affect the amount of altruistic and egoistic behavior impinging on the parent's kin, and parent and offspring are expected to view such behavior differently. That some teaching beneficial to the offspring transpires during human socialization can be taken for granted, and one would expect no conflict if socialization involved *only* teaching beneficial to the offspring. According to the theory presented here, socialization is a process by which parents attempt to mold each offspring in order to increase their own inclusive fitness, while each offspring is selected to resist some of the molding and to attempt to mold the behavior of its parents (and siblings) in order to increase its inclusive fitness. Conflict during socialization need not be viewed solely as conflict between the culture of the parent and the biology of the child; it can also be viewed as conflict between the biology of the parent and the biology of the child. Since teaching (as opposed to molding) is expected to be recognized by offspring as being in their own self-interest, parents would be expected to overemphasize their role as teachers in order to minimize resistance in their young. According to this view then, the prevailing concept of socialization is to some extent a view one would expect adults to entertain and disseminate.

Parent-offspring conflict may extend to behavior that is not on the surface either altruistic or selfish but which has consequences that can be so classified. The amount of energy a child consumes during the day, and the way in which the child consumes this energy, are not matters of indifference to the parent when the parent is supplying that energy, and when the way in which the child consumes the energy affects its ability to act altruistically in the future. For example, when parent and child disagree over when the child should go to sleep, one expects in general the parent to favor early bedtime, since the parent anticipates that this will decrease the offspring's demands on parental resources the following day. Likewise, one expects the parent to favor serious and useful expenditures of energy by the child (such as tending the family chickens, or studying) over frivolous and unnecessary expenditures (such as playing cards)—the former are either altruistic in themselves, or they prepare the offspring for future altruism. In short, we expect the offspring to perceive some behavior, that the parent favors, as being dull, unpleasant, moral, or any combination of these. One must at least entertain the assumption that the child would find such behavior more enjoyable if in fact the behavior maximized the offspring's inclusive fitness.

CONFLICT OVER THE ADULT REPRODUCTIVE ROLE OF THE OFFSPRING

As a special case of the preceding argument, it is clear that under certain conditions conflict is expected between parent and offspring over the adult reproductive role of the offspring. To take the extreme case, it follows at once from Hamilton's (1964) work that individuals who choose not to reproduce (such as celibate priests) are not necessarily acting counter to their genetic self-interest. One need merely assume that the nonreproducer thereby increases the reproductive success of relatives by an amount which, when devalued by the relevant degrees of relatedness, is greater than the nonreproducer would have achieved on his own. This kind of explanation has been developed in some detail to explain nonreproductives in the haplodiploid Hymenoptera (Hamilton, 1972). What is clear from the present argument, however, is that it is even more likely that the nonreproducer will thereby increase his *parents'* inclusive fitness than that he will increase his own. This follows because his parents are expected to value the increased reproductive success of kin relatively more than he is.

If the benefits of nonreproducing are assumed, for simplicity, to accrue only to full siblings and if the costs of nonreproducing are defined as the surviving offspring the nonreproducer would have produced had he or she chosen to reproduce, then parent-offspring conflict over whether the offspring should reproduce is expected whenever $C<B<2C$. Assuming it is sometimes possible for parents to predict while an offspring is still young what the cost and benefit of its not reproducing will be, the parents would be selected to mold the offspring toward not reproducing whenever $B>C$. Two kinds of nonreproductives are expected: those who are thereby increasing their own inclusive fitness $(B>2C)$ and those who are thereby lowering their own inclusive fitness but increasing that of their parents $(C<B<2C)$. The first kind is expected to be as happy and content as living creatures ever are, but the second is expected to show internal conflict over its adult role and to express ambivalence over the past, particularly over the behavior and influence of its parents. I emphasize that it is not necessary for parents to be conscious of molding an offspring toward nonreproduction in order for such molding to occur and to increase the parent's inclusive fitness. It remains to be explored to what extent the etiology of sexual preferences (such as homosexuality) which tend to interfere with reproduction can be explained in terms of the present argument.

Assuming that parent and offspring agree that the offspring should reproduce, disagreement is still possible over the form of that reproduction. Whether an individual attempts to produce few offspring or many is a decision that affects that individual's opportunities for kin-directed altruism, so that parent and offspring may disagree over the optimal reproductive effort of the offspring. Since in humans an individual's choice of mate may affect his or her ability to render altruistic behavior toward relatives, mate choice is not expected to be a matter of indifference to the parents. Parents are expected to encourage their offspring to choose a mate that will enlarge the offspring's altruism toward kin. For example, when a man marries his cousin, he increases (other things being equal) his contacts with relatives, since the immediate kin of his wife will also be related to him, and marriage will normally lead to greater contact with her immediate kin. One therefore might expect human parents to show a tendency to encourage their offspring to marry more closely related individuals (e.g., cousins) than the offspring would prefer. Parents may also use an offspring's marriage to cement an alliance with an unrelated family or group, and insofar as such an alliance is beneficial to kin of the parent in addition to the offspring itself, parents are expected to encourage such marriages more often than the offspring would prefer. Finally, parents will more strongly discourage marriage by their offspring to individuals the local society defines as pariahs, because such unions are likely to besmirch the reputation of close kin as well.

Because parents may be selected to employ parental investment itself as an incentive to induce greater offspring altruism, parent-offspring conflict may include situations in which the offspring attempts to terminate the period of PI *before* the parent wishes to. For example, where the parent is selected to retain one or more offspring as permanent "helpers at the nest" (Skutch, 1961), that is, permanent nonreproductives who help their parents raise additional offspring (or help those offspring to reproduce), the parent may be selected to give additional investment in order to tie the offspring to the parent. In this situation, selection on the offspring may favor any urge toward independence which overcomes the offspring's impulse toward additional investment (with its hidden cost of additional dependency). In short, in species in which kin-directed altruism is important, parent-offspring conflict may include situations in which the offspring wants *less* than the parent is selected to give as well as the more common situation in which the offspring attempts to garner *more* PI than the parent is selected to give.

Parent-offspring relations early in ontogeny can affect the later adult reproductive role of the offspring. A parent can influence the altruistic and egoistic tendencies of its offspring whenever it has influence over any variable that affects the costs and benefits associated with altruistic and egoistic behavior. For example, if becoming a permanent nonreproductive, helping one's siblings, is more likely to increase one's inclusive fitness when one is small in size relative to one's sibling (as appears to be true in some polistine wasps: Eberhard, 1969), then parents can influence the proportion of their offspring who become helpers by altering the size distribution of their offspring. Parent-offspring conflict over early PI may itself involve parent-offspring conflict over the eventual reproductive role of the offspring. This theoretical possibility may be relevant to human psychology if parental decision to mold an offspring into being a nonreproductive involves differential investment as well as psychological manipulation.

THE ROLE OF PARENTAL EXPERIENCE IN PARENT-OFFSPRING CONFLICT

It cannot be supposed that all parent-offspring conflict results from the conflict in the way in which the parent's and the offspring's inclusive fitnesses are maximized. Some conflict also results, ironically because of an overlap in the interests of parent and young. When circumstances change, altering the benefits and costs associated with some offspring behavior, both the parent and the offspring are selected to alter the offspring's behavior appropriately. That is, the parent is selected to mold the appropriate change in the offspring's behavior, and if parental molding is successful, it will strongly reduce the selection pressure on the offspring to change its behavior spontaneously. Since the parent is likely to discover the changing circumstances as a result of its own experience, one expects tendencies toward parental molding to appear, and spread, before the parallel tendencies appear in the offspring. Once parents commonly mold the appropriate offspring behavior, selection still favors genes leading toward voluntary offspring behavior, since such a developmental avenue is presumably more efficient and more certain than that involving parental manipulation. But the selection pressure for the appropriate offspring genes should be weak, and if circumstances change at a faster rate than this selection operates, there is the possibility of continued parent-offspring conflict resulting from the greater experience of the parent.

If the conflict described above actually occurs, then (as mentioned in an earlier section) selection will favor a tendency for parents to overemphasize their experience in all situations, and for the offspring to differentiate between those situations in which greater parental experience is real and those situations in which such experience is merely claimed in order to manipulate the offspring.

APPENDIX: THE OFFSPRING'S EQUILIBRIAL SEX RATIO

Let the cost of producing a female be one unit of investment, and let the cost of producing a male be x units, where x is larger than one. Let the expected reproductive success of a female be one unit of RS. Let the sex ratio produced be 1:y (males:females), where y is larger than one. At this sex ratio the expected RS of a male is y units of RS, so that, in being made a male instead of a female, an offspring gains y–1 units of RS. But the offspring also thereby deprives its mother of x–1 units of investment. The offspring's equilibrial sex ratio is that sex ratio at which the offspring's gain in RS in being made a male (y–1) is exactly offset by its loss in inclusive fitness which results because it thereby deprives its mother of x–1 units of investment. The mother would have allocated these units in such a way as to achieve a 1:y sex ratio, that is, she would have allocated $x/(x+y)$ of the units to males and $y/(x+y)$ of the units to females. In short, she would have produced $(x-1)/(x+y)$ sons, which would have achieved RS of $y(x-1)/(x+y)$, and she would have produced $y(x-1)/(x+y)$ daughters, which would have achieved RS of $y(x-1)/(x+y)$. The offspring is expected to devalue this loss by the offspring's r_o to its displaced siblings. Hence, the offspring's equilibrial sex ratio results when

$$y - 1 = \frac{r_o y (x - 1)}{x + y} + \frac{r_o y (x - 1)}{x + y}$$

$$= (2 r_o y) \frac{x - 1}{x + y}$$

Rearranging gives

$$y^2 + y(x - 2 r_o x + 2 r_o - 1) - x = 0$$
$$y^2 + (x - 1)(1 - 2 r_o) y - x = 0$$

The general solution for this quadratic equation is

$$y = \frac{-(x - 1)(1 - 2 r_o)}{2} + \frac{\sqrt{(x - 1)^2 (1 - 2 r_o)^2 + 4x}}{2}$$

Where $r_o = \frac{1}{2}$, the equation reduces to $y = \sqrt{x}$. In other words, when the offspring displaces full siblings (as is probably often the case), the offspring's equilibrial sex ratio is 1:$\sqrt{x}$, while the parent's equilibrial sex ratio is 1:x. These values, as well as the offspring's equilibrial sex ratio where $r_o = \frac{1}{4}$, are plotted in Figure 4. The same general solution holds if parents invest more in females by a factor of x, except that the resulting sex ratios are then reversed (e.g., $\sqrt{x}$:1 instead of 1:$\sqrt{x}$).

REFERENCES

Alexander, G. 1960. Maternal behaviour in the Merino ewe. Anim. Prod. 3:105–114.
DeVore, I. 1963. Mother-infant relations in free-ranging baboons, pp. 305–335. *In* H. Rheingold [ed.], Maternal behavior in mammals. Wiley, N.Y.
Drury, W. H., and W. J. Smith. 1968. Defense of feeding areas by adult Herring Gulls and intrusion by young. Evolution 22:193–201.
Eberhard, M. J. W. 1969. The social biology of polistine wasps, Misc. Publ. Mus. Zool. Univ. Mich. 140:1–101.

Elliott, B. 1969. Life history of the Red Warbler. Wilson Bull. 81:184–195.

Ewbank, R. 1964. Observations on the suckling habits of twin lambs. Anim. Behav. 12:34–37.

Ewbank, R. 1967. Nursing and suckling behaviour amongst Clun Forest ewes and lambs. Anim. Behav. 15:251–258.

Fisher, R. A. 1930. The genetical theory of natural selection. Clarendon, Oxford.

Gill, J. C., and W. Thomson. 1956. Observations on the behavior of suckling pigs. Anim. Behav. 4:46–51.

Hamilton, W. D. 1964. The genetical evolution of social behavior. J. Theoret. Biol. 7:1–52.

Hamilton, W. D. 1971. The genetical evolution of social behavior, p. 23–39. Reprinted, with addendum. In G. C. Williams [ed.], Group selection. Aldine-Atherton, Chicago.

Hamilton, W. D. 1972. Altruism and related phenomena, mainly in social insects. Annu. Rev. Ecol. Syst. 3:193–232.

Hinde, R. A., and Y. Spencer-Booth. 1967. The behaviour of socially living rhesus monkeys in their first two and a half years. Anim. Behav. 15:169–196.

Hinde, R. A., and Y. Spencer-Booth. 1971. Effects of brief separation from mother on rhesus monkeys. Science 173:111–118.

Hinde, R. A., and L. M. Davies. 1972a. Changes in mother-infant relationship after separation in rhesus monkeys. Nature 239:41–42.

Hinde, R. A., and L. M. Davies. 1972b. Removing infant rhesus from mother for 13 days compared with removing mother from infant. J. Child Psychol. Psychiat. 13:227–237.

Jay, P. 1963. Mother-infant relations in langurs, p. 282–304. In H. Rheingold [ed.], Maternal behaviour in mammals. Wiley, N.Y.

Le Boeuf, B. J., R. J. Whiting, and R. F. Gantt. 1972. Perinatal behavior of northern elephant seal females and their young. Behaviour 43:121–156.

Munro, J. 1956. Observations on the suckling behaviour of young lambs. Anim. Behav. 4:34–36.

Mussen, P. H., J. J. Conger, and J. Kagan. 1969. Child development and personality. 3rd ed. Harper and Row, N.Y.

Rheingold, H. 1963. Maternal behavior in the dog, p. 169–202. In H. Rheingold [ed.], Maternal behavior in mammals. Wiley, N.Y.

Rosenblatt, J. S., and D. S. Lehrman. 1963. Maternal behavior of the laboratory rat, p. 8–57. In H. Rheingold [ed.], Maternal behavior in mammals. Wiley, N.Y.

Rosenblum, L. A. 1971. The ontogeny of mother-infant relations in macaques, p. 315–367. In H. Moltz [ed.], The ontogeny of vertebrate behavior. Academic Press, N.Y.

Rowe, E. G. 1947. The breeding biology of Aquila verreauxi Lesson. Ibis 89:576–606.

Schaller, G. B. 1964. Breeding behavior of the White Pelican at Yellowstone Lake, Wyoming. Condor 66:3–23.

Schneirla, T. C., J. S. Rosenblatt, and E. Tobach. 1963. Maternal behavior in the cat, p. 122–168. In H. Rheingold [ed.], Maternal behavior in mammals. Wiley, N.Y.

Skutch, A. F. 1961. Helpers among birds. Condor 63:198–226.

Struhsaker, T. T. 1971. Social behaviour of mother and infant vervet monkeys (Cercopithecus aethiops). Anim. Behav. 19:233–250.

Trivers, R. L. 1971. The evolution of reciprocal altruism. Quart. Rev. Biol. 46:35–57.

Trivers, R. L. 1972. Parental investment and sexual selection, p. 136–179. In B. Campbell [ed.], Sexual selection and the descent of man, 1871–1971. Aldine-Atherton, Chicago.

Wallace, L. R. 1948. The growth of lambs before and after birth in relation to the level of nutrition. J. Agri. Sci. 38:93–153.

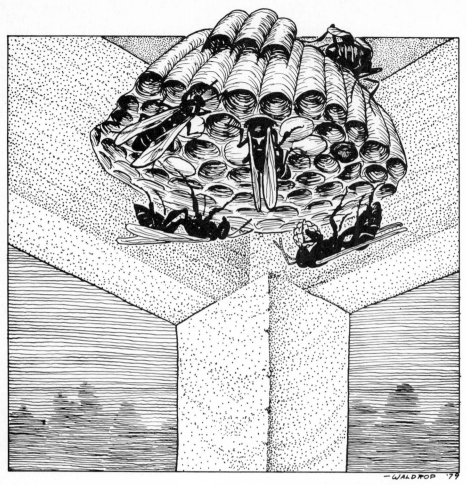

Part Two

Social Insects

I will not here enter on these several cases but will confine myself to one special difficulty, which at first appeared to me insuperable, and actually fatal to the whole theory. I allude to the neuters or sterile females in insect-communities; for these neuters often differ widely in instinct and in structure from both the males and fertile females, and yet, from being sterile, they cannot propagate their kind.

This difficulty, though appearing insuperable, is lessened, or, as I believe, disappears, when it is remembered that selection may be applied to the family, as well as the individual, and may thus gain the desired end.

Charles Darwin
On the Origin of Species*

Treatments of sociobiology in the news media and popular press tend to focus largely on human aspects. Occasionally, brief mention is made of apparent convincing concordance between some specific hypothesis in sociobiology and the available data on social insects, especially social Hymenoptera. In his writings on the subject, E.

*On the Origin of Species by Means of Natural Selection, John Murray, London, 1859.

O. Wilson has repeatedly stressed parallels between insect and human sociality. Less critical and less knowledgeable writers have followed this lead, so that statements appear to the effect that sociobiology (in a restrictive sense, meaning genetic control of social behavior) must be valid for humans because it is valid for social insects. This is not a general argument implying that genetics is involved in behavior as it is in human hair color or ant setae number; instead it is more circumscribed in inferring that particular genetic (breeding) systems establish patterns of inclusive fitness that dictate specific social behaviors in certain settings. The argument for insects is not trivial, for, if the sufficiency of inclusive fitness models in explaining insect social behaviors is to be taken as a model to infer parallels in human social behaviors, then a full understanding and fair evaluation of the role of inclusive fitness in insect sociality is clearly called for.

Hymenoptera have long been seen as out of the ordinary in terms of sociality. Truly social (eusocial) insects are characterized specifically by cooperative brood care, an overlap of generations, and separation into reproductive and nonreproductive castes. Eusociality has evolved numerous times in Hymenoptera: once or perhaps twice in ants, at least once in wasps, and apparently repeatedly in bees. The exact number of occurrences in bees can only be approximated (reversals in social evolution may also have occurred), but estimates of up to fourteen independent evolutions of hymenopteran sociality are not unreasonable.

In all other insect orders eusociality has evolved only once—in the termites (Isoptera). Social development equal in complexity to that in social Hymenoptera and Isoptera is found elsewhere among animals only in the higher social vertebrates. The exclusive restriction of advanced sociality in lower animals to termites and, conspicuously, Hymenoptera strongly suggests that these insects possess unique features that foster social evolution. Several independent hypotheses have been advanced in relation to the evolution of social behavior in Hymenoptera. Among these, W. D. Hamilton's inclusive fitness model has, in particular, been the stimulus for statements specifying analogies between social evolution in insects and vertebrates, including man. This stems from the general applicability of inclusive fitness concepts: particular patterns of relatedness can conceivably greatly facilitate the evolution of social behaviors. Hamilton identified a facet of hymenopteran biology, haplodiploidy, as being especially contributory to such facilitation.

All Hymenoptera are haplodiploid. That is, females are produced from fertilized ova and so are typical diploids. Males, on the other hand, are parthenogenetically produced from unfertilized ova and so are haploid. Spermatogenesis in males does not involve reduction division, so all sperm from any single male are identical (excepting mutation). Daughters of the same father thus receive identical sets of paternal chromosomes, resulting in a higher coefficient of relationship (Sewall Wright's r) between full sib females than between mother and offspring or between sister and brother. Hamilton suggested that female hymenopterans might therefore enhance their inclusive fitness more easily by contributing to the rearing of full sib females than by reproducing offspring. Haplodiploidy, he suggested, could, via inclusive fitness, uniquely predispose Hymenoptera to sociality. Social structure in hymenopteran colonies is in accord with this hypothesis: workers in Hymenoptera devote their efforts only as members of labor sororities. Males of social hymenopteran species, with a few trivial exceptions, contribute nothing to the labor of the colony.

Specific objections to Hamilton's haplodiploidy hypothesis have been voiced. Multiple insemination of a reproductive female or polygyny in a colony can effectively eliminate the haplodiploid bias in inclusive fitness. Other insects are haplodiploid (including thrips, whiteflies, and others), but are not eusocial. Termites are eusocial but are diplo-diploid. Inclusive fitness benefits under haplodiploidy can be maximized only if worker investment is biased in favor of reproductive female sibs as opposed to equal investment in reproductive sibs of both sexes. These and other pros and cons of the haplodiploidy hypothesis are discussed in papers included in this section of the reader.

The first two papers in this section are pre-Hamiltonian and clearly indicate that interest and research in hymenopteran social evolution is both long-standing and based on a substantial body of natural history data. The work by H. E. Evans on wasps has been augmented but little altered by subsequent research. The paper by C. D. Michener on bees varies slightly in some aspects from its author's present views, but the general concepts are still valid. (A more recent but much longer synopsis on bee sociality was presented by Michener in the 1969 *Annual Review of Entomology;* that paper, in turn, was expanded into his superb 1974 treatise, *The Social Behavior of Bees.*)

The third paper is a further extract from W. D. Hamilton's 1964 work that was extracted in part in the preceding section of this volume. The passage presented here shows in detail the particular advantages, under haplodiploidy, that accrue through inclusive fitness to worker female hymenopterans. The passage also addresses aspects of social insect biology that can be interpreted in light of the inclusive fitness theory. This passage, in particular, is the starting point for arguments developed subsequently by other authors that social Hymenoptera express a unique model system that validates inclusive fitness as a paradigm for analysis of sociality in other species, including man. M. J. West-Eberhard, in the continuation of her paper begun in the preceding section discusses Hamilton's theory and compares and contrasts it with other, less widely promulgated theories of social evolution in Hymenoptera.

The paper by R. L. Trivers and H. Hare, which follows in this section, deserves very careful attention. Perhaps more than any other single work, it has been invoked as support for assertions that inclusive fitness must be the primary motive force in vertebrate (including human) sociality, because more than any other work it appears to validate the haplodiploidy/inclusive fitness hypothesis for social insects. J. Krebs and R. M. May, in a review in *Nature* in 1976, credit Trivers and Hare's paper as having "put the capstone to an edifice that draws together genetic principles and Darwin's theory of natural selection toward explaining the evolution of social insects." A major *Time* article on sociobiology in 1977 noted that the Trivers and Hare work is "the strongest evidence to date that organisms act as if they understand the underlying genes." Such opinions have been widely and uncritically repeated. The following paper in this section, then, is no less important than that by Trivers and Hare, but it unfortunately has been less widely cited. In it, R. D. Alexander and P. W. Sherman examine the Trivers and Hare paper in detail, and they find serious shortcomings in it. They specify problems with the data, analysis, and interpretation presented by Trivers and Hare. They suggest, in fact, that an alternate hypothesis, competition for mates among genetic relatives, more conservatively accommodates the data given by Trivers and Hare. The next paper in this section, by K. M. Noonan, presents quantitative data from a single field study that do not support the haplodiploidy hypothesis.

H. E. Evans, in the closing paper reprinted here, attempts to place the haplodiploidy/inclusive fitness hypothesis into perspective. He feels that genetic factors, including perhaps haplodiploidy, have been but one of a suite of factors involved in social evolution. Other factors include (but certainly are not limited to) parasite pressure and adaptive radiation in nesting behavior. Assessment of the relative importance of these various contributors to social evolution is a challenge that remains for the future.

The Evolution of Social Life in Wasps

Howard E. Evans
Cornell University

The term wasp embraces a great array of hymenopterous insects, most of which are "solitary" while a few are "subsocial" or "social." It is useful to distinguish thirteen steps leading from the simple behavior of the Scolioidea to the complex behavior of the social Vespidae. Examples can be cited of genera which represent each level of social evolution, and it seems possible that forms now at step thirteen (such as Vespinae) may have passed through each of the other steps in sequence.

Briefly, these steps are as follows: (1) prey is paralyzed and egg laid upon it; (2) prey is stung, dragged into a hole, and egg laid; (3) prey is stung, a nest is dug, and prey is placed in nest and egg laid, the nest then being closed; (4) nest is made first, prey obtained, placed in nest, egg laid; (5) same, but several more prey added after egg is laid; (6) same, but provisioning is progressive; (7) egg is laid in empty cell before provisioning begins; (8) food is macerated and fed directly to larva; (9) life of female is prolonged to overlap that of some of offspring; (10) trophallaxis; females feed offspring other than their own; (11) egg laying done by one female; original offspring all female; (12) worker caste well defined, intermediates common; differential feeding of larvae; (13) worker caste differs morphologically from queen; intermediates uncommon or absent.

The term wasp embraces a great array of hymenopterous insects which exhibit much variation both in structure and in biology. Even the most conservative classification must recognize at least five superfamilies for the wasps. The possible relationships of these five superfamilies are indicated in Fig. 1. While some may disagree with certain points in this phylogenetic tree, I think that most will agree that the Scolioidea are the most primitive, that the Bethyloidea, Vespoidea, and the ants are all derived independently from the Scolioidea, and that the pompiloid-sphecoid-apoid stock represents a single phyletic line also arising from the Scolioidea.

If we scan the wasps as a whole, we find that the vast majority are strictly solitary. A few might be termed "subsocial," and a few Vespidae may be justly termed "social." But neither the term subsocial nor the term social is capable of precise definition, and different authors use these terms with different shades of meaning. Actually we may define, with much greater precision, a series of steps— or rungs of the social ladder, if you wish—leading from strictly solitary forms to those which, by any standards, are social. More attention has been paid to the higher rungs of the ladder, but the lower rungs seem to me worthy of equal consideration.

Since the Scolioidea are at the base of our phylogenetic scheme, it is logical that we begin with them. The females of most Scolioidea search for beetle grubs in the

From *Proceedings Tenth International Congress of Entomology 2* (1956): 449–457. Reprinted by permission of the author.

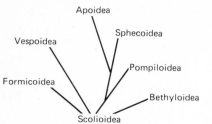

Figure 1

ground, sting them into temporary or permanent paralysis, lay their egg upon the grub, and leave the grub where it happens to be. This behavior hardly differs from that of many of the lower, parasitoid Hymenoptera from which the wasps are presumed to be derived. Some Scoliidae, however, move the grub into a more favorable situation in the soil, even into a prepared cell, before oviposition. This movement of the prey into a more suitable niche is, I submit, the very first step in the direction of the family association which we speak of as an insect society. There is, of course, no contact at all between mother and offspring, but at least the offspring is provided with temperature and moisture conditions which enable it to survive with greater certainty. The selective value of this new element in the behavior is, I think, obvious.

Since the Sciolioidea show little advance beyond this very simple manipulation of the prey, it is necessary to turn to another group, the Pompilidae or spider wasps (Fig. 2), which seem to be related on the one hand to the Scolioidea, and on the other hand to the Sphecoidea. All Pompilidae prey upon spiders. Some of them show hardly any advance in behavior over the Scolioidea. Wasps of the genus *Notocyphus*, for example, are said to sting certain spiders in their webs, lay their egg, and depart, the spider recovers from paralysis and goes about its business with the wasp larva developing like a parasitoid on its abdomen (Williams, 1928). In *Haploneurion apogonum*, Claude-Joseph (1930) reports that the spider is dragged into a beetle burrow in a bank, the egg laid upon it, and the cavity sealed off with debris. The vast majority of spider wasps have advanced one step further, and actually dig a simple nest in the ground in which the paralyzed spider is placed. I think it is appropriate to use the term *nest* for such a structure, even though the attachment of the wasp to the nest is very temporary. Certainly the possession of a nest is another important prerequisite for becoming social. The majority of genera of Pompilidae in both major subfamilies belong here, *Episyron, Pompilus, Pepsis, Calicurgus,* and many others—this is merely a selection of representative genera. A relatively few Pompilidae have attained, in step four, an important rearrangement in the sequence of behavior. These wasps prepare the nest first—either in the soil or of mud or plant fragments—then obtain their prey and lay their egg upon it. Many of these wasps make multicellular nests, and a single nest becomes the focal point of the activity of a female for her entire life. In two genera, *Macromeris* and *Paragenia,* several females tend to nest together—they may be sisters or mother and daughters (Wil-

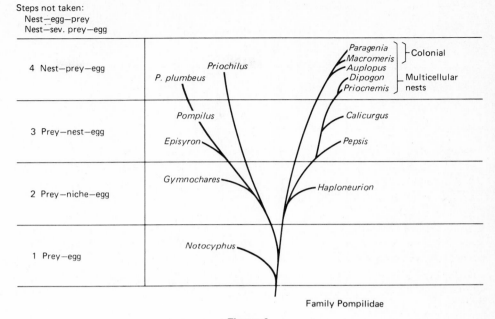

Figure 2

liams, 1919). Some of the cells are said to be used a second time. The females are said to act as individuals, exhibiting no notable cooperation or aggression. Williams' studies were made many years ago, and these wasps deserve much further study.

It is interesting to speculate why the Pompilidae have never progressed further up the social ladder, and which rungs in particular they have been unable to span. For one thing, they all use but a single spider in a cell, a distinctly primitive trait and one which makes progressive provisioning impossible. Further, the sequence nest-egg-prey, that is, the laying of the egg in the empty cell, which is characteristic of the social wasps, has never been attained.

Let us turn now to the superfamily Sphecoidea, a very large complex containing two families, the Ampulicidae and the Sphecidae (Fig. 3). The Ampulicidae are on a level with some of the Scoliidae and the primitive Pompilidae. They sting a cockroach, drag it to a suitable niche, lay an egg upon it, and seal up the niche. The most primitive Sphecidae are on a level with the majority of Pompilidae; *Priononyx,* for example, captures a grasshopper, then digs a nest, places the prey in it, lays the egg, and closes the nest. *Podalonia* does essentially the same with its cutworms. But nearly all Sphecidae prepare the nest first, as in *Palmodes,* and many, such as *Sphex,* add a number of additional prey to the cell after the first has been put in place and the egg laid upon it. The genus *Ammophila* is one of those very interesting genera which exhibit several different levels of specialization. Some species, such as *procera,* place a single caterpillar in the previously prepared cell and lay an egg upon it.

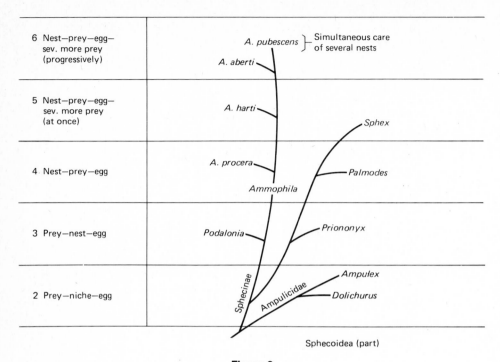

6 Nest—prey—egg—
   sev. more prey
   (progressively)

   A. pubescens ⎱ Simultaneous care
                   ⎰ of several nests
   A. aberti

5 Nest—prey—egg—
   sev. more prey
   (at once)

   A. harti

                                        Sphex

4 Nest—prey—egg

   A. procera

                        Palmodes

   Ammophila

3 Prey—nest—egg

   Podalonia

                    Priononyx

2 Prey—niche—egg

                                  Ampulex

   Sphecinae   *Ampulicidae*

                                  Dolichurus

Sphecoidea (part)

Figure 3

Others add several additional caterpillars to the cell, usually on the same day, but occasionally, if unfavorable weather intervenes, over several days. Thus, in *Ammophila harti,* there may occasionally be some accidental contact between mother and offspring. In some other species, typified by *Ammophila aberti,* the female lays her egg on the first caterpillar and then actually delays provisioning until just before hatching, after this bringing in caterpillars as required by the larva. This progressive provisioning, as it is called, involves considerable contact between mother and offspring; the mother inspects the nest each morning and receives stimuli emanating from the egg or larva which determine the course of her activity for the day. The European species *pubescens,* which has been studied by a number of workers, including particularly G. P. Baerends (1941), is known to care for several nests simultaneously, inspecting each active nest in the morning and provisioning in accordance with the needs of each larva as made known to her at the time of inspection.

Altogether *Ammophila* is a remarkable genus deserving much further study. But for further advance toward social life in the family we must turn to another group, the Bembicini (Fig. 4). We find even the most primitive of the Bembicini already ensconced on the fifth rung of the social ladder, with behavior essentially comparable to the genus *Sphex* and to such species of *Ammophila* as *harti.* The species of *Bicyrtes,* which prey upon stink bugs, occasionally, during unfavorable

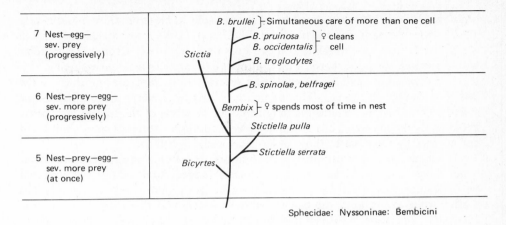

Figure 4

weather, do not complete their provisioning until after the egg has hatched. In some species of *Stictiella,* and in all species of *Bembix, Stictia,* and certain other genera omitted here, progressive provisioning is the rule. But note that some of these insects have achieved another important rearrangement in the sequence of behavior. They omit the first prey and lay the egg directly in the empty cell. This is an important economy in the life of the wasp, and presages the universal condition in the social wasps. These wasps of the genus *Bembix* have other very interesting traits. The females remain within the nest at all times when not actually feeding or provisioning; thus the nest is very definitely the focal point of the life of the females, and the female to some extent protects the larva from predation. Contacts between mother and offspring have been studied by Tsuneki (1951), using glass burrow and cells; he finds that the female places paralyzed flies close to the larva as needed, but that there is no trophallaxis, that is, no exchange of secretions between larva and adult. A few species of *Bembix* are known to clean out the cells of the remains of flies which have been consumed, thus reducing infestation by various inquilinous maggots and again presaging the condition in the social insects. Several species make nests of several cells, and one of these, the Chilean *brullei,* exhibits simultaneous care of more than one cell (Claude-Joseph, 1928). The egg is laid in the cell before provisioning of the previous cell is complete. Conceivably, the offspring may begin emerging before the mother dies, although whether or not this actually occurs in unknown.

The short life of the female in all Sphecidae seems to be one reason why none of them have become truly social. A second reason is that none of them macerate the prey before presenting it to the larva. Here are at least two rungs of the social ladder which the Sphecidae, for some reason, have been unable to climb.

Finally, let us turn to the Vespidae (Fig. 5). Wheeler (1928) lists four subfamilies of Vespidae as being solitary or subsocial, and five as being social. The curious thing is that even the most primitive forms are already well advanced beyond all Pompilidae and most Sphecidae. All build their nest and lay an egg in it before beginning to hunt prey; nearly all build several cells in close proximity; and nearly all use some building material in making their nest, in the lower forms mud and in the higher forms paper which they make from decaying wood. Everyone is familiar with *Eumenes,* the potter wasp, which, although it practices mass provisioning, lays its egg in the empty cell before capturing several caterpillars, placing them in the cell, and sealing off the top. This sequence of nest-egg-several prey, which is the starting point in the Vespidae, is only achieved by a few of the higher Sphecidae. Presumably the ancestors of the Vespidae went through a series of steps similar but not necessarily identical to those described for the Sphecidae.

Even within the most primitve subfamily, the Eumeninae, there are forms which advance to still higher rungs on the social ladder. Roubaud (1916) found that an African species of the genus *Rygchium* practices progressive provisioning. The mother wasp waits until the egg is ready to hatch and then brings in the first caterpillar; she inspects the cell periodically and brings in provisions slowly and as needed by the larva, finally closing the cell when the larva is ready to pupate. There is also a tendency in this species for the mother to care for two or more cells simultaneously. All of this is reminiscent of *Bembix brullei.*

Another related genus, *Synagris,* is even more interesting. This is an African genus and several species have been studied by Roubaud (1911, 1916). *Synagris spiniventris* is said to build mud cells in an irregular mass and to practice mass provisioning, much like *Eumenes* and most species of *Rygchium.* However, if food

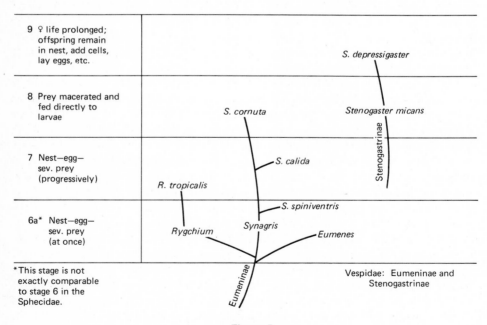

Figure 5

is scarce, due to weather conditions or other factors, the female may bring in caterpillars more slowly, completing provisioning when the larva is about three-fourths grown. Thus progressive provisioning is optional in this species. In another species, *calida,* progressive provisioning apparently is the rule. Still another species, *cornuta,* not only feeds the larva progressively, but actually chews up the caterpillar into a paste which it feeds directly into the mouth of the larva. Maceration of the prey is characteristic of all the truly social wasps and certainly deserves to be regarded as a new and very important step. It is the highest behavior achieved by any of the Eumeninae.

The Stenogastrinae are a poorly known group, consisting of a single genus occurring in the Oriental and Australian regions. So far as known, these insects all feed their larvae with what is described as a "gelatinous paste", presumably consisting of macerated prey and the secretions of the wasp. According to F. X. Williams (1919), some species are solitary, although the female attends several young simultaneously. Others, such as *depressigaster,* live in small colonies apparently consisting of a mother and several daughters. These daughters differ neither in structure or in function from the mother; they merely remain on the nest, adding cells, laying eggs, and caring for their own larvae. All of the Stenogastrinae make nests of paper; the nests are small, delicate, and often very odd in form.

In the Stenogastrinae we find for the first time that the life of the female is prolonged so as to overlap that of several of her offspring. Richards and Richards (1951) have suggested that in species which practice progressive provisioning and feed the larva directly, and where the demands of the larva at least partially determine how much food they receive, conditions are particularly favorable for the production of "over-fed" individuals which may be capable of living longer than they would otherwise.

I should like now to turn to the subfamily Polybiinae, one of the largest groups of Vespidae and mainly tropical in distribution (Fig. 6). The simplest type of behavior is exhibited by the African genus *Belonogaster* (Roubaud, 1916). These wasps have a number of structural specializations, and whether their behavior is truly primitive or specialized by reduction is difficult to say. At any rate they suggest a stage of evolution through which the bulk of the Polybiinae may have passed. The nests are small, simple, and suggestive of those of *Polistes;* the cells are lengthened and broadened as the larva grows, giving the nest a somewhat splayed-out appearance. These nests are inhabited by a small number of adults, both male and female, and the number of cells is usually around 50 or 60. The females are all identical structurally and physiologically; all of them mate and lay eggs, and none can be called workers. The nest is said to be founded by a single female which may be joined by other females at an early period of construction. As the offspring emerge, the females first remain on the nest for a few days and assist in the feeding of the larvae and in cleaning cells; later they hunt prey and bring in paper for the cells. Egg laying, in advanced colonies, is done mostly by the more mature females, although all the females are normally fecundated. Any given female does not restrict her nursing to her own offspring, but feeds any larva which needs food. The larvae produce a salivary secretion which is lapped up by the adults. Roubaud believed the feeding of the larvae by the adults was in response to this secretion by the larva. He called this phenomenon "ectrophobiosis", although Wheeler later used the more familiar term "trophallaxis". Both Roubaud and Wheeler considered trophallaxis extremely important in the evolution of social life in insects.

Recently the trophallaxis concept has been modified by some workers and even rejected altogether by others. One recent writer terms it a "combination of anthropomorphic thinking and Lamarkianism" (Schmieder, 1956). It is impossible to review the concept of trophallaxis here, but I believe I am safe in saying that in all Vespidae above this point, some interchange of fluids does occur between larva and adult.

I believe that we are fully justified in calling *Belonogaster* a "social" wasp. Whatever may be said about trophallaxis, the fact remains that in *Belonogaster* mother and daughters do co-operate in nest-building and brood-rearing, and individual wasps often feed larvae derived from eggs laid by other individuals. Richards considers the latter phenomenon the best criterion for considering a wasp as truly social.

The more familiar wasps of the genus *Polistes* actually represent only a slight advance over *Belonogaster*. Although *Polistes* is traditionally placed in a separate subfamily, some contemporary workers, including myself, feel that its characters are of only generic value, and that it really belongs with the Polybiine wasps. There are many species of *Polistes,* mostly in the tropics and subtropics, but a few have invaded the temperate regions. There seems to be much variation in biology in the different species, and it is impossible to review all the work of various authors on different species of *Polistes.* I would, however, like to review briefly some of Pardi's (1948) work on *Polistes gallica*.

The colonies of *Polistes gallica* are typically annual. The nest may be started in the spring by one fecundated female, but she is ordinarily soon joined by several others. Within this group of co-operating females a hierarchy or "peck-order" is soon established. Pardi has described the various types of contacts between females which result in the psychological dominance of one of them. Dissection of these individuals reveals a direct correlation between size of the ovaries and degree of dominance. This dominance is associated with a trophic advantage; the higher in the peck-order, the more food an individual is able to obtain from the social stomach. Dominants spend more time on the nest and assume most of the duties on the nest, and the top individual does most of the egg-laying. Due to their trophic advantage, the dominants show increasingly full development of the ovaries, while those of individuals lower in the hierarchy undergo regression. Thus there is but one effective queen. The offspring of this queen are females, similar to the queen but unfecundated and with reduced ovaries. These workers establish a social hierarchy based on age, and if the queen dies the top worker assumes the role of the queen, laying eggs which produce only males, of course. Well along in the active season, males are produced,

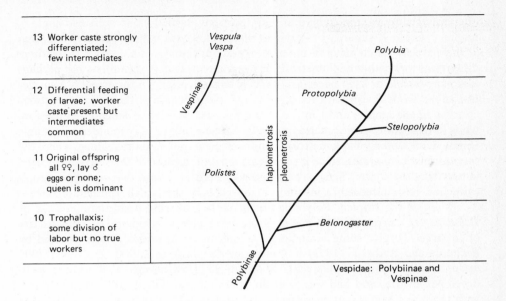

Figure 6

probably due to cyclical factors in the development of the queen, and some of the females are fecundated and overwinter to start the cycle in the spring. Strictly tropical species usually send out small swarms of females which may start new colonies immediately. It has never been clearly demonstrated that the workers of *Polistes,* such as they are, are the result of differential feeding in the larval stage.

The most important things which have occurred here are physiological matters which are not fully understood. The queen at first produces chiefly if not entirely diploid, fertilized eggs which give rise to females; these females act as workers either because of the psychological dominance of the queen, or because nutritional factors in the larval or adult stage do not permit full development of the ovaries, or because males are not present to effect fertilization (or perhaps all three). Rau (1939) has suggested that the so-called queens of *Polistes* are merely workers which have become inseminated and have survived the winter. *Polistes* seems to be something of a "key genus" in understanding the origins of social life in wasps. Unfortunately there are some contradictions in recent work on the genus. Khalifa (1953) failed to confirm the dominance theory. Deleurance (Richards, 1953) has shown that temperature has a direct relationship to the production of queens. When workers were kept warm at night, the grubs they were feeding turned into queens, suggesting that temperature somehow alters the physiology of the worker so that they give the grubs different food. This, of course, suggests that differential feeding of larvae does occur in *Polistes.*

In *Polistes* there is ordinarily only one effective, egg-laying queen, a condition often referred to as monogyny, but more porperly termed haplometrosis (single + mother). The vast majority of Polybiine wasps, however, exhibit pleometrosis, that is, there are several to many fecundated, egg-laying females in a single nest. Authors disagree as to whether haplometrosis or pleometrosis is more primitive, but perhaps it is not possible or even necessary to solve this dilemma. In the tropics, a species can afford to be lavish with its queens, and pleometrosis is the rule. In *Polistes,* colonies in the tropics and subtropics are founded by several fecundated females, while in temperate species such as *fuscatus,* colonies are usually founded by a single female. Undoubtedly haplometrosis is more efficient in temperate regions, where the queens must overwinter, since it represents a maximum use of those which succeed in surviving the winter. This may explain why *Polistes,* although essentially a tropical genus, has succeeded in invading many parts of the North Temperate Zone.

Most of the tropical Polybiinae build more elaborate nests than *Polistes* or *Belonogaster,* surrounded by one or more protective envelopes. The colonies are often large. To give some examples, a colony of *Protopolybia pumila* studied by Richards and Richards (1951) in Guiana contained over 21,000 cells. Over 7000 wasps were taken from this nest, of which 93 were queens, that is, had well-developed ovaries and had sperm in the spermatheca. About 2000 were workers, with more or less filamentous ovaries, and nearly 5000 were intermediates, having moderate-sized eggs in the ovaries, but no sperms. There were also 213 males in the nest. These authors were able to sort out the queens, after some experience, by the more swollen abdomens; later they found that queens had, on the average, longer wings and more hamuli.

This condition of many intermediates and no outstanding external differences between queens, intermediates, and workers, is presumably more primitive than the condition found in many species of *Polybia*. Whether or not differential feeding of larvae occurs in *Protopolybia* is uncertain; certainly it must occur in *Polybia,* where intermediates are uncommon and the queen often distinguishable by clear-cut morphological differences. One colony of *Polybia occidentalis* studied by Richards and Richards was found to have 596 wasps; 48 were queens and 548 were workers. There were no intermediates, and the queens differed from the workers in having a longer mesonotum, longer and wider first abdominal tergite, and fewer hamuli per millimeter of wing-length. Nothing is known, of course, about caste-determination in these insects, but Richards is probably right in stating that structural differences such as these can scarcely have any other explanation than differential feeding of the larvae. Queen cells, by the way, do not differ in any way from worker cells.

Richards and Richards have suggested that changes in the larva/worker ratio as the colony progresses may result in larvae automatically receiving more food and thereby producing queens. They have shown that, in general, the ratio of larvae to workers increases gradually to a certain point and then undergoes steady decline; it is during this decline in the larva/worker ratio that queens and males are produced. The paper of Richards and Richards on the social wasps of South America is replete with suggestive data of this sort, and I can only suggest that interested persons read their paper in detail.

The final group which deserve consideration are the common hornets and yellow-jackets, which form the subfamily Vespinae. These insects are more poorly known than might be expected. It is known that colonies ordinarily have only one queen, which is sharply differentiated in size from the workers and often differs in color pattern and in minor structural details. These queens are reared in special, large cells making up the last few combs in the nest. It seems logical to assume that the larvae in these cells receive a larger amount of food than those in smaller cells. The queens are capable of storing up considerable fat, and they are the only members of the colony which survive the winter. The Vespinae are basically a Holarctic group adapted for survival even, in some cases, close to the Arctic Circle. They are sharply differentiated from other Vespidae and probably evolved from some early vespid independently from the other subfamilies. The steps they went through to attain their lofty position on the social ladder are unknown and can only be deduced by analogy with other groups of Vespidae.

The recent work of Brian and Brian (1952) on *Vespula sylvestris* is particularly interesting. These workers studied several aspects of the social behaviour of this species, including trophallaxis. They found experimentally that the fluid secreted by the larvae actually was not attractive to adults. Apparently the larvae secrete excess water via the salivary glands, and the behavior patterns of the workers are such that they collect this fluid when they feed the larvae, so that it does not dampen the nest. They conclude that the trophallactic stage in the evolution of these insects, if it ever existed, has been superseded.

There is scarcely a group of wasps which could not bear much further study. In fact, speculation on the origin of social life seems to have far outstripped the observational data. While no group of wasps can be said to have attained the high degree of social evolution of certain of the bees and ants, the wasps deserve much further study for that very reason. I think we should not expect the steps in the evolution of bees and ants to be exactly the same as in the wasps. We are dealing with several different phyletic lines in which numerous parallelisms can be noted. Even in the Vespidae social life must have arisen at least twice; in the bees I believe it is supposed to have arisen more than twice independently. While the problem of the evolution of social life in insects is perennially interesting, I think we should be cautious about trying to find broad generalizations which will apply equally to all groups.

REFERENCES

Baerends, G. P. 1941. Fortpflanzungverhalten und Orientierung der Grabwespe *Ammophila campestris* Jur. *Tijdschr. Ent.* 84:68–275.

Brian, M. V., and A. D. Brian. 1952. The wasp, *Vespula sylvestris* Scopoli: feeding, foraging, and colony development. *Trans. R. Ent. Soc. London* 103:1–26.

Claude-Joseph, M. F. 1928. Recherches biologiques sur les prédateurs du Chili. *Ann. Sci. Nat., Zool.* (10)11:67–207.

Claude-Joseph, M. F. 1930. Recherches biologiques sur les prédateurs du Chili. *Ann. Sci. Nat., Zool.* (10)13:235–354.

Khalifa, A. 1953. Biological observation on *Polistes,* with special reference to stylopization. *Bull. Soc. Fouad ler Ent.* 37:371–404.

Pardi, L. 1948. Dominance in *Polistes* wasps. *Physiol. Zool.* 21:1–13.

Rau, P. 1939. Population studies in colonies of *Polistes* wasps, with remarks on the castes. *Ecology* 20:439–442.

Richards, O. W., and M. J. Richards. 1951. Observations on the social wasps of South America (Hymenoptera, Vespidae). *Trans. R. Ent. Soc. London* 102:1–170.

Richards, O. W. 1953. The social insects. London, *MacDonald.* 219 pp.

Roubaud, E. 1911. The natural history of the solitary wasps of the genus *Synagris. Smithson. Rpt.* 1910:507–525.

Roubaud, E. 1916. Recherches biologiques sur les guêpes solitaires et sociales d'Afrique. *Ann. Sci. Nat., Zool.* (10)1:1–160.

Schmieder, R. G. 1956. The world of bees, by Gilbert Nixon [book review]. *Ent. News* 67:82–83.

Tsuneki, K. 1954. The primitive social relationship found in the subsocial wasp, *Bembix niponica* Smith. *Insectes Sociaux* 1:192.

Wheeler, W. M. 1928. The social insects: their origin and evolution. New York, *Harcourt, Brace.* 378 pp.

Williams, F. X. 1919. Philippine wasp studies. *Bull. Exp. Sta. Hawaiian Sugar Planters Assoc., Ent. Ser.,* no. 14:186 pp.

Williams, F. X. 1928. Studies in tropical wasps—their hosts and associates. *Bull. Exp. Sta. Hawaiian Sugar Planters Assoc., Ent. Ser.,* no. 19:179 pp.

The Evolution of Social Behavior in Bees[1]

Charles D. Michener
University of Kansas, Lawrence

The thesis is developed that social behavior in bees (excluding the Allodape group) arose not through a series of steps involving larva-adult relationships as with wasps, ants and termites but through associations of adults to form semisocial groups and ultimately true societies. A series of steps in the establishment of social behavior in the Halictinæ is described, together with comparative information for the Apinæ. The similarities between social life in bees and that of ants, wasps and termites, provide noteworthy examples of convergence because the resemblances in behavior of terminal forms result from evolution through quite different intermediate steps.

INTRODUCTION

The usually accepted concept of the origin of social behavior[2] in insects is that it arose through a subsocial stage, i.e. an evolutionary stage in which progeny remain with the mother for a time and receive her protection or care, but in which the families break up, usually with the death of the mother, before the progeny mature. The idea, as explained by various authors, is that subsocial ancestral forms, as a result of (1) greater parental longevity (so that the mother coexists with her adult progeny), (2) trophallaxis and other mechanisms of integration to hold the colony together, (3) division of labor, and (4) establishment of morphologically different castes, gave rise to insect societies such as those of the termites, the ants, social wasps, and social bees. I have no reason to believe that this theory is incorrect for the termites, ants, and social (vespid) wasps. These insects all have societies in which intimate relations, including extensive and obvious trophallaxis, exist between young and adults, and various steps from solitary through subsocial to thoroughly social exist among vespoid wasps.

---

[1]Contribution number 942 from the Department of Entomology, University of Kansas, Lawrence.

[2]For comments on the meaning of this expression, see Michener, 1953. To clarify this and other terms as here used, the following definitions may be useful. *Social* insects occur in groups or colonies, in which one or both parents survive to cooperate with their young when the latter are mature, and in which division of labor occurs. *Semisocial* insects occur in groups or colonies consisting of individuals of the same generation (hence without parent-offspring relationship); division of labor (often weak or temporal) or cooperative activity occurs. *Subsocial* insects occur in groups or colonies in which one (or both) parents survive to protect or feed the young but die or leave the young before the latter reach maturity.

From *Proceedings Tenth International Congress of Entomology 2* (1956):441–447. Reprinted by permission of the author.

THE ALLODAPE GROUP

One group of bees is known in which evolution has resulted in subsocial family associations. This group consists of the genus *Allodape* and its relatives, occurring principally in southern Africa, but extending northeast as far as Formosa, and being replaced in Australia by *Exoneura*. The principal sources of information about behavior of these bees are works of Brauns (1926), Rayment (1951), and Skaife (1953). These bees belong to the Ceratinini, in the large family Apidæ, and are not related to social groups. In other Ceratinini *(Ceratina)* and in the related tribe Xylocopini *(Xylocopa)*, a long adult life is the rule, but like most bees, females of these groups construct series of cells, mass provisioning and closing them, and have no contact with their larvæ. However, because of their long lives, females of *Xylocopa* and *Ceratina* may still be making and provisioning new cells when their older progeny emerge as adults and it is common on opening nests of these bees to find an old female and several young adults. The latter presumably leave to establish new nests, as in other solitary bees. In *Allodape* and *Exoneura*, however, the females lay eggs in a group or arranged in various ways inside a burrow in a dead plant stem, and the larvæ, which are all together in a common space and do not occupy separate cells, are fed from day to day. In some species the larvæ are fed individually; in other cases a common food mass is provided from which all the larvæ feed. When young the larvæ are usually fed a clear liquid secreted by the females; later much pollen is included in the diet. In some species, however, even very young larvæ feed on a rather dry pollen mixture which is placed among the eggs before they hatch. The females may establish new nests singly but commonly several adults (up to at least 14) remain together in the parental nest. Apparently all the females (sisters) lay eggs and indiscriminately care for the developing larvæ, making no distinction between their own progeny and those of their sisters. They carry feces of larvæ out of the nest as they are voided. When nests are disturbed the bees carry the larvæ deeper into the burrow, like ants. The adult bees exchange food among themselves and mouth the eggs and larvæ. It is common for the adult female progeny to care for and feed their younger siblings after the mothers are dead.

It would seem that we have here a subsocial type of existence which, when several females cooperate in a single nest, is also semisocial, and because of the long life of the adult females, verges on social because of the association of adults of two generations. However there is no evidence of division of labor or of castes.

HALICTINE AND APINE SOCIETIES

The existence of a type of behavior like that of *Allodape* and *Exoneura* might seem to strengthen the usual concept of the origin of social behavior in bees through a subsocial stage. However, I think it clear that there is another series of evolutionary steps through which social behavior has arisen in the halictine and apine bees.

In these groups social behavior cannot have arisen from a subsocial stage, because (except for the presumably independently specialized Bombini and Apini) all of them practice mass provisioning, sealing each cell after it is provisioned and the egg laid. Therefore they cannot see or touch their progeny as larvæ; only among those that are actually social and have long-lived females or queens do the mothers live with their progeny and then it is only the mature offspring that associate with their mother.

For this reason it seems likely that the incipient stages of establishment of social behavior did not consist of families of a mother and her immature progeny, as among the vespid wasps and almost certainly also among the ancestors of ants and termites. Instead the relationship must have evolved among adult insects. The lack of larva-adult trophallaxis, so conspicuous in termites, ants, and wasps and also probably in the *Allodape-Exoneura* group, is another reason for believing that the social organization among most bees was established among groups of adults. Finally, among halictine bees, every stage in the establishment of social behavior can be found, without anything suggestive of the subsocial conditions found among wasps or in *Allodape* and *Exoneura*.

The Halictinæ and Apinæ are quite unrelated subfamilies of bees, as a glance at a dendrogram showing bee relationships will show (see Michener, 1944). However, there are good reasons to think that from the viewpoint of a study of social evolution, the two groups complement one another. They appear to have evolved in parallel fashion, but one progressed much farther than the other. In the enormous subfamily Halictinæ one finds every intergradation, among several evolutionary lines, from thoroughly solitary bees to tiny colonies with one or a few queens and several workers. Because of the great number of genera and species in this group, various combinations of behavioral characters are becoming known; we are just scratching the surface in this field.[3] In the Apinæ we find one tribe, the tropical American Euglossini, which contains solitary species as well as species in which numerous females nest together, placing their cells in a common cavity, but probably without division of labor or caste differentiation. This relatively small tribe, specialized at least in various morphological features, is little known behaviorally for nests are rarely found. However, some of the evolutionary steps which have now been more thoroughly studied in the Halictinæ probably occur among Euglossini. The rest of the subfamily Apinæ, however, has progressed beyond the social level of any known Halictinæ, having larger colonies and greater differentiation of the castes. In view of the difficulties of studying Euglossini and the small number of existing groups in this tribe, it appears that the best way to study the evolution of social

[3]For their aid in gathering information on the biology of halictine bees in the United States, Costa Rica, and Brazil, I wish to thank Mr. Alvaro Wille and Mr. Howell V. Daly of the University of Kansas and Prof. Rudolf B. Lange of the Museu Paranaénse. The results of these joint studies have yet to be completely analysed and prepared for publication but have served as a basis for some of the comments in this paper.

behavior among bees is to investigate halictines to learn about the initial steps and apines (tribes Bombini, Meliponini, Apini) for subsequent stages. It should be remembered that the various steps in the evolution of social life described below are not, in reality, steps in a phylogenetic series but are existing types of behavior probably similar in certain basic aspects to the stages through which the ancestors of the more highly evolved social bees passed.

Since behavior of the higher social bees is relatively well known, the emphasis in the remainder of this paper is on the initial stages of social behavior found in the Halictinæ; only enough about behavior of social Apinæ has been included to provide comparisons with less socialized forms. The literature citations are in no way exhaustive; they are intended largely as a guide to more recent papers.

AGGREGATIONS AND DEFENSE

As is well known, in many bees (a majority of the species) the nests, each made by a single female, are isolated. Primitively they are holes in the ground made by the female bee herself, although in many groups the nests are made in sticks, wood, or pre-existing cavities. Some ground nesting bees in the Halictidæ and in the related families Colletidæ and Andrenidæ, instead of scattering nests seemingly at random in suitable soil, form aggregations of nests, sometimes diffuse and at other times very dense. Students of bee biology have often wondered if such aggregations result (1) from an innate tendency of the bees to nest in groups (perhaps explainable as a tendency for progeny to return to the vicinity of the parental nest) or (2) from undetected environmental factors which make the areas of the aggregations more favorable than adjacent areas. The latter possibility is difficult to eliminate, but a recent study (Michener, Lange, Bigarella, and Salamuni, 1957) of nesting sites of various burrowing bees in a series of banks near Curatiba, Brazil, although showing the importance of various factors of soil, exposure, etc., indicated clearly that the aggregations of some species could not be explained by any environmental factor studied. They were, therefore, presumed to result from a tendency of the bees to aggregate. Malyshev (1926), for example, also concluded that aggregations of *Andrena vaga* Panzer resulted from a tendency of bees to return to the parental nest area to construct their new nests.

The possible significance of aggregations of nests, whatever their reason for existence, in the establishment of social behavior was recently shown for *Andrena erythronii* Robertson (Michener and Rettenmeyer, 1956). In this burrowing bee, when the ground in the areas of aggregation is moist and soft, each bee makes its own nest independent from those of others. But after prolonged dry periods bees establishing new nests spend much time attempting to dig through the hard soil crust and occasionally enter instead the loose soil which fills the burrows of pre-existing nests. In a few cases we observed two females using the same nest at the same time, although we never saw an encounter between two such bees. Excavation indicated that the bees used jointly only the main burrow and that each made her own branch burrows and cells at the bottom of the nest. This illustrates one means by which aggregation of nests may result in joint use of a single burrow. The likelihood of such occurrences in bees which do not form nest aggregations is almost nil.

The habit of joint use of one entrance burrow has become established in certain species of *Andrena,* e.g., *A. bucephala* Stephens (Perkins, 1919). In this species dozens of females can be seen going in and out of a single nest entrance. Similar behavior has been reported for scattered species in various other groups of bees (e.g., Custer, 1918, for *Melissodes obliqua* Say, one of the Anthophorinæ which has from one to eight females per nest). Too little is known of these cases to indicate what advantages might accrue to the bees except reduction in burrow making.

In the halictines, solitary species and species with nest aggregations also occur; from the standpoint of our account, the next significant step is found in such species as *Pseudaga-postemon divaricatus* (Vachal). In this species a single female sometimes establishes a nest and works alone. However, from two to forty females usually use a single entrance burrow. Sometimes these females are probably merely bees that remain in and re-use the parental nest but in other cases females from various parental nests may join in a new burrow. This is possible because the nests occur in groups. Each female probably makes her own lateral burrows and provisions her own cells. In every such semisocial nest there was always or almost always a female blocking the entrance with her head during warm weather. This guard was not always the same bee; the individual concerned varied from hour to hour and day to day. Guards back into the nest where the burrow is broader to allow entrance or exit of other bees, but were seen to effectively guard the nest against mutillids on two or three occasions. Thus bees in the common nest have the advantage of having to dig only one main burrow (instead of one per female bee as with solitary individuals and species), but perhaps more important, have the advantage of protection against intruders. Solitary individuals have to leave their nests unguarded while foraging, and do not remain at the entrance even when in the nest.

A similar state of affairs has been noted in *Lasioglossum (Choralictus) stultum* (Cresson). In this species overwintering queens establish nests in the spring. When one is alone the nest is never guarded but when two or more queens occupy the same nest, one is usually guarding the entrance during the warm part of the day. After workers are produced in nests of this species, one of them is almost always at the entrance during the day although very hot sun may force the guard back out of sight into the burrow.

This type of guarding, with a bee plugging the entrance with its head, is common to all Halictinæ known to me and described by others that have nests containing several bees; it also occurs in those Meliponini (e.g. *Melipona*) that have small nest entrances. Other social Apinæ usually have nest entrances large enough to be guarded by several bees. Of course the larger the colony the more effective the guarding, probably, in true social bees.

In the Halictinæ there does not appear to be any effective system for preventing bees of the same species from nearby nests (in the case of nest aggregations) from entering the wrong nest. We have noted this repeatedly in *Lasiglossum (Chloralictus) versatum* (Robertson), a species that has small dense groups of nests. As these bees store no food outside of the brood cells, the entrance of such intruders is probably of no consequence. In the social Apinæ, where extensive food storage is the rule, intruders of the same species are an obvious potential source of loss and are normally attacked. Recent studies indicate that in *Apis* different colony odors, by which foreign bees can probably be recognized by guards, result from the different food sources of the colonies (see Ribbands, Kalmus and Nixon, 1952; Kohler, 1955). In the smaller colonies of *Bombus* it may be that foreign bees are somehow recognized as individuals. That this may be possible is shown by Free's (1955) recent demonstration of social hierarchies ("peck orders") in *Bombus* colonies.

CONTROL OF PHYSICAL ASPECTS OF ENVIRONMENT

Most of the solitary and primitively social bees have no obvious means of controlling environmental conditions such as temperature and humidity within the nest. In soil nesting species the burrow usually extends well below the level of the cells, which perhaps provides for drainage of excess water. In *Augochloropsis sparsilis* (Vachal) the cells are in a cluster and several burrows are often constructed from the margin of the cell cluster, curving under the cells close to their lower ends. In various unrelated halictines (including solitary as well as semisocial species), the cell cluster is more completely separated from the surrounding earth; this trend culminates in nests (e.g., of *Paroxystoglossa jocasta* (Schrottky) and *Megalopta insignis* Smith) in which the cell cluster is supported in its cavity in the soil only by a few slender pillars. In these nests it is usual for the earthen walls of the cells to be very thin, sometimes as little as 0.2 mm. in thickness. This system of providing an air space on all sides of the cells must have some significance and Verhoeff (1897) suggested that it might provide an opportunity for brooding of cells. In social Apinæ nests often are surrounded by layers of special materials (grass, feathers, etc. in *Bombus,* an involucre of resin and wax in many Meliponini) which serve for insulation. Most or all social Apinæ are able to reduce nest temperatures to a certain degree by fanning, and in *Apis mellifera* Linnæus the temperature can be raised by the metabolism of muscular activity.

DIVISION OF LABOR AND CASTES

In bees in which each female makes and provisions her own nest, there is no possibility of division of labor for each has to do all the diversified things necessary, such as digging, wax secretion, foraging, and egg-laying. When several females occupy a single burrow in a semisocial relationship, as in *Pseudagapostemon divaricatus,* the beginning of division of labor is possible. In that species each female is believed to make and provision her own cells, but as already explained, one guards the nest entrance while some of the others are working; the division of labor is very temporary, for later other individuals guard the nest entrance.

In some more highly semisocial halictine bees, such as *Augochloropsis sparsilis* (Vachal) or *Augochlorella aurata* (Smith), the division of labor is of greater importance. In these bees normally all the females are fertilized. We do not yet know whether all ordinarily lay eggs but certainly at any one time only one or two bees are in egg-laying condition in each nest. Two or three others may be collecting pollen but those in egg-laying condition do not or only rarely leave the nest. As in *Pseudagapostemon,* one bee (ordinarily not an egg-layer) guards the entrance. The pollen collectors may cooperate, all provisioning a single cell at the same time. There is evidence that in *Augochlorella* the egg-laying individuals are often younger than the pollen collectors but this is inconclusive and certainly is not true of *Augochloropsis,* in which it seems likely that pollen collectors may later cease foraging and become egg-layers. We thus have a well established temporal division of labor and well established integration of activities among foragers in these bees, although castes are entirely lacking.

A most interesting fact concerns the occasional female of *Augochloropsis sparsilis* which does not get fertilized. Few such individuals were found among some hundreds of females dissected. They had much worn mandibles and wings at a season when mated females were still not or little worn. This suggests the unfertilized individuals even in these workerless semisocial species may function like workers and suggests a behavioral preadaptation that would have made advantageous the establishment of a behavior pattern that leaves some females (workers) normally unmated.

In this same section of the Halictidæ species exist (e.g., *Augochlorella michælis* (Vachal), *Pseudogochlora nigromarginata* (Spinola)) in which unmated individuals which do most of the foraging can regularly be found in nests. Unfortunately, knowledge of these species is meager, although we do know that various workers of *A. michælis* cooperate in provisioning a single cell. No difference in size has been observed between such workers and egg laying individuals, although differences in ovary size are obvious on dissection.

In *Lasioglossum (Chloralictus) rhytidophorum* (Moure) distinguishable castes occur,[4] apparently it has definitely reached the social stage. The queens, *on the average,* are larger than the workers although no other external differences were found. The queens alone establish nests in the spring and rear a few workers. After this they rarely leave the nest. The queens, although long-lived compared to the workers, do not survive the entire summer and are replaced by other queens one or more times during the summer. Males are produced in much smaller numbers than females (unlike species mentioned in the preceding paragraphs) but are produced

[4]Interestingly, some other species of the same subgenus (e.g., *L.* (*C.*) *opacum* (Moure)) have no caste differentiation whatever and all females lay eggs.

throughout the season of activity. The fecundity of the queens must be somewhat higher than that of most bees, for they lay eggs over a long period, but the colonies never become very populous; four individuals is perhaps average size in summer and fall, and a dozen is very exceptional.

Lasioglossum (Chloralictus) stultum (Cresson) has a somewhat similar life history, but we believe that the overwintering queens which establish nests in the spring live through the entire summer, not being replaced by other queens. They are thus long-lived compared to those of *L. rhytidophorum* and in most nests only worker progeny are produced during spring and summer, males and new queens appearing in the fall. A few males, however, do appear during the summer months. The queen probably produces considerably more eggs than that of *L. rhytidophorum,* but colonies are normally small, usually not containing more than a dozen individuals at any one time except when two or three queens establish a nest jointly. *L. (Evylæus) malachurum* (Kirby) has an essentially similar life history except that the queen lays her eggs in batches so that there are two or three "broods" of workers and, in fall, a "brood" of reproductives, the total produced in one nest in the fall brood sometimes reaching 120 (see Noll, 1931;[5] Bonelli, 1948). Noll and Bonelli both believed that males in this species result from eggs laid by workers, and this may be true of *L. stultum.*

Bombus has a life history basically similar to that of *Lasioglossum stultum* described above. The fecundity of the queen is considerably higher; this is perhaps correlated with the more marked differentiation of the queen from the worker. However, in many species of *Bombus* intermediates between workers and queens exist, forming a graded series from the smallest worker to the queen. Colonies of several hundred bees are known. Even in the tropics, *Bombus* colonies last only about a year and are started by lone queens which at first do foraging and nest making as well as the egg laying.

In the Meliponini and Apini queens differ from workers in various striking morphological features, lack pollen collecting apparatus, live for several years, and do not start nests alone but must be accompanied by workers from the parent colony. Obviously, the principal characteristics of these queens could not have arisen in groups where the queen must forage in establishing her nest. In the Meliponini the new nesting sites are prepared in advance by workers (Kerr, 1951; Nogueira-Neto, 1954), cells and provisions are established there, and ultimately a young virgin queen flies to the new nest. Later she makes a mating flight with males from the parental or other nests. In the Apini, as is well known, the old queen with a swarm of workers leaves the nest, and after a few days establishes herself in a new place. The high fecundity and long life of the meliponine and apine queens give rise, in many species, to colonies of many thousands of individuals, although species of meliponines exist which normally have colonies of only a few dozen.

[5]It should be noted that Noll's interpretations of the life cycles of various South American halictines, based upon the literature, are seriously in error because he had no way to know of types of life histories such as that of *Pseudagapostemon divaricatus* mentioned above.

We have no knowledge how the castes are determined in the social Halictinæ , although it seems likely that the control is trophic. In *Trigona* (s.1.) in the Meliponini and in *Apis,* queens are produced in special large cells and are trophically determined.[6] In *Melipona* they are produced in normal cells among workers and are perhaps genetically determined (Kerr, 1950, 1950a, and previous papers).

Division of labor between queens and workers has been discussed above. That among workers of different ages appears as soon as workers are recognizable in the series. In *Lasioglossum rhytidophorum, sparsum,* etc., it is the younger workers that guard the nest entrance most of the time and older workers that do most of the foraging. The details of the activities within the nests are not known. In *Bombus,* in which size variation among workers is great, division of labor is not very sharp and is based on size as well as age; the smallest workers may never become foragers (Brian, 1952). In *Melipona* (see Kerr and Santos Neto, 1953) and *Apis* (see Lindauer, 1953) the workers pass through a series of stages in each of which a different activity predominates, although environmental conditions and the age distribution of the entire worker population of the colony play a significant modifying role.

INTEGRATIVE MECHANISMS

Nothing is known of integration in colonies of Halictinæ. Several experiments indicate tentatively that communication of food sources does not occur in *Lasioglossum* or *Augochloropsis.* The same is true of *Bombus* (Brian, 1952). In Meliponini (Kerr and Laidlaw, 1956) and especially in *Apis* communication of food sources is well developed. No doubt some type of communication is necessary to make possible the swarming method of nest multiplication found in Meliponini and Apini.

An integrative mechanism that has long been regarded as very important in other social insects is trophallaxis. As already explained, this seems to have played little if any role in the early evolution of bee societies, but for really large colonies such as those of Meliponini and Apini, a socially significant exchange of materials seems to have been independently evolved. Nixon and Ribbands (1952) gave an indication of the enormous extent of such food exchange by feeding radioactive syrup to six foragers of an *Apis* colony. One social importance of such an exchange would be maintenance of a uniform colony order (see Ribbands, Kalmus, and Nixon, 1952). The existence of a "queen substance", produced by the queen, is important in integrating various activities of the workers, as has been shown for *Apis* by Butler (1954). This is an interesting parallel to the "social hormones" of termites.

FOOD STORAGE AND FEEDING OF YOUNG

In the halictine bees food for adult consumption is not stored within the nest. In the social Apinæ food is stored in special honey and pollen pots or modified cocoons (Meliponini, Bombini) or in normal comb (Apini).

---

[6]It has long been claimed that *Apis dorsata* Fabricius does not have large queen cells but this is not true; see Viswanathan (1950).

Larval cells are mass provisioned and closed after an egg is laid in each in Halictinæ. The same is true in most Meliponini, although in that group the food mass is stratified so that the food of the larva changes with growth. In certain Meliponini (Rayment, 1932, 1935), however, the cells are partially provisioned although new food material is added later as the larva grows. In Bombini and Apini progressive feeding occurs, although it is so different in the two groups that it is presumed to have arisen independently. This conclusion is supported by the retention of mass provisioning in Euglossini, a group close to Bombini, and in most Meliponini, a group obviously closely allied to Apini. It is interesting to note that (excluding the *Allodape* group) only in the more highly specialized bees have larval-adult contacts, presumably so important in the establishment and maintenance of subsocial and social life in other insect groups, become possible.

POPULATION BIOLOGY

The principal work on population genetics of Hymenoptera is that of Kerr (1951). Most Hymenoptera (including the bees) have haploid males in which, figuratively, all genes must be exposed to the selective forces of the environment since they cannot be protected by their alleles as in diploid organisms. An interesting problem is to understand how, under these circumstances, populations can maintain the variability necessary to make possible adaption and evolution. Kerr shows that sex-limited genes having unfavorable effects in the female only, sex-limited genes having heterotic effects in the female, and non-limited genes having heterotic effects in the female could account for the variability.

In bees such as the semisocial and social halictines with very small colonies, the problems of population genetics are probably not much different from those of solitary bees. However, as bee colonies increase in size, and especially as they become permanent as in the Meliponini and Apini, the population biology changes. The number of reproductive individuals per unit area decreases enormously, so that we have a few individuals with long lives of sexual maturity instead of many short-lived individuals. Wide dispersal of reproductives would be expected to lead to a high degree of inbreeding; the numerous sex-limited lethals and doubtless other matters make inbreeding unfavorable (Mackensen, 1955). Various behavioral mechanisms seem to have evolved in connection with reduction of inbreeding. These include mating in flight at a distance from the nest, powerful flight of males, and the fact that males can successfully enter hives other than their own.

REFERENCES

Bonelli, Bruno. 1948. Osservazioni biologiche sull *"Halictus malachurus"* K., *Boll. Istituto Ent. Univ. Bologna* 17:22–42.

Brauns, H. 1926. A contribution to the knowledge of the genus *Allodape* Lep. & Serv., order Hymenoptera, section Apidæ. *Ann. South African Mus.* 23:417–434.

Brian, Anne D. 1952. Division of labour and foraging in *Bombus agrorum* Fabricius. *Jour. Animal Ecol.* 21:223–240.

Butler, G. G. 1954. The method and importance of the recognition by a colony of honey-bees (A. *mellifera* L.) of the presence of its queen. *Trans. Royal Ent. Soc. London* 105:11–29.

Custer, Clarence P. 1928. On the nesting habits of *Melissodes* Latr. (Hymenop.) *Canad. Ent.* 60:28–31.

Free, J. B. 1955. The behaviour of egg-laying workers of bumblebee colonies. *British Jour. Animal Behaviour* 3:147–153.

Kerr, Warwick E. 1950. Genetic determination of castes in *Melipona. Genetics* 35:143–152.

Kerr, Warwick E. 1950a. Evolution of caste determination in the genus *Melipona. Evolution* 4:7–13.

Kerr, Warwick E. 1951. Bases para o estudo da genética de populaçoes dos Hymenoptera em geral e dos Apinæ sociais em particular. *Anais Escola Sup. Agric. "Luiz de Querioz", Univ. Sao Paulo* 8:219–354.

Kerr, Warwick E., and Harry H. Laidlaw, Jr. 1956. General genetics of bees, 8:109–153. *Academic Press,* New York.

Kerr, Warwick E., and Gabriel R. dos Santos Neto. 1953. Contribuiçao para o conhecimento da bionomia dos Meliponini II. Divisao de trabalho entre as operarias de *Melipona quadrifasciata* Lep. *Ciencia e Cultura* 5:224–225.

Köhler, F. 1955. Wache und Volksduft im Bienenstaat. *Zeitschr. f. Bienenforschung* 3:57–63.

Lindauer, N. 1953. Division of labour in the honeybee colony. *Bee World* 34:63–73, 85–90.

Mackensen, Otto. 1955. Further studies on a lethal series in the honeybee. *Jour. Heredity* 46:72–74.

Malyshev, S. J. 1926. The nesting habits of *Andrena* F. (Hym., Apoidea). *Trav. Soc. Naturalistes Leningrad, Sec. Zool. Physiol.* 56(2):25–78. (In Russian).

Michener, Charles D. 1944. Comparative external morphology, phylogeny, and a classification of the bees (Hymenoptera). *Bull. Amer. Mus. Nat. Hist.* 82:151–326.

Michener, Charles D. 1953. Problems in the development of social behavior and communication among insects. *Trans. Kansas Acad. Sci.* 56:1–15.

Michener, Charles D., Rudolf B. Lange, Joao José Bigarella, and Riad Salamuni. 1958. Factors influencing the distribution of bees' nests in earth banks. *Ecology.* (In press)

Michener, Charles D., and Carl W. Rettenmeyer. 1956. The ethology of *Andrena erythronii* with comparative data on other species (Hymenoptera, Andrenidæ). *Univ. Kansas Sci. Bull.* 37:645–684.

Nixon, H. L., and C. R. Ribbands. 1952. Food transmission in the honey bee community, *Proc. Royal Soc.* 140(B):43–50.

Nogueira-Neto, P. 1954. Notas bionômicas sôbre Meliponíneos III—Sôbre a enxameagem (Hymenoptera-Apoidea). *Arq. Mus. Nac. (Rio)* 42:419–452.

Noll, Josef. 1931. Untersuchungen über die Zeugung und Staatenbildung des *Halictus malachurus* Kirby. *Zeitschr. f. Morphologie u. Okologie d. Tiere* 23:285–367, pls. I–III.

Perkins, R. C. L. 1919. The British species of *Andrena* and *Nomada. Trans. Ent. Soc. London* 1919:218–319. pls. XI–XV.

Rayment, Tarlton. 1932. The stingless bees of Australia. *Victorian Naturalist* 49:9–15, 39–43.

Rayment, Tarlton. 1935. A cluster of bees. *The Endeavour Press,* Sydney, pp. 1–752.

Rayment, Tarlton. 1951. Biology of the reed-bees. *Australian Zoologist* 11:285–313.

Ribbands, C. R., H. Kalmus, and H. L. Nixon. 1952. New evidence of communication in the honeybee colony. *Nature* 170:438.

Skaife, S. H. 1953. Subsocial bees of the genus *Allodape* Lep. & Serv. *Jour. Ent. Soc. South Africa* 16:1–16.

Verhoeff, C. 1897. Zur Lebensgeschichte der Gattung *Halictus (Anthophila)*, insbesondere einer Ubergangsform zu socialen Bienen. *Zool. Anz.* 20:369–393.

Viswanathan, H. 1950. Note on *Apis dorsata* queen cells. *Indian Bee Journal* 12:55.

The Genetical Evolution of Social Behaviour. II (*extract*)

W. D. Hamilton
Galton Laboratory, University College, London

COLONIES OF SOCIAL INSECTS

The colonies of the social insects are remarkable in having true genetic diversity in the cooperating individuals.

Caution is necessary in applying the present theory to Hymenoptera because of course their system of sex-determination gives their population genetics a peculiar pattern. But there seems to be no reason to doubt that the concept of inclusive fitness is still valid.

a A Hypothesis Concerning the Social Tendencies of the Hymenoptera

Using this concept it soon becomes evident that family relationships in Hymenoptera are potentially very favourable to the evolution of reproductive altruism.

If a female is fertilized by only one male all the sperm she receives is genetically identical. Thus, although the relationship of a mother to her daughters has the normal value of ½, the relationship between daughters is ¾. Consider a species where the female consecutively provisions and oviposits in cell after cell so that she is still at work when the first of her female offspring ecloses, leaves the nest and mates. Our principle tells us that even if this new adult had a nest ready constructed and vacant for her use she would prefer, other things being equal, returning to her mother's and provisioning a cell for the rearing of an extra sister to provisioning a cell for a daughter of her own. From this point of view therefore it seems not surprising that social life appears to have had several independent origins in this group of insects or that certain divisions of it, represented mainly by solitary species which do more or less approximate the model situation (e.g. most halictine bees), do show sporadic tendencies towards the matrifilial colony.

It may seem that if worker instincts were so favoured colony reproduction could never be achieved at all. However, this problem is more apparent than real. As soon as either the architectural difficulties of further adding to the nest, or a local shortage of food, or some other cumulative hindrance, makes the adding of a further bio-unit to the colony 1½ times more difficult than the creating of the first bio-unit of a new colony the females should tend to go off to found new colonies. Of course, in a more advanced state with differentiated workers, the existing workers would be expected to connive at the change-over to the production queens, which is, so to speak, the final object of their altruism. That in actual species the change-over anticipates the

From *The Journal of Theoretical Biology 7:* 28–43, 51. Reprinted with permission from The Journal of Theoretical Biology. Copyright by Academic Press Inc. (London) Ltd.

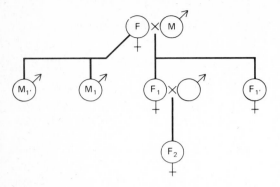

Figure 1   A hymenopteran pedigree.

onset of adverse conditions is not surprising since they must be to a large extent predictable. In Britain where winter sets the natural termination the vespine wasps round off their colony growth at about the time one would expect but some bumble-bees begin rather surprisingly early. If climatic termination were not in question and queen-production tended to come a little late so that the worker population had already risen above the number that could work efficiently on the nest workers might best serve their inclusive fitness by going off with the dispersing queens, despite the fact that in this case the special high relationship of workers to the progeny of the queen no longer holds. Descriptively this is roughly what happens in the meliponine bees (Moure, Nogueira-Neto & Kerr, 1956) and, apart from the serious complication of the swarms having many queens each, it seems to be what happens in the polybiine wasps. In *Apis,* as is well known, it is the old queen who goes off with some of her daughters, *leaving* a young queen together with sister workers. This oddity cannot be so easily derived in the imagination from semi-social antecedents in colony reproduction (it could come more readily from the habit of the whole colony absconding under adverse conditions) and like other peculiar features in honeybees it hints at a long and complicated background of social evolution. Of course as attempts to represent the actual course of evolution and its forms of selection the above outlines are in any case thoroughly naïve; they are merely intended to *illus-trate* certain possible courses which would accord with our principles.

The idea that the male-haploid system of sex-determination contributes to the peculiar tendency of the Hymenoptera towards social evolution is somewhat strengthened by considering other relationships which may be relevant.

Figure 1 shows a hymenopteran pedigree and Fig. 2 shows the coefficients of relationship between the individuals lettered on the pedigree.

The relationships concerning males are worked out by assuming each male to carry a "cipher" gene to make up his diploid pair, one "cipher" never being considered identical by descent with another. For all male relationships we then have

$$r = \tfrac{1}{2}c_1$$

where c_1 is the chance that the two have a replica each. The convenience of this procedure, which is arbitrary in the sense that some other value for the fundamental mother-son and father-daughter link would have given an equally coherent system, is that it results in male and female offspring having equal relationships to their mother which matches with the fact that when the sex-ratio is in its equilibrium condition individuals of opposite sex have equal reproductive values (see Bodmer & Edwards, 1960).

The relationships whose values are affected by polyandrous insemination of the female are indicated in Fig. 2 by asterisks. It will be seen that among those unaffected, because fertilization is not involved, are the relationships of a female to her son, $r = \tfrac{1}{2}$, and to her brother, $r = \tfrac{1}{4}$. According to our theory these values indicate that workers should be much less inclined to give up their male-producing in favour of the queen's than they are to give up their female-producing in favour of a singly-mated queen. Laying by workers is known to occur in each of the main social groups, bees, wasps and ants. The extent to which the practice occurs in normal colonies remains largely obscure; but in some species it is so prevalent that observers have been led to suggest that all the male members of the population are produced in this way (Wheeler, 1928, p. 220; Richards, 1953, p. 81). In fairness however,

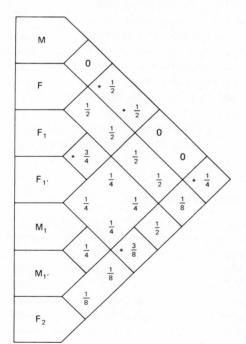

Figure 2 Coefficients of relationship for the pedigree of Fig. 1. Asterisks indicate the coefficients that would diminish in cases of polyandrous insemination assuming the fathership of particular offspring to be unknown. [*Ed. note:* Amended coefficients of relationship, reflecting directional assymmetries in relatedness, can be found in Table 1 of the Trivers and Hare paper on page 189.]

rather than emphasize this apparently detailed fit of our hypothesis, it should be pointed out that male-egg production by workers is in any case the simplest possible manifestation of an incipient selfish tendency since it does not require the complicated preliminary of mating.

Males are related to their brothers as well as to their sisters with $r = \frac{1}{4}$; their relationship to their daughters is $\frac{1}{2}$. Hence the favourable situation for the evolution of worker-like instincts cannot ever apply to males, and in conformity with this, working by males seems to be unknown in the group. Again however, it must be admitted that another explanation of the fact could be advanced: except for the faintest ambiguous suggestion in one genus (*Trypoxylon*, see Kirkpatrick, 1957, p. 254) there is not even any parental care by males even in the solitary nesting species, so that the evolution of worker behavior would have difficulties of initiation in this sex.

While this point must be fairly taken, nevertheless it may be that the male-haploid system is still the prime cause of the very different behaviour of males. It can be shown that it causes a selection pressure towards a sex-ratio which is markedly female-biassed. This may be seen as due to the fact that in the replacement of the gene pool in each generation the females have a bigger contribution to make than the males, so that, so long as the numerical deficiency of males has not gone too far, it is more profitable to produce females than males. And if a chronic deficiency of males does occur it is clear that the male sex will tend to evolve adaptations for polygamous mating which must be almost completely incompatible with the evolution of male parental care. The argument concerning the sex-ratio must properly take into account the relative expensiveness of producing the two sexes. Thus if individuals all incur the same expenditure irrespective of sex, which must be the case for instance with a bee which provisions a series of cells with equal amounts of food, the ratio is the well-known ratio $1 : 1 \cdot 618$; only when a male is merely half as expensive as a female does the ratio sink to the usual $1 : 1$. The argument does not apply, however, if there is thelytoky, polyembryony, etc. and it does not apply once a worker caste has come into existence. If worker laying takes place a more male-biassed ratio should prevail.

b Multiple-mating and Multiple-insemination in Hymenoptera

Following these considerations of sex-ratio, however, it is not surprising to find in most solitary and even moderately social Hymenoptera that the male carries more sperm than is necessary to fill the spermatheca of a single female. Generally it seems that he carries far more than enough. Possibly only in some very highly social species is multiple-insemination *necessary* to fill the spermatheca. This is an important point in favour of our hypothesis since it pre-disposes to the production of the production of the very highly intra-related families which the male-haploid system makes possible. But to what extent, over the range of groups and species, the females actually produce such families remains a large question. The literature contains many references to multiple matings by female Hymenoptera, spread over many of the major groups of the order. How frequently such multiple mating is accompanied by a significant degree of multiple insemination, and how the phenomena are distributed with respect to incipient, advanced or retrogressing social life are matters too wide and complex to be reviewed here. For the present it must suffice to quote the very small amount of work known to the author which bears directly on multiple insemi-nation.

Concerning female wild bees in general, Michener, Cross, Daly, Rettenmeyer & Willie (1955) state that: "Spermathecas with only a few sperms have not been found, in spite of some search, although specimens with the spermatheca only half-full are known." But in a survey of some Australian halictines, Michener (1960) found that on the whole the number of sperms in spermathecas was small in comparison with his experience of American halictines. Without knowledge of the quantity of sperms which the male can provide or of mating behaviour, one cannot be sure what this argues about multiple-insemination, but it suggests that it may be uncommon. Taken together with Michener's notable failure to find any small-ovaried worker-type bees, which according to him are a feature of most common halictines of other continents, this observation seems, therefore, against our hypothe-sis. But Michener notes as another general feature, the short adult life-span of the Australian bees and concludes that, "There is no evidence that any female lives long enough to encounter her adult progeny," which at least offers another possible reason why worker behaviour has failed to appear. Plateaux-Quénu (1959) thought queens of the quite highly social *Halictus marginatus* were probably multiply in-seminated because she found some queens towards the beginning of the period of fertilization with only partially filled spermathecae. Michener & Lange (1958a) present evidence that a female of the solitary (though gregarious-nesting) anthopho-rine bee *(Paratetrapedia oligotricha)* in Brazil, taken in copula, was engaged in receiving her second insemination, this apparently being the only direct evidence of such a thing in a primitive bee known to them at the time.

Multiple insemination of a high order effectively producing a progeny of multi-ple paternity seems to be firmly established for the honeybee (e.g. Taber & Wendel, 1958; Kerr, Zucchi, Nakadaira & Butolo, 1962). On the other hand, it would seem not to occur in the Meliponinae (Kerr *et al.,* 1962). It occurs in the socially very advanced fungus-growing ants, e.g. *Atta sexdens* (Kerr, 1961). But in another myr-micine of a different tribe I found no evidence but of single inseminations, using Kerr's sperm counting methods.

Suppose a female is mated by n males and they are respectively responsible for proportions

$$f_1, f_2, \ldots f_s, \ldots f_n, \left(\sum_s f_s = 1 \right),$$

of her female progeny. The average relationship between daughters is then

$$\tfrac{1}{2} \left(\tfrac{1}{2} + \sum_s f_s^2 \right).$$

In particular, if all males contribute equally we have

$$\bar{r} = \tfrac{1}{2}\left(\tfrac{1}{2} + \frac{1}{n} \right),$$

which is the lowest average relationship for a given value of n. If two males contribute equally we have $\bar{r} = \tfrac{1}{2}$ as for normal full-sibs. Clearly multiple-insemination will greatly weaken the tendency to evolve worker-like altruism and $n > 2$ in the model situation described above should prevent its incipience altogether. Using Taber & Wendel's estimate (1958) of $\bar{n} = 8$, which Kerr's different method roughly confirmed, we get $\bar{r} = 5/16$, which doubtless should be raised a little to allow for inequality in the contributions of the drones. It does seem at first rather surprising that altruism towards sisters so much *less* related than full sisters can be maintained at its observed pitch of perfection. But even the limiting value of $\bar{r}$ is no lower than ¼ and we may well imagine that once established the biological advantage of the social mode of reproduction, which is evidenced by the success of the social insects in general, proves sufficient to outweigh even a twofold higher value in personal offspring. It may also be argued that the firm establishment of highly differentiated trophogenic worker castes creates a gulf which a sexualized mutant is unlikely to cross successfully, especially when as in honeybees so much depends on the behaviour of the other workers. For example, a mutant sexualized worker of the honeybee will eclose from a worker cell and will therefore be small. Even if it secretes queen-substance it is unlikely to be as attractive as a proper queen and is likely to be killed. If it escapes it cannot found a colony on its own. Thus, if the trend to multiple insemination occurs after the firm establishment of the worker caste, its threat to colonial discipline is a rather remote one.

In species of social Hymenoptera which found their colonies through single fertilized females the difficulties and dangers of seeming to be royal are less important; but the mutant will still suffer handicaps from its probable small size and lack of food-reserves. In ants it will be further handicapped by its lack of wings. Nevertheless with ants there are strong indications that trends of worker sexualization have occurred in the evolution of the group (Haskins & Haskins, 1955; Michener & Michener, 1951, p. 126; Wheeler & Chapman, 1922; Wheeler, 1928, pp. 173–4). It may be remarked that the sexualized worker is likely to have a smaller spermatheca and so to restore single insemination, which will, according to our theory, restore the basis for re-evolving strong worker altruism.

An ability of females to lay unfertilized eggs which develop into females would open another possible avenue for selfish selection. Again, the menace will be greatest when multiple insemination of queens occurs, for then when a worker had inherited the causative gene from its father there would be a better chance, especially when the gene frequency was low, that it would have some normal worker sisters to help rear its offspring. In general, whether we are concerned with parthogenetic production of males or females we need only follow Sturtevant's (1938) argument and visualize the drastic or fatal over-production of sexual or egg-laying forms which would occur in the "son" or "daughter" colonies due to an egg-laying worker to see the potent counter-selection to which a fully penetrant causative gene will become exposed. Clearly the situation is worse for the gene when it is common than when it is rare so that an equilibrium is possible.

Female-to-female parthogenesis by workers does occur sporadically in honey-bees and shows geographical variation in its incidence. In the South African race, *Apis mellifera capensis* Esch., it seems that worker eggs always develop into females (see Kerr & Araujo, 1958).[†] But whether this is explicable as a selfish trait is rather doubtful. To be such the laying-workers would have to try to get their eggs cared for in queen-cells. Despite what Flanders (1962) seems to quote Onions as having stated—that in queenless hives "Uniparental workers do not construct either queen cells or drone cells," and that "a queenless colony gradually disintegrates"—Dr. Kerr informs me that these bees do eventually construct queen cells in an emergency and can thereby secure the perpetuation of their colony; but he found that they did so somewhat tardily compared to queenless colonies of the familiar honeybees. Of course for them, possessing this unusual ability, the need to initiate queen-rearing at once is not so urgent. Also in some other races diploid eggs laid in queen cells by workers in hopelessly queenless hives may sometimes be reared and so save their colonies from extinction (Butler, 1954, p. 58).

Female-to-female parthenogenesis is also present in various species of ants. For example in the ant *Oecophylla longinoda,* parthenogenesis of a clonal type seems to have become a normal mode in the reproduction of the colony (Ledoux, see Wilson, 1963). Here the workers and not the mother queen produce the new generation of queens, which is suggestive at least that the situation had its origin through the selection of a selfish trait.

c Termites

The special considerations which apply to the Hymenoptera do not seem to have been noticed by Williams & Williams (1957). The discussion which they base on their analysis of the full-sib relationship would, however, be applicable to the ter-mites where this relationship is ensured in the colony by having the queen attended by a single "king." Termites of both sexes have an equal relationship ($r = \frac{1}{2}$) to their siblings and their potential offspring. Thus the fact that both sexes "work" is just what we expect; we need only a bioeconomic argument to explain why restric-tion of fertility to a few members has proved most advantageous to the sibship as a whole. On this point the present theory can add little to previous discussions.

When either king or queen dies the worker castes rear a substitute or "neotene" from the eggs or young nymphs already present. The neotene mates with the surviv-

---

[†]Other interesting peculiarities reported for this race are its mild temperament and the presence in workers of large queen-like spermathecae. However Dr. Kerr tells me that he has checked that laying-workers do not have sperm in their spermathecae.

ing parent. The progeny which come from such a mating will still be related to the old workers with $r = \frac{1}{2}$. They will be related among themselves by $r = \frac{5}{8}$. They will also tend to be highly homozygous and such matings are in fact said to be somewhat infertile.

It is surprising, however, if increasing the tendencies to social cohesion by such close inbreeding can ever pay off as a long-term policy against the disadvantages of decreasing adaptive flexibility. That it may be a successful short-term policy for a species is perhaps indicated by the frequency of mention of brother-sister mating in the literature on social insects; but these statements are not always based on very firm evidence.

d Pleometrosis and Association; Population Viscosity in the Social Insects

However it does seem necessary to invoke at least a mild inbreeding if we are to explain some of the phenomena of the social insects—and indeed of animal sociability in general—by means of this theory. The type of inbreeding which we have in mind is that which results from a high viscosity of population or from its actual subdivision into small quasi-endogamous groups.

In some ants (e.g. *Iridomyrmex humilis*), at least one species of stingless bee (*Melipona schencki,* see Kerr, 1949 and orally) and apparently most species of wasps of the sub-family Polybiinae it is normal to have at least several "queens" engaged in egg-laying in each nest. This phenomenon is known as pleometrosis. Colony reproduction is by swarming with several or many fertilized females—potential queens—in each swarm. Clearly this social mode presents a problem to our theory. Continuing cycle after cycle colonies can come into existence in which some individuals are almost unrelated to one another. Such situations should be commoner the higher the number of founding queens, but less common in so far as there is any positive assortment of true sisters in the swarms. They would be very favourable to the selection of genes causing selfish behaviour and this in turn would be expected to lower the efficiency of social life and to reduce the species. Yet though selfish behaviour is certainly not absent—witness the large proportion of unfertilized wasps in egg-laying condition (Richards & Richards, 1951), and the common occurrence of dominance behaviour—it does not seem to do the colonies much harm and the species concerned are highly successful in many cases. For example, the genus *Polybia* includes several very abundant species in the Neotropics and has obviously undergone considerable speciation with the whole system in working order.

Wasps of the widespread genus *Polistes,* doubtfully placed in a separate sub-family from the Polybiinae, present a rather similar problem. In this case it seems that there is usually or always only a single principal egg-layer on the nest; she dominates the others and they succeed in laying only a few eggs if any (e.g. Gervet, 1962). But with many of the species and races that inhabit warmer lands it is common for the initial building of the nest to be the work of two or more fertilized queen-sized wasps. This phenomenon has been called "association" (Richards &

Richards, 1951). Even at this stage the dominant wasp does least work and probably all the egg-laying, and, probably due to their more arduous and dangerous lives, the auxiliaries (as the subordinate queen-like wasps are called) tend to disappear in the course of time so that a queen assisted by her daughter workers becomes the normal situation later on. Here it is the ready acceptance of non-reproductive roles by the auxiliaries that we have difficulty in explaining. There is good reason to believe that the initial nest-founding company is *usually* composed of sisters (Rau, 1940; personal observations on *Polistes versicolor*), which brings the phenomenon closely into line with the pleometrosis of the polybiines. But is is doubtful if the wasps have any personal recognition of their sisters and if a wasp did arrive from far away it is probable that it would be accepted by the company provided it showed submission to the one or two highest ranking wasps. Dominance order does sometimes change and an accepted stranger has before it the prospect of rising in rank and ultimately subduing or driving off the queen. Thus an innocent rendering of assistance is not always easy to distinguish from an attempt at usurpation as Rau has pointed out, so that the readiness to accept "help" is really just as puzzling as the disinterested assistance which some of the auxiliaries undoubtedly do render.

The geographic distribution of the association phenomenon in *Polistes* is striking (Yoshikawa, 1957). We may state it as a general, though by no means unbroken, rule that northern species approximate to the vespine mode of colony foundation and tropical species to the polybiine to the extent above described. The single species *Polistes gallicus* illustrates the tendency well. At the northern edge of its range in Europe its females usually found nests alone. In Italy and Southern France the females found nests in companies; while in North Africa the species is said to found colonies by swarming with workers (see Richards & Richards, 1951). We here suggest two hypotheses which could bring these facts into conformity with our general theory.

The first posits a general higher viscosity of the tropical populations. This will cause, through inbreeding, all coefficients of relationship to have higher actual values than we would get taking into account only connections through the past one or two generations. And it will also increase the tendency for casual neighbours to be related, which is clearly of potential importance for the association phenomenon.

Populations of *Polistes* certainly are very viscous. Generally the wasps have a strong attachment to their place of birth (Rau, 1940), and like to found nests near the parental nest. They are weak flyers. And they do show a very pronounced tendency to local variation. But whether these remarks apply any more strongly to tropical than to temperate populations I do not know. Polybiine wasps seem to be weaker flyers than vespines and also have indications of a tendency for swarms to build not far from the parent nest. Polybiines also show much geographical variation.

By its very nature the so-called temperate climate may tend to force a greater degree of vagrancy on the insects inhabiting it, both through its pronounced seasons and its seasonal irregularities. A discussion of this idea from a similar biological

point of view can be found in Wynne-Edwards (1962, p. 463). As one further factor
relevant at least to *Polistes* we suggest that if, as seems probable, the genus is of
tropical origin the northern species will be derived from former races which themselves tended to be made up of vagrant colonist wasps which had flown north. Thus
there would have been selection for wasps willing and able to found nests alone; and
in general, in the course of such a spreading colonization, a species would be
expected to shed some of its co-operative adaptations. But if the spread was very
slow, as it may well have been, these factors would hardly apply.

The second hypothesis appeals to the lack of marked seasons in the tropics
causing a lack of synchronism in the breeding activity of insects. This will tend to
cause inbreeding because it scarifies the mating population. Thus a Polybiine nest
may be in active production of sexual wasps when its nearest neighbours are not and
its progeny may therefore be more inclined to mate among themselves. The same
doubtless applies to *Polistes* in a really equable tropic environment and with *Polistes*
we again have an important correlative effect that when a nest-founding wasp
accepts an adventive helper the chance that she is a sister is also increased. However,
with *Polistes,* multiple-queen nest founding does occur even where the wasps are
constrained by the climate to follow a definite seasonal cycle. Queens may come
together in the spring after hibernation to found their colonies. Rau (1940) records
some interesting observations on *P. annularis* in the United States showing the
variability of its nesting behaviour and he mentions his general experience that the
hibernated queens return to the old nest for a short time before going off to found
nests. Such behaviour should help to ensure that in cases of associative founding the
co-foundresses are sisters. The cases of hibernating yet associating *Polistes* would
seem to dismiss any hypothesis that the differences we have noted between northern
and tropical wasps is due solely to factors following from the necessity for hibernation. In *Vespula,* queens do often hibernate in the parental nest and yet do not show
association in nest-founding.

To the extent that they are valid, the above hypotheses would also help to
extenuate previously discussed difficulties concerning the maintenance of reproductive altruism despite multiple insemination of queens. It may be remarked that
although modern work rather indicates that its breeding system is far from viscous
the honeybee does seem to maintain local races quite readily. With *Atta sexdens* I
have noticed that males and females come to earth from their nuptial flight in local
concentrations, but whether these are associated each with an established colony or
represent some wider nuptial gathering is not clear.

e   Aggressiveness

The aggressiveness of the workers of social insects towards disturbers of their nest
is one of the most conspicuous features of their altruism. The barbed sting and the
function of sting autotomy are physical parallels of the traits of temperament. The
correlation of these characters with sterilization does seem to hold very well

throughout the social Hymenoptera. Queens are always timid and reluctant to use their stings compared to workers. In *Polistes,* workers, unless very young, are more aggressive than auxiliaries, and auxiliaries more than the reigning queen. Races of honeybees in which laying workers occur more frequently or appear more readily when the hive becomes queenless are generally milder than the races where they are less prevalent (Sakagami & Akahira, 1958, 1959; Kerr & Araujo, 1958). Polybiine wasps, pleometrotic and lacking pronounced caste differences, are generally somewhat less fierce than vespines.

However, aggressiveness is also clearly a function of the size of the colony, or perhaps even more of the worker : queen ratio. This applies not only to particular colonies as they grow larger but also in a general way to variation in mature colony size between species. This effect too is not very surprising, for, to take the extreme case, we can see that it is only when its nest is overpopulated and its services in other directions superfluous that the worker can afford to throw its life away. Typically the vespines have the higher worker : queen ratio, so that from this point of view as well, it is not surprising that the polybiines are generally speaking milder wasps. It is interesting to learn that even in the limited north-south range covered by the islands of Japan, *Polistes* shows in this respect as well its previously noted tendency to bridge the two types. Yoshikawa (1962) gives an interesting comparison of northern and southern Japanese species and it is seen that northern species are both fiercer and have the larger colonies. Iwata (quoted by Yoshikawa) believes that the fierceness is a function of the colony size. Although no properly associative *Polistes* occur in Japan, Yoshikawa (1957) has found a case of temporary association in a southern species, suggesting a slight or vestigial tendency. Perhaps this factor may play a part in the difference in fierceness. Existence of auxiliaries would seem incompatible with a high degree of worker differentiation and will therefore tend to counter the development of high worker altruism. But just why it appears to be also incompatible with higher worker : queen ratios is not entirely clear.

f Usurpation

Its made or half-made nest is obviously a valuable property to a queen bee, wasp or ant. If it is ready provisioned or staffed by workers and set for the rearing of sexual brood it is even more valuable. It is therefore not surprising that usurpation has become a major evolutionary and behavioural issue with the nesting Hymenoptera.

On the one hand we have the great array of parasites. Often, especially in bees and wasps, the host and parasite species seem to be closely related, suggesting that the habit arose out of petty intra-specific usurpation. But the present theory indicates considerable difficulties for the sympatric emergence of a parasitic race. Unless the evolving complex of characters could include a strong tendency to vagrancy the usurper would in too many cases destroy the genes on which its own behaviour was founded. One allopatric race invading the territory of another with at least partial reproductive barriers already present should create a more promising situation for progress in usurper-instincts. A situation like this, involving occasional parasitism, is suggested for two species of *Bombus* in Britain (Free & Butler, 1959, p. 77). Plateaux-Quénu (1960) has observed a half-provisioned nest of *Halictus marginatus* being used by a female of *H. malachurus.* Both these species are social on about the same level as *Bombus.*

On the other hand, we have the sensitivity about adventive females which is so widespread in the nesting Hymenoptera, including the parasites themselves. According to Plateaux-Quénu, conspecific usurpation is frequently attempted, albeit before the appearance of the workers, in the nest aggregations of *Halictus malachurus* and sometimes succeeds. A successful conspecific usurpation, strongly resisted has actually been observed in *Polistes fadwigae* by Yoshikawa (1955) and I have observed what was probably an attempt, persistent but unsuccessful, in *P. versicolor.* Something similar seems to have been seen by Kirkpatrick (1957, p. 277) with *P. canadensis*†. And with the same species I have found that if a dominant wasp is transferred from one nest to another a mortal fight, usually with the reigning dominant, begins immediately; whereas a young worker similarly transferred may sometimes be accepted and, perhaps because of its submissiveness, seldom receives so severe an attack. Extreme suspicion concerning wasps which approach the nest in a wavering uncertain manner sometimes prevents a genuine member of the colony from rejoining it, at least for some time, in *P. canadensis.* This is especially apt to happen with young wasps, perhaps returning from their first flight; and it may be a rather paradoxical result of such a reception that they sometimes end up working on a nearby nest not their own. Possibly it is the danger of usurpation, joint with that of parasitoids, that keeps so large a proportion of a *Polistes* colony idle on the nest when one would have thought they could be much more usefully employed out foraging.

As the very existence of association necessitates, antagonistic behaviour is not so marked in the very early stages of nest-founding: then, with *Polistes versicolor,* a considerable amount of swapping of wasps may take place from week to week within a local group of initiated nests—for example all those located around the buildings of a household and usually not far from a last year's abandoned nest from which very likely all or most of the wasps are derived. The same sort of thing has been noted by Ferton (1901) for *P. gallicus* and by Rau (1940) for *P. annularis.* But even at this stage fights are sometimes seen severe enough for the combatants to fall off the nest.

In these associative *Polistes* the great variation in the degree of association—from lone nest-founding to companies of 12 or more crowded on and about a tiny nest-initial—the frequent abandonment of young nests, the quarrels, the manifest concern about adventive wasps, combine to create an impression which is very

---

† In the light of observations of Sakagami & Fukushima (1957) an alternative interpretation that one is concerned with an attempt to thieve larvae for food in these cases, should be borne in mind. But I have not seen thieving in either *P. versicolor* or *P. canadensis* even in artificial situations that should encourage it. It would in any case be normally very difficult to perform in associative species.

reminiscent of the breeding affairs of the South American cuckoos *Crotophaga ani* and *Guira guira* as described by Davis (1940 a, b). In their broad features the situations are indeed so similar as to suggest similar trends of selection must be at work in populations similarly patterned with respect to relationship. In these birds, much as in *Polistes,* we have a basic ability to rear young independently complicated by a tendency of some birds to assist altruistically (perhaps most marked in *Crotophaga*) and of others to play the cuckoo (most marked in *Guira,* which also sometimes parasitises other birds). A striking difference from *Polistes* of course is the presence of males, playing parts in close parity with those of females. And the systems also differ in that usually several birds succeed in laying in the communal nest, which is more like what is found with certain primitively social xylocopine bees (see, e.g. Michener, 1958) than like *Polistes.* When the clutch becomes very large through this cause a large proportion of eggs may fail to hatch. Eggs are sometimes taken out and dropped. Such action by a particular bird might serve to increase the proportion of its own eggs in the clutch. For all the seeming confusion and inefficiency these birds are, like *Polistes versicolor* and *P. canadensis* in the same area, widespread, and apparently successful.

g Pleometrosis in Halictinae

The social halictine bees closely parallel the systems found in *Polistes.* Worker populations are of comparable size. The state of affairs found in *Augochloropsis sparsilis* (Michener & Lange, 1958b) and in *Lasioglossum inconspicuum* (Michener & Wille, 1961) shows that these species have a class closely corresponding to the auxiliaries of warm-climate *Polistes.* But since at least some of the halictine nests are pleometrotic it seems more probable that some of their auxiliaries become layers later on rather than dying young as workers as they tend to do in *Polistes.* Probably only a minority of the species of Halictinae have any trace of a worker caste and the group also differs in the wide range of types of sociability which their tunnel-nesting encourages. For instance, quite a common situation with burrowing bees, both Halictinae and others, is for several females to be using a common entrance tunnel while each owns a separate branch tunnel further back.

Michener (1958) has recently suggested that the road to sociability and the development of a worker caste has lain in this group through a stage like this followed by a stage like that found in *Augochloropsis sparsilis.* This we are inclined to doubt since even if the nest-system users are for some reason always sisters the genetic relation of sister eggs will always be twice that of niece eggs irrespective of multiple insemination, so that on the present theory social evolution via the matrifilial colony always offers the easier route to worker altruism. Hymenopteran societies in which the queen (or queens) have auxiliaries but not, later, filial workers, seem in fact to be unknown. The classical theory concerning the evolution of the social insects has always posited a wide overlap of generations allowing mother and daughters to co-exist in the imaginal state as one of the preconditions for the evolution of this kind of sociability, and it is surely significant that it is never observed where this condition is lacking, as it might well be if genetic interest in nieces were sufficient to encourage reproductive altruism†. That such altruism could arise through genetic interest in the offspring of unrelated bees sharing the same excavation, as Michener actually suggests, seems to me incredible.

h Tunnel-guarding by bees

There is however another important type of social behaviour to which Michener has re-drawn attention which might well arise on the basis of much lower relationships. One of the potential advantages when two or more females share a common entrance tunnel is that the entrance can be defended against parasites by a single bee, leaving the others free to forage. Instincts for guarding a narrow entrance seem to be widespread in the nest-excavating bees and also occur in Meliponinae (Michener, 1958). Michener has seen females of *Pseudogapostemon divaricatus,* a workerless but entrance sharing species, apparently taking turns at the duty and he and other observers have seen guard bees of this and other species repulse mutillids (Michener, 1958, 1960; Michener & Wille, 1961) and parasite bees (Michener & Wille, 1961). The menace of intruding parasites may give such co-operation a very high advantage. But it would seem that once established the system should give an even higher advantage to the sporadic "shirker", so that it is a little difficult to see how guarding could become perfect. Perhaps it is not. One may however construct a simple imaginary system that would render it so: the bees could evolve an instinct which allowed them to leave duty at the nest entrance only on the stimulus of another recognized tenant coming in, or better, of another bee coming up from behind; this would ensure that there was always a bee on duty or at least somewhere in the nest system. By going out when supposed to be on duty, a bee would jeopardize her own brood as much as, if not more than, the broods of the others, so that selection would tend to stabilize the instinct. Interestingly Claude-Joseph and Rayment both have claimed to have observed guarding on this system, but Michener (1960) is inclined to doubt these claims because his careful observations on *P. divaricatus* in Brazil had revealed that the behaviour was more irregular than might appear at first sight, bees remaining on guard for some time and allowing others to go out past them. In a highly pleometrotic nest-system, shirking might be relatively easier and safer for the isolated social deviant but the spells of guard-duty demanded would also be much shorter and therefore the selective incentive to shirking much less. Nevertheless, even if it is possible to account for the evolution of guard-instincts without a basis of relationship between the bees, it is hard to see how other socially disruptive practices, such as robbing within the nest-system, could fail to evolve unless a bee's co-tenants were also usually the carriers of some part of its inclusive fitness.

† As regards the traces of similar sociability that exist in birds, with *Crotophaga* and *Guira,* present evidence suggests the possibility of both aunt-like and sister-like altruism, although just how widely genetical relationship may range within groups is not known. Other recorded cases in birds suggest *immature* progeny helping the mother to rear subsequent broods (Skutch, 1935). These immatures would doubtless reproduce normally later on.

REFERENCES

Bodmer, W. F. & Edwards, A. W. F. (1960). *Annu. hum. Genet.* 24, 239.
Butler, C. G. (1954). "The World of the Honeybee". London: Collins.
Davis, D. E. (1940a). *Auk* 57, 179.
Davis D. E. (1940b). *Auk* 57, 472.
Ferton, C. (1901). *Ann. Soc. ent. Fr.* 70, no. 1, 83.
Flanders, S. E. (1962). *Insectes Sociaux,* 9, 375.
Free, J. B. & Butler, C. G. (1959). "Bumblebees". London: Collins.
Gervet, J. (1962). *Insectes Sociaux,* 9, 231.
Haskins, C. P. & Haskins, E. F. (1955). *Insectes Sociaux,* 2, 115.
Kerr, W. E. (1949). *O Solo,* 41, 39.
Kerr, W. E. (1961). *Rev. bras. Biol.* 21, 45.
Kerr, W. E. & Araujo, V. de P. (1958). *Garcia de Orta,* 6, 53.
Kerr, W. E., Zucchi, R., Nakadaira, J. T. & Butolo, J. E. (1962). *J. N. Y. ent. Soc.* 70, 265.
Kirkpatrick, T. W. (1957). "Insect Life in the Tropics". London: Longmans.
Michener, C. D. (1958). *Proc. Tenth Int. Congr. Entom. Montreal,* 2, 441.
Michener, C. D. (1960). *J. Kans. ent. Soc.* 33, 85.
Michener, C. D., Cross, E. A., Daly, H. V., Rettenmeyer, C. W. & Wille, A. (1955). *Insectes Sociaux,* 2, 237.
Michener, C. D. & Lange, R. B. (1958a). *Kans. Univ. Sci. Bull.* 35, 69.
Michener, C. D. & Lange, R. B. (1958b). *Science,* 127, 1046.
Michener, C. D. & Michener, M. H. (1951). "American Social Insects". New York: Van Nostrand.
Michener, C. D. & Wille, A. (1961). *Kans. Univ. Sci. Bull.* 42, 1123.
Moure, J. S., Nogueira-Neto, P. & Kerr, W. E. (1956). *Proc. Tenth Int. Congr. Entom. Montreal,* 2, 481.
Plateaux-Quénu, C. (1959). *Ann. Biol.* 35, 327.
Plateaux-Quénu, C. (1960). *Insectes Sociaux,* 7, 349.
Rau, P. (1940). *Ann. ent. Soc. Amer.* 33, 617.
Richards, O. W. (1953). "The Social Insects". London: Macdonald.
Richards, O. W. & Richards, M. J. (1951). *Trans. R. ent. Soc. Lond.* 102, 1.
Sakagami, S. F. & Akahira, Y. (1958). *Kontyu,* 26, 103.
Sakagami, S. F. & Akahira, Y. (1959). *Evolution,* 14, 29.
Sakagami, S. F. & Fukushima, K. (1957). *J. Kans. ent. Soc.* 30.
Sturtevant, A. H. (1938). *Quart. Rev. Biol.* 13, 74.
Wheeler, W. M. (1928). "The Social Insects". New York: Harcourt, Brace & Co.
Wheeler, W. M. & Chapman, J. W. (1922). *Psyche,* 29, 203.
Williams, G. C. & Williams, D. C. (1957). *Evolution,* 11, 32.
Wilson, E. O. (1963). *Ann. Rev. Ent.* 8, 345.
Yoshikawa, K. (1955). *Insectes Sociaux,* 2, 255.
Yoshikawa, K. (1957). *Mushi,* 30, 37.
Yoshikawa, K. (1962). *J. Biol., Osaka City University,* 13, 19.

The Evolution of Social Behavior by Kin Selection (*concluding part*)

Mary Jane West Eberhard
Department of Biology, Universidad del Valle, Cali, Colombia, and
Smithsonian Tropical Research Institute, Balboa, Canal Zone

A synthesis of current ideas on the evolution of insect sociality shows how mutualism, parental manipulation, and kin selection could all have operated, either in conjunction or independently, to produce extreme altruism (worker sterility) starting with different kinds of primitive groups. A kin-selection interpretation of insect sociality is given which differs from that of Hamilton in not relying on extraordinary high relatedness among the members of a colony. The evolution of a reproductive division of labor in insects probably involved differences in reproductive capacity among adults in primitively social groups of relatives, making it profitable, in terms of inclusive fitness, for some (namely, the reproductively inferior individuals) to become altruistic helpers.

THE ORIGIN OF EXTREME ALTRUISM IN INSECTS

In terms of altruistic behavior the most social animals by far are insects. In all of the more than 24,000 known species of eusocial (i.e., possessing a worker caste) wasps, ants, bees, and termites, at least some of the brood of each reproductive female (queen) is made up of complete altruists—individuals (workers) whose entire lifetime reproductive effort is dedicated to rearing the young of others, and for whom group living is absolutely obligatory. The variety and exaggeration of social traits among insects offer an ample testing ground for any general theory of social behavior.

According to the view traditional in entomology, the reproductive division of labor originated when the mother of a subsocial group (a mother with her own young) become so long-lived as to cause a generational overlap and lead to a society in which the offspring would help the mother rather than go off on their own. This traditional account (Darwin, 1859; Wheeler, 1928) implied that the mother, or family, is the relevant unit of selection in bringing this about, since the evolution of sterility is obviously impossible by classical selection operating on workers (in terms of individual fitness).

In recent years there have been three major new interpretations of the evolution of insect sociality, each of them involving one of the three hypotheses applied to altruism in the previous section—kin selection, reciprocity, and parental manipulation. Each of these hypotheses will be discussed separately below. A fourth kind of explanation often referred to involves selection at the level of the colony: namely,

From *The Quarterly Review of Biology 50:* 22–33. Reprinted by permission of the author and *The Quarterly Review of Biology.*

colonies with specialized workers and reproductives out-reproduce (presumably in terms of daughter colonies) colonies without those specialized groups, in much the same way that a multicellular organism with specialized organs might do better than one not having a division of labor among its cells. The last hypothesis (colony control) has seldom been clearly set forth as an explanation of the *origin* of sterile castes. It has mainly served to explain how, given a group with some individuals specializing as workers and others as reproductives, the two castes can develop morphological and behavioral adaptations contributing to the success of the group as a unit. Selection at the level of colony, or "family," was first mentioned by Darwin (1859), is inherent in the "supraorganism" concepts of Wheeler (1911) and Emerson (1959), and was recently cited by Wilson (1971) as the most feasible explanation for the evolution of insect altruism (although Wilson did not explicitly choose it over the kin-selection hypothesis discussed at length in the same book, and he sometimes —p. 342—acknowledged that the queen is the "ultimate focus" of selection).

"Colony-level selection" is an undesirable term even when it implies selection on mothers, since it is certain to be understood by some readers to imply selection operating at a level higher than the individual—e.g., on groups or populations, a generally unjustified interpretation (see Introduction). Both "colony-level selection" and the old "supraorganism" concept have in common the error of considering the workers as extensions of the queen's soma, an idea which fails to acknowledge the quite important fact that, unlike a multicellular organism, an insect colony contains a number of genetically different individuals who must be considered actual or potential reproductive competitors.

The Three-Quarter-Relatedness (Haplodiploidy) Hypothesis

Hamilton introduced the idea of inclusive fitness in 1963, and with it the novelty of being able to consider the evolution of sterility from the individual daughter's point of view. He argued that the frequent occurrence of social altruism among the Hymenoptera may be owing to the great advantage to workers (in terms of inclusive fitness) of helping their mothers rear their sisters ($r_{AB,} = ¾$) rather than of reproducing on their own ($r_{AB,} = ½$). The unusually high relatedness of female hymanopterans and their sisters (¾, vs. the more common ½ for diploid organism) is the consequence of the haploidy of hymenopteran males, that makes all the paternal genes of sisters identical instead of only half identical (providing the mother has mated only once) (see Hamilton, 1964b).

Three objections are commonly raised regarding the ¾-relatedness argument: (1) that such (matri-filial) sociality is not prominent in other haplodiploid groups; (2) that comparable altruism has been achieved by workers of diploid species (termites) or in other social groups for which $r_{AB,}$ is less than ¾; and (3) that the observed occurrence of multiple mating among the social Hymenoptera means that the relatedness of sisters is sometimes lower than ¾ (for example, two matings would reduce the relatedness of sisters to ⅜, and would eliminate in one stroke the advantage in terms of r alone, of rearing sisters rather than daughters) (see reviews by

Hamilton, 1964b, 1972; Wilson, 1971; Lin and Michener, 1972; and Alexander, 1974). A fourth point is usually overlooked, namely, the fact that the extraordinary ¾-relatedness applies only among *females*. Hymenopteran sisters are unusually highly related ($r = $ ¾), but the relatedness of sisters and brothers is unusually low (¼); and if the queen's brood contains equal numbers of each sex the average worker/brood relatedness is only ½—the same as r for diploid siblings. So unless there has been some mechanism for assuring that more aid goes to the females than to the males of the queen's brood, the unusual ¾-relatedness of hymenopteran sisters cannot have been responsible for the frequent evolution of matrifilial societies in the Hymenoptera as Hamilton suggested (Trivers, unpubl.). Hamilton (1972) in fact discussed the point that this asymmetry in the relatedness of haplodiploid siblings should mean that workers would be comparatively unwilling to help rear brothers, and would be inclined to replace the queen's male-producing eggs with their own; but there is so far little evidence that workers do in fact channel more aid to the females of the immature brood.

These considerations place severe limitations on the situations in which the ¾-relatedness could have been important in hymenopteran social evolution. Not only would there have to have been temporal and spatial overlap of generations, but also a limitation to single matings on the part of females and separation of or discrimination between the male and female broods. One cannot rule out the possibility that these conditions were satisfied. Since eusociality (worker sterility) has arisen only a few times in all the history of all the many thousands of species of Hymenoptera, exceptional (improbable) conditions could very well have been involved. Even if multiple mating were to prove universal among *eusocial* Hymenoptera, it is conceivable that one or more of the several origins of eusociality among insects occurred in species already having single matings at that stage in their history. Indeed, multiple mating may have evolved secondarily in some social Hymenoptera to supply the extra sperms needed to fertilize the huge number of eggs produced by specialized queens. Spatial or temporal separation of the two sexes in the brood is also conceivable, although so far it is unknown in the few studied primitively social species. Workers do commonly lay (unfertilized) male-producing eggs in many social species. Information concerning this phenomenon has been recently reviewed by Wilson (1971), Lin and Michener (1972), and Hamilton (1972). Theoretically, given a perfect 50:50 sex ratio, all a worker has to do to capitalize on its 3/4-relatedness with its sisters is to lay one male egg, and thus raise her average relatedness with the brood slightly above that with her own offspring.

Lin and Michener (1972) construed the persistence of male production by workers to be evidence *against* kin selection, and concluded that "the larger the productivity of the joiner or worker, the less relevant is the coefficient of relationship to an understanding of the evolution of the worker caste" (p. 142). Their conclusion that eusocial colonies (by definition those having workers with reduced reproductivity) "without altruism are possible if male production by workers is important enough" (p. 132) involves the mistaken idea that the workers can be viewed as a group whose collective productivity can be summed and compared with that of the queen(s), the altruism of the sterile working workers somehow being cancelled out by the productivity of the others (for laying "workers" do not simultaneously work—Lin and Michener, 1972). Even if every worker is seen as reproducing during some period of her life, she could not recompense the potential offspring she lost in assisting the mother, unless the colony is visualized as somehow perfectly mutualistic, in which case it would not usually be called "eusocial."

Although the ¾-relatedness of hymenopteran sisters offers a dramatic hypothetical illustration of how kin selection can operate, it is unfortunate that Hamilton and others have allowed the whole case for kin selection in the social Hymenoptera to rest on this point. As has been pointed out repeatedly in this paper, kin selection involves not only relatedness but the benefit/cost ratio (K) of the changes in fitness incurred by beneficiary and donor. A discussion of multiple mating in highly social species is seen to be quite beside the point when one realizes that the number of times the mother mates is of little or no consequence to a daughter once she is sterile— even workers capable of laying eggs certainly have a greatly reduced individual reproductive capacity compared to that of their mothers, making K very high (if the altruist is completely sterile K approaches infinity). Thus, the more general kin-selection argument cannot be demolished by any of the above four arguments, since they all concern relatedness alone. Hamilton himself has not fully used the complete theory in its own defence. Although he has devoted much attention to factors that tend to raise relatedness, he has tended to neglect factors that would raise the benefit/cost ratio.

I believe it would be wise to replace the ¾-relatedness argument with a kin-selection hypothesis less heavily dependent on relatedness alone. It should consider factors that make altruism more profitable than selfishness even at $r = ¼$ (the lowest average r possible among offspring of a single mother), including such parameters as the potential (sacrificed) fitness or reproductive capacity of the altruistic worker, and the effect of her aid on the mother's reproduction. Individual differences in reproductive capacity among the members of a brood may have been of great significance in the evolution of worker sterility, as will be discussed below.

The Semisocial Hypothesis

Michener (1958) has suggested that "semisocial" groups, composed of differentially reproductive females of the same generation, have been important ancestors of the eusocial societies of bees, and has proposed the semisocial route to sociality as an alternative to the subsocial route (by which the original group is a single female and her offspring). This idea was originally proposed (Michener, 1958) in a form contradictory with the (later) genetical theory, involving as it did a "division of labor" among possibly unrelated females. However, in the examples cited by Michener (1958)—those for which sufficient geneological information and long-term individual histories could be inferred—a *reproductive* division of labor (as distinct from a non-reproductive one involving temporary specialization in foraging or guarding) appeared only among matrifilial societies or semisocial groups frequently consisting of sisters. Thus, at its most critical pass—the transition from selfish to altruistic behavior—the semisocial route does not differ from the subsocial route. Although the semisocial route is therefore not strictly an "alternative" to the subsocial route regarding the kind of group in which altruism actually originates, this hypothesis introduces two important points regarding the evolution of insect sociality: (1) that factors other than degree of relatedness, such as the necessity for cooperative defense against parasites and predators (Michener, 1958; Lin, 1964), probably favored group living and mutual beneficence with or without kinship; and (2) that such groups are common among the Hymenoptera and represent a class of pre-eusocial behavior different in important ways from isolated subsocial females, and hence offering a different situation in which social evolution might occur. Hamilton (1964b, 1972) has regarded the subsocial route as more likely than the semisocial, mainly on the basis of his objection to the suggestion of sociality among unrelated females (an aspect now less emphasized by Michener—see Lin and Michener, 1972); and Michener considers the "kin-selection" hypothesis (3/4-relatedness hypothesis) inadequate to explain altruism among semisocial groups of somewhat distant relatives (Lin and Michener, 1972). This "controversy" evaporates once it is realized that such factors as parasite-predator pressure raise the value of K and hence lower the value of r necessary for altruistic behavior by kin selection. So Michener's basic hypothesis in its present form (Lin and Michener, 1972) is not incompatible with the gentical theory.

Viewed in terms of the theory being presented here, mutualistic (cooperating) groups like those described by Michener represent one response (cooperation and reciprocity) to the same conditions (conditions producing difficulty for solitary individuals), which given a different population structure (family groups rather than more gentically diffuse aggregations) might produce a reproductive division of labor (altruism). One would expect that, given a group of selfish cooperators, the advantage of cooperating with relatives rather than nonrelatives and thereby of contributing simultaneously to self and kin might lead to a localization of families within the larger aggregation. This could set the scene for the evolution of a highly developed reproductive division of labor through kin selection (see Lin and Michener, 1972), maternal control, or both (Alexander, 1974—see below).

The Maternal-Control Hypothesis

Alexander (1974) has recently proposed a maternal-control hypothesis as an alternative to Hamilton's explanation of insect sociality. He argues that selection among reproductive females could favor using some offspring to help rear others in the same way that some mammals advantageously resorb some fetuses in order better to nourish others and that some insects use a portion of their eggs (trophic eggs) as food for older young. According to this hypothesis a sterile worker is, in effect, a grown-up trophic egg—it has been reared to adulthood but is likewise sacrificed in favor of its siblings; and mothers with some altruistic brood do better in competition than those who produce only selfish offspring. Major points supporting this hypothesis as applied to insects are as follows (after Alexander, 1974).

1 Maternal control solves the problem of the initial spread of altruism (because of the increased fitness of mothers with an altruistic brood), which cannot benefit an altruist by kin selection unless the beneficiary also carries the allele for altruism—a condition that would not hold for the original (mutant) altruist.

2 The origin of (diploid) termite eusociality, a "problem" for Hamilton's hypothesis because the ¾-relatedness hypothesis does not apply to diploid organisms, can be explained by supposing that the young originally stayed in the parental nest in the hope of using that costly resource for themselves, and thereby gave the parents (a monogamous pair) the opportunity to use them as helpers.

3 No insects are known to tend their offspring to adulthood and overlap with them without having sterile castes, a situation suggesting that it is selection on mother-offspring interactions rather than sibling interactions that is involved in eusociality.

4 Workers have apparently not evolved the ability to discriminate between sibs and half-sibs among the brood of a mother who has mated more than once, as they might be expected to under kin selection. The maternal control hypothesis predicts the absence of such discrimination, since all members of the brood have the same value from the mother's point of view.

5 The absence of male workers in the Hymenoptera is easily explained by selection on mothers, since female Hymenoptera can commonly control the sex of their offspring and hence produce as many as necessary of the sex best suited to altruism (in this case the females, hymenopteran males rarely contributing to the care of young).

6 Modes of caste determination among eusocial insects are evidence of maternal control, since they usually involve the direct or indirect influence of the queen during the preadult (larval) period.

7 The question (raised by Hamilton, 1972) of why the queen honeybee has a specialized sting that is used exclusively to kill a close relative (sister) can be explained by selection on the mother, who, once she has provided a certain number of workers, might find it more desirable to have only one daughter queen survive if that for some reason would increase the total reproductive efficiency of her descendents.

8 The faculative altruism of subordinate *Polistes* females which inhabit new spring nests (in the absence of the mother) can be explained if queens gain by producing daughters who cooperate in certain conditions at the expense of all but a single dominant reproducing queen (also a daughter) and thus can build new nests more swiftly. This situation offers an example of imposed altruism performed in the absence of the individual favored, for obviously the old (mother) queen need not be present at nest founding for such daughter altruism to evolve because of the superior reproduction of females having such broods.

Alexander (1974) has recently discussed Hamilton's explanations of various characteristics of eusocial behavior. He finds maternal manipulation a "more compelling" explanation. However, his discussion refers mainly to the ¾-relatedness hypothesis. If a broader view of kin selection is taken—one that comprehends changes in fitness, and not just relatedness—plausible kin-selection arguments can be provided on each of the above eight points, independent of the problematical ¾ -relatedness idea. The following parallel sets of arguments illustrate how parental control and kin selection are often suggested by exactly the same data.

1   The initial spread of altruism can be explained within the bounds of kin-selection theory if altruism is facultative and is directed only toward reproductively superior relatives, as seems to be the case in certain social wasps and bumblebees (see discussion of dominance relations, above). If the original (mutant) facultative altruist happens to be a superior reproductive individual (has a high potential classical fitness), her altruism would not be expressed phenotypically. She would produce a large brood of likewise facultatively altruistic young who could then engage in profitable facultative altruism among themselves, and thereby cause the allele to spread through the enhanced reproduction of beneficiaries. If she should happen to be a reproductively inferior individual (although not completely sterile), she would engage in temporary or part-time altruism toward superior relatives when $K > K_t$, while also producing her own smaller brood of young likely to bear the allele for facultative altruism. In the first case, the allele would be spread but not expressed by its original bearer; in the second case, it would be selected against for one generation only. Dominance interactions (see above) among cohabiting individuals could have been a preadaptation enabling facultative altruists to know when to give aid and to whom.

2   Kin selection on offspring would also favor altruistic aid to termite parents in the circumstances specified by Alexander. The threshold for advantageous altruism (K_t) is then low because the parents are monogamous and monogamy assures that all young are full siblings $(r_{AB,} = \frac{1}{2})$. The parent who already possesses a nest and mate (high potential benefit) is in a good position to capitalize on aid; and the offspring is in a relatively poor position to reproduce on its own, not having an established nest or mate, and therefore has little to lose by becoming at least temporarily altruistic.

3   An association between overlap of generations and sterile castes would likewise support a kin-selection interpretation, which also points to mother-offspring relations, not sibling interactions, as being of primary importance in the evolution of insect sociality (for the young of the worker's mother are more closely related to a worker than are the offspring of her siblings). [Actually, an overlap of generations without worker sterility is known to occur among wasps: *Macromeris violacea* and *Stenogaster depressigaster,* Williams, 1919; *Trigonopsis cameronii,* Eberhard, 1974; *Zethus miniatus,* West Eberhard, in prep., but that fact neither supports nor detracts from either hypothesis.]

4   The ability to make fine distinctions among variously related close relatives is not expected to be an inevitable consequence of kin selection, which should be able to produce a degree of altruism appropriate to to the average within-group relatedness. Inability to distinguish sibs from half-sibs, if it is observed, may simply indicate the difficulty of evolving a dependable discriminating cue (worker/brood relatedness even with multiple mating varies *continuously* from 0 to 1.0). Such discrimination is possible even with maternal control of altruisim as long as it does not hurt the mother (i.e., as long as the entire brood is still adequately cared for). So presence or absence of this ability does not really distinguish between the two hypotheses.

5 The threshold for becoming a mother-aiding altruist by kin selection is twice as high for males as for females ($K_t = 2.0$ and 1.0, respectively); and the threshold value is less likely to be reached by males because of their relative lack of preadaptions for the efficient performance of aid (worker duties). It seems likely that hymenopteran males could develop worker-like behavior if it were to their advantage, in terms of inclusive fitness, to do so. I have seen male Hymenoptera carry out every common worker duty except bringing prey and building material to the nest. *Polistes* males forage (for themselves) at flowers and return to the nest site, feed larvae, and fan (part of nest temperature regulation) (West Eberhard, 1969); *Trigonopsis* males stationed on a nest will chase approaching predators (ants) (Eberhard, 1974); and the male of an unidentified *Trypoxylon* species applied mud (brought by a female) to the nest (pers. obs.). Alexander (1974) suggests that a "genetic revolution" would be required to make hymenopteran males into workers, but moderate reform might be sufficient.

6 Maternal control of caste in *eusocial* species does not eliminate the possibility that worker altruism *originated* by daughter choice (kin selection), since once worker sterility or partial sterility had evolved the daughter would be trapped by her low personal reproductive capacity into agreeing with the best interests of her mother regarding caste ratios (K for workerness from the sterile daughter's point of view stays well above K_t—the denominator of K approaches 0—as long as the queen, whose offspring are the daughter's closest available relatives, is reproducing). Furthermore, K_t for imposing mother-aiding altruism on sisters is the same (0.5) as it is for imposing altruism on daughters from the queen's point of view, so a queen and her workers have no conflict of interest regarding the situations in which brood females should be made into workers rather than queens.

7 When factors other than close relatedness are considered, one would not expect closely matched superbeneficiaries such as honeybee queens to behave altruistically toward each other even if they are sisters. It is in the best interests of a highly specialized reproductive individual, poorly equipped to give aid, to reproduce on her own; and her own offspring are worth more to her ($r = \frac{1}{2}$) than are her sister's offspring ($r = \frac{3}{8}$).

8 A kin selection explanation of subordinate workerness in *Polistes* has already been discussed above (see West Eberhard, 1969).

Both sets of explanations seem tenable. It is difficult to choose between them because the conditions favoring each hypothesis overlap (see Table 1), and the two kinds of selection are not mutually exclusive (they can operate either alone or together to produce the same result). One conclusion that can be drawn from the above parallel analyses is that the wishes of mother and daughter often coincide. It is possible, at least theoretically, to define exactly when they agree (when K is less than 0.5 or is greater than 1.0); and also to show that under certain conditions (when K falls between 0.5 and 1.0), there is a conflict of interest between them, selection on the mother favoring daughter altruism and selection on the daughter opposing it.

The problem of a mother-daughter conflict of interest is critical in understanding the evolution of insect sociality. Unless there is a saltatory increase in K, conflict is inevitable as K changes from the low values that favor solitary or selfish reproduction to the higher values that favor altruism. Such a stage must have occurred during the multiple evolutions of insect sociality, and a similar situation is created in the normal ontogeny of colonies if a queen's reproductive powers decline as she grows old. In theory, selection on daughters can favor an escape from maternally imposed altruism when there is a conflict of interest. In practice, escape is virtually impossible to demonstrate, since knowing whether to call a given instance of behavior (e.g., oviposition by workers on the maternal nest) "escape from maternal control" or "agreement between mother and daughter" depends on knowing the *precise* value of K for that situation (0.51 would give one answer, 0.50 the other), and the calculation of K involves such unmeasurable parameters as the fitness a worker *would have* if she reproduced on her own, or that a particular queen would have without aid.

The interpretation of male production by workers illustrates the complexity of this problem. It is common (some say almost universal—see Hamilton, 1972; Lin and Michener, 1972) for workers to lay eggs, even among highly social insects. Hamilton (1972) cited this as evidence of worker control of altruism, and Alexander (1974) has shown how it could occur by selection on mothers. Either one or both interpretations could be right, depending on the value of K in a given case. When K is greater than 2.0, male production by the mother is favored by selection on both mother and daughter. This condition—the daughter's aid enabling a queen to produce more than twice as many males as the daughter could—must often be met in eusocial colonies, considering the relatively poor trophic and reproductive condition of most unfertilized females (workers), which characteristically have lower dominance or food-getting status (or both), reduced fat reserves, and rudimentary ovaries compared to queens (in wasps, Richards and Richards, 1951; in ants, Wilson, 1971; in bees, Michener, 1969). At values of K between 0.5 and 2.0, there would be disagreement between mother and daughter regarding which should produce males, each preferring to do it herself; and at K lower than 0.5, male production by workers would be favored by selection on both mothers and daughters, for example, if the mother's reproductive powers were declining severely (as might occur in ageing females), or if the available workers had brought the mother (queen) to her maximum possible reproductive rate.

Lin and Michener (1972) pointed out another context in which selection on queens might sometimes promote male production by workers. It would shorten the generation time for the expression of male-transmitted genes and hence increase the rate of evolution (the speed of responding to changed conditions) of the queen's male descendents. However, their added suggestion that the queen "will transmit more genes to subsequent generations by devoting that productivity to diploid females rather than haploid males" (p. 154) is erroneous. Although it is true that a diploid female has twice as many genes as a haploid male, only half of them come from the queen, the other (paternal) half coming from the queen's mate.

Interpretation of worker oviposition is further complicated by the fact that workers, being unmated females, produce only males. Hence the advantageousness of doing so (and to the mothers of allowing it) is affected not only by the reproductive condition of the queen, but also by the sex ratio in the population as a whole, and the fact that daughter-produced males compete with the queen's own sons (see Alexander, 1974). One situation in which worker oviposition should commonly occur by selection on both mothers and daughters is following the death or disappearance of the mother queen, when worker-brood relatedness, dropping from ½ to ⅜, makes daughter altruism less desirable from both points of view.

I know of at least one example in the social Hymenoptera which seems to indicate that the daughters behave according to their own advantage rather than the mother's. Following the death or disappearance of a queen *Polistes canadensis,* the daughters fight among themselves for possession of the colony, and cause an almost complete cessation of reproductive activity (egg-laying and nest enlargement) for as long as five weeks, after which the defeated females go off and found new colonies (West Eberhard, 1969). Evidently the stakes are high from the daughters' point of view, inasmuch as starting a new colony may be relatively risky and expensive, whereas conquest of the old colony means inheriting both a nest and a staff of workers; but the mother would clearly be at an advantage were any one of the evidently closely matched daughters to take over the original nest, while the others began new ones without delay. (A staunch maternal manipulationist could possibly argue that the mother would benefit enough by the dominant female taking over the nest that selection in her favor would justify or compensate for such long and costly fighting).

This example raises the question of how far into future generations maternal control could be expected to operate. Projection of a parent's best interests into the future would certainly be limited by lack of foresight into changing conditions, which must often make it advantageous to leave even immediate descendents a wider range of choice and flexibility. However, there are clear examples of parents manipulating their broods in ways that do tend to maximize production of grandchildren rather than of offspring, e.g., the fattening of reproductive offspring beyond the degree necessary for mere survival, so as to make them superior reproductives (of grandchildren) even when that means rearing fewer of them. This raises the further general question of just what it is that selection maximizes—whether number of children, grandchildren, great-grandchildren, or nth descendents (see Alexander, 1974)—and it shows another way in which classical fitness is an inadequate measure of an individual's total reproductive (genetic) contribution. Inclusive fitness can include effects on future generations but does not specify how many generations should be included. In threshold cases of hymenopteran sociality there must sometimes be a reduction in mean fitness of the offspring—a paradox for classical theory (Hamilton, pers. commun.).

Conclusion: A Synthesis

Although the above hypotheses are presented by their respective authors as separate and independent theories, all three of them are perhaps best seen as appreciations of historically neglected factors in the evolution of insect sociality—as new insights, not as mutually exclusive theories. There is no reason, as I have argued, why Hamiltonian kin selection, Michenerian mutualism, and Alexanderian parental manipulation cannot all have contributed simultaneously or sequentially to produce the evolution of sterile castes; and it seems fruitless, *in making generalizations,* to argue in favor of one idea to the exclusion of the others (although this may be an important question in discussing a particular well-studied case). Rather, it seems necessary to acknowledge that all three sets of hypothetical factors could have operated, either alone or in some combination, especially in view of the fact that the several origins of worker sterility could each have arisen in a different combination of circumstances, making a uniform explanation impossible.

How, then, are we to visualize the steps leading to eusociality in insects, given this set of three possibly interacting hypotheses? Beginning with a solitary female who does not overlap in time or space with her adult offspring, four kinds of primitive groups of adults might conceivably form: a patrifilial group (parents and adult offspring), formed when parents become longlived and adult offspring remain in the parental nest; a filial group, of adult siblings remaining together without the parents; an extended family group, containing variously related adults who tend to stay in the same place generation after generation; and a "semisocial" group of non-relatives (or quite distant relatives) occupying the same nest or nesting area.

Unreciprocated reproductive altruism of the kind found in eusocial insects (worker sterility) can evolve only if the beneficiary is a relative or group of relatives (see Alexander, 1974). This will ordinarily mean that it originates among relatives. So the formation of patrifilial, and filial, and extended family groups can be considered preadaptations for eusociality. What about semisocial groups of non-relatives? The only kinds of beneficence that can evolve in such groups are reciprocal altruism and cooperation. Could mutualism among non-relatives ever represent a significant step toward eusociality? I think it could, since the occurrence of cooperation and reciprocal altruism is likely to lead to the formation of subgroups of relatives in which cheating is less important, and this, in turn, could lead to the evolution of unreciprocated altruism by kin selection or parental manipulation. So, if the primitive group is composed of mutualistic non-relatives, an extra step is involved in reaching the stage in which eusociality can evolve.

Whether by maternal control or daughter choice, altruism performed unequally by different members of a filial, patrifilial, or other kin group is only likely to evolve if it is the temporarily or permanently inferior reproductives in the group who become altruistic. In the case of maternal control, mothers for whom offspring with inferior reproductive potential are effective altruists are likely to win over those for whom superior reproductives are sacrificed, or for whom the altruism is performed irrespective of reproductive capacity. Likewise, in the case of altruism by daughter choice, altruistic dedication of superior reproductives to aiding inferior reproductives would be highly disadvantageous to the altruists and possibly even to the beneficiaries (if close relatives) and there should be some mechanism guaranteeing that it not occur (see discussion of the function of dominance interactions, above). Thus, *a linkage of reproductive inferiority and altruistic behavior is expected to evolve* especially among social organisms in which altruism is very costly in terms of personal fitness (in contrast to low cost altruism, which is theoretically more likely in well-off individuals—see above). Exceptions might occur during emergencies, e.g., when the mother's life or a large portion of her reproductive investment (such as nest, or brood) is endangered unless help is recruited, even if that means the sacrificing or volunteering of a superior individual. But inferior ones should still become altruistic first.

Differences in reproductive capacity among the members of a brood may thus represent an important preadaptation for eusociality. Such differences could originate because of incidental or regularly occurring differences in diet, environment (temperature, or other seasonal conditions), genetic makeup, social conditions (e.g., sibling competition) during ontogeny, or various combinations of these. Or they could be the result of maternal manipulation of these factors, as Alexander (1974) has suggested. Whatever their origin, these differences could have the effect of forcing altruism by daughter choice (kin selection), through lowering the daughter's personal potential fitness so that it is more advantageous to her to become a helper (either of sisters or mother) rather than to reproduce on her own. Thus eusociality could sometimes be the product of a combination of parental manipulation and kin selection, initiated by maternal manipulation of reproductive capacity and concluded by the daughter's subsequent adaptation (as a helper) to her altered capacity for independent reproduction.

Kin selection, mutualism, and parental manipulation may not represent an exhaustive list of the possible contexts in which eusociality can evolve. One obvious additional possibility is that altruism might sometimes be imposed by selection operating on relatives other than parents, e.g., siblings or aunts, as already discussed in the section on imposed altruism.

A LIMIT TO SELFISHNESS

The majority of social interactions, even among close kin, are probably competitive rather than beneficent in nature. Indeed, as Alexander (1974) has pointed out, an individual's closest relatives are his closest competitors because of their proximity and dependence on the same, often limited, resources.

Although the present discussion has dealt mainly with beneficent social behavior, this biological view of sociality suggests certain limits to selfishness, as Hamilton (1964a, b; 1970) has already pointed out. Ecological and social (intragroup) competition among individuals should follow the same rule applied to beneficent behavior. It will be selected for if it contributes to the inclusive fitness of the performer. Accordingly, selfish behavior that causes excessive harm to a neighbor, or exacts more than the performer can use is selected against—precisely, when the kinship component of inclusive fitness becomes negative and exceeds the personal benefit of the act. Expectations regarding harmful and spiteful behavior have been formally considered by Hamilton (1970) and shown to conform generally to the predictions of the genetical theory.

LIST OF LITERATURE

Alexander, R. D. 1974. The evolution of social behavior. *Ann. Rev. Syst. Ecol.,* 4:325–383.

Darwin, C. D. 1859. *On the Origin of Species. A Facsimile of the First Edition* (1967). Harvard Univ. Press, Cambridge.

Eberhard, W. G. 1974. The natural history and behaviour of *Trigonopsis cameronii* Kohl (Sphecidae). *Trans. Roy. Ent. Soc. London,* 125(3):295–328.

Emerson, A. E. 1959. Social insects. *Ecyclopaedia Britannica,* 20:871–878.

Hamilton, W. D. 1964a. The genetical theory of social behaviour. I. *J. Theoret. Biol.,* 7:1–16.

———. 1964b. The gentical theory of social behaviour. II. *J. Theoret. Biol.,* 7:17–52.

———. 1970. Selfish and spiteful behaviour in an evolutionary model. *Nature,* 228:1218–1220.

———. 1972. Altruism and related phenomena, mainly in the social insects. *Ann. Rev. Syst. Ecol.,* 3:193–232.

Lin, N. 1964. Increased parasitic pressure as a major factor in the evolution of social behavior in halictine bees. *Insectes Soc.,* 11:187–192.

Lin, N., and C. D. Michener. 1972. Evolution of sociality in insects. *Quart. Rev. Biol.,* 47:131–159.

Michener, C. D. 1958. The evolution of social behavior in bees. *Proc. Tenth Int. Congr. Ent.,* Montreal, 2: 441-447.

———. 1969. Comparative social behavior of bees. *Ann. Rev. Entomol.,* 14:299–342.

Richards, O. W. and M. J. Richards. 1951. Observations on the social wasps of South America (Hymenoptera, Vespidae). *Trans. Roy. Ent. Soc. London,* 102:1–167.

West Eberhard, M. J. 1969. The social biology of polistine wasps. *Univ. Mich. Mus. Zool. Misc. Publ.,* 140:1–101.

Wheeler, W. M. 1911. The ant-colony as an organism. *J. Morphol.,* 22:307–325.

———. 1928. *The Social Insects: Their Origin and Evolution.* Kegan Paul, Trench, Trubner and Co., London.

Williams, F. X. 1919. Phillippine wasp studies. *Bull. Exp. Sta. Hawaiian Sugar Planters' Assoc.,* No. 114:1–186.

Wilson, E. O. 1971. *The Insect Societies.* Belknap Press, Cambridge.

Haplodiploidy and the Evolution of the Social Insects

Robert L. Trivers
Hope Hare
Museum of Comparative Zoology, Harvard University

In 1964 Hamilton (*1*) proposed a general theory for the way in which kinship is expected to affect social behavior. An important modification of Darwin's theory of natural selection, it specified the conditions under which an organism is selected to perform an altruistic act toward a related individual. It likewise specified the conditions under which an individual is selected to forego a selfish act because of the act's negative consequences on the reproductive success of relatives. Broad in scope, the theory provided an explanation for most instances of altruistic behavior, and it promised to provide the basis for a biological theory of the family.

Although many facts from diploid organisms (and some quantitative data) are explained by Hamilton's theory (*2–4*), the theory has received its main support from the study of the social insects, in particular the social Hymenoptera (ants, bees, wasps). Because species of the Hymenoptera are haplodiploid (males, haploid; females, diploid), there exist asymmetries in the way in which individuals are related to each other, so that predictions based on these asymmetries can be tested in the absence of quantitative measures of reproductive success. A set of such predictions has been advanced (*1, 5, 6*), but heavy reliance on pairwise comparisons of degrees of relatedness has obscured some of the more striking implications of haplodiploidy. These emerge when kinship theory is combined with Fisher's sex ratio theory (*7–9*) in such a way as to predict, under a variety of conditions, the ratio of investment in the two sexes, a social parameter which can be measured with sufficient precision to test the proposed theory. Such a test leads us, in turn, to a new theory concerning the evolution of worker-queen relations in the social Hymenoptera. If the work we describe is approximately valid, it lends support to the view that social behavior has evolved not only in response to a large array of ecologically defined selection pressures (*4, 5, 10*) but also according to some simple, underlying social and genetical principles.

Supported by the Harry Frank Guggenheim Foundation. For the use of specimens we thank M. V. Brian, A. Buschinger, G. Eickwort, Y. Hirashima, D. H. Janzen, K. V. Krombein, O. Lomholdt, C. D. Michener, M. Talbot, P. Torchio, and E. O. Wilson. For the use of unpublished data we thank M. V. Brian, A. Buschinger, G. Eickwort, G. W. Elmes, D. H. Janzen, K. V. Krombein, O. Lomholdt, L. Passera, W. A. Sands, M. Talbot, and P. Torchio. We thank K. V. Krombein, M. Talbot, and E. O. Wilson for generous and unstinting aid. For additional help we thank W. L. Brown, B. Hölldobler, S. Hyman, P. Hurd, J. Pickering, M. L. Roonwal, J. Scott, L. S. Trivers, and K. Strickler Vinson. For detailed comments on this article we thank R. D. Alexander, G. Eickwort and K. Eickwort, C. D. Michener, and P. Torchio.

This article is dedicated to Ernst Mayr on the occasion of his retirement from the Harvard faculty.

HAMILTON'S KINSHIP THEORY

An altruistic act is defined as one that harms the organism performing the act while benefiting some other individual, harm and benefit being measured in terms of reproductive success (RS). Genes inducing such behavior in their bearers will be positively selected if the recipient of the altruism is sufficiently closely related so that the genes themselves enjoy a net benefit. The conditional probability that a second individual has a given gene if a related individual is known to have the gene is called the degree of relatedness, or r (*11*). For natural selection to favor an altruistic act directed at a relative, the benefit of the act times the altruist's r to the relative must be greater than the cost of the act. Likewise, an individual is selected to forego a selfish act if its cost to a relative times the relevant r is greater than the benefit to the actor. The rules for calulating r's are straightforward in both diploid and haplodiploid species, even under inbreeding (*12*). If in calculating the selective value of a gene one computes its effect on the RS of the individual bearing it and adds to this its effects on the RS of related individuals, devalued by the relevant r's, then one has computed what Hamilton (*1*) calls inclusive fitness. Kinship theory asserts that each living creature is selected to attempt throughout its lifetime to maximize its own inclusive fitness.

In sexually reproducing species the offspring's inclusive fitness and the parent's are maximized in similar, but not identical, ways (*1, 6, 8*). This has the obvious consequence that parent and offspring are expected to show conflict over each other's altruistic and egoistic tendencies. Neither party is expected to see its interests fully realized, and data on both the existence and form of parent-offspring conflict appear to support this view (*6, 8, 13*). Since a human being typically grows to maturity dependent on a family whose members divide among themselves many resources critical to reproduction, the processes of human psychological development are expected to be strongly affected by kin interactions and designed strongly to affect such interactions. For this reason, kinship theory appears to be a necessary component of any functional theory of human psychological development.

DEGREES OF RELATEDNESS IN HAPLODIPLOID SPECIES

The social Hymenoptera account for nearly 2 percent of all described animal species, and they are characterized by a series of unusual traits. (i) They display extreme forms of altruism through the repeated evolution of sterile or near-sterile castes of workers. These workers typically help their mothers to reproduce (eusociality), but sometimes work for their sisters (semisociality) (*14*) or less related individuals. (ii) The altruism is sex limited: only females are workers, all males are reproductives. (iii) There are striking lapses of altruism, especially worker-queen conflict over the laying of male-producing eggs and worker-male conflict over the amount of investment males receive. (iv) All species are haplodiploid, that is, females develop from fertilized eggs and are diploid, while males develop from unfertilized eggs and are haploid. Hamilton (*1*) was the first to realize that all four traits might be related and that haplodiploidy could be used to explain the other three. Especially in his 1972 article (*6*) he demonstrated how 200 years of scientific work on the social insects stood to be reorganized around his kinship theory.

In haplodiploid species every sperm cell produced by a male has all his genes, while each egg produced by a female has (as in a diploid species) only half of her genes. Because any daughter of a male contains a full set of his genes, sisters related through both parents are unusually closely related ($r = \frac{3}{4}$). The most important r's, under outbreeding, are summarized in Table 1. By pairing relationships that differ in r, a number of predictions have been advanced, and some of these seem at first to explain the unusual traits of the social Hymenoptera. (i) A female is more related to her full sisters than she is to her own children, she "therefore easily evolves an inclination to work in the maternal nest rather than start her own" (*6*). (ii) By contrast, a male is more related to his daughters ($r = 1$) than to his siblings ($r = \frac{1}{2}$). "Thus, a male is not expected to evolve worker instincts" (*6*). (iii) A female is more related to her own sons than to her brothers. "Thus, workers are expected to be comparatively reluctant to 'work' on the rearing of brothers, and if circumstances allow, inclined to replace the queen's male eggs with their own" (*6*). Since females are more closely related to their sisters than to their brothers, they are expected to be "more altruistic in their behavior toward their sisters and less so toward their brothers" (*5*).

That this system of pairwise comparisons needs refinement is apparent when both sexes are treated together. For example, a female is related to her sisters by $\frac{3}{4}$, but she is related to her brothers by only $\frac{1}{4}$; if she does equal work on the two sexes, as expected under outbreeding (*6, 9*), then her average effective r to her siblings ($\frac{1}{2}$) is the same as that to her offspring. In short, haplodiploidy in itself introduces no bias toward the evolution of eusociality. For this reason, Hamilton (*6*) added the requirement that "the sex ratio or some ability to discriminate allows the worker to work mainly in rearing sisters," and he pointed out that inbreeding should be accompanied in haplodiploid species by female-biased sex ratios [or, better put, by female-biased ratios of investment (*9*)]. As long as F, the inbreeding coeffi-

Table 1 Degrees of Relatedness Between a Female (or a Male) and Her (or His) Close Relatives in a Haplodiploid Species, Assuming Complete Outbreeding. For the Effects of Inbreeding See Hamilton (6).

Relation	Female	Male
Mother	1/2	1 ⎫ av. = 1/2
Father	1/2	0 ⎭
Full sister	3/4 ⎫ av. = 1/2	1/2
Brother	1/4 ⎭	1/2
Daughter	1/2	1 ⎫ av. = 1/2
Son	1/2	0 ⎭

cient, is larger than 0, a female is more related to a daughter than to a son by a factor of $(1 + 3F)/(1 + F)$, so that she is selected to produce a similarly biased ratio of investment (6). Since this unique effect of inbreeding does not render eusociality more likely—a female's average effective r to her siblings remains, under inbreeding, the same as that to her offspring (15)—we suggest that Hamilton's requirement be amended to read: the asymmetrical degrees of relatedness in haplodiploid species predispose daughters to the evolution of eusocial behavior, provided that they are able to capitalize on the asymmetries, either by producing more females than the queen would prefer, or by gaining partial or complete control of the genetics of male production. The logic for this requirement is given below, along with some of its consequences.

CAPITALIZING ON THE ASYMMETRICAL DEGREES OF RELATEDNESS

In haplodiploid species, a female is symmetrically related to her own offspring (by sex of offspring) but asymmetrically related to her siblings, while a male is symmetrically related to his siblings but asymmetrically related to his own offspring. It is the male parent and the female offspring who can exploit the asymmetrical r's (for personal gain in inclusive fitness); but there is not much scope for such behavior in males (16), while the females can exploit the r's by investing resources disproportionately in sisters compared to brothers or by investing in sisters and sons (or sisters and nephews) instead of sons and daughters.

   1 *Skewing the colony's investment toward reproductive females and away from males.* Imagine a solitary, outbred species in which a newly adult female can choose between working to rear her own offspring and working to rear her mother's (but not both). Assuming that such a female is equally efficient at the two kinds of work, she will enjoy an increase in inclusive fitness by raising siblings in place of offspring as long as she invests more in her sisters than in her brothers—thereby trading, so to speak, r's of ¼ for r's of ¾. For example, by working only on sisters instead of offspring, her initial gain in inclusive fitness would be 50 percent per unit invested. Were this altruism to spread such that all reproductives each generation are reared by their sisters, in a ratio controlled by the sisters, we expect three times as much to be invested in females as in males, for at this ratio of investment (1:3) the expected RS of a male is three times that of a female, per unit investment, exactly canceling out the workers' greater relatedness to their sisters. Were the mother to control the ratio of investment, it would equilibrate at 1:1, so that in eusocial species in which all reproductives are produced by the queen but reared by their sisters, strong mother-daughter conflict is expected regarding the ratio of investment, and a measurement of the ratio of investment is a measure of the relative power of the two parties (17).
   2 *Denying to the queen the production of males.* Imagine a solitary outbred species in which a newly adult female can choose between working to rear some of

her own offspring and some of her mother's. Other things being equal, she would prefer to rear sons and sisters. A second female who had to choose between solitary life and helping this sister would choose the latter, since she would then trade r's of ½ for r's of ¾ and ⅜. The mother would benefit by this arrangement, since she would gain daughters in place of granddaughters, but she would benefit more if she could induce daughters to work for her without producing any sons of their own, so that strong worker-queen conflict is expected over who lays the male-producing eggs.

Likewise, there should be conflict between the workers over who produces male eggs, but such conflict is expected to be less intense than similar sister-sister conflict in diploid species. Were the arrangement to spread, such that in each generation all female reproductives are daughters of the queen and all males are her grandsons (by laying workers), then if the nonlaying workers control the ratio of investment, we expect a 1:1 ratio. Although a worker is twice as related to a sister (¾) as to a nephew (⅜), a male is in turn twice as valuable, per unit investment, as a female reproductive. This is because he will father female reproductives ($r = 1$) and males (by a laying worker) ($r = ½$), while a female will (like her mother) produce female reproductives ($r = ½$) and males by laying workers ($r = ¼$). Since (¾) (½ + ¼) = (⅜) (1 + ½), the workers' preferred ratio of investment is 1:1 (*18*). It is trivial to show that a queen also prefers a 1:1 ratio of investment, but if laying workers control the ratio of investment, then we expect a 4:3 ratio (since a laying worker is related to her sons by ½ and to her sisters by ¾). The important general point to bear in mind is that laying workers introduce an extra meiotic event into the production of males, and this extra event automatically raises the value of a male relative to a female reproductive.

3 *The intermediate cases.* When some fraction, p, of the males in each generation is produced by the queen, and the remainder, $1 - p$, by laying workers, then the equilibrial ratios of investment can be calculated as long as one assumes that p remains relatively constant from one generation to the next and that within a colony individuals prefer to allocate resources to the two sexes according to their average r to members of the two sexes. With these two assumptions, it is relatively easy to show (*19*) that under queen control the equilibrial ratio of investment, x, results when

$$x = \frac{(3-p)(1+p)}{(3+p)}$$

while under worker control it results when

$$x = \frac{(3-p)^2}{3(3+p)}$$

and under laying worker control when

$$x = \frac{2(3-p)(2-p)}{3(3+p)}$$

The three competing optimums are presented in Fig. 1. Even if the queen produces as few as one-third of the males, there is a substantial difference between expected ratios depending on who is assumed to control that ratio. Once the queen produces at least two-thirds of the males, workers prefer a ratio of investment of at least 1:2.

4 *The effects of inbreeding.* The above considerations are modified slightly under inbreeding. As long as $F < 1$, the relevant r's remain asymmetrical so that daughters can exploit them as they can under outbreeding. But inbreeding does reduce the asymmetries so that the payoffs associated with the various options become more alike as F approaches 1 (*6*). This means that the higher the value of F, the less likely is the evolution of eusocial behavior. At $F = 1$ and $p = 1$ (that is, complete inbreeding and complete maternal control of male egg production), both the workers and the queen prefer 1:2 ratios of investment, and no conflict is expected over any of the colony's activities. For $p = 1$, the equilibrial ratios of investment are given as a function of differing values of F in Fig. 2. The important point regarding ratios of investment is that such ratios are never expected to be more female biased than 1:2 on the effects of inbreeding alone. All values between 1:2 and 1:3 must reflect worker performances for sisters over brothers. Values more female biased than 1:3 are only expected where extreme patterns of dispersal occur (*9*).

Although Hamilton has given us an admirable treatment of the possible role of inbreeding in the evolution of the social Hymenoptera (*6*), we believe its usual role has been negligible, so that the assumption of outbreeding is usually valid. Because the strong selection pressures for producing diverse young act against inbreeding in the same way in which they act against parthenogenesis (*20*), outbreeding should, like sexual reproduction, have strong positive value in most species. In addition, outbreeding is more easily associated with eusociality than is inbreeding, so that the solitary Hymenoptera should typically show larger values of F than the social species. Most of the evidence we shall later present is consistent with this view of inbreeding.

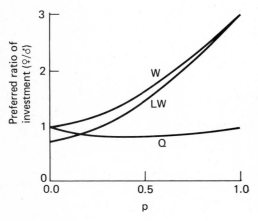

Figure 1 The preferred ratio of investment within eusocial Hymenoptera colonies for the three interested parties, the queen (*Q*), a laying worker (*LW*), and the nonlaying workers (*W*), as a function of the fraction of male-producing eggs laid by the queen (*p*), where the remainder are laid by a single laying worker. Note that queen-worker disagreement over the ratio of investment increases as *p* approaches 1.

5   *The early evolution of eusociality.*   Imagine for a moment that daughters are unable to reproduce within their mother's nest, so that they can choose between working there and rearing their own offspring. As pointed out above, they should naturally choose to work for their mother as long as they can preferentially invest in their sisters. Of course the spread of such a preference for sisters should naturally lead to a female-biased ratio of investment, and such a biased ratio raises the value of males, thereby altering the payoffs associated with the daughters' options. The precise genetical analysis is both tedious and complex. Instead, by imagining that the ratio of investment in our incipiently eusocial species is undergoing a steady change, it is easy to give an approximate outline of the relevant selection pressures.

Initially, a female-biased ratio of investment favors mothers who increase the number of their sons, but such behavior should select for workers who respond to sex ratios facultatively, working only when their mothers agree, in effect, to specialize in the production of daughters. As the ratio of investment passes the 1:1.5 mark,

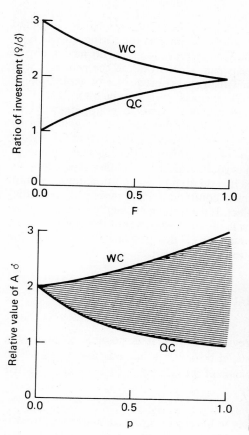

Figure 2   The equilibrial ratio of investment as a function of inbreeding coefficient, *F*, assuming that the queen lays all of the male-producing eggs. Abbreviations: *QC*, queen control of the ratio of investment; *WC*, worker control.

Figure 3   The relative value of a male (based on his expected genetic contribution to future generations) compared to the value of a female, per unit investment, as a function of *p*, depending on whether the queen controls the ratio of investment (*QC*), the nonlaying workers control the ratio of investment (*WC*), or the ratio of investment is jointly controlled (shaded area). Only under the unlikely assumption of complete queen control of the ratio of investment (and male production) is the value of a male, per unit investment, equal to that of a female.

a selection pressure appears for workers to work on sons rather than sisters, either on their own or (if we relax our initial requirement) within the maternal nest. If this does not stop the biasing process, the ratio of investment may pass 1:2 at which point workers are favored to concentrate on nephews in preference to sisters, intensifying selection for a return to less biased ratios. In short, one never expects a 1:3 ratio of investment as an early consequence of a eusocial trend. Instead, one expects that a polymorphism will naturally develop; some large, strifeless nests will specialize in the production of female reproductives and many solitary and small semisocial nests will specialize in the production of males. Such a polymorphism gives to eusocial colonies the evolutionary time to evolve the efficiencies which may eliminate entirely solitary nests in favor of large nests which produce the female reproductives and all the males by a mixture of queen and laying worker contributions.

A second consequence of the imagined early polymorphism is the sharp reduction in the value of males produced in the previous generation. Imagine that fertilized queens overwinter singly and begin new nests in the spring. Some produce daughters who are destined to remain with their mothers to work on rearing female reproductives. Others produce daughters destined to produce sons of their own. Because males are produced from unfertilized eggs, the polymorphism has rendered males superfluous in the first spring generation. As long as the spring queens typically live long enough to produce all the female reproductives, no new sperm is required in the spring and hence all queens can concentrate on the production of daughters to the virtual exclusion of sons. This trivial consequence of haplodiploidy is well documented for so-called primitively eusocial bees (see below).

6   *Summary.*   It appears that there are two, partly overlapping ways by which haplodiploid daughters may be expected to evolve eusocial behavior. Either of these ways tends to bias the ratio of investment toward females, so that this theory can be tested by finding out whether ratios of investment in the eusocial Hymenoptera are typically female biased compared to such ratios in the solitary Hymenoptera. So far as we know, no other theory makes this prediction. In addition, under certain conditions 1:3 ratios are expected to be fairly common, so that more precise predictions can be tested along with the main effect. If inbreeding in usually a minor factor, then the most important variable to know is the relative power of the queen and the workers to affect the two parameters over which disagreement is expected: the frequency of laying workers and the ratio of investment.

FUNDAMENTAL BIAS BY SEX IN SOCIAL BEHAVIOR OF HYMENOPTERA

With the analysis developed in the previous section, it is possible to present a consistent set of predictions regarding social behavior in haplodiploid species. The most important predictions, along with some of the relevant evidence, are presented here.

1   If and only if workers are assumed to be able to capitalize on the asymmetrical r's in haplodiploid species, does one expect in these species a bias toward

eusociality (the evolution of worker castes). If females do not respond appropriately to the asymmetrical r's, then their average effective r to their siblings will be the same as that to their own offspring. But if they respond in either of the two ways outlined above, their average r to their siblings will rise above that to their offspring. In short, a bias toward eusociality in the haplodiploid Hymenoptera is contingent upon the discriminatory capacities of the workers. The expectation of this bias does not depend on the assumption that the first workers showed appropriate discriminatory behavior; as long as workers evolved such behavior, their working was more likely to remain adaptive (in the face of fluctuating conditions). Once eusociality appears, it is more likely to endure in haplodiploid than diploid species.

Although species of diploid insects are apparently far more numerous than species of haplodiploid insects, eusociality has evolved only once (the termites) in diploid insects but more than 11 times independently in the Hymenoptera (*5, 10*). Incipient eusociality, in which an individual helps its parents for one or more years but not usually for life, has evolved repeatedly in mammals but with no bias toward female helpers. In birds, helpers at the nest are usually, but not always, males (*21*), presumably because the expected RS of a young male is typically less than that of his same-aged sister (*22*). Helpers in social carnivores may be male or female (*23, 24*).

2   The same bias toward eusociality can be demonstrated assuming multiple insemination of the queen (compared to multiple insemination in diploid organisms). If the queen is inseminated twice equally, then the average r between a female and her sister will be ½ and between a female and her brother, ¼. The average of these two will be ⅜, which is the same average r between siblings in a diploid species, given the same pattern of insemination. For any multiple insemination, it is trivial to show that a female's average r to her siblings is the same in haplodiploid as in diploid species. But females can still capitalize on the asymmetrical r's. Multiple inseminations remove this possibility only if each daughter is fathered by a different, unrelated male, and if workers are unable to produce any sons. (This same extreme requirement is necessary if the predictions that follow are also to be invalidated through multiple inseminations.) It is, of course, obvious that multiple inseminations render the evolution of worker habits less likely in both haplodiploid and diploid species.

No data exist which would permit one to compare the frequency of multiple inseminations in diploid and haplodiploid insects. What data exist suggest that multiple insemination is infrequent in both groups. In addition, it appears likely that multiple insemination has evolved in the social Hymenoptera as a response to eusociality: a social insect queen may produce tens of millions of workers in her lifetime, overtaxing the spermatogenic capacity of a single male (*1, 25*). As long as there is a tendency for sperm to clump according to father, as expected (*26*), there will be a tendency, despite the multiple insemination, for r's between sisters within a colony at any moment to be near ¾. The important point is that multiple insemination should not be treated as an independent parameter.

3   Females are more likely to evolve worker habits than are males. Once females evolve worker habits, a strong bias against the evolution of male workers at once develops. In addition, there develops a bias against males investing in their offspring. A male is unable to exploit the asymmetrical r's to his own advantage.

He is equally related to his brothers as to his sisters, so he gains nothing by the overproduction of either sex. Likewise, he is unable to produce eggs himself. Since in haplodiploid species a male is no more related to his mate's offspring than to his own siblings, no initial bias in such species (compared to diploid species) is expected either toward or away from male worker habits. (A slight degree of inbreeding introduces a slight bias against male workers.) Female workers are expected to exploit the asymmetrical r's and once they do so, in either of the two available ways, the expected RS of a male rises relative to that of a reproductive female, so that the evolution of male workers becomes relatively less likely. If, for example, all males arise from worker-laid eggs, then the expected RS of a male (per unit investment) is twice that of a reproductive female, so that a male would have to be more than twice as effective a worker (gram for gram) as a female in order for selection to favor his helping in the nest (27). In general, when the ratio of investment is controlled by the workers, a male's expected RS is $6/(3-p)$ times that of a reproductive female (where p is the fraction of males that come from queen-laid eggs). If the ratio of investment is completely controlled by the queen, then the male's expected RS per unit investment is $2/(1+p)$ times that of a female. For both worker and queen control of the ratio of investment, and for all intermediate cases, the relative RS of a male is given in Fig. 3. Only under the unlikely condition of complete queen domination of both male production and the ratio of investment is the expected RS of a male equal to that of a female. Under all other conditions the greater expected RS of a male makes helping behavior and altruism relatively unlikely. In addition, except under complete, or near complete, queen control of the ratio of investment, male parental investment becomes less likely, since a male is expected to inseminate more than one female (per unit investment in him).

In contrast to the termites (all species of which have both male and female workers), there are no species of Hymenoptera that have castes of male workers (5). Indeed, with one or two exceptions (5, 28–31), males have never been seen to contribute anything positive to the colony from which they originate. Again in contrast to the termites, males from social species of Hymenoptera have never been seen to contribute to the colonies that result from their sexual unions, yet rudimentary male parental investment occurs in some solitary species of Hymenoptera (32, 33).

4 No matter who produces the males or who controls the ratio of investment, greater conflict is expected between the workers and the males than between the workers and the reproductive females. Such worker-male conflict is expected to be especially intense where workers control the ratio of investment. If the queen produces all of the males and also controls the ratio of investment (at 1:1), then workers are expected to value their sisters three times as much as their brothers, while each male and each reproductive female values itself twice as much as other reproductives (averaging males and females). Males will then have to work harder to gain appropriate care than will reproductive females. Of course, worker preferences for sisters ought inevitably to lead to a biased ratio of investment. If workers gain their preferred ratio of investment (as a function of p), then they will value reproductives of the two sexes equally; but a male will value himself more relative to his siblings than will a reproductive female relative to her siblings (by approximately the amount shown in Fig. 3) (*27*), so that selection will more strongly favor male efforts (compared to female efforts) to gain more investment than workers are selected to give, leading to increased worker-male conflict. The argument extends to the intermediate situations as well, but worker-male conflict should be most intense under worker control of the ratio of investment (Fig. 3).

Male-worker conflict appears to be widespread in the social Hymenoptera. For example, male *Mischocyttarus drewseni* mob workers more intensely than do female reproductives, and males are more selfish in their behavior toward larvae (*31*). Shortly after they eclose, males may be chased from the nest (and killed if they resist), while females are fed in both *Polistes* and *Bombus* (*34*). In times of food shortage *Camponotus* workers first cannibalize males before turning to female reproductives (*28*). *Tetramorium* males are apparently starved after they eclose while reproductive females are intensively fed (*35*).

5   Either laying workers, or a biased ratio of investment in the reproductives, or both, are expected in all eusocial Hymenoptera. Where there are no laying workers, the ratio of investment is expected to approach 1:3 (male to female). In other species, the ratio of investment is expected to correlate with *p*. For reasons outlined earlier, it will be beneficial to the workers if they can produce some or all of the males (but none of the females) or if they can bias the ratio of investment toward their reproductive sisters. Although it is advantageous for the queen to prevent both of these possibilities, there is no reason to suppose that the queen can completely override the maneuvers of her daughters. In the absence of laying workers, one expects a ratio of investment biased toward 1:3. As shown earlier, the lower the proportion (*p*) of males who come from queen-laid eggs, the more nearly the nonlaying workers prefer a 1:1 ratio of investment.

A number of species are known to have laying workers (*1, 5, 6*) but the contribution of these laying workers to the total of males is usually unknown, and most species remain completely unstudied in this regard. It is sometimes supposed that workers must lay male-producing eggs (if they lay any) since they are assumed to be unfertilized, but it is preferable to argue that they remain unfertilized because there is usually no gain in being able to produce daughters. Even wingless, worker-like female ants are fertilized in species lacking winged queens (*36, 37*), and in some primitively eusocial bees a significant percentage of workers are regularly fertilized; yet fertilized workers have well-developed ovaries no more often than do unfertilized workers (*38*), suggesting the absence of a selection pressure to produce daughters when the queen is functioning. The ratio of investment in eusocial Hymenoptera is discussed below.

6   The early evolution of eusociality should be characterized by the lengthening of the queen's life so as to produce several generations. Males are expected to be infrequent in the early generations and frequent during the queen's terminal generation. The early evolution of eusociality should be characterized by a polymorphism in which some nests consist of queens and their daughters specializing in the production of female reproductives and other nests consist of daughters, singly or in small groups, producing male reproductives. Such a social grouping actually consists of two generations (in addition to the queen): the generation of adult workers and the generation of adult reproductives whom they rear. If all queens

survive to produce the female reproductives, then there will be no value to any males produced along with the generation of workers. Of course, additional generations of workers can be inserted, so that an early eusocial hymenopteran species easily comes to resemble the summer parthenogenetic generations of aphids culminating in the fall production of sexuals.

The correlations proposed are among the most clear-cut in the detailed literature on the early evolution of eusociality in bees (*10*). For example, the series of eusocial halictine bees, *Lasioglossum zephyrum, L. versatum, L. imitatum,* and *L. malachurum,* shows "progressively increasing differences in size and in ovarian development between castes, decreasing frequency of worker mating, increasing queen longevity, and decreasing spring and early summer male production" (*39*).

7   A bias toward the evolution of semisociality (females helping their sister raise her offspring) is expected in haplodiploid species (compared to diploid species). A haplodiploid female is related to her sister's offspring by $r = \frac{3}{8}$ and to her own by $r = \frac{1}{2}$, while a diploid female is related to her sister's offspring by $r = \frac{1}{4}$ and to her own by $r = \frac{1}{2}$, so that, other things being equal, semisociality is more likely in haplodiploid than diploid species. As with eusociality, the bias still persists even if the female is inseminated more than once, as long as each of her daughters is not inseminated by a different male. A male is related to his sibling's offspring by $r = \frac{1}{4}$ and to his mate's by $r = \frac{1}{2}$, so that he is less likely to evolve semisocial habits than are his sisters, but no less likely than males in diploid species. No biased ratio of investment is expected in purely semisocial species.

Semisocial habits (involving females) have evolved independently in the Hymenoptera even more often than have eusocial habits (*5*), yet they have not evolved, so far as is known, in the diploid insects. No semisocial behavior is known in haplodiploid males, but their adult behavior is virtually unstudied. Semisocial habits have evolved several times in birds and mammals, more commonly among brothers than among sisters (*2, 23, 40*).

RATIO OF INVESTMENT IN MONOGYNOUS ANTS

In the system outlined above, the critical prediction is that workers will bias the ratio of investment toward females whenever some or all of the males come from the queen-laid eggs. Since in ants workers feed and care for the reproductives from the time the reproductives are laid as eggs until they leave the nest as adults and since there are usually hundreds of workers (or more) per queen, it is difficult to see how an ant queen could prevent her daughters from producing almost the ratio of investment that maximizes the workers' inclusive fitness. In some ants, such as *Atta* and *Solenopsis* (*5*), all males appear to be produced by the queen, and in other monogynous ants (single queen per nest) laying workers appear to be a relatively uncommon source of males (compared to eusocial bees and wasps) (*41*), so that the ratio of investment in ants should often approach 1:3. This prediction can be tested by ascertaining the sex ratio of reproductives (alates) commonly produced by a species and correcting these data by an estimate of the relative cost (to a colony) of a female alate compared to a male.

There exist good data on the sex ratio of alates for about 20 ant species, based on complete nests dug up during the time when alates were present in the nest. Ideally, nests should be dug up after all alate forms have pupated (since pupae can be sexed while larvae cannot) but before any of the alates have flown (since one sex may fly earlier than the other). Such data exist, primarily from the pioneering population studies of Talbot (*42*). Sex ratios so obtained do not differ from sex ratios for the same species based on all nests (*42*), so data on complete nests dug up anytime were used (*43*). The number of alates counted, the number of nests from which they came, and the sex ratio for monogynous ants (including two slave-making species) are presented in Table 2. The quality of the data (based on sample sizes) varies widely (*44*). The sex ratio varies over a 20-fold range (compare *Formica pallidefulva* and *Prenolepis imparis*).

Since in monogynous species workers invest in the reproductives almost exclusively by feeding them, the relative dry weight of a mature male and female alate was taken as a good estimate of their relative cost (*45, 46*). Dry weights for males and females and the dry weight ratio (female to male) are presented in Table 2. Multiplying the sex ratio by the dry weight ratio gives an estimate of the relative investment in the two sexes (Table 2). This estimate should be approximately valid for monogynous and slave-making species but not, as explained below, for polygynous species.

For 21 monogynous ant species, the sex ratio of alates is plotted against their relative dry weight in Fig. 4A. The points tend to scatter around the 1:3 line of investment instead of the 1:1. The data are fitted by a linear regression in which

$$y = 0.33x - 0.1$$

The slope of this line is not significantly different from a 1:3 slope, but it deviates in a highly significant manner from a 1:1 slope ($P \ll .01$). In fact, all species are biased toward investment in females, and the least biased species show a 1:1.57 ratio of investment. The geometric mean ratio of investment for all species is 1:3.45 (range 1.57 to 8.88). The scatter around the 1:3 line appears partly to reflect sample size. For example, five of the six species with the best data show a range of only 2.99 to 4.14 (geometric mean = 3.36) (*47*). The other species (*Acromyrmex octospinosus*) has a ratio of investment of 1.59. It is the only species with a value of p estimated to be lower than 1 ($p = 0.63$), so that its expected ratio, under worker control, is only 1.94. There is a strong inverse relationship ($P \ll .01; t$-test) between the number of males produced and the relative size of a male (compared to a female). This inverse relation is predicted by Fisher's sex ratio theory (*9*), and, so far as we know, these are the first data—from any group of organisms—demonstrating this relation.

It would be valuable to refine our measure of relative cost. Minor biases are expected from a number of sources. Females contain relatively less water than do males (*35, 45*), they are richer in calories per gram than are males (*35, 48*), they are larger than males and therefore consume relatively less oxygen per unit weight (*49*), and they apparently require less energy (per unit weight) during development

Table 2 The Sex Ratios of Reproductives (males/females) from Natural Nests of 21 Monogynous Species of Ants and Two Slave-Making Species (indicated by s), Along with the Mean Dry Weights of Male and Female Reproductives, the Dry Weight Ratio, and the Inverse of the Ratio of Investment (inverse of 1:3 ratio = 3)

Species	Reproductives counted (no.)	Nests (no.)	Sex ratio	Weight-F (mg)	S.D.	Weight-M (mg)	S.D.	Weight ratio (F/M)	Inverse ratio of investment	Reference
				Subfamily: Formicinae						
Camponotus ferrugineus	1,854	6	1.29	41.18	7.39	6.32	0.50	6.52	5.05	(99)
C. herculeanus	6,300	1*	2.50	56.5^d	11.1	10.6^d	2.4	5.33	2.15	(100)
C. pennsylvanicus	1,249	4	0.77	59.5^f	11.5	8.7^c	3.3	6.84	8.88	(99)
Formica pallidefulva	2,278	31	0.44	14.4^c	1.7	7.9^c	1.2	1.82	4.14	(101)
Prenolepis imparis	1,994	11	8.36	12.7^L		0.509		25.4	3.04	(102)
				Subfamily: Myrmicinae						
Acromyrmex octospinosus	4,490	10	0.9	19.66^b	3.5	7.87	2.74	2.50	2.78	(103)
Aphaenogaster rudis	361	14	5.45	6.1^j		0.48^j		12.71	2.32	(104)
A. treatae	2,024	12	1.55	9.1^f		0.9^f		10.1	6.52	(105)
Atta bisphaerica	35,249	5	3.18					8.00	2.52	(106)
A. laevigata	22,723	6	2.87	263.9^a		31.5	2.7	8.37	2.91	(106)
A. sexdens	119,936	7	4.90	264.7^h	100.8	34.5^h	9.6	7.67	1.57	(106)
Harpagoxenus sublaevis(s)	2,459	58	1.38	0.59^L		0.34^L		1.73	(1.25)s	(36, 55)
Leptothorax ambiguus	169	12	0.82	0.63^d		0.10^k		6.30	7.68	(56)
L. curvispinosus	1,113	82	1.40	0.68^L		0.15^L		4.53	3.24	(57)
L. duloticus(s)	1,620	96	2.31	0.20		0.10		2.0	(0.87)s	(54)
L. longispinosus	206	12	0.62	0.54		0.11^c		4.90	7.90	(56, 57)
Myrmecina americana	226	10	1.19	0.55^d		0.21^d		2.62	2.20	(56)
M. schencki	795	10	0.31	2.0^d		1.0^f		2.00	6.45	(107)
M. sulcinodis	1,114	21	1.15	2.2	0.29	1.2	0.10	1.83	1.59	(108)
Solenopsis invicta	200,491	†	1.00	7.4^g		2.1		3.52	3.52	(50)
Stenamma brevicorne	235	10	0.90	0.88^d	0.06	0.36^d	0.09	2.44	2.71	(56)
S. diecki	391	9	1.30	0.52^c	0.06	0.15^c	0.01	3.46	2.66	(56)
Tetramorium caespitum	73,389	126	1.34	6.0		1.5		4.00	2.99	(109)

Note Blanks indicate lack of data. Weights are based on dried specimens in the collections of the Museum of Comparative Zoology, Harvard University, except where otherwise stated in the references. The mean weights are based on sample size of five individuals except where noted with the following superscripts: a = 1; b = 2; c = 3; d = 4; e = 6; f = 8; g = 9; h = 10; i = 14; j = 15; k = 20; L = 30; m = 66.

* Hölldobler (28) also estimated the sex ratio in 15 to 20 additional nests. It ranged between 2 and 3.

† Hundreds of nests (50).

than do males (35). Peakin's detailed study permits an overall estimate of the relationship between relative dry weight and relative caloric cost; for *Tetramorium caespitum,* females appear to be three-fourths as expensive as suggested by relative dry weight at the time of swarming (35), so that the ratio of investment based on caloric cost for this species would be 1:2.25 (instead of 1:2.98 as given in Table 2). The need for something like a three-fourths correction also appears likely from the pattern of our investment data: a mean ratio of 3.45 for all species, a mean of 3.36 for the five best studied species, and a 3.54 ratio for the single best studied species, *Solenopsis invicta (50),* which lacks laying workers and which is certainly typically outbred. In short, real ratios of investment in monogynous ants appear to be near 1:3 and certainly larger than 1:2.25.

To confirm the contention that the 1:3 ratio of investment in monogynous ants results from the asymmetrical preferences of the workers, a series of tests is possible, involving species of ants in which the workers are unrelated to the brood they rear (slave-making ants), species of ants in which winged females receive investment in addition to their body weight which males do not receive (polygynous ants), diploid species with workers (termites), haplodiploid species without workers (solitary bees and wasps), and other haplodiploid species with workers (eusocial bees and wasps). Data on the ratio of investment in these species are presented in the following sections.

RATIO OF INVESTMENT IN SLAVE-MAKING ANTS

In slave-making ants, the queen's brood is reared not by her own daughters but by slaves, workers of other species stolen from their own nests while pupae or larvae (5). The slave-making workers spend their time slave-raiding, and they typically capture several times their own number in slaves. The slaves feed and care for the slave-making queen and her brood. The slaves are, of course, unrelated to the brood they rear and should have no stake in the ratio of investment they produce. The queen, as always, prefers a 1:1 ratio of investment, and in slave-making species she should be able to see her own preferred ratio realized (51–53).

The only slave-making ants for which we have found sex ratio data are *Leptothorax duloticus (54)* and *Harpagoxenus sublaevis (36, 55),* two closely related species who prey on other *Leptothorax* species. Fortunately, the data themselves are excellent, being based on large and unbiased samples, and permit a comparison with equally good data from a closely related species that is not slave-making, *L. curvispinosus (56, 57),* and with less detailed data from two other closely related species that are not slave-makers (Table 2). The sex ratio is plotted as a function of relative dry weight for all five species in Fig. 4B. In contrast to these three species, the ratio of investment in both slave-makers is close to 1:1 and the geometric mean for the two is 1.00. Each slave-maker has a lower ratio of investment than all other monogynous species shown in Table 2, a highly significant deviation ($P < .001$) toward a

1:1 ratio. In *L. duloticus* sexual dimorphism is reduced (through reduction in size of the female) and yet the relative number of males is increased (*58*).

   Leptothorax duloticus enslaves mostly *L. curvispinosus* workers, who in their own nests produce a ratio of investment of about 1:3. Since the slaves eclose as adults in a strange nest and go to work caring for the brood as if it were their mother's, why do they not attempt to produce the 1:3 ratio of investment typical of their own nests? When *duloticus* first began enslaving *curvispinosus,* the slaves presumably produced a 1:3 ratio of investment in the *duloticus* nest, but selection then favored the *duloticus* queen—by whatever means—biasing the ratio of investment back toward 1:1, and selection did not favor any countermove by the slaves. In giving up care of the brood in order to raid for slaves, the *duloticus* workers presumably gained sufficient increase in their inclusive fitness to compensate for the loss of their control over the ratio of investment (*59*).

RATIO OF INVESTMENT IN POLYGYNOUS ANTS

In polygynous ant species, polygynous nests arise when a queen permits one or more of her fertilized daughters to settle within her nest (*60, 61*). Large polygynous nests may contain granddaughter queens and even later generation queens. Polygynous nests introduce a bias in the sex ratio because the inclusion of reproductive daughters in the maternal nest increases the relative cost of female reproductive compared to that of a male (*62*).

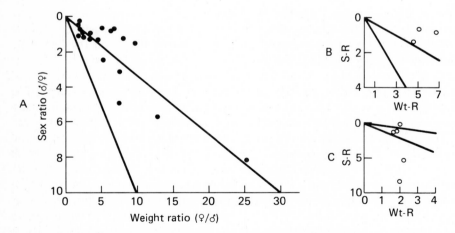

Figure 4   The sex ratio (male/female) of reproductives (alates) is plotted as a function of the adult dry weight ratio (female/male) for various ant species (Table 2). Lines showing 1:1 and 1:3 ratios of investment are drawn for comparison. (A) All monogynous species. (B) Two slave-making species (x) and three closely related nonslave makers (*Leptothorax*). (C) Five species of *Myrmica* (from top to bottom) *M. schencki, M. sulcinodis, M. ruginodis, M. sabuleti,* and *M. rubra.*

If a reproductive daughter is permitted to settle within or near the maternal nest when unrelated females would not be so permitted, then one must assume that the daughter thereby inflicts a cost on her mother (measured in terms of reproductive success) which her mother permits because of the associated benefit for the daughter. This cost can be treated as a component of investment and raises the relative cost of a reproductive female. If we assume outbreeding, the male mates with a female who forces the same cost (with its associated benefit) on her mother, so that a male gains the same benefit without inflicting a cost on his mother (*63*). In short, in polygynous ants we expect the ratio of investment, as measured by relative dry weight, to be biased toward males. This appears to be true for seven polygynous species with the appropriate data (Table 3). There are also several indications of male-biased ratios of investment in polygynous *Formica* (*64*). Likewise, two polygynous *Pseudomyrmex* have less female-biased ratios of investment than do two monogynous species (*65*). The more daughters that are permitted to settle in this fashion, the greater will be the relative cost of an individual reproductive female, so that a positive correlation is expected between the degree of polygyny (as measured by the number of queens in a typical nest) and the ratio of investment based on relative dry weight. The most interesting genus in this regard is *Myrmica* (Fig. 4C). Two species are monogynous, *M. schencki* and *M. sulcinodis,* the latter with many laying workers (Table 2). Two are polygynous, *M. rubra* and *M. sabuleti,* with 5 and 15 queens per nest, respectively (Table 3). The third species, *M. ruginodis,* is both monogynous and polygynous (Table 3) (*66*). The ratios of investment for these species are ordered exactly according to the parameters we have outlined (see Fig. 4C).

RATIO OF INVESTMENT IN TERMITES

Termites are diploid. In the absence of inbreeding, one expects all colony members, queen and king, female and male workers, to prefer equal investment in reproductives of the two sexes. This is true as long as the colony is monogynous but is not true if the queen is capable of producing some of her daughters by parthenogenesis. Unfortunately, there are almost no data on termite sex ratios and, with one exception (*67, 68*), none based on complete nests. In addition, it is difficult to get specimens to weigh. We have used two kinds of data. (i) Roonwal and his associates gathered sex ratio data, based on naturally occurring swarms, for four species and also ascertained wet and dry weights for male and female alates (*69*). (ii) Sands sampled between two and four nests for five species of *Trinervitermes* and also provided weights (*67, 70*). The data from the two sources are plotted in Fig. 5. The geometric mean ratio of investment for these nine species of termites is 1.62, which is significantly closer to 1:1 than are the ratios for monogynous ants ($P < .001$; t-test). There is no significant difference between the termite mean and that of the slave-making ants, a result consistent with the expectation that they be almost equal. However, the termite data are thin enough that they neither strongly support nor contradict our arguments.

Table 3 The Sex Ratio, Weight Ratio, and Inverse Ratio of Investment for Polygynous Ant Species

Species	Sex ratio	Weight-F (mg)	S.D.	Weight-M (mg)	S.D.	Weight ratio (F/M)	Inverse ratio of investment	Reference
Crematogaster mimosae	12	4.79[a]	0.62	0.46[a]	0.01	10.4	0.87	(110)
C. nigriceps	6	2.4[b]	0.03	0.57[b]	0.07	4.2	0.70	(110)
Iridomyrmex humilis							0.1	(111)
Myrmica rubra	8.37	2.2	0.21	1.1[c]	0.24	2.02	0.25	(51, 112)
M. ruginodis	1.11	1.87	0.29	1.14	0.18	1.61	1.45	(66)
Polygynous	6.71						0.24	
Monogynous	0.92						1.75	
M. sabuleti	5.18	2.2	0.08	1.0	0.23	2.20	0.42	(51, 112)
Pheidole pallidula	6.2	3.35		0.6		5.58	0.9	(113)
Tetraponera penzegi	1.8	0.93[a]	0.01	0.48[a]	0.10	1.94	1.1	(110)

a = sample size of 2; b = 3; c = 6.

Table 4 The Sex Ratio (males/females) from Natural Nests of Solitary Species of Bees and Wasps, Along with Adult Dry Weight of Males and Females of These Species

Species	Offspring counted (no.)	Sex ratio	Weight-F (mg)	S.D.	Weight-M (mg)	S.D.	Reference
Solitary bees							
Agapostemon nasutus	87	2.11	9.7	2.7	6.4	0.6	(114)
Anthophora abrupta	169	1.64	58.0	10.7	36.7	1.6	(115)
A. edwardsii	225	1.48	49.0[a]	2.9	36.6[a]	3.2	(116)
A. flexipes	200	1.50	17.3	2.6	15.1	1.5	(117)
A. occidentalis	241	1.06	89.7	3.7	51.1	6.3	(118)
A. peritomae	70	1.00	23.8[b]	4.1	10.1	1.7	(119)
Chilicola ashmeadi	84	2.82	0.8	0.06	0.5	0.05	(120)
Euplusia surinamensis	297	1.44	148.7	18.7	123.6	31.0	(121)
Hoplitis anthocopoides	351	1.95	11.6	1.6	12.3	2.7	(122)
Nomia melanderi	500	1.01	25.5	5.5	31.9	3.3	(123)
Osmia excavata	2,820	1.69	24.9	4.8	16.3	1.6	(124)
Pseudagapostemon divaricatus	222	1.61					(125)
Solitary wasps							
Antodynerus flavescens	200	1.56	22.2	2.5	14.6	2.8	(126)
Chalybion bengalense	183	1.47	19.6	5.9	8.7	2.8	(126)
Ectemnius paucimaculatus	169	1.82	4.0	1.7	3.0	1.2	(127)
Passaloecus eremita	114	0.70	3.4	0.9	1.6	0.3	(128)
Sceliphron spirifex	144	0.95					(83)

Note Blanks indicate lack of data. The mean weight for each sex is based on a sample size of five with three exceptions.

a = sample size of 2; b = sample size of 3.

RATIO OF INVESTMENT IN SOLITARY BEES AND WASPS

In solitary (nonparasitic) bees and wasps, an adult female commonly builds a cell and provisions the cell with prey or with pollen and nectar. In each cell, she lays either a haploid (male) egg or a diploid (female) egg. In the absence of inbreeding, one expects the typical adult female to invest equally in the two sexes (*9*).

Natural Nests

In most solitary bees and wasps, males emerge from and leave their nests earlier than do females (*32*). In some species the pupal stage itself is known to be shorter in males (*71*). In addition, female cells are commonly deposited first in twig-nesting species. Because of these sex differences, sex ratio data based on nests collected during the flying season are expected to be biased toward females, as indeed they appear to be (*72*). By contrast, unbiased data are expected if nests are gathered before any adults have emerged and if the contents are sexed after all larvae have pupated (since larvae can usually not be sexed). We have found such data (with a sample size of 70 or more) for 17 species (Table 4). Since we have no data on cell size or amount of provisions for individuals of either sex, we have again used relative adult dry weight as a measure of the relative cost of a male and a female. Males tend to be smaller than females and more numerous in most species sampled (Table 4). The sex ratio as a function of the dry weight ratio is plotted in Fig. 6. Although there is no tendency for relatively smaller males to be produced in relatively greater numbers, the ratio of investment in solitary bees and wasps in significantly closer to 1:1 than is true in monogynous ants. The geometric mean for all solitary species is 1:1.07. The two species which deviate most from 1:1 are among the three species with the smallest sample size (115 or less).

These data from natural nests can be supplemented by data from trap-nests (in which artificial nesting sites, usually holes bored in wood, are offered in the field and

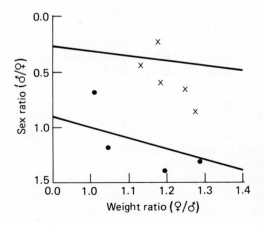

Figure 5 The sex ratio of reproductives is plotted against the dry weight ratio for termites. Data from Roonwal *et al.* (*69*), (closed circles); data from Sands (*67, 70*) (x). The 1:1 and 1:3 lines are drawn as in Fig. 4.

their contents later reared to maturity). Most such nests consist of a linear series of cells each separated by a partition of mud. The advantage of these data is that they are more numerous than natural data and they can be correlated with direct measures of the relative cost of producing the two sexes. Trap-nests may, however, introduce their own biases, for many bees and wasps prefer to produce the smaller sex (usually males) in smaller diameter holes (73) so that the sex ratio obtained will partly reflect the size distribution of the borings that are presented. Even where the appropriate boring sizes are offered, the data may still be biased if the size distribution of the borings does not exactly match the relative frequency of different size borings in nature. But there is no strong reason in advance to assume that trap-nests will have a systematic bias against any one sex (74) so that strong variance in sex ratio is expected from species to species but no systematic bias.

Trap-nests and the Measurement of Relative Cost

Krombein (32) has done the bulk of all published trap-nesting work, using the same trapping procedure in a series of localities to capture more than 100 species of solitary bees and wasps. For 27 species (Table 5) with a sample of 70 or more adults captured and reared to maturity (75), Krombein provided the sex of the individuals as well as their average cell dimensions. From these dimensions we have calculated the mean relative cell volume (female to male) for each species (Table 5). In addition, Krombein removed from his trap-nesting collection five typical individuals of each sex for each of the 30 species (76) (Table 5). We weighed the specimens and from these weights we have calculated dry weight ratios (female to male) for the same species. Comparison of these data reveals that relative volumes and relative weights are usually greater than one (females occupy more space than males and weigh more).

Since dry weight is partly a measure of the amount of food given and cell volume is a direct measure of the space allotted (77), the relative cell volume and the relative weight of the two sexes (female to male) can be considered partly independent measures of the substitution value of a female (in units of males). In addition, since Krombein's impression is that male and female cells were both stuffed full with prey (78, 79), relative cell volume is probably a good measure of relative amount of food provided. As would be expected, relative dry weight and relative volume are highly correlated, but there is a systematic tendency for females to weigh more than would be expected on the basis of cell volume (Table 5). That this discrepancy is real was confirmed by comparing the weights of our specimens with the volume of the cells they inhabited; weight per unit volume ratios are consistently biased toward females; the mean value for wasps is 1.37, and for bees it is 1.33 (80). Either these wasps and bees allot more space (per unit provisions) for their sons than for their daughters or else development is more expensive in males.

For five species of wasps, Krombein (32) counted the number of caterpillars in a sample of cells that later gave rise to either female or male wasps. On the basis of these data we have calculated the relative number of caterpillars stored in a female cell compared to a male cell. For all five species, this direct measure of provisioning is almost identical to the measure of relative cell volume (*81*). This is consistent with Krombein's impression that there was no average difference in the size of caterpillars stored in the two kinds of cells (*78*). To check this impression we weighed the contents of 24 cells of *Euodynerus foraminatus apopkensis;* these were cells whose wasps failed to develop but for which Krombein could reliably infer the sex of the intended wasp (*82*). For these 24 cells the mean relative weight of provisions (2.05) is very close to the mean relative cell volume (1.81) (*82*). These are virtually the only data available permitting a comparison of provisioning ratios with either cell volume ratios or adult weight ratios (*83, 84*). The only direct measure of developmental cost for any of the Hymenoptera suggests that development may indeed be more expensive in males; during pupation male ants *(Tetramorium)* lose about 30 percent of their caloric value while females, although similar in size, lose only about 15 percent of theirs (*35, 85*).

The sex ratio was plotted as a function of relative cell volume for 20 species of wasps (Fig. 7; data from Table 5). Although there is considerable scatter, the species are closer to a 1:1 ratio of investment than to a 1:3. The data are fitted by the linear regression

$$y = 1.1x - 0.34$$

There is a significant tendency ($P < .01$) for sex ratio and relative cost to be inversely related. The mean ratio of investment based on cell volume is 1.39 for wasps and 1.28 for bees. The ratio based on dry weight is 1.92 for wasps and 2.11 for bees. Similar data have been analyzed from the work of Danks (*86*) who combined data from natural nests with data from stems of plants made available to wasps and bees. The ratio of investment in these species approximates 1:1 (Fig. 8).

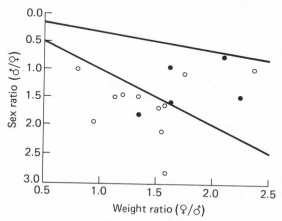

Figure 6 The sex ratio as a function of the dry weight ratio for species of solitary bees (open circles) and solitary wasps (closed circles). Data are from natural nests (Table 4). The 1:1 and 1:3 lines are drawn as in Fig. 4.

Taken together the available data from solitary bees and wasps support the expectation that ratios of investment in the solitary Hymenoptera are typically near 1:1 and no greater than 1:2. When an individual son is relatively less costly than an individual daughter, relatively more sons tend to be produced. Trap-nests should permit more precise measures of relative cost than presented here (87).

RATIO OF INVESTMENT IN SOCIAL BEES AND WASPS

Like ants, eusocial bees and wasps are expected to show ratios of investment biased toward females. Since laying workers are known to be an important source of males in some species of bees and wasps (10), ratios of investment in social bees and wasps are not, in general, expected to be as biased toward females as in ants (Fig. 1). Unfortunately, it is much more difficult to ascertain the ratio of investment in social bees and wasps than in either ants or solitary bees and wasps. To tell workers from reproductives requires careful, time-consuming behavioral and morphological studies, and these yield too few sex ratio data for our purposes (88). In addition, since female reproductives are hard to distinguish from workers, it is difficult to get an accurate estimate of the relative cost of a reproductive female (compared to a male). We limit ourselves here to detailed data available for bumblebees (*Bombus*) and the closely related parasite (*Psithyrus*).

A temperate bumblebee colony survives for only a season (10), the fertilized females overwintering alone. Reproductive females are produced in late summer at a time when few or no workers are being produced. Young queens remain on the nest for considerable periods where they are readily distinguished from workers. By marking emerging queens and males, Webb (34, 89) gathered extensive sex ratio data for five species of *Bombus* (and one parasite, *Psithyrus*). These data are presented in Table 6, along with mean weights of male and female reproductives. The sex ratios are all biased in favor of males, and this appears to be general in *Bombus* (90). Ratios of investment for the five species lie between 1:1.2 and 1:3.1.

Psithyrus variabilis is a parasite on *Bombus americanorum* (34, 89). A *Psithyrus* queen invades a *Bombus* nest, destroys the host larvae, and rears her own young using the food stores of her host and considerable help from the host workers (34, 89). If the *Psithyrus* queen is able to control the ratio of investment then one expects a 1:1 ratio and not the 1:2 ratio one observes (Table 6). Compared to ratios for the five species of *Bombus,* the ratio in *Psithyrus* is certainly not biased toward 1:1 (as expected), but it is difficult to compare the ratios directly, since mean *Psithyrus* female weight is based entirely on queens caught in the fall while each of the mean *Bombus* female weights is based largely on females caught in the spring after hibernation (and hence weight loss).

EVOLUTION OF WORKER-QUEEN CONFLICT

The information we have reviewed forms an interesting pattern. In monogynous ants the queen appears to produce most or all of the males and the workers apparently

Table 5 The Sex Ratio (male/female), Weight Ratio (female/male), Cell Volume Ratio (female/male), and Weight Per Volume Ratio (female/male) for the Species of Solitary Wasps and Bees Studied by Krombein (32)

Superfamily, family, and species	Adults reared (no.)	Sex ratio	Cell volume ratio (F/M)	Weight-F (mg)	S.D.	Weight-M (mg)	S.D.	Weight ratio (F/M)	Weight per volume ratio
Vespidae									
Vespoidea (wasps)									
Monobia quadridens	227	0.89	1.39	68.2	10.5	35.4	11.8	1.93	1.52
Euodynerus foraminatus foraminatus	96	2.56	1.70	19.0[b]	3.4	12.8	3.4	1.49	1.01
E. f. apopkensis	1,551	2.30	1.69	22.9	2.6	11.0	3.0	2.07	1.33
E. megaera	240	0.67	1.74	28.2	2.9	12.9	2.0	2.22	1.28
Pachodynerus erynnis	240	0.71	0.91	28.0	7.2	12.6[b]	2.3	2.16	3.32
Ancistrocerus antilope antilope	375	1.88	1.48	30.1	4.3	15.8	1.5	1.90	2.0
A. campestris	83	1.77	1.62	18.9	3.6	9.0	2.3	2.10	1.15
A. catskill	189	0.97	1.39	15.5	2.9	6.8	1.2	2.28	1.38
A. tigris	114	0.27	1.53	11.9[b]	2.6	5.0[b]	0.9	2.37	1.85
Symmorphus cristatus	114	1.04	1.20	6.6[a]	0.64	3.4[b]	0.96	1.92	1.12
Stenodynerus krombeini	69	0.86	0.95	9.8	1.5	9.1	1.9	1.07	1.26
S. lineatifrons	92	0.46	0.63	10.5[b]	1.4	5.4[b]	1.4	1.95	1.95
S. saecularis	149	0.69	0.77	17.3[b]	3.8	12.5	2.1	1.39	1.25
S. toltecus	82	0.71	1.34						

Pompilidae									
Dipogon sayi	107	0.41	1.05	10.2[b]		3.0	0.67	3.46	3.46
Sphecidae									
Trypargilum tridentatum tridentatum	332	0.77	0.90	9.1	2.2	10.1	2.3	0.90	0.77
T. clavatum	314	0.89	1.00	11.8	2.0	7.9	1.3	1.50	1.01
T. johannis	72	1.18	1.38	17.3	3.8	13.8	1.8	1.26	0.82
T. striatum	349	1.60	1.80	24.7	4.1	19.0	3.9	1.30	1.03
Trypoxylon frigidum	82	0.71	1.16	2.0[b]	0.24	1.4	0.37	1.40	0.98

Apoidea (bees)

Megachilidae									
Anthidium maculosum	78	0.3	1.0	34.4	3.6	37.0	6.4	0.93	2.38
Prochelostoma philadelphi	85	0.25		3.7[b]	0.38	3.3	1.0	1.11	1.14
Ashmeadiella meliloti	136	0.64	1.5	6.5	0.55	2.8	0.62	2.31	0.97
A. occipitalis	845	0.31	1.29	14.9[b]	3.6	7.1	2.6	2.10	1.29
Osmia lignaria lignaria	732	2.08	1.49	35.1	4.7	14.7	2.3	2.42	
O. pumila	315	0.38	1.24	9.4	1.6	5.1	1.6	1.84	1.23
Megachile gentilis	290	5.04	1.0	18.7	2.0	12.8	2.5	1.46	
M. mendica	208	2.71	1.0	33.2	6.8	16.7	3.3	1.99	

Note The weight per volume ratio is based only on the cell volumes of those specimens that were weighed. By contrast the cell volume ratio is based on the cell dimensions of all individuals reared. The sex ratio and number of adults reared includes a few individuals whose sex was inferred (*75*). The species are presented in the order in which Krombein (*32*) presents them.
a = sample size of 2; b = sample size of 4.

control the rate of investment. Where our information is most reliable, this certainly appears to be true (for example, *Solenopsis invicta,* Table 2). The repeated evolution in ants (*5*) of trophic eggs (eggs produced to feed other ants) suggests that in some groups of ants male production by workers was formerly more important than it is now, the queen having regained control of male production and forced a new function on worker-laid eggs. The ant species with the greatest known worker

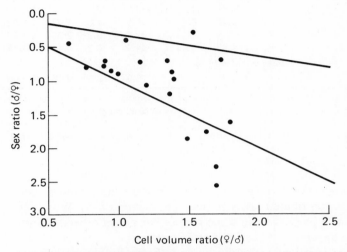

Figure 7   The sex ratio as a function of the cell volume ratio (female/male) for species of solitary wasps trap-nested by Krombein (*32*) (Table 5).

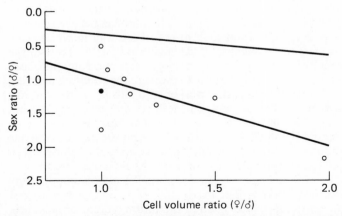

Figure 8   The sex ratio as a function of the cell volume ratio for species of solitary wasps (open circles) and bees (closed circle). Natural nests and trap-nests combined by Danks (*86*).

Table 6 The Ratio of Investment in *Bombus* and Its Parasite, *Psithyrus*

Species	Reproductives counted (no.)	Colonies (no.)	Sex ratio	Weight-F (mg)	S.D.	Weight-M (mg)	S.D.	Weight ratio (F/M)	Ratio of investment
			Species of Bombus						
B. americanorum	1,780	25	1.52	274.9[c]	32.0	82.4	27.4	4.17	1:2.74
B. auricomus	302	12	1.14	330.3[a]	10.2	136.3	22.8	2.42	1:2.12
B. fraternus	268	4	1.34	315.2[b]	95.28	195.1	32.6	1.62	1:1.21
B. griseocollis	887	20	1.72	207.3[b]	27.1	102.4	8.9	2.02	1:1.17
B. impatiens	351	5	1.42	234.8[d]	106.9	54.9	20.2	4.44	1:3.13
			Species of Psithyrus						
P. variabilis	290	4	0.91	164.8[a]	29.0	79.9	19.6	2.06	1:2.06

Note The sex ratio data are from Webb (*34*). For *Bombus* the weights of females are based entirely on specimens caught in the spring, while *Psithyrus* females were all caught in the fall (before hibernation).

The mean weight for males is based on a sample size of five individuals. For females: a = 2 individuals; b = 3; c = 4; d = 6.

contribution to male production is polygynous (*91*). In some monogynous social bees and wasps, workers contribute heavily to male production (*5, 6*). Why is the queen able to control male production in some species but not in others? Why in monogynous ants is she apparently powerless to affect the ratio of investment (Fig. 4A)? In answering these questions we outline here a theory for the evolution of worker-queen conflict.

1 *The asymmetry in aggressive encounters between queen and worker.* Aggressive encounters involve violence or the threat of violence. Where two combatants are related, each is expected to adjust its behavior according to the possibility of lowering its inclusive fitness by harming a relative (*92*). In a conflict between a queen and a laying worker, there is an important asymmetry in the way in which each individual is expected to view the possibility of damaging the other. To take the extreme case, early in the life of a large, perennial monogynous ant colony the queen could kill a daughter and we would barely be able to measure the resulting decrease in either party's inclusive fitness. By contrast, a worker who kills her mother harms her own inclusive fitness in three different ways. She destroys the one highly specialized egg layer in the colony. She destroys the one individual capable of producing reproductive females to whom the worker is related by ¾. And she destroys the one individual capable of producing new workers (and hence keeping the colony alive). In short, the worker inflicts a catastrophic loss on her own inclusive fitness.

In such situations there is a large bias in favor of the queen winning any aggressive encounter with her workers. The bias in favor of the queen is largest where the colony is expected to reproduce again in the future (perennial colonies), where there is no alternate, closely related reproductive to whom the workers can attach themselves (for example, monogynous ants), where the queen is strongly specialized as an egg layer, and where the ratio of investment is controlled by the queen (since this decreases the expected RS of the males produced when the queen is destroyed, assuming only males can still be produced). Aggression, as we shall see, is expected to have an important influence on male production but little or none on the ratio of investment.

2 *The relevance of aggression to the production of males.* Within a colony a small number of acts result in the laying of the male-producing eggs for a season. If the queen can be present, at or soon after these events, then her advantage in aggressive encounters should permit her to destroy worker-laid eggs, provided that she can recognize such eggs. Alternatively, if she can detect other potential egg layers, she may be able to attack them directly. To discriminate worker-laid eggs from her own, the queen must see them being laid, find them in places or circumstances where her own eggs are not, or learn to discriminate the two kinds of eggs. There is evidence for all three kinds of discrimination (*5, 10, 34, 93*). In particular, Gervet (*93*) has shown that *Polistes* females antennate the first several eggs they lay and may eat one or two. When deprived of this experience, a female does not develop the capacity to discrimate strange eggs from her own. Regardless of experience, the female does not destroy eggs that are more than 3 hours old. In short, the mechanisms are known by which a queen can easily discriminate against many worker-laid eggs. In addition, it is difficult to see how a worker could become an effective laying worker yet conceal this fact from the queen. West Eberhard (*34*) has suggested that in *Polistes* a female will fail to destroy an egg if she does not have one herself to lay, so that both the capacity to produce male eggs and to destroy those of the queen must depend on how often a laying worker is fed (and how rarely she feeds others). This, in turn, ought to depend on how attractive such an individual is to other workers or how aggressively she begs from them (without herself being altruistic). Queens should be selected to be aggressive toward workers attractive to others and to be aggressive toward begging workers who are themselves not altruistic. In summary, deception cannot save either the laying worker or most of her eggs.

3 *Annual versus perennial colonies.* In an annual bumblebee colony, killing the queen at the time when male eggs are being laid should not in itself lower the eventual output of the colony by much because, once male production begins, no more workers are produced anyway, and the colony does not survive beyond the production of reproductives. Of course if workers are unfertilized, the entire production of the altered colony must consist of males; but if workers control the ratio of investment then the males' expected RS must equal that of a similar mass of females, so that initially there is only a slight selection pressure against killing the queen. However, it cannot be assumed that the total production of the altered colony will equal that of the colony with the queen intact, for more conflict is expected in the altered colony (*94*), especially if it is large and no one individual can dominate all others. In summary, worker production of males is much more likely in annual colonies than during most of the life of perennial colonies, but there still remains some bias in favor of the queen.

It is noteworthy that worker-queen conflict and reciprocal egg-eating have been known in the annual colonies of bumblebees since the 19th century, but male production is only known to occur largely by laying workers in one species, *Bombus atratus,* which is perennial. According to our theory, male production by the queen in ants is associated with the perennial colonies typical of this group.

4   *The relationship between polygyny and laying workers.*   If workers easily lose in fights with their mother because of her unique reproductive role, then polygynous societies where the several queens are close relatives should be characterized by workers who are much more willing to risk injuring their mother than workers in monogynous colonies are (*95*). Although it would be preferable to gain one's way without harming one's mother, injuring her is associated with less drastic effects on the workers' inclusive fitness since they can at least transfer their work to close relatives. We thus predict that polygyny should be associated with laying workers. Arguing from a hypothesized association between inbreeding and polygyny, Hamilton (*6*) came to the opposite conclusion (*96*); but he admitted that the only available evidence shows an association between being polygynous and having laying workers produce many of the males (*91*).

5   *Conflict over the ratio of investment.*   Laying the male-producing eggs can be achieved by a small number of acts, but the ratio of investment (which includes all that goes into rearing the reproductives) results from thousands upon thousands of acts. In addition, the queen—via egg destruction—can often aggressively dominate male production, but it is much more difficult aggressively to impose a ratio of investment. By laying more male eggs than the workers would prefer, the queen may begin with a sex ratio that would, without intervention, lead to equal investment. But the workers care for the eggs and with care goes the power to destroy. The queen may guard her male eggs, but once they hatch they will need care from workers (*97*). As the larvae grow, execution of excess males becomes increasingly inefficient and underfeeding more likely. Consistent with this argument is the discovery that adult male ants lose weight while their reproductive sisters are being fattened up (*35*).

If workers can evolve the ability to estimate the ratio of investment within their colony, then they will be able to counteract the queen's maneuvers more efficiently and more precisely. In other words, the capacity to measure and produce a given ratio of investment (which may involve coordinating the activities of millions of workers) must lie within the workers. Perhaps the special cognitive strains of being a haplodiploid worker account in part for the enlargement of the brain in the social Hymenoptera in contrast to its diminution in the termites (*6*).

6   *The concept of offspring power.*   The data that we have gathered are inconsistent with the notion of complete parental domination (*13*). The female daughters of monogynous ant queens appear to completely dominate their mothers where the ratio of investment is concerned, while she enjoys in the same species nearly complete domination of the genetics of male production. The queen's royal status (highly protected, completely cared for, and the recipient of much altruism and deference) flows from her unique genetic role, but this role does not give her royal powers—at least not where care for her offspring is concerned (the ratio of investment). Instead, the relevant principle is more like: to those who do the work shall be delegated the authority over how such work is allocated. But our slave-making data show that this cannot be a general principle. Likewise, we have no data that would show whether the reproductives in the system get more investment than either the queen or her working daughters prefer. However, Brian has made the remarkable discovery that workers in *Myrmica rubra* have to actively bite larvae in order to decrease the number that develop into reproductives (*98*), and this is reminiscent of the inefficiencies of weaning conflict in mammals. Instead of supporting a general principle predicting who shall dominate situations of conflict, our work supports the notion that there is no inherent tendency for evolution to favor any particular party in situations of conflict.

SUMMARY

Hamilton (*1*) was apparently the first to appreciate that the synthesis of Mendelian genetics with Darwin's theory of natural selection had profound implications for social theory. In particular, insofar as almost all social behavior is either selfish or altruistic (or has such effects), genetical reasoning suggests that an individual's social behavior should be adjusted to his or her degree of relatedness, *r*, to all individuals affected by the behavior. We call this theory kinship theory.

The social insects provide a critical test of Hamilton's kinship theory. When such theory is combined with the sex ratio theory of Fisher (*9*), a body of consistent predictions emerges regarding the haplodiploid Hymenoptera. The evolution of female workers helping their mother reproduce is more likely in the Hymenoptera than in diploid groups, provided that such workers lay some of the male-producing eggs or bias the ratio of investment toward reproductive females. Once eusocial colonies appear, certain biases by sex in these colonies are expected to evolve. In general, but especially in eusocial ants, the ratio of investment should be biased in favor of females, and in ants it is expected to equilibrate at 1:3 (male to female). We present evidence from 20 species that the ratio of investment in monogynous ants is, indeed, about 1:3, and we subject this discovery to a series of tests. As expected, the slavemaking ants produce a ratio of investment of 1:1, polygynous ants produce many more males than expected on the basis of relative dry weight alone, solitary bees and wasps produce a ratio of investment near 1:1 (and no greater than 1:2), and the social bumblebees produce ratios of investment between 1:1 and 1:3. In addition, sex ratios in monogynous ants and in trap-nested wasps are, as predicted by Fisher, inversely related to the relative cost in these species of producing a male instead of a female. Taken together, these data provide quantitative evidence in support of kinship theory, sex ratio theory, the assumption that the offspring is capable of acting counter to its parents' best interests, and the supposition that haplodiploidy has played a unique role in the evolution of the social insects.

Finally, we outline a theory for the evolution of worker-queen conflict, a theory which explains the queen's advantage in competition over male-producing workers and the workers' advantage regarding the ratio of investment. The theory uses the asymmetries of haplodiploidy to explain how the evolved outcome of parent-offspring conflict in the social Hymenoptera is expected to be a function of certain social and life history parameters.

REFERENCES AND NOTES

1   W. D. Hamilton, *J. Theor. Biol.* **7**, 1 (1964); J. B. S. Haldane, *Nature (London) New Biol.* **18**, 34 (1955); G. C. Williams and D. C. Williams, *Evolution* **11**, 32 (1957).

2   J. Maynard Smith and M. G. Ridpath, *Am. Nat.* **106**, 447 (1972).

3   G. E. Woolfenden, *Auk* **92**, 1 (1975); I. C. R. Rowley, *Emu* **64**, 251 (1965).

4   E. O. Wilson, *Sociobiology* (Harvard Univ. Press, Cambridge, Mass., 1975).

5   ———. *The Insect Societies* (Harvard Univ. Press, Cambridge, Mass., 1971).

6   W. D. Hamilton, *Annu. Rev. Ecol. Syst.* **3**, 193 (1972).

7   R. L. Trivers, in *Sexual Selection and the Descent of Man 1871–1971,* B. Campbell, Ed. (Aldine, Chicago, 1972), pp. 136–179.

8   ———, *Am. Zool.* **14**, 249 (1974).

9   R. A. Fisher, *The Genetical Theory of Natural Selection* (Clarendon, Oxford, 1930). In diploid organisms (in the absence of inbreeding) natural selection favors equal investment in the two sexes. Where investment in a typical male produced equals investment in a typical female, natural selection favors the production of a 50:50 sex ratio—regardless of differential mortality by sex after the period of parental investment. For a definition of parental investment, see Trivers (*7*). For preferred sex ratios under inbreeding, see W. D. Hamilton, *Science* **156**, 477 (1967). In the absence of inbreeding, Fisher's argument applies to haplodiploid species. For the effects of inbreeding on the parents' preferred sex ratio in haplodiploid species, see Hamilton (*6*). Hamilton's argument on this point must be modified for species with laying workers, as pointed out to us by J. Pickering, Harvard Biology Department. For the offspring's preferred sex ratio (and the male parent's) in typical diploid species see Trivers (*8*).

10 C. D. Michener, *The Social Behavior of the Bees* (Harvard Univ. Press, Cambridge, Mass, 1974).

11 Slightly more precise formulations are found in Hamilton (*6*). Under inbreeding, r must be redefined to take into account the probability that an individual will have two copies of an allele that is identical by descent.

12 Several of the degrees of relatedness in Hamilton (*1*) and Wilson (*5*) are in error. For corrections, see W. D. Hamilton, in *Group Selection,* G. C. Williams, Ed. (Aldine, Chicago, 1971); R. H. Crozier, *Am. Nat.* **104**, 216 (1970); and (*6*).

13 By contrast, R. D. Alexander [*Annu. Rev. Ecol. Syst.* **5**, 325 (1974)] has argued that offspring should naturally act in their parents' best interests, but, in our opinion, neither the arguments presented nor the evidence available support this viewpoint. For example, the spread of alleles conferring selfish behavior on offspring may reduce the eventual reproductive success of both parent and offspring but this is not an argument against the spread of such alleles (although it is an argument for choosing a mate who was selfless when young). Similarly, the ability of the parent to respond to offspring selfishness by harsh retaliation is limited by the parent's growing investment in an offspring, as well as by the offspring's growing independence of the parent (*8*). Alexander interprets the apparent conflict in parent-offspring relations as an efficient system by which the two parties communicate regarding the optimal parental strategy, but this view fails to answer three questions (*6, 8*): (i) Why is such a system of communication not vulnerable to the kinds of

deceit already described for vertebrates and social insects? (ii) In what way are kicking, biting, and screaming, or reciprocal egg-eating, efficient systems of communication? (iii) And finally, if conflict occurs because of different estimates of the same parameters, why are parent and offspring estimates predictably biased in favor of the estimator? Total parental domination has also been argued by M. T. Ghiselin, *The Economy of Nature and the Evolution of Sex* (Univ. of California Press, Berkeley, 1974). See also R. L. Trivers, *Science* **186**, 525 (1974); W. D. Hamilton, *Q. Rev. Biol.* **50**, 175 (1975). For an introduction to kinship theory, see M. J. West Eberhard, *ibid.*, p. 1.

14 C. D. Michener, *Annu. Rev. Entomol.* **14**, 299 (1969). For a review of the literature on the social insects, see Wilson (*5*). For a discussion of the important "primitively eusocial" bees, see Michener (*10*).

15 This point was first brought to our attention by D. M. Windsor of the Smithsonian Tropical Research Institute. Windsor independently derived many of our conclusions.

16 Because a male typically invests nothing in the offspring, his only avenue to a biased sex ratio of investment is through his sperm. These are selected to wriggle through to fatherhood more often than the potential mother would prefer, thereby selecting for a spermatotheca under subtle spinctral control. Since any success of such sperm automatically raises the value to mothers of producing sons, it is difficult to imagine how spermal ingenuity would compete with mother-power for long.

17 This assumes that such species are typically outbred and that queens are actually or effectively singly inseminated (as when sperm of successive fathers are highly clumped). All full sisters agree among themselves on the preferred ratio of investment, so that the mother's power is pitted against that of a united three-fourths sisterhood.

18 J. Pickering, personal communication.

19 It is desirable to solve the equation $r_M \times$ the expected $RS_M = r_F \times$ the expected RS_F, where r_M is the r of an interested party (workers) to reproductive males and the expected RS_M is the expected RS of a male (per unit effort), measured by both the number of females he is expected to inseminate and by his average r to his mates' offspring. From the nonlaying workers' standpoint (where x is the ratio of investment in males compared to females) the equation reads

$$\left(\frac{3-p}{8}\right)\left(1 + \frac{1-p}{2}\right) = \frac{3x}{4}\left(\frac{1}{2} + \frac{1+p}{4}\right)$$

20 See G. C. Williams, *Sex and Evolution* (Princeton Univ. Press, Princeton, N.J., 1975). Inbreeding also decreases heterozygosity. The large degree of genetic variability that is found within sexual species supports Williams' arguments as well as the claim that inbreeding is usually trivial. For further evidence, see R. C. Lewontin, *The Genetic Basis of Evolutionary Change* (Columbia Univ. Press, New York, 1974).

21 A. F. Skutch, *Condor* **63**, 198 (1961); J. L. Brown, *Am. Zool.* **14**, 63 (1974).

22 C. J. Ralph and C. A. Pearson, *Condor* **73**, 77 (1971).

23 G. B. Schaller, *The Serengeti Lion* (Univ. of Chicago Press, Chicago, 1972).

24 L. D. Mech, *The Wolf* (Natural History Press, New York, 1970); J. Van Lawick-Goodall and H. Van Lawick, *Innocent Killers* (Houghton Mifflin, Boston, 1971).

25 Selection would not necessarily favor the production of a male capable of fertilizing all of a queen's daughters, because the cost of such a male to those that produce him may outweigh his benefits to them.

26 G. A. Parker, *Biol. Rev. Cambridge Philos. Soc.* **45**, 525 (1970); S. Taber, *J. Econ. Entomol.* **48**, 552 (1955).

27 A male's *r* to reproductives that he might help rear (his siblings) will also change as a function of *p*, as will a female's; but the difference between the two is slight, especially if there is more than one laying worker per nest. When only one laying worker produces all of the males in each nest, a male is more related (than is a female) to other reproductives in the nest by a factor of 10:9. (With additional laying workers, this factor approaches 1.0.) In general, with a single laying worker per nest the average *r* of a male to reproductives divided by the average *r* of a female to reproductives is

$$2(2p^2 - 3p + 5) / (9 - p)$$

This value varies between 1.11 and 0.93.

28 B. Hölldobler, personal communication.

29 ———, *Z. Angew. Entomol.* **49**, 337 (1962).

30 ———, *Z. Vgl. Physiol.* **52**, 430 (1966). Males apparently feed each other more often than they feed reproductive females or workers (*28*), and this bias is exactly consistent with the greater expected RS of males assuming workers are able to bias the ratio of investment or lay some of the male-producing eggs (Fig. 3). Hamilton (*6*) is apparently mistaken in supposing that *Camponotus* tend to inbreed (*29*).

31 R. L. Jeanne, *Bull. Mus. Comp. Zool. Harv. Univ.* **144**, 63 (1972).

32 K. Krombein, *Trap-nesting Wasps and Bees: Life Histories, Nests and Associates* (Smithsonian Press, Washington, D.C. 1967).

33 D. J. Peckham, F. E. Kurczewski, D. B. Peckham, *Ann. Entomol. Soc. Am.* **66**, 647 (1973); R. M. Bohart and P. M. Marsh, *Pan-Pac. Entomol.* **36**, 115 (1960); C. G. Hartman, *Entomol. News* **55**, 7 (1944); M. N. Paetzel, *Pan-Pac. Entomol.* **49**, 26 (1973). For *Trypargilum,* see also Krombein (*32*).

34 M. J. West Eberhard, *Misc. Publ. Mus. Zool. Univ. Mich.* **140** (1969); M. C. Webb III, thesis, University of Nebraska (1961). Alternatively, as both authors suggest, the workers may be guarding against inbreeding.

35 G. J. Peakin, *Ekol. Pol.* **20**, 55 (1972).

36 A Buschinger, *Insectes Soc.* **15**, 89 (1968).

37 ———, *Zool. Anz.* **186**, 242 (1971); C. P. Haskins and R. M. Whelden, *Psyche* **72**, 87 (1965). Thus, there is no inherent block to sexual reproduction by workers.

38 Reviewed in S. F. Sakagami and K. Hayashida, *J. Fac. Sci. Hokkaido Univ. Ser. VI Zool.* **16**, 413 (1968). Comparison of 12 primitively eusocial bees reveals no correlation between the percentage of workers with ovarial development and the percentage of workers that are inseminated. Within *Lasioglossum duplex* at least, there is a weak tendency for inseminated females to show some ovarial development. Insemination of workers may be useful if the queen weakens or dies.

39 Each of the subgenera of primitively eusocial bees reviewed by Michener (*10*) shows some or all of these trends, but quantitative data are still too weak to permit detailed correlations between numbers of males produced, degree of worker insemination, and frequency of worker supersedure.

40 C. R. Watts and A. W. Stokes, *Sci. Am.* **224**, 112 (June 1971).

41 For example, in *Aphaenogaster rudis* workers are capable of producing males when the queen is dead, but when she is alive she apparently produces most or all of the males [R. H. Crozier, *Isozyme Bull.* **7**, 18 (1974)].

42 This is true for *Leptothorax curvispinosus, L. duloticus,* and *Prenolepis imparis* (data separated by M. Talbot).

43 For one monogynous species *(Camponotus herculeanus)* we used data on alates counted while leaving the nest. For another species (*Tetramorium caespitum*), reproductives were removed from the nests each year, leaving the nests intact so that they could be sampled in succeeding years (each year's sampling of a given nest is counted as a separate nest).

44 There is stong variance between nests in the sex ratio produced. Small nests within some species apparently tend to produce males (*35*). Producing one sex at a time may be a ploy to reduce male selfishness, assuming that males are sensitive to the sex ratio of reproductives within a nest (since they will typically value other males more than female reproductives).

45 Relative dry weight was chosen (instead of relative wet weight), on the assumption that water is relatively inexpensive to an ant colony. For several species, the dry weights were found by collecting live alates, killing, drying, and weighing them. (Alates were dried for 1 hour at 275°F; additional drying had no effect on dry weight.) For most of the rest of the species, we weighed dried specimens in the collection of the Museum of Comparative Zoology (Harvard), and we normally weighed five individuals of each sex. For five species (Table 2), specimens preserved in alcohol were dried and weighed. Although two authorities on ants guessed that females would lose relatively more weight while being dried, the reverse was invariably true: males commonly lose about two-thirds of their weight, while females lose somewhat less than half of theirs. Thus the wet weight ratio is larger than the dry weight ratio by a mean factor of 1:1.7 (geometric mean for seven species, range, 1.4 to 1.9). Since it is unlikely that water has no cost to the colony, the true relative cost may lie between the dry weight ratio and the wet weight ratio but closer to the dry weight ratio.

46 A number of methodological safeguards were used. All sex ratio data were gathered in ignorance of the relative cost of the two sexes. For each species weighed, H. H. weighed male and female specimens (usually singly) on a Mettler balance scale, type B6 (precision to ± 0.01 mg). Whenever we chose specimens to weigh from a larger sample, they were chosen without knowledge of the relevant sex ratio. More than half of the specimens weighed were sent to us by other scientists in response to our request for five specimens of each sex that were typical by size. None of the scientists knew of the predictions being tested.

47 In our opinion the six monogynous species with the best data are *Formica pallidefulva, Leptothorax curvispinosus, Myrmica sulcinodis, Prenolepis imparis, Solenopsis invicta,* and *Tetramorium caespitum.*

48 Bomb calorimetry was performed for us by the Warf Institute (Madison, Wis.) with an estimated accuracy of ± 10 percent. Each female sample was slightly higher in calories per gram than the comparable male sample. Two species of *Camponotus:* male, 4.8 kcal/g, female (incomplete burns), 5.15 kcal/g. Composite males of *Myrmica emeryana, Aphaenogaster rudis,* and *Pogonomyrmex barbatus,* 5.16 kcal/g. Female *Myrmica emeryana,* 5.19 kcal/g, *Aphaenogaster rudis* (incomplete burns), 6.62 kcal/g, and *Pogonomyrmex barbatus,* 6.29 kcal/g.

49 R. G. Wiegert and D. C. Coleman, *BioScience* **20**, 663 (1970).

50 W. L. Morrill, *Environ. Entomol.* **3**, 265 (1974); personal communication; G. P. Markin and J. H. Dillier, *Ann. Entomol. Soc. Am.* **64**, 562 (1971).

51 M. V. Brian, *Ekol. Pol.* **20**, 43 (1972).

52 L. Passera, personal communication.

53 This prediction should also hold for parasitic ants (*5*) except that such species are likely to practice adelphogamy, resulting in a strong bias toward females (*6, 9*). Ratios of investment in parastic ants do appear to be biased toward females (*6*). *Sifolinia laurae* females are larger than males and more numerous (*51*). The same is true of *Plagiolepis xene* (*52*). As is consistent with the hypothesis of adelphogamy, nearly every nest of *P. xene* that was examined by Passera (8 of 11) produced at least one or two males.

54 As in *Leptothorax curvispinosus,* nests consisted of individual acorns and other nesting places in which *Leptothorax duloticus* were found. For additional information on *L. duloticus,* see M. Talbot, *Ecology* **38**, 449 (1957); L. G. Wesson, *Bull. Brooklyn Entomol. Soc.* **35**, 73 (1940); E. O. Wilson, *Evolution* **29**, 108 (1975).

55 A. Buschinger, personal communication. Buschinger sent us specimens stored in alcohol which we dried and weighed. For additional information on the biology of the species, see A. Buschinger, *Insectes Soc.* **13**, 5 (1966); *ibid.,* p. 311; *Zool. Anz.* **187**, 184 (1971).

56 M. Talbot, unpublished data gathered at the E. S. George Reserve, Pinckney, Mich. All specimens were sent in alcohol by Talbot and dried and weighed by us.

57 A. E. Headley, *Ann. Entomol. Soc. Am.* **36**, 743 (1943) (10 nests); M. Talbot (*56*) (72 nests). For additional observations on the species, see E. O. Wilson, *Ann. Entomol. Soc. Am.* **67**, 777 (1974); *ibid.,* p. 781.

58 The dry weight of the slave-making queen may be reduced because she founds a colony by expropriating a nest of the slave species; hence she may need little in fat reserves.

59 In nests of both *Leptothorax duloticus* and *Harpagoxenus sublaevis* the slaves greatly outnumber the slave-makers (*36, 55, 56*). The slaves gather all of the food and do all of the nest and brood care.

60 D. H. Janzen, *J. Anim. Ecol.* **42**, 727 (1973).

61 Polygynous nests, usually temporary, may also arise when young queens (perhaps sisters) work together to found a new colony [C. Baroni-Urbani, *Zool. Anz.* **181**, 269 (1968)]. Queens and workers are not expected to agree on relative merits of monogyny and polygyny. Workers are more likely to favor a reproductive sister joining the nest than is the queen, and in at least one ant species, *Camponotus herculeanus,* polygynous queens are tolerated by workers but act aggressively

among themselves (*29*). By contrast, two related females are more likely to agree to continue the polygyny, and polygyny between founding females often ends when the first workers eclose [N. Waloff, *Insectes Soc.* **4,** 391 (1957)]. For detailed studies of any polygyny, see A. Bushinger, thesis. Würzburg University (1967).

62 Inclusion of reproductive daughters in the nest also changes the average *r* between workers and the male and female reproductives that they finally rear. Insofar as workers are rearing the offspring of someone other than their mother, they will tend to prefer a 1:1 ratio of investment.

63 This is a general argument. In any species in which the offspring of one sex, after the end of period of parental investment, inflict a cost on their parents not inflicted by offspring of the opposite sex, then the inflicting sex will be produced in smaller numbers than expected on the basis of parental investment. The argument holds in reverse for altruistic behavior performed by offspring of one sex. This suggests a simple way to measure whether helpers at the nest (for example, in birds) are really helping or are inflicting a net cost on their parents [A. Zahavi, *Ibis* **116,** 84 (1974); J. Brown, *Ibid.* **117,** 243 (1975)], or are helping only enough to make up for costs they are inflicting. The sex ratio that is produced should show appropriate biases. This argument may explain some of the sex ratio variation in bird species with helpers.

64 The following polygynous *Formica* appear to have male-biased ratios of invest-ment: *F. obscuriventris* [M. Talbot, *Anim. Behav.* **12,** 154 (1964)]; *F. ulkei* and *F. obscuripes* [————, *Am. Midl. Nat.* **61,** 124 (1959)]; *F. opaciventris* [G. Sherba, *J.N.Y. Entomol. Soc.* **69,** 71 (1961)]. See also M. Ito and S. Imamura, *J. Fac. Sci. Hokkaido Univ. Ser. VI Zool.* **19,** 681 (1974). Relative dry weight (F/M) in *For-mica* is typically lower than 2:1.

65 D. H. Janzen, *Science* **188,** 936 (1975). The ratio of investment was based on a single nest for each species.

66 G. W. Elmes, personal communication: 21 nests were monogynous (2130 reproduc-tives), four were polygynous (293 reproductives). Polygynous queens were mi-crogynes (average, eight to a nest).

67 W. A. Sands, personal communication.

68 *Neotermes connexus* (sex ratio 2791:912; 55 nests were examined): H. A. Bess, in Biology of Termites, K. Krishna and F. M. Weesner, Eds. (Academic Press, New York, 1970), vol. 2. We have been unable to get specimens to weigh, but it is unlikely that females are more than 1.5 times as heavy as males (*67*).

69 M. L. Roonwal and S. C. Verma, *Ann. Arid Zone* **12,** 107 (1973); M. L. Roonwal and N. S. Rathore, *ibid.* **11,** 92 (1972). For one species, *Microcerotermes raja,* the dry weight ratio was calculated from Roonwal and Verma's linear measurements of the alates. A termite swarm consists of individuals who are just departing their nests.

70 W. A. Sands, *Insectes Soc.* **12,** 117 (1965). We thank W. A. Sands and M. T. Pearce of the Centre for Overseas Pest Research, London, England, for the use of their unpublished data on *Trinervitermes.* Specimens stored in ethanol were weighed after being dried for 1 minute on filter paper. For the five species of *Trinervitermes,* the sex ratios and the dry weight ratios are as follows.

	Sex ratio	Weight ratio
T. trinervius	61:136	1.15
T. germinatus	230:347	1.25
T. togoensis	60:101	1.18
T. oeconomus	95:114	1.27
T. occidentalis	52:214	1.18

Although the sex ratio data are sparse they are consistent with other indications of a female biased sex ratio. For nomenclatural changes see W. A. Sands, *Bull. Br. Mus. (Nat. Hist.) Entomol. Suppl.* **4** (1965).

71 S. D. Jayakar and H. Spurway, *J. Bombay Nat. Hist. Soc.* **61**, 662 (1964).

72 Data from the following studies are likely to be biased in this fashion: K. A. Stockhammer, *J. Kans. Entomol. Soc.* **39**, 157 (1966); R. P. Kapil and S. Kumar, *J. Res. Punjab Agric. Univ.* **6**, 359 (1969); C. D. Michener, W. B. Kerfoot, W. Ramirez, *J. Kans. Entomol. Soc.* **39**, 245 (1966).

73 The depth of the holes available may also affect the sex ratio produced, as in *Megachile rotundata* [H. S. Gerber and E. C. Klostermeyer, *Science* **167**, 82 (1970)].

74 There is usually considerably greater mortality in trap-nests than in nature. If the mortality is differential by sex, then the sex ratio of adults when eclosing misrepresents the sex ratio at the time of parental investment (when the eggs were laid). In general, species with little or no male parental investment (such as bees and wasps) are expected to show differential male mortality (*7*).

75 Plus *Stenodynerus krombeini* ($N = 69$). For some species, Krombein (*32*) was able to infer sex for some of the individuals who failed to develop and for these species the sex ratio we have used is based on all individuals reared plus those whose sex was inferred. Inclusion of individuals whose sex was inferred has only a slight (and nonsystematic) effect on the sex ratio measured.

76 All individuals were reared by Krombein (*32*) in trap-nests and were killed and pinned shortly after eclosing.

77 Weighted equally by the two dimensions, cell length and cross-sectional area.

78 K. V. Krombein, personal communication.

79 Also relevant to relative cost are features such as cell position and hence time of parental investment, cell partition width, and associated intercallary cells. Neither partition width nor associated intercallary cells appear to differ strikingly by sex (*32*), but female cells are often deeper in the nests; that is, they are the first to be occupied and the last to be vacated. The effect of these factors on relative cost is not clear.

80 This is also true for a larger sample (15 individuals of each sex) of *Euodynerus foraminatus apopkensis* (Table 5). Cell dimensions were not available for many of the specimens on which mean weights were based, thus Krombein picked out additional specimens to permit the measure of weight per unit volume.

81 For the five species, the provisioning ratio (sample size given in parentheses) and the cell volume ratio are: *Monobia quadridens* 1.38 (9), 1.39, *Euodynerus foraminatus apopkensis* 1.75 (77), 1.69; *E. megaera* 1.76 (9), 1.74; *E. schwarzi* 2.29 (11), 2.37; and *Ancistrocerus antilope* 1.21 (17), 1.48.

82 The caterpillars were removed from alcohol and dried for 18 hours before being weighed. Because the contents of some cells were lumped, it is not possible to calculate variances in the measures. Sample size: 8 females, 14 males, and 2 uncertain individuals that are likely to be males. For the same species (sample of 2 males and 2 females) the weight ratio of provisions (1.41) is very near the volume ratio of provisions (1.44) [J. T. Medler, *Ann. Entomol. Soc. Am.* **57**, 56 (1964)].

83 E. White, *J. Anim. Ecol.* **31**, 317 (1962). The weight ratio is based on White's data.

84 In *Osmia rufa* the provisioning ratio (1.3), based on the number of provisioning trips required to fill up two male cells and two female cells, was the same as the volume ratio (1.3), but not the same as the adult weight ratio (for all individuals, 1.7) The sex ratio was 1.4 [A. Raw, *Trans. R. Entomol. Soc. London* **124**, 213 (1972)]. in *O. lignaria* the peak larval weight ratio (1.4) is the same as the weight ratio of provisions consumed [M. D. Levin. *J. Kans. Entomol. Soc.* **39**, 524 (1966)]. In *Sphecius speciosus* the adult weight ratio (2.4) is almost identical to the provisioning weight ratio (2.3) but the latter was only estimated [R. Dow, *Ann. Entomol. Soc. Am.* **35**, 310 (1942)]. In *Sceliphron spirifex* (*83*) the provisioning ratio is about 1.6 while male and female cell volumes are nearly identical, but this species is a mud dauber and does not build cells end to end in a limited space.

85 In *Megachile rotundata* the dry weight ratio for adults is only slightly greater (3 to 8 percent) than the wet weight ratio of larvae for three independent samples (*73*).

86 H. V. Danks, *Trans. R. Entomol. Soc. London* **122**, 323 (1971), Relative cell volumes are based on relative cell length alone since this is the only cell dimension that Danks supplies. For one of his species *(Cemonus lethifer)* Danks also provides weights of prepupae. The prepupal weight ratio ($N = 252$) is 1.29, slightly greater than the cell volume ratio (1.12).

87 In particular, prey that is stored must be weighed as well as counted. In addition, by watching females provision cells, one can measure the time spent in provisioning cells of different sizes.

88 For example, Jeanne (*31*) and West Eberhard (*34*) give sex ratio limited by small samples. C. D. Michener [*Bull. Am. Mus. Nat. His.* **145**, 221 (1971)] gives detailed sex ratio data for allodapine bees but it is very difficult to separate workers from reproductives in these bees. For other data, see Michener (*10*).

89 Since males leave the nest before young queens do, Webb's data probably slightly underestimate the number of males produced.

90 J. B. Free and C. G. Butler [*Bumblebees* (Collins, London, 1959)] give an estimate of 2:1 for the sex ratio in *Bombus* generally.

91 *Myrmica rubra* (Table 3) [M. V. Brian, *Insectes Soc.* **16**, 249 (1969)].

92 W. D. Hamilton, in *Man and Beast: Comparative Social Behavior* (Smithsonian Press, Washington, D.C. 1971). For the expected effects on aggressive behavior of asymmetries in the payoffs, see G. A. Parker, *J. Theor. Biol.* **47**, 223 (1974).

93 J. Gervet, *Insectes Soc.* **9**, 343 (1964).

94 Conflict is expected because each worker would prefer to produce sons rather than nephews. This conflict is also expected when the queen is alive, but workers then agree on the production of sisters which is the major part of their work.

95 The acacia trees that are host to ant colonies of *Pseudomyrmex* show a similar bias.

Queens of monogynous species are protected within heavily fortified thorns, while queens of polygynous species occupy less protected ones (*60*).

96 For species such as *Myrmica rubra* polygyny apparently results when fertilized daughters are permitted to return to the colony of their origin. It is not known whether such females mate with close relatives. That inbreeding should be associated with laying workers is not a strong argument. Queens will be less antagonistic toward eggs laid by workers, but there will also be less gain for the workers.

97 The queen may be able to influence the ratio of investment in mass provisioning social bees because investment occurs at the time of egg laying.

98 M. V. Brian. *Colloq. Int. C.N.R.S.* **173**, 1 (1967).

99 J. L. Pricer, *Biol. Bull. (Woods Hole)* **14**, 177 (1908). *Camponotus ferrugineus* specimens were captured in Delaware and killed and weighed by us (after drying) on 10 April 1975. *Camponotus pennsylvanicus* females were captured and killed in Stoughton, Mass., on 10 June 1974, dried, and weighed. (Males came from the Museum of Comparative Zoology collection.)

100 B. Hölldobler and U. Maschwitz, Z. *Vgl. Physiol.* **50**, 551 (1965).

101 M. Talbot, *Ecology* **29**, 316 (1948).

102 ———, *ibid.* **24**, 31 (1943). *Prenolepis* reproductives overwinter as alates in the nest. Specimens were collected in mid-May while swarming in Lexington, Mass.

103 T. Lewis, *Trans. R. Entomol. Soc. London* **127**, 51 (1975).

104 M. Talbot, *Ann. Entomol. Soc. Am.* **44**, 302, (1951); A. E. Headley, *ibid., * **42**, 265 (1949). Specimens were collected from the nest 21 July 1974 at Blue Hills, Mass.

105 M. Talbot, *Contrib. Lab. Vertebr. Biol. Univ. Mich.* **69**, 1 (1954). Specimens collected 18 July 1974 at Wellfleet, Mass.

106 M. Autuori, *Arq. Inst. Biol. Sao Paulo* 19, 325 (1950). No specimens were available for *A. bisphaerica,* so an approximate weight ratio of 8.0 was inferred from weights of the other two *Atta.*

107 M. Talbot, *Ann. Entomol. Soc. Am.* **38**, 365 (1945).

108 G. W. Elmes, *Oecologio (Berlin)* **15**, 337 (1974). At least 223 of the 596 males were apparently produced by laying workers, so that the ratio of investment is expected to lie near 1:2 (rather than 1:3).

109 M. V. Brian, personal communication; ———, G. Elmes, A. F. Kelly. *J. Anim. Ecol.* **36**, 337 (1967). Weights (at swarming) are from Peakin (35).

110 B. Hocking, *Trans. R. Entomol. Soc. London* **122**, 211 (1970).

111 G. P. Markin, *Ann. Entomol. Soc. Am.* **63**, 1238 (1970). Each month of the year four nests were sampled at random and the contents were weighed.

112 G. W. Elmes, *J. Anim. Ecol.* **42**, 761 (1973).

113 Twenty-three nests, 1852 reproductives (*52*).

114 G. C. Eickwort and K. R. Eickwort, *J. Kans. Entomol. Soc.* **42**, 421 (1969).

115 T. H. Frison, *Trans. Am. Entomol. Soc. (Phila.)* **48**, 137 (1922).

116 R. W. Thorp, *Am. Midl. Nat.* **82**, 321 (1969).

117 P. F. Torchio and N. N. Youssef, *J. Kans. Entomol. Soc.* **41**, 289 (1968).

118 J. C. Porter, *Iowa State J. Sci.* **26**, 23 (1951).

119 P. F. Torchio, *Los Ang. Cty. Mus. Contrib. Sci.* **206**, 1 (1971).

120 G. C. Eickwort, *J. Kans. Entomol. Soc.* **40**, 42 (1967).

121 D. H. Janzen, personal communication.

122 G. C. Eickwort sexed pupae and prepupae in nests found prior to adult emergence in May 1972. He was unable to sex 27 prepupae. For additional data, see G. C. Eickwort, *Search* **3**, 1 (1973).

123 P. F. Torchio, personal communication.

124 Y. Hirashima, *Sci. Bull. Fac. Agric. Kyushu Univ.* **16**, 481 (1958).

125 C. D. Michener and R. B. Lange, *Ann. Entomol. Soc. Am.* **51**, 155 (1958).

126 S. D. Jayakar and H. Spurway, *Nature (London)* **212**, 306 (1966).

127 K. V. Krombein, *Proc. Biol. Soc. Wash.* **77**, 73 (1964).

128 O. Lomholdt, *Vidensk. Medd. Dan. Naturhist. Foren. Kbh.* **136**, 29 (1973).

Local Mate Competition and Parental Investment in Social Insects

Richard D. Alexander
Paul W. Sherman
Museum of Zoology, University of Michigan
Department of Zoology, University of California, Berkeley

Kinship theory (*1*) and sex ratio theory (*2*) were used by Trivers and Hare (*3*) to predict the relative investments in reproductive males and females by various eusocial insects and their nonsocial relatives. They suggested that in eusocial species with haplodiploid sex determination, queens gain by a 1:1 (male:female) investment in reproductive offspring, while their sterile worker offspring gain by a 1:3 investment among reproductive siblings, and that (*3*, p. 250) ". . . a measurement of the ratio of investment is a measure of the relative power of the two parties . . ." From their measurements of investment patterns in various species, Trivers and Hare concluded that in single-queen (monogynous) ants, the investment pattern is "near 1:3," while in nonsocial bees and wasps, which lack sterile castes, the investment pattern "approximates 1:1." Their interpretation is that the interests of the workers are more nearly realized than are those of the queen. In support of this interpretation they also cite investment ratios from multiple-queen (polygynous) ants, slave-making ants, termites, and bumblebees. Their conclusions have been multiply cited (*4*).

We argue here that, on the contrary, (i) Trivers and Hare's predictions of 1:1 and 1:3 investment patterns are inappropriate for the insect groups they analyzed, (ii) they did not demonstrate such patterns, (iii) their data are not explained by their hypothesis, and (iv) their data for the most part conform to an alternative hypothesis, that is, Hamilton's (*5*) hypothesis of "local mate competition" (mating rivalry among close relatives), which they mention (*3*, footnotes, 9, 53, and 96 and p. 251) but do not apply.

Trivers and Hare's predictions depend upon (i) monogamy or effective monogamy among laying females, (ii) inability of workers to lay eggs, and (iii) outbreeding without effects from local mate competition (LMC) (*6*). However, multiple matings by females, worker oviposition, and local mate competition may actually be typical of haplodiploid insects rather than rare or absent among them, as Trivers and Hare may have assumed in drawing their conclusions (*3*, p. 261).

We thank David P. Cowan for permission to use unpublished information and Robert K. Colwell for generous assistance with statistical interpretations. We also thank Gerald Borgia, Kent L. Fiala, R. Glenn Ford, Katharine M. Noonan, George F. Oster, and Edward D. Rothman for assistance. The Miller Foundation at the University of California, Berkeley, supported P.W.S.

MULTIPLE MATINGS BY QUEENS

Multiple matings by queens of eusocial Hymenoptera have frequently been reported (*7-10*); Wilson, for example, cites multiple matings for eight species of eusocial Hymenoptera but only two instances in which it is believed that single mating by queens is the rule. (Obviously, multiple mating is easier to document than single mating.)

Multiple insemination has two effects. First, it reduces the predicted female bias in preferred investment ratios among sterile workers. In species with haplodiploid sex determination, full sisters share an average of ¾ of their genes identical by (immediate) descent (IBD). If a female mates with n different males and uses their sperm randomly, her daughters average ($¼ + ½n$) alike (*1*). On the basis of Trivers and Hare's approach, the worker offspring of a female who mates twice and uses the sperm of the males randomly maximize their reproduction by an investment pattern of 1:2. This is because they share, on the average, only twice as many genes IBD with their sisters as with their brothers, rather than three times as many, as under monogamy. If the sperm of the different mates of one female tend to clump separately, as is likely (*11*), the workers' interests are more female-biased than if the sperm do not clump; but with multiple matings by their queen the workers' interests would reach Trivers and Hare's 1:3 prediction only if workers were never required to tend half siblings, a condition we consider unlikely (*12*).

Multiple matings do not alter the relationship of a female's worker offspring to their brothers, which remains at ¼. The mother is, in all cases, ½ like each offspring (in genes IBD), male or female.

Multiple mating by queens also produces mixed broods of full siblings and half siblings. This creates a potential for the expression of differences in reproductive interests within the brood. Only by using the sperm from one male (that is, being effectively monogamous) might a queen avoid reproductive differences of interest among her worker offspring. Even an abrupt transition from use of one male's sperm to use of another male's sperm would not cause quite the same effect as monogamy, since some workers would be required to tend less closely related siblings during the period of transition between the sperm of different males.

It would be interesting to know how changes in sperm use correlate with swarming in insects like honeybees, in which the old queen departs to a new nest site, leaving some of her worker offspring behind with a new queen, their sister. This new queen could be either a full sibling or a half sibling of the workers rearing her, depending on sperm use. Since half sisters average only ¼ alike, workers with a half sister as their queen tend juveniles averaging only ⅛ like them. Also, workers tending the offspring of a full sister or a half sister share their sister queen's interest in the ratio of investment in the sexes, since workers are equally related to their nieces and nephews.

WORKER OVIPOSITION

In some eusocial insects, workers are known to lay eggs. Wilson notes in (*10*, p. 333) that "Worker oviposition is widespread in the ants, from the primitive Myrmeciinae to the advanced Myrmicinae, Dolichoderinae, and Formicinae. . . . By feeding queens of *Myrmica* P^{32} and thus labeling their eggs, Brian (1968) was able to show that the workers lay in the presence of the queens and that most males are derived from worker-laid eggs" (*13*). Sex ratio data are sensitive to variations in the number of unfertilized laying females. There are several ways in which unfertilized females may become egg-layers in haplodiploid species: as workers in slave-making species which take over colonies, as microgynes or secondary reproductives in their mother's nest, as mated queens who have used all of their sperm, as unfertilized queens, as laying workers in a nest with a normal queen, or as laying workers when the queen is lost. One way to correct for this factor would be to eliminate from consideration all nests that produced only males; another would be to assume that, if nests that produce all males are included, then, in terms of Trivers and Hare's hypothesis, unless proportions of unfertilized laying individuals have been consistent enough for fertilized queens to adjust sex ratios in their broods accordingly, the data are male-biased.

When some workers lay eggs, the workers do not collectively share the same genetic interests, so that complex questions are raised about how individual, short-lived workers could function to achieve their "preferred" investment pattern in the sex ratio of reproductives produced by the colony as a whole. This problem is particularly evident in ants, in which a worker may live a maximum of 1 to 3 years while the queen lives for several times as long (*10*, pp. 426–430) and the colony, moreover, often produces only males while it is small, and only females (or both sexes) later (*3*, footnote 44, p. 262). Many workers in such colonies only interact with one sex of reproductives and, indeed, many workers in social insects probably fail to interact with any reproductives at all (for example, workers in the *Formica rufa* group; *10*, p. 163). Any analogy with the somatic cells of a metazoan producing a sex ratio in their gametes breaks down when eusocial workers in a colony do not have identical genetic interests, as in cases when workers lay eggs or when queens mate with more than one male (*14*).

Interpreting Trivers and Hare's discussion of this problem is difficult since they assume (*3*, figure 1 caption) that their "p" represents the ". . . fraction of male-producing eggs laid by the queen (p), where the remainder are laid by a *single* laying worker" (emphasis added). What Trivers and Hare envision as the "preferred" sex ratios of the three "interested parties" (that is, the queen, the laying workers, and the nonlaying workers), if most or all workers have the potentiality of laying eggs, is unclear, in spite of their explanation (*3*, note 19, p. 261). For example, if at least some workers are able to produce sons, the problem becomes one of understanding how a laying worker would apportion her male-directed beneficence among brothers (produced by her mother and, on average, ¼ like her in genes IBD), nephews, ⅛ to ¼ like her, and her own sons, ½ like her.

Trivers and Hare appear to avoid specifying these preferences for each species by assuming that few, if any, laying workers exist. They state (*3*, p. 254), "In some ants, such as *Atta* and *Solenopsis* . . . all males appear to be produced by the queen, and in other monogynous ants (single queen per nest) laying workers appear to be a relatively uncommon source of males (compared to eusocial bees and wasps) . . . so that the ratio of investment in ants should often approach 1:3." In view of the information presented above, the uncommonness of oviposition by females lacking sperm and thus the appropriateness of this prediction is open to question.

LOCAL MATE COMPETITION

Local mate competition refers to mating rivalry among genetic relatives. Its effects may derive from such competition not only between siblings or between parent and offspring, but also among more distant relatives, for mates that may be either related or unrelated to those competing for them. In one extreme, if all of a parent's daughters are fertilized only by their brothers, parents will benefit by producing only enough males to fully inseminate all their daughters. For "insects having usual sibmating," Hamilton (*5*) cites sex ratios within broods which vary from 1:2 to 1:46; males in such species, moreover, are usually smaller than females.

As evidenced by likelihood of sibling or parent-offspring matings, LMC may be widespread among both social and non-social haplodiploid insects (*15–17*) as, apparently, are the predicted female-biased investment patterns (*18–20*). Trivers and Hare's data from monogynous ants, for example, range from 1:1.57 to 1:8.88 with a geometric mean investment ratio of 1:3.45 (the arithmetic mean is 1:3.94). For "five of the six species with the best data" (*3*, p. 254) the range is 2.99 to 4.14, with a geometric mean of 3.36 (arithmetic mean, 3.39), essentially the entire range of variation thus falling outside the predictions of their hypothesis, even if the queens involved were monogamous and there were no unfertilized laying females. At least one ant species known to mate within the family (*21*) appears to produce investment patterns like those found by Trivers and Hare. We have been able to find satisfactory information regarding the likelihood of intrafamilial mating rivalry for only one ant species listed by them (*3*, table 2, p. 254), *Myrmica schencki*. In this species, sibling matings are appropriately suspected (*17, 18*) and the investment ratio is 6.45 (*3*, table 2). Since a hypothesis (other than inadequate data) exists to explain investment ratios greater than 1:3, findings in this range do not support Trivers and Hare's argument.

We examined Trivers and Hare's list of nonsocial Hymenoptera (*3*, table 4) for possible variations in effects from LMC. We considered that species in which individuals nest solitarily and siblings mature together are most likely to undergo such effects, thus to have female-biased investment patterns. By contrast group-nesting species (or solitary nesters which deposit their eggs singly) should be less affected by LMC and thus should have investment patterns nearer 1:1. Four species in the first category [13th, 14th, 16th, and 17th in the list in (3, table 4)] averaged an investment pattern of 1:1.81; in the second category (that is, all the rest with complete data) 12 species averaged 1:0.99. The direction of the difference is thus as predicted, and the two distributions differ significantly ($P < .03$, t-test).

Because they are the offspring of single reproductives, most eusocial insect colonies are like nonsocial solitary-nesting species in which siblings mature together. In other words, according to our classification of nonsocial species, eusocial insects are likely to have female-biased investment patterns as a result of LMC (see also 18–20). If the 12 nonsocial species least likely to be affected by LMC are removed from Trivers and Hare's nonsocial list, the remaining nonsocial species have an average investment pattern almost identical to that of all of their social species combined.

We infer that effects from LMC may be rather common and that these effects are most obvious among the Hymenoptera, whose haplodiploid system of sex determination makes them particularly capable of reducing deleterious consequences by sex ratio adjustments. Haplodiploidy also occurs in beetles and mites with "usual sibmating" (5). Together with Borgia (22) we hypothesize that haplodiploidy may actually spread and be maintained as a consequence of LMC.

NONSOCIAL, TRAPNESTED BEES AND WASPS

Trivers and Hare suggest that ratios of investment in nonsocial trapnested bees and wasps support their hypothesis that female-biased investment ratios in eusocial species result from worker domination. They state (3, p. 258), "Although there is considerable scatter, the species are closer to a 1:1 ratio of investment than to a 1:3." We do not believe that ratios of investment in nonsocial species trapnested by Krombein (23) can legitimately be used in this context for two reasons. First, patterns reported by Krombein plainly depended on the manner of trapnesting. He put out nests of various diameters, and sex ratios varied dramatically with nest bore: the larger the bore, the higher the percentage of females—with the smallest cavities sometimes having all males, the largest all females. Overall investment patterns obviously depended on the proportions of nests of each size that Krombein put out, and the significance of the size range he used would vary among species of differing body sizes. Thus, we disagree with Trivers and Hare's conclusion (3, p. 257) that no systematic bias is expected.

Second, Krombein usually bundled trapnests together, most often in groups of six. He thereby created a situation resembling colony breeding, in which outbreeding is likely. Should trapnested species be able to adjust sex ratios accordingly, 1:1 investments in the situation created by Krombein would not properly describe the investments of this group of Hymenoptera. D. P. Cowan (unpublished data) has discovered that, when females of *Euodynerus foraminatus* (Vespidae: Eumeninae) are trapnested in groups, they bias the sex ratios of their broods toward males more than when trapnested singly; data for this species were obtained by Krombein and used by Trivers and Hare (*3*, table 5). The possibility that trapnesting Hymenoptera may generally be able to vary the ratios of investment according to the likelihood of LMC indicates that trapnesting bee and wasp data currently available cannot be used to test the outcome of parent-offspring conflict.

POLYGYNOUS ANTS

Trivers and Hare suggested that polygynous ant colonies are collections of the daughters or granddaughters of a single queen, living in association with their queen mother. Even though this may not always be the case (*24*), they predicted male-biased investment patterns (*3*, p. 256) among polygynous species because (*3*, p. 255) "If a reproductive daughter is permitted to settle within or near the maternal nest when unrelated females would not be so permitted, then one must assume that the daughter thereby inflicts a cost on her mother ... This cost can be treated as a component of investment and raises the relative cost of a reproductive female." This argument is apparently derived form a consideration of *Acacia* ants (*25*), in which multiple colonies are founded on one tree by apparently unrelated queens, with each queen then behaving so as to replace, if possible, the other queens with her daughters. It may be more appropriate to view *Acacia* ant aggregations as groups of monogynous colonies rather than as a polygynous colony. In addition, it is probably inappropriate to view polygynous ants generally as parallels to the peculiar *Acacia* ant situation, in which the small colonies inhabit different hollow thorns. A queen of a subterranean species, for example, who allows her daughter to remain in her nest as an incipient queen, may be preparing a replacement for herself; further, a pair of sister queens in one nest is not appropriate to Trivers and Hare's interpretation, in spite of their footnote 61 (*3*, p. 262).

Trivers and Hare cite investment ratios from five species in the genus *Myrmica* as support for their polygynous ant hypothesis. In terms of decreasing female-bias in investment ratios, the five *Myrmica* species are ordered (*3*, figure 4C and p. 256): *M. schencki, M. sulcinodis, M. ruginodis, M. sabuleti,* and *M. rubra.* Trivers and Hare state (p. 256) that "The ratios of investment for these species are ordered exactly according to the parameters we have outlined (see Fig. 4C)."

We suggest that this ordering might be the result of several other factors, not taken into account by Trivers and Hare. For example, *M. schencki* probably mates within the family (*17, 18*), and it has the most female-biased investment ratio in the genus (1:6.45). Since unfertilized females can only produce males in haplodiploid species, oviposition by varying numbers of such females will tend to bias population-wide investment ratios toward males. Thus, it is important to know what proportions of nests in the polygynous sample produced only males, a factor that Trivers and Hare do not take into account despite their footnote 44 (*3*, p. 262). From data they used (*3*, tables 2 and 3), in *M. sulcinodis* 13 of 21 colonies produced only males while 1 produced only females (*26*), in *M. sabuleti* 25 of 35 colonies produced only males and none produced only females (*27*), and in *M. rubra* 9 of 11 colonies produced only males while none produced only females (*27*). Similar data for *M. ruginodis* are unpublished (*3*, footnote 66, p. 262).

Myrmica rubra, the species with the least female-biased investment ratio in the polygynous ant series, deserves further consideration. For this species, Brian (*27*, p. 50) noted that the colonies he studied were ". . . subject to disturbance by the trampling of cattle . . . causing colonies to be . . . difficult to retain . . . for study for more than a few years." If *M. rubra* tends to produce only males when colonies are young (see above), this, and not the number of queens, may well explain the low investment ratio (4:1) recorded for this species by Trivers and Hare and therefore its ranking in their polygynous ant series. *M. rubra* is also one of the species for which there is evidence of population-wide mate competition (*10*, p. 38).

SLAVE-MAKING ANTS

Trivers and Hare believe that their analysis of slave-making ants supports their hypothesis because they found investments showing "a highly significant deviation ($P < .001$) toward a 1:1 ratio" (*3*, p. 255) (apparently meaning significantly less than 1:3). Slave workers, they argue, have lost the ability to produce 1:3 investments in the nests of queens of slave-making species, who have evolved to extract from the slaves their preferred 1:1 investment. Slave-making workers, they suppose, must gain more by bringing to their nests slaves that will help their mothers produce a 1:1 investment than by remaining as workers themselves and producing their "preferred" 1:3 ratio; Trivers and Hare do not identify the nature of this gain. Their data on slave-makers are, like those on other species, averages from many colonies (in this case, 58 for *Harpagoxenus sublaevis* and 96 for *Leptothorax duloticus*) and standard deviations in sex ratios are not given. This is important because Wilson (*10*, p. 370) notes that in *H. sublaevis* "morphologically complete queens are relatively scarce," and that in a closely related species, *H. americana*, 16 of 32 colonies examined were populated exclusively by slave-making workers and their slaves. Worker queens are likely to be unfertilized, therefore able to produce only males, potentially creating male biases in samples of investment ratios which are unrelated to Trivers and Hare's explanation.

Regarding the likelihood of LMC among slave-makers, Wilson notes (*10*, p. 324) that "The exact extent of true brother-sister mating is unknown . . . in the only test of this kind of which I am aware, Wesson (1939) did find that the queens and males of the dulotic ant *Harpagoxenus americanus* prefer to mate with unrelated individuals." Wesson (*28*) also reported a sex ratio of 1.9:1 for 19 colonies of this species, including 11 colonies with laying workers. *H. sublaevis,* a closely related slave-maker, was reported (*3,* table 2) to have a sex ratio of 1.38:1 and the second least female-biased investment ratio (1.25) listed. Wilson also notes (*10,* p. 370) that "The rather fragmentary information available suggests that *L. duloticus* is basically similar to *Harpagoxenus* in its biology." The other slave-maker listed by Trivers and Hare, *L. duloticus,* invests the least in females of any formicid (0.87). At least these facts indicate that insufficient information was provided. At most, they suggest that the apparent bias toward 1:1 investments by the two slave-making species is due to different causes from those which Trivers and Hare postulate (that is, unfertilized queens or population-wide mate competition).

Trivers and Hare separate their data on slave-making ants from those on ants that are not slave-making (*3,* figure 4B), and those on polygynous ants from those on monogynous ants (*3,* figures 4C and 4A). The basis for their conclusions about formicid investment ratios (and those of all other social and nonsocial groups as well) are their tests of whether or not these separated sets of data resemble 1:1 or 1:3 investment slopes (but see below). In no case do they test whether or not these sets of data actually differ from one another. In contrast to this treatment, they consolidate, respectively, all data for termites (*3,* figure 5), all data for trapnested nonsocial Hymenoptera (*3,* figures 7 and 8), and all data for naturally nesting nonsocial Hymenoptera (*3,* figure 6). It is not clear to us, however, that the data in (*3,* figures 5–8) are any more unitary than are those in (*3,* figures 4A–C), if those in the latter case are appropriately combined (*3,* figures 4, A and B, and 4, A and C).

TERMITES

The termites may represent Trivers and Hare's most important comparison, since Isoptera do not have haplodiploid sex determination. This means that, according to Trivers and Hare's approach, termite investment ratios should be 1:1. Unfortunately, the data are scant, consisting of figures for nine species from two genera (*3,* figure 5). Trivers and Hare combine these data and obtain a geometric mean ratio of 1:1.62 (arithmetic mean, 1:1.91). They describe this (*3,* p. 256) as not significantly different from the slave-making ant data but different from the monogynous ant data.

We believe that a closer look at these data is warranted for two reasons. First, the two sets of data for different genera average, respectively, just more than 1:1 and 1:2.5, values not remarkably different from those reported for various social and nonsocial Hymenoptera. The two sets of data, moreover, differ from one another ($P < .05$; t-test). Second, if we use the same kind of test that Trivers and Hare used, the combined termite data are significantly biased toward 1:3 (that is, are different from 1:1). The implication is that the same factor or factors may influence investment ratios in both the Isoptera and the Hymenoptera.

Conceivably, the differences between termite genera and the wide scatter in all investment ratio data may be due to variations in LMC. Since termite eusociality has been attributed to inbreeding, (20, 29), it may not be unreasonable to assume that some species undergo LMC. If they do, and if female-biased investment ratios reflect this fact, we still do not know how any diploid species accomplishes such adjustment. Several possibilities are apparent, such as sex-differential destruction of gametes or juveniles, or sex-differential adjustments of investment in individual offspring. Termites, however, possess a means of adjusting investment in the sexes that may be unique and may have been important in their evolving eusociality. Unlike Hymenoptera, the nonreproductive casts of termites include both sexes, and, as with hymenopteran females, whether or not a given juvenile of either sex will be reproductive or nonreproductive is determined only when the juvenile is already partly grown—in termites it may already be an effective worker. This means that a termite colony has a continuing reservoir of nonreproductive juveniles of both sexes from which numbers and proportions of reproductives that are appropriate to any given circumstance be drawn. Apparently, no other species share this remarkable attribute.

PROBLEMS WITH INTERPRETING DATA

Selection of Specimens

All investment ratio data presented by Trivers and Hare may be consistently biased away from 1:1 because of the method of gathering them. They state (3, footnote 46, p. 262) that "More than half of the specimens weighed were sent to us by other scientists in response to our request for five specimens of each sex that were typical by size." If, as may be likely, cooperating scientists tended to pick males and females which did not resemble each other (that is, were "typically" male or female), and if females weigh more than males do, a consistent bias might well be introduced.

Grouping of Data

Wide variation in the original sex ratio data on which Trivers and Hare's article is based make the consistent use of grouped data unacceptable. As an example of the original data from which the authors draw their conclusions, consider their use of investment patterns of *Prenolepis imparis* (3, lower dot, figure 4; also, table 2). Their inverse investment ratio is based on sex ratios of 11 colonies of this species. In the article from which these data are drawn (30), information is reported for 20 colonies, only 12 of which possessed reproductives (a total of 2009). Trivers and Hare used 11 of the 12. Of the 12 colonies, one had males only (162), one had females only (15), one had a strongly female-biased ratio (9 males: 26 females), and nine had male-biased ratios, varying from 1.9:1 to 21:1. The sex ratio of six colonies dug up at Tiffin, Ohio, was 5.8:1, and that of the six from St. Charles, Missouri, was 8.7:1. These data were apparently averaged to produce a sex ratio of 8.36:1 (3, table 2).

Intraspecific Variation

Sample sizes of 1 to 66 were used in a single table (*3*, table 2) for weight-ratio measurements; what determined each sample size is not indicated. For most weight data, standard deviations are not given and are needed. The need for such is illustrated by data from the genus *Atta*. For *Atta sexdens* females, the standard deviation is almost 40 percent of the mean weight of the ten females sampled; nonetheless, the weight ratio of *A. laevigata* is based on a sample of six, five of which are males. For *Solenopsis invicta*, the sex ratio is based on a sample of 200,491, while the weight ratio sample size was 14 (again, no standard deviation is given for the weight of either sex). In addition, sample sizes are sometimes omitted from tables (for example, *3*, table 3) as are weight ratios and inverse investment ratios (for example, table 4).

Inappropriateness of Regression Analyses

Trivers and Hare presented and analyzed their data with regressions. Unless a systematic deviation in variance is corrected for, however, their linear regression analyses are inappropriate. Because they computed sex ratios by dividing the number of males by the number of females, their figure 4 and the others are asymmetric: when males outnumber females, the points are widely spread out; but when females outnumber males, the points are clustered between 1 and 0. This has two consequences. First, as the proportion of males increases, the total possible variance around any predicted line (1:1 or 1:3) also increases, thus violating an assumption of linear regression analysis; where "p" is the proportion of males, "q" is the proportion of females, and "n" is the sample size, the variance of the quantity "males/females" is non-homogeneously distributed as (p/nq^3) (*31*). Second, this means that even investment ratios as far different from the hypothesized 1:3 ratio as 1:7.9 and 1:8.88 are caused, in their graphs, to appear to support the 1:3 hypothesis.

Trivers and Hare draw their conclusions exclusively from testing such questions as whether or not a set of investment ratios "approximates 1:1" (*3*, p. 258) or is "biased toward females" (*3*, p. 258) (or males, *3*, p. 259); whether or not the results were "significantly different from a 1:3 slope" (*3*, p. 254); whether they "tend to scatter around the 1:3 line of investment instead of the 1:1" (*3*, p. 254); or whether or not termite investment ratios (*3*, p. 256) or those of solitary bees and wasps (*3*, p. 257) were "significantly closer to 1:1 than are the ratios for monogynous ants. . . ." The answers to such questions could be conclusive if the postulated investments of 1:1 and 1:3 were appropriate, if the hypotheses advanced were the only ones that could account for the data, and if regression analyses were appropriate. Since none of these preconditions is met, a reanalysis of their data seems warranted. Using principal components analysis (*32*) on total investment in females as a function of total investment in males, we estimated 95 percent confidence intervals for investment ratios. This treatment revealed that only monogynous ants' investments and those of all nonsocial, non-trapnested bees and wasps combined (but see above) differ. If the 95 percent confidence intervals are used, investment ratios of monogynous ants, termites, bumblebees, and nonsocial trapnested bees and wasps all overlap.

That almost every set of data presented by Trivers and Hare has an overall female bias implies some cause other than that, under haplodiploidy, worker interests are being realized. The wide scatter in their data is also prejudicial to their hypothesis in view of the apparent precision of their procedure of weighing adults in species in which juveniles are tended or provisioned to adulthood (that is, weighing them at termination of parental care) (2). Both the variability in their data and female biases beyond their predictions, on the other hand, support a hypothesis of varying amounts of LMC.

QUANTIFYING EFFECTS OF LOCAL MATE COMPETITION

Local mate competition, as Hamilton (5) used the term, refers to competition among genetic relatives for mates. Its effects are to devalue the competing individuals as contributions to the inclusive fitness of other relatives, including parents. These effects may be sexually symmetrical or asymmetrical. At least three means exist by which they may be alleviated. In most organisms, dispersal of potentially competing relatives may reduce or eliminate effects of LMC. Sexually asymmetrical effects may be alleviated by parents adjusting investments in the two sexes of their offspring. Among humans, marriage rules may be employed by collectives of interested, powerful relatives in fashions which reduce devaluations of kin as a result of LMC.

Quantification of the effects of LMC obviously is complex and must proceed along several different lines. Here we suggest only a few (see also 5). In most species, sexual competition is more severe among males than among females, with the possible outcome that brothers will devalue the parental effort invested in them when they compete for the same mate (or mates). In one kind of extreme, if a female produced in her brood two sons that competed solely with each other for every mate secured by either of them, the two sons would be of no more value to her than a single son. If they competed solely with each other for half the mates secured by both of them, they would be worth ¾ as much as two sons who never competed.

When brothers simultaneously compete for a female also being competed for by nonsibling males, whether or not they are devalued for their participation depends upon their effect on the likelihood that one of their mother's sons will secure the copulation; if their simultaneous presence doubles the chances, they are not devalued. If they cooperate in some fashion so as to more than double the chances of one of their mother's sons being successful, their individual values to their mother will be enhanced.

It is commonly assumed that Fisher's explanation of sex ratio selection (2) always holds in outbreeding populations, only failing when inbreeding occurs. But consanguineous matings can occur without effects from LMC, and vice versa. One reason for the confusion of inbreeding with LMC may be that when matings are frequent between siblings, brothers are likely to compete with each other for copulations with their sisters. If all matings are between siblings and if males do not invest parentally, a mother will partition her investment optimally between the sexes when she produces the minimum number of males necessary to inseminate her daughters fully and when the investment in these males is barely sufficient to enable them to accomplish this insemination. Because dispersal tends to reduce the likelihood that brothers will compete for mates, species in which premating dispersal occurs are not usually thought to be affected by LMC. This is not necessarily true. For example, brother-brother competition may not be unlikely in species among which males gather at crowded leks within which most females in the vicinity are inseminated, as in honeybees (*33*).

We emphasize that even competition for mates between rather distant relatives, such as cousins, may be deleterious to near and distant relatives of both. The question, for any species, seems to be whether or not cost-effective means are available for reducing these deleterious consequences.

CONCLUSIONS

The idea of testing the power of individuals (for example, a parent) against the collective power of groups of individuals (for example, a brood of similarly related offspring), as Trivers and Hare have attempted to do, is of broad significance in understanding the levels in the hierarchy of life at which natural selection has most consistently been effective. Current theory in evolutionary genetics seems, temporarily at least, to have taken the direction of supposing that selection is effective essentially only at the genic level, despite arguments to the contrary (*34*), the evident integrity of the genome, even in sexual organisms, and the widespread opinion that "the primary focus of evolution by natural selection is the individual" (*35*, p. 7).

We believe that because Trivers and Hare did not consider any hypotheses other than their own to explain the ratios of investment in the two sexes by social and nonsocial insects, and because of the manner in which they gathered and interpreted data, the significance of their arguments is diminished. Their data may possibly reflect the existence of both local mate competition and parent-offspring conflict. However, while ample evidence implicates the former hypothesis, in light of the reservations we outline, there is yet little or none to support the latter. The conclusion, therefore, that in modern eusocial Hymenoptera the workers' interests are being realized contrary to their queen's interest, is at least premature.

SUMMARY

Efforts to develop formulas for contrasting genetic interests of workers and queens in social Hymenoptera are complicated by many factors, including multiple matings by queens, oviposition by unmated females, and mating rivalry among genetic relatives (Hamilton's "local mate competition"). Because of haplodiploid sex determination in Hymenoptera, when such influences are absent, queens benefit from 1:1 sex ratios of investment (male:female) in reproductive offspring, workers from 1:3 ratios among reproductive siblings. Reports of variable ratios, including many well above 1:3, and female biases in nonsocial Hymenoptera and diplodiploid termites, implicate local mate competition and raises questions about previous interpretations that workers have their way.

REFERENCES AND NOTES

1   W. D. Hamilton, *J. Theor. Biol.* **7**, 1 (1964).
2   R. A. Fisher, *The Genetical Theory of Natural Selection* (Clarendon, Oxford, 1930).
3   R. L. Trivers and H. Hare, *Science* **191**, 249 (1976).
4   E. O. Wilson, *Sociobiology* (Harvard Univ. Press, Cambridge, Mass. 1975); in *Insects, Science, and Society,* D. Pimentel, Ed. (Academic Press, New York, 1975), pp. 25–31; J. Krebs and R. M. May, *Nature (London)* **260**, 9 (1976); R. Dawkins, *The Selfish Gene* (Oxford Univ. Press, Oxford, 1976); and others.
5   W. D. Hamilton, *Science* **156**, 477, (1967).
6   Hamilton has noted that "Fisher's principle" of the sex ratio (*5*, p. 477) ". . . is restricted to the actually unusual case of population-wide competition for mates." Trivers and Hare imply, by contrast, that population-wide competition is usual by stating (*3*, p. 251): "Values more female biased than 1 : 3 are only expected where extreme patterns of dispersal occur . . ." Trivers and Hare also state (in our opinion, erroneously) (*3*, p. 251) "The important point regarding ratios of investment is that such ratios are never expected to be more female biased than 1 : 2 on the effects of inbreeding alone. All values between 1 : 2 and 1 : 3 must reflect worker performances [*sic* : preferences?] for sisters over brothers."
7   For examples, see H. St. J. K. Donisthorpe, *British Ants: Their Life-History and Classification* (Routledge, London, ed. 2, 1927), p. 115.
8   W. C. Roberts, *Glean. Bee Cult.* **72**, 255 (1944).
9   F. Ruttner, *Bee World* **37**, 3 (1956); S. Tabor III, *J. Econ. Entomol.* **47**, 995 (1954); G. A. Parker, *Biol. Rev. Cambridge Philos. Soc.* **45**, 525 (1970); F. Ruttner, J. Woyke, N. Koeniger, *J. Apic. Res.* **12**, 21 (1973); J. Woyke, *ibid.* **14**, 153 (1975).
10 E. O. Wilson, *The Insect Societies* (Belknap, Cambridge, Mass., 1971), p. 330 and references therein.
11 S. Taber III [*J. Econ. Entomol.* **48**, 522, (1955)] found that proportions of offspring from multiply mated queen honeybees sampled weekly did not form a homogeneous binomial series. Although his data suggest that *Apis mellifera* sperm clump to some extent, it is also true that the progeny of at least two mating types appeared in every group of workers he sampled; Roberts (*8*) obtained similar results in a parallel experiment. Further, Taber's figure 1 (p. 525) suggests that the process of "switching" from predominant use of one type of sperm to predominant use of another lasts 3 to 5 weeks. Unless workers always discriminate between their half siblings and their full siblings, Taber's report suggests that they are consistently required to tend both.

12 The only possibility of the occurrence of this situation appears to be in a hypothetical species in which a polyandrous queen herself tends her first offspring by a second male during the transition between use of the sperm of different males.

13 See also M. V. Brian, *Insectes Soc.* **16**, 249 (1969). Wilson's 1968 reference to Brian is "Regulation of Sexual Production in an Ant Society," *Colloques Internationaux du Centre National de la Recherche Scientifique, Paris,* No. 173, pp. 61–76 (1967).

14 See also M. J. West-Eberhard, *Q. Rev. Biol.* **50**, 1 (1976).

15 Sibling matings are appropriately suspected in the various ant species with wingless males and with wingless or partially winged microgyne females, as well as in species in which mating occurs in the nest. For examples, see Donisthorpe (*7,* pp. 78, 86, 102, 107, 123, 129); H. St. J. K. Donisthorpe, *The Guests of British Ants: Their Habits and Life-Histories* (Routledge, London 1927), p. 82. Although P. B. Kannowski [*Insectes Soc.* **6**, 115 (1959)] concludes that "intranidal mating is an exceptional process, not a normal one," he reports numerous apparent instances among bog ants in Michigan; see also L. Passera, *ibid.* **15**, 327 (1968); P. B. Kannowski, *Symp. Genet, Biol. Ital.* **12**, 74 (1963); E. O. Wilson (*10*).

16 J. H. Sudd, *An Introduction to the Behavior of Ants* (St. Martin's, New York, 1967).

17 M. Talbot, *Am. Midl. Nat.* **34**, 504 (1945).

18 See Trivers and Hare's data (*3*). In species known to mate in the nest, moreover, sex ratios are female-biased. Such sex ratio skews probably indicate female-biased investment ratios since, according to Trivers and Hare, female ants are from 1.73 to 25.4 times heavier than conspecific males. Thus, for *Monomorium pharaonis,* Sudd in (*16*, p. 140) states that "Many other crevice-nesters, including *Monomorium pharaonis,* also mate in the nest." See also M. A. Bellevoye, *Insect Life* **2**, 230 (1890). In describing the mating flight activities of *Myrmica schencki,* Talbot in (*17*) states that "winged ants stayed close to the nests and never flew in numbers . . . ," and she concludes that ". . . contrary to the procedure for *Lasius* and *Prenolepis*" (in which she had reported conspicuous mating flights) "*Myrmica* produced more females than males."

19 A female-biased sex ratio has been reported for *M. pharaonis* (range between nests is 1 : 1.1 to 1 : 5.3) by A. D. Peacock, *Entomol. Mon. Mag.* **87**, 185 (1951).

20 W. D. Hamilton, *Annu. Rev. Ecol. Syst.* **3**, 204 (footnote) (1972).

21 We attempted to compute the investment ratio for *Monomorium pharaonis,* a species in which brothers likely compete with each other for mates (*10*, pp. 40–41; see also *18, 19*). We used a mean sex ratio of 1 : 2.19 (*19*). We did not have specimens to weigh, nor could we find published weights for reproductives of this species. Therefore, we used the body length ratio given by D. W. Hall and I. C. Smith [*Entomol. Mon. Mag.* **87**, 217 (1951)] as an indicator of the difference in size between males and females; this ratio is 1 : 1.39. Taken together, these data yielding a probable inverse investment ratio near 4.43 (5.84, using body lengths cubed), figures well within the range of many species listed by Trivers and Hare in Table 2 (*3*). Because *Monomorium pharaonis* found nests by swarming (*10*), the actual investment in females is somewhat higher (if one regards workers accompanying a new queen as part of the investment in her).

22 G. Borgia, in preparation. M. J. West Eberhard has pointed out to us that LMC may have promoted evolution of eusociality in haplodiploid species because female biases within broods would increase the average relationship between an incipient worker and her siblings. Similarly, LMC may reduce numbers of laying workers by devaluing males.

23 K. V. Krombein, *Trap-nesting Wasps and Bees: Life Histories, Nests and Associates* (Smithsonian Institution Press, Washington, D.C., 1967).

24 Wilson (*10*, p. 324) states that "We also understand very little of the adaptive significance of polygyny, and, more importantly, the degree of kinship of queens that live together in polygynous colonies. A definitive judgment cannot be made until more data are available on these subjects."

25 See *3*, footnote 60, p. 262; D. H. Janzen, *J. Anim. Ecol.* **42**, 727 (1973); *10*, pp. 51–55.

26 G. W. Elmes, *Oecologia (Berlin)* **15**, 337 (1974).

27 M. V. Brian, *Ekol. Pol.* **20**, 43 (1972).

28 L. G. Wesson, Jr., *Trans. Am. Entomol. Soc. (Philadelphia)* **65**, 97, (1939).

29 N. Lin and C. D. Michener, *Q. Rev. Biol.* **47**, 131 (1972).

30 M. Talbot, *Ecology* **24**, 31 (1943).

31 E. D. Rothman, personal communication.

32 R. R. Sokal and F. J. Rohlf, *Biometry* (Freeman, San Francisco, 1969), pp. 526– 532. In our analysis, the ordinate (I_f) = number of females X mean female weight, abscissa (I_m) = number of males X mean male weight; investment ratios are I_f/I_m. Since a logarithmic transformation of both I_f and I_m is necessary to produce normality, I_f/I_m is the antilogarithm of the intercept for the first principal component line, with the origin at (I_m, I_f). Confidence intervals are found from the intersections of the ordinate with the 95 percent confidence elipse for the bivariate mean.

33 C. Zmarlicki and R. A. Morse, *J. Apic. Res.* **2**, 64 (1963); G. E. Strang, *J. Econ. Entomol.* **63**, 641 (1970).

34 I. Franklin and R. C. Lewontin, *Genetics* **65**, 707 (1970); E. Mayr, *Biol. Zentralbl.* **94**, 377 (1975).

35 R.C. Lewontin, *Annu. Rev. Ecol. Syst.* **1**, 1 (1970).

Sex Ratio of Parental Investment in Colonies of the Social Wasp *Polistes fuscatus*

Katharine M. Noonan
Museum of Zoology, University of Michigan

Field estimates of parental investment in the two sexes in the social paper wasp *Polistes fuscatus* indicate that the mother's interests, rather than those of her worker offspring, are realized. Local competition for mates seemed to be absent, and the population investment ratio was not significantly different from 1:1. Workers are not more closely related to the brood they tend than they would be to their own offspring. The 3/4 relationship between sisters in haplodiploid species cannot account for the maintenance of eusociality in this case.

The sex ratio of parental investment in social wasp colonies bears on three current problems in social behavior: the importance of haplodiploidy in the evolution of hymenopteran eusociality (*1*), the resolution of queen-worker conflict in eusocial haplodiploid species (*2*), and the extent to which local mate competition favors female-biased sex ratios (*3, 4*). I now present data from field observations of colon-ies of the social paper wasp *Polistes fuscatus,* which suggest that when competition for mates is population-wide, the sex ratio of investment in reproductives is near 1:1.

Several features of *Polistes* social biology facilitate collecting data on behavior and sex ratios. Nests are founded annually by from one to several overwintered, inseminated females. The unenveloped nests allow direct observation of the behavior of individuals, including egg-laying, egg-eating, foraging, fighting, and mating. Workers emerge in midsummer, and reproductives in the late summer and fall. There are distinct behavioral (but no reliable morphological) differences between workers and reproductive females. The virtual lack of temporal overlap in their emergence, however, makes it possible to estimate sex ratios of reproductive individuals without extensive behavioral observations. The abundant nests are localized around houses and farm buildings, where mating and hibernation occur. It is possible, therefore, to gather sex ratio data for a sample of nests contributing to a local breeding population.

I collected sex ratio data for 17 of 20 nests known in a locality in southeastern Michigan. I determined the onset of emergence of reproductive females by observing daily the behavior of individuals on three of the nests. Foreign wasps were not

I thank J. Ehret, L. Frey, and C. Rosen for assistance in collecting data; R. D. Alexander, G. Borgia, D. P. Cowan, M. J. West Eberhard, T. E. Moore, D. Queller, D. Smith, and P. W. Sherman for comments on the manuscript; and the Theodore Roosevelt Memorial Fund and the University of Michigan for financial assistance.

permitted on the nest by workers. From the emergence of the first males and reproductive females to the end of the season, all new individuals on the nests were marked and recorded by sex every other day. While on the nests, wasps were marked with Testor's enamel, a procedure that did not seem to disrupt nest activities severely. The interval between markings was less than the average time spent by both males and females on the natal nest after eclosion, 4.7 days for males and 8.5 days for females (5). Any bias from individuals missed would probably underestimate investment in males.

To measure parental investment in each sex, one would need to know not only sex ratios but the time and energy spent plus risks taken by parents in behalf of male and female offspring, all of which would diminish their ability to invest in future offspring. I estimated the sex ratio of parental investment on nests by multiplying the sex ratio estimates by the relative wet weights (male divided by female) of 16 males and 23 females eclosing in the laboratory from a nest recently collected in the field. In addition to suffering from the general inadequacy of inferring parental investment from weights, this value probably underestimates investment in females, which stay longer on the parental nest and hence eat more after eclosion than do males. The females weighted 143 ± 3 mg, and the males weighed 135 ± 4 mg, yielding a wet weight ratio of 0.94 (6). Presumably, males were somewhat less than 94 percent as expensive as females to produce.

Table 1 gives the computed estimates of the sex ratio of parental investment for the 17 nests and for the population as a whole (7). Parental investment ratios were tested for deviation from 1:1 and 1:3 by comparing the observed sex ratios with sex ratios that would yield the theoretical investment ratios. The population investment ratio was not significantly different from 1:1 (χ^2 test, $P < .35$) but was significantly different from 1:3 ($P < .001$). Eight of the 17 nests produced investment ratios that deviated significantly from 1:1 ($P < .05$).

Fisher's theory of sex ratio selection (8) predicts that, when competition for mates is population-wide, parents will evolve to invest equally in the two sexes. Hamilton (3) showed that competition for mates within broods favors female-biased sex ratios of parental investment because the reproductive value of sons to their parents decreases when sons compete among themselves for females that one or a few of them could inseminate (3, 4, 9). I investigated the extent of mating among siblings by directly observing interactions on nests and by examining the spermathecae of females at various times after they eclosed. I observed one nest continuously during daylight hours when the wasps were active, from 10 August through 18 August 1976 (80 hours total). This was the time of peak abundance of males on nests. Males mounted females but rarely attached their genitalia. The evidence from dissections supported my impression that this behavior did not result in insemination: (i) Fourteen reproductive females captured as they left the nest for the first time were not inseminated. (ii) Two females collected 9 and 11 days after their eclosion were not inseminated. (iii) Only 2 of 29 reproductive females [distinguished from workers and foundresses by their thick fat deposits and lack of wing wear (10)] collected on nests in mid-September were inseminated. These data suggest that mating among siblings does not occur on the parental nest.

Mating aggregations, sometimes of more than 100 individuals, form near crevices and on tall sunlit structures such as buildings, telephone poles, and trees. Of 15 females collected from crevices in the fall, 11 were inseminated. Marked progeny of different nests appeared to mix freely (*11*), which suggests that Fisher's (*8*) assumption of population-wide competition for mates was met.

Fisher's theory (*8*) also assumes symmetry in the relatedness of parents to their male and female offspring. In the social Hymenoptera, queens are related to both sons and daughters by ½. Workers, which invest parentally in their mother's brood, are related to sisters by ¾ (if the queen mated only once) and to brothers by only ¼ because of the haplodiploid system of inheritance. Hamilton (*1*) argued that haplodiploidy predisposed the Hymenoptera to the evolution of sterile workers because females are potentially more closely related to their mother's brood than to their own offspring. Trivers and Hare (*2*) pointed out that this special relationship pertains only when colonial investment in reproductive members is female-biased. They suggested that opportunities for hymenopteran workers to capitalize on the asymmetry in their relatedness to brothers and sisters by investing preferentially in sisters may have increased the likelihood that eusociality would persist once it evolved. On this basis, they predicted that sex ratios of parental investment in eusocial hymenopteran colonies will be female-biased in a ratio of 1:3, unless laying workers contribute substantially to the male brood.

I observed the behavior of foundresses, workers, and reproductive offspring over the colony cycle on 20 nests from May through September 1974 through 1976 (approximately 400 hours). During 150 hours of observation in July, when workers and queens were on nests and reproductive broods were being produced, I did not see workers lay or eat eggs while the original queen was on the nest. Owen (*12*) and West Eberhard (*5*), in studies on the same population, also noted the absence of egg-laying and egg-eating by workers. Approximately half of 52 subordinate foundresses on multiple-foundress nests were also present while reproductive broods were being produced, but they contributed little to them. It appears that the reproductives reared on nests are chiefly offspring of the foundress queen.

Because queens are symmetrically related to male and female brood, and workers are not, their reproductive interests conflict in regard to the sex ratio of parental investment. This conflict has been linked to the broader issues of parent-offspring conflict and the origins of eusociality. Trivers and Hare (*2*) argued that workers should control the pattern of colony investment because they are the primary caretakers of the brood. They predicted that the way in which workers achieve their preferred ratio will depend on the cost to their inclusive fitnesses of confronting the queen aggressively. If a queen dies in such a fight, the workers lose a specialized egg-layer and source of closely related female eggs. They argued that this cost is less drastic in multiple-queen than in single-queen colonies because, there, workers can shift their investment to offspring of a closely related substitute queen. When workers can lay eggs nearly as well as the queen, as in *Polistes,* these arguments do not apply. The drop in worker relatedness to the brood after the queen's death is, in fact, greater in multiple- than single-queen colonies *(13).*

In contrast to Trivers and Hare *(2),* Alexander *(14)* and Trivers *(15)* have viewed the evolution of parent-offspring conflict in general as an uneven match favoring the parent. Alexander *(14)* has argued that parental care evolves so as to maximize the lifetime reproductive success of parents, not the inclusive fitnesses of particular offspring or sets of offspring. Thus, throughout the evolution of eusocial insect colonies, selection would have operated on queens to check tendencies in workers to maximize their inclusive fitnesses at the queen's expense. According to this argument, parents evolve to maximize their inclusive fitnesses, at the expense of offspring if necessary, and they will usually be able to achieve this end.

The almost exact coincidence of the population investment ratio with 1:1, and its significant departure from 1:3, in the absence of sibling mating competition on the nest, suggest that in *P. fuscatus* the queen's interests, rather than those of her worker daughters, are realized. Workers are not more closely related to the brood they tend than they would be to their own offspring. Haplodiploidy, therefore, cannot explain the maintenance of eusociality in this species *(2).* Kin selection *(16),* however (considering costs and benefits of altruistic behavior as well as the genetic relatedness of interactants), remains a possible explanation of worker altruism.

Although eight of the nests produced investment ratios significantly different from 1:1, they exactly canceled one another's effects on the investment ratio in the population as a whole. Therefore, their queens and workers should have suffered no counterselection on the basis of the devaluation of the more numerous sex *(8).*

A population-wide investment ratio of 1:1 might result from a balance between nests that are male- and female-biased in their investment patterns. For example, if certain proportions of nests are consistently orphaned before reproductive female eggs are produced, thus producing only males, queens might be selected to produce a female-biased investment ratio. They could thereby take advantage of the increase in reproductive value of females caused by the excess of males. This did not seem to be the case in the populations I studied. The queens of male-biased nests survived well beyond the time when the reproductive brood is usually complete. Nor was there any evidence of a worker's laying eggs in two of the male-biased nests that were observed regularly during July, the month of peak egg production *(5).* On one female-biased nest observed regularly, I saw no unusual strife between the queen and the workers nor any sign that the queen was dominated by the workers.

For several reasons, *P. fuscatus* colonies might be more likely to produce a 1:1 investment ratio than other species discussed by Trivers and Hare *(2).* The number of workers is small, usually less than 40. Workers are therefore less likely to realize their optimal sex ratio of parental investment by confronting the queen *(17).* Colonies are annual, and workers are reared almost entirely by foundresses. Queens are thus in a position to manipulate worker options by feeding them less as larvae than they might prefer. Queens probably mate multiply, so that the asymmetry in workers relatedness to brothers and sisters may be less than 1:3. The tendency for colonies

Table 1 The Sex Ratio of Parental Investment in Reproductives on Single- and Multiple-Foundress Nests in _P. fuscatus_

Reproductives marked (proportion)	Males: females (No.)	Investment ratio (male: female)
	Single-foundress nests	
0.8	40:80	1:2.12*
1.0	19:12	1:0.67
0.7	4:9	1:2.39
0.8	7:10	1:1.52
1.0	26:35	1:1.43
0.9	15:12	1:0.85
1.0	11:11	1:1.06
0.9	4:5	1:1.33
0.8	17:11	1:0.69
0.9	30:8	1:0.28*
0.8	7:15	1:2.27*
0.8	5:15	1:3.19*
	Multiple-foundress nests	
0.8	23:10	1:0.46*
0.9	123:82	1:0.71*
0.9	69:39	1:0.60*
0.5	4:5	1:1.33
0.9	20:36	1:1.91*
	Entire population	
	424:395	1:0.99

Note All sex ratio estimates were multiplied by a single estimate of the ratio of parental investment per individual of each sex [from wet weight at eclosion (6)]. Sex ratios are based on the number of male and female reproductives marked on each nest. It was usually not possible to mark every individual eclosing, as indicated by nest maps. The proportion of reproductives marked is estimated for each nest.

*Significantly different from an investment ratio of 1:1 (χ^2 test, $P < .05$).

to produce males earlier than reproductive females increases the expense to workers of modifying the colonial investment ratio in their own interests. When workers eclose, few female eggs and larvae are present. The males have usually completed part of their development and, therefore, have a higher reproductive value than contemporary eggs. This increases the costs to workers of discriminating against males or of replacing them with the workers' own male eggs (18–20).

Other characteristics of _Polistes_ colonies make it more likely that workers will realize their optimal investment pattern. Because colonies are annual and there is only one reproductive brood, it may be easier for workers to assess the colony investment ratio and adjust their parental effort to optimize their inclusive fitnesses. Workers do not lay while the original queen is on the nest, so they should be strongly selected to bias their parental investment in favor of females.

REFERENCES AND NOTES

1 W. D. Hamilton, *J. Theor. Biol.* **7**, 1 (1964); *ibid.*, p. 17 (1964).
2 R. L. Trivers and H. Hare, *Science* **191**, 249 (1976).
3 W. D. Hamilton, *ibid.* **156**, 447(1967).
4 R. D. Alexander and P. W. Sherman, *ibid.* **196**, 494(1977).
5 M. J. West Eberhard, *Misc. Publ. Mus. Zool. Univ. Mich.* 140(1969).
6 Wide variation in the relative wet weight per individual of each sex produced on nests would undermine my estimates of the sex ratio of parental investment. Relative weights for a large sample of nests, needed to estimate the variance, were not obtained. Relative wing length data collected for 15 nests in 1974 suggest that inter-nest variation in this respect is not great. Wing length correlated significantly with body length in both sexes [males: $r^2 = .86$; females: $r^2 = .76$ (*5*)]. Wing length ratios ranged from 93 percent to 106 percent (males divided by females) averaging 98 ± 3 percent.
7 Estimating the population investment ratio by counting progeny of a random sample of nests departs from the χ^2 test's assumption of independent observations (here, individuals) when nests differ significantly from one another in their investment ratios. Sex differences in mortality and visibility, however, are likely to introduce errors in estimation after the termination of parental care. Thus, sex ratio data reported in the literature are often based on sampling by brood [for example (*2*); H. Howe, *Ecology* **57**, 1195 (1976); M. F. Willson, *Ecol. Monogr.* **36**, 51(1966)]. The higher the proportion of all broods sampled, the smaller the effect of nonindependent sampling on the estimate. In view of the high proportion of known nests sampled in my study (0.85), the error introduced into the analysis by this departure from the assumptions is probably slight.
   Significant heterogeneity in investment patterns occurred in the pooled sample of nests (χ^2, $P < .001$). The proximate mechanisms by which differences in the sex ratio of parental investment are effected were not apparent in this study. I would expect them to be environmental cues at the time of egg-laying, which would influence queens to fertilize varying proportions of their eggs. It is possible, for example, that certain investment skews are associated with early or late production of reproductive offspring, the size of the worker force at a critical time, or the number of laying subordinate foundresses present. The precise control over the sex ratio afforded queens by haplodiploidy might allow them to track variations in the optimal sex ratio for their broods more closely than diplo-diploid parents. The long hazardous period of parental investment, with varying degrees of help from subordinate foundresses, and the production of sterile workers before any reproductive offspring undoubtedly increases the variety in circumstances to which egg-laying queens might respond.
   Whatever its proximal causes, heterogeneity in investment ratios among parents is predictable from sex-ratio theory. Fisher (*8*) argued that selection favors a particular ratio of investment in the population as a whole. Heterogeneity in the contributions of individual parents will not be selected against so long as the population investment ratio stays at its optimal value [(J. F. Crow and M. Kimura, *An Introduction to Population Genetics Theory* (Harper & Row, Evanston, 1970)].
8 R. A. Fisher, *The Genetical Theory of Natural Selection* (Dover, New York, 1958).
9 J. Maynard Smith, in preparation.
10 K. R. Eickwort, *Insectes Soc.* **16**, 67(1969a).

11 On four occasions, males from two different parental nests were seen together in the vicinity of mating aggregations. On one occasion, progeny of at least four nests were seen together in a crevice where courtship and mating occurred.

12 J. Owen, thesis, University of Michigan (1962).

13 If the queen dies on a multiple-queen nest and is replaced by a sister, the workers must rear cousins instead of brothers and sisters. Their relatedness to the brood falls from 1/2 (assuming monogamy and a 1:1 sex ratio) to 3/16. If the queen dies on a single-queen nest and is replaced by a worker daughter, leaving the rest of the workers to rear nieces and nephews, the relatedness of the workers to the brood falls only half as much, from ½ to ⅜. Although such a nest would produce only males (because workers are uninseminated), it would have to flood the local breeding population with offspring to the point that male reproductive value was halved for the workers to suffer the same reproductive loss as the workers on the multiple-queen nest.

14 R. D. Alexander, *Am. Zool.* **12**, 648(1972); *Annu. Rev. Ecol. Syst.* **5**, 325(1974); in preparation.

15 R. L. Trivers, *Am. Zool.* **14**, 249(1974).

16 G. C. Williams and D. C. Williams, *Evolution* **11**, 32(1957); M. J. West Eberhard, *Q. Rev. Biol.* **50**, 1(1975).

17 Mechanisms by which workers could forcibly affect the investment ratio are (i) by physically excluding the queen from cells after she has laid in them so she cannot eat or replace eggs or even assess the sex ratio of a brood and (ii) by keeping the queen from distributing food unequally to larvae, perhaps by preventing her from feeding them at all.

18 Colonies of *Polistes metricus* also produce males earlier than reproductive females [Metcalf and Whitt (*19*); Metcalf (*20*)]. Metcalf notes that this increases the expense to workers of discriminating against the queen's sons. Queens in *P. metricus* populations mate at least twice, using sperm from the two inseminations in a ratio of 9:1 (*19*). The sex ratio of investment in populations near Urbana, Ill., is approximately 1:1 (*20*).

19 R. A. Metcalf and G. S. Whitt, *Behav. Ecol. Sociobiol.* **2**, 339(1977).

20 R. A. Metcalf, thesis, Harvard University (1975).

Extrinsic versus Intrinsic Factors in the Evolution of Insect Sociality

Howard E. Evans
Department of Zoology and Entomology, Colorado State University,
Fort Collins

Over the past few years, there has been a veritable flood of speculation regarding the evolution of social behavior, especially in Hymenoptera. A partial list of papers might include Lin and Michener (1972), Alexander (1974), West Eberhard (1975), and Trivers and Hare (1976). The major stimulus to these authors was in every case the provocative theory of kin selection and its apparent special application to Hymenoptera, as propounded by Hamilton (1964, 1972) and made widely known especially through the stimulating books of E. O. Wilson (1971, 1975).

Stated baldly, the fact that male Hymenoptera are haploid results in a closer genetic similarity among daughters than would be the case if they were diploid, since genes derived from the father are all alike. Has this provided the major preadaptation for the development of sterile castes among Hymenoptera, since females have a greater relatedness to sisters than they would have to their own daughters if mated —hence, paradoxically, might increase their Darwinian fitness by sacrificing reproductive behavior in favor of caring for their younger sisters?

The literature relating to this attractive concept has recently become so vast that an erudite ant, were she able to grasp it at all, would surely become a hopeless psychotic. A termite, with her cellulose-digesting intestinal symbionts, might better be able to handle it. If an excuse be needed for still another contribution (and I think it is), I would say that in all fields of biology one needs, now and then, to ask whether current theory, however satisfying, provides a clear view of reality.

FEATURES OF WASP BEHAVIOR

Since ants and bees are modified wasps, we may reasonably turn to the wasps for prototypes of sociality. In fact the wasps provide unusually fine instances of progression from strictly solitary forms to highly evolved and fully social insects. Evidently, examples of intermediate stages have been able to compete successfully since their origin or have evolved at a slower rate than social wasps, ants, and bees.

There was a remarkably diverse wasp fauna in the Cretaceous, roughly 100 million years ago. Representatives of all major groups were present, including spe-

Several persons have commented on various drafts of this manuscript, but I would especially like to thank Mary Jane West Eberhard, John Alcock, and Darryl T. Gwynne for their many helpful suggestions.

From *BioScience 27:* 613–617. Reprinted, with permission, from the September 1977 *BioScience* published by the American Institute of Biological Sciences.

cialized forms, which suggest that much adaptive radiation had already occurred (Evans 1973a, Rasnitsyn 1975). Behavioral diversity may well have rivaled that of contemporary wasps. In the modern fauna, one is able to select genera which appear to represent specific stages in the evolution of sociality and to speculate regarding the selection pressures that appear to have guided the evolution of each stage.

Wasps are believed to have evolved from generalized "parasitoid" Hymenoptera, and members of this group are known from the preceding geologic period, the Jurassic. Female parasitoids seek out a host arthropod and lay their egg on or in it via a slender ovipositor; some species also inject a substance that causes temporary paralysis of the host. The host may be free-living (e.g., caterpillars) or may live in some concealed situation (e.g., in galls, tree trunks, etc.). The parasitoids form an enormously successful group in the modern fauna, a group of great interest at the present time, since we have become aware of ecological havoc sometimes caused by the indiscriminate use of chemical insecticides. One specialist has speculated that there may be a million species of ichneumon wasps (only one of several groups of parasitoids), but he was surely carried away by his enthusiasm.

The larvae of parasitoids are subject to much mortality as a result of secondary parasitism, competition among parasites in the same host, or premature death of the host when it is eaten by a bird or seized and carried off by a digger wasp. Hence, it is not surprising that among this vast assemblage of insects there arose a stock, the aculeates or "stinging Hymenoptera," that evolved the capacity to paralyze the host permanently and to carry it to a place of concealment. At first, this was probably no more than some kind of preexisting crevice in the soil or in wood; at a later stage, a closure of soil or detritus was provided; and at a still later stage, a simple nest-cell was constructed which was provisioned and closed off with a firm barrier.

There are existing species of wasps that exhibit each of these stages (see, e.g., Evans and West Eberhard 1970, chapter 3). Within the nest-cell of a hymenopteran, the egg, larva, and pupa are able to develop with less danger of parasitism, predation by birds or mammals, and so forth. Yet, this step was apparently taken only once in the Hymenoptera; the wasps appear to be a monophyletic group, and the evidence is fairly clear that ants and bees evolved from now-extinct groups of wasps. This is perhaps not surprising, as the evolution of a wasp from a parasitoid involved novel adaptions in many structural, behavioral, and physiological features. In brief, the aculeates came to occupy an entirely new adaptive zone and soon evolved to occupy a number of major subzones.

Many generalized wasps still make their nest after capturing prey and use a single prey to provision the nest (e.g., Pompilidae, spider wasps), an inheritance from parasitoid ancestors. But this involves subduing a prey approximately their own size and allowing it to remain unprotected while the female digs a nest; here the prey may be attacked by ants, tiger beetles, and the like. The majority of wasps prepare the nest first and provision it with several smaller prey, which can be quickly stung and carried to the nest. Many digger wasps (Sphecidae) have evolved novel methods of prey carriage, holding the prey in flight with the middle or hind legs or even on the sting or on special devices at the end of the abdomen. Unlike other groups of wasps, these wasps are able to close the nest entrance when they leave and reenter it later without depositing their prey, since their mandibles and front legs are free, and these are the structures needed for opening and for other manipulations of the substrate (Evans 1963).

Still other adaptations have been developed by certain groups of wasps. For example, some lay the egg in the empty cell before bringing in any prey. This, I believe, greatly reduces the possibility of introducing maggots of miltogrammine flies, which are deposited on the prey as they are brought into the nest and which commonly destroy the egg of the wasp. Also, some of the more advanced wasps are "progressive provisioners," that is, they bring in prey over a period of several days, as the larva grows. In these species, the female has many contacts with the larva and remains within the nest when not feeding or hunting, undoubtedly providing added protection against intruders.

Each of these steps appears to provide greater protection from parasites and predators. Although much more evidence would be welcome, such evidence as exists is consistent with these hypotheses. For example, in the cicada killer, *Sphecius speciosus,* a mass-provisioner that carries very large prey and lays the egg on the prey, mortality of larvae as high as 50% has been reported. In this case, miltogrammine flies were largely responsible. This is a group that (like some others) has evolved specialized behavior that takes advantage of new opportunities in the adaptive zone of the aculeates. In contrast, some species of *Bembix* (which belong to the same subfamily as *Sphecius*) appear to be well "ahead" of their parasites. These wasps are progressive provisioners that lay the egg in the empty cell, and parasitism by miltogrammine flies has been reduced virtually to zero (Evans 1966).

NESTS OF WASPS AND BEES

As the wasps evolved as a group, factors other than predator and parasite avoidance, of course, played a role. Nests are most readily dug in a soft, friable substrate, but sand is not available everywhere and in many places is uninhabitable as a result of flooding or blowing. Thus, it was advantageous to be able to dig in firmer substrates, to occupy hollow twigs, or to build aerial nests of mud, paper, or other substances. Adaptive radiation in the nesting behavior of aculeates has been dramatic but cannot be reviewed here. Suffice it to say that digging in firm substrates or building aerial nests consumes much more time and causes much more wear of body parts than preparing simple nests in friable soil.

Hence, the building of multicellular nests evolved. But such nests, with numerous adjacent cells, are especially prone to attack by various hole-searching parasites such as cuckoo wasps, mutillids, and certain miltogrammine flies. Thus, a fair number of nonsocial wasps making multicellular nests occupy these communally, providing a measure of protection from these natural enemies and from nest usurpers because of the frequent blocking of the burrow by fortuitous guards (see, e.g., Evans et al. 1976). It may well be that communal nests evolved from temporary associations of siblings recently emerged from the parental burrow, as described for *Philanthus gibbosus* (Evans 1973b). In the related solitary wasp, *Cerceris rubida,* the mother may live beyond the time of emergence of her daughters, and the resulting society may exhibit a measure of division of labor, including the sharing of "guard duty" at the nest entrance (Grandi 1944). Newly emerged wasps are not reproductively mature, and even mature adults are not continuously occupied in building or foraging. By assuming the relatively inert role of a guard, individuals are at the same time gaining genetic advantage by enhancing the success of other individuals having many of the same genes. Communal use of burrows by nonsiblings (but members of the same population) is probable in some wasps and is well documented in certain bees (Lin and Michener 1972). There need be no reproductive sacrifices among individuals in such mutualistic groupings; indeed the fitness of each individual may be increased by the mere presence of others.

A closer look at the bees seems in order at this point, since these insects exhibit almost every conceivable form of communal nesting and presociality, and the evidence suggests that true sterile worker castes have evolved independently several times in this superfamily (Michener 1974). Michener and his co-workers have strongly supported the importance of parasite pressure in the early stages of social evolution. They say, for example, that "it is the need for defense that makes colonies advantageous," but "selection appears to favor reduced sociality and solitary behavior in the absence of natural enemies" (Lin and Michener 1972). The belief that social evolution may be reversed under these conditions is supported by the fact that small colonies and lone individuals are reproductively more efficient (Michener 1969). I would maintain that natural enemies may play a major role in all stages of social (and solitary) evolution, even to the extent of producing the elaborate nests of many of the higher bees and wasps (e.g., Jeanne 1975).

Michener and Brothers (1974) have recently described the behavior of females in associations of the primitively social halictid bee *Dialictus zephyrus.* One female "nudges" and "backs" much more frequently than other females, thus presumably retarding ovarian growth of these females as well as prodding them into guarding positions or drawing them into parts of the nest where there are stimuli for cell construction and provisioning; the "queen" also eats eggs laid by subordinates. Their provocative paper is titled "Were Workers of Eusocial Hymenoptera Initially Altruistic or Oppressed?"

Dominance interactions have been described in a number of bees and wasps. Behavioral dominance of queen bumblebees over their daughters has been known since 1902 (see Wilson 1971). Dominance of alpha foundresses of *Polistes* wasps over joiners and daughters is also well known (Pardi 1948, West Eberhard 1969). Dominance interactions of at least a rudimentary kind have been observed in nonsocial wasps such as *Philanthus gibbosus* and *Cerceris rubida* (cited above).

In advanced social insects (such as the honeybee), behavioral dominance has been replaced by pheromonal dominance. In each instance, the dominant female is presumably able to increase her fitness by means of (a) providing guards, which decrease the ease of entry of parasites, and/or (b) obtaining assistance in nest construction and provisioning. The theoretical basis of parental manipulation of offspring has recently been reviewed by Alexander (1974).

INTRINSIC FACTORS

Clearly it is impossible to separate extrinsic factors (such as parasite pressure) from intrinsic (genetic) factors at any stage of this analysis. Explaining the decline and eventual loss of reproductive ability is the crux of the matter, and it is here that relatedness and the possible contribution of haplodiploidy have justly been emphasized. If Hamilton's (1964) concept of inclusive fitness makes sense (as, of course, it does), every organism will behave so as to enhance the proportion of its own genes in the next generation, even when these genes are borne by another individual, so long as the cost does not exceed the gain. As Wilson (1975) quips, an organism is only DNA's way of making more DNA.

It is clear that altered degrees of relationship are not the only consequence of haplodiploidy, as Lin and Michener (1972) have pointed out. For example, female hymenopterans are able to control the sex of their progeny by release or nonrelease of sperm from the spermathecae, permitting the skewed sex ratios observed in many Hymenoptera, both solitary and social (e.g., Hamilton 1967, Michener 1969). In solitary bees and wasps, in which the males are smaller than the females, it is common for the female to prepare cells of two sizes: large cells containing much food and a fertilized egg and small cells containing less food and an unfertilized egg (Evans 1971, Krombein 1967). In progressive provisioners, it is to the female's advantage to gauge the amount of prey in accordance with the sex of the offspring. Thus, I do not agree with Crozier (1977) that there is no selective advantage in nonsocial females being able to distinguish the sex of offspring. Since the castes of social Hymenoptera are largely trophogenically based, the ability to control both the sex of the progeny and the amount of food provided seems to me to involve preadaptations of major importance.

But to return to the importance of haplodiploidy in influencing degrees of relationship, Trivers and Hare (1976) have recently proposed a means of discriminating between the effects of haplodiploidy and parental dominance or "exploitation" of offspring. Trivers and Hare argue that the queen will favor a 1 : 1 investment in the sex of fertile offspring since she is equally related to her sons and daughters, but workers will favor a 3 : 1 investment of fertile sisters to brothers since (because of haplodiploidy) their genetic similarity to their sisters is ¾ and to their brothers is ¼. Trivers and Hare selected their examples from several species of ants that appear to exhibit the relatively uncommon combination of single queens and nonlaying workers. The ratio of investment in these species (females/males) was found to vary from 1.57 to 8.88, a significant departure from 1.0. With such a carefully selected sample, one might have hoped for less scatter. And one might have hoped for data from a broader spectrum of social insects, including less highly evolved forms, or even such advanced species as the honeybee, in which the production of drones invariably exceeds that of queens in terms of numbers and is surely at least equal in terms of weight. In a colony having a single queen that has mated only once, the new queens are also sisters of the workers, yet they opt for reproduction even though they will share fewer genes with their offspring than they share with their sisters. In theory, workers should indeed try to produce a large brood of sisters who are reproductives; but their own spinsterhood is imposed by the dominance of the queen, either through behavior or, more commonly, through pheromones.

Yet, paradoxically, it is difficult to find species of social insects having a single queen who has mated only once and in which the workers do not at least sometimes lay eggs (which, of course, are haploid and male-producing). The vast majority of social insects are tropical or subtropical, where polygyny (multiple queens) is the rule rather than the exception. Indeed, monogyny seems especially characteristic of species occurring in temperate or cold climates and may be a secondary adaptation for permitting maximum colony foundation from those mated females that survive the winter. The relative rarity of monogyny, and the frequency of multiple-mated queens and of laying workers, suggests that in fact the unusual relationships said to be imposed by haplodiploidy are rarely approached in nature and have minimal influence on behavior over and above that predictable from inclusive fitness alone.

Hamilton (1964), Trivers and Hare (1976), and others have made much of the fact that "females are more likely to evolve worker habits than are males." Surely one does not need elaborate ratiocination or genetic juggling to demonstrate this fact. Male insects, with minor exceptions, play no role beyond copulation. As West Eberhard (1975) points out, male Hymenoptera lack preadaptations for worker duties though in fact there are occasional instances of males serving as guards or performing other functions at the nest.

That male termites do function as workers is a consequence of the fact that these insects require intestinal symbionts in order to digest cellulose, and these symbionts must be obtained by anal trophallaxis from other individuals. The male must be socialized or must starve in infancy. Protagonists of haplodiploidy tend to be embarrassed by the termites, which are diploid but in which the queens of some species exceed those of any hymenopteran in terms of worker-subsidized egg production. They take solace in the fact that sociality arose "only once" in the termites but "11 times" in the Hymenoptera, which comprise only "6% of all insects" (Krebs and May 1976).

Unfortunately, neither of these figures will stand up under scrutiny. Wilson (1971) has stated that 15% of living insects belong to the Hymenoptera, a percentage I consider unrealistically low considering the vast number of parasitoids yet undescribed. We really have little idea how many times sociality arose. Michener (1974) pointed out that primitive levels of sociality are easily reversed, and, in fact, simple forms of sociality may have evolved a great many times in halictid bees. Also, there are at least two major cases in which we do not know if sociality was characteristic of a common ancestor or was independently achieved in derivative groups (in the wasps and the higher bees).

These matters may, in fact, be of little importance. The aculeate Hymenoptera form a monophyletic group of relatively recent origin in terms of geologic time. The termites evolved from a much more ancient group, the cockroaches, and any solitary or subsocial species that may have existed are long since extinct. The presocial cockroach *Cryptocercus* is surely not directly ancestral to termites, though its intestinal symbionts are similar. Who can say how many times social behavior may have arisen in this group of insects?

CONCLUSIONS

All groups of social insects are best represented in the tropics and subtropics. Among tropical Hymenoptera, multiple queens are the rule rather than the exception, and the presence of queen-worker intermediates and of laying workers is also common. Tropical climates more readily permit overlap of generations, and the intensity of competition and predation in warmer parts of the globe must also play a major role in the evolution of social systems.

Perhaps we are too much influenced by study of temperate species having rather simple mother-offspring associations. A better model of incipient sociality might be that provided by, for example, *Trigonopsis cameronii* (Eberhard 1972). In this species, several females may work together on a common nest, building and provisioning their own cells but cooperating in driving away ants, supplying mud to back and sides of the communal nest, and "stealing" prey from nestmates only under certain conditions of need. Nestmates are undoubtedly close relatives, part of a localized and inbred population, a common condition in Hymenoptera because of restrictions in suitable nesting sites. A similar situation, involving unrelated individuals in species having less stringent nesting requirements, might result in social parasitism, also a very common phenomenon among Hymenoptera.

Trigonopsis is by no means unique. Nests of *Microstigmus comes,* a member of the same family (Sphecidae), may contain as many as 18 adults who cooperate in defense and building (Matthews 1968). In this instance, dissection of females showed that one female did most of the egg-laying. Aggregations of cooperating females of two generations, without worker sterility, are known in a number of tropical wasps of at least three familes (West Eberhard 1975, p. 27). That *Microstigmus* has evolved at least partial worker sterility surely reflects the fact that selection for greater division of labor (as a result of extrinsic factors such as the need for more effective nest defense) has pushed the species over the "eusociality threshold" (Wilson 1976). That is, individual females stand to gain more in terms of their genetic contribution to the next generation by becoming workers than by risking their own genes in an inadequately defended nest.

If sociality arose in simple family groups of mother and offspring, the mother having mated only once and the workers never laying eggs, then the "enhancement of kin selection by haplodiploidy" may, indeed, add "a decisive amount to the bias toward eusocial evolution" (Wilson 1976). I agree with Wilson that some means of weighing the importance of diverse factors influencing the origin of sociality in various groups would be most desirable. I do not agree that Trivers and Hare's data on investment ratios either disprove the concept of parental manipulation or demonstrate that haplodiploidy must be invoked ad nauseam in discussing these matters. Least of all do I agree with Krebs and May (1976) that "Trivers and Hare's paper ... puts the capstone on an edifice that draws together genetic principles and Darwin's theory of natural selection toward explaining the evolution of the social insects." Though provocative (in both senses of that word), their paper does nothing of the kind.[1]

Hymenoptera evolved social systems by way of a series of steps not taken by other groups of insects and in which extrinsic factors, especially parasite pressure and adaptive radiation in nesting behavior, played a major role. Any social animal, of whatever group, must first of all have a nest and exhibit brood care. These steps were taken by few groups of insects other than Hymenoptera (though several other groups exhibit haplodiploidy!). The Hymenoptera form a fairly recent entry into the sweepstakes of evolution, and it is not surprising that these insects have developed novel ways of surviving and flourishing in a world dominated by the flowering plants, the mammals and birds, and a great diversity of insects that had already filled many available niches. That extended, polygynous families are so prevalent reflects needs for colony defense and for a large group of foragers able to gather adequate food in an already crowded world.

Documentation of the crossing of the eusociality threshold in various groups still has a long way to go, but the problem is more likely to yield to quantitative field studies of primitively social species (especially in the tropics), with due consideration for extrinsic factors such as natural enemies and competitors, than it is to further manipulation of ratios of relationships and investments.

REFERENCES CITED

Alexander, R. D. 1974. The evolution of social behavior. *Annu. Rev. Ecol. Syst.* 5: 325–383.
Crozier, R. H. 1977. Evolutionary genetics of the Hymenoptera. *Annu. Rev. Entomol.* 22: 263–288.
Eberhard, W. G. 1972. Altruistic behavior in a sphecid wasp: support for kin selection theory. *Science* 172: 1390–1391.

[1]Since this paper was originally written an important critique of Trivers and Hare's paper has been published by R. D. Alexander and P. W. Sherman (*Science* 196: 494–500, 29 April 1977). These authors argue that Trivers and Hare failed to demonstrate the investment patterns claimed and that their data for the most part conform to an alternative hypothesis, namely mating rivalry among close relatives. This paper should be consulted for an in-depth analysis of Trivers and Hare's paper.

Evans, H. E. 1963. The evolution of prey-carrying mechanisms in wasps. *Evolution* 16: 468–483.

———. 1966. *The Comparative Ethology and Evolution of Sand Wasps.* Harvard University Press, Cambridge, Mass.

———. 1971. Observations on the nesting behavior of wasps of the tribe Cercerini. *J. Kansas Entomol. Soc.* 44: 500–523.

———. 1973a. Cretaceous aculeate wasps from Taimyr, Siberia (Hymenoptera). *Psyche* 80: 166–178.

———. 1973b. Burrow sharing and nest transfer in the digger wasp *Philanthus gibbosus* (Fabricius). *Anim. Beh.* 21: 302–308.

Evans, H. E., R. W. Matthews, J. Alcock, and M. A. Fritz, 1976. Notes on the nests and prey of two subspecies of *Cerceris rufimana* Taschenberg (Hymenoptera: Sphecidae: Cercerini). *J. Kansas Entomol. Soc.* 49: 126–132.

Evans, H. E., and M. J. West Eberhard. 1970. *The Wasps.* University of Michigan Press, Ann Arbor.

Grandi, G. 1944. Un interessante caso di socialita negli Sfecidi. *Mem. Accad. Sci. Inst. Bologna* (10)1: 1–6.

Hamilton, W. D. 1964. The genetical evolution of social behaviour, I and II. *J. Theoret. Biol.* 7: 1–52.

———. 1967. Extraordinary sex ratios. *Science* 156: 477–488.

———. 1972. Altruism and related phenomena, mainly in social insects. *Annu. Rev. Ecol. Syst.* 3: 193–232.

Jeanne, R. L. 1975. The adaptiveness of social wasp nest architecture. *Q. Rev. Biol.* 50: 267–287.

Krebs, J., and R. M. May. 1976. Social insects and the evolution of altruism. *Nature* 260: 9–10.

Krombein, K. V. 1967. *Trap-Nesting Wasps and Bees: Life Histories, Nests, and Associates.* Smithsonian Press, Washington, D.C.

Lin, N., and C. D. Michener. 1972. Evolution of sociality in insects. *Q. Rev. Biol.* 47: 131–159.

Matthews, R. W. 1968. *Microstigmus comes:* sociality in a sphecid wasp. *Science* 160: 787–788.

Michener, C. D. 1969. Comparative social behavior of bees. *Annu. Rev. Entomol.* 14: 299–342.

———. 1974. *The Social Behavior of the Bees.* Harvard University Press, Cambridge, Mass.

Michener, C. D., and D. J. Brothers. 1974. Were workers of eusocial Hymenoptera initially altruistic or oppressed? *Proc. Natl. Acad. Sci. USA* 71: 671–674.

Pardi, L. 1948. Dominance order in *Polistes* wasps. *Physiol. Zool.* 21: 1–13.

Rasnitsyn, A. P. 1975. Hymenoptera Apocrita of Mesozoic. *Trans. Palaeontol. Inst. Acad. Sci. USSR:* 1–132.

Trivers, R. L., and H. Hare. 1976. Haplodiploidy and the evolution of the social insects. *Science* 191: 249–263.

West Eberhard, M. J. 1969. The social biology of polistine wasps. *Misc. Publ. Mus. Zool. Univ. Mich.* No. 140, 101 pp.

———. 1975. The evolution of social behavior by kin selection. *Q. Rev. Biol.* 50: 1–33.

Wilson, E. O. 1971. *The Insect Societies.* Harvard University Press, Cambridge, Mass.

———. 1975. *Sociobiology. The New Synthesis.* Harvard University Press, Cambridge, Mass.

———. 1976. Some central problems of sociobiology. *Soc. Sci. Inform.* 14: 5–18.

WALDROP '79

Part Three

Social Higher
Vertebrates

But as time went on the gopher began to be a little impatient, for no female appeared. He sat in the entrance of his hole in the morning and made penetrating squeaks that are inaudible to the human ear but can be heard deep in the earth by other gophers. And still no female appeared. Finally in a sweat of impatience he went up across the track until he found another gopher hole. He squeaked provocatively in the entrance. He heard a rustling and smelled female and then out of the hole came an old battle-torn bull gopher who mauled and bit him so badly that he crept home and lay in his great chamber for three days recovering and he lost two toes from one front paw from that fight.

John Steinbeck
Cannery Row *

If the inclusive fitness concept is a cornerstone of sociobiology, then perhaps a second, coequal cornerstone involves the extensive, carefully detailed studies pioneered by David Lack, and pursued by many researchers over the past several

*Viking Press, New York, 1945.

decades, that demonstrate the relation between population variables and environments of higher vertebrates, especially birds. No animals are more familiar to the average person than are birds and mammals that are locally common and frequently seen. Social behavior in these animals is varied, sophisticated, and complex. Cerebral hypertrophy has led to individual variations in behavior and to plasticity in responses to stimuli of a degree unapproached even in the most highly evolved social insects. Analogies and homologies between social behavior in birds and mammals and in humans are more readily perceived and agree much more closely in detail than do any similarities, real or imagined, between insects and human beings. We are, after all, mammals, and our uniqueness as a species is a conundrum that we, as assessors of our own condition, can never resolve.

The variety of higher vertebrate social behaviors includes many aspects that have been profitably examined and extensively treated, but which, for reasons of economy, are not covered here. These include aggregations of nonreproductives for defense or for resource exploitation, ontogeny of social behaviors, interspecific social interactions, and communication. Social phenomena treated in papers reprinted here include sexual selection and mating systems.

The first selection, G. H. Orians, develops a model for mating systems. Essential features of the model are gamete dimorphism, habitat variability, and individual choice. A series of predictions based on the model primarily addresses polygynous mating systems, with examples drawn for the most part from birds. Agreement between Orians's predictions and known avian breeding systems is generally good. In the following paper, however, K. Ralls addresses sexual dimorphism and mating systems in mammals and finds that existing data do not agree in detail with Orians's model. Ralls discusses differences between mammalian and avian strategies. She indicates factors that should be incorporated into a more comprehensive model for mammals. J. H. Crook, J. E. Ellis, and J. D. Goss-Custard, in the third selection presented here, examine mammalian social systems as a function of external environmental variables and of species parameters. They argue the need for detailed field studies in developing models of social systems. The fourth selection, by C. R. Cox and B. J. LeBoeuf, presents data from a field study with speculation on the extent to which females of various species might be active participants in the process of sexual selection.

Breeding aggregations of birds are conspicuous social units; nesting colonies of many thousands of marine birds are spectacular, extreme examples. Smaller communal aggregations of passerine species are less dramatic but are drawing increased attention from students of social behavior and evolution. Ecological and breeding system correlates of colonial and communal social systems suggest that these may be ideal model systems for analysis of vertebrate sociality. A paper by J. L. Brown, reprinted here, discusses ecological correlates of communality and the evolution of altruism in jays.

On the Evolution of Mating Systems in Birds and Mammals

Gordon H. Orians
Department of Zoology, University of Washington, Seattle

Mating systems and the selective factors that molded them have had an important place in the history of the theory of natural selection. Darwin (1871) himself gave considerable thought to the nature of sexual selection and its consequences for sexual dimorphism and mating patterns. He proposed two major forces in the evolution of sexual differences. First, that the fighting and display among males for the possession of females, which is especially prominent among mammals, accounted for the evolution of secondary sexual characteristics, such as horns and antlers, which are useful in battle. This aspect of sexual selection has been generally accepted. Second, Darwin suggested that the extreme development of plumage characters among males of some birds, such as pheasants and birds of paradise—features which did not seem of use in intermale combat—could be explained as being due to the cumulative effects of sexual preference exerted by the females at the time of mating. This aspect of his theory of sexual selection was challenged by a number of workers, but Fisher (1958) clearly showed that the notion of female choice is reasonable, notwithstanding the fact that direct evidence was then scarce for species other than man.

More recently, mating systems and sexual dimorphism have been assigned an important role in the theory of Wynne-Edwards (1962) as a device for regulating the reproductive output of populations. According to Wynne-Edwards, polygyny is one of a series of restrictive population adaptations arising through group selection which controls populations by reducing collective fecundity. He argues (1962, p. 515) that this restriction of breeding activity is possible because the territorial males of polygynous and promiscuous species can be fully informed about their own reproductive activity and, if the species engages in displays at communal mating grounds, of the total of matings performed by the group as well. These males could be conditioned to respond by becoming sexually inactive when an appropriate number of matings had taken place. The value of polygyny and group displays would lie in the fact that the assessment of total reproductive output by the population would be much easier than with a monogamous mating system in which the individuals are spaced out through the environment. He further suggested (1962, p. 525) that a balanced sex ratio would be maintained in nonmonogamous species because it would facilitate more intensive intermale competition and thereby provide a more sensitive index of population density and total reproductive output.

Valuable suggestions for improvement of the manuscript were provided by Henry S. Horn, Robert H. MacArthur, Dennis R. Paulson, Jared Verner, and Edwin O. Willis. My fieldwork on blackbird social organization has been supported by funds from the National Science Foundation.

This theory would best be tested by direct demonstration of the processes that are postulated to occur. For example, if females of polygynous species are unable to mate because males withhold coition after a certain number of copulations have been achieved, if low-ranking males do not attempt to solicit copulations after the quota has been reached, or if females are not receptive to their advances if they are made, then confidence in the theory would be strengthened.

Such evidence is extremely difficult to gather in the field, but there are now available data from a number of intensively studied polygynous species of birds, indicating that all females which appear in the breeding areas are able to obtain males and raise young. Jared Verner (personal communication) has not found any evidence for unmated females in the long-billed marsh wren (*Telmatodytes palustris*), and my own intensive work on red-winged blackbirds (*Agelaius phoeniceus*) and yellow-headed blackbirds (*Xanthocephalus xanthocephalus*) has failed to reveal a nonbreeding population of females in either of these species. In both species, there is a large and readily observable floating population of males. In the great-tailed grackle (*Quiscalus mexicanus*), a highly promiscuous species, adult males remain in full breeding condition and continue to attempt copulations after all females are nesting and are no longer receptive (Selander 1965). Therefore, in these species if there is some mechanism for limiting reproductive output, it must be due either to the failure of more females to present themselves at the breeding grounds or to a lowered effort per reproducing individual. At present, there is no evidence from any species that males withhold coition from receptive females.

It is the purpose of this paper to present an alternative theory of mating systems among birds and mammals which is based upon the assumption that the evolution of mate-selection behavior by individuals of both sexes has been influenced primarily by the consequences of these choices for individual fitness. The model is based upon mate-selection processes that can be observed directly in the field, and it is capable of generating a set of predictions which can be tested against the general mating patterns of broad groups of species for which there are no detailed observations of the factors influencing mating behavior.

A NATURAL SELECTION MODEL OF MATING SYSTEMS

This model is built upon the work of a number of people, especially Maynard Smith (1958), Verner (1964), Verner and Willson (1966), Lack (1968), and Willson and Pianka (1963), to which I have added some original ideas. Existing knowledge of the mating patterns of birds and mammals has been summarized by Lack (1968) and Eisenberg (1966), respectively. All theories of sexual selection involve an element of choice, and mine is no exception. In order for discrimination to be selected for, it is necessary that (*a*) the acceptance of one mate generally precludes the acceptance of another, and (*b*) the failure to accept one mate will be followed by an opportunity to mate with other individuals with such a high probability that the loss in reproductive output resulting from rejection of a potential mate is, on the average, less than the average gains that can be realized by obtaining a mate of superior fitness (Fisher 1958, p. 144).

The first condition is met by both sexes of many species and by females in virtually all species. Basically, a female produces gametes with a large amount of stored energy, while a male produces gametes with a complete set of genetic instructions but no significant amount of stored energy. Consequently, the number of gametes that can be produced by males is potentially, and in most cases actually, very large. On the other hand, the number of eggs produced by females is ultimately limited by the amount of energy that can be mobilized for their production or subsequent care. It follows that males can be expected to increase the number of offspring they produce by mating with more than one female, but females should not have more offspring by successive matings with more than one male unless one male were to provide insufficient gametes to fertilize all the eggs, an unlikely condition (Maynard Smith 1958, p. 146).

For the same reason, errors in mate selection are more serious for females than for males. An interspecific mating that produced inviable or sterile offspring might claim the entire season's gamete production for a female, while the male could have erred to the extent of no more than a few minutes and a few readily replaced gametes.

The inescapable conclusion is that mate selection will be practiced whenever sensory capabilities and locomotor abilities permit it and that females will, in the vast majority of cases, exercise a stronger preference. It is a well-known fact that males of many species court rather indiscriminately and can, especially when deprived of sexual activity for some time, be induced to mate with remarkably incomplete stimulus objects. Such behavior could not have evolved if errors were strongly selected against among males. For this reason, the following model assumes that females make a choice among available males. Since polygyny must always be advantageous to males, its presence or absence must depend primarily upon the advantages or disadvantages to the females.

I also assume that the environment inhabited by a species is variable and that mean reproductive success uncomplicated by density effects is correlated with this variation in quality of the habitat. For the purposes of graphic presentation, environments are treated as though they can be ordered linearly with respect to their intrinsic quality, as measured by reproductive success, but this is not essential to the argument. A model based upon these assumptions is presented in figure 1.

There are two bases upon which female choice could be made. The first, already mentioned, is the genetic quality of the male, that is, the nature of the genes that will be given to the offspring from a mating with that male. Given the existence of such differences, female choice must inevitably be under strong selection, since those females mating with more fit males will thereby produce offspring that are more fit, on the average, than females mating with less fit males. Therefore, females should evolve to be especially responsive to those morphological and/or behavioral traits of males which reflect their fitness (Fisher 1958, p. 151).

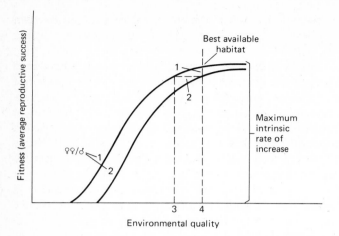

Figure 1 Graphic model of conditions necessary for the evolution of polygynous mating patterns. Average reproductive success is assumed to be correlated with environmental differences and females are assumed to choose their mates from available males. The distance *1* is the difference in fitness between females mated monogamously and females mated bigamously in the same environment; the distance *2* is the *polygyny threshold*, which is the minimum difference in quality of habitat held by males in the same general region sufficient to make bigamous matings by females favored by natural selection.

In many species, however, the role of the male in reproduction is more extensive, involving provision of food for the offspring, possession of a territory within which resources can be gathered, protection against predation or inclement weather, and so forth. In these cases, I expect selection by the females to be influenced also by the quality of the territory and the probability that the male is capable of and disposed toward taking an active role in the care and defense of the offspring. The model accommodates both cases.

The model assumes that mean reproductive success is correlated with the quality of the environment in which the individuals are living. The exact shape of the function is immaterial as long as the slope is everywhere positive. Given this condition, the best strategy for a female is to mate with a male on the best quality habitat and to rear her offspring, with or without his help, in that environment. However, as more individuals settle in these optimal environments, the average reproductive success will be expected to drop for three major reasons. First, the more individuals that are exploiting a given environment, the greater the likelihood that reduction of resources will adversely influence reproductive success. Second, the higher density of individuals may attract more predators, thereby increasing the probability of nest destruction. Third, if the male does play a role in the care of the offspring and females settle at a greater density than the males, then the aid of the male will have to be shared among the females, each getting less than if the male were able to devote his full attention to the offspring of one of them. For this reason, a curve representing the average reproductive success of females mated to males having more than one mate is drawn below the curve for females involved in monogamous matings.

Whatever the relative positions of these two curves, a situation may eventually be reached at which the quality of habitat on the territories of unmated males is such that the expected reproductive success of a newly arriving female is higher if she attempts to mate with a male already with one female but on a superior-quality habitat, rather than mating with an unmated male on poorer habitat. The difference in quality of habitats occupied by mated and unmated males required to make a bigamous mating advantageous for a female may be designated the *polygyny threshold* (Verner and Willson 1966), and polygyny is expected to evolve only when this situation regularly presents itself to the females of a species.

It follows that the likelihood that polygyny will evolve is influenced by all factors which determine how broad a range of environmental conditions will be occupied by the individuals of a species. For example, if the territories of the males of a species are nearly equal in quality and there are still unpaired males available, it is unlikely that the mean reproductive success of females attempting bigamous matings would be higher. Similarly, all factors that influence the amount of difference in mean reproductive success of females in monogamous and bigamous matings in equivalent environments will affect the likelihood that polygyny will evolve. More specifically, the greater the difference, that is, the farther apart the two curves are, the farther to the left will lie the polygyny threshold, and there must be greater differences in habitat quality for polygyny to pay for the females. Conversely, with less difference, that is, closer curves, a smaller difference in habitat will push part of the population to the left of the polygyny threshold.

a *Factors promoting occupancy of habitats differing widely in quality:* The existence of individuals to the left of the polygyny threshold will be facilitated by (1) low mortality rates during the nonbreeding season, so that not all individuals can be accommodated in the better areas, and (2) the existence of large differences in the quality of habitats actually occupied by the species.

b *Factors influencing the differences in average reproductive success of monogamously and bigamously mated females:* A major factor affecting the differences in reproductive success of females will be the role of the male in the care of the offspring. If his role is limited to the provision of genetic information, that is, if the male provides no food, territory, or protection, the success of the females will not be affected by the number of other females that have mated with the male unless his fertility declines with successive matings. Thus, in the limiting case of no male parental care, the two curves become congruent, and the mating choice by the females is based strictly upon the genotype of the male. A high degree of promiscuity is to be expected in such species.

Even if the male also cares for the offspring, in which case the number of other females he already has is a major factor in female choice, there are conditions which tend to minimize the reduction in reproductive success attendant upon polygynous matings. For example, if the successive females of a male are staggered in their breeding so that the periods of dependence of their offspring overlap little or not at all, more support from the male could be available (Verner 1964). This should give selective advantage to two different forms of female behavior. The first is the attempt to exclude additional females from the territory of the male until such time as the overlap in dependency periods of the young would be minimized, and second, the avoidance by newly arriving females of territories in which a prior female was just beginning to breed.

Another factor influencing the difference in reproductive success of monogamously and bigamously mated females is the nature of the food resources present in the area. If the food for the young is not being replenished during the breeding period, the individuals breeding earliest should experience the best foraging conditions, while later-breeding individuals are exploiting an already depressed supply. However, if the recruitment to the food supply is considerable during the breeding period, conditions for later breeders may be no worse (or may even be better) than conditions for earlier breeders. Therefore, other things being equal, species exploiting food supplies that are continually renewed are more likely to cross the polygyny threshold.

The above arguments all assume that the number of offspring being raised by a female (or pair) has evolved under the influence of natural selection to correspond to that which, on the average, is the largest number for which sufficient energy can be mobilized. The theoretical basis for this assumption and the supporting empirical data have been extensively summarized by Lack (1954, p. 21-44). However, in some species the number of offspring produced is strongly influenced by other factors. In such cases, the existence of male parental care may be of little consequence, and mate choice should be made primarily or strictly on the basis of phenotype and territory quality. Cases in which this situation may be operative will be discussed later.

The model implies the existence of several processes which can be directly observed in nature. For example, it should be true that females mate with already mated males when unmated males are readily available and perceived by the females. Evidence that this is true has been gathered for the long-billed marsh wren (Verner 1964), the red-winged blackbird, and the yellow-headed blackbird (Orians, unpublished observations). The great variations in number of females mated with different males in other polygynous species are suggestive of the widespread occurrence of this phenomenon. Verner has also shown that the number of females attracted to a male long-billed marsh wren is correlated with the features of his territory relatable to the available food.

The model also predicts that there should not be a negative correlation between average reproductive success per female and number of females mated with a given male, since females are assumed to enter polygynous matings only when it is advantageous for them to do so. This prediction has been verified for the red-winged blackbird (Haigh 1968).

The model does not require a skewed sex ratio in the breeding population for the initiation and evolution of polygynous mating patterns. This is important because there are theoretical reasons for expecting a sex ratio near equality when the young become independent in most species (Fisher 1958; Kolman 1960) and because sex ratios at the time of fledging are near equality in all polygynous species so far investigated (Haigh 1968; Selander 1960, 1961; Williams 1940).

Using the postulates upon which the polygyny model was erected, a series of seven predictions about mating patterns can be made. These predictions are subject to direct verification or falsification. Current knowledge of mating patterns among mammals, though by no means complete, is extensive enough that I can reasonably assess the goodness of the predictions. Moreover, the predictions from the model serve to draw attention to those cases which would be most rewarding of further study. Though predictions of wide application can be made, I restrict my present consideration to birds and mammals, the groups with which I am most familiar.

1 *Polyandry should be rare among all animal groups.* This prediction follows directly from the basic attributes of maleness and femaleness. A female could presumably increase her reproductive output if several males could be induced to care for her offspring, but such a situation would in most cases be sufficiently disadvantageous to the males to cause the evolution of male behavior patterns that would prevent the system from evolving. However, once a basic sexual role reversal had evolved in a species, males might profit by associating themselves with females on better territories, thus leading to polyandry.

The actual incidence of polyandry among birds and mammals is difficult to assess. Among mammals. Eisenberg (1966) reviewed several polygynous or promiscuous mating patterns but found no good case of a simultaneous association of a female with more than one male. Among birds the situation is confused by the fact that there has been a tendency to assume polyandry in all those species with a reversal of sexual roles. Most such species are tropical and subtropical in distribution and are not well known ecologically, making comparisons even more difficult. For example, it was formerly believed that the phalaropes (Phalaropodidae) were polyandrous, but recent data indicate that, though incubation and care of the young are exclusively the role of the males, the species are nonetheless monogamous (Höhn 1967). However, there is good evidence of polyandry for at least some species in five groups of birds, all with precocial young: the button quails (Turnicidae), painted snipe (Rostratulidae), jacanas (Jacanidae), tinamous (Tinamidae) and rails (Rallidae). Details in all these cases are summarized by Lack (1968).

Among rheas (Rheidae), emus (Dromiceidae), cassowaries (Casuariidae), kiwis (Apterygidae), tinamous and button quails, the males normally incubate the eggs and care for the young, but most species are apparently monogamous. In the best-studied species, the brushland tinamou (*Nothoprocta cinerascens*), the males defend territories while the females travel in small groups. Several females lay eggs in a single nest, but each female may mate with several males in rapid succession (Lancaster 1964). The classification of this type of pattern is somewhat ambiguous since the male may have several females at once, but each female may nevertheless mate with several different males during the laying of a single "clutch" of eggs. A clearer case of polyandry with a reversal of parental role is provided by the pheasant-tailed jacana (*Hydrophasianus chirurgus*) (Hoffmann 1949).

The evolution of sexual role reversal in birds may have had its origins in a monogamous system with equal sharing of parental care by the two sexes. In many such species, the males incubate first while the females recover the energy lost during egg production. Under such circumstances, especially among species with precocial young, if the females were able to obtain enough energy to produce more eggs, it would be advantageous to mate with another male were one available. It would also be advantageous for the incubating males to induce other females to mate with them and deposit their eggs in the nests, so that the tinamou type of system could readily evolve. A further advantage of such a system is that the length of time the nest is available to be destroyed by predators is reduced, since a full clutch of eggs is placed in the nest in a shorter period of time than if a single female were doing all the laying.

2   *Monogamy should be relatively rare among mammals but should be the predominant mating pattern among birds.*   The physiology of mammalian reproduction dictates a minor role of the male in the care of the offspring, whereas among birds the only activity for which males are not equally adept as females is egg laying. This prediction is readily verified. In his extensive review of mammalian social organization, Eisenberg (1966) pointed out that there are very few cases of known monogamy among mammals, the apparent exceptions being the marmosets (Callithricidae), gibbons (Hylobatinae), beavers (Castoridae), the hooded seal (*Cystophora cristata*), the only pinniped known to form a stable family unit, and a number of terrestrial carnivores, such as foxes, badgers, and viverrids. The situation is more difficult to determine among large ungulates, but temporary pair bonds that are apparently monogamous may form in hyraxes *(Dendrohyrax)*, rhinoceroses, and some deer *(Capreolus capreolus, Odocoileus)*.

The mammals among which monogamy is probably the most prevalent are the terrestrial carnivores, and they provide the most prominent exception to the generalization that the role of the male is limited or nonexistent in the care of offspring. For a carnivore, capturing food is a difficult task, and males can and do make kills and deliver the prey to either the female, who converts it to milk, or to the young once they are old enough to be able to ingest meat. It is difficult to imagine a comparable role for a male herbivore.

In contrast, monogamy is the prevalent mating pattern in the majority of bird species in virtually all families and orders. Assuming that all hummingbirds are promiscuous, Lack (1968) surmises that about 91% of all bird species are monogamous. Given the properties of the model, this is to be expected; but polygyny and promiscuity do exist among birds, and the model, if it is to be generally useful, must provide predictions capable of explaining those cases. Because polygyny should seldom evolve among birds, this group provides a particularly useful test case for the validity of the model. Fortunately, the mating patterns of birds are well enough known to allow tests of the predictions in most cases.

3   *Polygyny should evolve more readily among precocial birds than among altricial species.*   This prediction follows from the ability of many precocial young to find their own food and be relatively independent of the provisioning activities

of the adults. This decreases the potential role of the male. There are species with precocial young, such as gulls, in which the young, though able to run around actively at birth, are not able to forage for themselves. These species are not included in this prediction.

This prediction is only partially fulfilled in nature. Polygynous and promiscuous species are numerous among upland game birds (Phasianidae, Tetraonidae) and there are a few species among the shorebirds (ruff, *Philomachus pugnax;* buff-breasted sandpiper, *Tryngites subruficollis;* pectoral sandpiper, *Erolia melanotos;* and great snipe, *Capella media*), but most members of the Charadriidae (plovers) and Scolopacidae (sandpipers) are monogamous (Lack 1968, p. 116). Polygyny is also rare in the Anatidae (swans, geese, and ducks). In many of the monogamous species, both sexes take an active role in the care of the young, leading them to suitable foraging areas and keeping on the alert for predators. In geese the male defends the nest and young from predators, but in most species of ducks the female alone cares for the young, and yet monogamous pair bonding seems to be the rule. It is significant that the known exceptions among ducks are all tropical species (Lack 1968, p. 123), suggesting that perhaps the prevalence of monogamy among high latitude species may be the result of the advantage of pair formation on the wintering ground and rapid initiation of breeding which give a stronger advantage to monogamy for the males than would otherwise be the case.

4 *Polygyny is likely to evolve in species with altricial young that nest in marshes.* The marsh environment possesses several features that make it more likely that the polygyny threshold will be crossed than in any other environment. First, the range in productivity of marshes greatly exceeds that found in upland habitats (Verner and Willson 1966). Differences of over tenfold are not unusual in aquatic environments, whereas the difference between the most productive and least productive woods is much less. Moreover, great differences in productivity in a terrestrial environment are likely to result in a sufficiently altered vegetational profile to cause a change in species rather than the occupation of a broad gradient by one species (L. L. Wolf, personal communication). In marshes, however, productivity differences are not necessarily associated with vegetation structure, and striking changes in vegetational features regularly occur within the span of a few years (Weller and Spatcher 1965), so that opportunities for evolving species that occupy only a small segment of the marsh vegetation pattern are more limited than in terrestrial environments.

The food supply for insectivorous birds in marshes is often rapidly renewed. Many of the breeding passerine birds of marshes exploit primarily the emerging individuals of insects with aquatic larval and terrestrial adult stages. These insects are vulnerable for only a few hours during their lives, and those not taken on the day they emerge are mostly unavailable on subsequent days. Therefore, the supply of food on a given day is not significantly affected by the number of insects removed from the system on previous days but rather upon those factors that regulate the size of the emergence on that particular day. In contrast, the supply of insects on the foliage of trees and shrubs may be seriously depleted by the foraging activities of birds, which lowers the expected reproductive success of later arriving individuals.

In a review of the mating systems of North American passerines, Verner and

Wilson (1966) demostrated that, though marsh-nesting species constitute only a small fraction of the total species (about 5%), eight of the 15 polygynous species breed in marshes. Polygyny is also prevalent among the marsh-nesting weaverbirds (Ploceidae) in Africa (Crook 1963, 1964). Also, the only known nonpasserine species with altricial young that is regularly polygynous is the bittern *(Botaurus stellaris)*, a marsh-nesting species (Gaukler and Kraus 1965).

   5 *Polygyny should be more prevalent among species inhabiting early succes-sional habitats.*   Like marshes, early successional terrestrial vegetation changes rapidly, thus discouraging the evolution of species adapted specifically to minor variants of it. In addition, there are reasons for suspecting that variations in food supply in early successional sites might be considerable. Early successional plants are characterized by rapid growth and the apportionment of large amounts of energy to reproduction. They probably also devote less energy, on the average, to antiher-bivore devices than plants of later successional stages. Accordingly, they should be vulnerable to insect attack when found, and may owe their success in part to the fact that many patches escape detection. If this is true, patches of early successional vegetation should consist of some not yet found by insects, therefore containing relatively little food, and others supporting large populations of grazing insects. Five of the 15 regularly polygynous species of North American passerines breed in prairie or savannah habitats (Verner and Willson 1966; Zimmerman 1966), and some of them, notably the dickcissel *(Spiza americana)* and the bobolink *(Dolichonyx oryzivorus)* are restricted to the very early successional stages of grassland vegetation (Zimmerman 1966). Differential food supply and its possible correlation with the number of females per male in different patches of early successional vegetation has never been measured, but it should not be difficult to do so.

   6 *Polygyny should be more prevalent among species in which feeding areas are widespread, but nesting sites are restricted.*   If nest sites are restricted and a single male holds several of them, it should be advantageous for females to mate with such males even if they are already mated, particularly if the alternative is accepting an inferior site or no site at all. Two of the polygynous passerines of North America, the house wren *(Troglodytes aedon)* and the winter wren *(T. troglodytes)*, nest in cavities but are unable to excavate their own, and the same is true of the polygynous pied flycatcher *(Muscicapa hypoleuca)* of Europe (Curio 1959; von Haartman 1954). This may also be the explanation of the prevalence of polygyny among savannah species of weaverbirds in Africa and Asia (Crook 1962, 1963, 1964), since these are species that feed in grassland but require trees for their nests.

   7 *Polygyny and promiscuity should be more prevalent among species in which clutch size is strongly influenced by factors other than the number of offspring that can be supported by the parents.*   Clutches smaller than the number of young the parents can feed successfully might occur in species in which the adults feed primar-ily on low-energy food sources such as pulpy fruits and nectar which, though sufficient for maintenance energy, are not good for egg production. This supposition is supported by the fact that hummingbirds, unlike most avian species, lay no more than two eggs in all geographical areas and do not show the latitudinal gradient in clutch size characteristic of most birds. In addition, high predation rates may select against high feeding rates in tropical environments, reducing clutches below what the parents could feed (Skutch 1949). Finally, in stable environments competitive ability may demand considerable time expenditure (Cody 1966), so that foraging time is reduced and males may spend all or most of their time at these activities. If any of these factors are operating, the contribution of the male to reproductive success by means of food delivery to the nestlings would be decreased, and conditions favorable for polygyny would be created.

> This prediction cannot be tested directly at present, but it is noteworthy, as pointed out by Snow (1963), that polygyny or promiscuity associated with lek displays in the tropics occur only among fruit and nectar-eating birds such as hummingbirds, manakins (Snow 1962a, 1962b), cotingas (Snow 1961; Gilliard 1962), birds of paradise (Iredale 1950) and bowerbirds (Marshall 1954; Gilliard 1959a, 1959b), and not among insectivorous species, including insectivorous species in the same families, all of which are apparently monogamous. Only one of the lek species has been studied in detail (Snow 1962a, 1962b), and it was shown that fruits supporting the adults could not have been in short supply during the breeding season, but the effects of this kind of food source on egg production and nature of the food delivered to the young are completely unknown. There is evidence from the bowerbirds that frugivorous species feed their young on insects (Marshall 1954). Conversely, obligatory fruit eaters, such as parrots, have extremely long nestling periods, suggesting that rapid nestling growth and a fruit diet are mutually incompatible.

CONSEQUENCES OF THE EVOLUTION OF POLYGYNY

If polygynous mating systems evolve from monogamous ones as a result of the existence of choice situations in which it is advantageous for females to select mates already having at least one mate, the very existence of this choice system creates other selective forces that further influence the mating pattern and the morphology of the sexes.

First, in polygynous birds, there should be very keen competition among males for the better-quality territories, because possession of a high-quality territory is likely to result in the attraction of more than one female. The increased intermale competition for good areas should lead to stronger selection for secondary sexual characteristics useful in these contests. The existence of these characteristics, as indicated earlier, is well known among mammals, and Selander (1958) has demonstrated a strong correlation between the amount of sexual dimorphism in size and the degree of polygyny and promiscuity in mating pattern among American blackbirds (Icteridae). Great dimorphism in size is also characteristic of the polygynous marsh-nesting weaverbirds in Africa, the males even showing remarkable convergence toward the plumage patterns shown by males of polygynous species of icterids.

Nevertheless, unless the species are continually evolving to become more highly dimorphic, there must be counterselection against the more dimorphic individuals that stabilizes the degree of dimorphism at its present value. There are two obvious candidates for this counterselection. The first is predation, since the males are rendered exceedingly conspicuous by both their appearance and their behavior patterns. The second derives from the adverse ecological effects of larger size. In polygynous species, females are presumably not normally under selection for size other than that dictated by their basic ecological relationships with their environment (Amadon 1959). The greater the degree to which males depart from the presumably optimal size of the females, the more poorly adapted they should be for general existence, unless by their increased size they are able to exploit food resources not available to the smaller females. To date the only demonstration of a higher mortality rate during the nonbreeding season for males of a highly dimorphic species is that of Selander (1965) for the great-tailed grackle in south-central Texas. Sexing birds returning to communal roosts by examination of greatly enlarged photographs, Selander was able to show that males died at about twice the rate of the females during the winter. He also observed that the large tails of the males interfered with flying in strong winds, and that extremely strong winds completely prevented males from flying, while females were still able to navigate, though with difficulty.

Contrary to the theory of Wynne-Edwards, the model developed here predicts delayed maturation on the part of the males but not of females. Unless females are capable of preventing other females from settling in the area, all females should be able to obtain mates and reproduce. In fact, it should be extremely difficult for females to exclude other females from the territory of their mate. During the nest-building and egg-laying periods, defense of the area is easy; but once incubation has begun, eviction of a persistent intruder can only be accomplished at the expense of chilling and possible loss of the clutch of eggs. It is highly unlikely that the adverse effects of the second female could be so great as to select for such behavior. Moreover, by the time the first female is already incubating, the potential period of overlap in time when young are being fed is already minimized.

On the other hand, the strong competition among males for suitable territories and the failure of males with poor territories to obtain mates at all should produce a floating population of nonbreeding males. Such floating populations are known to be characteristic of a number of polygynous species of birds. Assuming that older and more experienced birds will be at an advantage in competition for territories, the chances of success for younger birds should be very low. If attempts to obtain territories result in higher mortality rates of the young birds and probability of success is sufficiently low, individuals making vigorous attempts might be selected against and delayed maturation would result. Selander (1965) gives a more detailed development of this argument. In the red-winged blackbird, first-year males do not acquire the full adult plumage, their testes develop later in the spring and do not reach the size characteristic of older males (Wright and Wright 1944), and they usually do not breed, though they may do so if the supply of adult males is reduced in some manner (Orians, unpublished field data).

SUMMARY

Predictions from a theory assuming mate selection on the part of females, which maximizes reproductive success of individuals, are found to accord closely, though not completely, with known mating patterns. These predictions are that (1) polyandry should be rare, (2) polygyny should be more common among mammals than among birds, (3) polygyny should be more prevalent among precocial than among altricial birds, (4) conditions for polygyny should be met in marshes more regularly than among terrestrial environments, (5) polygyny should be more prevalent among species of early successional habitats, (6) polygyny should be more prevalent among species in which feeding areas are widespread but nesting sites are restricted, and (7) polygyny should evolve more readily among species in which clutch size is strongly influenced by factors other than the ability of the adults to provide food for the young. Most cases of polygyny in birds, a group in which monogamy is the most common mating pattern, can be explained on the basis of the model, and those cases not apparently fitting into the predictions are clearly indicated. Thus, there is no need at present to invoke more complicated and restrictive mechanisms to explain the mating patterns known to exist.

LITERATURE CITED

Amadon, D. 1959. The significance of sexual differences in size among birds. Amer. Phil. Soc., Proc. 103:531–536.

Cody, M. L. 1966. A general theory of clutch size. Evolution 20:174–184.

Crook, J. H. 1962. The adaptive significance of pair formation types in weaver birds. Symposia (Zool. Soc. London) 8:57–70.

———. 1963. Monogamy, polygamy, and food supply. Discovery 24:35–41.

———. 1964. The evolution of social organization and visual communication in the weaver birds (Ploceinae). Behaviour (Suppl 10):1–178.

Curio, E. 1959. Verhaltenstudien am Trauerschnäpper. Z. Tierpsychol. 3:1–118.

Darwin, C. 1871. The descent of man and selection in relation to sex. Appleton, New York. 2 Vol.

Eisenberg, J. F. 1966. The social organizations of mammals. Handbuch der Zoologie. Walter de Gruyter, Berlin. 8 (39):1–92.

Fisher, R. A. 1958. The genetical theory of natural selection. Dover, New York. 291 p.

Gaukler, A., and M. Kraus. 1965. Zur Brutbiologie der grossen Rohrdommel (*Botaurus stellaris*). Vogelwelt 86:129–146.

Gilliard, E. T. 1959a. Notes on the courtship behavior of the blue-backed manakin (*Chiroxiphia pareola*). Amer. Mus. Novitates. No. 1942:1–19.

———. 1959b. A comparative analysis of courtship movements in closely allied bowerbirds of the genus *Chlamydera*. Amer. Mus. Novitates. No. 1936:1–8.

———. 1962. On the breeding behavior of the cock-of-the-rock (Aves, *Rupicola rupicola*). Amer. Mus. Natur. Hist. Bull. 124:31–65.

Haartman, L. von. 1954. Der Trauerfliegenschnäpper. III. Die Nahrungsbiologie. Acta Zool. Fennica 83:1–96.

Haigh, C. R. 1968. Sexual dimorphism, sex ratios, and polygyny in the red-winged blackbird. Ph.D. thesis. Univ. Washington. Seattle. 116 p.

Hoffman, A. 1949. Über die Brutpflege des polyandrischen Wasserfasans, *Hydrophasianus chirurgus* (Scop.). Zool. Jahrb. (Syst.), 78:367–403.

Höhn, E. O. 1967. Observations on the breeding biology of Wilson's phalarope (*Steganopus tricolor*) in central Alberta. Auk 84:220–244.

Iredale, T. 1950. Birds of paradise and bower birds. Georgian H., Melbourne. 239 p.

Kolman, W. A. 1960. The mechanism of natural selection for the sex ratio. Amer. Natur. 94:373–377

Lack, D. 1954. The natural regulation of animal numbers. Clarendon, Oxford. 343 p.

———. 1968. Ecological adaptations for breeding in birds. Methuen, London. 409 p.

Lancaster, D. A. 1964. Biology of the brushland tinamou, *Nothoprocta cinerascens.* Amer. Mus. Natur. Hist. Bull. 127:270–314.

Marshall, A. J. 1954. Bower-birds. Clarendon, Oxford. 208 p.

Maynard Smith, J. 1958. The theory of evolution. Penguin, Harmondsworth. 320 p.

Selander, R. K. 1958. Age determination and molt in the boat-tailed grackle. Condor 60:355–376.

———. 1960. Sex ratio of nestling and clutch size in the boat-tailed grackle. Condor 62:34–44.

———. 1961. Supplemental data on the sex ratio of nestling boat-tailed grackles. Condor 63:504.

———. 1965. On mating systems and sexual selection. Amer. Natur. 99:129–141.

Skutch, A. F. 1949. Do tropical birds rear as many young as they can nourish? Ibis 91:430–455.

Snow, B. K. 1961. Notes on the behavior of three cotingidae. Auk 78:150–161.

Snow, D. W. 1962*a*. A field study of the black and white manakin, *Manacus manacus,* in Trinidad. Zoologica 47:60–104.

———. 1962*b*. A field study of the golden-headed manakin, *Pipra erythrocephala,* in Trinidad. W. I. Zoologica 47:183–198.

———. 1963. The evolution of manakin displays, p. 553–561. *In* 13th Int. Ornithological Congr. Proc., Ithaca, N.Y., 1962.

Verner, J. 1964. Evolution of polygamy in the long-billed marsh wren. Evolution 18: 252–261.

Verner, J., and M. F. Willson. 1966. The influence of habitats on mating systems of North American passerine birds. Ecology 47:143–147.

Weller, M. W., and C. S. Spatcher. 1965. Role of habitat in the distribution and abundance of marsh birds. Iowa State Univ. Agr. Home Econ. Exp. Sta. Spec. Rep. No. 43.

Williams, J. F. 1940. The sex ratio in nestling eastern red-wings. Wilson Bull. 52:267–277.

Willson, M. F., and E. R. Pianka. 1963. Sexual selection, sex ratio, and mating system. Amer. Natur. 97:405–407.

Wright, P. L., and M. H. Wright. 1944. The reproductive cycle of the male red-winged blackbird. Condor 46:46–59.

Wynne-Edwards, V. C. 1962. Animal dispersion in relation to social behavior. Oliver & Boyd, Edinburgh. 653 p.

Zimmerman, J. L. 1966. Polygyny in the dickcissel. Auk 83:534–546.

Sexual Dimorphism in Mammals:
Avian Models and Unanswered Questions

Katherine Ralls
Office of Zoological Research, National Zoological Park,
Smithsonian Institution, Washington, D.C.

The degree of sexual dimorphism found in mammals ranges from species in which females are larger than males (Ralls 1976a) to those in which males are much larger than females and possess striking secondary sexual characteristics which females lack. Although some work has been done on mammals, principally pinnipeds (Bartholomew 1970; Stirling 1975) and primates (Crook 1972), current theories as to the ultimate causes of this variation in sexual dimorphism were developed largely by workers most familiar with the natural history of passerine birds (Verner and Willson 1966; Orians 1969).

Sexual selection is generally believed to be the principal cause of sexual dimorphism. Trivers (1972) extended earlier ideas and proposed that parental investment is the key factor influencing sexual selection. According to his model, the sex which makes a smaller parental investment in its offspring will compete for mates and be subject to sexual selection. If most sexual dimorphism is due to sexual selection, the degree of sexual dimorphism should in turn be correlated with the relative parental investments of the sexes. Ecological factors, such as the abundance and distribution of food, which influence the degree of sexual selection are pictured as operating mainly by influencing parental investment.

Recent reviews apply this body of theory to all vertebrates (Wilson 1975; Brown 1975). This paper points out some reasons why it applies less well to mammals than to passerines, attempts to evaluate the importance of parental investment in governing the degree of sexual selection in mammals, and makes some alternative predictions as to the probable relative importance of various factors in influencing the evolution of mating systems and sexual dimorphism in mammals. It also discusses the difficulty of measuring male parental investment and contribution to zygotes.

VARIABLES

Sexual Dimorphism

I will consider primarily sexual dimorphism in size, as this is the most common form in mammals and the one most often implied when the term is used without explicit

I thank the American Association of University Women, the Radcliffe Institute, and the Smithsonian Institution for financial support, and Richard W. Thorington, Jr., for his frequent encouragement and help in many ways. The following colleagues criticized versions of the manuscript and/or contributed helpful ideas and information: Jack Bradbury, Robert L. Brownell, Jr., John Eisenberg, Roger Gentry, Patricia Gowaty, Steven Green, Charles O. Handley, Jr., Robert S. Hoffmann, Frances James, Peter Jarman, David Kessler, Devra Kleiman, Lawrence Slobodkin, Ian Stirling, Richard W. Thorington, Jr., Christen Wemmer, Haven Wiley, and Mary F. Willson.

definition. Some of the difficulties of measuring sexual dimorphism are discussed in Ralls (1976a).

It is important to distinguish between sexual dimorphism in size and in other secondary sexual characteristics. The degree of sexual dimorphism in coloration and in structures used in displays or as weapons may be more closely related to the intensity of sexual selection than is the degree of sexual dimorphism in size. While sexual selection may well be the most important pressure affecting color or structures in males, it is but one of the pressures affecting size. These other pressures and those affecting female size, such as neonate and/or litter size, all contribute to the final degree of sexual dimorphism in size.

Studies of the extent to which sexual dimorphism in size correlates with sexual dimorphism in other secondary sexual characteristics are badly needed. The strength of this correlation appears to vary a great deal. Lowther (1975) found no correlation between the degree of sexual dimorphism in size and in plumage in the avian family Icteridae. A preliminary report by Leutenegger and Kelly (1975) on the anthropoid primates indicates that in this group sexual dimorphism in canine tooth size is indeed more closely related to the presumed intensity of sexual selection on males than is sexual dimorphism in body size. However, Gautier-Hion (1975) found a good correlation between sexual dimorphism in size and canine length in several cercopithecids as did Orlosky (1973) in cebids. Geist (1974) states that horn size and body size tend to evolve in parallel in ungulates.

The modal size and degree of sexual dimorphism in each of the mammalian orders is shown in table 1. Although a tabulation at this level is necessarily an oversimplification, it is nevertheless of heuristic value. Most species of mammals are small and not extremely dimorphic.

In 16 of the 20 orders, the degree of sexual dimorphism shown by most species is small to moderate. When dimorphism occurs, males are usually larger than females except in the Mysticeti and Lagomorpha, in which females are larger than males in all or the majority of species, and the Chiroptera, in which a larger size in females is very common (Ralls 1976a).

The orders in which extreme cases of sexual dimorphism favoring males, defined as a ratio of average male to female weights greater than 1.6, occur are marked with an asterisk in table 1. Some cases occur in orders in which the modal degree of sexual dimorphism is small to moderate; usually these cases are concentrated in only a single family of the order. Examples include the Macropididae in the Marsupialia, Pteropidae in the Chiroptera, Physeteridae in the Odontoceti, and Mustelidae in the Carnivora. The most extreme cases in these families are probably the great red kangaroo, *Megaleia rufa* (Frith and Calaby 1969), the hammer-headed bat, *Hypsignathus monstrosus* (J. Bradbury, personal communication, 1976), the sperm whale, *Physeter catodon* (Bryden 1972), and weasels such as *Mustela erminea* (Hall 1951).

Most of the extreme cases, however, occur in the four orders in which it is difficult to specify a prevailing mode of sexual dimorphism: Primates, Pinnipedia,

Table 1 Number of Genera and Species, Size, and Sexual Dimorphism in Size in Mammalian Orders

Order*	No. of recent genera†	No. of recent species†	Modal size category‡	Modal degree of sexual dimorphism §
Monotremata	3	6	S	M
Marsupialia*	81	242	S	M
Insectivora	77	406	S	M
Dermoptera	1	2	S	M
Chiroptera*	173	875	S	M, ♀♀?
Primates*	47	166	L	V
Edentata	14	31	L	M
Pholidota	1	8	S	M
Lagomorpha	9	63	S	M, ♀♀
Rodentia	354	1,687	S	M
Mysticeti	5	10	L	M, ♀♀
Odontoceti*	33	74	L	M
Carnivora*	96	253	S	M
Pinnipedia*	20	31	L	V
Tubulidentata	1	1	L	M
Proboscidea*	2	2	L	V
Hyracoidea	3	11	S	M
Sirenia	3	5	L	M
Perissodactyla	6	16	L	M
Artiodactyla*	75	171	L	V

  * Orders in which extreme cases of sexual dimorphism favoring males have evolved. Extreme dimorphism is defined as a ratio of male to female weight exceeding 1.6.

  † After Anderson and Jones 1967.

  ‡ After Bourlière (1975), with the addition of the nonterrestrial orders. Size categories: S = adult weight less than 3 kg, L = adult weight more than 5 kg.

  § Dimorphism categories: M = small to moderate in all or the majority of species, males probably larger in most cases of dimorphism; M, ♀♀ = small to moderate in all or the majority of species, females larger in most cases of dimorphism. V = variable, degree of dimorphism so variable that it is difficult to specify a prevailing mode.

Proboscidea, and Artiodactyla. Examples are the baboons, *Papio,* the orangutan, *Pongo pygmaeus,* and the gorilla, *Gorilla gorilla* (Crook 1972; Eckhardt 1975; Schaller 1963); the fur seals and sea lions (Otariidae) and elephant seals, *Mirounga* (Bryden 1972); the African elephant, *Loxodonta africanus* (Laws, Parker, and Johnstone 1975); and the nyala, *Tragelaphus angasi* (Tello and Van Gelder 1975). The most extreme cases in mammals, such as the northern fur seal, *Callorhinus ursinus* (Scheffer and Wilke 1953), far exceed those in birds (Ralls 1976b).

Sexual Selection

Sexual selection is usually divided into two processes: intrasexual selection, in which members of one sex compete to mate with members of the other, and intersexual or epigamic selection, in which members of one sex choose to mate with members of the other. In practice, the two aspects cannot always be separated and Fisher

(1930) argued that, when a selective advantage is linked to a secondary sexual characteristic, there will be simultaneous selection on the other sex in favor of those who prefer the advantageous type. However, most discussions of sexual selection in mammals have stressed the importance of intrasexual selection, e.g., "among mammals the role of agressive male behavior tends to be more important than that of female choice" (Brown 1975, p.160).

A variety of field and laboratory observations suggest that the importance of epigamic selection in mammals may have been underestimated. Female mountain gorillas, chimpanzees, *Pan troglodytes,* and African wild dogs, *Lycaon pictus,* transfer between groups more frequently than males, reversing what is thought to be the usual mammalian pattern (Harcourt, Steward, and Fossy 1976; Kawanaka and Nishida 1975; Frame and Frame 1976). Apparently, the female chooses whether to stay with a particular male or group of males or join another group. Both wild and captive female gorillas initiate sexual activity, males being relatively passive, and captive females are selective in their choice of sexual partners (Schaller 1963; Nadler 1976). Richard (1974) presents evidence on female choice in sifaka, *Propithecus verreauxi.*

Lincoln and Guinness (1973) claim that female red deer, *Cervus elaphus,* play an active role in forming the rutting groups and that a hind in estrus may select a particular stag and move to it. Female bighorn sheep, *Ovis canadensis,* seem to prefer to mate with large-horned males (Geist 1971). Estrous domestic ewes allowed to choose between several tethered rams most often approached those with the best mating records (Lindsay and Robinson 1961). Female fallow deer, *Dama dama,* congregate around territorial rutting bucks (Chaplin and White 1970; Chapman and Chapman 1975). Female pronghorn antelope, *Antilocapra americana,* prefer to mate with territorial rather than nonterritorial males (Kitchen 1974). Female Uganda kob, *Adenota kob,* and Kafue lechwe, *Kobus leche,* presumably choose particular territorial males on the lek (Buechner 1974; Schuster 1976) and the same may also occur in other antelope in which the territories are less tightly concentrated.

In deer mice, *Peromyscus leucopus,* each sex is caught most readily in traps baited with the odor of the other sex, indicating that mate selection may not be entirely an active seeking process on the part of males but may involve some male seeking by females (Mazdzer, Capone, and Drickamer 1976). Laboratory data on "proceptivity" (female initiative in sexual behavior) in female rodents suggest that this may be true for other species as well (Beach 1976). Female preference for particular males has been experimentally demonstrated in domestic dogs (Beach and Le Boeuf 1967) and macaques, *Macaca* (Dixson et al. 1973; Eaton 1973; Lindburg 1975). However, workers who have studied pinnipeds almost unanimously report that there is no evidence for female choice in this order (Peterson 1968) and there is some quite strong evidence against it in northern fur seals (R. Gentry, personal communication, 1977). Cox and Le Boeuf (1977) have suggested a mechanism by which female elephant seals may increase their chances of mating with dominant males without directly choosing such males. Females protest vigorously when males attempt to copulate, thus inciting competition among all nearby males.

Brown (1975) suggests that it is possible to distinguish a group of species in which sexual selection consists primarily of intrasexual selection (the "male dominance and competitive mating" type) and a group in which it consists primarily of epigamic selection (the "male adornments and female choice" type). Female preferences for individual males are supposedly weak or difficult to detect in the first group. It seems unlikely that a clear-cut dichotomy really exists, as much of the evidence suggesting female choice in mammals is from species where intrasexual selection appears to be quite strong.

At least at the present level of knowledge, it is not possible to predict the roles played by the sexes either from the social system or the degree of sexual dimorphism. For example, both hamadryas, *Papio hamadryas,* and gelada *(Theropithecus gelada)* baboons are extremely dimorphic and live in stable harems. However, young gelada males may start to cultivate the attention of juvenile females within a harem without attracting the attention of the adult harem male, while the young hamadryas male has to begin by kidnapping young females. Similarly, gelada harem males do not solicit new females; rather, it is the females that choose harems to join (Gartlan 1973; Dunbar and Dunbar 1975). The hamadryas females appear to be captured by males and do not have the opportunity to express a preference (Kummer 1968).

The indiscriminate use of the terms harem and harem master (Brown 1975; Wilson 1975) is a legacy of early misconceptions of the social structure of most highly polygynous mammals. Several field observers have stressed that it is extremely misleading to use harem and harem master with respect to pinnipeds (Peterson 1968; Gentry 1975*a*, 1975*b*; Marlow 1975) and the same is true with respect to most antelopes (Estes 1974). Peterson (1968, p. 36) comments on pinniped breeding groups:

> The misconceptions regarding the harems of pinnipeds seem to be a result of superficial investigations. To a casual observer, the males of several species do indeed seem to have stable groups of females within their territories. . . . In the otarids, especially, it might appear that each male is controlling one of the aggregations of females. When the animals are individually marked, however, it soon becomes clear . . . that females may move through these harems fairly easily, and that the groups result more from the gregariousness of the females than from the efforts of the "harem master." . . . Bulls of several species chase females that attempt to leave the aggregations within their territories, and in dimorphic species, such as fur seals where the male is much larger than the female, a bull may lift a female and throw her back into his territory. . . . But there are too many females per territory and they are too agile for the bulls. I have watched female fur seals move through five harems in less than one hour.

Early casual observations of antelopes also suggested that most species formed stable harems. However, field studies of such species as the impala, *Aepyceros melampus,* have usually shown that their breeding groups consist of a mosaic of male territories through which female groups of unfixed membership wander almost at will (Jarman 1974; Jarman and Jarman 1974). The home range of a typical female impala covers about 10 male territories. Female mobility has also been described in the rutting groups of the red deer: "In contrast to the restricted movements of the stags controlling the harems, the hinds are able to move between the different rutting groups" (Lincoln and Guinness 1973, p. 486).

Although ethologists have not formally defined the scientific meaning of harem, two dictionaries define it as a "group of females led by and mated to one male" (Random House Unabridged Dictionary) and a "group of females controlled by one male" (Webster's Third New International Dictionary). These definitions suggest that the term might properly be applied to a mammalian social unit that consisted of a stable group of one dominant male and several females persisting throughout at least one breeding season. Mammalian breeding groups meeting these criteria do exist; for example, those of the hamadryas baboon (Kummer 1968) and the vicuna, *Vicugna vicugna* (Franklin 1974). Those of most polygynous mammals do not, however, due to the movement of females between groups and the lack of male control. It would seem best to use a neutral term with no behavioral implications, such as breeding group or one-male group in most cases and restrict the use of harem to those few species in which long-term group stability and male control actually exist.

The terms monogamy and polygyny are presently used in two distinct senses. They may be defined by the nature of the bonds between the sexes, as follows: polyandry = one female has bonds with several males; monogamy = one female has a bond with one male; polygyny = several females have bonds with one male; promiscuous = no bonds between the sexes. This system is much used by ornithologists; Selander (1972) offers a more elaborate version. It is difficult to use when discussing the mammals as a whole, however, due to the large number of non-monogamous species, the lack of agreement on an operational definition of a bond in these species, and the lack of detailed studies of their social behavior. Alternatively, the terms may be part of a classification based on genetic criteria, as follows: polyandry = more males than females contribute gametes to zygotes; monogamy = males and females contribute gametes to zygotes in equal numbers; polygyny = more females than males contribute gametes to zygotes (Wiley 1974a). I will follow this classification. Fortunately, it is the relative genetic contributions of the sexes which presumably affect the evolution of sexual dimorphism, regardless of the exact nature of the bonds between the sexes. Under this system, promiscuous species are considered polygynous. Birdsall and Nash (1973) claim that deer mice, *Peromyscus maniculatus*, are polyandrous, since the individual young in a litter often have different fathers. However, they did not establish that more males than females contribute gametes to zygotes.

The intensity of intrasexual selection in a species should be proportional to the ratio of the lifetime number of offspring sired by a highly successful male compared to the number born by a highly successful female in her lifetime. Although the data needed to calculate this ratio are available for only a few mammalian species, such as the northern elephant seal, *Mirounga angustirostris* (Le Boeuf 1974), it is clear that it will tend to be smallest in monogamous species and tend to increase with increasing degrees of polygyny. Due to the lack of adequate data on the actual contributions of individual males to zygotes in most species, it is necessary to estimate this from behavioral observations. The use of observations such as long-term association and bonding between individual males and females to identify the monogamous species is probably not a serious source of error. Estimating the degree of polygyny from behavioral observations, however, is often exceedingly difficult and may lead to large errors.

Species may be polygynous in the absence of easily recognized groups containing one male and several females. For example, the mountain lion, *Felis concolor,* is usually solitary. Since a male's territory encompasses the territories of several females, however, the species is polygynous (Seidensticker et al. 1973).

This dispersed form of polygyny is much more difficult to detect than that seen in the African lion, *Panthera leo,* in which males and females are often associated; it may be widespread in mammals, however, as it has been reported in a variety of species including rodents (Brown 1966), cervids (Dubost 1970), prosimians (Charles-Dominique 1972), and mustelids (Lockie 1966).

Even if it is established that a species has a breeding sex ratio of one male to some number of females, determining the actual degree to which individual males contribute to zygotes, and the number of offspring a male can potentially sire, may still be very difficult. Changes in the membership of a group of females associated with a given male may be frequent and extensive (Peterson 1968; Jarman 1974; Jarman and Jarman 1974; Lincoln and Guinness 1973; Bradbury, in press). The relationship between the degree of turnover in female groups and the expected degree of sexual dimorphism is unexplored.

Estimating male contribution to zygotes is further complicated in many species because of the turnover in males holding territories. In the impala, for example, about one-third of the adult males hold territory at a time. Females spend most time in territories containing the best resources; this places strenuous demands on the males holding these territories and turnover on them is more frequent than on other territories (Jarman and Jarman 1974). Males who lose territories join bachelor groups and work their way up the hierarchy in these groups before attempting to regain territory. Similar problems arise with pinnipeds. For example, the observed ratio of breeding males to females in the northern fur seal of about 1:20 has led to the characterization of this species as the most highly polygynous pinniped. Since the annual rate of turnover in breeding males is much higher than in females, however, the ratio of zygote-contributing males to females is likely to be lower (Peterson 1968). Furthermore, males are selectively harvested from the population and a ratio lower than 1:20 might have occurred under undisturbed conditions.

When the social group contains several adult males, it is necessary to estimate the proportion of young sired by each. It is usually assumed that the males of such species are arranged in a dominance hierarchy, and that the highest ranking males sire the most offspring (Wilson 1975; Brown 1975), but some workers question this hypothesis (see Kolata 1976).

A common technique for estimating the proportion of young sired by each male is to count the number of times each male copulates during some period of observation. Difficulties arise, however, because males of high and low status are often not equally visible to a human observer. For example, it has often been reported that high-ranking rhesus macaques, *Macaca mulatta,* mate more frequently than low-ranking males. But an observer may easily fail to note some of the copulations of low-ranking and solitary males because they tend to be more secretive and peripheral than high-ranking males. Drickamer (1974) found that when he corrected his data on copulation frequencies to account for the relative observability of males of high and low status there were no significant differences between them. Similarly, Missakian (1973) suggests that mating activity of mother-son pairs may often be overlooked because it is less conspicuous than typical consort behavior. Eaton (1974) found no relationship between dominance scores and several measures of sexual behavior in the males of a captive troop of Japanese macaques; Enomoto (1974) found no correlation between number of copulations and rank order among the high-status males of a wild troop.

Ascertaining the relationship between frequency of copulation and actual paternity presents additional problems. For example, it is often stated that high-ranking male primates have priority of access to females at the height of estrus and thus sire the majority of young. Rowell (1974, p. 149), however, in an important review of the concept of social dominance, concluded that "the evidence for priority of access to receptive females is equivocal, especially when access to ripe ova rather than access to receptive females is considered, since the latter do not always contain the former. . . . Estrus is not necessarily associated with ovulation in rhesus monkeys (Loy 1970) and Conaway and Koford (1965) found that high ranking males preempted the more attractive older females in the group for most of the breeding season—continuing to consort with them exclusively while they were already pregnant, and so siring fewer offspring than their sexual activity might suggest."

The priority of access model was formulated mathematically by Altmann (1962) and has been most carefully tested by Hausfater (1975) on yellow baboons, *Papio cynocephalus.* His data did not support the hypothesis that first-ranking males have higher reproductive success than lower ranking males. However, male rank did account for 56% of the variance in proportion of copulations among males.

The only study which determined the actual number of offspring sired by each male of a primate troop is that of Duvall et al. (1976) on the rhesus monkey, *Macaca mulatta.* Paternity was ascertained by analysis of serum proteins, red cell enzymes, and leucocyte antigens. The alpha male did not father all, or even most, of the 29 infants born during the 2-year study. In fact, he could not have fathered more than seven, which was not significantly different from the number expected by chance. The male which had both the most known (eight) and the most possible (10) offspring was of low rank during 1 year of the study and of middle rank the other.

As with territorial species, it is very difficult to estimate the degree of lifetime differential reproductive success in species with multimale groups, as an individual male does not occupy a given rank for very long. As Hausfater (1975) comments:

. . .data on the total lifetime reproductive success for even a single individual nonhuman primate are not presently available. It may be, for example, that every adult male baboon in his lifetime occupies each dominance rank for the same amount of time as does every other male. If so, then, in the long run, all males would be expected to have an equal total lifetime reproductive success. Even if, as is more likely, males differ in the sequence of ranks that they occupy and in the duration of rank occupancy, the total lifespan reproductive success of all males may still be equal . . . to achieve any given level of reproductive success, a male may either occupy second rank and reproduce at a high rate for a short period of time or occupy fifth rank and reproduce at a low rate for a longer period of time.

It does not seem likely that the total life-span reproductive success of all males is equal; the point is that evidence to rule out this hypothesis in primates is still lacking.

In mammals which have more than one offspring at a time, the problem of ascertaining paternity is further complicated because the members of a single litter may have different fathers. Birdsall and Nash (1973) have shown that this occurs in a large proportion of litters in the deer mouse.

Parental Investment

Parental investment is defined as "any investment by the parent in an individual offspring that increases the offspring's chance of surviving (and hence reproductive success) at the cost of the parent's ability to invest in other offspring" (Trivers 1972, p. 139). Male parental care is relatively rare in mammals (Spencer-Booth 1970) and the overall variation in male parental investment from species to species is greater than that of female parental investment, making it particularly important to assess the degree of male parental investment. Unfortunately, parental investment is presently impossible to measure.

The magnitude of a given parental investment is proportional to the degree to which it decreases the parent's ability to invest in other existing or hypothetical future offspring. For some forms of parental investment, such as feeding or transporting the young, measures of the time or energy devoted to the activity may reflect the amount of investment rather well. In other cases some fraction of the time and energy devoted to an activity would seem an appropriate measure of the parental investment it represents. For example, territorial defense by males is an indirect form of parental investment when it preserves resources for females rearing young sired by the male. Because territorial defense is usually a multipurpose activity, however, and provides other benefits to the male performing it, only some unknown proportion of the time and energy devoted to it should be considered parental investment. It is clearly not possible to measure some forms of parental investment, such as defense of the young, in time or energy units at all. The magnitude of a parental investment involving defense of the young would seem to be related to the degree of risk of injury or death rather than to the amount of time or energy required for the actual behavior.

Trivers's model will remain untestable in any precise way until some agreement is reached on the best way to quantify each type of parental behavior and on how to estimate the degree of parental investment a given amount of each behavior represents. It is therefore important to devise some system to estimate the amount of male parental investment shown by a given mammalian species. Kleiman (1977) has made a first attempt.

It seems unlikely, however, that the degree of male parental investment can be considered a unitary variable with regard to the evolution of sexual dimorphism. Some forms of male parental investment, such as direct care of the young, do seem to set limits to the degree of sexual selection upon males and thus favor little or no sexual dimorphism. Both defense of the young and defense of a territory often involve selective advantages for large size in males and may be associated with pronounced sexual dimorphism favoring males. Indeed, the role of the male in defense has often been considered the primary reason that males of many Old World primates are considerably larger than females (DeVore 1963).

RELATIONSHIPS AMONG THE VARIABLES

If there are associations among the degrees of sexual dimorphism, parental investment, and sexual selection (as implied from the breeding system) in mammals, they should be very evident in the extreme cases. I will therefore briefly review present knowledge of the associations between the extreme forms of these variables.

Sexual Dimorphism and Male Parental Investment

In general, species in which males make a very large parental investment show little sexual dimorphism, in spite of the advantages of large males in defense (Kleiman 1977), and the males of extremely dimorphic species make small parental investments. However, the males of most mammalian species make small parental investments, and only a small proportion of these species are extremely sexually dimorphic. There are many more species which show little sexual dimorphism in which male parental investment is very small, particularly in the orders Insectivora, Chiroptera, and Rodentia. It can be seen from table 1 that these orders comprise the majority of mammalian species.

Parental Investment and Breeding System

Monogamous species tend to show unusually large male parental investments. Male parental investment also occurs in some nonmonogamous species but it tends to be smaller than in the monogamous species, or it occurs in a highly specific and individualistic way rather than a species-typical one (Kleiman 1977).

The majority of mammalian species are nonmonogamous ones in which males make a small parental investment. The degree of polygyny is not known for most species but is probably modest; relatively few show the extreme degrees of polygyny exhibited by some of the bovids and pinnipeds. In general, the males of highly polygynous species make little parental investment, although interception of sharks, which was interpreted as defense of pups, has been reported in the Galapagos sea lion, *Zalophus californianus wollebaeki* (Barlow 1972, 1974*a*, 1974*b*).

Sexual Dimorphism and Breeding System

Monogamous species in general show little sexual dimorphism (Kleiman 1977). The hooded seal, *Cystophora cristata*, is reportedly monogamous yet males are considerably larger than females (Mansfield 1963; Olds 1950; Oritsland 1970). Nonmonogamous species which show little sexual dimorphism are extremely numerous in the orders Insectivora, Chiroptera, and Rodentia (table 1).

The correlation between degree of polygyny and degree of sexual dimorphism is undoubtedly better in some mammalian taxa than others, as is the case in birds (Selander 1972). Unfortunately it has never been evaluated for the three orders which comprise at least 70% of recent mammals: the insectivores, bats, and rodents. There are polygynous species, such as the plains and mountain zebras, *Equus quagga* and *E. zebra*, which are undimorphic, but the ratio of females to males in these species is only about 5:1 (Klingel 1967, 1968). The Weddell seal, *Leptonychotes weddelli* (Erikson and Hofman 1974; Bertram 1940; Mansfield 1958; Stirling 1971), and some bats (Bradbury, in press) are polygynous but females are larger than males.

Some pinnipeds such as the gray seal and the walrus, *Odobenus rosmarus*, are more dimorphic than would be expected from their breeding systems. The discrepancy posed by these species has been dealt with by postulating that they now copulate more frequently in the water than they did in the past. A few males can monopolize the females less successfully if copulation occurs in the water, and hence the degree of polygyny in these species may now be less than it was during the period when the sexual dimorphism supposedly evolved (Bertram 1940; Repenning 1976). The orangutan is also much more dimorphic than would be expected from its breeding system, and MacKinnon (1974) accounts for this in a similar manner by postulating that the extreme sexual dimorphism is a relict of former times when large males enjoyed more of a reproductive advantage than they do today. Such hypotheses, while perhaps plausible, are impossible to test, and it might be productive to explore the possible role of selective pressures other than sexual selection in these cases. Several small weasels are extremely dimorphic but modestly polygynous at most. Niche separation may be particularly important in these cases (Brown and Lasiewski 1972) and the tendency toward seasonal geographical segregation of the sexes found in some otariids suggests that this factor may play a role in pinnipeds as well.

Consideration of these associations between the extreme forms of the variables allows an estimate of the chances that one would be correct in predicting that a species exhibited an extreme form of one variable if it were known that it exhibited an extreme form of another. This is instructive because the success with which the first member of such a pair could be predicted from the second is often quite different from the success with which the second could be predicted from the first. For example, monogamy is a good predictor of little sexual dimorphism but little sexual dimorphism is a poor predictor of monogamy, because the set of mammalian species which shows little sexual dimorphism includes but is much larger than the set which is monogamous.

In table 2 the extreme forms of the three variables are listed in pairs and the value of each member of the pair as a predictor of the other is roughly judged as either "very good," "good," or "poor." In light of the lack of knowledge about many mammalian species and the previously discussed difficulties in measuring the variables, it is obvious that some of these judgments may be in error. Nevertheless, I believe they accurately reflect the current state of mammalogical opinion and are of considerable heuristic value.

EVOLUTION OF SEXUAL DIMORPHISM IN MAMMALS

There is a high predictability both from monogamy to little sexual dimorphism and from extreme polygyny to extreme sexual dimorphism. Thus the breeding system, at least in the extreme cases, is a good predictor of the degree of sexual dimorphism and the concept of sexual selection can account for a good deal of the variability in degree of sexual dimorphism found in mammals.

Parental investment, however, does not seem to be the key variable governing the degree of sexual selection in mammals. Although a large male parental investment is a good predictor of both monogamy and little sexual dimorphism, a small male parental investment is a poor predictor of extreme polygyny and sexual dimorphism. There must be other important factors which oppose the evolution of extreme

Table 2 Estimates of the Predictability Relationships Among the Extreme Forms of Male Parental Investment, Breeding System, and Sexual Dimorphism in Mammals

A	Predictability	B
Large male parental investment	$a-b$ = good; $b-a$ = very good	Monogamy
Monogamy	$a-b$ = very good; $b-a$ = poor	Little sexual dimorphism
Large male parental investment	$a-b$ = good; $b-a$ = poor	Little sexual dimorphism
Small male parental investment	$a-b$ = poor; $b-a$ = good	Extreme polygony
Extreme polygyny	$a-b$ = very good; $b-a$ = very good	Extreme sexual dimorphism
Small male parental investment	$a-b$ = poor; $b-a$ = good	Extreme sexual dimorphism

Note E.g., given that a species is known to be monogamous, the likelihood that the prediction that it shows little sexual dimorphism would be correct is very good. However, given that a species shows little sexual dimorphism, the likelihood that the prediction that it is monogamous would be correct is poor.

polygyny and sexual dimorphism in mammals. The nature of these factors may vary from taxon to taxon and they have not been investigated for most groups. In general, they appear to act by increasing the spacing or mobility of females or favoring a short breeding season. The quality and dispersion of food resources could plausibly oppose polygyny by favoring dispersion of females. Jarman (1974) argues that the highly nutritious and widely dispersed food items utilized by forest antelopes act in this fashion. Owen-Smith (1975) suggests that dispersed food resources account for the absence of extreme polygyny and sexual dimorphism in the white rhinoceros, *Ceratotherium simum,* a species in which males make a minimal parental investment.

In the pinnipeds, the most important variables seem to be whether or not copulation occurs on land, whether parturition occurs on land, land-fast ice, or pack ice, and the length of the pupping, and hence mating, season. Their influence has been pointed out by Stirling (1975) and his views are summarized below as an example of the probable importance of factors other than male parental investment.

Male parental investment is very low in the majority of pinniped species, yet some have evolved extreme polygyny and sexual dimorphism while others have not. Extreme polygyny tends to develop only in species, such as the sea lions and fur seals, in which both parturition and copulation occur on land, and the mating season is prolonged. On land, females are often closely spaced because of their reduced mobility and the relatively small amount of suitable pupping habitat. Extreme polygyny has not evolved in species, such as the common seal, *Phoca vitulina,* and the monk seals, genus *Monachus,* which give birth on land but copulate primarily in the water. The mobility of seals in the water and the difficulty of maintaining aquatic territories may be important in these cases.

Another factor, in addition to aquatic copulation, works against the development of polygyny in species such as the harp seal, *P. groenlandicus,* and the crab-eater seal, *Lobodon carcinophagus,* which give birth on pack ice: females disperse more on ice than they do on land and the habitat is unstable. Winds and currents suddenly break up the ice and widely disperse groups of females. No pagophilic pinniped is known to show extreme polygyny and some are believed monogamous. There must be strong selection for a brief synchronized period of parturition and copulation in these species. Pups born late would be subject to severe mortality when the ice breaks up and females coming into estrus late in the season might be physically dispersed before they could mate. For those pack-ice species on which good data exist, most mating occurs within a 10-day period. A small number of males might not be physically capable of impregnating the entire female population within such a short period while warding off other males.

Species which give birth on land-fast ice may be expected to be intermediate between those which breed on land and those which breed on the unstable pack ice. The best-studied is the Weddell seal, *Leptonychotes weddelli.* The dispersion of females in this species seems dependent on the number of holes in the ice because only a limited number of females can use a single access hole. Copulation occurs in the water under the ice. Males appear to defend underwater territories but are unable to achieve the degree of polygyny found in species which give birth and copulate on land, and the mating season may last several weeks although it remains highly synchronized on a seasonal basis.

Kleiman (1977) has identified two forms of monogamy in mammals. She classifies monogamous species which are most often seen singly or in pairs as showing Type I or facultative monogamy, and monogamous species typically seen in families as showing Type II or obligate monogamy. A large male parental investment is found only in species showing obligate monogamy and it is only this type which is successfully predicted by models based on passerine data. It seems likely that facultative monogamy evolves when the kinds of factors discussed above, which set constraints on the number of females available to successful males, are exceedingly strong. This seems to be the case in the pinnipeds, in which all of the species and subspecies in which monogamy has been reported show the facultative type.

Although the "Orians-Verner" model for the evolution of polygyny may apply in part to some mammalian species, such as the yellow-bellied marmot, *Marmota flaviventris* (Downhower and Armitage 1971), it is inadequate as a general explanation of the evolution of polygyny in mammals, because most species do not meet one or more of its assumptions. First, it assumes that the need for male parental care is the main factor opposing the evolution of polygyny, which is often not the case. Second, it assumes that females choose to mate with particular males. Although this may be true of more mammalian species than is generally supposed, there is evidence that it is not true in some species, such as the hamadryas baboon and polygynous pinnipeds. Finally, it assumes that a female raises her young on the resources contained in the territory of the male with which she mates and this is not true of many highly polygynous species.

The territories of male antelopes, for example, except for a few small species such as the dik-dik, *Madoqua kirki,* serve only as part of their mating strategy and are thus not functionally equivalent to those of most passerine birds (Hendrichs and Hendrichs 1971; Jarman 1974; Estes 1974). The model might be applicable to pinnipeds if one regarded choice pupping habitat as analogous to abundant food resources (J. Bradbury, personal communication, 1976). Such an interpretation, however, would require that the males arrive first on the rookeries and establish territories before the arrival of the females. Although this occurs in some species, such as the northern fur seal, *Callorhinus ursinus* (Peterson 1968), it does not occur in others such as the grey seal, *Halichoerus grypus* (Hewer 1974), and the California sea lion, *Zalophus californianus* (Odell 1975).

Precocial young are thought to facilitate the evolution of polygyny in vertebrates by reducing the need for male parental investment (Wilson 1975). However, because male parental investment in many mammalian taxa consists only of copulation, it would appear impossible for it to be affected by how precocial the young are. A brief consideration of what is known about the distribution of precocial young in the Mammalia indicates little correlation between the degree of precociality and the degree of polygyny. All species of bovids, cervids, cetaceans, pinnipeds, perissodactyls, and caviomorph rodents have precocial young, yet breeding systems within these groups vary enormously. In pinnipeds, the least precocial young occur in the species with the greatest degree of polygyny, i.e., Otariids (I. Stirling, personal communication, 1977). The most precocial young among the African bovids are found in one of the less dimorphic groups, the Alcelaphini (Estes 1974). Conversely, the young of the Chiroptera are all somewhat more altricial, although the degree of development at birth varies (Gould 1975), yet the species of bats show a full range of breeding systems from monogamy to extreme polygyny (Bradbury, in press). In the family Leporidae, the hares have precocial young while the rabbits do not, yet hares do not tend to be more polygynous than rabbits.

The emphasis on progeny-rearing strategies by the males of many passerine species led ornithologists to develop theories which stressed the influence of the degree of male parental care on the evolution of mating systems and sexual dimorphism. However, passerines are, in several respects, an unusual group and may not be well suited to serve as models for other vertebrate taxa, particularly those which emphasize mating strategies. The passerine radiation filled a series of niches which could only be occupied by species of small body size. The small size of the females dictated a small egg, which in turn resulted in altricial young. Therefore, females typically require male assistance to rear young successfully and about 90% of living avian species are monogamous (Lack 1968).

In larger birds with herbivorous diets and precocial young, such as grouse, there is much less male parental care, monogamy is less common, and males tend to emphasize mating strategies. Wiley (1974a) points out that the degree of male parental investment is insufficient to explain the evolution of polygyny and sexual dimorphism in these avian taxa.

The relative importance of progeny rearing and of mating strategies varies among mammalian taxa just as it does among avian taxa. However, mammals as a whole clearly tend to resemble grouse rather than passerines in this respect. Male parental care is relatively rare and fewer than 3% of the species are monogamous (Kleiman 1977). The basic reproductive characteristics of internal gestation and lactation make it possible for a female mammal to rear her young successfully alone under a wide range of environmental conditions and the "mother-family," not the pair, is the fundamental unit of mammalian society (Eisenberg 1966, and in press).

Polygyny in grouse is correlated with later onset of reproduction in males than in females, a condition for which Wiley (1974a) has coined the fitting term "sexual bimaturism." This led him to develop a two-factor theory in which the evolution of polygyny depends on the balance between the advantages of dual parental care and the advantages of sexual bimaturism (Wiley 1974a, 1974b). Because of the relative emphasis on mating strategies in mammals, the advantages of sexual bimaturism may play a correspondingly large role in the evolution of mammalian mating systems. Polygyny is known to be associated with marked sexual bimaturism in many ungulates (Estes 1974) and pinnipeds (Peterson 1968; Bryden 1972). However, the majority of mammals probably show some sexual bimaturism and the relationship between the degree of sexual bimaturism and degree of sexual dimorphism remains to be critically examined. Wiley's model, while more appropriate for most mammals than the Orians-Verner model, is probably still too simple. An adequate model will certainly have to incorporate factors other than a large male parental investment which oppose the evolution of polygyny.

Another factor which will have to be included in an adequate model is body size. Although the influence of this variable is not well understood, it is apparent from tables 1 and 2 that extreme sexual dimorphism evolves much more frequently in large species of mammals than in small ones. Most extremely dimorphic species are large and most occur in orders in which the modal species size is large: Primates, Pinnipedia, Proboscidea, and Artiodactyla. In the Marsupialia and the Chiroptera, the extremely dimorphic species are found in the families which have the largest modal species size in their orders.

The question of whether or not sexual dimorphism in size tends to increase with increasing body size in individual mammalian taxa has not been systematically investigated. Although Rensch (1950, 1959) claims that this is the general rule in the animal kingdom, he found that it was not true for several pairs of related European mammalian genera and suggested that the hypothesis should be tested on a larger mammalian sample.

In grouse, large body size and greater sexual dimorphism are correlated with sexual bimaturism and the evolution of polygyny is inseparable from the evolution of large body size (Wiley 1974a). Wiley argues that larger size might contribute to the evolution of deferred reproduction. Body size has also been shown to be related in some taxa to the nutritional value and dispersion of the food items utilized. The highly nutritious and widely dispersed food items used by forest antelopes favor both a small body size and a dispersed social organization which makes a high degree of polygyny impossible (Jarman 1974). Large body size is generally correlated with long life span (Kurtén 1953; Sacher 1975) and it has also been argued that longevity will favor the evolution of polygyny (Elliott 1975).

Although the predictability between extreme sexual dimorphism and extreme polygyny is good in both directions, the association between degree of polygyny and degree of sexual dimorphism seems loose enough to indicate that sexual selection cannot account for all the variation in sexual dimorphism. An additional paradigm seems needed.

Variations in the degree of sexual dimorphism have traditionally been interpreted in terms of the factors affecting the size of the males. Recently, however, several workers have suggested new approaches by focusing on the factors affecting female size. Downhower (1976), arguing from simple bioenergetic considerations, concludes that, in a fluctuating environment, smaller female birds are likely to breed sooner and more often than larger ones. His hypothesis provides an alternate interpretation of the general condition of larger size in males, at least in temperate species. Sexual selection could then amplify the degree of dimorphism in some species.

Hamilton (1975), studying sexual dimorphism in American Indians, concluded that selective pressures affecting female size—pregnancy, lactation, and childbirth—may be more powerful determinants of sexual dimorphism in human populations than those which affect males. She concluded that small size was advantageous to women when food supplies were not ample during lactation. Ralls (1976a) considered the mammalian species in which females are larger than males and concluded that selective pressures in favor of larger females, but not sexual selection on females, were involved in many cases. An additional paradigm may already be in the making!

SUMMARY

Current models for the evolution of polygyny and sexual dimorphism are largely derived from data on passerine birds. These models are less appropriate for taxa such as mammals, in which males emphasize mating strategies, than for those such as passerines, in which males emphasize progeny-rearing strategies. The Orians-Verner model is inadequate as a general explanation of the evolution of polygyny in mammals because many species do not meet one or more of its assumptions: that the need for male parental care is the main factor opposing the evolution of polygyny; that females choose to mate with particular males; and that the female raises her young on the resources contained in the territory of the male with which she mates. A two-factor model incorporating the concept of sexual bimaturism, developed by Wiley for grouse, is more appropriate for many mammals but still too simple.

In mammals, large male parental investment is a good predictor of both monogamy and reduced sexual dimorphism, but small male investment is a poor predictor of extreme polygyny and increased sexual dimorphism. Thus, large male parental investment is only one of the important factors which oppose the evolution of polygyny. An adequate mammalian model will have to include another set of factors which oppose the evolution of polygyny by increasing the spacing or mobility of females. It will also have to explain why sexual dimorphism has evolved more frequently in large mammals than in small ones.

Sexual selection cannot account for all the variation in degree of sexual dimorphism found in mammals. An emerging paradigm based on the consideration of bioenergetic constraints and the factors affecting female size promises new insight.

LITERATURE CITED

Altmann, S. A. 1962. A field study of the sociobiology of the rhesus monkey, *Macaca mulatta.* Ann. N.Y. Acad. Sci. 102:338–435.

Anderson, S., and J. Knox Jones, Jr., eds. 1967. Recent mammals of the world. Ronald Press, New York.

Barlow, G. W. 1972. A paternal role for bulls of the Galapagos Islands sea lion. Evolution 26:307–310.

———. 1974a. A paternal role in Galapagos sea lions. Evolution 28:433–476.

————. 1974*b*. Galapagos sea lions are paternal. Evolution 28:476–478.

Bartholomew, G. A. 1970. A model for the evolution of pinniped polygyny. Evolution 24: 546–559.

Beach, F. A. 1976. Sexual attractivity, proceptivity, and receptivity in female mammals. Hormones and Behav. 7:104–138.

Beach, F. A., and B. J. Le Boeuf. 1967. Coital behavior in dogs. I. Preferential mating in the bitch. Anim. Behav. 15:546–558.

Bertram, G. C. L. 1940. The biology of Weddell and crabeater seals with a study of the comparative behavior of the Pinnipedia. British Graham Land Expedition 1934-1937. Sci. Rep. 1 (1): 1–139.

Birdsall, D. A., and D. Nash. 1973. Occurrence of successful multiple insemination of females in natural populations of deer mice (*Peromyscus maniculatus*). Evolution 27:106–110.

Bourliere, F. 1975. Mammals, small and large: the ecological implications of size. Pages 1–8 *in* F. B. Golley, K. Petrusewiez, and L. Ryszkowski, eds. Small mammals: their productivity and population dynamics. International Biological Programme 5. Cambridge University Press, Cambridge.

Bradbury, J. In press. Social organization and communication. *In* W. A. Wismatt, ed. Biology of bats. Academic Press, New York.

Brown, J. H., and R. C. Lasiewski. 1972. Metabolism of weasels: the cost of being long and thin. Ecology 53:939–943.

Brown, J. L. 1975. The evolution of behavior. Norton, New York.

Brown, L. E. 1966. Home range and movement of small mammals. Symp. Zool. Soc. Lond. 18:111–142.

Bryden, M. M. 1972. Growth and development of marine mammals. Pages 1–79 *in* R. J. Harrison, ed. Functional anatomy of Marine mammals. Vol. 1. Academic Press, New York.

Buechner, H. K. 1974. Implications of social behavior in the management of Uganda kob. Pages 853–870 *in* V. Geist and F. Walther, eds. The behavior of ungulates and its relation to management. IUCN Pub., N.S., no. 24, vol. 2.

Chaplin, R. E., and R. W. White. 1970. The sexual cycle and associated behavior patterns in the fallow deer. Deer 2:561–565.

Chapman, D., and N. Chapman. 1975. Fallow deer. Terence Dalton, Lavenham and Suffolk.

Charles-Dominique, P. 1972. Ecologie et vie sociale de *Galago demidovii*. Pages 7–41 *in* P. Charles-Dominique and R. D. Martin, eds. Behavior and ecology of nocturnal prosimians. Advances in Ethology 9. Paul Parey, Berlin.

Conaway, C. H., and C. B. Koford. 1965. Estrous cycles and mating behavior in a free ranging herd of rhesus monkeys. J. Mammal. 45:577–588.

Cox, C. R., and B. J. Le Boeuf. 1977. Female incitation of male competition: a mechanism in sexual selection. Amer. Natur. 111:317–335.

Crook, J. H. 1972. Sexual selection, dimorphism, and social organization in the primates. Pages 231–281 *in* B. Campbell, ed. Sexual selection and the descent of man, 1871-1971. Aldine, Chicago.

DeVore, I. 1963. Comparative ecology and behavior of monkeys and apes. Pages 301–319 *in* S. L. Washburn, ed. Classification and human evolution. Viking Fund Pub. no. 37. Wenner-Gren Foundation, New York.

Dixson, A. F., G. J. Everitt, J. Herbert, S. M. Rugman, and D. M. Scruton. 1973. Hormonal and other determinants of sexual attractiveness and receptivity in rhesus and talapoin monkeys. Pages 36–63 *in* C. H. Phoenix, ed. Primate reproductive behavior. Symposium of the 4th International Congress of Primatology. Vol. 2. Karger, Basel.

Downhower, J. F. 1976. Darwin's finches and the evolution of sexual dimorphism in body size. Nature 263:558–563.

Downhower, J. F., and K. B. Armitage. 1971. The yellow-bellied marmot and the evolution of polygamy. Amer. Natur. 105:355–370.

Drickamer, L. C. 1974. Social rank, observability, and sexual behavior of rhesus monkeys (*Macaca mulatta*). J. Reprod. Fertility 37:117–120.

Dubost, G. 1970. L'organisation spatiale et sociale de *Muntiacus reevesi* Ogilby 1839 en semi-liberte. Mammalia 34:331–355.

Dunbar, R., and P. Dunbar. 1975. Social dynamics of gelada baboons. Contributions to Primatology. Vol. 6. Karger, Basel.

Duvall, S. W., I. S. Bernstein, and T. P. Gordon. 1976. Paternity and status in a rhesus monkey group. J. Reprod. Fertility 47:25–31.

Eaton, G. G. 1973. Social and endocrine determinants of sexual behavior in simian and prosimian females. Pages 20–35 *in* C. H. Phoenix, ed. Primate reproductive behavior, Symposium of the 4th International Congress of Primatology. Vol. 2. Karger, Basel.

————. 1974. Male dominance and aggression in Japanese macaque reproduction. Pages 287–298 *in* W. Montagna and W. A. Sadler, eds. Reproductive behavior. Plenum, New York.

Eckhardt, R. B. 1975. The relative body weights of Bornean and Sumatran orangutans. Amer. J. Phys. Anthropol. 42:349–350.

Eisenberg, J. F. 1966. The social organizations of mammals. Handb. Zool.8(39):1–92.

————. In press. The evolution of the reproductive unit in the Mammalia. *In* J. Rosenblatt and B. Komisaruk, eds. Lehrman memorial symposium. No. 1. Plenum, New York.

Elliott, P. F. 1975. Longevity and the evolution of polygamy. Amer. Natur. 109:281–287.

Enomoto, T. 1974. The sexual behavior of Japanese monkeys. J. Hum. Evol. 3:351–372.

Erikson, A. W., and R. J. Hofman. 1974. Antarctic seals. Pages 4–13 *in* S. G. Brown et al., eds. Antarctic mammals. Antarctic map folio series no. 18. American Geographical Society, New York.

Estes, R. 1974. Social organization of the African Bovidae. Pages 166–205 *in* V. Geist and F. Walther, eds. The behavior of ungulates and its relation to management. IUCN Pub., N.S., no. 24, vol. 1.

Fisher, R. A. 1930. The genetical theory of natural selection. Clarendon, Oxford.

Frame, L. H., and G. W. Frame. 1976. Female African wild dogs emigrate. Nature 263:227–229.

Franklin, W. L. 1974. The social behavior of the vicuna. Pages 477–487 *in* V. Geist and F. Walther, eds. The behavior of ungulates and its relation to management. IUCN Pub., N.S., no. 24, vol. 1.

Frith, H. J., and J. H. Calaby. 1969. Kangaroos C. Hurst, London.

Gartlan, J. S. 1973. Influences of phylogeny and ecology on variations in the group organization of primates. Pages 88–101 *in* E. W. Menzel, Jr., ed. Precultural primate behavior. Symposium of the 4th International Congress of Primatology. Vol. 1. Karger, Basel.

Gautier-Hion, A. 1975. Dimorphisme sexuel et organisation sociale chez les cercopithécinés forestiers Africains. Mammalia 39:365–374.

Geist, V. 1971. Mountain sheep: a study in behavior and evolution. University of Chicago Press, Chicago.

———. 1974. On the relationship of ecology and behavior in the evolution of ungulates: theoretical considerations. Pages 235–246 *in* V. Geist and F. Walther, eds. The behavior of ungulates and its relation to management. IUCN Pub., N.S., no. 24, vol. 1.

Gentry, R. L. 1975*a*. Comparative social behavior of eared seals. Rapports Procés-Verbaux. Réunions Conseil Int. Exploration Mer 169:189–194.

———. 1975*b*. The validity of the "harem" concept in fur seals. Abstr., conferences on the Biology and Conservation of Marine Mammals, University of California at Santa Cruz, December 4–7.

Gould, E. 1975. Neonatal vocalizations of bats in eight genera. J. Mammal. 56:15–29.

Hall, E. R. 1951. American weasels. Univ. Kansas Publ. Mus. Natur. Hist. 4:1–466.

Hamilton, M. 1975. Variations in the sexual dimorphism of skeletal size in five populations of Amer-indians. Ph.D. diss. University of Michigan.

Harcourt, A. H., K. S. Stewart, and D. Fossy. 1976. Male emigration and female transfer in wild mountain gorilla. Nature 263:226–227.

Hausfater, G. 1975. Dominance and reproduction in baboons (*Papio cynocephalus*). Contrib. Primatology 7:1–150.

Hendrichs, H., and U. Hendrichs. 1971. Dikdik und Elephanten. Ökologie und Soziologie zweier afrikanischer Huftiere. R. Piper, Munich.

Hewer, H. R. 1974. British seals. Collins, London.

Jarman, P. 1974. The social organization of antelope in relation to their ecology. Behavior 48:215–267.

Jarman, P., and M. V. Jarman. 1974. Impala behaviour and its relevance to management. Pages 871–881 *in* V. Geist and F. Walther, eds. The behavior of ungulates and its relation to management. IUCN Pub., N.S., no. 24, vol. 2.

Kawanaka, K., and T. Nishida. 1975. Recent advances in the study of inter-unit-group relationships and social structure of wild chimpanzees of the Mahali mountains. Pages 173–186 *in* S. Kondo, M. Kawai, A. Ehara, and S. Kawamura, eds. Proceedings of the Symposium of the 5th International Congress of Primatology. Japan Science Press, Tokyo.

Kitchen, D. W. 1974. Social behavior and ecology of the pronghorn. Wildlife Monogr. 38: 1–96.

Kleiman, D. G. 1977. Monogamy in mammals. Quart. Rev. Biol. 52(1):39–69.

Klingel, H. 1967. Soziale Organisation und Verhalten freilebender Steppen-zebras (*Equus quagga*). Z. Tierpsychol. 24:580–624.

———. 1968. Soziale Organisation und Verhaltensweisen von Hartmann-und Bergzebras (*Equus zebra hartmannae* und *Equus zebra zebra*). Z. Tierpsychol. 25:76–88.

Kolata, G. B. 1976. Primate behavior: sex and the dominant male. Science 191:55–56.

Kummer, H. 1968. Social organization of Hamadryas baboons. University of Chicago Press, Chicago.

Kurtén, B. 1953. On the variation and population dynamics of fossil and recent mammal populations. Acta Zool. Fenn. 76:1–22.

Lack, D. 1968. Ecological adaptations for breeding in birds. Methuen, London.

Laws, R. M., I. S. C. Parker, and R. C. B. Johnstone. 1975. Elephants and their habitats. Clarendon, Oxford.

Le Boeuf, B. J. 1974. Male-male competition and reproductive success in elephant seals. Amer. Zool. 14:163-176.

Leutenegger, W., and J. T. Kelly. 1975. Relationship of sexual dimorphism in canine size and body size to social, behavioral, and ecological correlates in anthropoid primates. Amer. J. Phys. Anthropol. 42:314 (abstr.).

Lincoln, G. A., and F. E. Guinness. 1973. The sexual significance of the rut in red deer. J. Reprod. Fertility (suppl.) 19:475–489.

Lindburg, D. 1975. Mate selection in rhesus monkey (*Macaca mulatta*). Amer. J. Phys. Anthropol. 42:315 (abstr.).

Lindsay, D. R., and T. J. Robinson. 1961. Studies on the efficiency of mating in the sheep. II. The effect of freedom of rams, paddock size, and age of ewes. J. Agr. Sci. 57: 141–145.

Lockie, J. D. 1966. Territory in small carnivores. Symp. Zool. Soc. Lond. 18:143–165.

Lowther, P. 1975. Geographic and ecological variation in the family Icteridae. Wilson Bull. 87:481–495.

Loy, J. 1970. Peri-menstrual sexual behavior among rhesus monkeys. Folia Primatologica 13:286–297.

MacKinnon, J. 1974. The behavior and ecology of wild orang-utans (*Pongo pygmaeus*). Anim. Behav. 22:3–74.

Mansfield, A. W. 1958. The breeding behavior and reproductive cycle of the Weddell seal (*Leptonychotes weddelli* Lesson). Sci. Rep. Falkland Island Depend. Surv. 18:1–41.

———. 1963. Seals of artic and eastern Canada. Bull. Fishery Res. Board Can. 137:1–30.

Marlow, B. J. 1975. The comparative behavior of the Australasian sea lions, *Neophoca cinerea* and *Phocarctos hookeri* (Pinnipedia: Otariidae). Mammalia 39:159–230.

Mazdzer, E., M. R. Capone, and L. C. Drickamer. 1976. Conspecific odors and trappability of deer mice (*Peromyscus leucopus noveboracensis*). J. Mammal. 57:607–609.

Missakian, E. A. 1973. Genealogical mating activity in free-ranging groups of rhesus monkeys (*Macaca mulatta*) on Cayo Santiago. Behavior 45:225–241.

Nadler, R. D. 1976. Sexual behavior of captive lowland gorillas. Arch. Sexual Behav. 5: 487–502.

Odell, D. K. 1975. Breeding biology of the California sea lion, *Zalophus californianus*. Rapports Procès-Verbaux. Réunions Conseil Int. Exploration Mer 169:296–302.

Olds, J. M. 1950. Notes on the hood seal (*Cystophora cristata*). J. Mammal. 31:450–452.

Orians, G. H. 1969. On the evolution of mating systems in birds and mammals. Amer. Natur. 103:589–603.

Øritsland, T. 1970. Sealing and seal research in the south-west Atlantic pack ice, Sept.-Oct. 1964. Pages 367–370 *in* N. W. Holdgate, ed. Antarctic ecology. Vol. 1. Academic Press, New York.

Orlosky, F. 1973. Comparative dental morphology of extant and extinct Cebidae. Ph.D. diss. University of Washington.

Owen-Smith, R. N. 1975. The social ethology of the white rhinoceros, *Ceralotherium simum* (Burchell 1817). Z. Tierpsychol. 38:337–384.

Peterson, R. S. 1968. Social behavior in pinnipeds with particular reference to the northern fur seal. Pages 3–53 *in* R. S. Harrison et al., eds. The behavior and physiology of pinnipeds. Appleton-Century-Crofts, New York.

Ralls, K. 1976a. Mammals in which females are larger than males. Quart. Rev. Biol. 51: 245–276.

————. 1976*b*. Extremes of sexual dimorphism in size in birds. Wilson Bull. 88:149–150.

Rensch, B. 1950. Die Abhängigkeit der relativen Sexualdifferenz von Körpergrössee. Bonn Zool. Bei. 1:58–69.

————.1959. Evolution above the species level. Wiley, New York.

Repenning, C. A. 1976. Adaptive evolution of sea lions and walruses. Syst. Zool. 25:375–390.

Richard, A. 1974. Patterns of mating in *Propithecus verreauxi verreauxi*. Pages 49-74 *in* R. D. Martin, G. A. Doyle, and A. G. Walker, eds. Prosimian biology. Duckworth, London.

Rowell, T. 1974. The concept of social dominance. Behav. Biol. 11:131-154.

Sacher, G. A. 1975. Maturation and longevity in relation to cranial capacity in hominid evolution. Pages 417–441 *in* R. Tuttle, ed. Primate functional morphology and evolution. Mouton, The Hague.

Schaller, G. B. 1963. The mountain gorilla. University of Chicago Press, Chicago.

Scheffer, V. B., and F. Wilke. 1953. Relative growth in the northern fur seal. Growth 17:129–145.

Schuster, R. 1976. Lekking behavior in Kafue lechwe. Science 192:1240–1242.

Seidensticker, J. C., IV, M. C. Hornocker, M. V. Wiles, and J. P. Messick. 1973. Mountain lion social organization in the Idaho Primitive area. Wildlife Monogr. 35:1–60.

Selander, R. K. 1972. Sexual selection and dimorphism in birds. Pages 180–230 *in* B. G. Campbell, ed. Sexual selection and the descent of man. 1871-1971. Aldine, Chicago.

Spencer-Booth, Y. 1970. The relationship between mammalian young and conspecifics other than mothers and peers: a review. Pages 119–194 *in* D. S. Lehrman, R. A. Hinde, and E. Shaw, eds. Advances in the study of behavior. Vol. 3. Academic Press, New York.

Stirling, I. 1971. Population aspects of Weddell seal harvesting in McMurdo Sound, Antarctica. Polar Rec. 15:633–667.

————. 1975. Factors affecting the evolution of social behavior in the Pinnipedia. Rapports Procès-Verbaux Réunions Conseil Int. Exploration Mer 169:205–212.

Tello, J. L. P. L., and R. G. Van Gelder. 1975. The natural history of nyala *Tragelaphus angasi* (Mammalia, Bovidae) in Mozambique. Bull. Amer. Mus. Natur. Hist. 155:321–386.

Trivers, R. L. 1972. Parental investment and sexual selection. Pages 136-179 *in* B. Campbell, ed. Sexual selection and the descent of man, 1871-1971. Aldine, Chicago.

Verner, J., and M. F. Willson. 1966. The influence of habitats on mating systems of North American passerine birds. Ecology 47:143–147.

Wiley, R. 1974*a*. Evolution of social organization and life history patterns among grouse. Quart. Rev. Biol. 49:201–227.

————. 1974*b*. Effects of delayed reproduction on survival, fecundity, and the rate of population increase. Amer. Natur. 108:705–709.

Wilson, E. O. 1975. Sociobiology. Harvard University Press, Cambridge, Mass.

Mammalian Social Systems: Structure and Function

J. H. Crook, J. E. Ellis &
J. D. Goss-Custard
Psychology Department, University of Bristol, England

Mammalian societies are complex socio-ecological systems controlled by the interactions of numerous internal constraints and external factors. We present a simple model describing these systems functionally in terms of the adaptive behavioural strategies for resource exploitation, predation avoidance and mating and rearing of young to maturity shown by the individuals that comprise them. The relations between species-specific limitations on the range of potential individual social behaviour and the environmental variables to which the system is responsive are analysed and hypotheses from correlational and analytical field studies examined. We advocate the continued development of sophisticated systems-analytical approaches to societal analysis taking into account the contrasting informational provenance of factors of different types. This is preferred to either an over-emphasis on environmental determination or excessively formalised neo-Darwinian modelling based on assumptions from genetics and selection theory alone.

A major objective in the study of mammalian societies is to develop an understanding of the way in which, through evolution, species characteristics and environmental forces have interacted to shape the structure and dynamics of these diverse and complex systems. Such an understanding should make it possible to state how a society operates and to predict how changes in intrinsic (species) or extrinsic (environmental) characteristics may affect social organizations and the relations between individuals.

Mammalian societies are complex systems, influenced and modified by the interactions of numerous external forces and internal constraints. In order to understand them, we need to work toward the development of social systems models which will incorporate this inherent complexity and yet produce realistic simulations of both the structure at one time and dynamic change through time. In working toward this goal, the following procedures need to be undertaken, although not necessarily in the sequence suggested here:

1 Identifying: (a) The principal social system variables which between them describe the structure of a social system (e.g. group size and dispersion, inter-

Manuscript preparation supported in part by National Science Foundation Grant GB-41233X to the Grassland Biome, U.S. International Biological Program, for 'Analysis of Structure, Function, and Utilization of Grassland Ecosystems.' We are grateful to Robert Hinde and Martin Daly for critical evaluations of the text in preparation.

From *Animal Behavior 24:* 261–274. Reprinted by permission of Bailliere Tindall and the author.

individual relations) (Fig. 1). (b) The external environmental variables which produce changes in social structure and dynamics (e.g. dispersion of food; predators).
(c) The species parameters which affect the flexibility of social structure and dynamics (e.g. mobility and body size may determine ranging capacity).

    2   An assessment of how, in relation to the environment, the system expresses
the life-support and reproductive strategies of the individuals comprising it.

    3   The development of conceptual models suggesting how, with respect to
these functions, the various environmental and species characteristics interact to
determine the described structure and underlying dynamics of the society.

    4   The proposal and testing of hypotheses derived from these conceptual mod-
els.

    5   The conversion of the conceptual models (incorporating the surviving hy-
potheses) into mathemetical models which may then be used as tools for predicting
the social effects of changes in environmental variables or species parameters.

The initial steps (1–3) form the major topics of this paper. The first sections
identify what appear to be the principal variables in each of the three 'boxes' shown
in Fig. 1. Later sections are concerned with interactions among these variables and
are related to a classification of mammal social systems. In doing this, we hope to
set out a framework for future studies of mammalian social systems, and through
some simple models, to generate tentative hypotheses about the adaptive significance
of mammalian societies.

FUNCTIONAL SUB-SYSTEMS IN A SOCIETY

Individuals of a mammalian species neither disperse nor relate to one another
randomly. Rather they are found in characteristic patterns of population dispersion,
grouping and ranging and form relationships varying in number, complexity and
duration. These patterns we refer to as social structure. Structure is both maintained
and changed by processes of interindividual behaviour; these we refer to as social
dynamics (Crook & Goss-Custard 1972). Both dispersion patterns and relating are
mediated by individual behaviours comprising a communication system.

    We argue that particular social structures arise because they provide an optimal
context within which the individuals comprising them carry out vital functions.
These, on a minimal count, include (i) resource exploitation, (ii) predator avoidance,
(iii) mating and rearing. Behavioural adaptations maximizing an individual's reproductive success, survival and the survival of offspring to maturity we describe here
as 'strategies'. These include strategies comprising the behavioural determinants of
the social structures with which we are concerned. We analyse social structure here
in terms of sub-systems within which individuals achieve the main vital functions.
If desired, resource-exploitation can itself be sub-divided into, for example, food and
non-food resources, although for our present purpose it adds little to do so.

    These four functions may all be carried out within the same social structure,
as in the gibbon's (*Hylobates lar*) monogamous, single-male family group. Often,

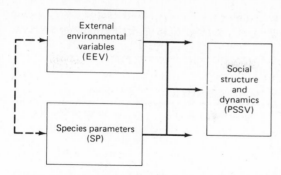

Figure 1 External environmental variables (EEV) interact with species parameters (SP, e.g. morphological and physiological characteristics) to determine social structure (measured as the principal social system variables (PSSV) and social dynamics (changes in PSSV over time)). The dotted arrow takes note of the fact that EEV's also affect SP but on a slower (evolutionary) time scale than the effects on PSSV's which may change within the life-span of an individual, through learning.

however, different activities occur within different sub-groupings within a society. In hamadryas baboons (*Papio hamadryas*) for example, rearing of the young is primarily the job of a single individual, the mother. Mating takes place within a mating group or harem of one to five females dominated by a single male. Predator-avoidance is a coordinated function of the whole troop. Resource-exploitation may be accomplished by a lone individual, by a single harem group, or within the context of an extremely large troop, depending upon the density and dispersion of resources (Kummer 1968).

The ways in which the vital functions are satisfied in different species or populations of the same species comprise an organization of strategies that interact in various ways. In some species the strategic solutions occur in spatially or temporally separated social units. In others they are convoluted into complex systems based on a compromise (Hinde & Tinbergen 1958) arising from conflicting needs and which represent the optimal strategy for individuals within the system as a whole. The total system amounts to the adaptive 'grade' of a species population in relation to its habitat (Crook 1964).

The division of a society into functional sub-systems is useful analytically in that it helps to focus attention on environmental variables and species parameters which are likely to be particularly important in the accomplishment of a particular function, but which may have little influence on the accomplishment of others. For instance, one species parameter, the maturation rate of the young, provides critical constraints on the structure of the mating and rearing sub-systems, but may be less critical in determining the structure of the resource-exploitation group. It must be remembered, however, that these sub-systems do not exist in isolation but are fully integrated and that individuals usually operate within several sub-systems simultaneously (Ellis, in preparation (a)). What appear to be the main parameters or variables in each are described now and are summarized in Table I.

Table I Matrix of Some Important External Environmental Variables (EEV), Species Parameters (SP), and Principal Social System Variables (PSSV), by Functional Sub-systems

	Resource-exploitation and predation avoidance sub-systems	Mating sub-system	Rearing sub-system
EEV	Resource density, resource distribution, density of predators	Resource distribution	Resource seasonality
SP	Mobility potential, susceptibility to predation	Role of male in rearing	Role of male in rearing, maturation rate of young
PSSV	Group size and stability, cover utilization, range exclusivity	Duration of male-female bond, no. females mated/males	Duration of the male-female bond, duration of the female-offspring bond

PRINCIPAL SOCIAL SYSTEM VARIABLES

Mating Sub-systems

Each sub-system can be usefully described at this stage by quantifying a relatively small number of principal social system variables. For instance, a mating group can be described by: (1) enumerating the number of females with which each male consorts during a breeding season (if mating is seasonal) and (2) noting the duration of the male-female bond. Although other variables will also require consideration in due course, four mating systems can be defined on this two-variable basis: (a) Monogamous pairs: single female per male; lengthy male-female bonds. (b) Monogamous mating with brief pairing; single female per male; short-term bonds. (c) Simultaneous polygamy: more than one female per male; lengthy male-female bonds. (d) Serial polygamy: more than one female per male; sequential short-term bonds. Number of females and males in group forming the potential mating pool.

Similar descriptions can be consructed for each of the other functional subgroupings utilizing identified variables which form foci of attention in current literature. We have no doubt that future studies in detail will identify further or more subtle variables and extend our account with an appropriate increase in sophistication.

Rearing Sub-systems

Rearing sub-systems can be described by: (1) relating whether or not the male remains with the female while she rears the young (i.e. the duration of the male-female bond) and (2) determining if the young remain with the female past weaning and if so, for how long (i.e. the duration of the female-young bond). Rearing sub-systems arising from variations in these two principal social variables are shown in Table II as follows:

Males do not assist:

a Males provide no assistance during rearing and do not remain with females, young leave mother at weaning (i.e. Ia).

b Same as (Ia) except that young remain with mother until subsequent young are born.

Table II   Classification of Mammalian Social Systems

Sociotype	Rearing strategy	Mating strategy	Grouping and dispersion strategy	Examples
	System variables: 1. Male's presence in rearing group. 2. Duration of male's presence. 3. Duration of mother-infant (M-I) bond.	System variables: 1. Number of female consorts per male. 2. Duration of male-female bond.	System variables: 1. Group size. 2. Group stability. 3. Refuge utilization. 4. Range exclusivity.	
Ia	Male absent from rearing group.	Promiscuous matings.	Single M-I unit, males and juveniles also range individually. Refuge (cache or nest-based) system, exclusive ranges.	Tree squirrels. Gophers.
Ib	Same as Ia. Longer M-I bond.	Same as Ia.	Similar to Ia except that ranges are not exclusive.	Bush-babies.
Ic	Same as Ia. M-I bond persists past weaning.	Promiscuous matings, brief copulatory meetings. Males may enter female herds or females may visit mating territory of male.	M-I units join together in large herds. Males may form separate herds or remain solitary. No refuges. M-I herds free-ranging. Solitary males may have exclusive ranges.	Elephants Kob.
IIb	Males present with rearing group, but only in loose association, not bonded.	Promiscuous; brief copulatory meetings within-in groups.	M-I units, males and independent juveniles remain together in groups. Non-exclusive ranges.	Some bats. Badgers.
IIb	Same as IIa.	Same as IIa.	Same as IIa, except non-refuge based, free-ranging.	Bison, Wildebeest.

Table II (Continued)

Sociotype	Rearing strategy	Mating strategy	Grouping and dispersion strategy	Examples
IIIa	Male present in rearing group.	Harem; several females per male, membership varies through the season. Some male-female bonds may be re-established in successive years but not necessarily so.	Individual harem groups during breeding season, may gather into colonies—break up after breeding season. Refuge based. Non-exclusive foraging range.	Seals.
IIIb	Same as IIIa.	Same as IIIa.	Exclusive rearing and breeding sites; units grouped into colonies, each unit with an exclusive foraging range. May be maintained outside breeding season.	Rabbits, Prairie dogs
IVa	Male remains with rearing (M-I) group, usually for more than one season. M-I bond lasts from 1 to several seasons.	Mated pairs.	Refuge-based groups may include offspring from successive seasons. Ranges may be exclusive or non-exclusive.	Beavers.
IVb	Same as IVa.	Same as IVa.	Same as IVa except non-refuge based.	Marmosets, Gibbon, Titi.
IVc	Same as IVa.	Same as IVa but looser relations between mates.	Several 'family' groups may join together, otherwise, same as IVa, and IVb.	Wolves, hunting dogs, Hyaenas.
IVd	Same as IVa.	Harem groups of long duration.	'Excess' males may form independent groups or may be integrated within rearing-mating groups. 'Herding' of basic harem groups may occur. May or may not be refuge-based. May or may not maintain exclusive ranges.	Horse, Vicuña, Patas monkey, Blue monkey, Gelada baboon Hamadryas baboon.
IVe	Same as IVa.	Multimale groups with several females of long duration.	Same as IVd except all males are integrated male-female groups; no 'excess' males. Herding of basic units not known to occur.	Papio baboons, other than hamadryas, Vervet monkeys, macaques.

    c Same as (Ia) except that young remain with the dam long past weaning and after the birth of subsequent young.

Males do assist:

    a Males remain with the females during rearing and provide some assistance in the form of feeding or protection for the dam and young, the young mature rapidly and leave the family group at weaning. Male assistance is most frequently associated with slow maturation of the young.

    b Same as above except that young leave prior to birth of subsequent offspring. This would be the same as IIa if several litters are born annually; however, it differs from it where only a single litter is produced annually and young overwinter with adults (beavers).

    c Males remain with females during rearing (i.e. III-IV in Table): young remain with the pair-bonded parents long past weaning, dependence usually decreasing slowly with age. Adult-young bond is frequently maintained after the birth of subsequent offspring. In some rare cases the attendant young may carry subsequent offspring and thus participate in care (marmoset).

Resource-exploitation and Predator-avoidance Sub-system

The structure and strategy of resource-exploitation sub-systems can be described in terms of: (1) group size, (2) group stability, (3) refuge or cover utilization, and (4) range exclusivity. However, all but the last of these may also express predator-avoidance. Thus, except in specific instances where there is evidence for assuming that these social variables are determined either by resource-exploitation strategies or by predator-avoidance strategies, they are currently most economically considered as the products of both and discussed as grouping and dispersion strategies.

    a *Group size and stability.* The potential variation in group size ranges from one to the size of the population deme. Group stability may range from considerable mobility of membership through steady or periodic changes in size or composition over time to complete group stability.

    b *Refuge or cover utilization.* One method of classifying cover utilization may be based on the frequency of use. Many mammals utilize cover on a continuous or daily basis. Others use dens or cover only when caring for young, while many with precocious young never use cover or refuges. There are then three refuge-utilization categories: (1) continuous refuge-users, where the refuge also contains the required resources for forage, (2) temporary refuge-users where foraging may (also) occur elsewhere, and (3) free-ranging types without consistent use of protective refuges.

    c *Range exclusivity.* This term is used to avoid the connotations inherent in 'territoriality'. Thus, it is possible to say that an individual's range is used either exclusively by that individual, or a cohesive group of individuals, (e.g. vicuna), or the range is non-exclusive and other individuals (or other groups) also have access to the resources within the range (e.g. Barbary macaques). If a temporal component is included there are: (i) non-exclusive ranges, (ii) temporarily-exclusive ranges, and (iii) permanently-exclusive ranges.

If the principal system variables describing a social structure are identified and if the functions of the system are defined, the next appropriate step is to attempt to determine the relations between the external environmental variables and the constraining species parameters which give the society its structure (Fig. 1).

Species Characteristics

Comparative analysis of social structures often suggests a phyletic ordering. For example, among mammals the simple system of isolated females living in more or less exclusive yet contiguous ranges, themselves distributed within the larger ranges of equally exclusive males is frequent among forms, such as the Insectivores, commonly considered to be primitive. The more elaborate organizations of monkey troops or wildebeeste herds appear derived from such simple beginnings. Although the direction of change is not always easily examined or determined, wherever a range of social systems is found within a taxon an adaptive radiation in relation to ecology may be suspected (Eisenberg 1966; Eisenberg, Muckinhirn & Rudran 1972; Crook 1970; Jarman 1974). Changes in characteristics during cladogenetic divergence may allow new options on social organization to be realized. For example, animals whose size limits mobility may not be able to congregate into large groups since it may not be possible for them to forage over the large distances that may be required once such large groups form. An increase in body size however releases the species from such a constraint. In this sense new 'options' in social evolution become possible. Likewise structures maintained through practice of elaborate social skills are unlikely to be found among mammals which possess relatively primitive brains.

We argue here that both gross morphological features such as body size and more subtle features such as brain neurology related to learning capacity and social flexibility may often be more resistant to evolutionary change than many characteristics of behaviour and relationship. This is because it seems likely that stabilizing selection on a genetically determined trait will tend to make it conservative and more resistant to change under selection pressure than characteristics controlled by information of more diverse provenance. The rates of evolutionary change probably differ for different classes of character. We suspect, with Struhsaker (1969), that traits with long phylogenetic history in a species are likely to act as constraints on changes within systems of which they are a part. Furthermore, in cases of societal convergence the behaviour mediating social organization is likely to show differences providing indications of phylogenetic sources.

In the organization of functions such as rearing or resource-exploitation a number of species morphological and physiological characteristics may limit the kinds of strategies and social structures that might be developed. For instance, an important constraint operating on the form of a rearing strategy may be the maturation rate of the young. We suspect that maturation rate is likely to be a more conservative trait than other characteristics related to it. Thus among species where maturation is slow the duration of the mother-infant bond is, of necessity, lengthy.

However, we admit that in the examination of behavioural correlations the attribution of dependency to a variable is often difficult since it is rarely clear which characteristic is the more resistant to change. For example, where feeding and caring for the young so occupy the mother as to make them both susceptible to predators, or where the female alone is unable to provide sufficient food for her offspring, the male may remain with his mate or mates to assist in rearing. While the adaptiveness of the correlation seems clear, the causal relation between such traits (as to which may necessitate or facilitate the other) has rarely been resolved in thorough investigations.

Admitting these difficulties, which arise in part from the current state of knowledge, we would none the less like to propose a preliminary list of some species parameters which appear to act as constraints on the kinds of social structure that a species may adopt. These are: (1) The duration of the nutritional dependency of young upon adults (i.e. the maturation rate). As an extension of this the duration of psycho-social dependency in socially complex mammals such as carnivores and primates may also need consideration. (2) The susceptibility of the species to predation. (3) The mobility potential of the species in terms of its capacity for ranging in given habitats. (4) The feeding and foraging behaviour of the species (e.g. digging and dental equipment and use, etc.).

These species characteristics are intermediate parameters in that they are the consequences of specific combinations of more basic characteristics. For example susceptibility to predation depends upon basic species characteristics such as size, speed, and weaponry. Ultimately, these basic characteristics must be considered as the crucial species parameters; however, for the present purposes, the intermediate characteristics are a useful preliminary categorization for the development of our argument.

EXTERNAL (ENVIRONMENTAL) VARIABLES

The constraints imposed by the characteristics of the species on the range of social 'options' open to it interact with a number of environmental variables to determine the actual social structure. These environmental variables include: (1) Resource density (resources including all forms of food, water, cover, etc.); (2) the temporal distribution of resources; (3) the spatial distribution of resources, and (4) the density, distribution and mode of hunting of relevant predators in the environment.

Among recent papers Hamilton & Watt (1970) have discussed in particular the effect on resource exploitation of the adoption of a regular refuge. Crook (1972) analyses the possible relations between the social organizations of terrestrial primates and spatial and temporal fluctuations in the dispersion of patchily distributed food. Jarman (1974) relates different types of grazing and browsing requirements to ungulate social systems. Kleiman & Eisenberg (1973) discuss the socio-ecology of carnivores and Ward & Zahavi (1973) show how refuging combined with gregarious behaviour and a 'dispersal system' could operate in information transfer, facilitating effective exploitation of limited resources by birds. Clutton-Brock (1974) and Rich-ard (1974), studying colobine monkeys and Sifakas respectively, both show how a detailed analysis of the distribution of dietary items allows the formulation of hypotheses at a finer level than that available to Crook & Gartlan in 1966. They also show how such refinement is related to the need for careful empirical studies in the formulation and testing of sophisticated models.

Up to this point we have suggested that our three sub-systems operate within the social system and have proposed first a list of some principal social system variables by which the society can be described and second a list of species and environmental variables which may be important determining factors. We now propose to relate these three sets of variables into a classification scheme of mammal social systems which, of necessity, involves assumptions about what appear to be the important relationships determining the overall form. The scheme (Table II) is derived from an extensive survey of information available on mammals. Our scheme uses the differences in rearing strategies as a prime criterion for distinguishing sociotypes. This is because this sub-system seems particularly conservative, less flexible and least directly responsive to environmental fluctuation. This is probably because of the high level of innate characteristics involved in its determination. We discuss each functional strategy in turn.

Rearing Strategies

Male's presence in the rearing group. The survey of mammal social systems reveals the great importance of the rearing conditions in determining the kind of system that evolves. The basic rearing unit is that of mother-infant (M-I). Since only the mother can provide the milk essential for the young mammal's early survival and growth, this bond is universal in mammalian societies. We may postulate that the male is acceptable to the female and will stay with this basic unit through gestation and rearing only if his presence significantly enhances the survival of their offspring. This seems likely, since merely to mate the male probably needs to stay with the female for only a short time. Hence, we can assume that in general the male staying with his mate and progeny is a rearing strategy; the case that this is a mating strategy being much weaker (Goss-Custard, Dunbar & Aldrich-Blake 1972).

There are a number of ways in which the presence of the male may aid the survival of his young, the particular form of this advantage depending on species characteristics and ecology. Being relatively free from directly caring for the young, he can devote time and energy to protecting resources within an exclusive feeding range and preventing other animals taking the food his own young may find, actually providing food for the offspring (canids), looking out for danger, and in some cases, taking necessary defensive steps. There seems to be little reason why the male's familiarity with an area should exceed that of the female, so this is not necessarily a factor promoting male presence in the rearing group. In one-male units of the hamadryas baboon, however, it is possible that the males pay greater attention to topographical changes than do their dependents so that the life experience of old males may be of especial value to a group. In this species males appear to determine the routes taken in foraging more than in the gelada baboon where older females play an important role (Kummer 1968; Dunbar 1974). In this latter species the prime significance of the male to the reproductive unit appears to be in relation to reducing the frequency of aggression between females and in preventing a high frequency of incursions from non-reproductive males. In addition, he probaly performs functions in protecting the young from possible predators.

Within multi-male groups of animals such as baboons where males do not play a role in bringing food for the young, they may none the less be important in child care. While it remains uncertain how far the hierarchy of the males regulate differential access to females in oestrus, it seems certain that the collective policing of the group maintains its stability in the face of recurrent quarrels. Furthermore, the males show collective care of young irrespective of paternity in relation to both fights within the group and to predation risks. Collective caring has presumably arisen due to the close genealogical relationship of the males concerned, and the operation of kin selection. The actual occurrence of large multi-male groups must be considered in relation to ecology and resource distribution (see below). The association of several adult males in a hierarchy none the less expresses an important adaptation ensuring care during rearing through collective male operations. This type of association is therefore to an important degree concerned with the rearing strategies of the group members. The agonistic buffering that occurs within Barbary Macaques whereby relations between males are regulated, and antagonistic encounters within the group probably reduced, may be an important extension of this trait. (See Crook 1975; Deag & Crook 1971).

Duration of the M-I bond. The time period during which the young are nutritionally dependent is likely to determine the length of the particular mother-infant bonds, as well as the male-female bonds if these exist. The bonds may be severed relatively early if the young become independent at weaning or later if this does not happen until the birth of the next young. In some cases, bonds may last over several seasons if the maturation rate of the young is very slow or if the dependency periods of young of several females overlap one another in time. We may assume that the adult-young bond will be maintained until the presence of the young significantly inhibits the survival of the adult or subsequent offspring or until the young male becomes a reproductive rival. (See Trivers 1972).

We have felt that the most illuminating way to classify rearing strategies is to specify four classes (Table II) based on (i) whether or not the male stays with his females and young, (ii) the duration of his presence, and (iii) the length of the female-young bond.

In type I the male does not stay with his female and young, but the mother-infant bond may be short or long-lived. In type II the males and females probably stay together but no particular bond is involved; rather, all individuals consort in the same group. We cannot in this case rule out benefits for the young accruing from the male's presence, but no specific relationships appear involved. Hence, we use the term 'association' to describe this state of affairs.

Male-female bonds lasting for one breeding season are classified in type III and in all cases each male has more than one female.

In type IV, the male-female bond lasts for more than one season and appears to evolve where the period of dependency of the young exceeds one season. The ratio of females to males varies greatly in this class which includes single male-single female pairs, stable one-male reproductive groups (i.e. 'harems') and the more-or-less stable multimale groups found in many primates (Crook & Gartlan 1966; Crook 1972). This type includes species whose male-female relationships within their stable groups are the most long-lasting and it is perhaps the most behaviourally complex of all the four rearing groups outlined in the table.

Mating Strategies

If males were completely free from rearing their young, we might generally expect each to pursue a promiscuous strategy since this would maximize the number of females that a male fertilizes. Males that behaved this way would contribute disproportionately to the gene-pool of succeeding generations. Strong intra- and inter-sexual selection would then be expected to operate in this vital and highly competitive activity (e.g. Darwin 1871; Fisher 1929; Huxley 1938a, b; Smith 1962; Goss-Custard et al. 1972; Crook 1972, 1975; Trivers 1972).

The form that the mating sub-system takes varies considerably and probably relates to the species characteristics and ecology. The important species characteristic seems to be whether or not the males contribute to rearing the young. In type I, for example, where the male does not help rear the young and where immobile young in a nest or a food cache limits the freedom of movement of the females, males may take a territory which overlaps as many female ranges as possible (Goss-Custard et al. 1972; Crook, in press). Here the defence of an area may ensure the male more exclusive access to the females contained therein. In these cases, the males that are unable to obtain a territory within the area most utilized by females are excluded and live in peripheral areas with reduced access to females (Charles-Dominique & Martin 1972). In another case, males may sometimes take territories that have a continuous throughput of wandering females, as in the hartebeest (Gosling 1974). Here the territory may ensure its owner undisturbed access to as many females as possible.

In the case of the Uganda kob (Buechner 1961) the males come together and display in locally concentrated territories of small extent resembling the arenas of lekking birds such as ruff or sage-grouse (Hogan-Warburg 1966; Wiley 1973). These 'leks' are situated in areas used by the females for foraging.

In herding type II species, no direct male help occurs and inter- and intra-sexual selection is likely to be intense. Males are likely to differ markedly in the numbers of females they fertilize and certainly, very striking weapons and displays have also evolved in some of these animals.

In type III the males stay with their females and young in general, we think, to contribute to their survival, although the ways in which this is achieved may not always be obvious. An alternative case could be made that since the male cannot predict when a female will come into oestrus, the male's best strategy might be to collect every available female for himself. However, as pointed out by Goss-Custard et al. (1972) there are many problems with this view, so that interpreting the long-term bond between males and females as a mating strategy is not convincing.

In situations where the male can contribute to the survival of several young from several females we might expect long-lasting harems to develop, as they have done commonly in the class III and IV species. In these cases, inter- and intra-sexual selection is again likely to be strong, since by mating with more females, a male can contribute disproportionately to the genepool of succeeding generations.

Grouping and Dispersion Strategies

Resources and Their Effects on Groupings

i *Refuge utilization.* Anything which forces the animals to forage out radially from some more-or-less fixed point or refuge seems to have a great influence on social structure (Hamilton & Watt 1970). The reasons for having such a fixed site are numerous and depend on the animal's ecology and characteristics. Undoubtedly, all animals benefit from accumulating knowledge of the local area so that staying in a suitable place, once discovered, may be an advantage (Kummer 1971), but returning regularly to the same site imposes important constraints. Thus, Smith (1968) proposes that tree squirrels live solitarily because individuals place their food in a cache. Were pairs or larger groups to evolve, much greater areas would have to be searched for food with a consequent increase in the amount of energy expended in foraging.

In other cases, immobile young may require a nest, or a safe resting place may impose a locus on daily activity. In some cases, a locus of this kind might evolve as a means by which an individual may discover the whereabouts of undiscovered food from the experience of its conspecifics. This 'information centre' idea has been discussed in relation to birds (Ward & Zahavi 1973) and may also apply to wide-ranging socially refuging mammal species such as bats that utilize a patchy and fluctuating food supply.

In cases such as this the primary function of social refuging may lie in information exchange concerned with reducing energy expenditure in the daily search for food in foraging. The protective site that is actually used may then evolve secondarily as a necessary adaptation to increased predation that results from the attraction of predators to a large assemblage of potential prey.

Selection favouring congregational behaviour for information exchange (whether at a protective site necessary for sleep or brood care or periodically at non-protected sites, e.g. water holes, etc.) is likely to arise when resources are heterogeneous and dispersed patchily both spatially and temporally. Congregation at sleeping sites generates a 'dispersal system' (Crook 1953) centred upon the refuge itself. In general this results in a heavily exploited zone nearest the locus and a gradient in the intensity of resource-exploitation that diminishes with distance. One might expect that on the average an individual or group foraging afar may be as able to replenish its energy expenditure of foraging as an individual or group foraging near the locus, finding less food but expending less energy in travelling there to collect it. Seasonal fluctuation in the overall abundance of nourishment may, however, periodically impose so great a range on individuals that energy expenditure exceeds the returns. Such a system must then break and an alternative strategy such as nomadism may arise (see Hamilton & Watt 1970; Crook 1972).

ii *Range exclusivity.*   Brown (1964) introduced an important idea concerning the circumstances in which exclusive use of areas will occur. He proposed that, assuming competition for some limited resources exists, it will be an advantage to defend an area only if an adequate supply of that resource (usually food) is found in an area small enough to defend economically. This may occur under a number of circumstances of food density and distribution. For instance, a food supply that is relatively dense yet highly clumped may allow exclusive ranges to evolve if suitable food patches always occur close enough together for the individual (or group) to have at least one available throughout a period long enough to make defence of its range worthwhile. Similarly, relatively evenly dispersed food supplies may be defendable in the same way. On the other hand, clumped food sources that are widely spaced and irregular in occurrence relative to the species' 'cruising' range may be simply undefendable as, indeed, may very sparse but more evenly dispersed supplies. The outcome seems likely to depend on the relationship between the overall density and dispersion of the resources on the one hand and the ranging abilities of the animal in question on the other. In general, defendability is likely to correlate with more-or-less 'evenly-dispersed' resources whereas more-or-less spatially and temporally 'heterogeneous' supplies are unlikely to be defended. The terms 'homogeneous' and 'heterogeneous' are used in this paper although we recognize that they don't fully express the condition under which range exclusivity and overlap respectively are likely to evolve.

In free-ranging species we may assume that there will be a selective advantage in an individual restricting its activities to a limited home range because of the advantages accruing from acquaintance with an area (e.g. sites of resources and places particularly dangerous from predators). Since the animals have to locate food and water continually, individuals utilizing heterogeneous resources have to range over an area large enough to contain available resources, at least in some regions, at all times. This might necessitate huge ranges in some highly mobile species that do not have a refuge-based foraging system. Since many individuals may be utilizing the same area, the possibility for large associations (e.g. herds of bison) exists if there is a selective pressure, such as predation or a need for more efficient food utilization (Ellis, in preparation (b)), which favours it.

Hence we assume that, where possible, animals maintain exclusive ranges to maintain a competed resource for themselves and that nonexclusive ranges result from the necessity of sharing resources that are uneconomical or impossible to defend. If there are major differences in the distribution of resources over time (seasonally) or in the distribution of two or more resources in space relative to the 'cruising range' of the species, range exclusivity is unlikely unless the resources are effectively homogeneous for periods of time sufficient for mating and rearing. In the latter case, seasonal exclusivity may be expected. So, in general, the major subdivision of range use into exclusive and non-exclusive ranges seems to be related to the nature and distribution of the resources, as it does in birds (Crook 1965).

iii *Group size and stability.* Contrasts in resource distribution illustrate the way in which species ecology may influence the size and stability of a social group. A male may be able to improve the chances of survival of his young if he defends an exclusive area in which some competed resource is thereby maintained for just his offspring and their mother(s). The resource density in the area that a male can defend economically may then determine the size of the group. In some cases, the male may be able to defend a range which provides sufficient for just one female and young (e.g. gibbons, Ellefson 1968), while in others it may be possible for him to provide for several (e.g. blue monkey, Aldrich-Blake 1970). In contrast, a patchily distributed resource where large individual ranges are necessary may result in the common use of a range by several mating groups which together form large herds.

If we assume that group stability depends on resource stability (Estes 1969) and that the number of animals in a particular area depends largely on the density of resources in that area, four broad categories of group size and stability can be identified. If resource distribution changes with time or varies spatially, unstable groups are likely. If the resource density is high, large, unstable groups (e.g. gelada baboon, Brook 1966) are likely; if not, small ones may evolve (e.g. chimpanzee, Reynolds & Reynolds 1965). With temporal and spatial homegeneity of resources, stable groups of any composition may evolve. Again, group size is likely to correlate with resource density.

Predation and Its Effect on Grouping

i *Refuge use.* The extent and kind of predation in conjunction with the possibility of adopting antipredator strategies other than through social means is likely to have a considerable influence on social systems. It can be assumed that animals particularly susceptible to predation will use cover continuously, or at least sleep in some form of refuge, but those which can readily avoid predation by fleeing or fighting will not seek refuge. The species parameter assumed to determine refuge use is the susceptibility of adults and young to predation. Hence, if the adults require cover to avoid predation, continuous or frequent cover and perhaps refuge use would be expected, as occurs in many small, ground living animals. If only the young require cover, temporary refuging during rearing would be expected. If neither adults nor young require cover, complete free-ranging becomes possible.

ii *Group composition and size.* One reason for a male staying with his females and young is that his presence may increase their safety. Whether or not this is likely will depend on basic characteristics of the animal in relation to the hunting characteristics of the predators. For instance, highly mobile patas monkeys in relatively treeless savannah pursued by fast-running predators may benefit from the male adopting the role of look-out (Hall 1965). However, small animals that rely on a nocturnal existence under dense cover may not benefit in this way. In these cases, the presence of the male would not add anything to the survival chances of the female and young, which are probably hidden in a camouflaged nest anyway.

The possibility of active defence may also favour the presence of males, e.g. chimpanzes, baboons. In other cases, large associations of the herd kind may be effective in avoiding predation in situations in which large numbers of animals range widely over huge areas (e.g. bison). In these cases, large associations in which males do not directly help only their own young, may be more effective than smaller, more vulnerable, family or harem groups. The ways by which temporal and spatial grouping may reduce predation risk are discussed for example by Hamilton (1971), Goss-Custard et al. (1972), Crook (1972), Vine (1971), Lazarus (1972), and with reference to the formation of poly-specific associations, by Gartlan & Struhsaker (1972). In general the presence of conspecifics provides both a type of cover reducing the probability of an individual's capture and also increased collective vigilance. Synchronization of births has the same effect on survival of individual young.

TOWARDS SOCIO-ECOLOGICAL MODELS BASED ON DETAILED FIELD STUDY

The environmental conditions determining shifts from one-male to multi-male re-productive groups in primates have been discussed in the formulation of Crook's (1972) simple models which attempt to account for the socio-ecological relations underlying these types of grouping. Recent studies illustrate (i) the number and subtlety of the factors which need to be considered in field work if advances in theory are to be made, (ii) the complex nature of the interaction between such factors and their variability between species and populations of the same species, (iii) the refined nature of the effects of ecological contrasts on social behaviour and (iv) the fact that, rather than simple correlations of traits, we are now comparing systems.

In a specific case, Clutton-Brock's (1974) comparison of two African *Colobus* species indicates the subtle habitat contrasts that possibly underlie societal differ-ences. Black and white colobus seem able to survive on a diet of mature leaves when only these are available. They can thus live in dry forest areas with marked seasonal-ity and are able to survive on the products of a small number of species providing an acceptable diet throughout the year. Relatively small areas of forest could support a considerable number of animals. The small troop size of this species may permit it to minimize ranging and thus to increase the defensibility of the range through some form of territorial behaviour. The reduction of adult male reproductives to one, may express the extreme sexual competition within such small groups and, futher-more, have adaptive consequences in making a high proportion of the food available to females and young (Crook 1972).

The red colobus, by contrast, evidently requires a high proportion of shoots, flowers and fruit throughout the year. The species is found in wetter forests where suitable food becomes available on different trees sporadically in space and time. A large range is required to provide sufficient supplies of acceptable food all the year. This range size is unlikely to allow easy territorial defence so that larger wide ranging groups are preferred. Futhermore these may increase protection from predators. The presence of several male reproductives will tend to favour group defence, as well as providing additional strategic functions (see above). The colobus story will however, need further extension since the sub-species of red colobus living in the Tana river valley is now known to have one-male groups living in small territories. Clive Marsh (personal communication) believes that these also are explicable in terms of contrasting patterns of dietary availability.

Richard (1974) in her *Propithecus* study in Madagascar compares arid and humid forest populations of the same lemur species. Her findings and her explanatory hypotheses resemble those of Clutton-Brock strikingly in form. Her arid country animals showed range exclusivity and group territorial behaviour while her forest animals showed considerable overlap in group ranging. She suggests that the latter is associated with little periodic variation in abundance while in the former there is a greater seasonal fluctuation in overall abundance even though items are similarly dispersed. In this case a strategy of range reservation, even when food is not lacking, provides adequate resources later when stocks are low. In the first case the dispersion of dietary items necessitates range overlap and, while groups tend to avoid one another, range exclusion has not developed.

Richard adds, however, that she attributes some variance between her groups to a randomizing effect of contrasting traditions of local behaviour and remains unsure how far the observed contrasts might not be accounted for in this way. She was unable to correlate important components of behavioural variance with the ecological variables she examined. Under what conditions such behavioural randomization would obscure valid socio-ecological correlations or generate societal structures unrelated to underlying ecology remains to be determined. It seems unlikely, however, that traditions of societal functioning will prove any more independent of ecology than did the apparently 'arbitrary' cases of ritualization in bird displays studied in the 1930s. However, the complexity of the interacting determinants in these societies may render clear explanation difficult to obtain.

DISCUSSION

Early attempts to relate interspecific differences in social organization in birds and mammals to ecology were initially successful because the choice of level at which socio-ecological variance was examined and the categories chosen for comparison were appropriate. Furthermore, the patterns of relationship were often repeated at different taxonomic levels. With more advanced and socially complex mammals, experience has shown that the levels of comparison and the choice of categories need to be more finely defined than was at first possible. With an increase in information available, differences within categories become close to those between categories, thus requiring that boundaries between categories and their number be redefined, so that finer resolution may be obtained. Current studies do not represent a break from earlier comparative work using grosser categories but rather their continuation.

Furthermore, now that effective socio-ecological modelling has become possible, comparisons are made more between systems than between sets of statically conceived socio-ecological grades. The method of broad correlation between habitat and society remains the only approach initially available when knowledge of a group of animals is sparse.

Parallel evolution of taxonomically distinct stocks necessarily involves convergent modification of characteristics initially different. The degree of apparent convergence becomes a function of the way in which changes in phylogenetically separated traits produce likeness. For example, similarities between gelada and hamadryas baboon social structures are mediated by social processes which a detailed analysis shows to be very different in the two cases and doubtless dependent on contrasting phylogenetic inheritance. However, the parallelism at the gross level may remain meaningful enough, the interest simply shifting to the way in which convergent modification has occurred. A focus dwelling only on the details of interaction would obscure the interest of the convergence. Thus gross similarities in structure and ecology may be based on those more subtle interspecific differences in organization and dynamics that may represent, as Clutton-Brock (1974) argues, different methods of overcoming the same or similar ecological problems.

In this paper we have treated broad problems of socio-ecology in the Class Mammalia as a whole. Clearly the knowledge available varies enormously from order to order, yet, in spite of the approximations this imposes, repeatable patterns emerge that demand analysis and explanation. It seems possible that socio-ecological systems analysis will provide important clarification of these issues. Even so, in those species in which intra-specific variation between populations is dependent on acquired and traditional behaviours we need to be aware that processes of socio-cultural change may obscure the ecological base. Again, here, only the more sophisticated treatment of the variables involved will identify the extent to which ecology is relegated to a less-directive role in societal evolution.

Naturally, it has not been our intention to review all the existing hypotheses that could relate mammalian social structure to ecology and species characteristics. Rather, we have presented a few generalizations and a classification scheme that we hope will have heuristic value in organizing our knowledge of these systems a little more extensively than has been attempted so far. It is of necessity somewhat abbreviated, but the major social-system types appear to be represented.

We have set forth a number of assumptions about how certain environmental variables and species parameters interact to determine social variables. Consequently, social structures have been generated and related to social functions. We stress that these relationships should be considered as working hypotheses to guide further study. It is beyond the scope of this paper to expand on these hypotheses, although one of these has been dealt with elsewhere (Ellis, in preparation). It is obvious that these extremely simple models and working hypotheses will require considerable elaboration based on new quantitative field study before they will be suitable for conversion to mathematical models of mammalian societies. None the less, the work of Hamilton & Watt (1970) and Vine (1971) indicates ways in which this may be attempted, and the recent field studies quoted show the type of data analysis and inference to which such models must be anchored. We feel that the study of mammalian social organizations has progressed to the point where the impact of environmental variables and species parameters on the formation of social structures may be investigated empirically. Progress seems more likely to come from such a research orientation than from a continued emphasis on the more general studies of social organization which have brought us to this point.

REFERENCES

Aldrich-Blake, F. P. G. (1970). The ecology and behaviour of the blue monkey *Cercopithecus mitis stuhlmani.* Ph.D. Dissertation, Briston, England: Bristol University Library.

Brown, J. L. (1964). The evolution of diversity in avian territorial systems. *Wilson Bull.,* **76,** 160–169.

Buechner, H. K. (1961). Territorial behaviour in Uganda kob. *Science, N.Y.,* **133,** 698–699.

Charles-Dominique, P. & Martin, R. D. (1972). Behaviour and ecology of nocturnal prosimians. Field Studies in Gabon and Madagascar. *Fortschr. Verhaltensforsch Zugleich Z. Tierpsychol. Beih.* Heft 9. (*Adv. Ethol.* Supplements to *J. Comp. Ethol.* Issue 9) Berlin, West Germany: Paul Parey. 89 pp.

Clutton-Brock, T. H. (1974). Primate social organisation and ecology. *Nature, Lond.,* **250,** 539–542.

Crook, J. H. (1953). An observational study of the gulls of Southhampton water. *Br. Birds,* **46,** 385–397.

Crook, J. H. (1964). The evolution of social organisation and visual communication in weaver birds (Ploceinae). *Behaviour Monograph,* **10;** Leiden: Brill.

Crook, J. H. (1965). The adaptive significance of avian social organisations. *Symp. Zool. Soc. Lond.,* **14,** 181–218.

Crook, J. H. (1966). Gelada baboon herd structure and movement: a comparative report. *Symp. Zool. Soc. Lond.,* **18,** 237–258.

Crook, J. H. (1970). The socio-ecology of primates. In: *Social Behaviour in Birds and Mammals* (ed. by J. H. Crook). London: Academic Press.

Crook, J. H. (1972). Sexual selection, dimorphism, and social organisation in the primates. In: *Sexual Selection and the Descent of Man* (Ed. by B. G. Campbell). Chicago: Aldine.

Crook, J. H. (in press). On the integration of gender strategies in mammalian social systems. In: *The Memorial Symposium for D. Lehrmann* (Ed. by J. Rosenblatt). Rutgers University.

Crook, J. H. & Gartlan, S. S. (1966). Evolution of primate societies. *Nature, Lond.,* **210,** 1200–1203.

Crook, J. H. & Goss-Custard, J. D. (1972). Social ethology. *Ann. Rev. Psychol.,* **23,** 277–312.

Darwin, C. (1871). *The Descent of Man and Selection in Relation to Sex.* London: John Murray.

Deag, J. M. & Crook. J. H. (1971). Social behaviour and 'agonistic buffering' in the wild Barbary macaque. *Macaca sylvana* L. *Folia Primatol.,* **15,** 183–200.

Dunbar, R. (1974). Ph.D. Thesis. Bristol University Library. In press. *Bibliotheca Primatologica.*

Ellefson, J. O. (1968). Territorial behaviour in the common white-handed gibbon, *Hylobates lar* Linn. In: *Primates: Studies in Adaptation and Variability* (Ed. by P. Jay), pp. 180–199. New York: Holt, Rinehart & Winston.

Ellis, J. E. (In preparation) (a). Systems in primate societies.

Ellis, J. E. (In preparation) (b). The social implications of resource distribution.

Eisenberg, J. F. (1966). The social organisation of mammals. *Handb. Zool.,* **10,** 1–92.

Eisenberg, J. F., Muckinhirn, N. A. & Rudran, R., (1972). The relation between ecology and social structure in primates. *Science, N.Y.,* **176,** 863–874.

Estes, R. D. (1969). Territorial behaviour of the wildebeest (*Connochaetes taurinus* Burchell, 1823). *Z. Tierpsychol.,* **26,** 284–370.

Fisher, R. A. (1929). *The Genetical Theory of Natural Selection.* Oxford: Clarendon Press.

Gartlan, J. S. & Struhsaker, T. (1972). Polyspecific associations and niche separation of rain-forest anthropoids in Cameroon, W. Africa. *J. Zool.,* **168,** 221–265.

Gosling, L. M. (1974). The social ethology of Coke's hartebeest. *Alcelaphus busclaphus cokei.* Gunther. In: *The Behaviour of Ungulates and its Relation to Management.* IUCN.

Goss-Custard, J. D., Dunbar, R. I. M. & Aldrich-Blake, F. P. G. (1972). Survival, mating, and rearing strategies in the evolution of primate social structure. *Folia Primatol.,* **17,** 1–19.

Hall, H. R. L. (1965). Behaviour and ecology of the wild patas monkey *Erythrocebus patas* in Uganda. *J. Zool.,* **148,** 15–87.

Hamilton, W. D. (1971). Geometry for the selfish herd. *J. Theor. Biol.,* **31,** 295–311.

Hamilton, W. J., III & Watt, K. E. F. (1970). Refuging. *Ann. Rev. Ecol. Syst.,* **1,** 263–286.

Hinde, R. A. & Tinbergen, N. (1958). The comparative study of species-specific behaviour. In: *Behaviour and Evolution* (Ed. by A. Roe & G. G. Simpson). New Haven, Conn.: Yale University Press.

Hogan-Warburg, A. J. (1966). Social behaviour of the ruff, *Philomachus pugnax* L. *Ardea,* **54,** 109–229.

Huxley, J. S. (1938a). The present standing of the theory of sexual selection. In: *Evolution: Essays on Aspects of Evolutionary Biology* (Ed. by G. R. DeBeer). Oxford: The Clarendon Press.

Huxley, J. S. (1938b). Darwin's theory on sexual selection and the data subsumed by it in the light of recent research. *Am Nat.,* **72,** 416–433.

Jarman, P. J. (1974). The social organisation of antelope in relation to their ecology. *Behaviour,* **48,** 215–267.

Kleiman, D. & Eisenberg, J. F. (1973). Comparisons of canid and felid social systems from an evolutionary perspective. *Anim. Behav.,* **21,** 637–659.

Kummer, H. (1968). Social organization of hamadryas baboons. A field study. *Bibl. Primatol.,* No. 6. Basel: Karger.

Kummer, H. (1971). *Primate Societies.* Chicago: Aldine-Atherton.

Lazarus, J. (1972). Natural selecton and the functions of flocking in birds: A reply to Murton. *Ibis,* **114,** 556–558.

Reynolds, V. & Reynolds, F. (1965). Chimpanzees of the Budongo forest. In: *Primate Behavior* (Ed. by I. DeVore), pp. 368–424. New York: Holt, Rinehart & Winston.

Richard, A. (1974). Intra-specific variations in the social organisation and ecology of *Propithecus verreauxi. Folia. Primatol.,* **22,** 178–207.

Smith, C. C. (1968). The adaptive nature of social organization in the genus of tree squirrels *Tamiasciurus. Ecol. Monogr.,* **38,** 31–63.

Smith, J. M. (1962). Disruptive selection, polymorphism, and sympatric speciation. *Nature, Lond.,* **195,** 60.

Struhsaker, T. T. (1969). Correlates of ecology and social organisation among African cercopithecines. *Folia Primatol.,* **11,** 86–118.

Trivers, R. (1972). Parental investment and sexual selection. In: *Sexual Selection and the Descent of Man* (Ed. by B. Campbell). Chicago: Aldine.

Vine, I. (1971). The risk of visual detection and pursuit by a predator and the selective advantage of flocking behaviour. *J. Theor. Biol.,* **30,** 405–422.

Ward, P. & Zahavi, A. (1973). Importance of certain assemblages of birds as information centers for food finding. *Ibis,* **115,** 517–534.

Wiley, R. H. (1973). Territoriality and non-random mating in sage grouse *Centrocercus urophasianus. Anim. Behav. Monogr.*

Female Incitation of Male Competition: A Mechanism in Sexual Selection

Cathleen R. Cox
Department of Psychology, Stanford University
Burney J. Le Boeuf
Crown College, University of California, Santa Cruz

The role of the female in determining which male will sire her offspring was treated by Darwin (1871) in his theory of sexual selection. Fisher (1930) and Huxley (1938) saw two principles involved in sexual selection. Huxley termed behavioral interactions between males and females epigamic selection and behavioral interactions between members of the same sex (usually males) intrasexual selection. Female choice, which occurs when a female selects only one or a few among many male suitors, is an example of epigamic selection, and fighting among males to monopolize females, with the result being that some males breed more than others, is an example of intrasexual selection. The distinction between the two types of selection is often difficult to make. For example, if a female increases her fitness by choosing among male sexual partners she will outcompete females that do not choose. Darwin thought that both epigamic and intrasexual aspects of his theory helped to explain the evolution of striking differences between the sexes.

Females that discriminate between potential mates should be favored by selection because one-half of the genetic complement of their offspring comes from the father, and in some species, he also helps to rear the young. In other words, a female's reproductive success is tied up with her offspring whose fitness is in part determined by an unrelated male. Because reproductive success is not simply a matter of the number of offspring that an organism leaves but also a matter of the "quality or probable success of these offspring" (Fisher 1930, p. 143), the male that is chosen to be the other parent should be the most fit male available, i.e., the one whose genes will make the greatest contribution to the next generation relative to other available genes. In species where males invest little in the offspring beyond their sex cells, females should choose males on the basis of genotype alone. Where males engage in parental care, female choice should also involve the male's willingness and ability to be a good parent (Orians 1969; Trivers 1972). In several birds there is strong evidence that females choose males on territories which are rich in food (Hinde 1956; Verner 1964; Zimmerman 1966; Verner and Engelson 1970).

Field assistance was provided by Michael Bonnell, Kathy Panken, Mark Pierson, Joanne Reiter, and Nell Lee Stinson. We thank Kenneth Briggs, Gary Marshall, Andrew Moldenke, Leo Ortiz, and Paul Sherman for reviewing the first draft and Richard Alexander, Dale McCullough, and Robert Trivers for helpful comments. Supported in part by NSF grant BMS 74-01363A02 to B. J. Le Boeuf.

Williams (1975), however, disagrees with the idea that female discrimination should favor the genetically fittest male because, in his opinion, this would require an unrealistically high heritability of fitness.

Female choice has received less attention and is a more controversial subject than male-male competition (Ghiselin 1974). Perhaps the study of female choice has been neglected because it implied to Darwin "powers of discrimination and taste," attributes which are difficult to study. On the other hand, competition among males is more physical and obvious, and thus appears easier and more significant to investigate. Some say female choice is not as important an evolutionary force as Darwin thought (e.g., Wallace 1889; Huxley 1938; Lack 1968) but others disagree (e.g., Fisher 1930; Orians 1969). The fact is that pure epigamic selection is hard to document in the field (Wilson 1975). According to Trivers (1972), most studies have shown merely that females choose sexual partners that are sexually mature, of the right species, and of the right sex. It has proven more difficult to document subtle discriminations among many appropriate males. Even in lek-forming grouse, the ruff and other polybrachygynous birds (Selander 1972; Wiley 1973), and a few ungulates (Beuchner and Schloeth 1965; Leuthold 1966), where female choice has been demonstrated, little is known about the basis on which females choose.

In the broadest sense, female choice operates whenever a female influences what male will sire her offspring regardless of the means by which she brings this about. Investigators have tended to emphasize positive responses of the female as an indication of choice, i.e., moving toward the male or soliciting him. But moving away from a suitor or rejecting him can also be instrumental in determining with whom a female will mate. For example, copulatory mounts protested by a periestrous female may not simply be due to unreceptivity, as is often claimed, but may be contingent on the identity of the suitor. A bitch in heat may reject one male and a few seconds later accept a different male (Beach and Le Boeuf 1967; Le Boeuf 1967b). Similarly, moving away from courting males has often been interpreted as unreceptive behavior or as a female's attempt to avoid a sexually overeager male (Summers-Smith 1963). But this behavior may also allow the female to test the vigor, tenacity, and speed of the several males which pursue her, attributes which are probably correlated with fitness. Selection should favor that behavior of a female which results in a sexual union with optimal genetic consequences for her.

We describe one way in which a female can maximize the probability of mating with the "best male" without discriminating among males or choosing the best territory. She may incite males to compete for her and then mate with the winner. In many species, this may be the most direct strategy for insuring copulation with a mature male who has conquered his rivals and who, by mating with other females, has demonstrated his reproductive success. Trivers (1972) and Selander (1972) discuss the advantages to a female of mating with such a male.

Specifically, we describe how female elephant seals, *Mirounga angustirostris,* respond to copulatory attempts with loud vocalizations and vigorous escape movements. This behavior alerts nearby males who attempt to prevent the copulations of others. Competition ensues among males of varying social ranks with the result that mating is most likely to occur with the highest-ranking adult male. We discuss how a similar mechanism might operate in other species where several males compete simultaneously for a sexually receptive female.

The social organization and breeding behavior of elephant seals has been described in detail elsewhere (Bartholomew 1952; Le Boeuf and Peterson 1969; Le Boeuf 1972, 1974; Le Boeuf et al. 1972), so only those aspects of behavior relevant to the present paper will be reviewed here.

During the breeding season males fight and threaten each other to establish rank in a social hierarchy which determines access to females who clump together in one or more harems. A male displaces another by threat or overt attack. The subordinate avoids an encounter by retreating from a male that dominates him. Males prevent subordinates from approaching females and interrupt their copulatory attempts. The higher a male's social rank, the closer his physical proximity to females and the more frequently he interrupts the mounts of others; conversely, he is interrupted by others less frequently. Only the highest-ranking male, or alpha male, can mount females repeatedly without being displaced by a competitor. The correlation between social rank and reproductive success, as indicated by copulatory frequency, is high and positive (Le Boeuf 1974).

All males attempt to enter the harem and mate with females while at the same time attempting to keep other males out of it. The number of males in a harem is a function of its size. Only the alpha bull resides in a harem composed of less than 40 females. As the number of females in a harem increases, additional males gain entrance. For example, 10–15 males may be found in a harem of 300 females, and others may enter when the opportunity arises. When the harem is large, the alpha bull can no longer patrol the entire harem, so he compromises by dominating only one sector of it. The beta and gamma males, and so forth, occupy and defend increasingly smaller subsections of the harem. Low-ranking males are relegated to the periphery of the harem or beyond.

Females give birth to a single pup approximately 6 days after arrival on the rookery. The pup is nursed daily for about 28 days then weaned when the female returns to sea. Females copulate during the last few days of nursing before they depart. During estrus, defined here as the period between the first day and last day of copulation (the day of departure), a female may copulate several times with one or more males.

Males do not court or investigate the perineal region of the female prior to mounting. They mount from one side without any preliminaries and seemingly attempt to overpower the female who is less than half their size. Males use the great bulk and weight of their forequarters, a foreflipper clasp, and a neck bite to restrain the female. They mount females regardless of their stage in the estrous cycle: pregnant females, females giving birth, postparturient females, and estrous females. Only the frequency, not the form of these mating attempts, varies with the female's estrous cycle. A mount ends in one of three ways: (1) the male ceases to attempt copulation and the female is allowed to move away, (2) the mounter is moved from the female by the aggressive action of a more dominant male, or (3) intromission (copulation) occurs.

Females respond to male mounts by active protest or passive acceptance. We use the word "protest" simply as a term of convenience to describe the corpus of behavioral components which makes it difficult for the male to obtain penile intromission. A female protests by issuing a virtually continuous train of vocal threats (Bartholomew and Collias 1962) and by whipping her hindquarters vigorously from side to side. She may also direct sand-flipping movements of her foreflippers back and upward toward the male, nip his neck, or struggle to get away. Alternatively, the female may remain passive throughout the mount or she may facilitate intromission by spreading her hindflippers. Females do not court the male or solicit copulation. The conditions under which a female protests or acquiesces when mounted and the consequences of this behavior form the substance of this paper.

METHODS

The elephant seal colony at Año Nuevo Island, California (Le Boeuf et al. 1972, 1974), was observed during the 1975 breeding season. All observations were made from an elevated blind overlooking a sandy point occupied by a large harem of breeding females. At peak season, around January 26, approximately 550 females and 60 males resided on this beach, and an additional 40 males visited the area intermittently during the season.

Forty females, marked individually with paint or a bleaching agent (Le Boeuf and Peterson (1969), were observed during the daylight hours in the periods January 3–6, January 27–February 3, and February 11–21. All sexual interactions involving these females were recorded.

Twenty-three marked females did not copulate during the study period, so observations of their behavior cover only the period prior to the onset of estrus. Seventeen marked females were observed while in estrus; 14 were observed before and throughout estrus; three were observed only subsequent to the onset of estrus. Females were in estrus for 3–5 days.

When marked females were inactive, sexual interactions involving unmarked females in various stages of the estrous cycle were recorded. The estrous condition of unmarked females could be determined with certainty only if they were pregnant (nonestrous) or seen copulating (estrous).

All 180 males in the colony had names bleached on both sides of their bodies. Dominance relationships among males were known as well as the exact age of 20 males, which included the majority of the top-ranking individuals. When age was unknown it was estimated, a procedure which is accurate to within 1 yr (Le Boeuf 1974).

For analytical purposes, males were classified into one of four categories based on age, size, development of secondary sex characteristics and social rank.

   1   Subadult male 3 (SA3): 6–7 yr of age, about 3.6 m long, neck shield beginning to develop, and nose just beginning to dangle. A male who underwent puberty
in the previous year.
   2   Subadult male 4 (SA4): 7–8 yr of age, about 3.9 m long, incompletely
developed neck shield and nose. Well past puberty, but not quite fully grown.
   3   Adult male: fully grown male, 8–14+ yr of age, 4.2–4.8 m long with fully
developed neck shield and a dangling proboscis, approximately 0.3 m long.
   4   Alpha male: one of five adult males that dominated a subsection of the
crowded harem on the point beach in 1975. Although a dominance relationship
existed among these males, it was rarely expressed because of the large harem size.
Each male had more females than he could mate with in his own subsection so he
spent most of his time there and attempted to keep subordinates out.

   In addition to individual dominance relationships within each age category,
there existed age- and size-related dominance between categories; all adults dominated males in the SA4 category and the latter dominated all males in the SA3
category. It is important to note that all males present, regardless of their age,
attempted to mate with females. Although 5-yr-old, pubertal males are capable of
copulating, they were usually prevented from doing so by older, larger males.
   Each time a female was mounted the following was recorded: the date, time,
duration, and location of the episode; the identity, age category, and social rank of
the male; and the identity of the female. Most important, the behavioral response
of the female and interactions between the mounting male and males nearby which
followed were noted. We distinguished three categories of female response:

   1   Total protest: the female issues threat vocalizations, whips her hindquarters
from side to side, or tries to escape. This response continues throughout the duration
of the mount and is only terminated if the male dismounts or in the rare event that
he achieves insertion.
   2   Partial or initial protest: same as above except that the female protests
initially but stops doing so before the male dismounts or achieves insertion. The
duration of the protest phase was noted.
   3   No protest: the female emits none of the behavioral components of total
protest except that she may try to move away. Usually, she accepts the mount
passively. In some cases, she may spread her hindflippers in such a manner as to
facilitate insertion. A female may also call her pup (a radically different call than
the threat vocalization), flip sand, or nip at the male's neck.

   Where germane, we cite preliminary observations of female reproductive strategies made in 1974 as well as annual observations of elephant seal behavior made by
Le Boeuf since 1968.

RESULTS

Estrous as well as nonestrous females protest the majority of mounts attempted by
males. A total of 1,478 mounts were observed, of which 79.0% were protested for

the entire duration of each episode, 13.7% were partially protested, and 7.3% were not protested at all. All mounts ($N = 189$) directed to marked, known nonestrous females were totally protested. Of 271 mounts to marked females known to be in estrus, 62.7% were totally protested, 24.4% were partially protested, and 12.9% were not protested. Thus, protesting throughout the duration of a mount is not necessarily a sign of nonestrus, while no protest or partial protest is a reliable indication that the female is in estrus.

In early estrus, females protest virtually all mounts. As estrus proceeds, females stop protesting toward the end of a mount of long duration. No-protest responses begin increasing in frequency and are the most common response on the last day of estrus. Changes in the receptivity of 14 females observed before and throughout estrus are illustrated in figure 1. A trend away from protesting totally begins about 5–6 days prior to departure, i.e., when the earliest females begin coming into estrus. Some females began protesting only at the start of a mount, and a few of them did not protest at all. In 73 mounts directed to females subsequent to their first copulation on the first day of estrus, 67.1% were totally protested, 26.0% were partially protested, and 6.8% were not protested. Females accepted mounts more readily as estrus proceeded so that by the last day, the day of departure, passive acceptance was the most common response.

Males mounting estrous females are more likely to be driven off by nearby males when the female protests than when she does not. Only 25% of 108 mounts that were unprotested by estrous females were interrupted. In contrast, more than double this amount were interrupted when the estrous female totally protested (97/158 = 61.4%). Initially protested mounts were interrupted with about the same frequency as unprotested mounts (43/202 = 21.3%).

Young, small, and low-ranking males are interrupted most frequently and most quickly. The percentage of mounts by males from different age and social rank categories that were interrupted is shown in table 1. The younger a male and the lower his social rank, the more frequently he was prevented from copulating by other males. This relationship holds true regardless of the female's response, but the relationship was strongest when the female protested throughout the mount.

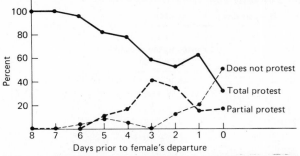

Figure 1 Percentage of mounts which 14 marked females protested totally, protested only initially, or did not protest at all. All females copulated for 3–5 days prior to departure.

Table 2 shows that the duration of mounts protested by females is also a function of the mounting male's age and social rank. Young, low-ranking males were interrupted more quickly ($F = 6.56$, df = 2 [alpha male group excluded because of small N], 564, $P < .01$) and, even when they were not moved by a dominant male, they did not persist in their copulatory attempts as long as older, higher-ranking males ($F = 4.57$, df = 3, 539, $P < .01$). When young, low-ranking males mounted a female it was apparent from their shifty eyes and nervous behavior that they were constantly monitoring the movements of nearby, larger males and were afraid of being attacked.

Even when mounts are not interrupted by dominant males, estrous females are most apt to respond with total protest if the mounter is an immature male. Data supporting this point are shown in table 3. All of the uninterrupted mounts of SA3 males were totally protested. In contrast, less than a third of the mounts of alpha males were protested totally. Table 3 also indicates that young males were least likely to encounter estrous females that did not protest. One explanation is that young males were unable to obtain access to nonprotesting females, usually females in the process of departing from the rookery. These females attracted a great deal of attention, and the most mature, high-ranking males on the periphery of the harem

Table 1 Mounts Interrupted by Males Following Various Types of Female Responses to Mounter

Age or social rank category of mounting male	Response of females		
	Total protest	Partial protest	No protest
Alpha	3/24 = 12	0/58 = 0	1/26 = 4
Adult	54/86 = 63	25/104 = 24	18/66 = 27
SA4	26/31 = 84	10/27 = 37	6/12 = 50
SA3	14/17 = 82	8/13 = 62	2/4 = 50

Note Proportion and percentage of interrupted mounts relative to total mounts is shown. All females were in estrus.

Table 2 Mean Duration and Standard Deviations of Male-Interrupted Mounts and Uninterrupted Mounts That Were Totally Protested by Esterous and Nonesterous Females (in seconds)

Age or social rank category of mounting males	Interrupted mounts ($N = 567$)	Uninterrupted mounts ($N = 543$)
Alpha	37.7 ± 11.6 ($N = 3$)	50.6 ± 71.0 ($N = 109$)
Adult	27.2 ± 39.2 ($N = 249$)	36.1 ± 56.4 ($N = 268$)
SA4	15.4 ± 21.7 ($N = 202$)	26.1 ± 40.6 ($N = 97$)
SA3	17.3 ± 29.4 ($N = 116$)	24.6 ± 36.6 ($N = 69$)

kept all of the younger, subordinate males away from them. Indeed, young males had a difficult time mounting any estrous female, as the number of mounts observed indicates. Older, dominant males prevented them from entering the harem, chased them out of it, or interfered with their attempts to mount females. Even when they were successful in eluding the guard of dominant males, the behavior of females made it difficult for them to copulate.

Mature, high-ranking males are most often involved in mounts in which the female's behavior changes from initial protest to passive acceptance. This point is supported by data in table 3. The distribution of partial protests favoring adult males is important because the first copulations of the majority of females occurred during mounts in which the female initially protested but then became passive. During the first copulations of 10 females observed, seven of them protested partially, one protested throughout the mount, and two did not protest.

Figure 2 shows that as estrus proceeded the mean duration of the protest phase of partially protested mounts decreased ($F = 4.29$, df $= 3,41$, $P < .01$).

What may account for the differential response of females to mounts by males varying in age and social rank? This outcome may be caused by the behavior of the mounting male, the female, or the interaction between them. Since adult males were dominated by fewer individuals than younger males and they were less likely to be interrupted (table 1), they had more time to persevere in attempting copulation (table 2). Their greater size seemed to help them to overpower and exhaust the protesting female. On the other hand, the adult males may not have induced a change in a female's behavior independent of her choice. It is possible that a female distinguished a high-ranking, mature male from others by the duration and vigor of his mounts and simply stopped protesting when mounted by the former. Trivers (1972 p. 167) points out that ". . . in many species females may guarantee reproductive success by mating with those males who are most vigorous in courtship, since this vigor may correlate with an adequate supply of sperm and a willingness to transfer it."

Females that protest mounts at the beginning of estrus increase the probability that their first copulation will be with the highest-ranking male in the vicinity. Figure 1 showed that the frequency of total protests was greatest at the beginning of a

Table 3   Responses of Marked Estrous Females to Mounts by Males Varying in Age or Social Rank

Age or social rank of mounting male	Mounts observed (N)	Totally protested (%)	Partially protested (%)	Not protested (%)
Alpha	74	37	43	20
Adult	70	49	34	17
SA4	9	78	22	0
SA3	4	100	0	0

Note Interrupted mounts are excluded.

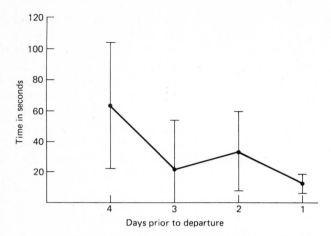

Figure 2   Mean duration (± 1 SD) of the protest phase of partially protested mounts.

female's estrous period. Table 1 showed that the protesting behavior of females alerts nearby males who threaten the subordinate mounter and prevent copulation. Thus, indirectly, the female's behavior reduces the probability of mating by younger males. The result is that the first copulations of 11 of 14 females were with the closest alpha male (we do not know who copulated at night but we assume from previous observations [Le Boeuf 1972] that daytime activity reflects accurately what goes on at night). Two females copulated for the first time with the beta male, and the remaining female copulated with a mature male with a social rank of 10, relative to all males on the beach.

A similar result was observed in 1970. There were 256 females in the harem at peak season and one male dominated the entire harem; the first copulations of 10 marked females were noted. Four females copulated first with the alpha bull, three with number 2, one with number 3, one with number 4, and one with an adult male ranked eighth in the social hierarchy. Thus, the four top-ranking bulls were responsible for 90% of the first copulations in this sample.

Females continued to copulate most frequently with high-ranking males up until the final day of estrus. Marked females copulated a total of 28 times between their first and last day of estrus. Fourteen copulations were with an alpha male, 11 were with adult males with social ranks between 2 and 10, two were with adults ranked lower than 10, and one was with a SA4 male. The same point is reinforced by considering which males mated most frequently. During the period February 11–21, the five alpha males copulated 27, 20, 17, 15, and 15 times, respectively. Only two other males, both fully grown and ranked just below the alphas, copulated as frequently as the least successful alpha males, 17 and 16 times, respectively. In general, the mating frequency of males declines with decreasing social rank (Le Boeuf 1974).

A previous study in the same area (Le Boeuf 1974) showed that the probability of a female mating with a high-ranking male depends in part on the number of females in the harem. As the number of females in the harem increased, more males copulated, including young, low-ranking, previously nonbreeding males. The latter were most successful when males dominant to them were fighting, mating, or sleeping. From the female point of view, an increasing harem size means that the odds of mating with a mature, high-ranking male decrease.

Females near the end of estrus rarely protest mounts and readily accept copulation with peripheral males. The behavior of females changed drastically on their last day of estrus (fig. 1). During the last hour or two on land, they were extremely receptive to all males. This was especially noticeable in their response to peripheral males as they moved out beyond the periphery of the harem on their way to the water. We interpret this change in behavior as a female's means of insuring fertilization.

Two aspects of male competition might lower a female's chances of becoming fertilized, an outcome that she will be selected to avoid. First, mounts and copulations in progress are interrupted frequently (see also Le Boeuf and Peterson 1969; Le Boeuf 1974), which brings up the possibility that all of the copulations of some females are incomplete. Second, the few males that monopolize breeding throughout the 6-wk-long season copulate repeatedly, both day and night, a state of affairs that might lower their fertility by causing a reduction in volume, concentration, and total number of spermatozoa. Under these circumstances, it is possible that some females are not fertilized despite having copulated several times. One might expect selection to favor females that gain insurance of pregnancy by copulating on the last day of estrus with a male who has not mated frequently in the past. However, such a union cannot occur in the harem because it is ruled by high-ranking males, all of whom copulate frequently. Accordingly, females should mate somewhere outside their sphere of influence.

Most females mate with a male on the harem's periphery as they leave the rookery on their return to sea. We observed 20 females leaving the harem during the 1975 study period; four of them were marked and had been observed copulating in the harem for 3–5 days prior to their departure. We assume that all other females had also been in estrus for several days prior to departure, based on numerous observations of departing females in previous years. Seventeen of the 20 females copulated near the water's edge or in the shallow water offshore.

Most females copulated with the highest-ranking adult male present among the 10–12 males on the periphery of the harem. These males adopted the strategy of pursuing departing females. The male that copulated was usually a low-ranking male relative to males in the harem and one who copulated infrequently, less than 10 times during the entire breeding season. Other peripheral males were also low-ranking adults or subadults. Copulations outside the harem were seldom interrupted. Only one out of every 10 mounts directed to departing females was protested. Only rarely did an alpha male in the harem follow a female as she departed, and this was only for a short distance and usually near the season's end when only a few females remained in the harem. Whereas alpha males were usually the first male with whom a female copulated, in only three out of 20 cases was he the last.

DISCUSSION

This study suggests that female elephant seals may influence the genotype of their offspring to their benefit in a simple and direct way without employing deliberate choice or esthetic criteria. By inciting males to compete for her, a female maximizes the probability of mating with a mature, high-ranking male. We assume that this type of individual is likely to be the most fit male of those that are available for several reasons. Few males survive to age 10 or more, the minimal age necessary to achieve a high social rank and dominate breeding (Le Boeuf 1974). The mortality rate of breeding age males on Año Nuevo Island is estimated to be 45% from one year to the next. The mortality rate of males prior to reaching age 8 is estimated to be 86%–97% of those born (see table 7 in Le Boeuf 1974). Accordingly, the probability of surviving to age 10 is very low. If mortality is partially a function of genotype, then males who have survived to maturity have demonstrated an important aspect of their fitness. Other atrributes possessed by high-ranking adults which are probably correlated with fitness are sound physiological condition, reflected by their ability to physically dominate other mature males, and sexual experience (see Selander [1972] and Trivers [1972] for a further discussion of the attributes of males whose fitness has been demonstrated).

The consequences of a female's protesting behavior can be expected to vary with the social context. In small harems containing less than 40 females, the alpha male can prevent all other males from approaching females, and consequently he alone mates with all of them (Le Boeuf 1974). In this situation, the female gets no benefit from inciting male competition; she mates with the highest-ranking male, the only one in the harem, regardless of what she does. Yet it has been our observation that females are as likely to protest mounts in small harems as in large ones. Protesting mounts seem to be "wired in" and not specific to social situations. This may be an adaptation to the social environment most frequently found on rookeries; the majority of females in the population breed in large harems containing up to several hundred females at peak season. It is in large harems that incitation of male competition should be of greatest benefit to females. As harem size increases more males enter the harem, and some of them are low-ranking, young males. In this context, the potential for competition and male variation in fitness will be greatest. A female that does not incite competition in a large harem runs the risk of being inseminated by a young male who may be no more fit than a noncompetitive "marginal" male (see Bartholomew 1970).

It is conceivable that females could detect high fitness in young males of low rank and mate with them as opposed to other young males. However, we think this is improbable, because copulations with young pubertal males are rarely concentrated in a few individuals. Furthermore, a few copulations at this age does not predict breeding success in adulthood, and, in retrospect, males who achieved high reproductive success in adulthood did not reveal their potential by copulating frequently as subadults (see table 6 in Le Boeuf 1974). Finally, even subadults who are somewhat successful in breeding are subject to the same high annual mortality rate as unsuccessful subadults.

The manner in which females incite males to compete for them must be clarified. One cannot distinguish whether females are simply protesting a copulation or attempting to incite noncopulating males to intervene and chase off a mounting male. From the observer's blind, it looks as if protesting females simply do not want to copulate, and this may be the case. The important thing is not the female's intentions or the observer's interpretation of them, but the *effect* of her behavior on nearby males. A blatant, squawking, wriggling, sandflipping female with a prospective suitor on top of her struggling to pin her down attracts the attention of all males in the vicinity. Since each male's reproductive success is a function of how many females he can keep inaccessible to other males (Williams 1975), one or more of the rivals interferes with the potential copulation. The female's behavior sets in motion a sequence of male movements. For example, a male dominant to the mounter may issue a vocal threat sufficient to move the mounter from the female. But before the aggressor can reach the female he is threatened and displaced by another male dominant to him. Several aggressive interactions involving other males may ensue, resulting in a considerable change in the spatial relationships of males in the area. Episodes like this usually end when the most dominant male in the area gets close to the female and prevents all other males from mounting her or he mounts her himself. Now the female's protests have no effect, for no male can displace the mounter. He attempts to copulate until he is successful or gives up trying and moves off of his own accord.

If females did not protest copulations, males would still compete for females and interfere with each other's copulations. The mating frequency of males would probably be roughly proportional to their social rank, i.e., most females would be inseminated by mature, high-ranking males. This is the pattern which emerges from females who do not protest when mounted. The effect of a female's protesting behavior is to intensify male-male competition and augment its consequences. Her behavior activates the social hierarchy; it literally wakes up sleeping males and prompts them to live up to their social positions. The result is that it is more difficult for young males to mate, and the breeding monopoly of a few adult males is increased. Female choice in birds which lek has a similar consequence, as Trivers (1972) has pointed out.

Selection should favor the most parsimonous mechanism that enables females to optimize their reproductive success. In elephant seals—when sexual dimorphism is great, the breeding season is short, a rigid social hierarchy exists among males, and females are continually accosted by numerous aggressive suitors—inciting competition seems to be the simplest, least complicated strategy for mating with the best male in the harem. Once a female joins a harem, this is one of the few things she can do to effect a "choice" of males.[1] In species where males fight for territories and the winner gets the most favorably situated one, the one that is richest in food, or the same one each time, the simplest strategy is for the female to select the best territory rather than the male since the greatest benefits will come with the territory. In dragonflies, *Plathemus lydia*, females oviposit at a time and place where the most fit males are available (Campanella and Wolf 1974). Female choice for a particular male based on certain criteria, what is sometimes called the "specific image" type of choice, should be relatively rare, occurring only in social systems where males do not compete for territories or for social rank which is important in mating.

As Darwin (1871) recognized, there are elements of intrasexual competition in both sexes, and the two processes do not operate independently of each other. The outcome of competition within each sex influences the distribution of reproductive success in the other sex. Male elephant seals compete to mate with as many females as possible; they show no signs of choosing among females. If one asumes that the first male to mate with a female is most apt to cause insemination, a good possibility in a mammal that gives birth to a single offspring, then males will be selected to try to mate with a female as early as possible, i.e., to try to rape females. This is the strong impression one gets observing mating in this species. But this strategy of males can work to the advantage of females. Because of the way elephant-seal society is structured, only a mature, high-ranking bull can rape a female, i.e., copulate despite total protest on the part of the female, and it is such a male, who has demonstrated his fitness, that a female is selected to "choose" to sire her offspring. Thus, it would benefit females to optimize the possibility of being raped! How might a female do this? How can a female maximize the probability that the first male to mate with her will be the alpha male? Since there is a limit to how many females an alpha male can inseminate and there is a good possibility that he is overworked (he may copulate as much as 13 times in 6 h with only 5–30-min intervals between matings (Le Boeuf 1972)), it would be advantageous for a female to mate with him early, when he is fresh and before his fertility or sexual interest starts to decline. Thus, we might expect females to compete among themselves to arrive early in the breeding season, to attempt to secure a position near the alpha male and to protest all mounts vigorously up to the point of penile intromission. We know that females who arrive early in the season form the center of the harem. They are more likely to copulate with the alpha male than females on the periphery, because the alpha male takes up a central position among the females. The more space a harem

---

[1]It is conceivable that arriving females exert choice over which harem to join since the fitness of the various alpha males might be expected to vary with the size of the harems defended. Alpha males in large harems might be more fit since they must defend their positions much more frequently and against more competition than alpha males in small harems. We do not know if females choose in this way, but it is known that once a female breeds in a particular harem she tends to return to it to breed in the future (Le Boeuf 1972).

occupies, the lower the probability that a female on the periphery will mate with the alpha male. Centrally located females are aggressive to females on the edge and keep them from entering the center of the harem, and early arriving females may prevent late arriving females from joining the harem (Christenson 1974). Although it is not clear what permits early-arriving, centrally located females to dominate later-arriving females, we suspect that the former are older and hence, as a group, dominant to the latter. Other factors, having to do with survival of the young, favor females that arrive early in the breeding season (Le Boeuf and Briggs 1977).

Females might be expected to incite male competition in numerous polygynous species. Since males in most polygynous species invest nothing in their offspring except genes, selection should favor females that screen males on the physical manifestation of these genes, i.e., physical superiority over other "sets of genes." This can be done most easily and is most apparent in societies where several males compete to mate with a female, a social hierarchy exists among males, and interference with mating occurs. These conditions exist in several species of fishes, lizards, toads, frogs, snakes, gallinaceous birds, carnivores, ungulates, and primates; we shall give representative illustrations from these animal groups below. As in elephant seals, we expect the behavior of these females to result in an increase in the probability of mating with a fit partner. If the first male to mate with a promiscuous female is most likely to inseminate her (a good possibility but admittedly an unknown), then we would expect females to incite competition most frequently during early estrus and less frequently or not at all toward the end of estrus.

Females may incite male competition by doing anything which alerts males in the area, causes them to compete among themselves to approach and copulate with the female, or causes them to prevent copulations by other males, particularly younger, subordinate males. A similar female strategy may be employed by some monogamous birds during pair bond formation. The signal may involve any sensory modality or combination of modalities.

Moving away from a suitor can be an effective visual signal for alerting nearby males. This is an essential component of courtship behavior in some ungulates, rodents, carnivores, and reptiles. Geist (1971) notes that female mountain sheep typically run away when mounted during the first week of the rut, and long chases ensue in which several males pursue the female. The ram follows when the female runs away, and ". . . such a chase will invariably catch the attention of other rams and they will hurry to intercept the female. Competition for the female is increased; the chances that a larger ram than the original one will be drawn to the chase is also increased, and the original ram's chances of siring offspring is reduced (p. 223)." A similar behavior pattern seems to occur in several other species of North American ungulates, e.g., the white tailed deer, *Odocoileus virginianus* (Newsom 1926) and bison, *Bison bison* (Dale Lott, personal communication). In black rats, *Rattus rattus*, females initially reject males by running away. Ewer (1971) observed that "if more than one male is present, they may all follow the female in a line, one behind the other." Following of the female is often interrupted while a dominant male chases off subordinates. Running away from a suitor is a reliable component of courtship in the estrous bitch and excites all dogs nearby to join in the chase (Le Boeuf 1967 a). Noble (1937) reports that many male snakes (notably the brown snake, *Storeria dekayi,* and the garter snake, *Thamnophis sirtalis* and *T. butleri*) are attracted to a moving female. Several males may give chase and jockey with each other for the copulatory position on the female's dorsum. Similar behavior has been observed in the terrestrial crab, *Coenobita pertatus* (Ernst Reese, personal communication).

Females may adopt unusual postures during locomotion to signal receptivity and provoke male competition. Magnuson and Prescott (1966) described the exaggerated, wobbling swimming exhibited by female Pacific bonito (*Sarda chiliensis* Cuvier) when ready to spawn. This display elicits following in a group of males who give lateral threat displays to each other and compete for a position immediately behind the female. Eventually, the female pairs with one male, they swim in a circle, and gametes are released.

Aerial chases in which females are pursued by several males are common elements in the courtship of many birds. Females initiate these chases in pintail ducks, *Anas acuta* (Smith 1968), the winter wren, *Troglodytes troglodytes* (Armstrong 1955), and in the sanderling, *Calidris alba* (Parmelee 1970).

Sounds made by females often trigger competition among males. In sage grouse, *Centrocercus urophasianus,* arriving females fly straight across the lek, and their quacking call stimulates males to strut on their territories (Wiley 1973). Nero (1956) reports that first-year male red-winged blackbirds *(Agelaius phoenicus)* often attempt to approach a resident female, but typically the female gives a loud, rapid, shrill call, accompanied by fluttering wingtips, to which the resident territorial male responds by flying up immediately and driving off the young male. Vocalizations by chimpanzees, *Pan troglodytes,* often cause dominant males to prevent subordinates from mounting or consorting with them. During copulation, a female emits loud, distinctive calls which attract males from a wide area who subsequently copulate with her (P. R. McGinnis, personal communication).

The behavior of many female insects attracts courting males. For example, the flight tone of the female mosquito, *Aedes aegypti* L., sets off the pursuit activity of males (Roth 1948). In honeybees there may be considerable intrasexual competition among drones swarming around flying queens (Gary 1963). However, it is not clear whether this is simply attracting a mate, inciting competition, or both. Indeed, it appears that most female insects exert less control over what male inseminates them than one finds in vertebrates. Because of the rapid development of most insects, females cannot cue on maturity, social rank, or sexual experience as an indication of fitness. (Alexander [1975] discusses other criteria which might figure in mate selection by females.) There seems to be more of a priority in insects to mate quickly as opposed to selectively.

In several species of ducks females incite their mates to attack strange drakes (e.g., Tinbergen 1958). If the stranger wins, the female may desert her mate and court the victor (Johnsgard 1968).

In polyandrous species where females court males to get them to invest in their eggs and rear offspring one would expect the sex role reversal to be complete (see Trivers 1972); males should incite competition among females. In Wilson's phala-rope, *Phalaropus tricolor,* Howe (1975) found that as soon as males arrive in the spring short flights, consisting of a male being pursued by several females, take place during pair formation. Males initiate the aerial chase by swooping down over swim-ming females, causing them to fly up and join the chase. This results in a larger group of pursuing females and a corresponding increase in competition among them.

Behavioral signals are but one means by which females can incite male competi-tion. Hormone-controlled morphological changes during the estrous cycle of some females advertises their receptivity in an undirected way and can produce the same effect. The color and turgidity of the perineal sex skin of many primates communi-cates the precise estrous condition of the female and determines male access to females. Although female baboons, *Papio ursinus,* may be mounted by young males early in the estrous cycle, at the time of maximal perineal swelling and redness, when ovulation occurs, mature males chase younger males away and they alone copulate (e.g., Hall and DeVore 1965). The advantage of this morphological signal over a behavioral one is that it stays on for a long time. In the baboon it is graded throughout the estrous cycle. Unlike a behavioral signal, it is an inflexible, perma-nent fixture. The female cannot avoid signaling her estrous condition to all males. The element common to both physical and behavioral signals of this kind is the consequence: the signaling female is most apt to be fertilized by a mature, high-ranking male. It seems that selection has so favored this outcome in many primates that females near ovulation would have a difficult time copulating with a young male even if they wanted to, for older males would prevent it. Similarly, some spawning fishes undergo a change in coloration which attracts males and causes them to compete for the female (e.g., the Blue Acara, *Aequidens pulcher* Steindachner; E. Shaw, personal communication).

It is well known that pheromones released automatically by some female mam-mals in estrus attract members of the opposite sex and remain effective for several days (e.g., urine of the domestic bitch in estrus). Minute amounts of a chemical substance released by the virgin silk moth, *Porthetria monacha,* attracts males from as far away as a few miles (Schneider 1969). Some female fishes release pheromones into the water, which attracts courting males (Tavolga 1956). However, it is not clear whether these chemical signals simply advertise a female's receptivity or whether they also incite males to compete, with the result being that the winner is most apt to fertilize the signaler. As in many insects, it may be simply a matter of first come, first served.

Finally, some females may affect the potential genotype of their offspring after mating has occurred. In insects in which sperm competition occurs within the reproductive tract of the female after several males have copulated, Parker (1970) reasons that the female might have evolved postmating mechanisms to influence which sperm will fertilize her eggs. The favoring of any sperm character over another within the female's reproductive tract would serve to intensify sperm competition, i.e., male competition.

Laboratory studies of the female's role in courtship are often misleading. Observations are usually restricted to a heterosexual pair in an enclosed area. The female is given no choice of partners. Elements of her behavior pattern which might normally function to signal other males to compete are apt to be misinterpreted as being irrelevant, a sign of solicitation, or an indication of unreceptivity, e.g., darting away, earwiggling, and tail vibrating in the laboratory rat, *Rattus norvegicus.* The most unnatural aspect of the standard laboratory study of courtship and mating is allowing one male uninterrupted access to an estrous female who cannot get away. This is like giving the male subject alpha-male status or his own territory. The male can force the issue without the threat of male interference. Some females are even killed by the male when they cannot get away (e.g., white-tailed deer [Severinghaus 1955]). In nature, this one-to-one situation is probably a rarity, since most vertebrates are polygynous.

In conclusion, we agree with the thrust of Fisher's statement (1930, p. 147) that some naturalists may have been overly concerned with the distinction between the two processes of sexual selection, especially the possibility that the female process involves will or choice, and this has detracted from the potentially more important study of the element common to both processes, i.e., competition between members of each sex.

SUMMARY

Females that mate with the most fit male available leave more viable offspring than females that mate with males of lesser fitness. We describe a mechanism by which females facilitate mating with a superior genotype, as reflected by age, social rank, and sexual experience, without exerting choice. Female elephant seals increase the probability of mating with a mature, high-ranking male by simply rejecting all copulatory attempts during early estrus. Females protest loudly when mounted; this signals all nearby males and activates the dominance hierarchy. The probability that the mounting male will be interrupted by another male is a function of the mounter's social rank. The lower his rank, the higher the probability of interruption. The result is that mature males of high social rank have more time and freedom to attempt copulation, and they succeed in doing most of the mating. The behavior of the female intensifies this monopoly by making it more difficult for young, subordinate males to copulate. A similar female strategy seems to operate in several species where the female is courted by several males. Influencing the genotype of her offspring is an important means by which a female can increase her inclusive fitness. This aspect of sexual selection has been neglected.

LITERATURE CITED

Alexander, R. D. 1975. Natural selection and specialized chorusing behavior in acoustical insects. Pages 35–77 *in* D. Pimentel, ed. Insects, science and society. Academic Press, New York.

Armstrong, E. A. 1955. The wren. Collins, London. 312 pp.

Bartholomew, G. A. 1952. Reproductive and social behavior of the northern elephant seal. Univ. California Pub. Zool. 47:369–372.

Bartholomew, G. A. 1970. A model for the evolution of pinniped polygyny. Evolution 24:546–559.

Bartholomew, G. A., and N. E. Collias. 1962. The role of vocalization in the social behavior of the northern elephant seal. Anim. Behav. 10:7–14.

Beach, F. A., and B. J. Le Boeuf. 1967. Coital behavior in dogs. I. Preferential mating in the bitch. Anim. Behav. 15:546–558.

Beuchner, H. K., and R. Schloeth. 1965. Ceremonial mating behavior in Uganda kob (*Adenota kob thomasi* Neuman). Z. Tierpsychol. 22:209–225.

Campanella, P. J., and L. L. Wolf, 1974. Temporal leks as a mating system in a temperate zone dragonfly (Odonata: Anisoptera) I. Plathemis lydia (Drury). Behavior 51:49–87.

Christenson, T. E. 1974. Aggressive and maternal behavior of the female northern elephant seal. Ph.D. diss. University of California, Berkeley. 57 pp.

Darwin, C. 1871. The descent of man and selection in relation to sex. Murray, London.

Ewer, R. R. 1971. The biology and behaviour of a free-living population of black rats *(Rattus rattus)*. Anim. Behav. Monogr. 4:125–174.

Fisher, R. A. 1930. The genetical theory of natural selection. Clarendon, Oxford.

Gary, N. E. 1963. Observations of mating behavior in the honeybee. J. Apicult. Res. 2:3–13.

Geist, V. 1971. Mountain sheep. University of Chicago Press, Chicago. 383 pp.

Ghiselin, M. T. 1974. The economy of nature and the evolution of sex. University of California Press, Berkeley. 346 pp.

Hall, K. R. L., and I. DeVore. 1965. Baboon social behavior. Pages 53–110 *in* Irven DeVore, ed. Primate behavior. Holt, Rinehart & Winston, New York.

Hinde, R. A. 1956. The biological significance of territories in birds. Ibis 98:340–369.

Howe, M. A. 1975. Social interactions in flocks of courting Wilson's Phalaropes *(Phalaropus tricolor)*. Condor 77:24–33.

Huxley, J. S. 1938. The present standing of the theory of sexual selection. Pages 11–42 *in* G. DeBeer, ed. Evolution. Oxford University Press, New York.

Johnsgard, P. A. 1968. Water fowl. University of Nebraska Press, Lincoln.

Lack, D. 1968. Ecological adaptations for breeding in birds. Methuen, London.

Le Boeuf, B. J. 1967a. Heterosexual attraction in dogs. Psychonomic Sci. 7:313–314.

———. 1967b. Interindividual associations in dogs. Behaviour 29:268–295.

———. 1972. Sexual behavior in the northern elephant seal. *Mirounga angustirostris* Behaviour 41:1–26.

———. 1974. Male-male competition and reproductive success in elephant seals. Amer. Zool. 14:163–176.

Le Boeuf, B. J., D. G. Ainley, and T. J. Lewis. 1974. Elephant seals on the Farallones: population structure of an incipient breeding colony. J. Mammal. 55:370–385.

Le Boeuf, B. J., and K. T. Briggs. 1977. The cost of living in a seal harem. Mammalia (in press).

Le Boeuf, B. J., and R. S. Peterson. 1969. Social status and mating activity in elephant seals. Science 163:91–93.

Le Boeuf, B. J., R. J. Whiting, and R. F. Gantt. 1972. Perinatal behavior of northern elephant seal females and their young. Behaviour 34:121–156.

Leuthold, W. 1966. Variations in territorial behavior of Uganda kob *Adenota kob thomasi* (Newmann 1896). Behaviour 27:215–258.

Magnuson, J. J., and J. H. Prescott. 1966. Courtship, locomotion, feeding, and miscellaneous behaviour of Pacific bonito (*Sarda chilieresis*). Anim. Behav. 14:54–67.

Nero, R. W. 1956. A behavior study of the red-winged blackbird. Wilson Bull. 68:129–150.

Newsom, W. M. 1926. White-tailed deer. Scribner's, New York.

Noble, G. K. 1937. The sense organs involved in the courtship of *Storeria, Thamnophis* and other snakes. Bull. Amer. Mus. Natur. Hist. 63:673–725.

Orians, G. H. 1969. On the evolution of mating systems in birds and mammals. Amer. Natur. 103:589–604.

Parker, G. A. 1970. Sperm competition and its evolutionary consequences in insects. Biol. Rev. Cambridge Phil. Soc. 45:525–567.

Parmelee, D. F. 1970. Breeding behavior of the sanderling in the Canadian high Arctic. Living Bird 9:97–146.

Roth, L. M. 1948. A study of mosquito behavior. An experimental laboratory study of the sexual behavior of *Aedes aegypti*. L. Amer. Midland Natur. 40:265.

Schneider, D. 1969. Insect olfaction: deciphering system for chemical messages. Science 163:1031–1036.

Selander, R. K. 1972. Sexual selection and dimorphism in birds. Pages 180–230 *in* B. Campbell, ed. Sexual selection and the descent of man, 1871–1971. Aldine, Chicago.

Severinghaus, C. W. 1955. Some observations on the breeding behavior of deer. New York Fish and Game J. 2:239–241.

Smith, R. I. 1968. The social aspects of reproductive behavior in the pintail. Auk 85:381-396.

Summers-Smith, D. 1963. The house sparrow. Collins, London.

Tavolga, W. N. 1956. Visual, chemical and sound stimuli as cues in the sex discriminating behavior of the gabrid fish, *Bathygobius sporator*. Zoologica 47:49–64.

Tinbergen, N. 1958. Curious naturalists. Doubleday, New York. 301 pp.

Trivers, R. L. 1972. Parental investment and sexual selection. Pages 136–179 *in* B. Campbell, ed. Sexual selection and the descent of man, 1871-1971. Aldine, Chicago. 378 pp.

Verner, J. 1964. Evolution of polygamy in the long-billed marsh wren. Evolution 18:252–261.

Verner, J., and Engelsen, G. H. 1970. Territories, multiple nest building, and polygyny in the long-billed marsh wren. Auk 87:557–567.

Wallace, A. R. 1889. Darwinism. Macmillan, London.

Wiley, R. H. 1973. Territoriality and non-random mating in sage grouse, *Centrocercus urophasianus*. Anim. Behav. Monogr. 6:85–169.

Williams, G. C. 1975. Sex and evolution. Princeton University Press, Princeton, N.J.

Wilson, E. O. 1975. Sociobiology. Belknap, Cambridge, Mass. 697 pp.

Zimmerman, J. L. 1966. Polygyny in the dickcissel. Auk 83:534–546.

Alternate Routes to Sociality in Jays—With a Theory for the Evolution of Altruism and Communal Breeding

Jerram L. Brown

Biology Department, University of Rochester

The social systems of New World species of jays are compared behaviorally and ecologically. Two lines leading to sociality are identified, one connecting the pair-in-territory system with the colonial system and a second connecting the pair-in-territory system with the communal system.

Ecological factors in the evolution of communal breeding and its associated altruistic behavior are considered mainly in the genus *Aphelocoma,* but other birds are treated briefly. Three principal origins of communality and altruism in birds are identified: from colonies, from a surplus of males, and by retention of young in the family, the latter being of greatest importance. The theory proposed for the evolution of communal breeding and altruism emphasizes three main processes: 1) K-selection, (2) kin selection, and (3) kin-group selection in the same chronological order.

This paper has two goals. First, a comparative survey of the social organization and ecology of 30 species of New World jays is attempted. Second, a general theory for the evolution of communal breeding and altruistic helping at the nest in birds is developed. Social organization will be viewed as resulting from natural selection acting on individuals and kinship groups.

A useful way of exploring social organization is to examine the social systems in a group of animals that is relatively homogenous in terms of its morphological adaptations yet inhabits a wide range of environments and exhibits a variety of social systems. When comparisons among species within such a group are combined with detailed analyses of the population ecology of selected species, insights into the evolutionary processes leading to diversity in social organization may result. A suitable group for such an analysis might be the Corvidae, the family of jays, crows, magpies, nutcrackers, and choughs, but the family is too large to review here (26 genera, 102 species) (Blake and Vaurie, 1962). I have limited my treatment of it to

The author's research was supported by research grant MH 16345 from the National Institute of Mental Health, U.S. Public Health Service. Field work on Mexican jays at the Southwestern Research Station in Arizona was made possible by the American Musuem of Natural History. I am indebted to M. Slatkin, W. D. Hamilton, R. P. Balda, J. W. Hardy, R. Pulliam, S. Emlen, H. Alvarez, F. A. Pitelka, D. Ligon, C. J. Vernon, and others for criticisms and help in the preparation of this paper. They are not to be blamed where I failed to follow their advice.

From *American Zoologist 14:* 63–80. Reprinted by permission of the American Society of Zoologists and the author.

a group to be referred to as the New World jays, all of which are listed in Table 1, and mainly to those species with which I am familiar. With the possible exception of the piñon jay (*Gymnorhinus cyanocephalus*) these species seem to form a natural group (Amadon, 1944*a*). The group includes a wide variety of social organizations, environments, and body sizes.

Jays, like corvids generally, tend to have generalized food habits, relying mainly on large arthropods, but also taking nuts and fruits in season. Food storage is well developed (Turcek and Kelso, 1968). Their plumage is colorful and sexually mono-morphic, the sexes being distinguishable in the field mainly by behavior. The New World jays comprise eight genera and have their center of abundance in Central America, having one genus in eastern United States, three in western United States, seven in southern Mexico, and two in South America.

PATTERNS OF SOCIALITY: COMPARATIVE STUDY

New World jays show a variety of social organizations, as summarized in Figure 1 and Table 1. Sociality has evolved in two distinct forms, the colonial and the communal. I will attempt to show that each of these extremely social types is connected through various intermediate species to the classical, all-purpose territo-rial type. The existence of these intermediate forms suggests that there have been

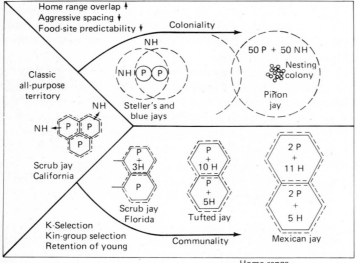

Figure 1   Alternate routes to sociality in jays. Sociality may be achieved by progressive overlapping of home ranges together with reduction of aggressive spacing, which results ultimately in a colonial social structure. Or it may be achieved through retention of the young in the territory for progres-sively longer periods, which results in a communal social structure.

two separate evolutionary lines of specialization, one connecting the all-purpose territorial and colonial types, and the other connecting the all-purpose territorial and communal types. There is no evidence from this comparative survey for direct links between the extreme colonial and communal forms, but there is no reliable information at all for at least nine species, and the present picture may well require revision as more information becomes available. The most common type of social organization in New World jays is the communal system (in the broad sense). Of 24 species and isolated populations for which adequate or sketchy information is available, 16 typically occur in family-sized groups during the breeding season, one is colonial, and 7 occur in pairs (Table 1). In this section I shall compare the intermediate and extreme forms in each line (Fig. 1). In the following section I shall examine the ecological determinants of communal systems and discuss some relevant selection pressures.

The Classical All-purpose Territory

The classical case of an all-purpose territory from which other jays are effectively excluded by aggressive behavior of the owner is represented by the California mainland populations of the scrub jay (*Aphelocoma coerulescens*). Although many nests of California scrub jays have been watched by numerous ornithologists over the years, no cases of helpers (as defined by Skutch, 1961) have been reported. At the nests of several color-banded pairs that I watched on the Berkeley campus and at the Hastings Natural History Reservation in Carmel Valley, 1957–60, no helpers were present.

An Evolutionary Route to Coloniality

There is only one colonial New World jay, the piñon jay. The following account of it is taken from the study by Balda and Bateman (1971). Colonies of piñon jays range up to a few hundred individuals. The nests are clumped. Foraging is done almost invariably in large, closely packed flocks which "roll" through the open, grassy woodland much like a winter flock of European starlings (*Sturnus vulgaris*). Spacing in the flocks through individual-distance mechanisms is apparently often absent. Aggressive behavior is notably rare. There is apparently no defense of the colony home range against other colonies (Balda, pers. comm.). Adults separate out from the flock at the inception of breeding, court, build nests, and feed their young as pairs. Helpers at the nest were essentially absent for the first two weeks after hatching. At some nests in Arizona a few adult helpers were seen during the last 4 or 5 days of the nestling period. First-year birds were not observed feeding nestlings (with one exception) (Balda, personal communication), and they were chased away by adults. Ligon (1971) saw no helpers at nests in New Mexico. After fledging, the contribution by helpers increased, although the young were still fed principally by the parents.

From the many points of difference between the scrub and the piñon jays, and between regularly spaced and colonial species, I would like to select one ecological factor of primary importance, namely, the home range of an individual. Scrub jays that I have studied in California and those observed by Hardy (1961) in New Mexico had home ranges of a few acres, while piñon jays in Arizona had home ranges of a few square miles, even though the body weights of the two species are about the same. The scrub jay defends all of its regular home range, while the piñon jay defends only its nest. Consequently, a pair of scrub jays shares a small foraging area with no other scrub jays, but a pair of piñon jays shares a large area with perhaps hundreds of others. Scrub jay populations expand by settling new areas, while piñon jay populations expand mainly by colony growth. The settling of new areas by piñon jays probably occurs during population crashes induced by nut crop failures, but this is poorly documented. Both species are prone to have "invasion years" (Bent, 1946; Westcott, 1969).

Just how far a species goes along the continuum between regular spacing and coloniality is probably determined by (i) the spatiotemporal pattern of food abundance, (ii) the probability that one small territory will supply everything needed, (iii) the intraspecific competition for resources and space, (iv) the energy costs and effectiveness of defense and foraging, and (v) susceptibility to predation.

An intermediate position on this continuum is occupied by the Steller's jay (*Cyanocitta stelleri*) (Brown, 1963a). Individuals of this species extend their foraging range far into home ranges of others, yet they maintain an area of dominance around their nest, which is not a territory as strictly defined (see Brown and Orians, 1970) but which results from aggressive competition. The areas of dominance of Steller's jays are relatively small compared to their home ranges, as shown in Figure 2. The Steller's jay is not in any sense of the word a colonial species, since its nests appear to be regularly spaced by means of the area of dominance around each. Its compromise system allows a pair to fly long distances to temporarily rich food supplies, such as acorn-bearing trees so long as it behaves subordinately while there, but still to retain priority of usage in a core area used for nesting and most foraging. The system allows individuals to gain some of the social advantages of flocking, such as in finding temporary, rich food sources and detecting predators and harassing them, without the susceptibility to predation of clumped nests. In short, the social system of the Steller's jay might be viewed as resulting from adaptations of individuals to an environment that is intermediate between conditions which favor coloniality and conditions which favor pairs in all purpose territories.

In the above discussion I have been concerned with social systems as reflections of individual adaptations to their environments. For this purpose it does not matter that the piñon, scrub, and Steller's jays are not a monophyletic group. Each is probably more closely related to another species than to the other two. The phylogenetic affinities of the piñon jay are especially uncertain, since in some respects it resembles a nutcracker rather than a jay (Hardy, 1969a; Balda and Bateman, 1971); it may be a link between jays and nutcrackers, a jay which has acquired nutcracker traits convergently, or a nutcracker which has acquired jay traits convergently. I also wish to disclaim any use of the comparative method to establish the direction of evolution in this discussion. Presumably selection could favor either direction on the continuum under discussion. And, of course, I do not mean to imply that piñon jays evolved from Steller's jays, and Steller's jays from scrub jays, nor the opposite.

Some Evolutionary Routes to Communal Breeding

According to Lack (1968, p. 72) in "true" communal or cooperative breeding, several adults help to feed one brood. Although it is as good a way as any to draw a line between communal and non-communal breeding, this usage eliminates many species with helpers at the nest from consideration. In looking for possible evolutionary origins of communal breeding I have found it useful to consider a wider spectrum of phenomena, including some which do not qualify as communal breeding by any conventional usage. I have considered as a potential precursor of "true" communality any system in which some kind of cooperation in breeding activities occurs between individuals other than a mated pair. In Table 2 the entire gamut is arranged according to hypothetical modes of origin. Within each type of origin I have arranged the cases B through F in order of their grade or level of evolutionary specialization for communal breeding. If it is assumed that a complex level must have evolved ultimately from a simpler level, each grade can be interpreted as having evolved from the preceding one and as being a preadaptation for the following one, if one exists. This is not to say that a lower grade cannot be derived from a higher one. The numbered categories within a grade are not intended to be ranked or ordered (e.g., I A 1, 2). Three types of origin, the colonial, the lek, and the male-surplus types apparently lead rather quickly to evolutionary dead ends so far as communal breeding is concerned. The fourth, or non-dispersal type, has led to the most extremely specialized modes of communal breeding known in birds. New World jays are well represented in the non-dispersal type but have only one species in the colonial type and none in the male-surplus or lek types. All the types will be at least briefly considered because they help place the jays in better perspective, but emphasis will be on the non-dispersal type.

Although it has been generally felt that communal social organizations have not arisen from colonial ones, since the pair is typically the basic social unit in colonial species and even in the lodge-builders (e.g., Crook, 1965), helpers feeding young at the nest have recently been discovered in a few colonial species, including the piñon jay. Such cases are rare, however. A colonial system provides many opportunities for an individual to feed young not its own. Often nests are located in the midst of hundreds or thousands of others of the same species, or young herd together into a dense creche containing hundreds of mobile young. Under such conditions adults may occasionally make a mistake and feed the wrong young, but it is amazingly rare. An adult which has lost its own young may be so primed for parental care that it helps to feed young not its own.

The helpers in the piñon jay and terns (Skutch, 1961) probably fall into the category of rather frequent accidents, but in the red-throated bee-eater (*Merops*

Table I Social Systems of New World Jays

Species	Range	Social unit	Helpers	Habitat	References
Gymnorhinus cyanocephalus, piñon j.	w. U.S.	C	Q	piñon woodland	1, 15
Cyanocitta cristata, blue j.	e. U.S.	P	N	deciduous woodland	2, 9, 14
Cyanocitta stelleri, Steller's j.	w. N. Amer.	P	N	evergreen forest	4, 5
Aphelocoma coerulescens, scrub j.	w. N. Amer.	P	N	scrub, chaparral	2, 3, 9
Aphelocoma coerulescens, scrub j.	Fla.	F	I	sand scrub	21
Aphelocoma ultramarina, Mexican j.	Mex., Ariz.	F	A	pine-oak woodland	3, 6, 7
Aphelocoma unicolor, unicolored j.	C. Amer.	F	??	cloud forest	16
Cyanolyca viridicyana, collared j.	n. S. Amer.	??	??	cloud forest	11
Cyanolyca pulchra, beautiful j.	Ecuad.-Col.	??	??	tropical, subtropical	
Cyanolyca cucullata, azure-hooded j.	S.L.P.-Pan.	F?	??	cloud forest	10, 28
Cyanolyca pumilo, black-throated j.	Chiap.-Hond.	F	??	cloud forest	10, 21, 28
Cyanolyca nana, dwarf j.	V.C.-Oax.	P	N	humid pine-oak	10, 13
Cyanolyca mirabilis, Omilteme j.	Guer.	P	N?	humid pine-oak	10, 28
Cyanolyca argentigula, silver-throated j.	C.R.-Pan.	??	??	high montane forest	12
Cissilopha melanocyanea, bushy-crested j.	Nicar.-Guat.	F	A	cloud-forest edges	12, 25
Cissilopha yucatanica, Yucatan j.	Yuc.-Guat.	F	A?	deciduous forest	25
Cissilopha sanblasiana, San Blas j.	Nay.-Guer.	F	A	tropical woodland	25
Cissilopha beecheii, Beechey's j.	Son.-Nay.	F?	??	subtropical woodland	
Cyanocorax caeruleus, azure j.	se. Brazil	??	??	warm, humid forest	11
Cyanocorax cyanomelas, purplish j.	e. S. Amer.	??	??		
Cyanocorax violaceus, violaceous j.	ne. S. Amer.	F?	??	warm evergreen forest	11
Cyanocorax cristatellus, curl-crested j.	Brazil	F?	??	tropical savanna	11

Species	Range			Habitat	References
Cyanocorax heilprini, azure-naped j.	Brazil, Venez.	??			11
Cyanocorax cayanus, Cayenne j.	ne. S. Amer.	??			11
Cyanocorax affinis, black-chested j.	C.R.-Venez.	P?	N?	lowland humid forest	11
Cyanocorax chrysops, plush-crested j.	e. S. Amer.	F?	??	heavy forest	11
Cyanocorax cyanopogon, white-naped j.	e. Brazil	??		heavy forest	11
Cyanocorax mystacalis, white-tailed j.	Ecuad.-Peru	??		mesquite woodland	11
Cyanocorax dickeyi, tufted j.	Son.-Nav.	F	I	humid, pine-oak barrancas	8
Cyanocorax yncas, green j. Mex.	Tex.-Hond.	P	??	tropical woodlands	2, 26, 28
Cyanocorax yncas, green j. Col., S. Amer.	S. Amer.	F	I or A	oak forest	27
Psilorhinus morio, brown j.	e. Mex.-Pan.	F	I	tropical forest	17, 18, 20
Calocitta formosa, magpie j.	w. Mex.	F	I	arid woods, savannas	18, 22

P = In pairs when nesting; unaccompanied by other adults or immatures; nests regularly dispersed.

C = In pairs when nesting; colonial; nests clumped.

F = In family-sized groups when nesting.

I = Immature helpers common at nests, but adult helpers absent.

A = Adult and immature helpers common at nests.

N = Helpers absent or only accidental at nests.

Q = Fledglings, and to a lesser extent nestlings, normally fed only by own parents, but commonly fed by parents not their own under some circumstances.

References:

1—Balda and Bateman (1971). 2—Bent (1946). 3—Brown (1963b). 4—Brown (1963a). 5—Brown (1964). 6—Brown (1970). 7—Brown (1972). 8—Crossin (1967). 9—Hardy (1961). 10—Hardy (1964). 11—Hardy (1969b). 12—Hardy (1969c). 13—Hardy (1971). 14—Laskey (1958). 15—Ligon (1971). 16—Pitelka (1951). 17—Selander (1959). 18—Skutch (1935). 19—Skutch (1953). 20—Skutch (1960). 21—Skutch (1967). 22—Wagner (1955). 23—Westcott (1970). 24—Woolfenden (personal communication).|25—Hardy (personal communication). 26—Sutton et al. (1950). 27—Humberto Alvarez (personal communication). 28—Pitelka (personal communication).

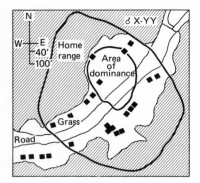
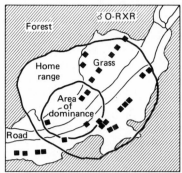

Figure 2 Home ranges and areas of dominance of two male Steller's jays in the breeding season of 1959. Notice that the area of dominance is much smaller than the home range. The areas of dominance are non-overlapping, but the home ranges of different individuals overlap extensively. For further details consult Brown 1963*a*. n = nest.

bulocki) helpers are regular (Fry, 1972). The ratio of 1.5 males per female favors the occurence of extra males at some of the nests in a colony. These helpers are usually one year old and are thought in most cases to be progeny of the same pair from the preceding year. Other colonial species of bee-eaters have similarly skewed sex ratios, and in some, helpers are known or suspected, but most have not been studied. Solitary species of bee-eaters have an even sex ratio and lack helpers. Thus, the communal bee-eaters combine elements of the three types of origins. They should cause us to have some reservations about the earlier conclusion that communal breeding did not evolve from colonial breeding. However, in the vast majority of colonial species selection seems to have favored selective feeding of one's own young by making possible exquisite abilities for individual recognition (Beer, 1971).

A variety of communal phenomena other than feeding the young has evolved in colonial species (A 1, 2), but in all these the contribution of each individual clearly aids its own offspring directly and involves no significant individual sacrifice. Participation in the communal phases of nest building in the social weaver (*Philetairus socius*) and monk parakeet (*Myiopsitta monachus*) is probably necessary to acquire ownership of a nesting compartment. The role of kin selection in such cases, if any, has not been explored, but since the colonies in these species are often quite large, the average coefficient of genetic relationship among colony members must be quite small, as can be appreciated from Figure 3.

Cooperative courtship, such as that in the ruff (*Philomachus pugnax*) and blue-backed manakin (*Chiroxiphia pareola*), is not communal breeding as generally conceived, but it involves an unusual kind of cooperation in the breeding cycle. Here again, the role of kinship, if any, remains to be explored, although it is known that in one case of group display the groups are composed of sibling males (wild turkey, *Meleagris gallopavo*) (Watts, 1968; Watts and Stokes, 1971).

An origin of communal breeding through an excess of males is indicated by the many cases of helpers at the nest summarized by Skutch (1961) in which the helpers

Table 2 Some Evolutionary Routes to Communal Breeding

I) Origin from colonies
  A) Communal activities other than feeding young
    1) Communal building of a single large nest or "lodge" or many burrows in which compartments are held by males or pairs. Social weaver, *Philetairus socius* (Friedman, 1950); buffalo weaver, *Bubalornis albirostris* (Crook, 1958); palm chat, *Dulus dominicus* (Wetmore and Swales, 1931); monk parrot, *Myiopsitta monachus* (Friedmann, 1935); African starling, *Creatophora cinerea* (Lack, 1968:72); bank swallow, *Riparia riparia* (Skutch, 1961).
    2) Communal guarding of young in a colony or creche. Some penguins and terns (Skutch, 1961).
  B) Helpers feed young at a small to moderate proportion of nests. Piñon jay (Balda and Bateman, 1971); *Merops bulocki* and some other bee-eaters (Fry, 1972); pied kingfishers, *Ceryle rudis* (Douthwaite in Fry, 1972); *Chaetura* swifts (Sick, 1959; Skutch, 1961).
  C) Helpers regular at most nests. Noisy miner, *Myzantha melancephala* (Dow, 1970); probably the bell miner, *Manorina melanophrys* (Swainson, 1970); some wood swallows, Artamidae (Harrison, 1969).
II) Origin from leks
  A) Feeding of young not involved.
    1) Cooperative courtship displays by males at a lek. Ruff, *Philomachus pugnax* (Hogan-Warburg, 1966); turkey, *Meleagris gallopavo* (Watts, 1968; Watts and Stokes, 1971); blue-backed manakin, *Chiroxipha pareola* (Snow, 1963).
  B) Feeding of young involved. No cases known.
III) Origin connected with surplus of males due to skewed sex ratio
  A) Feeding of young not involved. No cases known.
  B) Helpers feed young at a small to moderate proportion of nests. Superb blue wren, *Malurus cyaneus* (Rowley, 1965*b*); bushtit, *Psaltriparus minimus "melanotis"* (Skutch, 1961); pygmy and brown-headed nuthatches, *Sitta pygmaea, S. pusilla* (Norris, 1958); Tasmanian native hen, *Tribonyx morteirii* (Smith and Ridpath, 1972); colonial bee-eaters, Meropidae (Fry, 1972); colonial pied kingfishers, *Ceryle rudis* (Douthwaite in Fry, 1972).
  C) Helpers regular at most nests. No cases known.
IV) Origin by non-dispersal of young in species with all-purpose territories
  A) Feeding of young not involved. No clear cases.
  B) Helpers feed young at a small to moderate proportion of nests; helpers typically immatures.
    1) Most young of both sexes stay one year with parents before dispersal; some help feed siblings. Florida scrub jay, *Aphelocoma c. coerulescens* (Woolfenden, personal communication; Westcott, 1970); probably rufous-fronted thornbird, *Placellodomus rufifrons* (Skutch, 1969).
    2) Some young males stay with parents and help feed siblings; females disperse. Superb blue wren, *Malurus cyaneus* (Rowley, 1965*b*); kookaburra, *Dacelo gigas* (Parry in Fry, 1972).
  C) Helpers regular at most nests; helpers typically immatures of either sex; only one pair of breeding adults per territory. Tufted jay, *Cyanocorax dickeyi* (Crossin, 1967); brown jay, *Psilorhinus morio* (Skutch, 1935; Selander, 1959); probably magpie-jay, *Calocitta formosa* (Skutch, 1953).
  D) Similar to the preceding but with both adult and immature helpers and frequently with two or more breeding pairs; nest building and incubation by pairs at separate nests and without aid from helpers. Mexican jay, *Aphelocoma ultramarina* (Brown, 1963*b*, 1970, 1972).
  E) Similar to preceding but frequently two or more pairs share in building, laying, and incubating at one nest. Anis, Crotophaginae (Davis, 1942).
  F) Similar to preceding but no evidence of pairing within the flock. White-winged chough, *Corcorax melanorhamphus* (Rowley, 1965*a*).
V) Origin involves distastefulness
  A) Feeding of young not involved. No cases known.
  B) Helpers regular at moderate to large proportion of nests. Anis (*Crotophaga, Guira*). Highly speculative.

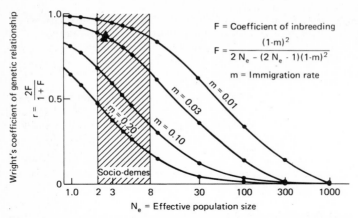

Figure 3 Relationship between average coefficient of genetic relationship, r, and effective population size, N_e, at various equilibria between the outbreeding effects of immigration, m, and the inbreeding effects of small population size. The range of socio-deme sizes found in Mexican jays is shaded. (A socio-deme is a deme that is bounded by social constraints; an eco-deme is bounded by ecological or geographical constraints.) The triangle marks the value of r that was estimated using uncorrected data from field observations; N_e was estimated as 2.6, immigration rate as 0.03, and r as 0.9. With a correction for overlapping generations N_e would be about 3.9 and r would be 0.8. The immigration rate per generation could be higher or lower than the yearly immigration rate, which has been used here as an estimate of the per generation rate.

are nearly always adult males. It was recently pointed out by Smith and Ridpath (1972) that this situation through kin selection should favor brothers helping each other, and this is usually the case in the Tasmanian native hen, in which the young are driven away by their parents before they can help with the next year's brood.

A fifth factor in Table 2, distastefulness, is highly speculative. It could lead to reduced dispersal of the members of a family in the manner described by Fisher in 1929 (1958, p. 177) and to increased survival rates deriving from the protection acquired by the occasional sacrifice of one member of a group, as in butterflies (Turner, 1971). As will be argued below, these factors in birds are conducive to the evolution of communal breeding. It is worth noting that anis are said to possess a "disagreeable odor" (Davis, 1940). Whether they actually are avoided by predators is a point which merits testing in the field and laboratory.

The most likely mode of origin of the advanced forms of communal breeding is by retention of young from earlier broods for longer and longer periods. The comparative series in the New World jays illustrates and supports this theory (Table 1, Fig. 1). The group contains species at various grades of specialization, the widest extremes being found within one small genus (*Aphelocoma*).

The lowest grades are found in the scrub jay. California mainland populations do not have helpers; territories are defended by pairs and young disperse from their parents in their first fall, often forming large flocks. Some at least breed in their first spring (personal observation). In contrast, in the isolated Florida populations studied by Woolfenden (personal communication) and Westcott (1970) young normally remained within their parental territory until their second year. Although they normally remained away from their parents in the territory, they occasionally acted as helpers. Thus, the first indications of communal breeding are accompanied by delayed reproduction and reduced dispersal. It is perhaps noteworthy that the total population in Florida is rather small and is dissected into demes by its occurence in small areas of thickets isolated from each other.

The next higher grades are characterized by the regular retention and non-dispersal of young which then regularly help feed the next generation raised by their parents. Each flock contains only one breeding pair, and the young presumably usually leave the flock as they mature. This condition has been studied in the tufted (*Cyanocorax dickeyi*) (Crossin, 1967) and brown jays (*Psilorhinus morio*) (Skutch, 1935, 1960; Selander, 1959) and probably occurs also in the magpie jay (*Calocitta formosa*) (Skutch, 1953).

The highest grade of communal breeding presently known in jays is represented by the Mexican jay (Brown, 1970, 1972). The genus *Cissilopha* also shows some of the same features, but few details of social organization for it are available (Hardy, 1969c; personal communication). In the Mexican jay the young continue to remain with their parents; when mature they breed in pairs in their home flock at separate nests and most individuals probably live their entire lives within their homeflock territory. Young do not attempt to pair and breed until the age of three years or more. At this grade, the delayed reproduction and reduced dispersal which was first noticed in the Florida scrub jay are carried to an extreme.

The highest grades of communal breeding have not been found in jays. These differ from the system of the Mexican jay by the participation of adult helpers in the nest building and incubation phases so that two or more pairs may build and lay in the same nest. Only once have I observed two females laying and incubating in one nest in the Mexican jay (unpublished), but in the anis (Davis, 1942) and the white-winged chough (Rowley, 1965a) this condition is fairly common. Paradoxically, the occurence of anis (Marchant, 1960) in pairs also seems to be more common than in the Mexican jay.

In brief, comparative study suggests that communal breeding may have originated in more than one way, and that the principal way probably involves retention of the young in the family in a unified, socially integrated flock. The plausibility of this evolutionary pathway to sociality in jays is strengthened by the existence of a series of species with intermediate degrees of specialization. Since communal behavior is so common among New World jays, the possibility must be taken seriously that in some cases breeding in isolated pairs may have evolved from breeding communally, rather than vice versa.

ECOLOGY AND NATURAL SELECTION IN COMMUNAL BREEDING

Comparative studies of behavior and social organization are useful for recognizing different grades of specialization and possible connecting links between them, but they do not reveal why evolution might have proceeded in one direction or another.

To gain insight into the selective forces involved, it is necessary to compare the ecology of related communal and non-communal species. In this section I shall use ecological information from my continuing study of the Mexican jay to develop hypotheses concerning the selection pressures promoting communal breeding in jays.

Old Theories: Climate and Geography

Various authors have remarked on the correlations between communal breeding and climate or geography. Rowley (1965b) regarded the social system of *Malurus cyaneus* in southeastern Australia as an adaptation to "widely varying climate." In a review of communal breeding Rowley (1968) suggested that dispersal of the annual crop of young is not so urgent where the winter (or non-breeding season) is not so rigorous as that in the Northern Hemisphere. Harrison (1969) considered that the likeliest common factor underlying the high frequency of communal breeding among species of Australian birds to be climate, mentioning aridity and unpredictability of rainfall. Fry (1972) pointed out the prevalence of communal breeding in "hot climates," as compared with the cool Temperate Zones of the world. None of these correlations is without numerous exceptions. I submit that there is one more basic, principal underlying cause of these correlations, namely, that communal breeders are nearly all non-migrant, permanent residents. It is well known that rather long migrations are characteristic of most species of birds north of the tropics but are comparatively rare in the tropics. Since it is better in terms of fitness for a helper to aid his parents than to aid strangers (Hamilton, 1963, 1964), we may expect the mixing of individuals on migration to select against helpers and communal breeding. Probably another deterrent to communal breeding in temperate and arctic-alpine areas is the greater frequency of *r*-selection in those areas than in the tropics (discussed further below).

Demographic Portrait of a Communal Breeder: Evidence for K-selection

Judging from its demography, the Mexican jay is relatively K-selected in the sense of MacArthur and Wilson (1967). This is made most apparent by comparing the Mexican jay to the closely related scrub jay and other north Temperate Zone jays (which are relatively *r*-selected).

A delay in the age of first breeding until about three years is the principal curtailment of reproduction in the Mexican jay. The Steller's jay (Brown, 1964) and blue jay (Hickey, 1952; Laskey, 1958) are known to breed in their first year as is the California scrub jay (Pitelka in Amadon, 1944b; Brown, personal observation), but the Florida scrub jay probably breeds first at two years of age (Amadon, 1944b; Westcott, 1970). Clutch size in the Arizona population of the Mexican jay is usually four or five, as it is in the Arizona subspecies of the scrub jay (Bent, 1946). Survival rates of Mexican jays one year old or older on my study area have been quite variable; they were at least .95 in 1969–70 ($n=20$), .42 in 1970–71 ($n=64$), and .80

in 1971–72 ($n=39$), for an average of .72. Corresponding data are not available for the scrub jay (but see Linsdale, 1949); however, Hickey's study of band returns for adult blue jays indicates survival rates of .55–.63. In a small sample ($n=22$) of paired adult Steller's jays a survival rate of at least .91 was recorded in one year (Brown 1963b), but this must have been exceptional. In British jays (*Garrulus glandarius*) Holyoak (1971) used ring recoveries to calculate survival rates in the first, second, and subsequent years as .60 ($n=89$), .45 ($n=53$), and .59 ($n=44$) respectively. Although few comparative data for jays are available, the Mexican jay seems to have a relatively high rate of survival, with the exception of the catastrophic winter of 1970–71. Demographic data for other communal breeders are vague or unavailable, but *Corcorax* delays reproduction until the age of four years (Rowley, 1965a), and *Malurus cyaneus* helpers delay reproduction for one year (Rowley, 1965b). In other communal jays reproduction is delayed at least a year and yearlings posses distinctive coloration (e.g., *Cyanocorax dickeyi, Psilorhinus, Calocitta, Cissilopha*).

Reduced Dispersal in Communal Breeders

The question of dispersal is an important one since according to the theory of Hamilton (1963, 1964) we should expect helpers (altruists) to be closely related to the parents and young that they help. The commonest origin of helpers seems to be for the young to remain with their parents when the young of non-communal species normally disperse away from their parents (Skutch, 1961; Lack, 1968; Rowley, 1968; Harrison, 1969). In New World jays this mode of origin of helpers has been demonstrated using color banding in the Mexican jay (Brown, 1972) and Florida scrub jay (Westcott, 1970). In *Psilorhinus* (Skutch, 1935, 1960), *Cyanocorax dickeyi* (Crossin, 1967), *Calocitta* (Skutch, 1953), and *Cissilopha beecheii* (Hardy, personal communication) the helpers are immature yearlings and yearlings associate with their presumed parents in family-sized groups. In some other social jays the yearlings associate with their presumed parents in family-sized groups, but the species have not yet been studied to confirm the occurrence of helpers or the relationship between helpers and parents, e.g., *Aphelocoma unicolor,* and various species of *Cyanolyca, Cyanocorax,* and *Cissilopha.* The evidence for the acquisition of helpers by non-dispersal and retention of young in the family is thus strong among New World jays.

In most of these communal species the young helpers presumably leave the family group upon attaining sexual maturity. Except in the Florida scrub jay (Westcott, 1970) nothing is known of this dispersal. In contrast, the offspring of Mexican jays are known to stay with their family even when mature. Dispersal away from a study area is, of course, difficult to detect, but dispersal into it can be observed. Flocks normally contain two breeding pairs and up to four have been recorded (Brown, 1963b, 1970, 1972). If dispersal occurs, movement into an area should average about equal to movement out of it, but one completely color-banded flock studied in four successive breeding seasons showed no immigrations. Recruitment to the breeding stock came from maturing individuals within the flock, and recruitment to the flock came from reproduction within the flock. In this and other flocks a large percentage of each age class present in one year is also present in the same flock the next year. Thus, non-dispersal can be documented for all age classes. Disappearances from the flock are of the magnitude attributable to mortality. Although over 100 nestlings and many adults have been banded over a wide area, no distant movements of dispersing birds have been detected despite good opportunities to detect them. Dispersal is not absent since occasional ($n=5$) transfers of individuals from one flock to an adjacent one have been recorded, but such events are rare and are not a regular and conspicuous yearly event, nor are they characteristic of any one age class.

The Role of Habitat

Communal breeders tend to have lower reproductive rates than their nearest non-communal relatives, mainly because so many individuals are helpers rather than breeders. Their relatively old age structure and low dispersal suggest that they are adapted for long-continued competitive conditions at population densities near their carrying capacities (K-selected) rather than for colonizing new or repetitively available habitats (r-selected). Consequently, we should expect to find communal breeding among species inhabiting stable, climax vegetation forms more frequently than among species characteristic of transient environments. I am not prepared to test this prediction by analyzing the habitat requirements of many species at this time, but a comparison between the scrub and Mexican jays illustrates the point. The scrub jay is widely distributed in western North America, where it inhabits a variety of habitats (Pitelka, 1951) including scrubby areas and chapparal, much of which is transient and created by forest fires. By contrast, the Mexican jay is found in pine-oak woodland, especially where it borders streams. The higher reproductive rate and wider dispersal of the scrub jay may be viewed as adaptations for finding and exploiting newly available suitable habitat. The Mexican jay is dependent on relatively mature woodland and is adapted for maintaining clans there; its powers of colonizing newly available habitat seem to be relatively low. In support of this, invasion years are a regular phenomenon in the non-communal scrub, Steller's, blue, and piñon jays, but they are unknown in the communal Mexican jay (Phillips et al, 1964; Westcott, 1969).

Quite a different influence of habitat might be in promoting conditions favorable for group selection, especially among kin groups. For example, certain anis (*Crotophaga ani, C. sulcirostris*) inhabit savanna habitat in which breeding was originally restricted mainly to scattered, small patches of trees surrounded by grassland. Davis (1942) felt that the use of small patches of trees for roosting and nesting by more than one pair facilitated the evolution of communal nesting by bringing individuals into contact with each other. This is true so far as it goes, but does not explain why a communal rather than a colonial social system based on pairs resulted. A population divided by habitat restrictions into small local groups of individuals is prone to inbreeding within groups. The resulting increase in genetic relatedness within groups might under certain conditions facilitate kin-group selection.

Inbreeding and Kin-Selection

Hamilton (1963, 1964) has pointed out a relationship between genes conferring altruistic or helping behavior and the degree of genetic relationship, r, between the helper and the recipient. If closeness of relationship has been an important factor in the evolution of actual examples of communal breeding, we should expect to find a high r among members of a communal group. A rough estimate of r within a flock can be obtained for the flocks of Mexican jays that I have studied.

It is desirable to estimate r between helpers and recipients, but this cannot yet be done. Since each individual behaves as both a helper and a breeder (recipient of aid) if he lives long enough, it is informative to estimate the average r among members of a flock regardless of individual status. Mexican jays begin acting as helpers when about one year old, but they do not begin to receive aid from helpers until they start to breed, which is at the age of three or four years. Their life expectancy after reaching breeding age is relatively high and for the sake of these calculations is assumed to be four years (which is consistent with the estimated survival rate of $s=.72$).

The coefficient of genetic relationship, r, can be determined from the coefficient of inbreeding, F, by the following formula:

$$r = \frac{2F}{1+F}$$

This formula has been derived from one given by Crow and Kimura (1970:79), namely,

$$r_{IJ} = \frac{2f_{IJ}}{\sqrt{(1+f_I)(1+f_J)}},$$

by assuming that $F = f_{IJ} = f_I = f_J$. Here f_{IJ} is the coefficient of inbreeding of the progeny of individuals I and J, and f_I and f_J are the inbreeding coefficients for I and J, while r_{IJ} is the coefficient of genetic relationship between I and J.

In a population that is subdivided into small flocks the resulting inbreeding within a flock is opposed by immigration. The value of F at equilibrium between the inbreeding effects of small population size and the diluting effects of immigration is given by the following formula from Li (1955, p. 305):

$$F = \frac{(1-m)^2}{2N_e - (2N_e - 1)(1-m)^2}$$

Here m is the proportion of immigrants in the breeding population and N_e is the effective population size.

The effective population size can be estimated from observations of the numbers of breeders in each flock, which are shown in Table 3. The mean number of breeders for seven flocks in 4 years ($n = 19$) was 2.6 individuals. Since jays have overlapping generations with iteroparous breeding and the equations are for discrete generations, corrections will be necessary. As a temporary and simple expedient, in the absence of adequate life-table data, I have used $N_e = 3.9$.

The immigration rate is difficult to estimate precisely because it is so small and because all or nearly all members of a flock must be color banded in order to detect an immigrant. Ideally the criterion for a bird to be classed as an immigrant would require that its original home flock be known to be different from the flock in question. This is usually not possible in the early years of a study of a long-lived species. The alternative which I have adopted is to count as immigrants only those jays who were not in the flock the preceding year. By this criterion there were no birds in the entire sample of 32 successful breeders (one or more young fledged) who were immigrants. If breeders and non-breeders of *all* age classes are tallied (see Table 4), the immigration rate is 5 immigrants in a sample of 149. Of these, one disappeared before breeding and the other four bred unsuccessfully. As a tentative estimate of immigration rate into the breeding population, I have taken 5/149 or 0.03 immigrants per year per flock. A correction for overlapping generations would raise this figure. On the other hand, corrections for the age of the immigrants (some of whom would be younger or older than a native just starting to breed) would lower the figure.

Using the estimates of 2.6 for N_e and 0.03 for m, F is estimated as 0.8 and r as 0.9 using $N_e = 3.9$, $r = 0.8$. Consequently, an altruistic jay would be more closely related to the young of a recipient flock member than to his own young if he were to mate at random outside the flock (in which case r to his own young would close to 0.5). Even if the average immigration rate or effective population size were doubled, r would still be greater than 0.5. These are preliminary estimates which will be revised when data on life-table statistics, sex ratios, population dynamics and geneologies are available. By way of comparison it may be noted that the highest value of F given by Cavalli-Sforza and Bodmer (1971, p. 352) for a human population is 0.04. Despite the crudity of the present method of calculation and the simplifying assumptions, it is evident that r in a flock of Mexican jays is very high.

Table 3   Estimate of N_e, Effective Population Size, in Flocks of Mexican Jays

Flock	1969	1970	1971	1972	Total
SWRS	4	4	3	3	14
Bryce	—	4	4	6	14
UC	2	2	0	2	6
Roth	—	2	0	2	4
Hillside	—	—	2	2	4
Corral	—	—	2	2	4
Acinom	—	4	—	—	4
Total	6	16	11	17	50

Only the number of individuals that reared young to the age of banding (16 days) is counted; the actual flock size is larger due to non-breeders and unsuccessful breeders. Mean = 2.6. n = 19. Ny = 2.6. N_e = 3.9. See text.

Table 4   Estimates of Yearly Immigration Rate in Flocks of Mexican Jays

Flock	1970	1971	1972	Total
SWRS	0/15	0/9	0/11	0/35
Bryce	0/13	0/11	0/10	0/34
UC	0/10	0/7	0/7	0/24
Bruhlman	0/7	—	—	0/7
Roth	1/14	0/10	0/6	1/30
Hillside	—	—	2/7	2/7
Corral	—	2/7	0/5	2/12
Total	1/59	2/44	2/46	5/149

The numerators represent the number of immigrants in each flock each year. The denominators represent the total number of individuals in the flock.

This virtually confirms for one population the prediction that can be made from Hamilton's theory that r should indeed be high in communal breeders that behave altruistically.

Territoriality and Competition among Kinship Groups: An Example of Kin-group Selection?

It seems likely from considerations summarized in the models presented by C. Smith (1968) and Horn (1968) that a regular dispersion of single individuals is the most economic dispersion pattern for individuals dependent on homogeneously distributed energy sources. Departures from regular dispersion toward clumping thus require explanation. The dispersion pattern of the Mexican jay is inefficient in comparison to regular dispersion to the extent that the paths of the foraging individuals overlap, and since they travel in a group, this must occur often. There are many advantages of sociality that might counteract this loss of efficiency, but I wish to confine my attention here to one.

If the habitat occupied by a species is dissected by topography and microclimate into areas that differ rather strongly in carrying capacity and productivity, then it will be advantageous for a flock to establish its territory in the most productive area. Behavior that has the effect of retaining the most productive area will be selected. This much is similar to the familiar case of all-purpose territories held by pairs. The critical difference in the Mexican jay is that because of the retention of offspring in the clan *the most productive territories of an area are handed down from generation to generation within the ownership of the same genetic lineages or clans.* The territory becomes the property of the clan genotype over generations, not just for the lifetime of the parents. The genotype of the clan is maintained by the high degree of inbreeding in the clan. The probability of handing down a good territory to one's own descendents is nearly 100 percent for a flock of Mexican jays. It is likely to be significantly lower in the scrub jay or other species in which there is a free-for-all scramble to fill vacancies when they occur and in which the young normally disperse widely in the population as an adaptation for finding territorial vacancies.

The communal system establishes the ground rules for competition among clan genotypes. Genotypes which successfully acquire and keep the best territories tend to produce more surviving young. Such flocks, being larger than others because of having more young, seem to have an advantage in defense against smaller flocks. They are thought to be more likely to survive the loss of some members and to be able to retain the territory in the lineage under adverse conditions. And they are probably more productive of individuals who disperse away from the flock, carrying its genes to other flocks or to establish new territories. Thus, the communal social system enables a form of *kin-group selection.*

One testable prediction of this theory is the following. If the theory is correct, territories should differ significantly in the breeding success of their occupants, and their rank order in terms of number of young produced should be similar from year to year. If it is incorrect, the rank order of territories in productivity of young should tend to vary randomly from year to year. With only three years of data it is too soon to make this test, but preliminary results are consistent with the theory.

Neoteny

At the level of the individual many of the changes described above have the characteristics of neoteny. Traits which are characteristic of the young are maintained in communal species long after they would have disappeared in a non-communal species. In the genus *Aphelocoma* this is evident in plumage, bill color, and behavior (Brown, 1963*b*). Young Mexican jays stay longer in the nest and are dependent on their parents longer than are young scrub jays. The most important developmental change in the evolution of communal breeding, namely the remaining of young in a non-breeding condition with their parents rather than dispersing and breeding, can also be viewed as a continuation into the adult state of a condition that in other species is characteristic of young.

Advantages in Reproduction

In some communal breeders (e.g., *Malurus cyaneus,* certain Timaliids, anis) the young from an early brood help to feed their siblings in a later brood during the same breeding season. This can free the parents from attending to the second brood and allow them to raise a third brood sooner. Similarly, yearling helpers with the first brood free the parents for a second brood sooner. This is clearly advantageous to the parents, particularly when the breeding season is short. However, it is unlikely to be a general explanation for communal breeding since many communal breeders are single-brooded. Among communal jays the Mexican, tufted, and brown jays are typically single-brooded, and regular double broods by the same color-banded female are unknown in any species.

The additional food supplied to the young by helpers must be considered to be an important aspect of communal breeding systems. Very likely in most cases helpers do allow more young to be raised than would be possible without them, simply because more individuals are feeding the young. But only in *Malurus* (Rowley, 1965 *b*), which is only a borderline communal breeder, has it been shown that the number of young raised *per individual* in the social unit is greater in enlarged units than in pairs (1.9 fledglings per adult in threesomes vs. 1.2 in pairs). Against this must be set the observations on *Merops* and *Tribonyx*. In *Merops* Fry (1972) found no difference in fledged young per individual between pairs without and with helpers (usually threesomes). Smith and Ridpath (1972) working with *Tribonyx,* also failed to find greater productivity per adult in pairs with helpers (again mostly threesomes) than in pairs without helpers.

Can the greater productivity of groups with helpers be viewed as a "solution" to the communal breeding problem? I think not. Such a hypothesis suggests that the principal advantages of communal breeding lie in enhanced yearly reproduction, but my observations on jays have revealed lower yearly reproductive rates in communal breeders and higher yearly survival rates compared with non-communal species. Perhaps this paradox can be explained as follows: Communal breeding raises reproductive success but only under certain conditions. These conditions are characterized by intense competition in a population that is always at or near carrying capacity and in which (one may speculate) young birds breeding as pairs are unlikely to be successful. Such conditions favor iteroparous reproduction and long life, especially among individuals and kin-groups inhabiting superior territories. They tend to favor reduced (delayed) reproduction and increased survival. Communal breeding may be viewed as an adaptation for competition under these conditions.

Only by the comparison of life tables for communal and related non-communal forms can the issue be resolved. We need to know the productivity of young per adult in communal vs. non-communal social units to assess reproduction. And we need to know the age-specific survival rates in communal and non-communal social units. Further field work on a variety of species will be necessary to provide a basis for generalization. Mathematical modeling of the alternatives might also be useful.

A SYNOPSIS OF THE HYPOTHESIZED ORIGIN AND MAINTENANCE OF COMMUNAL BREEDING AND ALTRUISM IN JAYS

Three phases in the evolution of communal breeding and altruism can be recognized: (i) *K-selection Phase*. The initial phase in the origin of communal breeding from a non-communal species probably involves a period of K-selection in which competition for living space in an environment continuously at carrying capacity and with few suitable vacant territories causes selection for greater competitive ability. This phase is more likely to occur in non-migratory species inhabiting a stable, mature vegetation form. Since older, experienced individuals with mates and territories are probably better able to compete under such conditions than young ones, an older age structure and greater iteroparity are favored. With fewer territorial vacancies available, the optimal reproductive strategy changes from one of producing many young who disperse widely to find vacancies to one of producing fewer young who by virtue of experience gained in a year or more of immature apprenticeship have a better chance of competing successfully for a territory, remaining on it, and reproducing successfully. Reduced dispersal in the preceding phase sets the stage for the next phase. (ii) *Kin-selection Phase.* Because of the close genetic relationship between parent and offspring, the young who actively help their parents to raise young during their apprenticeship are selected more strongly than those who do not help at all or who help distant relatives. If the probability of a newly maturing jay finding a territorial vacancy by dispersing becomes as low as the probability of the death of its parent of the same sex, then a strategy will be favored in which half of the young remain with their parents in a subordinate, helping condition but ready to breed should the parent disappear. As the chances of a dispersant finding a good territory decrease, the adaptive value of traits which aid in the retention of good territories by the family increases. Since this happens simultaneously with the pro-longed retention of young in the family, selection further reinforces the creation of family-owned territories because large families are likely to dominate small ones. This makes possible the third phase: (iii) *Kin-group-selection Phase.* If this trend continues, flock size and territory size increase, and more than one breeding pair may be tolerated in a territory. Inbreeding becomes more intense, and as the members of a flock become more nearly genetically uniform, the flock or clan becomes a more important genetic unit in natural selection. Ultimately selection comes to favor the most successful flock genotypes. Individual genotypes are selected mainly as the function harmoniously in a flock. Aggressiveness within the flock, selfishness and cheating might be selected against if they lowered flock productivity and competitive ability.

SOME TESTABLE PREDICTIONS OF THE PROPOSED THEORY

At the risk of some redundancy the following predictions are offered in the hope of stating briefly certain points which may be tested in future field investigations. When other communally breeding birds are studied the theory predicts them to have the characteristics listed, when compared with related non-communal species.

Correlates of K-selection

1 Delayed maturity in both sexes.
2 Lowered reproductive rate and increased survival rate.
3 Diminished dispersal. Dispersants are fewer in number and do not travel as far.
4 Not a regular, long-distance migrant; rarely a short-distance migrant.
5 Characteristically found in stable as opposed to transitional habitats.
6 Prominent density-dependent mortality.

Correlates of Kin-selection (in Temporary Groups and Families)

7 Helpers (altruists) are on the average closely related to recipients, and less so to non-recipients.

8 Helpers are found in small groups with adults, all of whom are kept together by strong social bonds.

9 Outsiders are strongly repelled, especially by larger flocks (territoriality).

Correlates of Kin-Group-Selection (in Groups which Last for Many Years)

10 Territories differ significantly in productivity. The rank order of flocks in respect to production of young will tend to remain the same from year to year.

11 Adaptations for retaining good territories in the same genetic lineage will be favored. The territory occupied by a flock will show little change in location, areas, and boundaries over intervals of many years. Larger flocks will show less change than smaller ones.

12 Genetically the future occupants of a territory are descended from the present occupants, especially for larger flocks. Genetic differences between flocks (and between demes created by local topography) will tend to remain the same from year to year.

13 Adaptations that reduce and formalize intra-flock conflict will be strengthened; intra-flock aggression should be inconspicuous.

14 Because territories are defended by flocks rather than pairs, there should be virtually no vacant territories of good quality.

REFERENCES

Amadon, D. 1944a. The genera of Corvidae and their relationships. Amer. Mus. Novitates (1251):1–21.

Amadon, D. 1944b. A preliminary life history study of the Florida jay, *Cyanocitta c. coerulescens.* Amer. Mus. Novitates (1252):1–22.

Balda, R. P., and G. C. Bateman. 1971. Flocking and annual cycle of the piñon jay, *Gymnorhinus cyanocephalus.* Condor 73:287–302, 494.

Beer, C. G. 1971. Individual recognition of voice in the social behavior of birds. Advan. Study Behav. 3:27–74.

Bent, A. C. 1946. Life histories of North American jays, crows, and titmice. U.S. Nat. Mus. Bull. 191:1–495.

Blake, E. R., and C. Vaurie. 1962. Family Corvidae, p. 204–282. *In* E. Mayr and J. C. Greenway, Jr. [ed.], Check-list of birds of the world. Mus. Comp. Zool., Cambridge, Mass.

Brown, J. L. 1963a. Aggressiveness, dominance and social organization in the Steller jay. Condor 65:460–484.

Brown, J. L. 1963b. Social organization and behavior of the Mexican jay. Condor 65:126–153.

Brown, J. L. 1964. The integration of agonistic behavior in the Steller's jay. Univ. Calif. Publ. Zool. 60:223–328.

Brown, J. L. 1970. Cooperative breeding and altruistic behavior in the Mexican jay, *Aphelocoma ultramarina.* Anim. Behav. 18:366–378.

Brown, J. L. 1972. Communal feeding of nestlings in the Mexican jay (*Aphelocoma ultramarina*): interflock comparisons. Anim. Behav. 20:395–402.

Brown, J. L., and G. H. Orians. 1970. Spacing patterns in mobile animals. Annu. Rev. Ecol. Syst. 1:239–262.

Cavalli-Sforza, L. L., and W. F. Bodmer. 1971. The genetics of human populations. Freeman, San Francisco.

Crook, J. H. 1958. Etudes sur le comportement social de *Bubalornis a. albirostris* (Vieillot). Alauda 26:161–195.

Crook, J. H. 1965. The adaptive significance of avian social organizations. Symp. Zool. Soc. London 14:181–218.

Crossin, R. S. 1967. The breeding biology of the tufted jay. Proc. West. Found. Vert. Zool. 1:265–297.

Crow, J. F., and M. Kimura. 1970. An introduction to population genetics theory. Harper and Row, N.Y.

Davis, D. E. 1940. Social nesting habits of *Guira guira.* Auk. 57:472–484.

Davis, D. E. 1942. The phylogeny of social nesting habits in the Crotophaginae. Quart. Rev. Biol. 17:115–134.

Dow, D. D. 1970. Communal behaviour of nesting noisy miners. Emu 70:131–134.

Fisher, R. A. 1958. The genetical theory of natural selection. Dover Publ., N.Y.

Friedmann, H. 1935. Bird societies, p. 142–182. *In* C. Murchison [ed.], Handbook of social psychology. Clark Univ. Press, Worchester, Mass.

Friedmann, H. 1950. The breeding habits of the weaver birds. A study in the biology of behaviour patterns. Annu. Rep. Smithson. Inst. 1949:292–316.

Fry, C. H. 1972. The social organization of bee-eaters (Meropidae) and cooperative breeding in hot-climate birds. Ibis 114:1–14.

Hamilton, W. D. 1963. The evolution of altruistic behavior. Amer. Natur. 97:354–356.

Hamilton, W. D. 1964. The genetical evolution of social behaviour. I and II. J. Theoret. Biol. 7:1–52.

Hardy, J. W. 1961. Studies in behavior and phylogeny of certain New World jays (Garrulinae). Univ. Kans. Sci. Bull. 42:13–149.

Hardy, J. W. 1964. Behavior, habitat and relationships of jays of the genus *Cyanolyca.* Occas. Pap. C. C. Adams Center Ecol. Stud. 11:1–14.

Hardy, J. W. 1969*a*. A taxonomic revision of the New World jays. Condor 71:360–375.

Hardy, J. W. 1969*b*. Habits and habitats of certain South American jays. Los Angeles Co. Mus. Contrib. Sci. (165):1–16.

Hardy, J. W. 1969*c*. Comparative ecology and evolutionary relationships of two Central American jays. Amer. Phil. Soc. Yearb. 1969:305–307.

Hardy, J. W. 1971. Habitat and habits of the dwarf jay, *Aphelocoma nana.* Wilson Bull. 83:5–30.

Harrison, C. J. O. 1969. Helpers at the nest in Australian passerine birds. Emu 69:30–40.

Hickey, J. J. 1952. Survival studies of banded birds. Special Scientific Report: Wildlife No. 15. U.S. Dept. Interior, Fish and Wildlife Service, Washington, D.C.

Hogan-Warburg, A. J. 1966. Social behavior of the ruff, *Philomachus pugnax* (L.). Ardea 54:109–229.

Holyoak, D. 1971. Movements and mortality of Corvidae. Bird Study 18:97–106.

Horn, H. S. 1968. The adaptive significance of colonial nesting in the Brewer's blackbird *Euphagus cyanocephalus*). Ecology 49:682–694.

Lack, D. 1968. Ecological adaptations for breeding in birds. Methuen, London.

Laskey, A. R. 1958. Blue jays at Nashville, Tennessee: movements, nesting, age. Bird-banding 29:211–218.

Li, C. C. 1955. Population genetics. Univ. Chicago Press, Chicago.

Ligon, J. D. 1971. Late summer-autumnal breeding of the piñon jay in New Mexico. Condor 73:147–153.

Linsdale, J. M. 1949. Survival in birds banded at the Hastings Reservation. Condor 51:88–96.

MacArthur, R. H., and E. O. Wilson. 1967. The theory of island biogeography. Monogr. Pop. Biol. 1:1–203.

Marchant, S. 1960. The breeding of some S. W. Ecuadorian birds. Ibis 102:349–382.

Norris, R. A. 1958. Comparative biosystematics and life history of the nuthatches *Sitta pygmaea* and *Sitta pusilla*. Univ. Calif. Publ. Zool. 56:119–300.

Phillips, A. R., J. Marshall, and G. Monson. 1964. The birds of Arizona. Univ. Arizona Press, Tucson.

Pitelka, F. A. 1951. Speciation and ecologic distribution in American jays of the genus *Aphelocoma*. Univ. Calif. Publ. Zool. 50:195–464.

Rowley, I. 1965a. White-winged choughs. Aust. Natur. Hist. 15:81–85.

Rowley, I. 1965b. The life history of the superb blue wren *Malurus cyaneus*. Emu 64:251–297.

Rowley, I. 1968. Communal species of Australian birds. Bonn. Zool. Beitr. 19:362–370.

Selander, R. K. 1959. Polymorphism in Mexican brown jays. Auk 76:385–417.

Sick, H. 1959. Notes on the biology of two Brazilian swifts, *Chaetura andrei* and *Chaetura cinereiventris*. Auk 76:471–477.

Skutch, A. F. 1935. Helpers at the nest. Auk 52:257–273.

Skutch, A. F. 1953. The white-throated magpie-jay. Wilson Bull. 65:68–74.

Skutch, A. F. 1960. Life histories of Central American birds. II. Pac. Coast Avif. (34):1–593.

Skutch, A. F. 1961. Helpers among birds. Condor 63:198–226.

Skutch, A. F. 1967. Life histories of Central American highland birds. Publ. Nuttall Ornithol. Club (7):1–213.

Skutch, A. F. 1969. A study of the rufous-fronted thornbird and associated birds. Wilson Bull. 81:5–43.

Smith, C. C. 1968. The adaptive nature of social organization in the genus of tree squirrels *Tamiasciurus*. Ecol. Monogr. 38:31–63.

Smith, J. M., and M. G. Ridpath. 1972. Wife sharing in the Tasmanian native hen, *Tribonyx mortierii:* a case of kin selection? Amer. Natur. 106:447–452.

Snow, D. W. 1963. The display of the blue-backed manakin, *Chiroxiphia pareola* in Tobago, W. I. Zoologica 48:167–176.

Sutton, G. M., R. B. Lea, and E. P. Edwards. 1950. Notes on the ranges and breeding habits of certain Mexican birds. Bird-banding 21:45–59.

Swainson, G. W. 1970. Co-operative rearing in the bell miner. Emu 70:183–188.

Turcek, F. J., and L. Kelso. 1968. Ecological aspects of food transportation and storage in the Corvidae. Comm. Behav. Biol. A 1:277–297.

Turner, J. R. G. 1971. Experiments on the demography of tropical butterflies. II. Longevity and home range behaviour in *Heliconius erato.* Biotropica 3:21–31.

Wagner, H. O. 1955. Bruthelfer unter den Vögeln. Veröff. Überseemus. Brehem Reihe A 2:327–330.

Watts, C. R. 1968. Rio Grande turkeys in the mating season. Trans. 33rd N. Amer. Wildl. Natur. Resources Conf., p. 205–210.

Watts, C. R., and A. W. Stokes. 1971. The social order of turkeys. Sci. Amer. 224(6): 112–118.

Westcott, P. W. 1969. Relationships among three species of jays wintering in southeastern Arizona. Condor 71:353–359.

Westcott, P. W. 1970. Ecology and behavior of the Florida scrub jay. Ph.D. Thesis. Univ. Florida.

Wetmore, A., and B. H. Swales. 1931. The birds of Haiti and the Dominican Republic. U.S. Nat. Mus. Bull. 155:345–352.

Part Four

Homo sapiens

What we believe of man *affects the behavior of men for it determines what each expects of the other. Theories of education, of political science, of economics, and the very policies of governments are based on implicit concepts of the nature of man.*

Leon Eisenberg
The "Human" Nature of Human Nature*

It is frequently observed that the origins of man are shrouded in antiquity. Anthropological discoveries in recent years have traced our lineage further back in time and have filled many gaps in preexisting knowledge. There are strong indications of coexistence with other anthropoids coupled with tantalizing suggestions of interspecies competition. But at this frontier of anthropology the data are cold and hard: a few teeth, a few bones, a few chips of stone. We may, in time, learn when and how we became *Homo,* but we can never know when and how we became human. The essence of humanity is to be aware of self and contemplative of being. It is pleasing

*Science 176: 123–128 (1972).

to speculate that *Homo* became human when he first began to contemplate his being.

Humanity, however one may define it, is nonetheless a derivative of specific behavioral and structural traits in some prehuman anthropoid stock. The nature of man may include attributes unique to our species, but an unweighted listing of characteristics would include a preponderance that are shared with other species. To what extent, then, is the nature of man truly unique, or, conversely, to what extent are we merely another species (albeit a remarkably successful one) in the catalog of earth's fauna?

Inquiry into the nature of man has been formalized in the writings of anthropology, sociology, psychology, and philosophy. Most of this vast literature is ethnocentric to such a degree that research on homologies with nonhuman species may be viewed as only a minor aspect of the larger inquiry. The true merit and relevance of such studies has, however, generated considerable debate and controversy. A relatively small number of investigators have repeatedly called attention to varied aspects of the biological basis of human nature. Sociobiology has been viewed by some critics as merely the most recent exposition of this long-held view that the biological basis of human nature merits full consideration. In that sense, then, sociobiology as applied to the study of human nature is not new. Some question arises, however, as to whether sociobiologists may not indeed offer either new methodologies or new insights relevant to existing issues and controversies. The answer seems to be a conditional yes on each point.

Sociobiology, defined broadly, calls for investigation of sociality by combined study of species attributes and environmental variables. Model building, hypothesis, and prediction have been employed to advantage in the study of animal sociality, as exemplified by papers in the preceding section of this reader. Analogous approaches to the study of some human social behaviors may well generate new understanding in established areas of inquiry. The work of Dyson-Hudson and Smith that is reprinted here exemplifies the possibility for fruitful research and synthesis of this kind.

A second contribution from sociobiology to the study of human nature may, to at least some extent, be truly novel. The paradigm of inclusive fitness has become a focal point of human sociobiology in the narrow sense of the term. Inclusive fitness models are now applied to analysis of social behaviors in preliterate societies, such as kinship analysis, aggression, and hypergamy. By extension, the same inclusive fitness models are also applied to analogous aspects of behavior in literate societies. These are the frontiers on which sociobiologists draw sharp criticism for venturing too far too fast with too few hard data. Samples of these criticisms are presented in the fifth section of this reader. Here, a paper by van den Berghe and Barash has been selected as illustrative of the application of inclusive fitness models to the study of human social systems.

Human Territoriality:
An Ecological Reassessment

Rada Dyson-Hudson
Eric Alden Smith
Cornell University

The question of human territoriality has frequently been debated, but most previous discussions have not sufficiently emphasized ecological variables as major factors determining territoriality. We argue that current theories in sociobiology, especially the model focusing on economic defendability of resources, need to be considered in analyzing human territoriality. According to this model, territoriality is expected to occur when critical resources are sufficiently abundant and predictable in space and time, so that costs of exclusive use and defense of an area are outweighed by the benefits gained from resource control. This model is developed, and then applied to several locally adapted human populations (Northern Ojibwa, Basin-Plateau Indians, and Karimojong). Variations in territorial responses for these groups seem to accord with the predictions of the economic defendability model.

The question of human territoriality has been the focus of much discussion and controversy (e.g., Crook 1973, Esser 1971). Discussions of human spatial organization have tended to polarize into an either-or situation: either humans are territorial by nature or they are not. At one extreme, Ardrey (1966:1) believes that territoriality is a genetically fixed form of behavior which has evolved in most species, including our own. Cohen (1976:55) believes in the existence of a fundamental "human tendency to achieve territorial control (whether instinctively or culturally derived)." On the other hand, evidence indicating a lack of rigid territoriality in many contemporary hunting and gathering groups has been viewed as supporting the argument that humans are not by nature territorial (Reynolds 1966:449).

Acknowledgments. We would like to thank the following people for reading and commenting on the manuscript: Ruth Buskirk, Steve Emlen, Lew Oring, and graduate students in the "Behavior Lunch Group," Section of Neurobiology and Behavior; Davydd Greenwood, Charles Hockett, Ilene Stern Wallace, and Bruce Winterhalder, of the Department of Anthropology, and Steve McRae, Department of Natural Resources, all of Cornell University; Brooke Thomas, Alan Swedlund, and graduate students in the Social Biology Seminar, Department of Anthropology, University of Massachusetts at Amherst; and William Durham, Departments of Anthropology and Human Biology, Stanford University. Marge Ciaschi efficiently and cheerfully typed the manuscript. R. Dyson-Hudson received aid from National Science Foundation grant GS 52307 during the period when this article was written. N. Dyson-Hudson, Department of Anthropology at the State University of New York, Binghamton, provided advice and comments on the section dealing with Karimojong Territoriality.

A version of this paper was read at a Symposium on Sociobiology at the American Anthropological Association's annual meeting in 1976. A longer version will appear in *Sociobiology and Human Social Organization,* N. Chagnon and W. Irons, eds. (in press, Cambridge, MA: Duxbury).

The territoriality controversy in anthropology has primarily focused on hunter-gatherers. King (1975, 1976) and Peterson (1975) are recent examples of a long line of anthropologists (e.g., Radcliffe-Brown 1930, Service 1962, Williams 1974) who argue that some form of territorial band is the optimum pattern of spatial organiza-tion for hunter-gatherers under all or most ecological conditions. Various authors (e.g., Lee and DeVore 1968, Damas 1969) have argued that a more flexible pattern of spatial organization and resource utilization is typical of hunter-gatherers. How-ever, both of these approaches overlook the diversity of hunter-gatherer social and territorial organization (Martin 1974) and fail to consider adequately the effects of different patterns of resource distribution on patterns of spatial organization. Even when variations in human spatial organization are noted, they are often presented as deviations from some natural norm or optimum.

Current research in sociobiology indicates an enormous complexity in animal territoriality which parallels the complexity of spatial organization found in human groups. Sociobiologists and ecologists have developed a general theory of economic defendability of resources in order to analyze the diversity of animal spatial organ-ization, which allows us to ask more interesting and sophisticated questions than those that have dominated discussions of human territoriality in the past.

We believe that the issue of human territoriality can be approached by analyz-ing anthropological data from a theoretically sound perspective, using the models developed by various biologists, and that this approach will be useful in explaining the diversity of human spatial organization. (These in fact parallel some of the ideas, implicit or explicit, in Steward's 1938 study of human ecology.) In particular, attention needs to be paid to the ecological contexts and consequences of human behavior in a much more extensive and rigorous fashion than has been typical of studies in either ecological anthropology or popular ethology. Rather than devoting our energies to such questions as "Is *Homo sapiens* an innately territorial species?" we suggest examining human resource defense and utilization within an adaptive framework.

The goal of this paper is to advance our understanding of the behavioral ecology of the human species with regard to resource defense and spatial organization, by analyzing some of the cross-cultural (multipopulational) data of anthropology in the theoretical framework of sociobiology (Wilson 1975) and evolutionary ecology (Crook 1970, Pianka 1974). First, some recent developments in the study of animal territoriality and resource utilization are briefly summarized, and a general model relating resource distribution to spatial organization is presented. Then we examine the relevance of these concepts for the human case by examining the predictions of the model in light of the evidence from several locally adapted populations, where relationships between the social organization and environmental parameters are more amenable to ecological analysis.

We do not intend to offer a general review of human territoriality here. Rather we wish to apply the ecological model presented in the following section to three selected examples as a preliminary test of its explanatory usefulness with respect to humans. The examples we have chosen are the Basin-Plateau Indians, consisting of several different groups in geographical proximity and sharing certain linguistic and cultural features but exploiting different microenvironments; the Northern Ojibwa Indians, showing significant changes over time in spatial organization and subsistence strategies; and the Karimojong of East Africa, illustrating the degree of complexity in spatial organization that can exist in a single human population at one point in time.

We define a territory as an area occupied more or less exclusively by an individual or group by means of repulsion through overt defense of some form of communication (see below). Personal space and territoriality are often lumped together, but in this paper we are concerned with the latter. The question of whether humans are innately aggressive is also often implicit or explicit in arguments about human territoriality. We will not deal with this aspect of the controversy (see Wilson 1971 and Durham 1976 for a discussion of this point).

ECOLOGICAL THEORY

While human territoriality has been a major issue for little over a decade, the study of animal territoriality in general (and of avian cases in particular) has a significantly longer history. Several general reviews are available (Burt 1943, Carpenter 1958, Hinde 1956, Klopfer 1969, Tinbergen 1957, Wilson 1975), so neither a history of the concept nor a listing of alternative definitions will be attempted here. Rather, we will attempt to demonstrate how current ecological approaches to the study of spatial organization shift attention away from older questions about territoriality (Is there a defended area or only mutual exclusivity? Is the tendency innate or learned?) to a focus on the critical parameters of resource distribution and economic defendability.

In the definition of what constitutes territoriality, much dispute has revolved around whether to emphasize *defense* of a particular area, or *exclusive use* of an area regardless of how it is maintained. In order to distinguish territoriality from cases where exclusive use is due solely to factors such as widely dispersed resources or very low density of individuals, we choose to adopt the definition used by E. O. Wilson (1975:256): a territory is "an area occupied more or less exclusively by an animal or group of animals by means of repulsion through overt defense or advertisement." This definition emphasizes the behavioral basis of territoriality without overemphasizing one possible mechanism of spacing (aggressive defense) at the expense of other possibilities (e.g., mutual avoidance based on olfactory or visual markings).

Before proceeding further, some prevalent misconceptions must be dealt with. First, it must be realized that the great amount of variability exhibited by animals in aspects of their territorial organization makes many generalizations misleading or invalid. This variability has been the source of much argument and confusion in the literature. Variability can be noted in *structural* (or definitional) categories, such as whether territories are exclusive or overlapping, defended or nondefended, geographically stable or somewhat mobile, or seasonal or permanent. Variability is equally apparent in *functional* characteristics of territories, in that many different patterns of resource utilization are involved (thus, biologists speak of feeding territories, mating territories, all-purpose territories, etc.).

A second major source of error is the conception of territoriality as an innate or species-specific trait. While this may be a valid view for some species (given an adequately sophisticated notion of "innate"), it is clearly mistaken for a wide range of species. Not only can territorial behavior come and go seasonally in many species (something which has long been recognized), but a local population may shift to or from a territorial system rapidly in direct response to nonseasonal alterations in resource distribution. Such variability has been documented in a number of populations recently. For example, artificial introduction of resource concentrations was followed by a shift from nomadic flock-foraging to strict territoriality in White Wagtails (Zahavi 1971). While studies of cynocephalus baboons in various habitats have generally disclosed a nonterritorial (home range) system, recent fieldwork on a population inhabiting a resource-rich swamp habitat revealed a case of exclusive and mutually defended territories (Hamilton et al. 1976). Ongoing studies of various species of nectar-feeding birds have elegantly demonstrated that individuals will shift to and from territorial defense of nectar sources as part of a strategy of maximizing energetic efficiency (Wolf and Hainsworth 1971, Gill and Wolf 1975). The lesson of these and other studies is that territoriality cannot profitably be viewed as an innately fixed and homologous drive found in a multitude of species.

While variability, functional diversity, and flexibility must be given due consideration in analyzing animal spatial organization, this does not mean that a general theory of territoriality is unattainable. With the discrediting of the simpler ethological conceptions of territoriality, theoretical modeling and empirical investigation are being guided by a cost-benefit model that focuses on *economic defendability* (Brown 1964).[1] According to this model, territorial behavior is expected when the costs of exclusive use and defense of an area are outweighed by the benefits gained from this pattern of resource utilization. Economic defendability is determined by the interaction of foraging behavior and territorial defense with the particular distributions in space and time of critical resources.

It should be noted that a number of possible measures may be employed in modeling economic defendability: time, energy, reproductive fitness, or even survival. For most purposes, in dealing with food resources, the use of energy-per-unit time to measure both costs and benefits would seem to be both valid and feasible, although with other types of resources different measures may be more suitable. For operationalizing and empirically measuring economic defendability ratios, we feel that energy is definitely superior to reproductive fitness. However, the underlying assumption of our reasoning is that adaptation (whether genetic or phenotypic) ultimately maximizes fitness and that the net rate of energy gain will tend to correlate highly with this ultimate measure (as discussed in Smith 1977). In other words, the model presented here assumes that: "The territorial strategy evolved is the one that maximizes the increment of fitness due to extraction of energy from the defended area, as compared with the loss of fitness due to the effort and perils of defense" (Wilson 1975:269).

Economic defendability has several components that interact to produce a cost-benefit ratio. The costs of territoriality include (1) the time, energy, and/or risk associated with defending an area; (2) the possible diversion of time and energy from other necessary activities; and (3) the possible negative consequences of relying on a spatially limited area for resources. The benefits of territoriality are simply those that result from exclusive access to critical resources; however, this benefit is conditioned by factor 3 (above) and is relative to alternative (nonterritorial) modes of resource utilization. For any case of territoriality, the ratio of benefits to costs should exceed 1.0 (and probably by a comfortable margin). It can also be argued that adaptive processes in the long run will tend to produce optimal results and, thus, that the benefit/cost ratio for a territorial system should have an average value greater than the nonterritorial alternatives available to the individual or group. However, this last expectation involves the assessment of a broad range of opportunity costs, and the economic defendability model is not sufficient for this pur-pose.

The cost-benefit ratio of a territorial strategy is highly dependent on the pattern of resource distribution, and it is this relationship which must be examined in attempting to account for the presence or absence of territorial organization in any population. For our purposes, the important parameters of resource distribution are predictability and abundance. Predictability has both a spatial component (predictability of location) and a temporal one (predictability in time). Abundance or density of a resource can be measured in several ways: in terms of average density over a broad area (the average for the territory or home range), as an average value within a particular type of microhabitat (within-patch density), and in terms of the fluctuation in density over time (the range of variability). While all these parameters of resource distribution will interact to determine the adaptive value of any foraging strategy, in the interests of clarity we will first consider each parameter separately in terms of the general model of economic defendability.

Resources that are predictable in their spatiotemporal distribution have greater economic defendability than unpredictable resources. A habitat where critical resources are predictable will be most efficiently exploited by a territorial system (holding other resource distribution parameters constant). Geometrical models of foraging indicate that it is more efficient (requires less foraging time or energy for a given amount of return) for individuals to disperse to mutually exclusive foraging areas when food resources tend toward a uniform distribution and are predictable (Horn 1968, Smith 1968). Unpredictability of resources results in lowered benefits of territorial defense (in terms of resources controlled), and, below a certain threshold, territoriality will be uneconomical or even unviable (Brown 1964).

With a sufficient degree of resource unpredictability, clumping of individuals (often termed coloniality for nonhuman species) is expected to occur. Under these situations, efficient resource utilization may depend on the pooling of information about the location of ephemeral resource concentrations. Information may be shared either passively, as in cases of observation and following of successful foragers (Horn 1968, Ward and Zahavi 1973), or actively (as in the case of chimpanzees who advertise finds of patchily distributed and asynchronously fruiting trees by drumming [Reynolds and Reynolds 1965:423]). As an illustration of some of these principles, among primates, the arboreal folivores (such as *Alouatta, Colobus,* and *Presbytis*) usually exhibit strong territoriality, in contrast with most frugivorous and omnivorous species (Bates 1970). This increased frequency of territoriality has been attributed in part to the high defendability of leaf resources, which can be very predictable in the tropics and subtropics (Brown and Orians 1970, Denham 1971, Crook 1972, Eisenberg et al. 1972).

Abundance or density of resources is a more relative parameter than predictability and must be related in each particular case to foraging bioenergetics and group size. In our model, resource density really means *effective* density, not absolute abundance. (Thus, a given area may have a higher biomass of small rodents than of large game, but a human group would probably capture a greater amount of the large game and with greater efficiency; in our terms, the large game would exist at a greater effective density in this example.) In general, increased average density of critical resources makes a territorial system more economically defendable, simply by reducing the area that needs to be defended and thus reducing defense costs. However, density of resources *within a patch* combined with a high degree of unpredictability reduces the economic advantage of territoriality. That is, with sufficient within-patch density and patch unpredictability, localized and ephemeral *superabundances* result, where the temporary glut of resources is more than can be consumed and thus is best shared (either actively or passively) rather than defended. Such a situation may be characteristic of the critical resources for various populations, such as insectivorous birds (Horn 1968, Emlen and Demong 1975), colonial seabirds feeding on dense and unpredictable concentrations of fish (Lack 1968:134 ff.), and chimpanzees foraging for patchily distributed fruit trees (Eisenberg et al. 1972).

Without delving further into theoretical complexities or specific cases, the formal relationships between the parameters of resource distribution discussed above and the economic defendability of different foraging strategies can be summarized schematically (Table I; a graphic version is given in Fig. 1). Note that predictability and abundance of resources interact to determine the adaptive value of different patterns of resource utilization. In summary, a territorial system is most likely under conditions of high density and predictability of critical resources. However, it must be noted that if a resource is so abundant that its availability or rate of capture is not in any way limiting to a population, then there is no benefit to be gained by its defense and territoriality is not expected to occur. With relatively scarce but still predictable resources, large home ranges with some degree of overlap would be expected. With unpredictability of resources above a certain threshold, a territorial tie to a fixed area is not economically defendable, and the degree of movement in foraging over a large area must increase (nomadism). Depending on the average density of the resources within a patch, unpredictable resources are most efficiently exploited by communal sharing of information (high average density) or by a high amount of dispersion (low average density). While this sort of simplified correlation between resource distributions and foraging strategy cannot do justice to the complexity of specific cases, we feel it provides a general framework for explaining the occurrence (or nonoccurrence) of territoriality that is far superior to many alternative formulations.

In the next section, we test the relevance of the economic defendability model for an understanding of human territorial behavior. Ideally, we should make a systematic survey of territorial behavior in a random sample of human societies. However, the nature of the data on human territoriality makes such a systematic survey difficult. The term "territory" and "territoriality" tends to be applied to hunter-gatherers and pastoralists, while what may be equivalent behavior among agriculturalists is described in terms of land tenure systems. Even when a group is described as territorial, the nature of the group, the means of territorial defense, and the distribution and abundance of resources, often are not specified. Therefore, to test the model, we selected two ethnographic studies of locally adapted populations which appeared to provide the requisite data for comparison with animal models and data from a third locally adapted population for which we have detailed firsthand information.

HUMAN TERRITORIALITY: THREE CASES

The variation in spatial organization in response to variations in resource distribution found in other animal species can also be seen with human populations. Our first example, the Basin-Plateau Indians, consists of several different groups in geographical proximity and sharing certain linguistic and cultural features but exploiting different microenvironments. The Northern Ojibwa Indians are more geographically, culturally, and ecologically unified, but here a detailed historical record shows significant changes over time in spatial organization and subsistence strategy. Following our examination of these hunter-gatherer cases, we present a more detailed study of the Karimojong of East Africa, illustrating the degree of complexity

Table I   Relationship Between Resource Distribution and Foraging Strategy

Resource distribution	Economic defendability	Resource utilization	Degree of nomadism
A. Unpredictable and Dense	Low	Info-sharing	High
B. Unpredictable and Scarce	Low	Dispersion	Very high
C. Predictable and Dense	High	Territoriality	Low
D. Predictable and Scarce	Fairly low	Home ranges	Low-medium

in spatial organization that can exist in a single human population at one point in time.

In applying the deductive argument of our general model of economic defendability, we will examine data for each particular case in a definite sequence. We will first consider the resource distribution for the area in question, delimiting as far as possible the abundance and predictability of key resources. Then we will turn to the patterns of resource utilization reported for the particular population (patterns of cooperative foraging, information sharing, competition, etc.). Finally, we will examine the spatial organization of the population, focusing on the degree of dispersal, nomadism, and territoriality. Our goal is to deterine whether the resource distribution parameters are related to the patterns of resource utilization and spatial organization of each case in the manner predicted by our general model.

Our examples, then, are not a representative sample but were chosen to illustrate various aspects of human territoriality; in this way we feel we can begin to test the economic defendability model in a broad manner and yet avoid the superficiality that would be entailed by a general review of human spatial organization in a paper of this length. In summary, our three examples were chosen to demonstrate intergroup variation for a single region (Basin-Plateau Indians), variation through time (Northern Ojibwa), and intragroup variation at one point in time (Karimojong).

Basin-Plateau Indians

Steward (1938) in his classic study of the indigenous populations of the Great Basin region of North America described great differences between groups in the degree

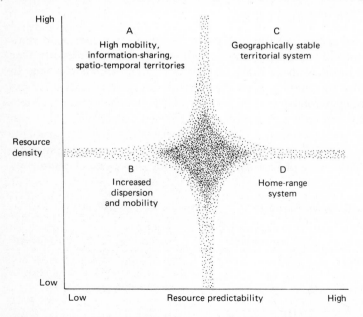

Figure 1 General predictions of the economic defendability model for spatial organization.

to which territories were delimited and defended.[2] Within the Great Basin and the adjoining Colorado and Columbian Plateau areas, Steward recognized four ethnolinguistic groups, of which three concern us here: Western Shoshoni, Southern Paiute, and Northern Shoshoni. In accordance with the model of economic defendability, we will analyze Steward's data by first examining the parameters of resource abundance and predictability. Then we will examine the patterns of resource distributions that maximize or optimize the efficiency of their utilization.

In the area inhabited by the Western Shoshoni (the Central Great Basin) the rainfall was low and patchy. The density of game and most plant foods was very low (Steward 1938:20,33). In terms of predictability, the usual pattern for arid regions held, in that both plant and animal resources "had in common the extremely important characteristics that the place and quantity of their occurrence from year to year were unpredictable, owing largely to variations in rainfall" (Steward 1955:105). Owing to the low primary productivity, game was exceedingly scarce, and large game did not live in herds. Small game, such as rodents, lizards, and insects, probably contributed more to the diet than large mammals (Steward 1938:33).

The Western Shoshoni lived primarily on plant foods, principally grass seeds and piñon nuts, although leaves, roots, and berries were also eaten. The grass seeds they depended on ripened sequentially from the lowlands to the highlands as the season progressed from spring to summer to fall. Steward (1938:19–20) described particular features of seed distribution as follows. First, particular grasses with edible seeds seldom occurred in dense patches, so that Shoshonean gathering techniques, which Steward considered to be reasonably efficient, did not provide great quantities. Second, because the harvest period in any locality was short and the seeds of most species fell off the plant within a few days or weeks of ripening, many were not harvested. Third, the location of patches of seed plants was unpredictable, as the abundance of seeds bears a close relationship to the distribution of rain-fall.

Piñon nuts (occurring in the Piñon-Juniper belt at 1,500 to 2,100 m.) were the major winter food of the Western Shoshoni. As this resource provided a major contribution to the diet, it is important to consider its distribution and abundance. In Steward's words:

> It is the most important single food species where it occurs, but harvests are unpredictable. Each tree yields but once in 3 or 4 years. In some years there is a good crop throughout the area, in some years virtually none. In other years, some localities yield nuts but others do not. When a good crop occurs, it is far more abundant than the local population can harvest. . . . The period during which they [the pine nuts] can be harvested is . . . 2 to 3 weeks, rarely longer [Steward 1938:27].

These local and short-lived concentrations of pine nuts can be viewed as temporary superabundances.

Western Shoshoni patterns of resource utilization and spatial organization can be analyzed as responses to characteristics of specific resources. The low average density of resources is reflected in a population density of approximately 0.13 people per square kilometer (0.05 people per square mile) (Steward 1938:49). Most hunting was carried out by solitary individuals, but any large game captured was distributed among groups of families sharing a camp. Cooperative hunting (antelope drives, rabbit net hunts) resulted in a higher per capita yield than solitary hunting. However, the effect on local prey populations was so drastic that such hunts could only be held on a very infrequent basis in any one locale (Steward 1938:33,231).

Grass seeds were collected by individual family units. Population dispersal was marked during the period of the year when grass seeds were the major food resource, since the low density of these resources made aggregation for foraging inefficient. "Participation of many persons in seed and root gathering not only failed to increase the per capita harvest, but it generally decreased it so greatly that individual families preferred to forage alone so as not to compete with other families" (Steward 1955:107). During this period, the population was also highly nomadic in response to the highly ephemeral and unpredictable nature of the major resource.

In the fall, the individual family gathering groups who happened to be nearby would converge on a piñon grove which was yielding a crop. They would gather as many nuts as possible and cache them for winter storage. Several families would spend the winter together in small "villages" at the site of these pine nut caches. The very erratic pattern of yields brought different families together at different places each fall, and the need to spend the winter at the cache meant that at their most sedentary time of year, no consistent group of families could amalgamate and establish either band or family ownership of piñon groves (Steward 1938:233).

Cooperation between families via information sharing is referred to frequently by Steward (1938:19, 27, 254, etc.). Thus, individual families often found out about the location of good piñon crops, patches of ripe seeds, locust concentrations, or rabbit drives being organized through word of mouth. Apparently this method played a major role in distributing the population with respect to local and ephemeral resource concentrations, although Steward does not discuss this in any quantitative detail.

In turning to the general model proposed earlier, we can locate the Western Shoshoni in Quadrant B (Fig. 1) for that portion of the year when they focused on collection of wild seeds; since these resources are both unpredictable and scarce, the most economical response is dispersion and nomadism (in this case at the family level). Piñon nuts, the main resource for the winter months, are unpredictable and ephemeral yet locally dense (a temporary superabundance), and thus the predicted utilization patterns involve nomadism, reduced dispersal, and a high degree of information sharing (Quadrant A). However, the factor of storage means that once harvested, these nuts are reliably available, leading to a sedentary period in the yearly round. In summary, the Western Shoshoni exhibited changes in degrees of nomadism and dispersal in general accordance with our model. Because of the distribution of critical resources, we argue that territoriality was an economically undefendable option. Steward's summary of the data he collected clearly supports this argument:

> The Shoshoni lacked any form of ownership of land or resources on it (except eagle nests). No group habitually or exclusively utilized any clearly defined territory for hunting, fishing, or seed gathering. . . . The sparse and erratic occurrence of vegetable foods required that territories exploited by different families and villages not only should vary from year to year but should greatly overlap. . . . Under such conditions, ownership of vegetable food resources would have been a disadvantage to everyone [Steward 1938:254].

In contrast to the Western Shoshoni, the Owens Valley Paiute lived in a circumscribed but much more productive area on the edge of the Great Basin. (The Owens Valley is formed by the eastern scarp of the Sierra Nevada and by the Inyo and White mountain ranges on the west.) Because of the steep topography, the local environment exhibited extreme zonation and diversity of resources, such that all necessary food could be obtained within a 32-km. radius of each settlement (Steward 1938:50). This zonation reduced the foraging area and thus increased effective density. In addition, the streams flowing from the Sierras meant a greater water supply in comparison with the area of the Western Shoshoni. A water supply derived from streams fed by snowmelt and aquifers presumably led to more abundant and predictable resources as compared to the regions where plant growth was solely dependent on patchy rainfall. The valley inhabitants increased resource predictability and density themselves by systematic irrigation of wild seed patches (Steward 1938:53). The greater resource density of the Owens Valley is attested to by the human population density (approximately 1.25 people per square kilometer, or 0.48 people per square mile) which is roughly ten times the average density of the Western Shoshoni.

Resource utilization patterns included communal hunts, meat redistribution within the local band, and the familiar pattern of family harvesting of plant foods. However, the Owens Valley Paiute, probably unique among the Indians of the Great Basin, lived year-round in permanent villages on tributaries of the Owens River. Groups of villages were organized into well defined bands which delimited and defended territories. The band territories were cross sections of the valley cutting across the valley and extending up the mountainsides. If necessary the territories were defended by small scale aggression (little bloodshed is reported), but primarily by social and supernatural sanction. Access to resources depended on band membership, although on occasion some nonmembers gained access. Piñon areas within the band territories were subdivided into family plots. According to Steward (1938:52), families defended their piñon plots against trespass but "often invited persons even of other bands, especially their relatives, to pick on their plots." The piñon-nut harvest was organized by the band chief.

Although Steward speaks of band-owned hunting territories, he makes it clear that this territorial organization was much more flexible than was the case with respect to plant resources. The two species of game which could be driven (jack rabbit and antelope) were hunted cooperatively within band territories. The hunts were under the direction of a hunting leader, and participation was usually limited to band members (Steward 1938:53). However, not all game was hunted by band members within their own territory. Some deer hunts involved the participation of several bands. In the southern part of the Owens Valley, bands did not claim hunting territories: "Men were permitted to hunt anywhere but naturally tended to restrict hunting to the mountains near their own villages. . . . [B]and ownership of hunting territory seems to fade out gradually from northern to southern Owens Valley" (Steward 1938:54). The fact that the Owens Valley Paiute were less territorial with respect to game than to plant resources can be explained by noting that game animals are highly mobile and, therefore, a more unpredictable resource than plant foods.

In summary, the greater predictability and density of resources in the Owens Valley as compared with the Western Shoshoni made the area economically defendable for this hunter-gatherer population. While territorial exclusiveness led to a reduced efficiency of capture for some types of resources, it apparently allowed an average increase in the individual rate of return for time and energy devoted to foraging: "The disruptive effect of the erratic yield of wild seeds, especially the pine nut, was outweighed by the importance of communally irrigated and therefore comparatively reliable seed patches in the valley" (Steward 1938:256).

The Northern Shoshoni were a third group of Basin-Plateau Indians studied by Steward. We will deal here only with those groups living on the northeastern rim of the Great Basin, in an area of somewhat higher rainfall and greater primary productivity. In the northern Great Basin (where rainfall is higher) the plant resources such as grass seeds would presumably be more predictable and less patchy than in the southern Great Basin where rainfall is lower.[3] However, Steward does not directly discuss the question of the distribution of the plant foods. He does note that the grazing in this area was sufficient for raising horses (while any horses which strayed into the area of the Western Shoshoni were killed and eaten because they competed directly with humans for food resources [Steward 1938:235]). The Northern Shoshoni used the horses to derive a substantial portion of their subsistence from buffalo hunting. Although the buffalo herds had a relatively low spatial predictability, they were a highly concentrated resource when encountered. We argue that the amount of available resources was increased by use of horses for search, pursuit, and transport of resources, especially buffalo but also plant foods.

The Northern Shoshoni pattern of resource utilization involved a seasonal sequence of subsistence strategies: buffalo hunting in summer; foraging for roots, berries, and game in the fall; and living primarily off the surplus buffalo meat in winter. The buffalo hunts involved the formation of large bands and a migration over the low passes in the Rocky Mountains to the Great Plains. According to Steward (1938:235), cooperative hunting of buffalo was a high-yield activity basic to Northern Shoshoni subsistence:

> The herds east of the Rocky Mountains were so large that several hundred persons were not only able to maintain themselves during the hunt but to cure sufficient meat to last

through much of the year. The hunts were cooperative because . . . the yield of a planned, concerted drive was so much greater than what individuals could procure alone.

These large migratory groups of hunters were also effective in defense against raids from other equestrian hunters. The return from the plains hunts was followed by a dispersal of individual families or small groups in order to forage for local resources prior to the onset of winter. Families then amalgamated again to live in winter villages in groups roughly the same in size and composition as the summer hunting parties. Clearly the horse was critical in allowing food to be gathered over a wide area and transported centrally, thus supporting large local groups. The large aggregations of people did not indicate high overall resource density: population density was low (2.1 to 0.08 people per square kilometer, or 0.8 to 0.03 people per square mile), despite the fact that much of the food (i. e., buffalo) was "imported" from another habitat.

The spatial organization of the Northern Shoshoni involved high mobility with aggregation for part of the year, mobility with dispersal for another part, and a fairly sedentary aggregation during the winter. Since the different seasonal patterns of subsistence occurred in two geographically separated regions, and focused on very different resources, we would not expect Northern Shoshoni spatial organization to be the same in the two zones. According to Steward (1938:237) the area used by Northern Shoshoni groups overlapped, and they were not territorial at any time of year.[4] Clearly this would be expected for the summer phase, since pursuing highly mobile herd animals on horseback is incompatible with territorial defense. During the fall dispersal, people seem to have focused on securing foods typical of the Great Basin as a whole, which were patchy in space and ephemeral in time (Steward 1938:235), and again territoriality would not be predicted. Steward indicated that other groups raided the Northern Shoshoni, but he does not specify the time of year, so it is not clear whether winter villages were defended against outsiders. It appears that the villagers were subsisting primarily on their caches and not depending on resources derived from the area adjacent to their settlements. However the food surpluses, horses, and goods, such as skins kept at the winter villages, would have been economically defendable and capturable items. We predict that large resource areas as such would not have been delimited and defended, but that the winter villages would have been. However, more evidence is needed on both resource use and spatial organization at this time of year in order adequately to test our model.

Northern Ojibwa

The analysis of territoriality in the Northern Algonkians (including the Northern Ojibwa) has a long history in anthropology, and both empirical and theoretical controversies have been frequent. There are basically two contending viewpoints on the origins of Northern Algonkian hunting territories. Some scholars, beginning with Speck (1915, 1923; Speck and Eiseley 1939; Cooper 1939; Hallowell 1949), argue that a territorial hunting system was an aboriginal adaptation to maximize the sustained yields from game, especially beaver. Others have presented evidence that territoriality was not aboriginal for the Northern Algonkians and in fact arose after fur trading had become established (Leacock 1954; Knight 1965; Bishop 1970, 1974). While this latter view is now generally accepted, disputes still arise over what factors are the major determinants of the shift to territorial systems of land use. Leacock has emphasized the role of acculturation and barter economy in encouraging the shift from cooperative group hunting to individualized trapping, suggesting that family territories were the result of competition for fur-bearing animals whose pelts were traded for food. Knight has countered this by noting that the East James Bay Cree spent over 250 years in contact with traders and participating in the trapping economy without developing territorial systems of land tenure. Contrary to Leacock, Knight (1965:36) argues that fur-bearing animal populations fluctuate drastically (as with many other subarctic animal species), and that, in addition, fluctuations of the trading economy (changes in prices, credit availability, trading post location, etc.) must also be considered in assessing the viability of a territorial system. In Knight's view:

> Until some stable and significant amount of income other than that from trapping and hunting was available to the band, long-run minimum conditions did not allow subarctic hunter-trappers to compartmentalize general band areas into permanently delineated tracts given over to the exclusive use of particular families, and still survive [1965:29].

Bishop (1970, 1974) reaches conclusions regarding Northern Ojibwa spatial organization that are not in accordance with either Knight's or Leacock's views. He argues that Northern Ojibwa groups adopted territorial systems of land tenure not primarily as a response to the individualistic barter economy nor in the context of reliance on store foods, but when (among other things), the depletion of large game forced a shift to the hunting of small nonmigratory species. We will use Bishop (1970, 1974) as the basis of our discussion of changes in Northern Ojibwa territoriality, because of the historical depth of his account and the detailed record of changes over time. However, as is generally true of ethnohistorical reconstructions, much information is lacking or incomplete in Bishop's account. For example there is little information about density of resources, the scale of large-game movements, and the cycles of fluctuations in numbers of small game. Furthermore, Bishop does not define territoriality clearly nor is he specific about the group associated with a particular piece of land and how territorial rights were defended. However, the information that Bishop does present about changes in Northern Ojibwa spatial organization with changes in resource utilization appears to fit the predictions derived from our model.

Originally the Northern Ojibwa were hunters and gatherers living in Canada east of Lake Superior. They expanded their range northward and westward over the last 400 years, changing their subsistence patterns as a result of this movement and of contact with Europeans (Bishop 1974:332). Their precontact food resources included moose, Virginia deer, woodland caribou, beaver, several species of fish, and a wide variety of vegetable produce. However, they depended primarily on two species of large game—caribou and moose. In the 1600s and 1700s, trading of furs for European manufactured goods and later for food became established, first through itinerant traders and later through established trading posts. Over a period of 300 years, the Ojibwa changed from dependence on wild foods to a primary dependence on foods obtained from trading posts in exchange for furs. Nonetheless, until recently Ojibwa subsistence primarily depended either directly or indirectly on animals which they hunted and trapped. During recent times the Northern Ojibwa increasingly have come to depend on money earned by new occupations (such as mine laborer and fishing guide) and on money provided by the Canadian government. Now almost half of the income of the group studied by Bishop is from government sources, and trapping contributes little to their subsistence.

Between 1730 and 1780, trade goods increasingly replaced aboriginal technology, and these goods were relatively cheap and easy to acquire. The trapping of fur-bearing animals, while important for trade, did not interfere with Northern Ojibwa hunting and gathering of foods, nor did the Ojibwa depend on trade for food (Bishop 1974:10). During the period from about 1780 to 1820, there was great competition between rival trading companies, resulting in many trading posts and the availability of cheap trade goods. At this time, the primary source of food for the Northern Ojibwa was large game, and trapping was opportunistic and involved great mobility. Reliance on a mobile animal like caribou favored a "more nomadic existence mitigating the formation of well defined territories since caribou migrations are not restricted by any artifically bounded regions" (Bishop 1974:209). Bishop (1974:289–292) found that among the Ojibwa of the Osnaburgh region, territorial ownership did not exist during this period. The hunting group returned to the same general area each year but possessed no exclusive rights to resources. Boundaries between the areas used by different hunting groups were not sharply demarcated. During this period, when large game was abundant, although the members of any particular band "tended to hunt in the same general region each year, resources belonged to those who came first, even when they were within the region inhabited by another band" (Bishop 1970:11).

By 1820 large game was depleted in the area studied by Bishop. As a result of the establishment of a trading monopoly by the Hudson's Bay Company in 1821, the exchange value of furs declined. Thus, at the same time that the Northern Ojibwa came to depend more on trading posts for food and other goods, the value of their furs decreased. Consequently, competition for fur-bearing animals became intense. With the decline of large game in the Northern Ojibwa area, subsistence depended primarily on small nonmigratory game, especially hare and fish (Bishop 1970:12, 1974:209). Following the disappearance of large game and the shift to hare and fish, archives for the area studied by Bishop document a decrease in the degree of mobility and the extent of area covered by the Ojibwa hunters (Bishop 1974:209–210). By the mid-19th centruy, Northern Ojibwa groups who were dependent on the fur trade and on small game had developed family hunting territories throughout most of Northern Ontario (Bishop 1974:94). Social sanctions against trespass apparently were an important aspect of defense of hunting territories (Bishop 1974:218–219). In summary, Bishop concludes that it was:

> ... The shift to small game, working in conjunction with a growing population in an area drastically depleted of the necessary peltry, that led to the emergence of hunting territories in Northern Ontario. . . . In the case of the Northern Ojibwa, the loss of large game, caribou and moose, and the forced reliance on hare and fish constituted the crucial factor in the development of family hunting territories [Bishop 1970:13].

From 1890 to 1945, the Northern Ojibwa dependence on trading posts continued to increase. Archival evidence indicates a decline in the rigidity of the territorial system during the first decade of this century in the area studied by Bishop. At this time, "rules against trespass had grown lax," and this change was "promoted by the return of large game, caribou and moose," animals "not confined by artificially bounded territories" (Bishop 1974:94). Bishop suggests that population growth and an increase in competition over furs led to a breakdown of social sanctions against poaching and trespass, and contributed to the decline in territoriality.

Today the Osnaburgh Ojibwa live in a village, and most of their income comes from wage labor and government assistance rather than trapping and trading. Indian trappers are now able to hire airplanes to transport them to their trapping territories (Bishop 1974:15). Also most forms of wage labor have taken men away from their community and family; and government-established schools interfere with traditional modes of subsistence. The present-day pattern of Ojibwa territorial organization is not discussed by Bishop, but clearly economic defendability of a particular area would be influenced by factors such as government regulations, enforcement of laws, and increased mobility with changing technology, as well as by the distribution and abundance of resources.

The evidence Bishop presents on the development of Northern Ojibwa territoriality seems to accord with the predictions of our model. Large game, such as caribou and moose, are highly mobile and therefore relatively unpredictable in space and time. While they were dependent on these animals as a major resource, the Northern Ojibwa did not defend territories, although the degree of nomadism and dispersal of Ojibwa hunting groups at this time is not well documented. After the virtual disappearance of large game, the Northern Ojibwa were forced to rely on small game species for their subsistence. Although this probably did not provide as abundant a subsistence base as the large game, the small game was less mobile and therefore more predictable in space, and the Ojibwa began to defend hunting territories. As indicated by our model, economic defendability of a resource area can develop even when resource abundance declines, as long as this decline is more than compensated for by increased predictability of key resources.

Karimojong

In the case of the Basin-Plateau Indians and the Ojibwa, territorial behavior occurs under ecological conditions similar to those in which territoriality occurs in other species. However, characterizing the behavior of a particular group as "territorial" or "not territorial" can sometimes conceal important aspects of their social organization. A particular human group may be described as being either territorial or nonterritorial depending on the resource which is being considered. Even human groups with subsistence economies use an enormous variety of resources at any given time. They utilize various food sources, each of which can be different with respect to such characteristics as predictability, abundance, mobility, and defendability. Human groups also use nonfood resources such as clay for pots, salt mines, iron ore for making tools, or wood for building and burning. Furthermore, people have manufactured resources such as homes, tools, irrigation works, and livestock corrals. It is not surprising, given this enormous diversity, that within the same human population some resources may not be defended, while others may be defended in various ways. For example, crops may be defended by exclusive ownership of a particular piece of land, livestock may be defended as they move through space, while deposits of clay for pots may not be defended at all. Furthermore, if a resource is defended by defense of a territory, the size of that territory and the people who are excluded from it can vary according to the resource under consideration. These points will be illustrated by a discussion of the spatial organization among the Karimojong living in northeastern Uganda. (More details of Karimojong subsistence strategies and social organization can be found in N. Dyson-Hudson 1966 and Dyson-Hudson and Dyson-Hudson 1969, 1970.)

Although the Karimojong have a great variety of resources ranging from personal ornaments to water sources, we will focus on the resources associated with the two distinct subsistence strategies which provide the major sources of food energy —cultivating plants, particularly sorghum, and husbanding livestock, particularly cattle. The growing sorghum is predictable in space, in that it grows where it is planted, in fields on the alluvial terraces along the central reaches of the major rivers. It is also predictable in time, in that the grain ripens four to five months after it is planted. Although the yield per acre varies enormously from less than 45 kilograms per hectare (250 pounds per acre) to over 185 kilograms per hectare (1,000 pounds per acre), growing sorghum clearly is a dense and predictable resource. After the harvest, sorghum is stored in granaries within stockaded settlements near the fields, and stored sorghum also is a dense resource which is predictable in time, space, and amount. If the harvested sorghum is sufficient to provide them with food, the women, young children, and old people remain in the permanent settlements year-round, and their main food is the sorghum stored in the settlements.

Both growing and stored sorghum are resources which are defended by the woman who grows the grain, with the help of her close kin. The land good for growing sorghum is limited in amount and is owned collectively by the people of the group of settlements near that land. Specific areas are allocated to individual women, and other people are excluded from cultivating that land by the woman and her husband, supported by other members of the settlement cluster should that become necessary. Growing crops are defended against livestock by fencing and by keeping herds under continuous observation. During the critical period when the grain is ripening, the cultivator and her kin take turns standing on platforms in the field from dawn to dusk, defending crops against birds and against people who might cut and steal the succulent stalks. Harvested grain is kept in individually owned granaries inside the stockade surrounding the settlement in which ten or more women and their close kin live. Each woman protects her own grain from animal pests, including rodents, termites, and weavils. Theft by other people is prevented by keeping a guard in the settlement or by ritual means. The guards often are old people who are physically infirm, and the ritual involves placing branches of a sacred tree at each entrance into the settlement to ensure that misfortune befalls any thief. A work diary of a Karimojong settlement clearly shows that defending crop resources against animal competitors—fencing fields, guarding livestock, shouting and throwing mud balls at birds trying to steal the ripening grain, and spreading the sorghum in the sun to kill insect pests—requires activities which entail large energy expenditures by people (R. Dyson-Hudson 1972). Defense of crop resources against other Karimojong involves primarily social constraints and has a very low energy cost.

In summary, density and predictability in time and space is high for growing sorghum and harvested grain and both are defended resources. Defense of agricultural crops against animal competitors requires great amounts of time and energy. Relatively little energy is devoted to defense of these resources against other Karimojong, because social controls are so effective. Control of access to garden land is through prior social exclusion rather than overt fighting, and disputes over the use of that garden land are rare. Harvested grain is also defended primarily through the fear of social disapproval and of divine intervention. The availability of a dense and predictable resource means that people dependent on that resource are not highly mobile.

The distribution, abundance, and predictability of the cattle/grazing land resource complex are very different from that of the agricultural land/crop complex. The cattle, which convert grazing into human food, can be considered to be predictable in time and space, in that the herdsmen remain associated with their cattle by moving with them. Cattle can also be considered to be an abundant resource in that herd size is adjusted so that all the herders caring for a particular herd can subsist on the food produced by that herd, by milking and drawing blood from living animals. Cattle are a defended resource, as would be predicted by our model. They are defended against enemies and predators by guarding them during the day (with spears and shields if necessary) and by corralling them at night. However, the defense of cattle does not involve delimiting and defending particular territories (except insofar as the corrals can be considered territories). The distribution and abundance of Karimojong cattle is a function of grazing land availability. The patterns of distribution and predictability of grazing lands are complex, and we will analyze in more detail their relation to Karimojong spatial organization.

Grazing land is very abundant and widespread in Karamoja. Except for perhaps 500 square kilometers occupied by mountains, the 6,437 kilometers of virtually all Karimojong tribal land can be used at some time for grazing. However, the suitability of a particular area for grazing cattle at a particular time depends both on the conditions of the vegetation and on the presence of a reliable water source within some 20 km. (since Karimojong cattle must drink at least every other day). During the rainy season there is ample water and grazing almost everywhere in the tribal area. During the dry season, areas of good grass within 20 km. of water are patchy and unpredictable in time, space, and duration. Localized and unpredictable dry season storms produce a highly nutritious flush of plant growth. The length of time that grazing is available in a particular area depends on the amount of moisture in the soil and the number of cattle grazing in that area, and cattle are moved to take advantage of areas of temporary abundance of grazing. The herdsmen construct temporary camps where the cattle can be protected at night from predators and human enemies. As compared with the women and old men who live primarily in the permanent settlements and eat mainly grain, the men and herd-boys associated with the cattle have a more mobile mode of life, in response to the low predictabil-ity of dry season grazing in space, time, and amount. Furthermore, the herders are more dispersed because of the relatively low density of plant resources and the long-er food chain involved in getting food from livestock rather than directly from plants.

Particular Karimojong do not defend specific grazing grounds. There is some tendency for members of a group of settlements to use the dry season waterholes nearest to their permanent settlements. Also, an individual herd-owner tends to graze his cattle in the same general area in successive dry seasons, presumably because he gains a more thorough knowledge of the environment. But there is no private ownership of grazing lands; all Karimojong have the right to graze every-where within the tribal area.

Because of the patchy and unpredictable nature of resources and the individual-ized pattern of herd movements, territorial ownership of fixed grazing areas is not a viable strategy. However, at a particular point in time the number of cattle grazing in an area can be regulated by social interactions. A herd-owner moving to a new grazing area must request permission of the people already herding in the area, who are organized into an ephemeral political unit termed a "camp cluster" (N. Dyson-Hudson 1966). These social interactions allow an exchange of information and can operate to regulate the number of herds in a particular area at a particular point in time in relation to the available resources. In times of severe shortage the people who are associated in the camp cluster may exclude other Karimojong from the area where they are grazing, or from sharing their water supply, and enforce the exclusion by fighting with sticks (N. Dyson-Hudson 1966:73, 255). However, informants emphasize that these fights occur only in times of extreme shortage, when an individual's survival would be jeopardized by sharing the grazing resources.

The economic defendability model seems to account adequately for the complex and varied spatial organization within the Karimojong tribe. The two resource complexes we have considered fall into different quadrants on the graph of our model (Fig. 1). Grazing resources are relatively unpredictable and of varying density (Quadrants B or A) and herdsmen, particularly during the dry season, are highly nomadic and dispersed, living in temporary camps and forming ephemeral but nonetheless important associations with other herdowners. Only in times of extreme scarcity do Karimojong herdsmen defend grazing areas, and the defended areas are those which have relatively abundant grazing at that particular point in time.

In contrast, agricultural resources are relatively dense and predictable in space and time (Quadrant C), and the women who practice agriculture are sedentary and live at a relatively high population density. Specific areas of agricultural land are delimited and defended, and the harvested crops are also defended both against pests and against other Karimojong. The predictability of agricultural yields from year to year is too low for a constant number of people to depend on crops, and the flexibility of Karimojong social organization, which allows people to move between permanent settlements and cattle camps, enables them to adjust to variations in the abundance of resources.

Despite the fact that (as predicted by our model) the Karimojong do not in general have territorial defense of grazing land against other Karimojong, they do defend their tribal grazing lands against non-Karimojong. Enemies who trespass into Karimojong land are killed with spears, and their cattle are taken. There is also active raiding across tribal boundaries.[5] This territorial defense cannot adequately be accounted for by our model, which does not take into account different responses to members of one's own group versus outsiders. Yet among human groups such differences are very common. A system of cooperative perimeter defense involving ethnic exclusion alters the costs and benefits of territoriality dramatically (Hamilton and Watt 1970:270–272), and this might help to account for Karimojong defense of territory at their tribal boundaries. An analysis of Karimojong territorial behavior taking into consideration ethnic identity, ethnic exclusion, symbolic communication, and cooperative perimeter defense is beyond the scope of this paper.

CONCLUSIONS

In our view, territoriality is a subset of resource-defense strategies, and resource defense is in turn an aspect of subsistence strategies. Clearly under some circumstances humans are territorial, in that they occupy certain areas more or less exclusively by means of repulsion through overt defense or through social interactions. But it is equally clear that although (as with all behaviors) the capacity to demark and defend territory must have some genetic basis, human territoriality is not a genetically fixed trait, in the sense of being a "fixed-action pattern," but rather a possible strategy individuals may be expected to choose when it is to their adaptive advantage to do so. Analyses arguing that territoriality is an evolutionary imperative, or conversely a political aberration of basic human nature, do not seem to us to have explanatory validity. We have argued that territoriality in humans is at least in part an adaptive response to environmental factors and, as such, is to be expected when critical resources are distributed so that exclusive use and defense of a resource area produces a net benefit in resource capture. Our model incorporates concepts derived from the study of spatial organization among other animal species. The notion that spatial organization is adaptively related to resource characteristics was developed independently in anthropology, although its formulation has not been as precise as that developed in sociobiology.[6]

Our analysis suggests that human territoriality can, as with other animal species, be fruitfully analyzed in terms of a general model of spatial organization that focuses on resource distributions and economic defendability. However, since humans use such a wide variety of resources, even a single population can exhibit a great range of responses with respect to different resources, and describing the behavior of a particular group as "territorial" or "nonterritorial" can therefore be overly simplistic. It is not enough to know if a particular group exhibits territorial behavior. Instead, it is necessary to discuss particular resources and determine if these resources are defended, how they are defended, the circumstances under which access to these resources is restricted, and which people or groups of people are allowed or denied access to resources.

Levins (1966) has noted that scientific models cannot simultaneously maximize generality, realism, and precision. If the model of ecological determinants of spatial organization presented in this paper has maximized anything, it has been generality and (to a lesser extent) realism. Of necessity, we have simplified our discussion by considering only a limited set of potential determinants. Other factors influencing spatial organization, such as group size, specific foraging strategies, competition, political organization, and nonfood resources, have not been considered in our model, which focuses exclusively on resource distribution. Our failure to achieve precision can be ascribed to two main factors: the necessity for simplification and the lack of quantitative and operational measures for critical variables.

The lack of quantitative data relevant to the parameters of our model is a serious problem, but its solution should not be conceptually difficult. Certainly, data on resource abundance, distribution in time and space, and utilization patterns can be collected in sufficient detail in the future, although they will be difficult to reconstruct from past studies. However, a more serious problem is presented by the absence of operational measures for key concepts such as predictability (but see Harpending and Davis 1977). In addition there are complexities in analyzing the energy costs of resource defense. The case of the Karimojong indicates that energy costs for resource defense can be extremely low when common values and beliefs make ritual sanctions rather than overt defense effective in preventing trespass. The low energy costs only hold true if outsiders not enculturated into the beliefs are excluded. Exclusion of outsiders can be accomplished, for example, by cooperative perimeter defense, which also has a relatively low individual energy cost. Thus the energy costs of resource defense strategies within groups and between groups can be quite different and need separate analysis.

If the model relating economic defendability to territoriality is to be more than a plausibility argument, hypotheses must be derived from this model and tested with good quantitative data. We hope that other researchers in human ecology will gather such data and begin tests of this and related models of optimal resource use. Adequate tests of the economic defendability model would utilize cases where quantitative measures of resource density and predictability vary, either within a group (through time, as with the Ojibwa, or for different resources classes, as with the Karimojong) or across groups who share similar technology and social organization (as with the Basin-Plateau Indian groups). This is the approach we have tried to take above, but because of inadequate data we have been forced to adopt a qualitative mode of argument. In addition, the model might also be tested by examining evidence for the null hypothesis. In particular, if it could be shown that clear-cut changes from nonterritorial systems of spatial organization to well defined territorial systems occur with any frequency without correlated increases in measures of resource density and/or predictability (holding technology and social organization constant and introducing no new key resources), the model as presented would have to be rejected. Until such tests are performed, however, we argue that the economic defendability model accounts for the available evidence in greater depth and extent than the alternative explanations of variations in human spatial organization.

NOTES

1   For something to be economic, a number of conditions must be present: ranked alternative values, insufficient alternative means, choice, and so on (D. G. Greenwood, personal communication). While some social scientists may feel that the use of this term in the context of animal behavior is inappropriate, we feel that the conditions listed above are, in fact, met. In any case "economic defendability" is a term that is widely used in the behavioral ecology literature and has a sufficiently clear meaning to justify its use in this context.

2   We are basing this description on Steward (1938, 1955). His model of Great Basin spatial organization has been both criticized (e.g., Service 1971, 1975; Williams 1974) and defended (e.g., Thomas 1972, 1973, 1974).

3   As a general meteorological rule, patchiness of rainfall is known to increase as the total average annual precipitation decreases.

4   In contrast, Service (1971:86) attributes territoriality to the Northern Shoshoni, stating that the mounted groups "monopolized the more fertile areas as pastures for their horses. They were grandly dominant over the other Indians, whom they scattered widely in small units and denied access to fishing sites and good hunting and gathering areas." However, the evidence for this view is not presented.

5 Despite enormous efforts by the Administration to prevent killing and cattle raiding, this was still a common pattern of behavior in the late 1950s.

6 A number of anthropologists have recently presented ecological analyses of human spatial organization, focusing especially on hunter-gatherer groups (e.g., Knight 1965, Damas 1969, Heinz 1972, Lee 1972, Williams 1974). As noted earlier, we feel that many discussions have assumed too much uniformity in resource distribution and, therefore, in optimum patterns of spatial organization. For example, Wilmsen, who takes a somewhat similar position to the one we espouse, generalizes (1973:8) that "plant foods, primarily in the form of roots, seeds, and nuts, are relatively stable and evenly distributed over suitable habitats" and are most effectively exploited by dispersal, which hardly seems to fit the Great Basin evidence we have summarized above. Wilmsen (1973:6) also seems to identify spatial unpredictability of resources (such as large game) with territoriality, when actually the model he presents defines the conditions under which clumping and cooperative foraging are optimal. Dumond (1972:296) has made perhaps the closest statement to our own view, although he does not develop a general model. In our view, anthropological analyses of hunter-gatherer spatial organization have made little progress since the fundamental insights of Steward (1938). This paper is an attempt to move beyond the generalities that currently dominate the literature toward the development of a general model that explains (rather than explains away) the *diversity* of human spatial organization.

REFERENCES CITED

Ardrey, Robert
 1966 The Territorial Imperative. New York: Atheneum.
Bates, B. C.
 1970 Territorial Behavior in Primates: A Review of Recent Field Studies. Primates 11:271-284.
Bishop, Charles A.
 1970 The Emergence of Hunting Territories among the Northern Ojibwa. Ethnology 9: 1-15.
 1974 The Northern Ojibwa and the Fur Trade: An Historical and Ecological Study. Toronto: Holt, Rinehart and Winston of Canada.
Brown, Jerram L.
 1964 The Evolution of Diversity in Avian Territorial Systems. Wilson Bulletin 76:160-169.
Brown, Jerram L., and G. H. Orians
 1970 Spacing Patterns in Mobile Animals. Annual Review of Ecology and Systematics 1:239-262.
Burt, W. H.
 1943 Territoriality and Home Range Concepts as Applied to Mammals. Journal of Mammalogy 24:346-352.
Carpenter, C. R.
 1958 Territoriality: A Review of Concepts and Problems. *In* Behavior and Evolution, A. Roe and G. G. Simpson, eds. Pp. 224-250. New Haven: Yale University Press.

Cohen, Erik
    1976   Environmental Orientations: A Multidimensional Approach to Social Ecology.
           Current Anthropology 17:49-70.
Cooper, J. M.
    1939   Is the Algonquian Family Hunting Ground System Pre-Columbian? American
           Anthropologist 41:66-90.
Crook, J. H.
    1970   Social Behavior and Ethology. *In* Social Behavior in Birds and Mammals, J. H.
           Crook, ed. Pp. xxi-xl. New York: Academic Press.
    1972   Sexual Selection, Dimorphism, and Social Organization in the Primates. *In* Sexual
           Selection and the Descent of Man, 1871-1971. B. G. Campbell, ed. Pp. 231-281. Chicago:
           Aldine.
    1973   The Nature and Function of Territorial Aggression. *In* Man and Aggression, Ash-
           ley Montagu, ed. Pp. 183-220. London: Oxford University Press.
Damas, David, ed.
    1969   Conference on Band Societies. National Museum of Canada, Bulletin 228.
Denham, W. W.
    1971   Energy Relations and Some Basic Properties of Primate Social Organization.
           American Anthropologist 73:77-95.
Dumond, Don E.
    1972   Population Growth and Political Centralization. *In* Population Growth: Anthropo-
           logical Implications. Brian Spooner, ed. Pp. 286-310. Cambridge, MA:MIT Press.
Durham, William H.
    1976   Resource Competition and Human Aggression: A Review of Primitive War. Quar-
           terly Review of Biology 51:385-415.
Dyson-Hudson, Neville
    1966   Karimojong Politics. London: Oxford University Press.
Dyson-Hudson, Rada
    1972   Pastoralism: Self-Image and Behavioral Reality. Journal of Asian and African
           Studies 7 (1-2):30-47. *Also in* Perspectives on Nomadism. William Irons and Neville
           Dyson-Hudson, eds. Leiden:Brill.
Dyson-Hudson, Rada, and Neville Dyson-Hudson
    1969   Subsistence Herding in Uganda. Scientific American 220 (2):76-89.
    1970   The Food Production System of a Semi-Nomadic Society: The Karimojong,
           Uganda. *In* African Food Production Systems: Cases and Theory. P. F. M. McLoughlin,
           ed. Pp. 91-124. Baltimore: Johns Hopkins Press.
Eisenberg, J. F., N. A. Muckenhirn, and R. Rudran
    1972   The Relation between Ecology and Social Structure in Primates. Science 176:863-
           874.
Emlen, Stephen T., and Natalie Demong
    1975   Adaptive Significance of Synchronized Breeding in a Colonial Bird: A New Hypoth-
           esis. Science 188:1029-1031.
Esser, A. H., ed.
    1971   Behavior and Environment: The Use of Space by Animals and Men. New York:
           Plenum.
Gill, F. B., and L. L. Wolf
    1975   Economics of Feeding Territoriality in the Golden-Winged Sunbird. Ecology 56:
           333-345.

Hallowell, A. Irving
1949 The Size of Algonkian Hunting Territories: A Function of Ecological Adjustment. American Anthropologist 51:35-45.

Hamilton, William J., III, Ruth F. Buskirk, and William H. Buskirk
1976 Defense of Space and Resources by Chacma (*Papio ursinus*) Baboon Troops in an African Desert and Swamp. Ecology 57:1264-1272.

Hamilton, William J., III, and K. E. F. Watt
1970 Refuging. Annual Review of Ecology and Systematics 1:263-286.

Harpending, Henry, and Herbert Davis
1977 Some Implications for Hunter-Gatherer Ecology Derived from the Spatial Structure of Resources. World Archaeology 8:275-283.

Heinz, H. J.
1972 Territoriality among the Bushmen in General and the !Ko in Particular. Anthropos 67: 405-416.

Hinde, Robert A.
1956 The Biological Significance of the Territories of Birds. Ibis 98:340-369.

Horn, Henry S.
1968 The Adaptive Significance of Colonial Nesting in the Brewers Blackbird (*Euphagus cyanocephalus*). Ecology 49:682-694.

King, Glenn E.
1975 Socioterritorial Units among Carnivores and Early Hominids. Journal of Anthropological Research 31:69-87.
1976 Society and Territory in Human Evolution. Journal of Evolution 5:323-332.

Klopfer, P. H.
1969 Habitats and Territories: A Study of the Use of Space by Animals. New York: Basic Books

Knight, Rolf
1965 A Re-examination of Hunting, Trapping, and Territoriality among the Northeastern Algonkian Indians. *In* Man, Culture, and Animals. Anthony Leeds and Andrew P. Vayda, eds. Pp. 27-42. American Association for the Advancement of Science Publication 78.

Lack, David
1968 Ecological Adaptations for Breeding in Birds. London: Methuen.

Leacock, Eleanor
1954 The Montagnais "Hunting Territory" and the Fur Trade. American Anthropological Association, Memoir 78.

Lee, Richard B.
1972 !Kung Spatial Organization: An Ecological and Historical Perspective. Human Ecology: 1:125-147.

Lee, Richard B., and Irven DeVore, eds.
1968 Man the Hunter. Chicago:Aldine.

Levins, Richard
1966 The Strategy of Model Building in Population Biology. American Scientist 54: 421-431.

Martin, M. K.
1974 The Foraging Adaptation—Uniformity or Diversity? Module in Anthropology, No. 56. Reading, MA:Addison-Wesley.

Peterson, Nicolas
    1975   Hunter-Gatherer Territoriality: The Perspective from Australia. American Anthropologist 77:53-68.
Pianka, Eric R.
    1974   Evolutionary Ecology. New York: Harper and Row.
Radcliffe-Brown, A. R.
    1930   The Social Organization of Australian Tribes. Oceania 1:34-63.
Reynolds, Vernon
    1966   Open Groups in Hominid Evolution. Man 1:441-452.
Reynolds, Vernon, and Francis Reynolds
    1965   Chimpanzees of the Budongo Forest. *In* Primate Behavior. Irven DeVore, ed. Pp. 368-424. New York: Holt, Rinehart and Winston.
Service, Elman R.
    1962   Primitive Social Organization. First ed. New York: Random House.
    1971   Primitive Social Organization. Second ed. New York: Random House.
    1975   Origins of the State and Civilization. New York: Norton.
Smith, C. C.
    1968   The Adaptive Nature of Social Organization in the Genus of Tree Squirrels *Tamiascirius.* Ecological Monographs 40:349-371.
Smith, Eric Alden
    1977   Adaptation and Energetic Efficiency: A General Model. Manuscript. Files of the author.
Speck, Frank G.
    1915   The Family Hunting Band as the Basis of Algonkian Social Organization. American Anthropologist 17:289-305.
    1923   Mistassini Hunting Territories in the Labrador Peninsula. American Anthropologist 25:452-471.
Speck, Frank G., and Loren C. Eiseley
    1939   The Significance of the Hunting Territory System of the Algonkian in Social Theory. American Anthropologist 41:269-280.
Steward, Julian H.
    1938   Basin-Plateau Aboriginal Sociopolitical Groups. Bureau of American Ethnology, Bull. 120.
    1955   The Great Basin Shoshonean Indians: An Example of a Family Level of Sociocultural Integration. *In* Theory of Culture Change. J. H. Steward. Pp. 101-121. Urbana: University of Illinois Press.
Thomas, David H.
    1972   Western Shoshone Ecology: Settlement Patterns and Beyond. *In* Great Basin Cultural Ecology: A Symposium. Don Folwer, ed. Pp. 135-154. Desert Research Institute, Reno, Publ. in Social Science, No. 8.
    1973   An Empirical Test for Steward's Model of Great Basin Settlement Patterns. American Antiquity 38:155-176.
    1974   An Archaeological Perspective on Shoshonean Bands. American Anthropologist 76:11-23.
Tinbergen, Niko
    1957   The Functions of Bird Territory. Bird Study 4:14-27.

Ward, P., and A. Zahavi
   1973   The Importance of Certain Assemblages of Birds as "Information-Centres" for
      Food-Finding. Ibis 115:517-534.
Williams, B. J.
   1974   A Model of Band Society. Society for American Archaeology, Memoir 29.
Wilmsen, Edwin N.
   1973   Interaction, Spacing Behavior, and the Organization of Hunting Bands. Journal of
      Anthropological Research 29:1-31.
Wilson, Edward O.
   1971   Competitive and Aggressive Behavior. *In* Man and Beast: Comparative Social
      Behavior. J. F. Eisenberg and W. S. Dillon, eds. Pp. 181-217. Washington:Smithsonian
      Institution Press.
   1975   Sociobiology: The New Synthesis. Cambridge, MA: Harvard University Press.
Wolf, L. L., and F. R. Hainsworth.
   1971   Time and Energy Budgets of Territorial Humming Birds. Ecology 52:980-988.
Zahavi, A.
   1971   The Social Behavior of the White Wagtail Wintering in Israel. Ibis 113:203-211.

Inclusive Fitness and Human Family Structure

Pierre L. van den Berghe
David P. Barash
University of Washington

The implications of sociobiology, and especially of "inclusive fitness" or "kin-selection" theory, to human family structures are explored. Kin-selection theory provides a model to formulate testable hypotheses predicting cooperation and conflict for categories of kinsmen; it also suggests an alternative way of looking at incest, endogamy, exogamy, rule of descent, and type of marriage in terms of such biological concepts as mating strategies, inclusive fitness, parental investment, and sexual dimorphism and bimaturism.

In the clutch of concepts recently developed by the nascent science of sociobiology, that of inclusive fitness is perhaps the most central for behavioral prediction, and its human applications beg exploring (Alexander 1971, 1975; Barash 1977; Hamilton 1964, 1975; Trivers 1971, 1972, 1974; Wilson 1975). Extending the classical Darwinian notion of fitness from the ability of the individual to pass on his genes directly through his own reproduction, inclusive fitness takes into account all the individuals in a population that carry, in varying proportions, ego's genes. Ego's fitness is thus enhanced not only through his own reproduction, but also, in varying degrees, through the reproduction of those who share his genes. Through the concept of inclusive fitness, seemingly self-defeating forms of behavior such as "altruism" become comprehensible and predictable. Ego may behave in such a way as to endanger his own survival for the benefit of alter, and thus reduce his direct individual fitness, but if alter is related to ego, ego's inclusive fitness is served by proxy through the survival of alter.

Inclusive-fitness theory, also known as "kin-selection" theory, goes on to predict that the probability of altruistic acts is a function of two factors: the degree of relatedness between altruist and beneficiary, and the benefit-cost ratio of the altruistic act to recipient and altruist. If r is the coefficient of relatedness between altruist and recipient and k the ratio of recipient benefit to altruist cost, altruistic behavior will be selected if: $k > 1/r$. In more general form, altruistic behavior is to be expected if $k > 1/\bar{r}$, where $\bar{r}$ is the mean r between the altruist and all the conspecifics with whom he interacts (Barash 1977). Accordingly, altruism is more likely as k is large and/or as $1/r$ is small. The former obtains when benefit to recipient is great and/or cost to altruist is small; i.e., altruism is more strongly selected as the recipient is in greater need or is more likely to profit from a given altruistic act. The latter obtains when r is large; i.e., altruism is more strongly selected in proportion as alter is more closely related to ego (more genes in common).

Note that this formulation makes no supposition as to cognitive processes or conscious intent. Altruism is considered only in terms of its consequences for the inclusive fitness of both altruist and recipient. The proximate mechanisms ensuring each behavior may and, in the human case, typically do include a combination of early experience, social learning, and direct, genetically mediated predispositions. Even where the first two factors predominate, as they well might in humans, genotype may influence differential susceptibility of the organism to produce a behavioral phenotype that maximizes ego's inclusive fitness. Kin-selection theory, in short, neither posits nor precludes conscious motivation and cognition (such as recognition of kin). It does not deny the importance of culture in humans (and of "tradition" in other higher vertebrates). Rather, it puts culture in the broader context of biological evolution.

"Altruism," in the last analysis, turns out to be the ultimate form of biological egoism, or, perhaps better, narcissism. We help those in whom we recognize ourselves and we do so in proportion as we (or, more precisely, our genes) are represented in others. Such is the fundamental principle of nepotism, one of the most pervasive forms of behavior in higher vertebrates, and most notably in our own species. Here we propose to examine the implications of kin selection and inclusive fitness in that universal from of human social organization, the family. Inclusive-fitness theory goes well beyond the family in its human applications, for many larger and more complex human groups are explicitly conceived of as extensions of the family, and are made up of individuals who are related or, at least, who think they are. Nations, ethnic groups, and phenotypically defined groups such as "races" are common examples of extensions of the familistic idiom. Such groups are referred to as big families, their leader as a father, their members as brothers and sisters, the basis of their solidarity as "blood," and so on. Whether the biological relatedness of group members is real or putative, it is probably no accident that kinlike groups can command more instantaneous and unreflecting loyalty and altruism, and, conversely, can confront each other with more unrelenting ferocity than more abstractly based groups, such as economic classes, professional associations, or other such congeries of people joined by rationally defined interests but not by shared genes. While some social scientists (Keyes 1976; Francis 1976) have recently defined nations and ethnic groups primarily as descent groups, few have drawn the biological implications of such a definition.

Here, however, we shall restrict ourselves to human groups that are defined by relations of marriage and filiation, that is, to nuclear or extended families and such larger kin-based groups as clans and lineages. Kinship analysis has a long and distinguished history in anthropology, and nearly all of it has been premised on the unique character of human marriage and kinship, and based on the formal structural properties of rules of residence, descent, exogamy, endogamy, preferential marriage, incest, jural authority, and the like. Our argument, on the other hand, is that sociobiology could add an important dimension to the analysis of the human family. Traditionally, anthropology's concern with exchange, reciprocity, kinship structure, and other social patterns has focused on their operations at the *group* level. Sociobiology, and inclusive-fitness theory in particular, represent a significant departure in that they emphasize functionality at the level of the *individual*—i.e., maximization of ego's inclusive fitness. Many human behaviors can profitably be viewed as strategies toward that end. For all our uniqueness as a species, and our cultural variations from group to group, our mating and reproductive systems are remarkably alike in their basic features, and very much what we would expect for the particular kind of higher vertebrate that we are. These species-wide regularities have long been recognized by anthropologists, and more or less taken for granted as "cultural universals" (Murdock 1949), but little attempt has been made until recently to draw their biological implications (Fox 1975; Parker 1976; Shepher 1972; Tiger and Fox 1971; Tiger and Shepher 1976). Following is a nonexhaustive list of characteristics of human family systems, seen in biological perspective.

   1   In all human societies, the most common small group consists of kin-related individuals. The minimum "typical" family consists of mated adults and their common subadult offspring. Most members of nearly all societies have themselves been raised and raise their own offspring in such groups. (The textbook exceptions like the Nayar of India or the Israeli Kibbutzim are *not* complete autonomous societies, but very special subgroups such as specialized castes or ideologically selective utopian communities.)

   Animals show a wide range of mating and rearing systems (see Crook, Ellis, and Goss-Custard 1976 for a recent classification) but in nearly all cases, r between individuals chosen at random within a mating and rearing group is higher than r̄, the average coefficient of relationship among members of the entire population (West Eberhard 1975). Primate mating and rearing systems vary widely; they include monogamy, various complex harem patterns, age-graded male-dominated troops, and multimale troops (Eisenberg, Muckenhirn, and Rudran 1972). In all cases, however, related individuals are more likely to interact with each other than with unrelated ones. For human as well as nonhuman animals, this has dual sociobiologic significance: with $r > \bar{r}$, ego can accrue inclusive fitness by assisting others within the social group; in addition, ego will gain fitness from the altruism of others, whose beneficence will also be potentiated by their mutual relatedness, since alter garners inclusive fitness by assisting ego.

   2   The relative stability of the human family is made possible by our propensity to form relatively enduring pair bonds. To be sure, we are not rigidly monogamous as some species are, and we engage in considerable premarital experimentation and extramarital forays, but we are also far from promiscuous, and our pair bonds tend to last for years rather than months, weeks, or days. This is especially true of those pair bonds which, by design or accident, produce offspring. Pair bonding in animals is associated most directly with the requirements of child-rearing. Accordingly, pair bonds are typically brief or absent in mammals (Eisenberg 1966), correlated with the unique adaptation of females to nourish their offspring. By contrast, over 90% of all birds species form extensive pair bonds (Crook 1965), correlated with the high metabolic demands of the fledglings, which select for a social system containing two adults, both of whom are committed to provisioning the young. In some ways, humans may approach the avian situation, in that the prolonged period of utter infant dependency may well have selected for human bonding systems in which males are involved in caring for their offspring, either directly or by supporting their mates.

3　Our species tends to show a preference for limited polygyny. Some three-fourths of all human societies (75.6% in Murdock's [1957] sample of 565 societies) permit polygyny, and most of them prefer it. Monogamous societies often have been polygynous in a more or less recent past, and typically their monogamy is a legal fiction. That is, legal monogamy is combined with various forms of institutionalized concubinage. Polyandry, on the other hand, is extremely rare (0.7% in Murdock's sample of four out of 565 societies) and linked to very special conditions, such as severe ecological conditions, or complex systems of hypergamy producing polygyny at the top of the social hierarchy and polyandry at the bottom. Polyandry, then, and to a lesser extent monogamy, seem to be exceptions and *pis-aller,* reluctant adaptations to special conditions. Monogamy appears to be an adaptation to an urban, industrial habitat where the productive role of women has been reduced, and where, therefore, polygyny and multiple fatherhood become too great burdens on men. Significantly, in the absence of special conditions (such as the high metabolic demands of birds), polygyny is the preferred system among nonhuman animals as well, and polyandry is extremely rare (Jenni 1974).

In the few cases of polyandrous mating in humans, kin-selection theory would lead one to expect that if several men shared a wife and contributed to the fitness of her offspring, they would want to maximize the probability of her children sharing genes with them. This probability would be maximized in the case of fraternal polyandry, i.e., of a set of brothers marrying a common woman whose children would thus be at least nephews if not sons.

The frequency of polyandry in humans is partly a function of definition. Murdock (1949) deplores the extension of the term to "sporadic instances of the association of several men with one woman in contravention of cultural norms, or to cases where a woman enjoys sexual privileges with the brothers of her husband, although she does not cooperate economically with them." He restricts the definition of polyandry to fully sanctioned marriage, and discovered only two cases in his 1949 sample of 250 societies: the Marquesans of Eastern Polynesia and the Toda of South India. Fraternal polyandry is the usual form among the Toda, and nonfraternal polyandry among the Marquesans. True polyandry (as distinguished from female promiscuity) seems as rare in other species as it is in humans, although it has been reported for the Tasmanian native hen, in its fraternal form (Barash 1977; Smith and Ridpath 1972).

Murdock, however, adds that "the extension of sexual rights of either partner in a marital union to his sibling-in-law of opposite sex is by no means a rare phenomenon." He found it present in "41 societies in our sample, or considerably more than half of those for which pertinent information is available." Somewhat related to fraternal polyandry as a way of "keeping women in the family" is the common practice of the levirate, or widow inheritance between brothers. Sororal polygyny is also a preferred type of marriage in a number of polygynous societies, making the children of co-wives each others' first cousins as well as half-siblings. Co-wives, who frequently contribute to the fitness of each others' children, are thereby taking care of nephews.

4   At sexual maturity, human offspring typically leave the family group in which they have been raised to establish a new family unit of their own. This makes for what anthropologists have called the "incest taboo" between parents and off-spring and between siblings, and this some have hailed as a unique human feature, indeed the very foundation of human culture (Levi-Strauss 1968). This dispersal of maturing offspring applies either to both sexes, giving rise to neolocal residence, or to one sex only, producing either virilocal or uxorilocal residence, depending on whether the boys or the girls, respectively, stay put. Increasingly, it is realized that offspring dispersal on the onset of sexual maturity, far from being a human monopoly, is, in fact, a common strategy of relatively unprolific higher vertebrates to maintain a certain level of heterozygosity and therefore genetic adaptiveness (Parker 1976). In addition, many nonhuman animals show inhibitions against sibling matings, because play patterns, established during infancy, interfere with copulatory behavior (Hill 1974). This phenomenon may also occur among humans (Shepher 1972). The proximate mechanism for sibling incest avoidance thus seems to be mere propinquity of raising during a critical period of early childhood, rather than biological relatedness as such. Since nursery groups, in humans as in many other species, tend to be close relatives, the evolutionary effect of reducing the likelihood of inbreeding would operate. A biological explanation of the incest taboo in humans in no way presupposes, as many social scientists have argued, a conscious recognition of the deleterious effects of inbreeding.

5   In all human societies, there is a clear asymmetry and complementary of gender roles, one salient aspect of which is parental care. Human females, as typical mammals, invest much more in their offspring than males. We have suggested elsewhere how behavioral characteristics such as polygyny and differential parental investment for males and females were linked to somatic and physiological characteristics such as sexual dimorphism and sexual bimaturism, not to mention more obvious aspects of the mammalian condition such as differential size and number of gametes produced by males and females, the energetic drain of gestation and lactation, and male-female differences in confidence of genetic relatedness to their purported offspring (Barash 1977; van den Berghe n.d.). Human females, as good mammals who produce a few, costly and therefore precious, offspring, are choosy about picking mates who will contribute maximally to their offspring's fitness, whereas males, whose production of offspring is virtually unlimited, are much less picky. Hence, the widespread occurrence in human societies of polygyny, hypergamy, and double standards of sexual morality. There is another related reason for the sexual double standard in such things as differential valuation of male and femlae virginity and differential condemnation of adultery: marital infidelity of the spouse can potentially reduce the fitness of the husband more than that of the wife. Women stand to lose much less if their husbands have children out of wedlock than vice-versa. This situation is not unique to humans (Barash 1976). Male ringdoves show less courtship and more aggression toward females whose behavior indicates that they have been courted, and possibly mated, by another male (Erickson and Zenone

1976). It should be added, however, that some mammals (ungulates, pinnipeds) are much more extreme than we are in sexual dimorphism, sexual bimaturism, polygyny, and differential parental investment, while others (rodents, most carnivores) are less so. On the whole, we tend to be toward the medium-low end of the mammalian spectrum on these characteristics.

Let us now examine more closely some of the features of human family structure, and suggest how these diverse features are most parsimoniously explained in terms of biological fitness in general, and kin-selection theory in particular. The most direct way of ensuring the survival of one's genes is, of course, to procreate and to see to the survival of one's offspring. Zero-population-growth advocates notwithstanding, most people in most societies have been "pronatalist," and have, in fact, reproduced at levels close to their biological potential. Until quite recently in a few industrial societies, it was mortality rather than restriction of natality that limited the growth rate of human populations. Kin-selection theory enables us to predict much more, however, than that most people want to breed. It also explains gender differences in both sexual and parental behavior. There is no human society that does not ascribe the bulk of the responsibility for raising children, at least until the age of five or six, to women. Even utopian societies like kibbutzim that have attempted to eliminate this sexual division of labor and that have institutionalized infant care, have been unsuccessful in freeing women of child care (Tiger and Shepher 1976).

For a woman, the successful raising of a single infant is essentially close to a full-time occupation for a couple of years, and continues to claim much attention and energy for several more years. For a man, it often means only a minor additional burden. To a limited extent, sexual roles can be modified in the direction of equalization of parental load, but even the most "liberated" husband cannot share pregnancy with his wife. In any case, most societies make no attempt to equalize parental care; they leave women holding the babies.

Among most vertebrates, female involvement with offspring is obligatory whereas male involvement is more facultative. For example, male hoary marmots typically do not interact substantially with their offspring. Rather, their social activities are concentrated in defending their females against neighboring males, while also attempting to steal copulations from neighboring females. However, at isolated colonies where males are unable to maximize their fitness by interacting with other adults, they become doting parents, enhancing their fitness via care of offspring (Barash 1975). Among orangutans, males on Sumatra typically associate with a female and her young, whereas on Borneo they defend territories and limit their interactions to other adult males (MacKinnon 1974). Significantly, predators and interspecific competitors are more abundant on Sumatra. In short, biology dictates that females bear the offspring, although environmental conditions can exert a powerful influence on the extent of male parental investment. Males and females are selected for differing patterns of parental care, and there is no reason to exempt *Homo sapiens* from this generalization (Barash 1976).

In addition, a woman will, at a maximum, produce some 400 fertile eggs in her lifetime, of which a dozen at most will grow up to reproductive age, while a man produces millions of sperm a day and can theoretically sire hundreds of children. Not surprisingly, females tend to go for quality, and males for quantity. This means, for women, to select as mates those men most likely to contribute to the fitness of their children, both in terms of physical and social attributes. A dual consequence of this female selection for quality and male selection for quantity if polygyny accompanied by hypergamy. Indeed, in practically all polygynous societies, the better off and the more socially and politically well-placed a man is, the more wives and/or concubines he is likely to have. It follows that, since a high-ranking polygynist's status group produces on the average no more than its share of women, most of his wives and concubines will come from social strata lower than his own. Polygyny and hypergamy, then, are two sides of the same biological coin: polygyny serves the male drive for quantity, while hypergamy fulfills the female search for quality.

There is another way of formulating the fundamental asymmetry of female and male reproductive strategies. For male mammals, the availability of nubile females is always a limiting factor to their fitness, whereas, for females, males are not such a limiting condition. In other words, the reproductively limiting condition for a species is the number of females, not the number of males. Females are always a scarce resource, and males an expendable one. Females can afford to be picky because there always are plenty of males available for mating. Males are quick to grab what females they can, because if they do not, some other male is sure to do so. Besides, a male's chances of successfully mating with other females are much less affected by his mating with one than are a female's chances of mating with other males. A human male can theoretically sire offspring with different women at hourly or at most daily intervals; a woman has to wait a year or even more under normal conditions of lactation. Clearly, the risks are far greater for females.

Biologists had long puzzled over the fact that among some bird species, such as red-winged blackbirds, dickcissels, and marsh wrens, some males are typically mated polygynously while others are bachelors. Given that males of these species do provide some assistance in provisioning their offspring, females seem to be acting against their best reproductive interests by forgoing the services of a bachelor in favor of being the second, third, or fourth mate of a polygynist. The answer appears to lie in the quality of resources (territory, in most cases) commanded by the males: when the habitat is sufficiently heterogeneous, some males may be defending a habitat of sufficient forage value or protection against predators such that femlaes are more fit mated polygynously on this habitat than they would be if mated monogamously on a poorer habitat (Orians 1969). Extrapolating to humans, we suggest that men are selected for engaging in male-male competition over resources appropriate to reproductive success, and that women are selected for preferring men who are successful in that endeavor. Any genetically influenced tendencies in these directions will necessarily be favored by natural selection.

It is true, of course, that social advantages of wealth, power, or rank need not, indeed often do not, coincide with physical superiority. Women in all societies have found a way of resolving this dilemma by marrying wealthy and powerful men while taking young and attractive ones as lovers: the object of the game is to have the husband assume parental obligations for the lover's children. Understandably, men in most societies do not take kindly to such female strategies on the part of their wives, though they are not averse to philandering with other men's wives. The solution to this moral dilemma is the double standard, independently invented in countless societies. In any case, ethnographic evidence points to different reproductive strategies on the part of men and women, and to a remarkable consistency in the institutionalized means of accommodating these biological predispositions.

The main objection which cultural determinists might make to this view of human reproductive strategies is that it conflicts with some ethnographic evidence. Our view implies that men compete with each other over women, and that women pick the winners. In most ethnographies, we read that it is men who swap their sisters for wives, often seemingly without consultation, much less consent, of the women involved (Lévi-Strauss 1968). It is true that men are politically dominant in all known human societies, and that their political power typically includes considerable control over women and children. This is as true in matrilineal as in patrilineal or bilateral descent societies. Marriage in most societies takes the form of a negotiated jural settlement between the kin group of the groom and that of the bride, and men publicly play the main role on each side.

However, this public, official, legal display is not necessarily an accurate reflection of how the marriage came about. Women *are* in fact often consulted, and may even play an active behind-the-scene role. Alternatively, the legal transaction may merely ratify a *de facto* union. In any case, one must be critical of the possible male bias of much ethnography, and of the tendency of mistaking public displays, official pronouncements, and legal fictions for actual behavior. Even in our own society, for instance, there is a fiction that the father of the bride "gives her away," but we know better. The point is that, in all societies, rape is the exception rather than the rule. Notwithstanding male dominance, female assent is a precondition to nearly all mating. Whether the assent is based on "love" or on "mercenary" motives is irrelevant if one regards female mating strategy in terms of fitness. Men have power, and hence control over resources. Women, as do the females of many other species, choose males with the best possible resources.

Furthermore, men do openly compete for women in most if not all societies. Many societies practice extensive premarital courtship and "try-outs." In many others, the accumulation of considerable property for the payment of "bridewealth" is a prerequisite to marriage. In others yet, an act of physical prowess in war or hunting, or a protracted period of military service, is required of the young man before he is considered marriageable. Much of male competition is ultimately translated into access to women—i.e., to fitness. An interesting test of this hypothesis would be to study the performance of male athletes, with and without the stimulus of nubile females as spectators. Equally interesting is the insistence of many coaches on pregame sexual abstinence for their male players. It has been suggested that the physical exertion of intercourse cannot have an appreciable debilitating effect on a young athlete in good condition, but it may well take a horny athlete to perform at his best.

Finally, the suitor must generally be acceptable to the bride's kinsmen, if not formally to the bride herself. The bride's kinsmen also have a biological interest in the fitness of the offspring, and typically choose a groom who will contribute to that fitness according to criteria that are congruent with a *female* reproductive strategy. In our cultural idiom, a father will seek a "good provider" for his daughter. Fathers are typically far choosier and critical of whom their daughters consort with, than is the case with their sons. Sons sow "wild oats"; daughters run the risk of being "ruined," i.e., inseminated by an unfit male, and thereby made undesirable to a fit one.

Kin-selection theory also provides a parsimonious way of accounting for nepotistic behavior and its various extensions to larger groups of putative or real descent, such as tribalism, racism, ethnocentrism, parochialism, nationalism, patriotism, or what sociologists generally call "particularism." Favoritism toward real or putative kin has been observed in practically all societies, and most societies seem to take it for granted. Some modern industrial societies, and a few agrarian societies like Imperial China, have attempted to combat various forms of particularism, such as racism, and ethnic or caste prejudice, and have tried to institutionalize impersonal norms of universalism in their bureaucratic organization, but nearly all such attempts have been insidiously and systematically subverted from within. Nepotism triumphs in the end, and most societies have been realistic enough not to try to stamp it out.

If inclusive-fitness theory told us no more than that we favor kin, it would not represent much of an advance over popular wisdom. We think, however, that it goes beyond that and that it can generate testable hypotheses, predicting not only favoritism but also conflicts between kinsmen. As we all know, kinsmen not only prefer each other over strangers, they are also capable of bitter feuding. A theory that is able to account for both of these ubiquitous facets of human behavior is obviously superior to a mere statement that they represent an unaccountable paradox.

Interestingly, several anthropologists have advanced notions which, though not based on biological kin selection, are fully congruent with it. Such, for instance, is Evans-Pritchard's concept of "fission and fusion" in his famous account of Nuer politics (1940). Though Evans-Pritchard accounts for the phenomenon in terms of the Nuer "segmentary lineage" structure, he states that lines of conflict in Nuer society are predictable depending on how close to each other the parties to a conflict are. That is, in a pyramidal structure of clans, lineages, and sublineages, and of localized communities corresponding to these kin units, the mobilization for con-flict occurs at the lowest level of the structure which the parties to the dispute do *not* share. Furthermore, the likelihood of settling a dispute, such as blood feud, through peaceful mediation is directly related to the genealogical closeness of the antagonists.

Sahlins' (1965) review of "reciprocity" is also notable for its parallelism to the expectations of sociobiolgy, and kin selection in particular. This is all the more striking as he recently assumed a very critical stance toward sociobiology (Sahlins 1976). Sahlins describes three basic patterns in the exchange of goods and services: "generalized," "balanced," and "negative" reciprocity, corresponding respectively to a one-way flow of beneficence from giver to receiver, a balance of tit-for-tat, and, finally, exploitative interaction. He then superimposes this reciprocity continuum upon the society's social structure, noting that generalized reciprocity is restricted to interactions within ego's household and, to a lesser extent, his lineage, whereas balanced reciprocity predominates within the village and to a lesser extent, the ethnic group. Finally, negative reciprocity characterizes interactions between ethnic groups.

Inclusive-fitness theory suggests that the reproductive interests of individuals overlap in proportion as their genotypes overlap. Accordingly, ego should favor close kin over more distant kin, and kin over nonkin; hence, "generalized reciprocity." Sahlins' "balanced reciprocity" corresponds almost exactly to the evolutionary biologist's "reciprocal altruism" (Trivers 1971) in that unreciprocated altruism toward nonrelatives would be selected against, as would cheating, when proximity makes it likely that interactions would be iterated. "Negative reciprocity," of course, is the expected interaction between nonrelatives when beneficent return in unlikely. Cultural determinists may argue that these patterns are describable as the result of early experience: we naturally favor those to whom we are exposed since childhood, and these individuals tend to be our relatives. Without disparaging the role of experience, we could inquire further: Why are human societies invariably organized such that relatives associate with each other? and also, Why does such association lead to preferential behavior? Kin selection suggests an underlying evolutionary basis for these universals in the organization of human family structure—they maximize the inclusive fitness of the participants.

Cultural determinists will immediately object that the determining factor is not biological relatedness as such, but the social recognition thereof in the kinship structure peculiar to a given group. Furthermore, they delight in pointing to the great diversity of kinship structures. Without wanting to open a sterile argument as to how diverse human kinship structures really are, there is enough diversity to allow for the testing of competing theories, or, perhaps better, for ascertaining how much of the variance each theory explains. Indeed, we suspect that the two theories are complementary rather than mutually exclusive; both biological relatedness *and* the greater social recognition of some lines of kinship at the expense of others combine to explain actual behavior.

At present, systematic data are not available to test these hypotheses, but the possibility of doing so clearly exists. The vast majority of the world's societies (70%

according to the sample in Murdock 1949) have opted for unilineal as distinguished from bilateral descent. That is, they have chosen to assign priority to one line of descent over all others for purposes of social organization. Patrilineal societies outnumber matrilineal ones by about two to one; but, in both cases, a single line of filiation determines membership in lineages and clans that are, by definition, mutually exclusive and all-encompassing. Every member of the society (except for recent immigrants) belongs to a given clan and a particular lineage and sublineage thereof, and can only belong to one unit at any given level of this segmentary structure.

Unilineal descent, whether parti- or matrilineal not only has the structural neatness that anthropological kinship theorists delight in; it also has the very tangible advantage of organizing an entire society on the basis of corporate kin groups that are unambiguous, exhaustive, and mutually exclusive in membership. This is obviously not possible beyond the nuclear family in bilateral descent societies (such as our own) which give approximately equal recognition to all lines of descent, since only full brothers and sisters have an identical group of ancestors. Unilineal descent, thus, can be seen as a cultural adaptation enabling up to millions of people to organize on the basis of biological kin selection. This tremendous organizational advantage is, of course, purchased at the cost of systematically favoring certain categories of kinsmen over others who are equally related but socially less relevant. Unilineal descent is more properly seen as a cultural modification of biological kin selection than as a negation of it.

In addition, the structural neatness of unilineal descent should not blind us to actual kinship behavior in those societies. In practically all societies, people know that they have two parents, four grandparents, and so on, and behave preferentially toward not only the members of their own clan and lineage, but also toward other relatives belonging to different lineages. This can and often does create conflicts between one's obligations toward distant relatives in one's own lineage and one's affective ties to close relatives belonging to other lineages. Indeed, the anthropological literature is full of such conflicts.

Matrilineal societies in particular are especially prone to create conflicts between mother's brother and father over ego. In matrilineal societies, jural authority over ego is vested in his mother's brother who belongs to his own lineage, not in his father who necessarily belongs to another lineage if the lineages are exogamous, as they typically are. There is a vast and distinguished anthropological literature on the peculiar position of mother's brothers who have greater rights over nephews than over their own offspring, and on the peculiar instability of matrilineal societies (Murdock 1949; Radcliffe-Brown 1952; A. Kuper 1976; Evans-Pritchard 1929; Goody 1959). Indeed, a number of matrilineal societies have been known and observed to shift over to patrilineal (or sometimes bilateral) descent, while there is not a single documented case of a shift from patrilineal to matrilineal descent. Inclusive-fitness theory suggests a plausible explanation: matrilineal societies systematically create conflict situations where a man is supposed to favor his nephews over his children, whereas neither patrilineal nor bilateral societies do. It is *possible* to devise social arrangements that buck human biology, but there is always a price, and those societies that go along with human biology have a competitive advantage.

There are two interesting further problems in this connection. The first is why matrilineal societies originated in the first instance. The most common explanation given here is the greater ease and reliability in establishing maternity as distinguished from paternity. Matrilineal descent, in short, solves the problem of uncertain paternity by having men invest in their uterine nephews rather than in doubtful offspring. If the probability of paternity falls below 0.25, one is better off investing in nephews who are related to ego by a factor of at least one-eighth. (If probability of paternity is low, then one cannot be sure that one's siblings are *full* siblings. Uterine nephews by a half-sister would only be related by a factor of one-eighth, as distinguished from one-quarter for children of a full sister.) It does indeed seem to be the case that matrilineal societies, compared to patrilineal ones, have conditions making for lower probabilities of paternity: premarital permissiveness for women, tolerance of adultery, frequency of divorce.

The second problem is that of male domination. Theoretically, matrilineal societies could be simple mirror images of patrilineal ones by giving jural authority to the mother. In fact, male domination is so universal in human societies that the incongruous position of the mother's brother has been created in *all* matrilineal societies at the considerable cost that we have just seen. Thus the matrilineal solution, by conforming to one aspect of our biogram (male domination) created dissonance in another. As such, it was less adequate a solution than patrilineality, and it is being selected out.

Aside from these problems inherent in matrilinearity, Hartung (1976) has recently suggested two positive biological advantages of patrilineal descent. One concerns that fact that a man is certain (barring mutations) to pass on intact to all his male descendants his Y chromosome. Since the Y chromosome has no homolog, it cannot recombine through crossing over, as the X chromosome can for females. A woman cannot be sure that either of her granddaughter's X chromosomes is hers, in the same way as a man can be sure of his son's son's single Y chromosome. Patrilineal descent thus insures a slightly greater certainty of biological relatedness than matrilineal descent.

The second of Hartung's arguments in favor of patrilineal descent concerns the inheritance of "wealth" (broadly defined to include socially transmitted skills). Males have greater *variability* in reproductive success than females. This is clearly evident in polygynous societies. It is also clear that wealth can contribute more to the reproductive success of males than of females, especially if it is invested in wives, as it typically is in most polygynous societies. Therefore, the accumulation of wealth favors patrilineality. The sociobiological argument fits in very well with the ethnographic evidence. In matrilineal societies, bridewealth payments are typically absent or fairly nominal, whereas, in patrilineal societies, they are typically quite substantial.

The "catch" to patrilineal descent, of course, is the uncertainty of paternity.

This, in turn, would lead one to expect that in patrilineal societies men have a far greater interest in controlling and monopolizing the sexual behavior of women than in matrilineal societies. Measured by such indices as premarital chastity and virginity (sometimes enforced by such extreme measures as infibulation and chastity belts), and sanctions against adultery (sometimes punishable by death, or by damages paid to the husband), patrilineal societies are notoriously stricter than matrilineal ones. Patrilineal societies are also notable for their propensity to keep women (and hence their reproductive power) within the patrilineage by such institutions as the levirate.

Undeniably, both patrilineal and matrilineal descent are *cultural,* not biological arrangements, and there is no question that human behavior must always be understood as the product of an interplay between biological, ecological, and sociocultural conditions. Our argument is only with social scientists who dogmatically assert the irrelevance of biology to our social behavior.

There are other recurrent conflicts between kinsmen that kin-selection theory can shed new light on. For example, it is only rarely appreciated, even by evolutionary biologists, that genetic relatedness and physical propinquity often coincide (Alexander 1974). Since competition is also greatest among neighbors, it follows that a degree of conflict will occur even among relatives, insofar as they compete for limited resources which contribute to fitness. Rules of primogeniture, or ultimogeniture, for example, are obvious cultural innovations to limit what might otherwise be ruinous competition among siblings. There also is commonly conflict between father and son over the acquisition of new wives in those polygynous societies where marriage is accompanied by extensive bridewealth payments. Many of these societies, such as are found among both Bantu and non-Bantu pastoralists and mixed pastoralists-agriculturalists in Eastern and Southern Africa, impose prolonged celibacy on young men during a lengthy period of military service. Such was the case, among many other societies, with the Masai, the Zulu, and the Swazi (H. Kuper 1952; Gluckman 1940).

With bridewealth payments often ranging from ten to 20 head of cattle, the number of wives that can be acquired is obviously limited, and since cattle ownership in those patrilineal societies goes in the male line, fathers and sons typically have to draw from the same herds to get wives. Inclusive-fitness theory will predict that fathers would rather get additional wives for themselves with whom to beget children ($r = \frac{1}{2}$) than wives for their sons, who will produce grandchildren ($r = \frac{1}{4}$). The calculus for sons is the precise opposite: they would rather have children ($r = \frac{1}{2}$) than half-siblings ($r = \frac{1}{4}$). Naturally, there is a competing hypothesis in terms of sexual gratification or economic benefits to explain the conflict. One test of inclusive-fitness theory would be to devise choice situations such as that ego would be given the option of one wife for himself versus, say, three for his sons. (Inclusive-fitness theory would predict that a ratio greater than two wives for alter to one for ego is necessary to overcome the fact that alter's children by such potential wife or wives would only be half as related to ego as would ego's children.) Very few Zulu or Masai fathers, we would expect, would opt to have one additional wife if the same bridewealth could secure three wives for their sons. In addition, the likelihood of producing successful offspring should influence the balance of choice in predictable ways: impotence, genetically transmitted defects, and/or economic incompetence should displace interest in acquisition of wives from ego to alter.

Other parent-child conflicts are likely to occur where the cost-benefit or relatedness ratio is asymmetrical. For instance, parents and offspring can be expected to disagree on the treatment of nephews/first cousins (Trivers 1974). Nephews share, on the average, one-fourth of their genes with their uncles or aunts, while first cousins share only one-eighth. Parents, then, by projecting their own feeling towards their nephews, might well expect their children to be more altruistic than the latter feel inclined. An interesting test here would be to see if, say, sheer frequency of interaction between cousins diminishes after the death of their respective parents (controlling for such obvious contaminating factors as geographical dispersal).

In his masterly treatise, Wilson (1975) suggests that the central problem of sociobiology is the relationship between populations and societies. He defines a population as a network of interbreeding conspecifics, and a society as a network of interacting conspecifics. Both populations and societies are bounded by areas of much lower frequencies of interbreeding or interactions. That is, the members of a species cluster in dense networks of ties separated by "no-animal's land," where ties are few and episodic. Such a conception of a society is quite similar to Radcliffe-Brown's, and indeed overlaps considerably with the anthropological treatment of marriage and kinship. Many anthropologists, and perhaps most cogently, Lévi-Strauss (1968), have stated that rules of endogamy and exogamy have, to a large extent, determined the structure of "primitive" societies, that is to say, of nearly all human societies for nearly all of human history. Interestingly, they determine not only social structure, but genetic structure as well.

In its simplest and most schematic form, a "primitive" society-population is composed of a larger group, *the* people, who interact and interbreed, and who are bounded by either implicit or explicit, preferential or prescriptive, rules of endogamy. The larger society-population is, in turn, made up of smaller exogamous kin groups (at a minimum, the nuclear family, at a maximum, clans with thousands of members). In the larger group, the boundaries of society and population roughly coincide: in the smaller component kin groups, society and population are mutually exclusive concepts. That is, the smaller groups are subsocieties, but exogamy prevents them from being subpopulations. Another way of expressing this relationship is to say that the network of interbreeding and interaction of the society as a whole is determined positively by the exogamy of its constituent kin subgroups, and negatively by the relative absence of ties (or by the presence of mostly aversive and hostile relationships) with other societies. Ingroup nepotism and altruism, and outgroup hostility and aversion are thus but the two sides of the same social reality. They define the very nature of a human society.

Similarly, rules of exogamy and endogamy are also two sides of the same coin.

Endogamy defines the boundaries of a society; exogamy makes for the internal cohesion of its subunits. Groups that swap women interact with each other and establish kin ties as well. On the one hand, exogamy limits inbreeding and thus favors the retention of sufficient heterozygosity to allow for biological adaptability. On the other hand, endogamy maintains sufficient relatedness in the larger society to preserve what sociologists have, following Durkheim (1933), called "social solidarity," and what sociobiologists now somewhat misleadingly term "altruism."

Modern industrial societies, or even complex agrarian societies, represent considerable elaboration on this simple schema, while at the same time retaining appreciable residues thereof. More and more human societies have in the last couple of millennia moved further and further away from our species-specific biogram, so much so that most social scientists have for several decades assumed our biology to be largely irrelevant to our behavior.

A sociobiologic perspective suggests at least one major departure from the mainstream of social science thinking. Despite several attempts at reductionism, especially psychological reductionism represented for instance by social behaviorism, much of sociological and anthropological thinking has treated social behavior as a level of phenomena largely abstractable from the behavior of individual actors. Herbert Spencer (1874) misapplied Darwinism by stating that society was an organism, or, indeed, a superorganism (whatever *that* meant). Durkheim (1951) followed suit by insisting that society was a reality *sui generis,* greater than the sum of its parts, and not reducible to the behavior of its members. Much of American anthropology treated culture as a disembodied superorganism, and British and French anthropology did much the same to social structure. Generations of graduate students have been told that reductionism was a dirty word, and should, therefore, be resisted.

Yet, the entire scientific enterprise is reductionist: it seeks more and more basic explanations for wider and wider ranges of phenomena. Sociobiology is obviously reductionist, and therein lies its seductiveness to some and its repulsiveness to others. It suggests that human social behavior must be understood as the product of a long evolutionary process in which we are but one species among many, albeit a very special one. It further suggests that important features of what we call social structure and culture are not mysteriously fulfilling certain individual needs of "functional prerequisites," but are merely shorthand descriptions for the behavior of individual organisms. Finally, it commits what, to many social scientists, is the ultimate insult: it asserts that at least some of our behavior is understandable without any reference to what we say, think, or feel. If the complex patterns of cooperation and conflict that we term societies are ultimately reducible to blobs of protoplasm jostling to pass on genes, then our fanciful ideological superstructures, including our scientific structures, must appear rather silly.

Of course, we do not claim that sociobiology is the ultimate or the best framework to understand all human behavior, nor even that it is true in any absolute sense. We are merely advocating an epistemology that calls for starting with the lowest and most general level of reductionism and seeing how much it explains, before going on to higher and less general levels. Biology is clearly not the ultimate level of reductionism: below biology are the levels of biochemistry and biophysics. At present, however, our knowledge gap is such that we can explain little of behavior in biochemical terms, and even less in biophysical terms. Conversely, there is much in human affairs that sociobiology can shed very little light on: it cannot, and probably never will, explain the French Revolution, the music of Bartok, or the meaning of Yom Kippur. Our contention is merely that, a century after Darwin, we have learned enough biology to try to apply it to behavior in general, social behavior in particular, and human social behavior most especially.

NOTES

1　There are two textbook exceptions. One is the Catholic belief in parthenogenesis, limited, of course, to one very special case. The other is the Trobrianders' alleged belief that sexual intercourse facilitates, but does not cause, pregnancy (Malinowski 1929). Since Malinowski is widely revered as the pioneer of the tradition of anthropological fieldwork, few of his colleagues have been irreverent enough to suggest that the Trobrianders were pulling his leg, but that possibility remains.
2　Even large unilineal kin groups such as clans and lineages with memberships running into hundreds or thousands, or indeed in a few cases, millions, are typically exogamous. Only about one-sixth of a sample of 175 patrilineal or matrilineal societies had nonexogamous kin groups (Murdock 1949).

REFERENCES CITED

Alexander, Richard D.
　1971　The Search for an Evolutionary Philosophy of Man. Proceedings of the Royal Society, Victoria 84:99–120.
　1974　The Evolution of Social Behavior. Annual Review of Ecology and Systematics 5:325–383.
　1975　The Search for a General Theory of Behavior. Behavioral Science 20:77–100.
Barash, David P.
　1975　Ecology of Paternal Behavior in the Hoary Marmot (*Marmota caligata*): An Evolutionary Interpretation. Journal of Mammalogy 56:612–615
　1976　Some Evolutionary Aspects of Parental Behavior in Animals and Man. American Journal of Psychology 89:195–217.
　1976　Male Response to Apparent Female Adultery in the Mountain Bluebird (*Sialia corrucoides*): An Evolutionary Interpretation. The American Naturalist. 110:1097–1101.
　1977　Sociobiology and Behavior. New York: Elsevier.
Crook, John H.
　1965　The Adaptive Significance of Avian Social Organizations. Symposia of the Zoological Society of London 18:237–258.
Crook, John H., J. E. Ellis, and J. D. Goss-Custard
　1976　Mammalian Social Systems: Structure and Function. Animal Behavior 24:261–274.

Durkheim, Emile
  1933   The Division of Labor in Society. New York: Macmillan.
  1951   Suicide. Glencoe: Free Press.
Eisenberg, John F.
  1966   The Social Organization of Mammals. Handbuch der Zoologie 10(7):1–92.
Eisenberg, John F., N. A. Muckenhirn, and R. Rudran
  1972   The Relation Between Ecology and Social Structure in Primates. Science 176:863–874.
Erickson, Carl J., and P. G. Zenone
  1976   Courtship Differences in Male Ring Doves: Avoidance of Cuckoldry? Science 192:1353–1354.
Evans-Pritchard, E. E.
  1929   The Study of Kinship in Primitive Society. Man 29:190–194.
  1940   The Nuer. Oxford: Clarendon Press.
Francis, E. K.
  1976   Interethnic Relations: An Essay in Sociological Theory. New York: Elsevier.
Fox, Robin, ed.
  1975   Biosocial Anthropology. New York: Wiley.
Gluckman, Max
  1940   The Kingdom of the Zulu. *In* African Politcal Systems. Meyer Fortes and E. E. Evans-Pritchard, eds. Pp. 25–55. London: Oxford University Press.
Goody, J. A. R.
  1959   The Mother's Brother and the Sister's Son in West Africa. Journal of the Royal Anthropological Institute 89:61–88.
Hamilton, W. D.
  1964   The Genetical Evolution of Social Behaviour. Journal of Theoretical Biology 7:1–52.
  1975   Innate Social Aptitudes of Man: An Approach from Evolutionary Genetics. *In* Biosocial Anthropology. Robin Fox, ed. Pp. 133–155. New York: Wiley.
Hartung, John
  1976   On Natural Selection and the Inheritance of Wealth. Current Anthropology 17:606–614.
Hill, James L.
  1974   Peremyscus: Effect of Early Pairing on Reproduction. Science 186:1042–1044.
Jenni, Donald A.
  1974   Evolution of Polyandry in Birds. American Zoologist 14:129–144.
Keyes, Charles F.
  1976   Towards a New Formulation of the Concept of Ethnic Group. Ethnicity 3:202–213.
Kuper, Adam
  1976   Radcliffe-Brown, Junod and the Mother's Brother in South Africa. Man 11:111–115.
Kuper, Hilda
  1952   The Swazi. *In* Ethnographic Survey of Africa: Southern Africa, Vol. 1. London: International African Institute.
Lévi-Strauss, Claude
  1968   The Elementary Structures of Kinship. Boston: Beacon Press.

MacKinnon, John
  1974   The Behaviour and Ecology of Wild Orang-utans (*Pongo pygmaeus*). Animal Behaviour 22:3–74.
Malinowski, Bronislaw
  1929   The Sexual Life of Savages in North-Western Melanesia. London: Routledge.
Maynard Smith, J., and M. G. Ridpath
  1972   Wife Sharing in the Tasmanian Native Hen, *Tribonyx mortierii:* A Case of Kin Selection? Journal of the American Naturalist 106(950):447–452.
Murdock, George P.
  1949   Social Structure. New York: Macmillan.
  1957   World Ethnographic Sample. American Anthropologist 59:664–687.
Orians, Gordon H.
  1969   On the Evolution of Mating Systems in Birds and Mammals. The American Naturalist 103:589–603.
Parker, Seymour
  1976   The Precultural Basis of the Incest Taboo: Toward a Biosocial Theory. American Anthropologist 73:285–305.
Radcliffe-Brown, Alfred R.
  1952   Structure and Function in Primitive Society. Glencoe: Free Press.
Sahlins, Marshall D.
  1965   On the Sociology of Primitive Exchange. *In* The Relevance of Models for Social Anthropology. M. Banton, ed. Pp. 139–236. London: Tavistock.
  1976   The Use and Abuse of Biology. Ann Arbor: University of Michigan Press.
Shepher, Joseph
  1972   Mate Selection Among Second Generation Kibbutz Adolescents and Adults. Archives of Sexual Behavior 1:293–307.
Spencer, Herbert
  1874   The Study of Sociology. London: Appleton.
Tiger, Lionel, and Robin Fox
  1971   The Imperial Animal. New York: Holt, Rinehart & Winston.
Tiger, Lionel, and Joseph Shepher
  1976   Women in the Kibbutz. New York: Harcourt, Brace, Jovanovich.
Trivers, R. L.
  1971   The Evolution of Reciprocal Altruism. Quarterly Review of Biology 46(4):35–57.
  1972   Parental Investment and Sexual Selection. *In* Sexual Selection and the Descent of Man, 1871–1971. B. Campbell, ed. Pp. 136–179. Chicago: Aldine.
  1974   Parent-Offspring Conflict. American Zoologist 14:249–264.
van den Berghe, Pierre L.
  n.d.   The Human Family: A Sociobiological Look. *In* Evolution of Human Social Behavior. Joan Lockard, ed. (Submitted for publication.)
West Eberhard, Mary J.
  1975   The Social Biology of Polistine Wasps. Quarterly Review of Biology 50:1–33.
Wilson, Edward O.
  1975   Sociobiology: The New Synthesis. Cambridge: Belknap Press.

Part Five

Ramifications

An eagerness to apply biological science to human affairs is a marked feature of the times. Gone are the days when the biologist was at best looked upon with amused tolerance; he is astonished to find himself called upon for advice, for leadership. He used to be pictured in the public prints as an absurd creature, his pockets bulging with snakes and newts—a harmless fellow, no doubt, but preposterous, objectionable. All that is changed. It has come to be recognized that man is a biological specimen, as much as are snakes and newts; his affairs are biological affairs, and must be carried on in accordance with sound biological principles. The uplifter hastens to secure the endorsement of the biologist for his particular remedy for human ills. The man in the street recognizes that if his practices are not biologically sound, they are not sound at all; the biological expert must set the seal of his approval upon them. Profound changes in practice are urged upon the world as pronouncements of biological science.

H. S. Jennings
*The Biological Basis of Human Nature**

*W. W. Norton & Co., New York, 1930.

E. O. Wilson's *Sociobiology: The New Synthesis* was widely publicized at the time of its introduction as a milestone treatise that signaled the birth of a new academic discipline. Such a proposition will inevitably draw close attention and invite both criticism and support. In this case, the unusually large amount of publicity given *Sociobiology* generated an unusually large published response. Both zealots and skeptics were easily identifiable. The lay press spotlighted the concept of a new discipline, while at least a few specialists commented (mostly among themselves) that sociobiology was merely a new name applied to an already established area of academic inquiry. Perhaps the majority of interested academicians warmly applauded *Sociobiology* as a significant contribution to the synthesis of existing knowledge, while they recognized that only historians of science, at some date well in the future, will be able to pinpoint the date of birth of a discipline.

The greatest part of *Sociobiology* concerns itself with sociality in animals other than man. Very little of this material has been subjected to any wider close scrutiny than that occurring in the specialized scholarly press. However, the last chapter of the volume, entitled "Man: From Sociobiology to Sociology," not only drew substantial publicity in the media, but also generated heated controversy. To the acknowledged surprise of *Sociobiology's* author, a small body of vocal and harsh critics took positions beyond being merely skeptics. The chapter on man was assailed as pseudoscience and as merely the most recent installment of a long series of works of advocacy that incorrectly invoke biological principles to validate particular patterns of human behavior. Many discussants, both pro and con, spoke at symposia throughout the country. Of the numerous published exchanges, none were more widely circulated nor, perhaps, more heated than that between *Sociobiology's* author, E. O. Wilson, and a Cambridge, Massachusetts, Marxist collective called the Sociobiology Study Group of Science for the People. One of those published exchanges is reprinted here. In the closing paper of this volume, P. H. Klopfer adds both historical and philosophical perspective to the sociobiology debate.

Sociobiology—Another Biological Determinism

Sociobiology Study Group of Science for the People

Biological determinism represents the claim that the present states of human societies are the specific result of biological forces and the biological "nature" of the human species. Determinist theories all describe a particular model of society which corresponds to the socioeconomic prejudices of the writer. It is then asserted that this pattern has arisen out of human biology and that present human social arrangements are either unchangeable or if altered will demand continued conscious social control because these changed conditions will be "unnatural." Moreover, such determinism provides a direct justification for the status quo as "natural," although some determinists dissociate themselves from some of the consequences of their arguments. The issue, however, is not the motivation of individual creators of determinist theories, but the way these theories operate as powerful forms of legitimation of past and present social institutions such as aggression, competition, domination of women by men, defense of national territory, individualism, and the appearance of a status and wealth hierarchy.

The earlier forms of determinism in the current wave have now been pretty well discredited. The claims that there is a high heritability of IQ, which implies both the unchangeability of IQ and a genetic difference between races or between social classes, have now been thoroughly debunked.

The simplistic forms of the human nature argument given by Lorenz, Ardrey, Tiger and Fox, and others have no scientific credit and have been scorned as works of "advocacy" by E. O. Wilson, whose own book, *Sociobiology: The New Synthesis,* is the manifesto of a new, more complex, version of biological determinism, no less a work of "advocacy" than its rejected predecessors. This book, whose first chapter is on "The Morality of the Gene," is intended to establish sociology as a branch of evolutionary biology, encompassing all human societies, past and present. Wilson believes that "sociology and the other social sciences, as well as the humanities, are the last branches of biology waiting to be included in the Modern Synthesis" (p. 4).

This is no mere academic exercise. For more than a century the idea that human social behavior is determined by evolutionary imperatives operating on inherited dispositions has been seized upon and widely entertained not so much for its alleged correspondence with reality as for its more obvious political value. Among the better

At the time of composition of this article the Sociobiology Study Group of Science for the People consisted of L. Allen, B. Beckwith, J. Beckwith, S. Chorover, D. Culver, N. Daniels, E. Dorfman, M. Duncan, E. Engelman, R. Fitten, K. Fuda, S. Gould, C. Gross, R. Hubbard, J. Hunt, (no relation to the editor of this volume), H. Inouye, M. Kotelchuck, B. Lange, A. Leeds, R. Levins, R. Lewontin, E. Loechler, B. Ludwig, C. Madansky, L. Miller, R. Morales, S. Motheral, K. Muzal, N. Ostrom, R. Pyeritz, A. Reingold, M. Rosenthal, M. Mersky, M. Wilson, and H. Schreier.

From *BioScience 26:* 182, 184–186. Reprinted, with permission, from the March 1976 *BioScience* published by the American Institute of Biological Sciences.

known examples are Herbert Spencer's argument in *Social Statics* (1851) that poverty and starvation were natural agents cleansing society of the unfit, and Konrad Lorenz's call in 1940 in Germany for "the extermination of elements of the population loaded with dregs," based upon his ethological theories.

In order to make their case, determinists construct a selective picture of human history, ethnography, and social relations. They misuse the basic concepts and facts of genetics and evolutionary theory, asserting things to be true that are totally unknown, ignoring whole aspects of the evolutionary process, asserting that conclusions follow from premises when they do not. Finally, they invent ad hoc hypotheses to take care of the contradictions and carry on a form of "scientific reasoning" that is untestable and leads to unfalsifiable hypotheses. What follows is a general examination of these elements in sociobiological theory, especially as elaborated in E. O. Wilson's *Sociobiology.*

A VERSION OF HUMAN NATURE

For the sociobiologist the first task is to delineate a model of human nature that is to be explained. Among Wilson's universal aspects of human nature are:

- territoriality and tribalism (pp. 564–565);

- indoctrinability—"Human beings are absurdly easy to indoctrinate—they *seek* it" (p. 562);

- spite and family chauvinism—"True spite is commonplace in human societies, undoubtedly because human beings are keenly aware of their own blood lines and have the intelligence to plot intrigue" (p. 119);

- reciprocal altruism (as opposed to true unselfishness)—"Human behavior abounds with reciprocal altruism," as for example, "aggressively moralistic behavior", "self-righteousness, gratitude and sympathy" (p. 120);

- blind faith—"Men would rather believe than know" (p. 561);

- warfare (p. 572) and genocide (p. 573)—"the most distinctive human qualities" emerged during the "autocatalytic phase of social evolution" which occurred through intertribal warfare, "genocide" and "genosorption."

The list is not exhaustive and is meant only to show how the outlines of human nature are viewed myopically, through the lens of modern Euro-American culture.

To construct such a view of human nature, Wilson must abstract himself totally from any historical or ethnographic perspective. His discussion of the economy of scarcity is an excellent example. An economy of relative scarcity and unequal distribution of rewards is stated to be an aspect of human nature:

"The members of human society sometimes cooperate closely in *insectan* fashion [our emphasis], but more frequently they compete for the limited resources allocated to their role sector. The best and the most entrepreneurial of the role-actors usually gain a disproportionate share of the rewards." (p. 554)

There is a great deal of ethnographic and historical description entirely contradicting this conception of social organization. It ignores, for example, the present and historical existence of societies not differentiated in any significant way by "role sectors"; without scarcities differentially induced by social institutions for different subpopulations of the society; not differentiated by lower and higher ranks and strata (Birket-Smith 1959; Fried 1967; Harris 1968; Krader 1968).

Realizing that history and ethnography do not support the universality of their description of human nature, sociobiologists claim that the exceptions are "temporary aberrations" or deviations. Thus, although genocidal warfare is (assertedly) universal, "it is to be expected that some isolated cultures will escape the process for generations at a time, in effect reverting temporarily to what ethnographers classify as a pacific state" (p. 574).

Another related ploy is the claim that ethnographers and historians have been too narrow in their definitions and have not realized that apparently contradictory evidence is really confirmatory.

"Anthropologists often discount territorial behavior as a general human attribute. This happens when the narrowest concept of the phenomenon is borrowed from zoology . . . it is necessary to define territory more broadly . . . animals respond to their neighbors in a highly variable manner. . . . the scale may run from open hostility . . . to oblique forms of advertisement or *no territorial behavior at all*" (our emphasis).
"If these qualifications are accepted it is reasonable to conclude that territoriality is a general trait of hunter gatherer societies." (pp. 564–565)

Wilson's view of aggression and warfare are subject to this ploy of all-embracing definition on the one hand and erroneous historical-ethnographic data on the other. "Primitive" warfare is rarely lethal to more than one or at most a few individuals in an episode of warfare, virtually without significance genetically or demographically (Livingstone 1968). Genocide was virtually unknown until state-organized societies appeared in history (as far as can be made out from the archeological and documentary records).

We have given only examples of the general advocacy method employed by sociobiologists in a procedure involving definitions which exclude nothing and the laying of Western conceptual categories onto "primitive" societies.

HUMANS AS ANIMALS—THE MEANING OF SIMILARITY

To support a biologistic explanation of human institutions it is useful to claim an evolutionary relationship between the nature of human social institutions and "social" behavior in other animals. Obviously sociobiologists would prefer to claim evolutionary homology, rather than simple analogy, as the basis for the similarity in behavior between humans and other animals; then they would have a prima facie case for genetic determination. In some sections of *Sociobiology*, Wilson attempts to do this by listing "universal" features of behavior in higher primates including humans. But claimed external similarity between humans and our closest relatives (which are by no means very close to us) does not imply genetic continuity. A behavior that may be genetically coded in a higher primate may be purely learned and widely spread among human cultures as a consequence of the enormous flexibility of our brain.

More often Wilson argues from evolutionary analogy. Such arguments operate on shaky grounds. They can never be used to assert genetic similarity, but they can serve as a plausibility argument for natural selection of human behavior by assuming that natural selection has operated on different genes in the two species but has produced convergent responses as independent adaptations to similar environments. The argument is not even worth considering unless the similarity is so precise that identical function cannot be reasonably denied, as in the classic case of evolutionary convergence—the eyes of vertebrates and octopuses. Here Wilson fails badly, for his favorite analogies arise by a twisted process of imposing human institutions on animals by metaphor, and then rederiving the human institutions as special cases of the more general phenomenon "discovered" in nature. In this way human institutions suddenly become "natural" and can be viewed as a product of evolution.

A classic example, long antedating *Sociobiology*, is "slavery" in ants. "Slavemaking" species capture the immature stages of "slave" species and bring them back to their own nests. When the captured workers hatch, they perform housekeeping tasks with no compulsion as if they were members of the captor species. Why is this "slavemaking" instead of "domestication"? Human slavery involves members of one's own species under continued compulsion. It is an economic institution in societies producing an economic surplus, with both slave and product as commodities in exchange. It has nothing to do with ants except by weak and meaningless analogy. Wilson expands the realm of these weak analogies (chapter 27) to find barter, division of labor, role playing, culture, ritual, religion, magic, esthetics, and tribalism among nonhumans. But if we insist upon seeing animals in the mirror of our own social arrangements, we cannot fail to find any human institutions we want among them.

GENETIC BASES OF BEHAVIOR

We can dispense with the direct evidence for a genetic basis of various human social forms in a single word, "None." The genetics of normal human behavior is in a rudimentary state because of the impossibility of reproducing particular human genotypes over and over, or of experimentally manipulating the environments of individuals or groups. There is no evidence that meets the elementary requirements of experimental design, that such traits as xenophobia, religion, ethics, social dominance, hierarchy formation, slavemaking, etc., are in any way coded specifically in the genes of human beings.

And indeed, Wilson offers no such evidence. Instead, he makes confused and contradictory statements about what is an essential element in the argument. If there are no genes for parent-offspring conflict, then there is no sense in talking about natural selection for this phenomenon. Thus, he speaks of "genetically programmed sexual and parent-offspring conflict" (p. 563), yet there is the "considerable technical problem of distinguishing behavioral elements and combinations that emerge . . . independently of learning and those that are shaped at least to some extent by learning" (p. 159). In fact, it cannot be done.

Elsewhere, the *capacity* to learn is stated to be genetic in the species, so that "it does not matter whether aggression is wholly innate or acquired partly or wholly by learning" (p. 255). But it does matter. If all that is genetically programmed into people is that "genes promoting flexibility in social behavior are strongly selected" (p. 549) and if "genes have given away most of their sovereignty" (p. 550), then biology and evolution give no insight into the human condition except the most trivial one, that the *possibility* of social behavior is part of human biology. However, in the next phrase Wilson reasserts the sovereignty of the genes because they "maintain a certain amount of influence in at least the behavioral qualities that underly the variations between cultures." It is stated as *fact* that genetical differences underly variations between cultures, when no evidence at all exists for this assertion and there is some considerable evidence against it.

Since sociobiologists can adduce no facts to support the genetic basis for human social behavior, they try two tacks. First, the suggestion of evolutionary homology between behavior in the human species and other animals, if correct, would imply a genetic basis in us. But the evidence for homology as opposed to analogy is very weak. Second, they postulate genes right and left and then go on to argue as if the genes were demonstrated facts. There are hypothetical altruist genes, conformer genes, spite genes, learning genes, homosexuality genes, and so on. An instance of the technique is on pages 554–555 of Wilson's book: "Dahlberg showed that *if* a single gene appears that is responsible for success and upward shift in status . . ." and "Furthermore, *there are many* Dahlberg genes . . ." (our emphases throughout). Or on page 562: "*If we assume* for argument that indoctrinability evolves . . ." and "Societies containing higher frequencies of conformer genes replace those that disappear . . ." (our emphasis). Or consult nearly any page of Trivers (1971) for many more examples.

Geneticists long ago abandoned the naive notion that there are genes for toes, genes for ankles, genes for the lower leg, genes for the kneecap, or the like. Yet sociobiologists break the totality of human social phenomena into arbitrary units, which they reify as "organs of behavior," postulating particular genes for each.

EVERYTHING IS ADAPTIVE

The next step in the sociobiological argument is to try to show that the hypothetical, genetically programmed behavior organs have evolved by natural selection. The assertion that all human behavior is or has been adaptive is an outdated expression of Darwinian evolutionary theory, characteristic of Darwin's 19th century defenders who felt it necessary to prove everything adaptive. It is a deeply conservative politics, not an understanding of modern evolutionary theory, that leads one to see the wonderful operation of adaptation in every feature of human social organization.

There is no hint in *Sociobiology* that at this very moment the scientific community of evolutionary geneticists is deeply split on the question of how important adaptive as opposed to random processes are in manifest evolution. More important, there is a strain in modern evolutionary thought, going back to Julian Huxley, that avoids much of the tortured logic required by extreme selectionism, by emphasizing allometry. Organs, not themselves under direct natural selection, may change because of their developmental links to other features that are under selection. Many aspects of human social organization, if not all, may be simply the consequence of increased plasticity of neurological response and cognitive capacity.

The major assertion of sociobiologists that human social structures exist because of their superior adaptive value is only an assumption for which no tests have even been proposed. The entire theory is so constructed that *no tests are possible*. The mode of explanation involves three postulated levels of the operation of natural selection: (1) classical individual selection to account for obviously self-serving behaviors; (2) kin selection to account for altruistic behaviors or submissive acts toward relatives; (3) reciprocal altruism to account for altruistic behaviors toward unrelated persons. All that remains is to make up a "just-so" story of adaptation with the appropriate form of selection acting. For some traits it is easy to invent a story. The "genes" for social dominance, aggression, entrepreneurship, successful deception, and so on will "obviously" be advantageous at the individual level. For example, evidence is presented (p. 288) that dominant males impregnate a disproportionate share of females in mice, baboons, and Yanamamo Indians. In fact, in the ethnographic literature there are numerous examples of groups whose political "leaders" do not have greater access to mates. In general it is hard to demonstrate a correlation of any of the sociobiologists' "adaptive" social behaviors with actual differential reproduction.

Other traits require more ingenuity. Homosexuality would seem to be at a reproductive disadvantage since "of course, homosexual men marry much less frequently and have far fewer children" (Dr. Kinsey disagreed, and what about homosexual women?). But a little ingenuity solves the problem: "The homosexual members of primitive societies may have functioned as helpers . . . [operated] with special efficiency in assisting close relatives" (p. 555). Kin selection saves the day when one's imagination for individual selection fails.

Only one more imaginative mechanism is needed to rationalize such phenomena as friendship, morality, patriotism, and submissiveness, even when the bonds do not involve relatives. The theory of reciprocal altruism (Trivers 1971) proposes that selection has operated such that risk taking and acts of kindness can be recognized and reciprocated so that the net fitness of both participants is increased.

The trouble with the whole system is that nothing is explained because everything is explained. If individuals are selfish, that is explained by simple individual selection. If, on the contrary, they are altruistic, it is kin selection or reciprocal altruism. If sexual identities are unambiguously heterosexual, individual fertility is increased. If, however, homosexuality is common, it is a result of kin selection. Sociobiologists give us no example that might conceivably contradict their scheme of perfect adaptation.

VARIATIONS OF CULTURES IN TIME AND SPACE

There does exist one possibility of tests of sociobiological hypotheses when they make specific *quantitative* predictions about rates of change of characters in time and about the degree of differentiation between populations of a species. Population genetics makes specific predictions about rates of change, and there are hard data on the degree of genetic differentiation between human populations for biochemical traits. Both the theoretical rates of *genetic* change in time and the observed *genetic* differentiation between populations are too small to agree with the very rapid changes that have occurred in human *cultures* historically and the very large *cultural* differences observed among contemporaneous populations. So, for example, the rise of Islam after the 7th century to supreme cultural and political power in the West, to its subsequent rapid decline after the 13th century (a cycle occupying fewer than 30 generations) was too rapid by orders of magnitude for any large change by natural selection. The same problem arises for the immense cultural differences between contemporary groups, since we know from the study of enzyme-specifying genes that there is very little genetic differentiation between nations and races.

Wilson acknowledges and deals with both of these dilemmas by a bold stroke: He invents a new phenomenon. It is the "multiplier effect" (pp. 11–13, 569–572), which postulates that very small differences in the frequency of hypothetical genes for altruism, conformity, indoctrinability, etc., could move a whole society from one cultural pattern to another. The only evidence offered for this "multiplier effect" is a description of differences in behavior between closely related species of insects and of baboons. There is, however, no evidence about the amount of *genetic* difference between these closely related species nor how many tens or hundreds of thousands of generations separate the members of these species pairs since their divergence. The multiplier effect, by which any arbitrary but unknown genetic difference can be converted to any cultural difference you please, is a pure invention of convenience without any evidence to support it. It has been created out of whole cloth to seal off the last aperture through which the theory might have been tested against the real world.

AN ALTERNATIVE VIEW

It is often stated by biological determinists that those who oppose them are "environmental determinists," who believe that the behavior of individuals is precisely determined by some sequence of environmental events in childhood. Such an assertion reveals the essential narrowness of viewpoint in determinist ideologies. First, they see the individual as the basic elements of determination and behavior, whereas society is simply the sum of all the individuals in it. But the truth is that the individual's social activity is to be understood only by first understanding social institutions. We cannot understand what it is to be a slave or a slave owner without first understanding the institution of slavery, which defines and creates both slave and owner.

Second, determinists assert that the evolution of societies is the result of changes in the frequencies of different sorts of individuals within them. But this confuses cause and effect. Societies evolve because social and economic activity alter the physical and social conditions in which these activities occur. Unique historical events, actions of some individuals, and the altering of consciousness of masses of people interact with social and economic forces to influence the timing, form, and even the possibility of particular changes; individuals are not totally autonomous units whose individual qualities determine the direction of social evolution. Feudal society did not pass away because some autonomous force increased the frequency of entrepreneurs. On the contrary, the economic activity of Western feudal society itself resulted in a change in economic relations which made serfs into peasants and then into landless industrial workers with all the immense changes in social institutions that were the result.

Finally, determinists assert that the possibility of change in social institutions is limited by the biological constraints on individuals. But we know of no relevant constraints placed on social processes by human biology. There is no evidence from ethnography, archeology, or history that would enable us to circumscribe the limits of possible human social organization. What history and ethnography do provide us with are the materials for building a theory that will itself be an instrument of social change.

REFERENCES CITED

Birket-Smith, K. 1959. *The Eskimos,* 2nd ed. Methuen, London.

Fried, M. 1967. *The Evolution of Political Society.* Random House, New York.

Harris, M. 1968. Law and order in egalitarian societies. Pages 369–391 in *Culture, Man and Nature.* Crowell, New York.

Krader, L. 1968. Government without the state. Pages 29–42 in *Formation of the State*. Prentice Hall, Englewood Cliffs, N.J.

Lorenz, K. 1940. Durch Domestikation verursachte Störungen arteigenen Verhaltens. Zeitschrift für angewandte Psychologie und Characterkunde 59:56–75. (As quoted in Cloud, W., 1973, Winners and Sinners. *The Sciences* 13:16–21).

Livingstone, F. 1968. The effects of warfare on the biology of the human species. Pages 3–15 in M. Fried, M. Harris, and R. Murphy, eds. *War: The Anthropology of Armed Conflict and Aggression*. Natural History Press, Garden City.

Spencer, H. 1851. *Social Statics*. Chapman, London.

Trivers, R. 1971. The evolution of reciprocal altruism. *Q. Rev. Biol.* 46:35–57.

Wilson, E. O. 1975. *Sociobiology: The New Synthesis*. Harvard University Press, Cambridge, Mass.

Academic Vigilantism and the Political Significance of Sociobiology

Edward O. Wilson
Museum of Comparative Zoology, Harvard University

The best response to a political attack of the kind exemplified by the preceding article, "Sociobiology—Another Biological Determinism," is perhaps no response at all. Some of my colleagues have offered that advice. But the problem is larger than the personal distress that this and earlier activities of the Science for the People group have caused me. The issue at hand, I submit, is vigilantism: the judgment of a work of science according to whether it conforms to the political convictions of the judges, who are self-appointed. The sentence for scientists found guilty is to be given a label and to be associated with past deeds that all decent persons will find repellent.

Thus, in a statement published earlier in *The New York Review of Books* (Allen et al. 1974), the Science for the People group characterized my book *Sociobiology: The New Synthesis* (Wilson 1975a) as the latest attempt to reinvigorate theories that in the past "provided an important basis for the enactment of sterilization laws and restrictive immigration laws by the United States between 1910 and 1930 and also for the eugenics policies which led to the establishment of gas chambers in Nazi Germany." To this malicious charge they added, "Wilson joins the long parade of biological determinists whose work has served to buttress the institutions of their society by exonerating them from responsibility for social problems." The tone of the present *BioScience* article is muted, but the innuendo is clear and remains the same.

This tactic, which has been employed by members of Science for the People against other scientists, throws the person criticized into the role of defendant and renders his ideas easier to discredit. Free and open discussion becomes difficult, as the critics continue to press their campaign, and the target struggles to clear his name. The problem is increased by difficulties in knowing with whom one is dealing. The statements are often published over long lists of names, shifts in committee membership occur through time, and the authors' names are withheld from some of the documents. (All have occurred during the present controversy.)

Despite the protean physical form taken by the Sociobiology Study Group of Science for the People, the belief system they promote is clear-cut and rigid. They postulate that human beings need only decide on the kind of society they wish, and then find the way to bring it into being. Such a vision can be justified if human social behavior proves to be infinitely malleable. In their earlier *New York Review* statement (Allen et al. 1975) the group therefore maintained that although eating, excret-

From *BioScience 26:* 183, 187–190. Reprinted, with permission, from the March 1976 *BioScience* published by the American Institute of Biological Sciences.

ing, and sleeping may be genetically determined, social behavior is entirely learned; this belief has been developed further in the *BioScience* article. In contrast, and regardless of all they have said, I am ideologically indifferent to the degree of determinism in human behavior. If human beings proved infinitely malleable, as they hope, then one could justify any social or economic arrangement according to his personal value system. If on the other hand, human beings proved completely fixed, then the status quo could be justified as unavoidable.

Few reasonable persons take the first extreme position and none the second. On the basis of objective evidence the truth appears to lie somewhere in between, closer to the environmentalist than to the genetic pole. That was my wholly empirical conclusion in *Sociobiology: The New Synthesis* and continues to be in later writings. There is no reasonable way that this generalization can be construed as a support of the status quo and continued injustice, as the Science for the People group have now, on four painful occasions, claimed. I have personally argued the opposite conclusion, most fully and explicitly in my *New York Times Magazine* article of 12 October 1975 (Wilson 1975b). The Science for the People group have not found it convenient to mention this part of my writings.

With the exception of the Science for the People group, all of the many biologists and social scientists whose reviews of *Sociobiology: The New Synthesis* I have seen understood the book correctly. None has read a reactionary political message into it, even though the reviewers represent a variety of personal political persuasions; and none has found my assessment of the degree of determinism in human social behavior out of line with the empirical evidence. The Science for the People group have utterly misrepresented the spirit and content of the portions of *Sociobiology* devoted to human beings. They have done so, it would seem, in order to have a conspicuous straw man against which their views can be favorably pitted, and to obscure the valid points in *Sociobiology* which do indeed threaten their own extreme position. Let me document this interpretation with responses to the specific criticisms made by the 35 cosigners.

RESPONSE TO CRITICISMS

First, it should be noted that *Sociobiology: The New Synthesis* is a large book, within which only chapter 27 and scattered paragraphs in earlier chapters refer to man. The main theses of sociobiology are based on studies of a myriad of animal species conducted by hundreds of investigators in various biological disciplines. It has been possible to derive propositions by the traditional postulational and deductive methods of theoretical science, and to test many of them rigorously by quantitative studies. One can cite the work on kin selection in social Hymenoptera, the elaboration of caste systems in social insects, the economic functions of vertebrate territories, the ecological causes of ungulate social behavior, the repertory size and transmission characteristics of communication systems, and others. These ideas and data provide the main thrust of general sociobiology.

In my book human sociobiology was approached tentatively and in a taxonomic rather than a political spirit. The final chapter opens with the following passage: "Let us now consider man in the free spirit of natural history, as though we were zoologists from another planet completing a catalog of social species on Earth. In this macroscopic view the humanities and social sciences shrink to specialized branches of biology; history, biography, and fiction are the research protocols of human ethology; and anthropology and sociology together constitute the sociobiology of a single primate species."

It is the intellectually viable contention of the final chapter that the sociobiological methods which have proved effective in the study of animals can be extended to human beings, even though our vastly more complex, flexible behavior will make the application technically more difficult. The degree of success cannot yet be predicted. Chapter 27 was intended to be a beginning rather than a conclusion, and other reviewers have so interpreted it. In it I have characterized the distinctive human traits as best I could from the literature of the social sciences, and I have offered a set of hypotheses about the evolution of the traits stated in a way that seemed to make them most susceptible to analysis by sociobiological methods.

The Science for the People group ignore this main thrust of the book. They cite piece by piece incorrectly, or out of context, and then add their own commentary to furnish me with a political attitude I do not have and the book with a general conclusion that is not there. The following examples cover nearly all of their points.

Roles

The 35 cosigners have me saying that role sectors, and thus certain forms of economic role behavior associated with role sectors, are universal in man. On pages 552 and 554, the reader will find that I did not include role sectors among the widespread or universal traits. What I said was that when role sectors occur, certain economic features are associated with them.

Territory

It is now well known that animal territories commonly vary in size and quality of defense according to habitat, season, and population density. Under some circumstances many species show no territorial behavior, but it is necessary for them to display the behavior under other, specified circumstances in order to be called territorial—an obvious condition. This is the reason I have called the human species territorial. No contradiction in definitions exists; the cosigners have made it appear to exist by simply deleting three key pieces from the quoted statement. Most human societies are territorial most of the time.

Warfare

In *Sociobiology* I presented widespread lethal warfare in early human groups as a working hypothesis, not as a fact, contrary to what the cosigners suggest. And it is a hypothesis wholly consistent with the evidence: military activity and territorial expansion have been concomitants throughout history and at all levels of social organization (Otterbein 1970), and they can hardly fail to have had significant demographic and genetic consequences.

Slavery and Other Terms

The cosigners state that I claim to have found barter, religion, magic, and tribalism among nonhumans. I have made no such claim. The cosigners do not like to see terms such as slavery, division of labor, and ritual used in both zoology and the social sciences. Do they wish also to expunge communication, dominance, monogamy, and parental care from the vocabulary of zoology?

Genetic Bases of Behavior

The cosigners claim that no evidence exists for the genetic basis of particular forms of social behavior. Their statement indicates that they do not use the same criteria as other biologists. To postulate the existence of genes for the diagnostic human traits is not to imply that there exists one gene for spite, another for homosexuality, and so on, as one might envision the inheritance of flower color or seed texture in garden peas. The tendency to develop such behaviors, in a distinctively human form, is part of an immensely complex social repertory which is undoubtedly dependent on large numbers of genes.

My emphasis in *Sociobiology* was on the most widespread, distinctive qualities of human behavior—"human nature" if you wish—and the possible reasons why the underlying genes are different from those affecting social behavior in other species. Certain forms of human social behavior, such as the facial expressions used to convey the basic emotions, are relatively inflexible and transcultural. Human expressions, in fact, are so similar to those of the higher cercopithecoid primates as to suggest the possible existence of true homology (*Sociobiology,* pp. 227–228). Other kinds of response, including those under the categories of aggression, sexuality, and conformity, are of course subject to great variation through differences in experience. But as plastic as these latter behaviors might seem to us, they still form only a small subset of the many versions found in social species as a whole. It seems inconceivable that human beings could be socialized into the distinctive patterns of, say, ring-tailed lemurs, hamadryas baboons, or gibbons, or vice versa. This is the ordinary criterion on which the expression "genetic control of human social behavior" in sociobiology is based. The main idea conveyed by the final chapter of my book is that such a comparison with other social species will place human behavior in a clearer evolutionary perspective.

With reference to genetic variation between human populations, there is no firm evidence. As usual, the cosigners misrepresent what I said. Here is their claim: "It is stated as a *fact* that genetical differences underlly variations between cultures, when no evidence at all exists for this assertion and there is some considerable evidence against it" (emphasis theirs). Here is what I really said, in the very sentences to which they allude (p. 550): "Even a small portion of this [genetic] variance invested in population differences *might* predispose societies toward cultural differences. At the very least, we should try to measure this amount. It is not valid to point to the absence of a behavioral trait in one or a few societies as conclusive evidence that the trait is environmentally induced and has no genetic disposition in man. The very opposite *could* be true" (italics newly added).

Adaptation versus Non-adaptation

The Science for the People group state that I believe all social behavior to be adaptive and hence "normal." This is so patently false that I am surprised the cosigners could bring themselves to say it. I have on the contrary discussed circumstances under which certain forms of animal social behavior become maladaptive, with examples and ways in which the deviations can be analyzed (pp. 33–34). With reference to human social behavior I have said (Wilson 1975b, an article well known to the cosigners): "When any genetic bias is demonstrated, it cannot be used to justify a continuing practice in present and future societies. Since most of us live in a radically new environment of our own making, the pursuit of such a practice would be bad biology; and like all bad biology, it would invite disaster." I then cited examples of maladaptive behavior in human beings. Furthermore, both R. L. Trivers and I have provided varieties of adaptation hypotheses that compete with each other and against the non-adaptation hypothesis, contrary to the assertion of the Science for the People group (see, e.g., *Sociobiology:* pp. 123–124, 309–311, 326–327, 416–418).

Cultural Evolution

The cosigners propose that "sociobiological hypotheses" can be tested by seeing whether certain short-term episodes in history, such as the rise and decline of Islam, occurred too rapidly to be due to genetic change. They conclude that the theory of population genetics excludes that possibility. I agree, and that is why neither I nor any other sociobiologist of my acquaintance has ever proposed such hypotheses. The examples I used in *Sociobiology* to make the same point are the origin of the slave society of Jamaica, the decline of the Ik in Uganda, the alteration of Irish society following the potato famine, and the shift in the Japanese authority structure follow-ing World War II (pp. 548–550). I see no reason why the subject was even brought up. (A fuller discussion of the rates of cultural evolution and the complementarity of cultural to genetic evolution can be found in pages 168–175 and 555–562 of *Sociobiology.*)

COMMENTS ON THE DEBATE

I now invite readers to check each of the pronouncements in the article by the 35 cosigners against the actual statements in my book, in the true context in which the statements were made. I suggest that they will encounter very little correspondence, and I am confident that they will be left with no doubt as to my true meaning.

How is it possible for the Science for the People group to misrepresent so consistently the content of a book, in contrast to all of the many other reviewers among their scientific colleagues? There is first the circumstance of the size and composition of the group. It has grown from 16, when it called itself The Genetic Engineering Group of Scientists and Engineers for Social and Political Action (in the magazine *Science for the People,* November 1975), to the present 35 now identified as the Sociobiology Study Group of Science for the People. The membership is heterogeneous: from the best count I can make there are eight professors in several fields of science in the Boston area; other members include at least one psychiatrist, a secondary school teacher, students and research assistants. Furthermore, in conformity with their political convictions the group really does believe in collective decision making and writing, so perhaps the result is not all that surprising. (In the issue of *Science for the People* just mentioned, the two main targets of criticism were myself, for biological determinism, and the Soviet Union, for revisionism.)

But the other, more important cause of the problem, and the reason I have not been able to find the matter as humorous as have some of my colleagues, is the remorseless zeal of the cosigners. By their own testimony they worked for months on the project. They appear to have been alarmed by the impact a critical success of the book might have on the acceptability of their own political views. One of the faculty members, in a *Harvard Crimson* interview on 3 November 1975, stated that the group was formed of persons who became interested "in breaking down the screen of approval" around the book. Clamorous denunciations followed during a closely packed series of lectures, work sessions, and release of printed statements. In October 1975 a second professorial member of the group drafted a 5,000-word position paper for *The New York Times* which characterized me as an ideologue and a privileged member of modern Western industrial society whose book attempts to preserve the status quo (*The New York Times,* 9 November 1975). Later the same person (who shares the identical privileges at Harvard) startled me even more by declaring that "Sociobiology is not a racist doctrine" but "any kind of genetic determinism can and does feed other kinds, including the belief that some races are superior to others" (*Harvard Crimson,* 3 December 1975).

The latter argument is identical to that advanced simultaneously by student members of the Harvard-Radcliffe Committee against Racism, who, citing the Science for the People statement for authority, did not hesitate to label the book "dangerously racist" in leaflets distributed through the Boston area. Both the logic and the accusation were false and hurtful, and at this point the matter was close to getting out of hand.

On various occasions and with only limited success the Harvard faculty has attempted to protect itself from activities of this kind. During an earlier, similar episode 100 of its members published a statement that "In an academic community the substitution of personal harassment for reasoned inquiry is intolerable. The openminded search for truth cannot proceed in an atmosphere of political intimidation." This is the melancholy principle which has been confirmed by the exchange now extended to *BioScience.* In the Boston area at the present time it has become difficult to conduct an open forum on human sociobiology, or even general sociobiology, without falling into the role of either prosecutor or defendant.

THE POLITICAL SIGNIFICANCE OF SOCIOBIOLOGY

Finally and briefly, let me express what I consider to be the real significance of human sociobiology for political and social thought. The question that science is now in a position to approach is the very origin and meaning of human values, from which all ethical pronouncements and much of political practice flow. Philosophers themselves have not explored the problem; traditional ethical philosophy begins with premises that are examined with reference to their consequences but not their origins. Thus, John Rawls opens his celebrated *A Theory of Justice* (1971) with a proposition he regards as beyond dispute: "In a just society the liberties of equal citizenship are taken as settled; the rights secured by justice are not subject to political bargaining or to the calculus of social interests." Robert Nozick launches his equally celebrated *Anarchy, State, and Utopia* (1974) with a similarly firm proposition: "Individuals have rights, and there are things no person or group may do to them (without violating their rights). So strong and far-reaching are these rights that they raise the question of what, if anything, the state and its officials may do."

These two premises are somewhat different in content, and they lead to radically different prescriptions. Rawls would allow rigid social control to secure as close an approach as possible to the equal distribution of society's rewards. Nozick sees the ideal society as one governed by a minimal state, empowered only to protect its citizens from force and fraud, and with unequal distribution of rewards wholly permissible. Rawls rejects the meritocracy; Nozick accepts it as desirable except in those cases where local communities voluntarily decide to experiment with egalitarianism.

Whether in conflict or agreement, where do such fundamental premises come from? What lies behind the intuition on which they are based? Contemporary philosophers have progressed no further that Sophocles' Antigone, who said of moral imperatives, "They were not born today or yesterday; they die not, and none knoweth whence they sprung."

At this point the 35 members of the Science for the People group also come to a halt. At the close of their essay they imply the central issue to be a decision about the kind of the society we want to live in; humanity can then find the way to bring this society into being. But which persons are the "we" who will decide, and whose moral precepts must thereby be validated? The group believe that all social behavior is learned and transmitted by culture. But if this is true, the value system by which "we" will decide social policy is created by the culture in which the most powerful decision makers were reared and hence must inevitably validate the status quo, the very condition which the Science for the People group reject. The solution to the conundrum must be that their premise of complete environmentalism is wrong.

The evidence that human nature is to some extent genetically influenced is in my opinion decisive. In the present space I can only suggest that the reader consider the facts presented in *Sociobiology* and in the very extensive primary literature on the subject, some of which is cited in this work. It follows that value systems are probably influenced, again to an unknown extent, by emotional responses programmed in the limbic system of the brain. The qualities that comprise human nature in the Maring of New Guinea as recognizably as they did in the Greeks at Troy are surely due in part to constraints within the unique human genotype. The challenge of human sociobiology, shared with the social sciences, is to measure the degree of these constraints and to infer their significance through the reconstruction of the evolutionary history of the mind. The enterprise is the logical complement to the continued study of cultural evolution.

Even if that formidable challenge is successfully met, however, it will still leave the ethical question: To what extent should the censors and motivators in the emotive centers of the brain be obeyed? Given that these controls deeply and unconsciously affect our moral decisions, how faithfully must they be consulted once they have been defined and assayed as a biological process? The answer must confront what appears to me to be the true human dilemma. We cannot follow the suggestions of the censors and motivators blindly. Although they are the source of our deepest and most compelling feelings, their genetic constraints evolved during the millions of years of prehistory, under conditions that to a large extent no longer exist. At some time in the future it will be necessary to decide how human we wish to remain, in this the ultimate biological sense, and to pick and choose consciously among the emotional guides we have inherited.

This dilemma should engender a sense of reserve about proposals for radical social change based on utopian intuition. To the extent that the biological interpretation noted here proves correct, men have rights that are innate, rooted in the ineradicable drives for survival and self-esteem, and these rights do not require the validation of ad hoc theoretical constructions produced by society. If culture is all that created human rights, as the extreme environmentalist position holds, then culture can equally well validate their removal. Even some philosophers of the radical left see this flaw in the position taken by Science for the People. Noam Chomsky, whose own linguistic research has provided evidence for the existence of genetic influence, considers extreme environmentalism to be a belief susceptible to dictatorships of both the left and the right:

One can easily see why reformers and revolutionaries should become radical environmentalists, and there is no doubt that concepts of immutable human nature can be and have been employed to erect barriers against social change and to defend established privilege. But a deeper look will show that the concept of the "empty organism," plastic and unstructured, apart from being false, also serves naturally as the support for the most reactionary social doctrines. If people are, in fact, malleable and plastic beings with no essential psychological nature, then why should they not be controlled and coerced by those who claim authority, special knowledge, and a unique insight into what is best for those less enlightened? . . . The principle that human nature, in its psychological aspects, is nothing more than a product of history and given social relations removes all barriers to coercion and manipulation by the powerful. This too, I think, may be a reason for its appeal to intellectual ideologists, of whatever political persuasion (Chomsky 1975, p. 132).

Chomsky and I, not to mention Herbert Marcuse (who has a similar belief in the biological conservatism of human nature), can scarcely be accused of having linked arms to preserve the status quo, and yet that would seem to follow from the strange logic employed by the Science for the People group.

In their corybantic attentions to sociobiology, the Science for the People group have committed what can be usefully termed the Fallacy of the Political Consequent. This is the assumption that political belief systems can be mapped one-on-one onto biological or psychological generalizations. Another particularly ironic example is the response to B. F. Skinner's writings. Skinner is a radical environmentalist, whose conclusions about human behavior are essentially indistinguishable from those of the Science for the People group. Yet the particular political conclusions he has drawn are anathema to the radical left, who reject them as elitist, reactionary, and so forth. The cause of the Fallacy of the Political Consequent is the failure to appreciate adequately that scientific theories and political ideas are both complex and tenuously linked, and that political ideas are shaped in good part by personal judgments lying outside the domain of scientific evaluation.

All political proposals, radical and otherwise, should be seriously received and debated. But whatever direction we choose to take in the future, social progress can only be enhanced, not impeded, by the deeper investigation of the genetic constraints of human nature, which will steadily replace rumor and folklore with testable knowledge. Nothing is to be gained by a dogmatic denial of the existence of the constraints or attempts to discourage public discussion of them. Knowledge humanely acquired and widely shared, related to human needs but kept free of political censorship, is the real science for the people.

REFERENCES CITED

Allen, E. et al. 1975. Against sociobiology. *The New York Review of Books,* 13 November.

Chomsky, N. 1975. *Reflections on Language.* Pantheon Books, Random House, New York.

Nozick, R. 1974. *Anarchy, State and Utopia.* Basic Books, New York.

Otterbein, K. F. 1970. *The Evolution of War.* Human Relations Area Files Press, New Haven, Conn.

Rawls, J. 1971. *A Theory of Justice.* Harvard University Press, Cambridge, Mass.

Wilson, E. O. 1975a. *Sociobiology: The New Synthesis.* Harvard University Press, Cambridge, Mass.

————. 1975b. Human decency is animal. *The New York Times Magazine,* 12 October, pp. 38–50.

Social Darwinism Lives! (Should It?)

Peter H. Klopfer
Duke University

Sociobiology has made a resurgence in recent years, but has become enmeshed in political controversy. Indeed much of the work in sociobiology has been used to justify repressive or racist measures. It is argued that the unfortunate alliance of some sociobiologists and politicians is a poor basis for discrediting the field itself; that a science of sociobiology is possible and, if we seek to know the nature of our social heritage (if any!), needs be vigorously pursued.

Sociologists may consider their specialty a child of this century, but it was nurtured and trained by Darwin's work a century earlier. Spencer [1], for instance, made use of Darwinian paradigms to develop and champion his sociological views, based upon economic and political *laissez faire*. Others, after Spencer, were more eclectic (and less consistent) embracing Darwinian biology when this suited their preconceptions, and otherwise ignoring it. One of the marvels of biology, as Margaret Mead has often said, is that it can provide examples to support any point of view! However, the development in the 20's, 30's, and 40's of a systematic approach to evolution, and particularly of comparative psychology, erected inhibitions to the selective use of Darwin's arguments and produced enough facts to somewhat discourage facile generalizing. The most recent two decades, however, have seen a remarkable return to the earlier 19th Century style of theorizing, i.e., the effort to explain human social phenomena through extrapolations from selected animals.

This modern effort in social biology has been heralded by ethologists, foremost among them the Nobelist, Konrad Lorenz, who had originally made his mark studying the displays of ducks. In two papers published in Germany in the early forties, Lorenz [2] applied his theory of releasors—a pattern of stimuli that inevitably and automatically elicit an innate response—to human morals and esthetics. Lorenz's argument proceeded as follows: In the evolution of morality, releasors for moral (and esthetic) behavior appear. These are unique to each race. Hybridization of races leads to a breakdown of the integrity of the releasors and a loss of appropriate response patterns. Since human morality and esthetic ideals are tied to particular releasing stimuli, hybridization between the human races will degrade morals and art. The model for this notion are the specific displays that stimulate sexual intercourse in ducks. When miscegenation does occasionally occur, the hybrid offspring shows displays so different from either parent as to be largely barred from effective sexual activity.

From *Yale Journal of Biology and Medicine 50*:77–84. Reprinted by permission of the *Yale Journal of Biology and Medicine* and the author.

The fact that the promulgation of such a view did political mischief might have been forgiven had Lorenz's notions been either inductively sound or factually correct. Parenthetically, let me add that some have argued that Lorenz's ideas should have been suppressed even if untainted by flawed logic and factual error, but that is a point to be returned to later. For now, enough to say that the reintroduction of what we may call "social Darwinism" (with apologies to poor, innocent Charles Darwin) was not associated with the world's most popular social movement.

Nonetheless, not too many years after the second World War, more Lorenzian-type tracts appeared, some of them highly sophisticated, by technically competent professionals—the anthropologist Coon [3], for instance, arguing a theory of multiple and independent origins of modern races of mankind—others, by writers of rather limited background in biology—Robert Ardrey [4] and his anecdotes on territoriality, for example. The flood continues, though now it is not rising undetected. Levees are being constructed. I distinguish a levee-builder from an intellectual opponent of social Darwinism in that the former, fearing the damage the flood can do, would prevent it with dams and sandbags, while the latter seeks the source of the waters so as to anticipate the flood and perhaps move to higher ground. Is the presence of a supernumerary Y chromosome in man associated with behavioral disorders? One could study this issue, seeking evidence that would test the null hypothesis; one could also refuse to allow the study or dissemination of the results on the grounds that prophecies of behavior are self-fulfilling and may thus be too dangerous to be admitted. It is not an easy choice.

This issue represents but one aspect of the dilemma of experimental sociobiology. When, to what extent, and how do studies of animal behavior—in particular, social behavior—contribute to an understanding of the social norms of man? The recent monumental study by E. O. Wilson [5], through the impetus it has given biosociology, no less through the controversy it has spawned, makes this a particularly topical issue (see Wade [6]).

One of the major difficulties in the interpretation of the behavior of other animals lies in the uniqueness of the sensory world of each species. Ironically, the man who is largely credited with the explicit recognition of this problem was one of Lorenz's intellectual mentors, von Uexküll [7]. Von Uexküll introduced the term "*Umwelt*" to ethology, as a label for the environment as perceived by members of a particular species. A profusion of white blossoms which present a uniform *Umwelt* to us, would appear rather more heterogenous to bees, whose eyes distinguish between white pigments that reflect or absorb U.V. The song of two wrens, indistinguishable to us, may sound very different to a mockingbird whose capacity for temporal resolution of sound exceeds ours. And what is an empty, desolate room to us could be packed with the scents and reassurances of nearby companions to a more olfactorily acute mammal. In short, the stimuli to which responses are made are often not self-evident, and may be identifiable only with difficulty.

While the differences between species in their *Umwelt* may seem to present largely technical difficulties, they suggest a comparable lack of correspondence between some of the functional or emotional correlates of superficially similar patterns of behavior. Therein lies a second, major difficulty.

To understand the emergence of, let us say, the cusp pattern of human teeth, the comparative anatomist relies upon the existence of parallels between function and structure. Fossils often provide an additional clue suggesting how structures have varied in time. Some ethologists, steeped in the tradition of comparative anatomy, have applied anatomic methods to behavior. Territorial behavior in man is homologized with territoriality in other forms and its *analagen* may then seem to become visible. Hear Lorenz [8] at his Nobel ceremony:

> As a pupil of the comparative anatomist and embryologist Ferdinand Hochstetter, I had the benefit of a very thorough instruction in the methodological procedure of distinguishing similarities caused by common descent from those due to parallel adaptation. In fact, the making of this distinction forms a great part of the comparative evolutionist's daily work. Perhaps I should mention here that this procedure has led me to the discovery which I personally consider to be my own most important contribution to science. Knowing animal behavior as I did, and being instructed in the methods of phylogenetic comparison as I was, I could not fail to discover that the very same methods of comparison, the same concepts of analogy and homology, are as applicable to characters of behavior as they are in those of morphology (p. 231).

There are many objections to this approach; mine have been often enough repeated, but the polemic can be allowed one more repetition:

1 The distinction between analogies and homologies is essential to the comparative approach, but the validity of this distinction is rarely, if ever, tested. The excretory organs of earthworms and men may appear similar only in function when viewed holistically; at the subcellular level their similarities may become structural as well. In short, the level or organization or "grain" of the investigator's perceptual field may determine whether two structures or behavior patterns are to be regarded as homologues or analogues [Klopfer, 9].

2 In a few instances it is possible to trace a direct causal relation between the presence and action of a specific locus on the DNA and a palpable, measurable structure. In a minute fraction of these cases a further link to a pattern of behavior may be forged. This is rare. Since most behavior patterns can remain fixed even when the muscles subserving them vary, the further link to DNA is likely more tenuous yet. Behavioral development is a process involving multiple-feedbacks between DNA, cellular, organismic, and external environment rather than the lineal unfolding of a preprogrammed design for particular neuro-muscular networks. It is a system of multiple controls, often admirably buffered so as to maintain a seeming constancy of output, but with numerous intertwining pathways of causality and control. Thus, the concept of the "evolution" or "heritability" of behavior is only metaphorically comparable to the notion of the heritability of a particular cusp-pattern [Lewontin, 10]. Behavior, itself, does not evolve, but merely changes.

If there is indeed more than one way to skin a cat, what does this say about the legitimacy of efforts to generalize behavioral studies? Is generalization suspect? Recall Lehrman's cautionary tale concerning Federal child care centers and mother- less monkeys. Studies by Harlow revealed that surrogate-reared rhesus macaques displayed severe behavioral deficits. *Ergo,* child care centers which encourage surro- gate-rearing are to be avoided. Later work by Kaufman and Rosenblum, with another macaque, showed this species accepting surrogate mothering happily. The two macaque species are more closely related *inter se* than is either to man [Lehr- man, 11].

Among the lemurs of the Duke Primate Facility are three species which have been the particular objects of my studies. Fig. 1 displays *Lemur catta;* it lives in the forests of Southern Madagascar, often alongside a second species, shown in Fig. 2., *Lemur fulvus.* These animals are remarkably similar in their morphology and eco- logical relations. *L. catta* mothers, however, readily hand-off their infants to other females in their troop utilizing baby-sitters even when the infants are no more than seventy-two hours old. *L. fulvus* mothers, in contrast, are much more zealous in their guardianship; as a general rule, the infant is almost a month old before being regularly cared for by a sitter. And now consider the third species, *Lemur variegatus* (Fig. 3), which leaves its infants alone in a nest, visiting only at intervals. The infant is rarely carried by the mother, and then only in the mouth [see Klopfer and Boskoff, 12].

Lest one believe that such major differences are merely reflecting a great taxo- nomic distance between the species, consider another subject of my work, the Toggenburg goat (Fig. 4). Several years' work and experience with over 100 individ- ual animals have revealed a very consistent pattern of maternal behavior. If the mother, immediately upon the birth of her infant, is allowed but a few minutes contact with it, a subsequent separation of 1–3 hours produces no permanent difficul- ties in re-acceptance. Denied this contact, even a separation of half an hour may lead to permanent rejection [Klopfer, 13]. We know some other details about the underly- ing mechanisms, but our most recent efforts to bare-all, failed totally. These efforts were made at a commercial goat diary, to which my colleagues, David Gubernick and Kathryn Jones, travelled in order to exploit the availability of a large number of animals. The control animals there did not conform to the usual pattern. This dairy herd consisted of half-breeds, still one species, of course, so we must now acknowledge that even intraspecific breed differences may be significant.

Where does this leave us? Is each species to be regarded as behaviorally unique, providing no basis for prediction of the nature of the next? This could be so, but as a matter of faith I prefer to assume there is a pattern which we have yet to perceive. The pattern is apparently not one that corresponds to taxonomic order. I suggest it may correspond to an economic order, and that it is to the province of cost-benefit accounting that we might turn.

The suppositions are simple enough. Whatever tactics pay may become fixed [note Hannon, 14]. "Pay-off," of course, must ultimately be interpreted in terms of

Figures 1–3 *Lemur catta, L. fulvus,* and *L. variegatus* at the Duke University Primate Facility. (By J. Wallace)—*L. f.* and *L. c.* (By K. Boskoff)—*L. v.*

genetic fitness. For many birds, laying a clutch of five rather than of three eggs ultimately fails to pay, because, on the average, the young from larger clutches are less better nourished and have a lower survivorship, with a smaller proportionate contribution to the next generation than young from smaller clutches [Lack, 15]. However, for species whose young feed themselves and whose food supplies impose no immediate limits, larger clutches pay better [Hutchinson, 16]. In short, outcomes are not always obvious, so while the supposition is simple, the determination of which tactic most increases fitness may not be.

The second supposition is that animals can respond phenotypically to new demands in advance of genotypic alterations. While there are obvious limits to this, men may learn to swim, but whales are unlikely to walk, we do have to assume that one particular mechanism—whether genotype, a limb, or a metabolic pathway—can come to subserve functions very different from those which selection originally favored.

The game is thus to determine what life-styles the demands and constraints of a particular habitat will favor, and to develop equations which include terms for such parameters as time-lags in responses to changed conditions, and morphological limitations to adaptation. The differences in mother-infant relations exemplified by my lemurs may then become explicable.

There are three general ways to play the game, several examples of which can be found in recent publications. Assume our goal to be an explanation for differences in degree of sociality. The first play entails listing broad principles, qualitatively stated but still operational and heuristic. Alexander [17], for instance, has generated a list of the advantages and disadvantages of living in a group rather than solitarily. Group life affords greater protection from predators (except where protection is provided by concealment), and may enhance accessibility of highly localized resources. At the same time, competition for resources may increase, and the transmission of diseases or parasites facilitated. In an effort to apply Alexander's various "rules," Hoogland and Sherman [18] examined a colonial bank swallow and found the colonial habit did indeed increase competition for nest sites and materials, as well as mates, that it led to more instances of misdirected parental care and also more sharing of ectoparasites. Greater protection from predation was also provided, however, so this benefit outweighed the other costs.

A second play is to focus more narrowly on those features which appear most pivotal with respect to the balance-of-payments. In the case of the swallows, this would be the benefit provided by protection from predation. Triesman [19] provides an illustration of this approach. He has examined the manner by which a predator detects potential prey. He then developed an abstract but testable variant of detection theory that predicts when the values of the governing parameters will prevent a prey organism from escaping. Pay-off for the prey then depends on promoting those specific conditions that preclude detection.

Finally, a third variant of the game, which will appeal to those more comfortable with equations than field glasses, is to construct wholly abstract models which

Figure 4 A rejecting caprine mother at the Duke University Field Station for Animal Behavior Studies.

identify the boundary conditions for certain forms of social grouping. J. Cohen's treatment of primate societies [20] illustrates this approach.

In short, a science of sociobiology may indeed be possible—the development of a theoretic framework within the compass of which we can predict and understand the varied manifestations of sociality. There remains the prospect than an encompassing theory, one which includes man, will suggest certain political actions, or argue against others. Equally plausible is the possibility that man will be shown so infinitely flexible as not to be biologically restricted to any particular social forms. Either way, we need to know the nature of our social heritage, if, indeed, we have one in any but an historical sense, and that harm from such revelations is no more inevitable that from any increase in knowledge. The partial knowledge that a species to species extrapolation provides is deceptive: we do well to shun that. Here I join the workers on the levee. But the bold efforts made by a few imaginative men [e.g., Wilson, 5; Emlen, S., 21] to explore the upper reaches of the waters, these we ought applaud. With such explorations we may yet find that the behavior of goats and lemurs can also reveal man.

REFERENCES

1. Spencer H: Principles of Psychology, Second edition. New York, Appleton & Co., 1896
2. Lorenz K: Durch Domestikation verursachte störungen arteigenen Verhaltens. Z Angew Psych Charakterk 59:2–81, 1940
3. Coon CS: The Origin of Races. New York, Alfred A. Knopf, Inc., 1962
4. Ardrey R: The Social Contract. New York, Atheneum Publishers, 1970
5. Wilson EO: Sociobiology. Cambridge, Mass., Harvard University Press, 1975
6. Wade N: Sociobiology: troubled birth for new discipline. Sci 191; 1151–1155, 1976
7. von Uexküll J: Umwelt und Innenwelt der Tiere. Berlin, Springer Verlag, 1921
8. Lorenz K: Analogy as a source of knowledge. Sci 185: 229–234, 1974
9. Klopfer PH: Evolution, behavior, language, Communication, Behavior and Evolution. Edited by E Simmel and M Hahn, New York, Academic Press, 1976, pp 7–21
10. Lewontin R: The Genetic Basis of Evolutionary Change. New York, Columbia University Press, 1974
11. Lehrman D: Behavioral science, engineering, and poetry. Biopsychology of Development. Edited by E Tobach, LR Aronson, E Shaw. New York, Academic Press, 1971, pp 459–471
12. Klopfer PH, Boskoff K: Maternal behavior in prosimians. The Study of Prosimian Behaviour. Edited by GA Doyle and RD Martin, New York, Academic Press, in press
13. Klopfer PH: Mother love: what turns it on? Am Sci 59: 404–407, 1971
14. Hannon B: Marginal product pricing in the ecosystem. Journal of Theor Biol 56: 253–268, 1976
15. Lack D: The Natural Regulation of Animal Numbers. New York, Oxford University Press, 1954
16. Hutchinson GE: Copepodology for the ornithologist. Ecology 32: 571–577, 1951
17. Alexander RD: The evolution of social behavior. Annu Rev Ecol Syst 5: 325–383, 1974
18. Hoogland JC, Sherman PW: Advantages and disadvantages of bank swallow coloniality. Ecol Monogr 46: 33–58, 1976
19. Triesman M: Predation and the evolution of gregariousness. Anim Behav 23: 779–825, 1975
20. Cohen JE: Casual Groups of Monkeys and Men: stochastic models of elemental social systems. Cambridge, Mass., Harvard University Press, 1971
21. Emlen S: An alternative case for sociobiology. Sci 192: 736–738, 1976

Index

RESERVE BOOK